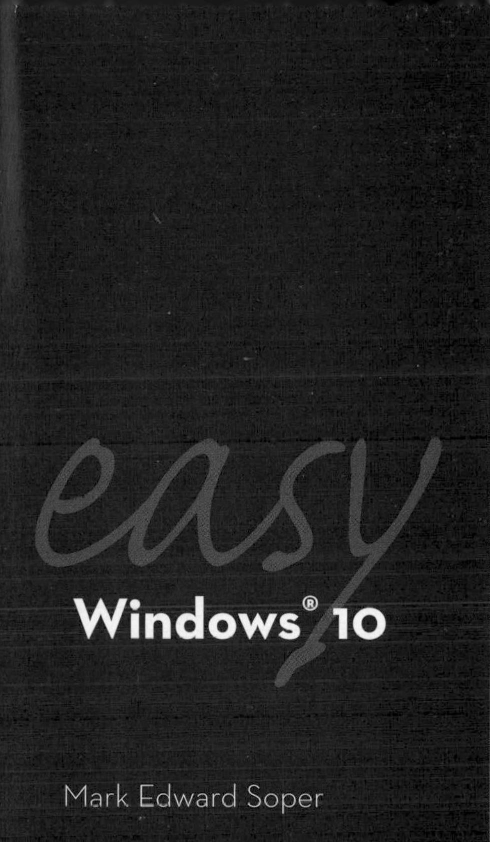

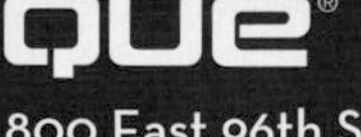

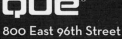

easy Windows® 10

Mark Edward Soper

QUE®
800 East 96th Street
Indianapolis, Indiana 46240

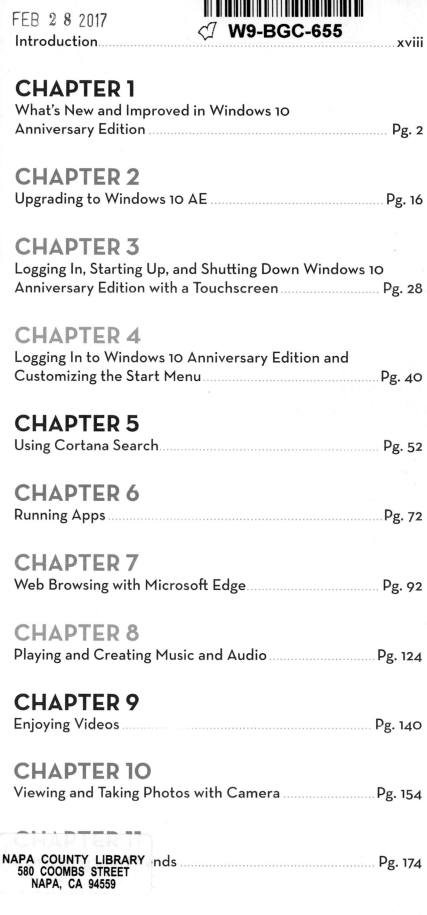

ONLINE CONTENT

Additional tasks are available to you at www.quepublishing.com/title/9780789756848. Click the Downloads tab to access the links to download the PDF file.

CONTENTS

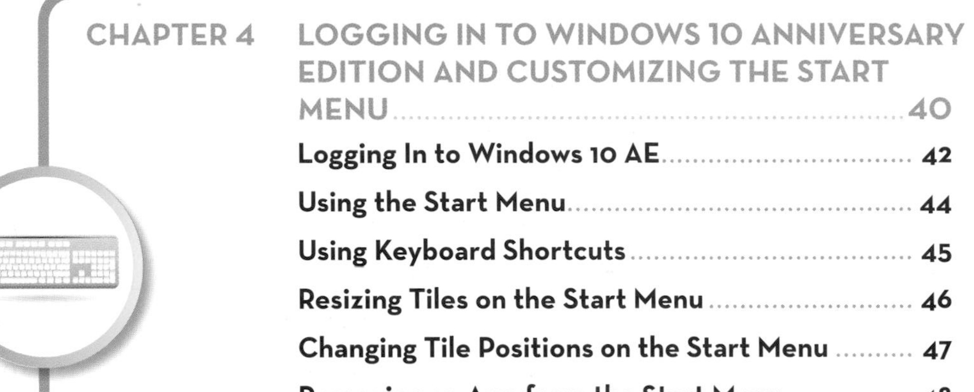

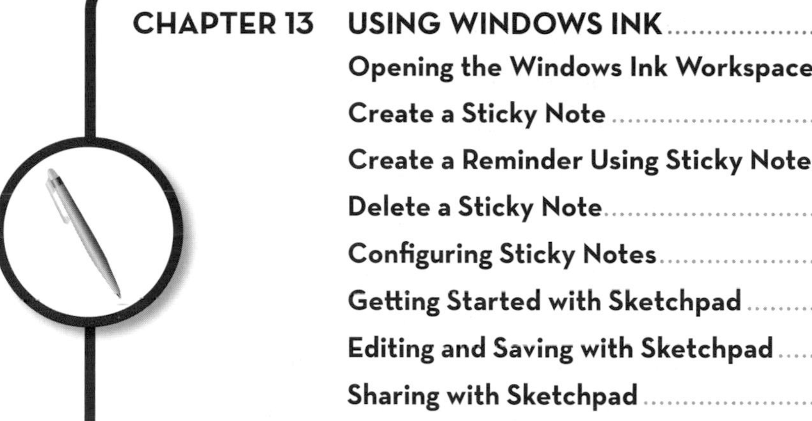

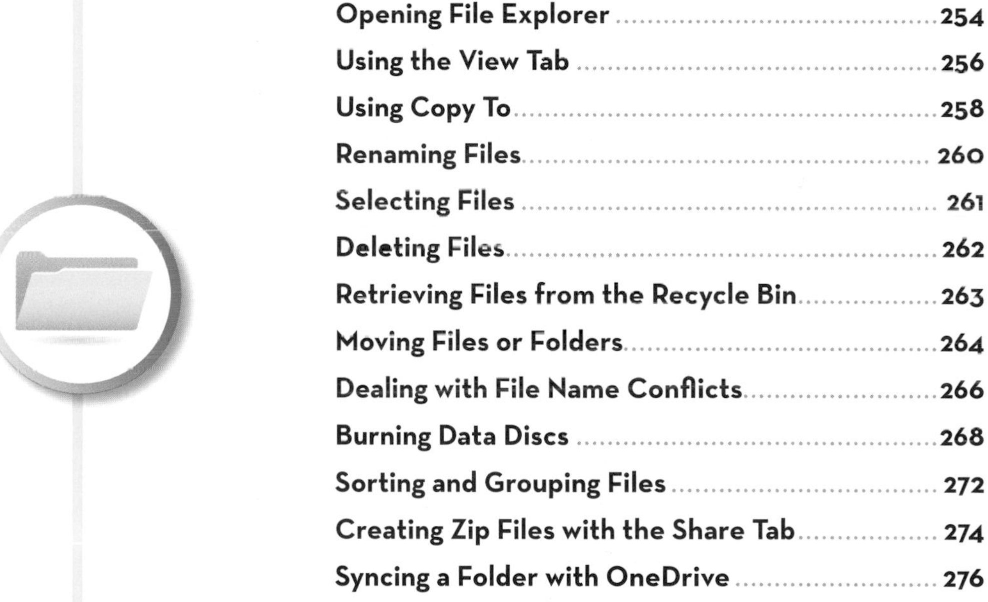

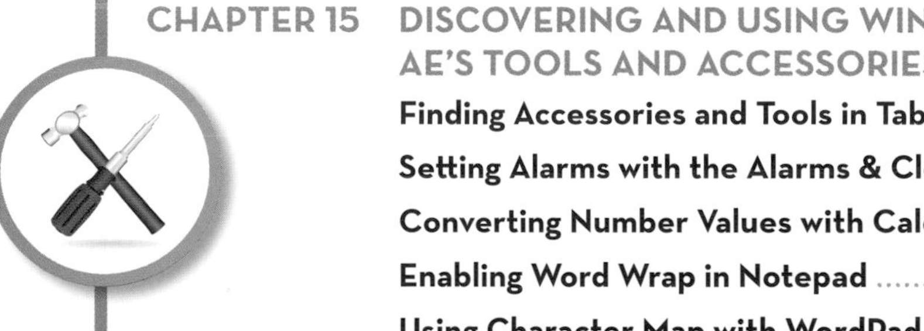

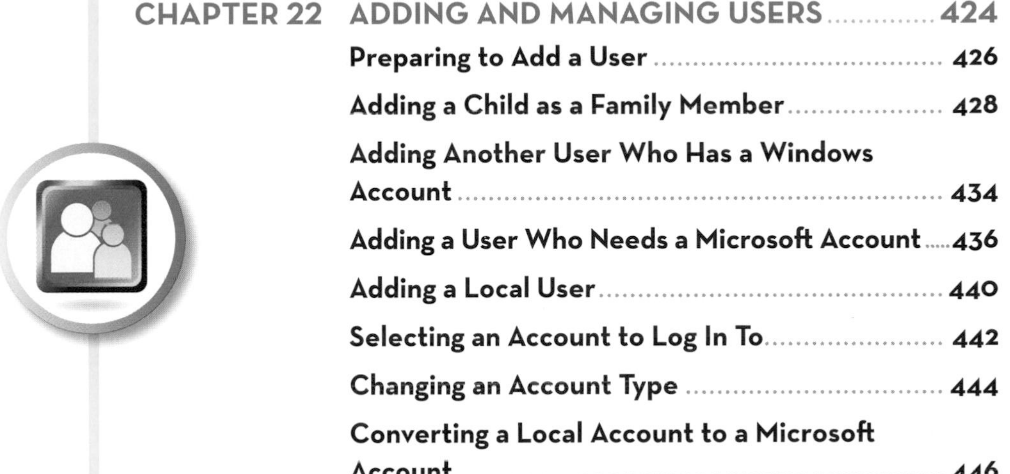

ONLINE CONTENT

Additional tasks are available to you at www.quepublishing.com/title/9780789756848. Click the Downloads tab to access the links to download the PDF file.

EASY WINDOWS® 10

ISBN-13: 978-0-7897-5684-8
ISBN-10: 0-7897-5684-6

Library of Congress Control Number: 2016962698

First Printing: February 2017

TRADEMARKS

All terms mentioned in this book that are known to be trademarks or service marks have been appropriately capitalized. Que Publishing cannot attest to the accuracy of this information. Use of a term in this book should not be regarded as affecting the validity of any trademark or service mark.

Windows is a registered trademark of Microsoft Corp.

WARNING AND DISCLAIMER

Every effort has been made to make this book as complete and as accurate as possible, but no warranty or fitness is implied. The information provided is on an "as is" basis. The author and the publisher shall have neither liability nor responsibility to any person or entity with respect to any loss or damages arising from the information contained in this book.

SPECIAL SALES

For information about buying this title in bulk quantities, or for special sales opportunities (which may include electronic versions; custom cover designs; and content particular to your business, training goals, marketing focus, or branding interests), please contact our corporate sales department at corpsales@pearsoned.com or (800) 382-3419.

For government sales inquiries, please contact governmentsales@pearsoned.com.

For questions about sales outside the U.S., please contact intlcs@pearson.com.

Editor-in-Chief
Greg Wiegand

Senior Acquisitions Editor
Laura Norman

Development Editor
Sherry Kinkoph Gunter

Managing Editor
Sandra Schroeder

Senior Project Editor
Tonya Simpson

Indexer
Ken Johnson

Proofreader
Gill Editorial Services

Technical Editor
Vince Avarello

Editorial Assistant
Cindy Teeters

Cover Designer
Chuti Prasertsith

Compositor
Bronkella Publishing

ABOUT THE AUTHOR

Mark Edward Soper has been using Microsoft Windows starting with version 1.0, and since 1992 he has taught thousands of computer troubleshooting and network students across the country how to use Windows as part of their work and everyday lives. Mark is the author of *Easy Windows 10*, *Easy Windows 8.1*, *Easy Windows 8*, *Easy Microsoft Windows 7*, *Teach Yourself Windows 7 in 10 Minutes*, and *Using Microsoft Windows Live*. Mark also has contributed to Que's *Special Edition Using* series on Windows Me, Windows XP, and Windows Vista, as well as *Easy Windows Vista* and *Windows 7 In Depth*. In addition, he has written two books about Windows Vista: *Maximum PC Microsoft Windows Vista Exposed* and *Unleashing Microsoft Windows Vista Media Center*.

When he's not teaching, learning, or writing about Microsoft Windows, Mark stays busy with many other technology-related activities. He was written three books on computer troubleshooting, including *The PC and Gadget Help Desk: A Do-It-Yourself Guide to Troubleshooting and Repairing*. He is a longtime contributor to *Upgrading and Repairing PCs*, working on the 11th through 18th, 20th, and subsequent editions. Mark has co-authored *Upgrading and Repairing Networks*, Fifth Edition, written several books on CompTIA A+ Certification (including two titles covering the 2016 exams), an occasional column on certification for Computerworld.com, and has written two books about digital photography: *Easy Digital Cameras* and *The Shot Doctor: The Amateur's Guide to Taking Great Digital Photos*. Mark also has become a video content provider for Que Publishing and InformIT and has posted many blog entries and articles at InformIT.com, MaximumPC.com, and other websites. He has also taught digital photography, digital imaging, and Microsoft Office for Ivy Tech Corporate College's southwest Indiana campus in Evansville, Indiana, and Windows and Microsoft Office for the University of Southern Indiana's continuing education department.

DEDICATION

To Katie, as you begin a new journey.

ACKNOWLEDGMENTS

This book might have my name on the cover, but plenty of people behind the scenes make it possible and provide the encouragement needed to create a useful and enjoyable work. Thank you for reading this book. Here are some of the people who helped make it possible.

My wife, Cheryl, is a modern-day Proverbs 31 woman. Her encouragement has helped me every moment since we first met. We celebrate 40 years of marriage this year, and more than that as a team. She is truly a gift from God.

I first saw Microsoft Windows back when it was a home for a simple paint program and a simple word-processing program that needed MS-DOS to work. Windows has come a long way, and here are some of the people who gave me the opportunity to learn about it.

Thanks go to Jim Peck and Mayer Rubin, for whom I taught thousands of students how to troubleshoot systems running Windows 3.1, 95, and 98; magazine editors Edie Rockwood and Ron Kobler, for assigning me to dig deeper into Windows; Ed Bott, who provided my first opportunity to contribute to a major Windows book; Scott Mueller, who asked me to help with *Upgrading and Repairing Windows*; Ivy Tech Corporate College and the University of Southern Indiana, for teaching opportunities; Bob Cowart and Brian Knittel, for helping continue my real-world Windows education. And, of course, the Microsoft family.

Thanks also to my family, both for their encouragement over the years and for the opportunity to explain various Windows features and fix things that go wrong.

I also want to thank the editorial and design team that Que put together for this book.

Many thanks to Greg Wiegand and Laura Norman for the opportunity to write another *Easy* series book, and thanks to Sherry Kinkoph-Gunter, Vince Averello, and Tonya Simpson. Thanks also to Cindy Teeters for keeping track of invoices and making sure payments were timely. I also want to thank contributing author Michael Miller for his work on the connecting with friends, home networking, and users chapters. Thanks also to Ken, Tricia, and Karen.

I have worked with Que Publishing and Pearson since 1999, and I'm looking forward to many more years—and books—together!

WE WANT TO HEAR FROM YOU!

As the reader of this book, *you* are our most important critic and commentator. We value your opinion and want to know what we're doing right, what we could do better, what areas you'd like to see us publish in, and any other words of wisdom you're willing to pass our way.

We welcome your comments. You can email or write to let us know what you did or didn't like about this book—as well as what we can do to make our books better.

Please note that we cannot help you with technical problems related to the topic of this book.

When you write, please be sure to include this book's title and author as well as your name and email address. We will carefully review your comments and share them with the author and editors who worked on the book.

Email: feedback@quepublishing.com

Mail: Que Publishing
ATTN: Reader Feedback
800 East 96th Street
Indianapolis, IN 46240 USA

READER SERVICES

Register your copy of *Easy Windows 10* at quepublishing.com for convenient access to downloads, updates, and corrections as they become available. To start the registration process, go to quepublishing.com/register and log in or create an account*. Enter the product ISBN, 9780789756848, and click Submit. When the process is complete, you will find any available bonus content under Registered Products.

*Be sure to check the box that you would like to hear from us to receive exclusive discounts on future editions of this product.

INTRODUCTION

WHY THIS BOOK WAS WRITTEN

Que Publishing's Easy series is famous for providing accurate, simple, step-by-step instructions for popular software and operating systems. Windows 10 Anniversary Edition (or AE for short) is the first major update to Windows 10, providing more features, superior management, and better ease of use for users with a keyboard and mouse, a touchscreen, or a convertible 2-in-1 device. To make Windows 10 AE work for you, *Easy Windows 10*, Second Edition is here to help you understand and use it. Whether you're a veteran Windows user or new to Windows and computers, there's a lot to learn, and we're here to help.

Easy Windows 10, Second Edition gives you a painless and enjoyable way to discover the essential features of Windows. We spent months with Windows 10 AE to discover its new and improved features and learn the best ways to show you what it does, and you get the benefit: an easy-to-read visual guide that gets you familiar with the latest Microsoft product in a hurry.

Your time is valuable, so we've concentrated our efforts on features you're likely to use every day. Our objective: to help you use Windows to make your computing life better, more productive, and even more fun.

HOW TO READ *EASY WINDOWS 10*, SECOND EDITION

So, what's the best way to read this book?

You have a few options, based on what you know about computers and Windows. Try one of these:

- Start at Chapter 1, "What's New and Improved in Windows 10 Anniversary Edition," and work your way through.
- Go straight to the chapters that look the most interesting.
- Hit the table of contents or the index and go directly to the sections that tell you stuff you don't know already.

Any of these methods will work—and to help you get a better feel for what's inside, here's a closer look at what's in each chapter.

BEYOND THE TABLE OF CONTENTS—WHAT'S INSIDE

Chapter 1, "What's New and Improved in Windows 10 Anniversary Edition," provides a quick overview of the most important new and improved features in Windows 10 AE, including Tablet mode, voice-enabled searches and reminders with Cortana, more powerful settings options, and more. If you're reading this book mainly to brush up on what's new and different, start here and follow the references to the chapters with more information.

Chapter 2, "Upgrading to Windows 10 AE," is designed for users of Windows 7 or Windows 8.1 who are upgrading to Windows 10 AE. This chapter covers the updating process and helps you make the best choices along the way.

Chapter 3, "Logging In, Starting Up, and Shutting Down Windows 10 Anniversary Edition with a Touchscreen," shows you how to log in to Windows 10 AE, how to use Tablet mode, how to find and launch programs from the Start or All Apps menu, how to use the touch keyboard or handwriting interface, how to use shortcut keys, how to lock and unlock your computer, and how to shut it down or put it into sleep mode.

Chapter 4, "Logging In to Windows 10 Anniversary Edition and Customizing the Start Menu," helps you understand how to use the Start menu, customize it, use keyboard shortcuts, lock and unlock your system from the keyboard, and shut it down or put it into sleep mode.

Chapter 5, "Using Cortana Search," provides step-by-step instructions on how to use Cortana in Desktop or Tablet modes, enable and use voice search, create and edit voice reminders, start apps by voice, add Cortana to iOS or Android mobile devices, and turn off Cortana.

Chapter 6, "Running Apps," shows you how to search for, run, switch between, change window size, and close desktop and Modern UI apps. You also learn how to snap windows and use jump lists.

Chapter 7, "Web Browsing with Microsoft Edge," helps you use powerful features such as Web Notes, Cortana integration, and new browser extensions that enable Edge to translate foreign-language pages and much more.

Chapter 8, "Playing and Creating Music and Audio," shows you how to manage and add to your digital music collection and create audio recordings using Groove Music and Voice Recorder.

Chapter 9, "Enjoying Videos," shows you how to manage and add to your digital video, TV, and movie collection using Video.

Chapter 10, "Viewing and Taking Photos with Camera," is your guide to the Camera and Photos apps. Whether you use your tablet's built-in webcam and backward-facing camera or a digital camera, you'll learn how to view and edit your pictures, change camera settings, and record video.

Chapter 11, "Connecting with Friends," shows you how to use the People, Facebook, Mail, Calendar, Skype Preview, and Notifications apps in Windows 10 AE to stay in touch with friends and family.

Chapter 12, "News, Weather, Sports, and Money," introduces you to key features in the new and improved News, Weather, Sports, and Money apps.

Chapter 13, "Using Windows Ink," introduces you to the new Windows Ink Workspace and its pen-enabled apps. Create notes, reminders, and simple drawings you can store and share.

Chapter 14, "Storing and Finding Your Files," helps you manage files, folders, and drives, burn data discs, copy/move files safely, and use OneDrive cloud storage.

Chapter 15, "Discovering and Using Windows 10 AE's Tools and Accessories," helps you use built-in apps such as Alarms & Clock, Calculator, Character Map, and Notepad.

Chapter 16, "Using the Windows Store," takes you on a tour of the preferred way to get free and commercial apps and media content for your device. Learn how to search for apps, download free apps, buy new apps, and uninstall apps.

Chapter 17, "Gaming," shows you how to build a gaming library from the Windows Store, connect to your Xbox One or Xbox One S, and connect to other users so you can stream games to your Windows device, record your best gaming moments, and compare achievements with friends.

Chapter 18, "Printing and Scanning," shows you how to use your printer, scanner, or multifunction device to print documents and photos on plain or photo paper, and how to scan documents and photos, too.

Chapter 19, "Managing Windows 10 AE," helps you master Windows 10 AE's improved Settings so you can add an additional display, manage devices, configure privacy settings, and much more.

Chapter 20, "Networking Your Home with HomeGroup," shows you how to connect to wireless networks and use the HomeGroup feature to set up and manage a network with Windows 7, Windows 8/8.1, and Windows 10 AE computers.

Chapter 21, "Customizing Windows," helps you make Windows look the way you want by tweaking the Start menu, desktop background, screen saver, time zone, and taskbar.

Chapter 22, "Adding and Managing Users," introduces you to different ways to set up a Windows login for users, how to add additional users, and how to create Child accounts for use with Microsoft Family parental controls.

Chapter 23, "Protecting Your System," shows you how to keep Windows 10 AE updated, protect your files with File History backups, use Notifications, and check for spyware and viruses with Windows Defender.

Chapter 24, "System Maintenance and Performance," helps you improve system speed and battery life, check disk capacity, solve disk errors, learn more about what Windows is doing by using Task Manager, and learn to use Reset and Troubleshooters to solve problems that can prevent your system from running properly.

Baffled by PC and Windows terminology? Check out the Glossary!

Also be sure to check out additional tasks available online at www.quepublishing.com/register.

Enjoy!

WHAT'S NEW AND IMPROVED IN WINDOWS 10 ANNIVERSARY EDITION

Windows 10 Anniversary Edition, or AE for short, brings even more improvements for both touch and mouse/keyboard users, including tablet mode, battery saver, voice-enabled scheduling with Cortana, and much more. In this chapter, you learn about these and other new and improved features.

Desktop mode Start menu
Touch mode Start menu
Creating a reminder with "Hey Cortana"
Using Screen Sketch
Using Cortana from the lock screen
Using Game DVR in the Xbox app
Life at a glance
Monday
7
Mail
Microsoft Edge
Photos
Cortana
Money
Recently added
Air Hockey
Most used
Movies & TV
Alarms & Clock
Camera
Maps
Windows PowerShell
WordPad
Suggested
Art of Coloring by Disney
Acrobat Reader DC
Remind you about this?
Reminder
Book study
6:30 PM
Today
Only once
Add a photo
Remind
Cancel
Ask me anything
Game DVR
On this PC
On Xbox Live
play my soundtracks playlist

IMPROVED TABLET MODE

Whether you use a tablet, a touchscreen computer with a mouse, or a non-touchscreen computer with a mouse, Windows 10 Anniversary Edition's improved Tablet mode helps you use Windows the way you prefer.

1. The Start menu in normal (desktop) mode.

2. When you disconnect or reconnect a keyboard from a convertible (2-in-1) device, Tablet mode can prompt you to select the mode you prefer.

Continued

TIP

Switching to Tablet Mode You can also switch to and from Tablet mode from the Windows 10 AE Action Center. ■

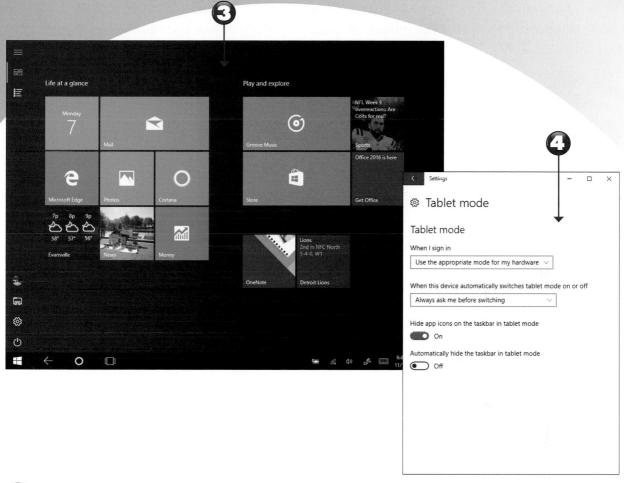

3 The Start menu in Tablet mode.

4 You can use Windows Settings to customize Tablet mode.

End

VOICE-ENHANCED CORTANA

In Windows 10 AE, the Cortana personal assistant is even more powerful. You can now talk to Cortana to create reminders and play music even when your computer is locked.

Start

1. After enabling "Hey Cortana" voice control through the Cortana settings menu, say, "Hey Cortana" into your computer's microphone.
2. Say "remind me" and the information, and Cortana will create a reminder for you.
3. Here's the new reminder, ready to edit or save.
4. You can also use Cortana from the lock screen when the Cortana prompt is displayed.

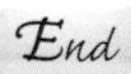

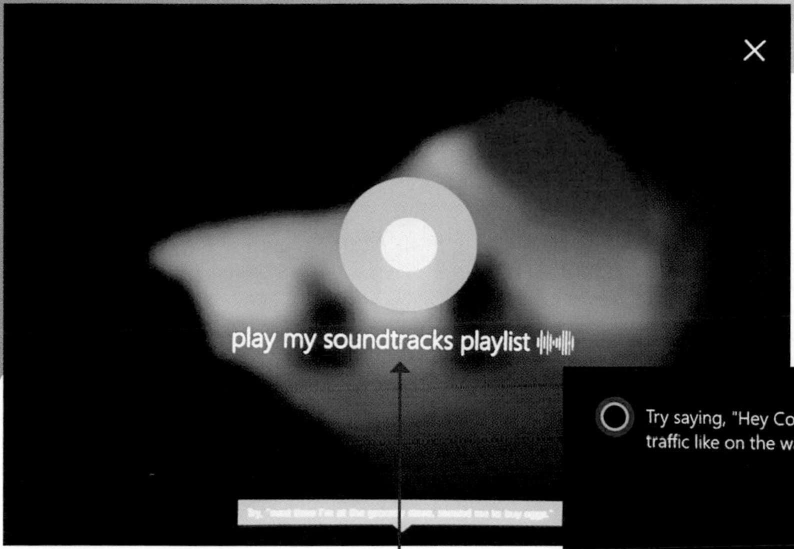

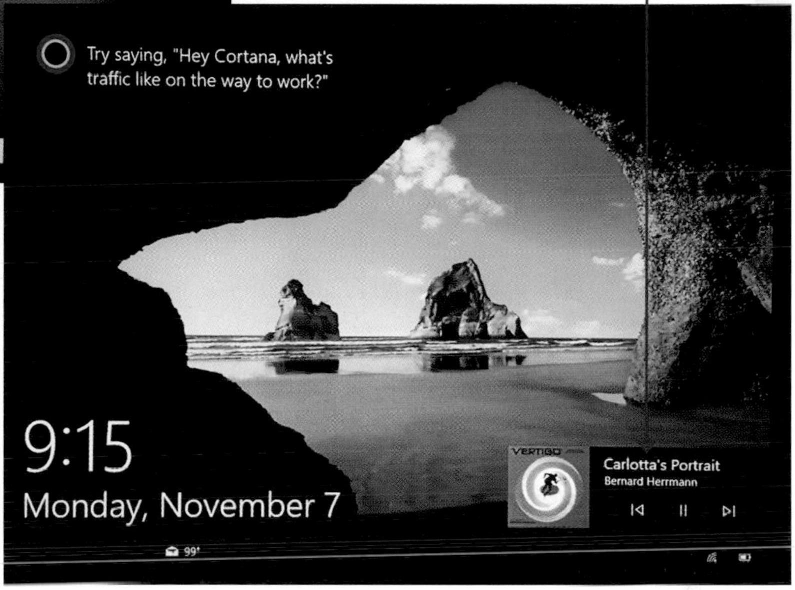

5. Say, “Hey Cortana” and continue saying what you want Cortana to do, such as play music.

6. Cortana starts playing the playlist requested in step 5.

End

NOTE

Enabling Cortana’s Speech Recognition In addition to enabling Cortana, make sure Cortana is configured to respond to “Hey Cortana” and to work from the lock screen. See Chapter 5, “Using Cortana Search,” to learn more about using Cortana. ■

IMPROVED TOUCHSCREEN-OPTIMIZED MENUS

If you have a touchscreen-enabled PC, you don't need to use Tablet mode to make menus easier to use. When you use your touchscreen, Windows 10 AE automatically optimizes some menus to make them easier to use with a touchscreen. For example, check out the taskbar properties menu as viewed with normal or touchscreen-friendly displays.

Start

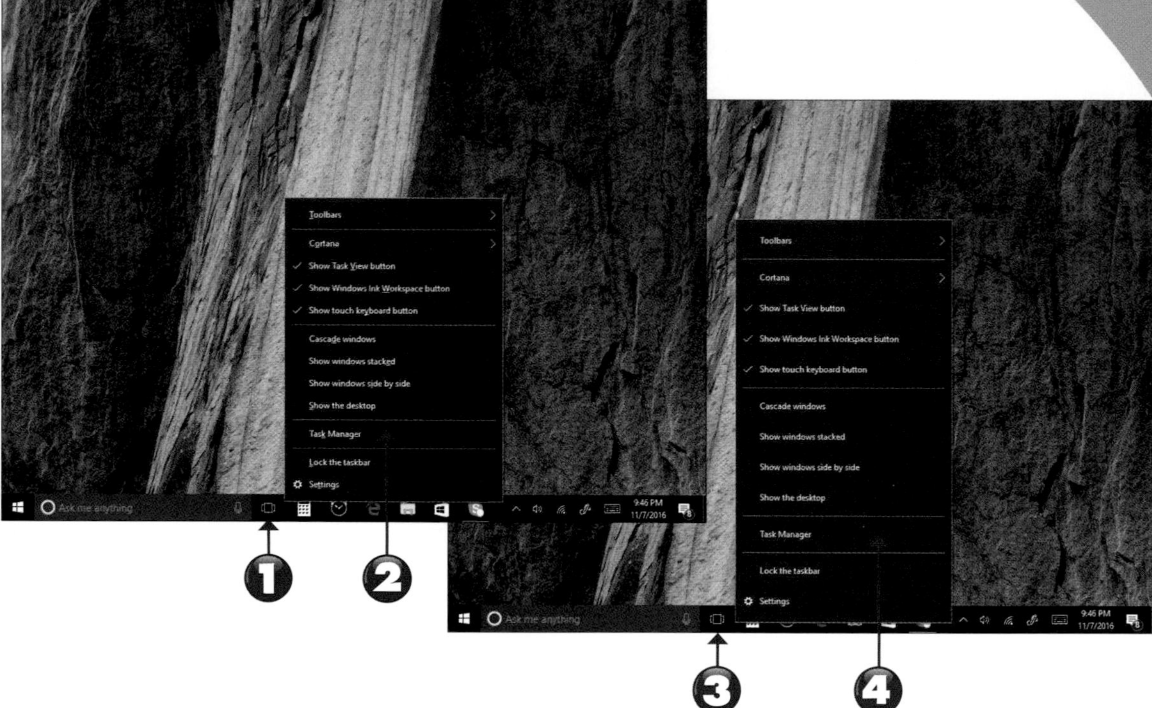

1. Right-click the taskbar with your mouse or touchpad to bring up the taskbar properties menu.
2. This menu displays normal menu spacing.
3. Press and hold on the taskbar using your touchscreen to bring up its properties sheet.
4. This menu displays touchscreen-friendly wide menu spacing.

End

NOTE

Discovering More Touchscreen Features See Chapter 3, "Logging In, Starting Up, and Shutting Down Windows 10 Anniversary Edition with a Touchscreen," to learn more about using your device's touchscreen. ■

EASIER MANAGEMENT WITH SETTINGS

Windows 10 AE's Settings provide you with more control than ever over how Windows works and looks. You can find all kinds of customizing options, controls for managing devices and apps, and much more among the Settings categories.

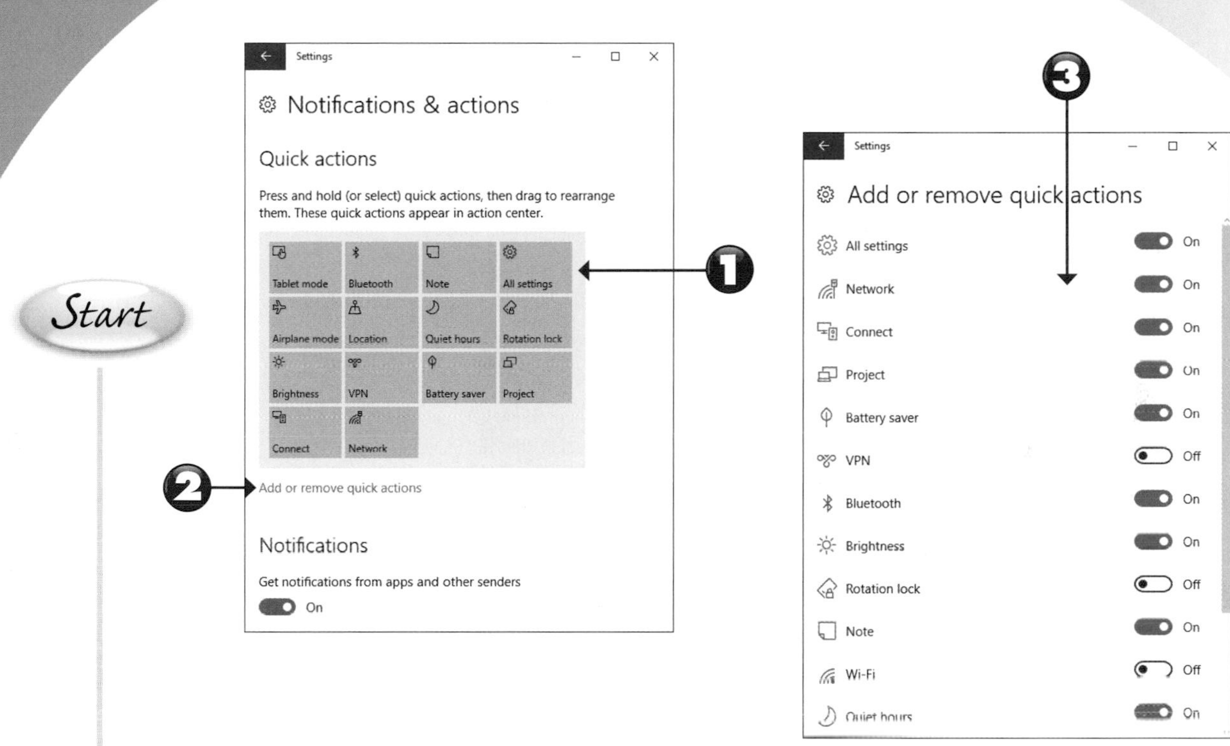

1. Windows Settings include options for controlling Quick Actions for quickly accessing the settings you use most often.

2. You can click or tap to customize the list.

3. Many of the settings available include push/click-to-drag controls to make configuring Windows 10 AE easy. You can click or drag to turn a control on or off.

End

NOTE

Discovering More Settings Learn more about customizing your system using Windows Settings in Chapter 19, "Managing Windows 10 AE." ■

NEW WINDOWS INK WORKSPACE

If you use a touchscreen laptop, tablet, or 2-in-1 convertible device, the new Windows Ink Workspace gives you several new tools for your touchscreen or stylus.

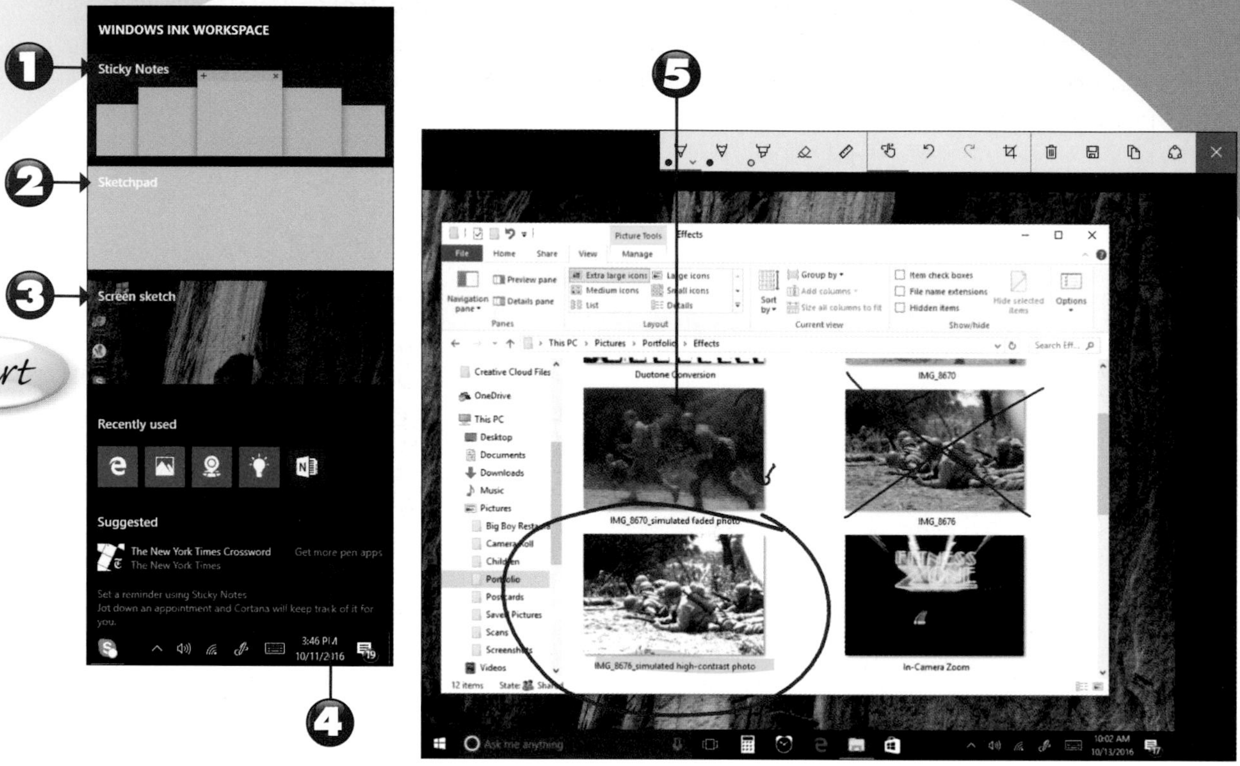

Start

1. Sticky Notes is back and now works with Cortana.
2. Create sketches with Sketchpad and save or share them.
3. Use Screen Sketch to create and mark up screen captures.
4. Get more pen apps from the Windows Store.
5. Using Screen Sketch to highlight photos for a project.

End

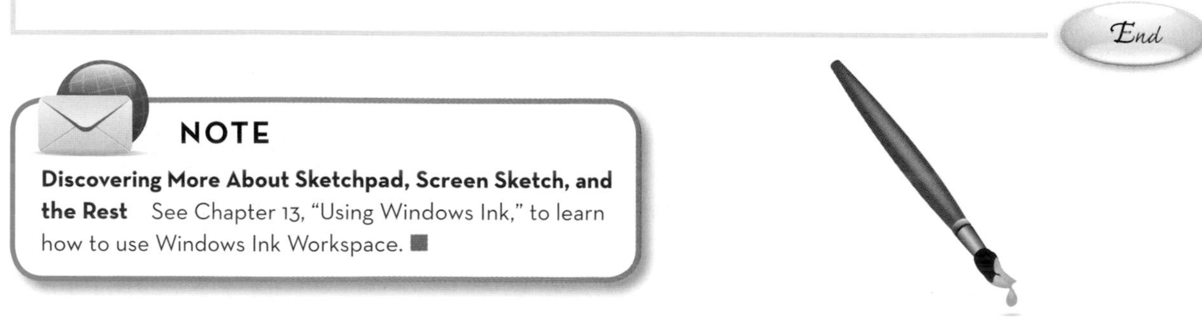

NOTE

Discovering More About Sketchpad, Screen Sketch, and the Rest See Chapter 13, "Using Windows Ink," to learn how to use Windows Ink Workspace. ■

NEW EXTENSION SUPPORT IN MICROSOFT EDGE WEB BROWSER

In Windows 10 AE, the Microsoft Edge web browser now includes support for extensions, which add additional features to your browser. Currently available extensions include the Microsoft Translator (for foreign-language websites); ad blocking; enhancements for Pinterest, Reddit, and other web services; and more. Add extensions with a quick visit to the Windows Store.

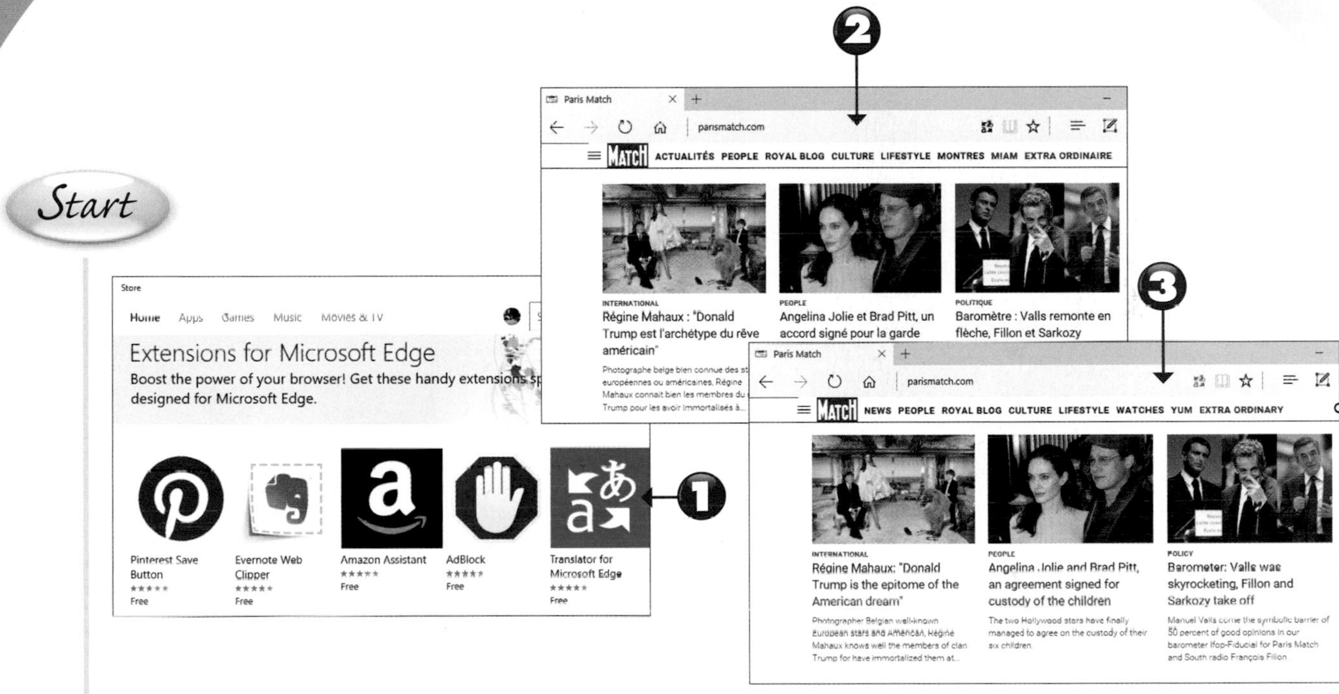

1. When you find an extension you want to use, you can install it on Microsoft Edge.
2. Here's an example of a French-language news page in Microsoft Edge that would benefit from a translation extension.
3. Here's the same page after translating with the Microsoft Translator for Microsoft Edge extension.

NOTE

Getting Up to Speed with Edge You can learn more about Microsoft Edge in Chapter 7, "Web Browsing with Microsoft Edge." ■

IMPROVED PHOTOS APP

Photos provides more information and easier access to picture locations and can now create slow-motion videos and pull still images from your videos.

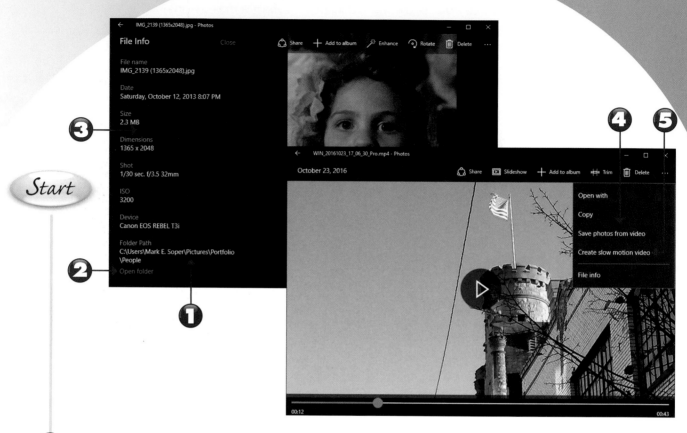

1. Where is this photo located? Photos tells you the full path to the file's location.
2. You can click or tap to go to that location.
3. Photos also lists exposure, camera, and file size information at a glance.
4. Do you need a still photo but have only a video file? You can use Photos to save a photo of any frame you choose.
5. You can also create a slow-motion video from any or all parts of your movie and save it as a new file.

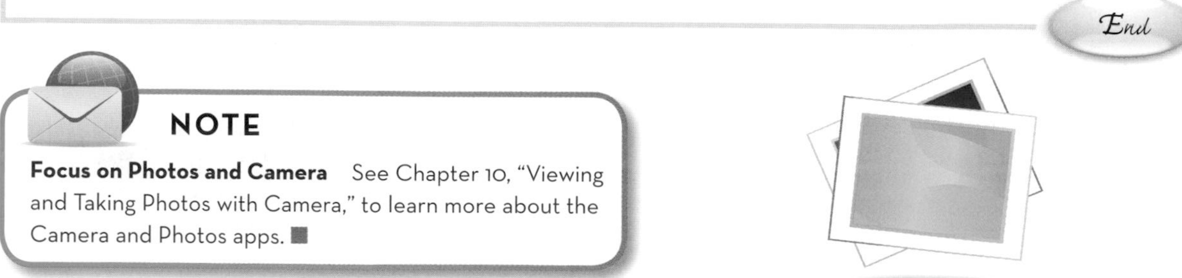

NOTE

Focus on Photos and Camera See Chapter 10, "Viewing and Taking Photos with Camera," to learn more about the Camera and Photos apps. ■

IMPROVED XBOX ONE GAMING SUPPORT

Combine Windows 10 AE with Xbox One or the new Xbox One S for 4K gaming and make gameplay more fun and more social.

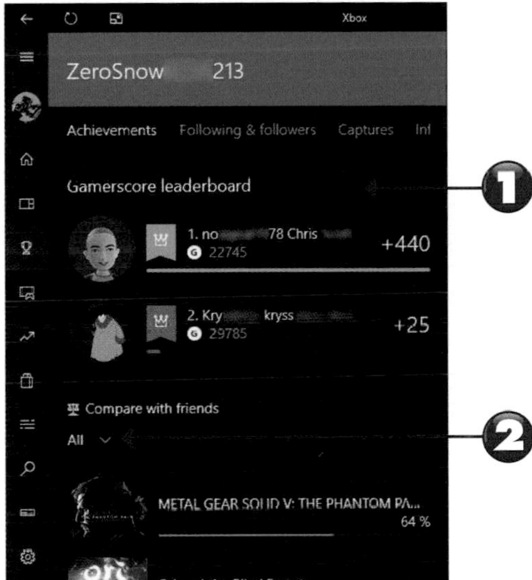

1. The Xbox app lets you view recent activity of friends you're connected to.
2. You can easily compare your scores with friends.
3. Use the improved Game DVR feature to capture, play, and share video clips from your PC or Xbox.

End

NOTE

Get Your Game On See Chapter 17, "Gaming," to learn more about the Gaming app. ■

IMPROVED ONEDRIVE CLOUD STORAGE

In Windows 10 AE, OneDrive provides easier management of your cloud storage.

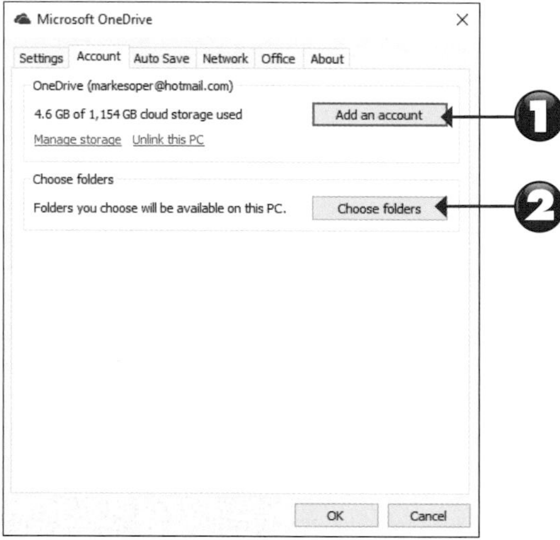

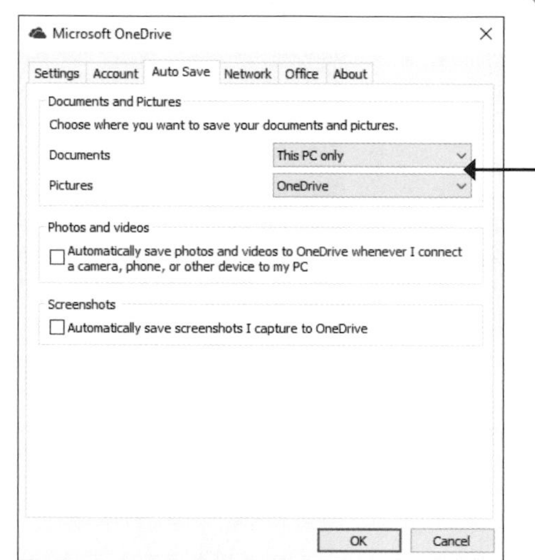

Start

1. Have a large OneDrive? Use the Account tab to "share the wealth" with another account.
2. Choose the OneDrive folders to sync with your device.
3. Use the Auto Save tab to place your choice of documents, pictures, photos, videos, and screenshots on OneDrive.

End

NOTE

Drive to Chapter 14 You can learn more about OneDrive and local storage in Windows 10 AE in Chapter 14, "Storing and Finding Your Files." ■

NEW GROOVE MUSIC

Windows 10 AE includes the new Groove Music app, bringing easy access to music stored locally or on the cloud and support for third-party streaming music apps.

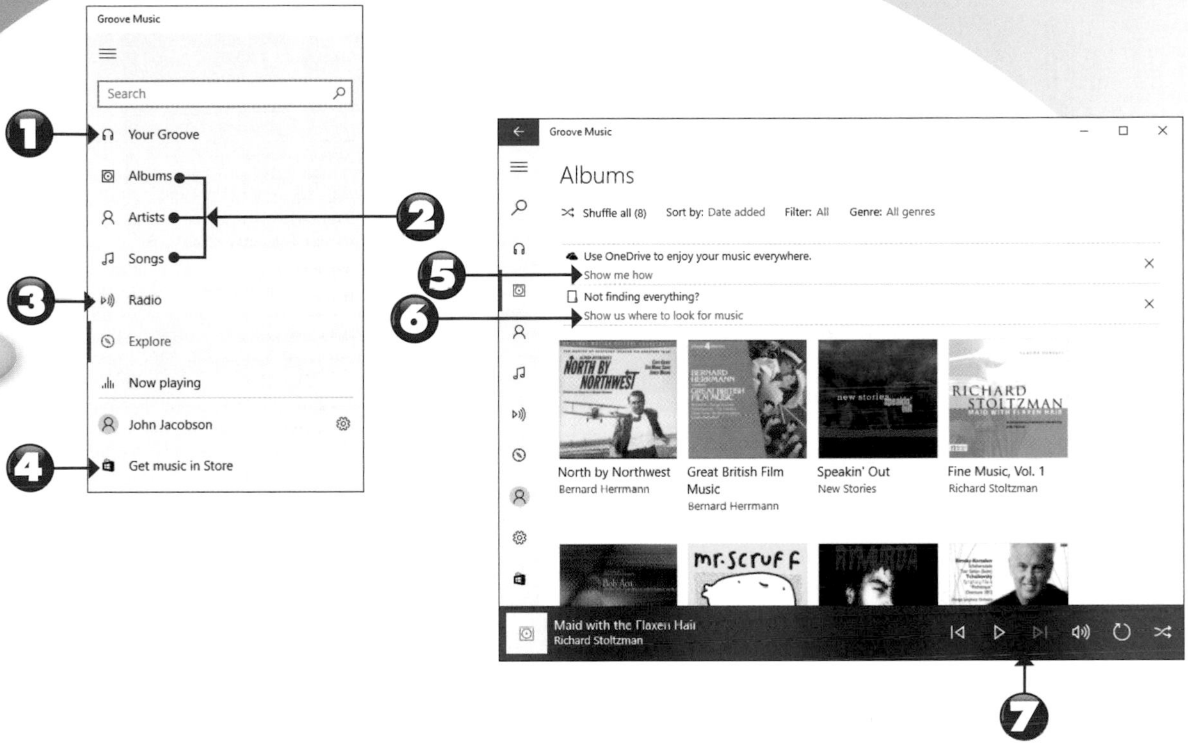

Start

1. You can use Your Groove to discover your recent songs.
2. Find music by albums, artists, or songs.
3. Sign up for a free trial of Groove Music Pass and create customized radio stations based on your favorites.
4. Want more music? Go directly to the Windows Store to shop for more.
5. Take your music with you everywhere by adding it to your OneDrive cloud storage.
6. Easily add more locations to find more music on your device or network.
7. Playback controls are always available in Groove Music.

NOTE

More Groove in Chapter 8 See Chapter 8, "Playing and Creating Music and Audio," to learn more about using Groove Music. ■

UPGRADING TO WINDOWS 10 AE

You can install Windows 10 Anniversary Edition (AE) as an upgrade to either Windows 7 or Windows 8.1, retaining your existing apps, settings, and personal data. You can purchase the software license and upgrade from Microsoft or from third-party vendors in two forms: a downloadable file or a USB flash drive that contains the upgrade files. In this chapter, we cover the process of upgrading to Windows 10 AE using the media creation tool to help you download the upgrade.

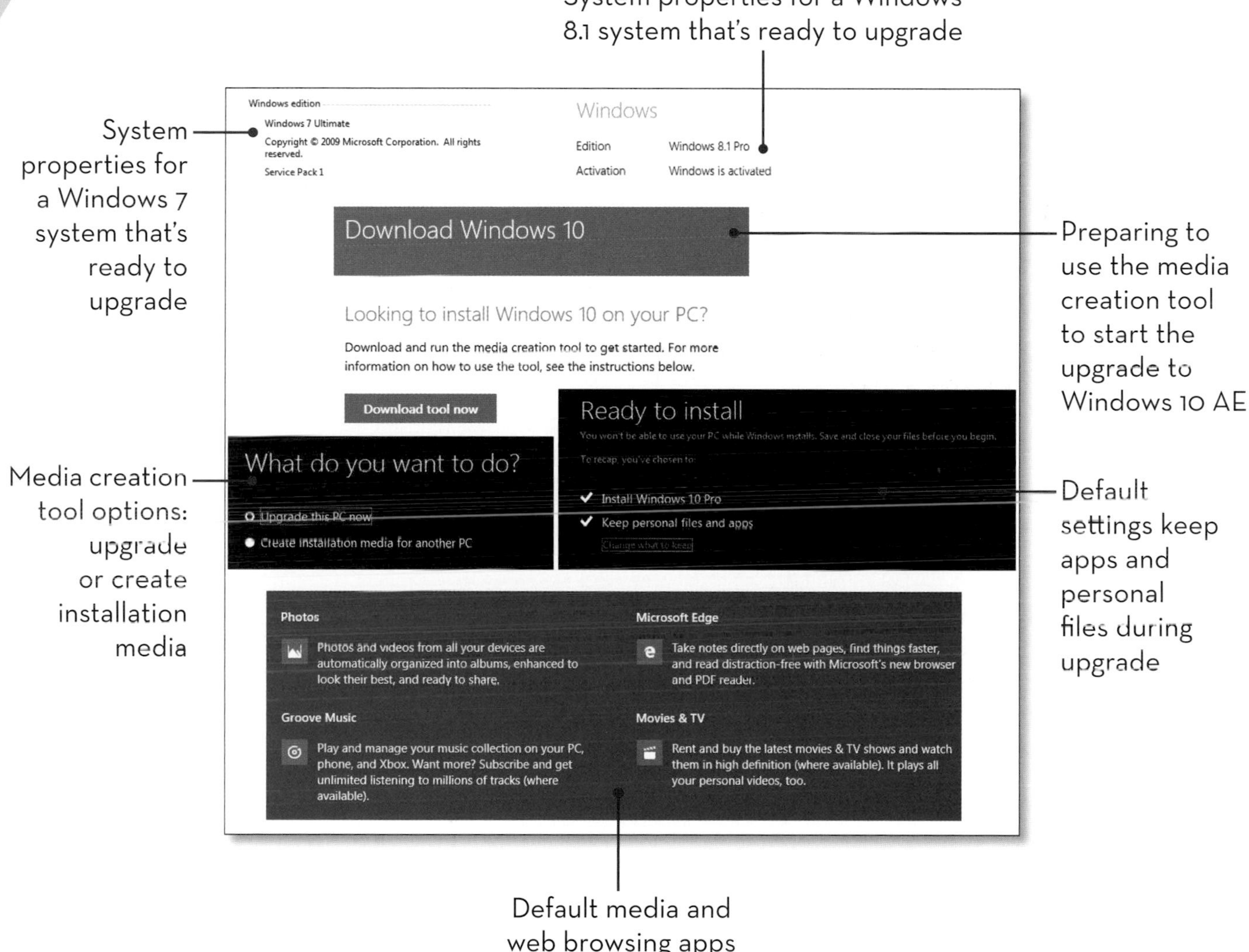
System properties for a Windows 8.1 system that's ready to upgrade
System properties for a Windows 7 system that's ready to upgrade
Windows edition
Windows 7 Ultimate
Copyright © 2009 Microsoft Corporation. All rights reserved.
Service Pack 1
Windows
Edition
Windows 8.1 Pro
Activation
Windows is activated
Download Windows 10
Preparing to use the media creation tool to start the upgrade to Windows 10 AE
Looking to install Windows 10 on your PC?
Download and run the media creation tool to get started. For more information on how to use the tool, see the instructions below.
Download tool now
Ready to install
Media creation tool options: upgrade or create installation media
What do you want to do?
Upgrade this PC now
Create installation media for another PC
Install Windows 10 Pro
Keep personal files and apps
Default settings keep apps and personal files during upgrade
Photos
Photos and videos from all your devices are automatically organized into albums, enhanced to look their best, and ready to share.
Microsoft Edge
Take notes directly on web pages, find things faster, and read distraction-free with Microsoft's new browser and PDF reader.
Groove Music
Play and manage your music collection on your PC, phone, and Xbox. Want more? Subscribe and get unlimited listening to millions of tracks (where available).
Movies & TV
Rent and buy the latest movies & TV shows and watch them in high definition (where available). It plays all your personal videos, too.
Default media and web browsing apps in Windows 10 AE

DETERMINING THE UPGRADE YOU NEED IN WINDOWS 7

Windows 10 AE is available in two versions: Windows 10 Home and Windows 10 Pro. Follow this procedure in Windows 7 to make sure you order the correct upgrade.

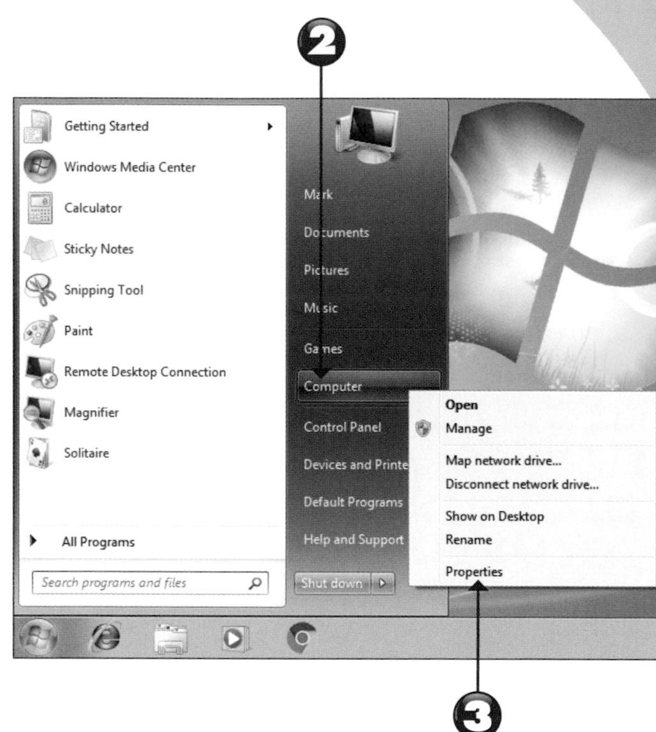

Start

1. Click or tap **Start**.
2. Right-click or press and hold **Computer**.
3. Click or tap **Properties**.

Continued

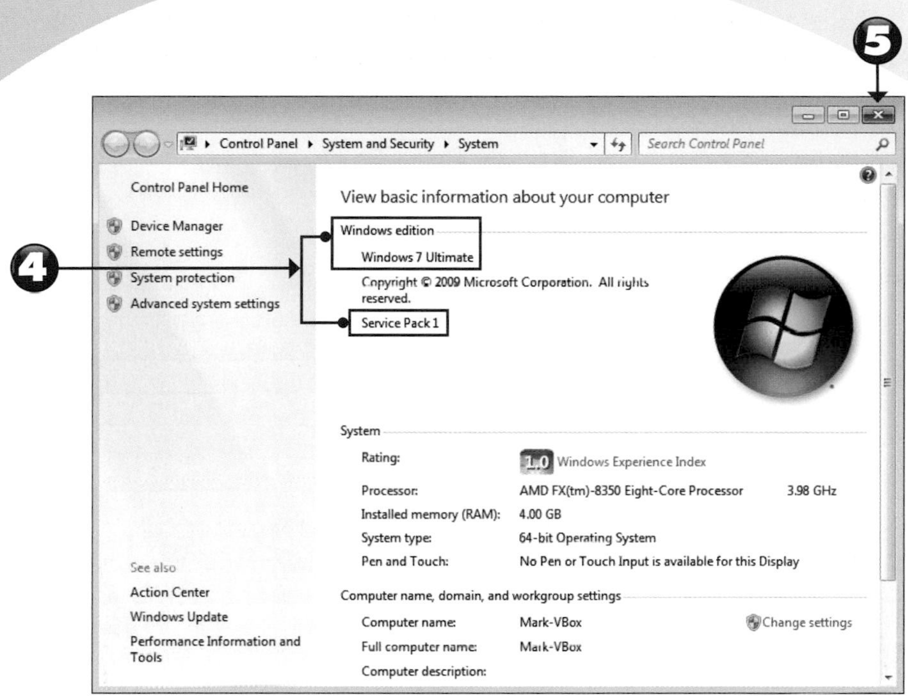

4 This system is running Windows 7 Ultimate with Service Pack 1.

5 Click **Close** to exit.

End

TIP

Which Windows 10 AE Version to Order? If your Windows 7 version is Windows 7 Ultimate or Professional, order Windows 10 Pro. If it is Windows 7 Home Premium or Home Basic, order Windows 10 Home. If it is Windows 7 Enterprise, upgrades are provided by the organization that supports the computer.

DETERMINING THE UPGRADE YOU NEED WITH WINDOWS 8.1

Windows 10 AE is available in two versions: Windows 10 Home and Windows 10 Pro. Follow this procedure in Windows 8.1 to make sure you order the correct upgrade.

Start

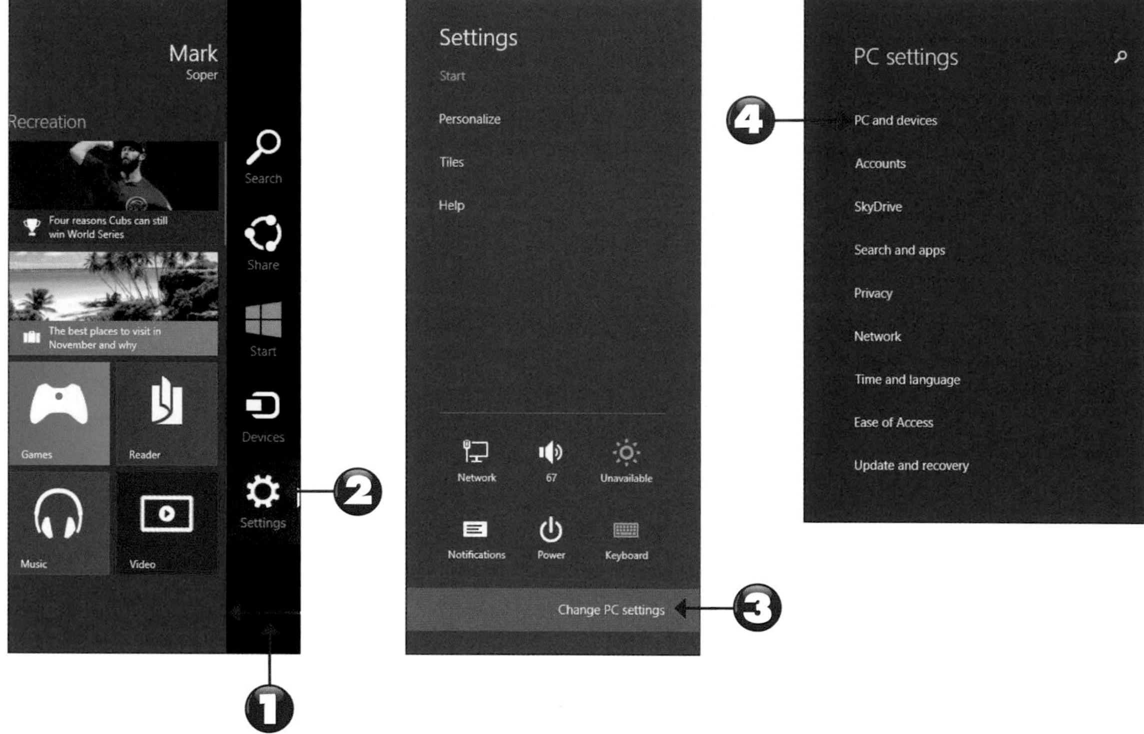

1. From the Start screen, point to the lower-right corner (mouse) or flick the right edge of the screen (touchscreen).
2. Click or tap **Settings**.
3. Click or tap **Change PC settings**.
4. Click or tap **PC and devices**.

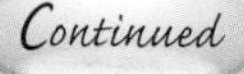

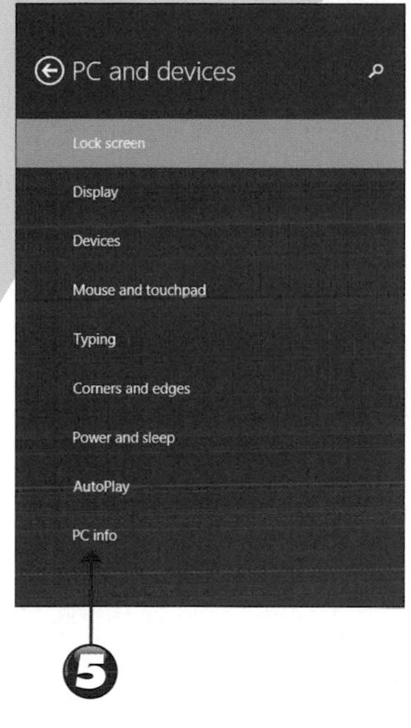

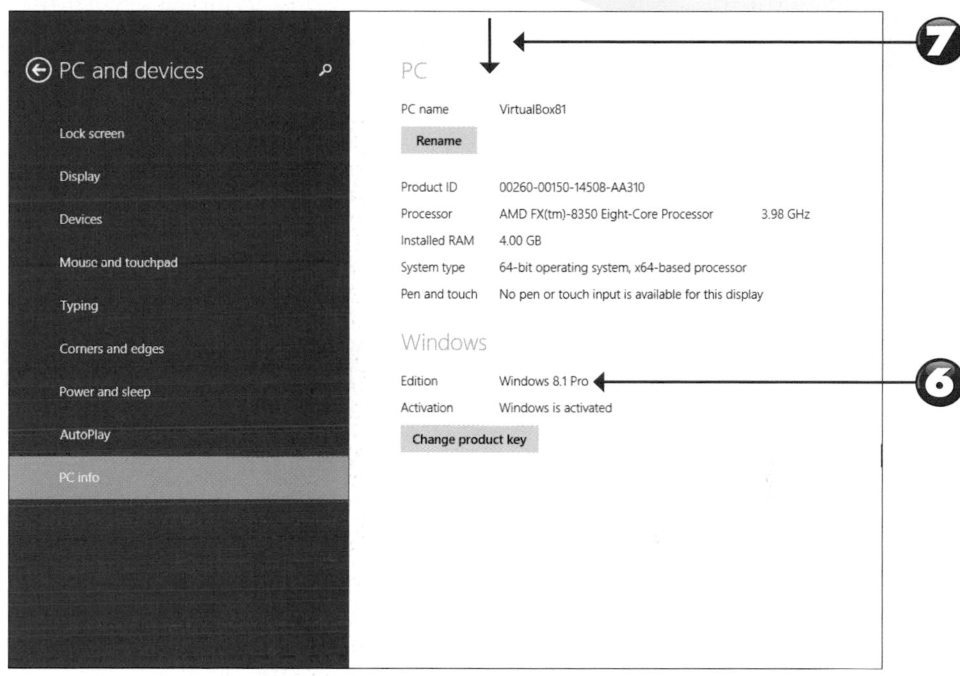

5 Click or tap **PC info**.

6 This computer is running Windows 8.1 Pro.

7 To close this window, click or press and drag at the top of the window and drag it down to the bottom of the screen until it disappears.

End

TIP

Which Windows 10 AE Version to Order? If your Windows 8.1 version is Windows 8.1 Pro, order Windows 10 Pro. If it is Windows 8.1 Home Premium or Home Basic, order Windows 10 Home. If you are still running Windows 8 Home or Pro, get the free upgrade to Windows 8.1 from the Windows Store before upgrading to Windows 10. If it is Windows 8 or 8.1 Enterprise, upgrades are provided by the organization that provides the computer.

INSTALLING THE UPGRADE WITH THE MEDIA CREATION TOOL

You must purchase a license for Windows 10 to install it, because the free upgrade offer ended in July 2016. When you purchase a license, you can use the Download Windows 10 web page to perform the upgrade process. Note that this discussion uses default settings. If you choose custom setup options later in the process, some steps will be different from those shown here.

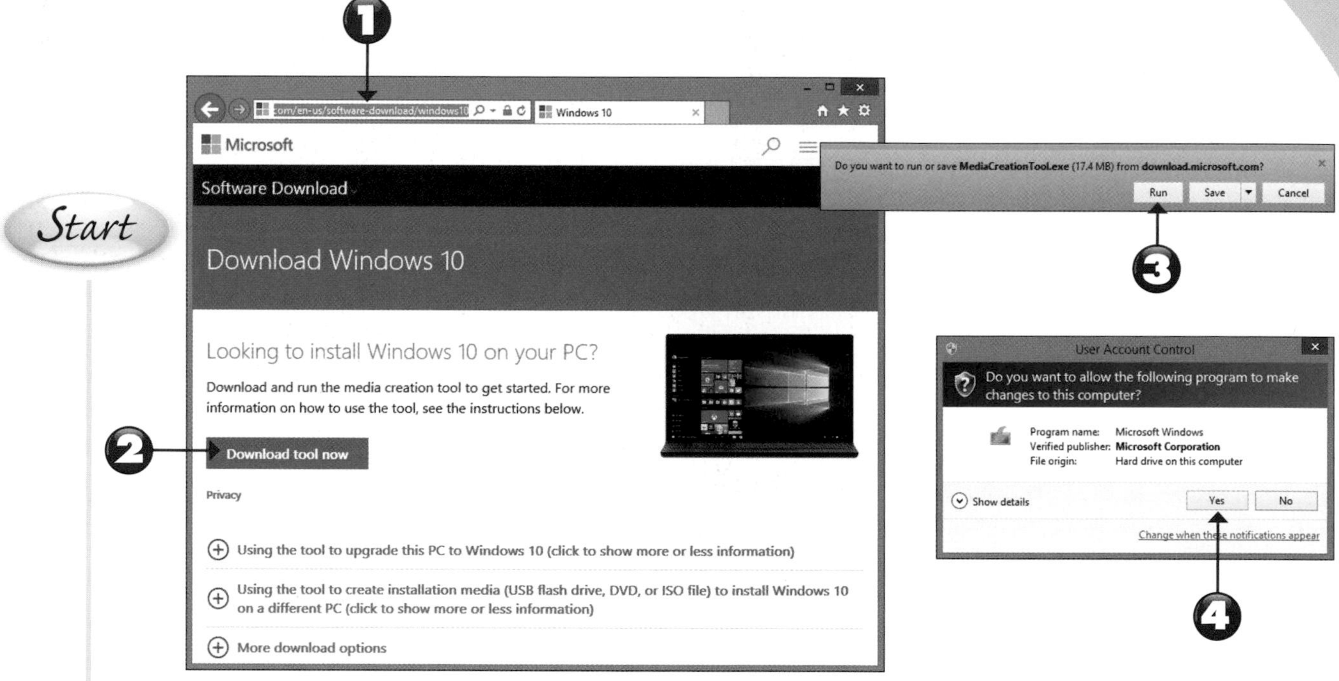

1. Open your web browser and go to https://www.microsoft.com/software-download/windows10.
2. Click or tap **Download tool now**.
3. Click or tap **Run** when prompted.
4. Click or tap **Yes** in the User Account Control dialog box.

Continued

NOTE

Creating Install Media When you reach step 6, you can choose to create installation media (USB flash drive or DVD) for another computer. Choose this option if you don't want to install Windows 10 AE on this computer right now.

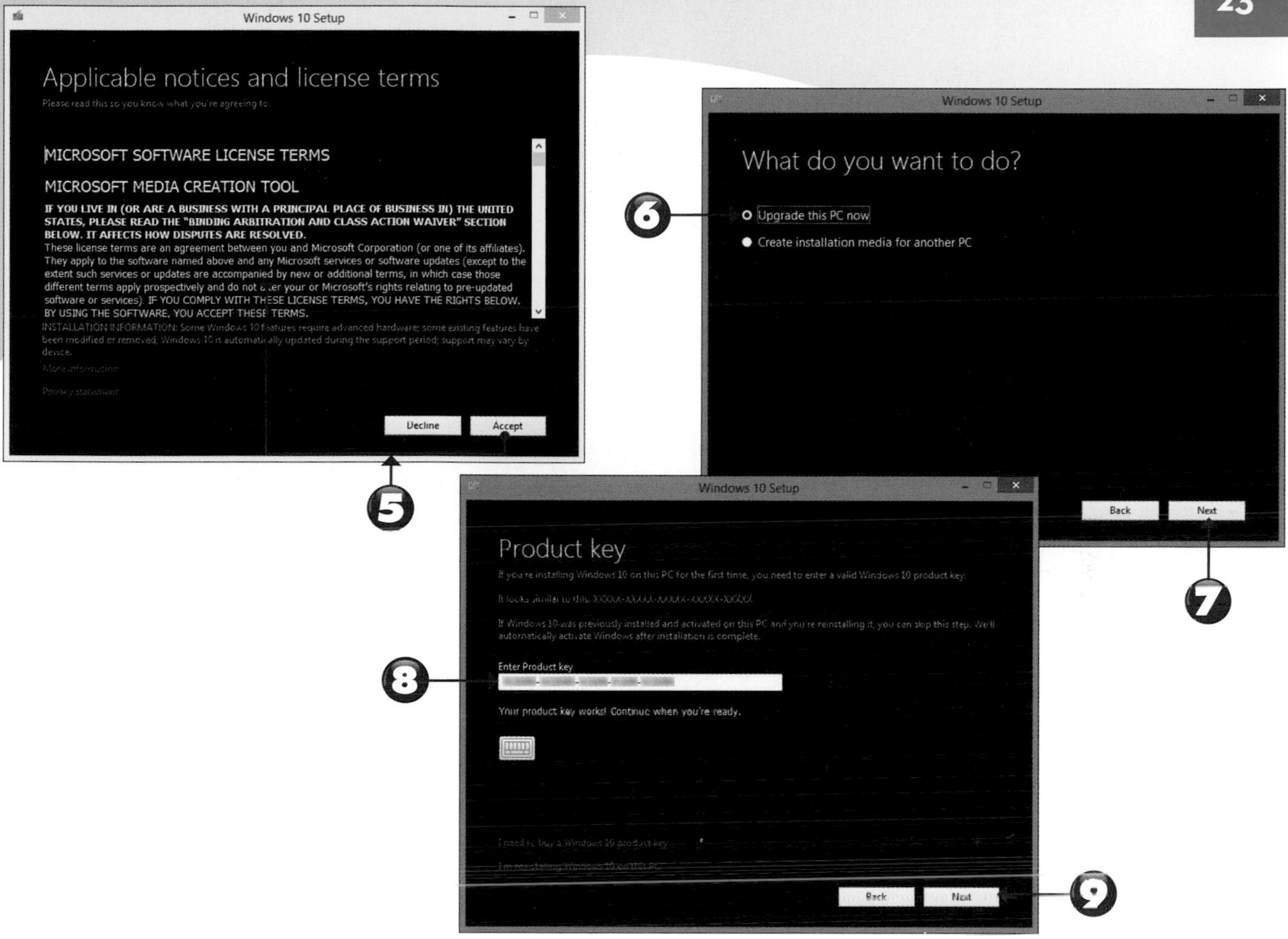

5 Review the agreement, and then click or tap **Accept**.

6 Click or tap **Upgrade this PC now**.

7 Click or tap **Next** to continue.

8 After Windows 10 is downloaded, you are prompted to provide the license key you received when you purchased Windows. For a new installation, enter it.

9 Click or tap **Next** to continue.

Continued

NOTE

Reinstalling Windows 10 When you reach step 8, if you have already installed and activated Windows 10 on this computer, choose **I'm reinstalling Windows 10 on this PC**. You can continue without entering your product key again.

NOTE

Forgot to Buy a Key? If you don't yet have a valid product key when you reach step 8, you can click or tap **I need to buy a Windows 10 product key**, and you will be directed to the Microsoft website for ordering.

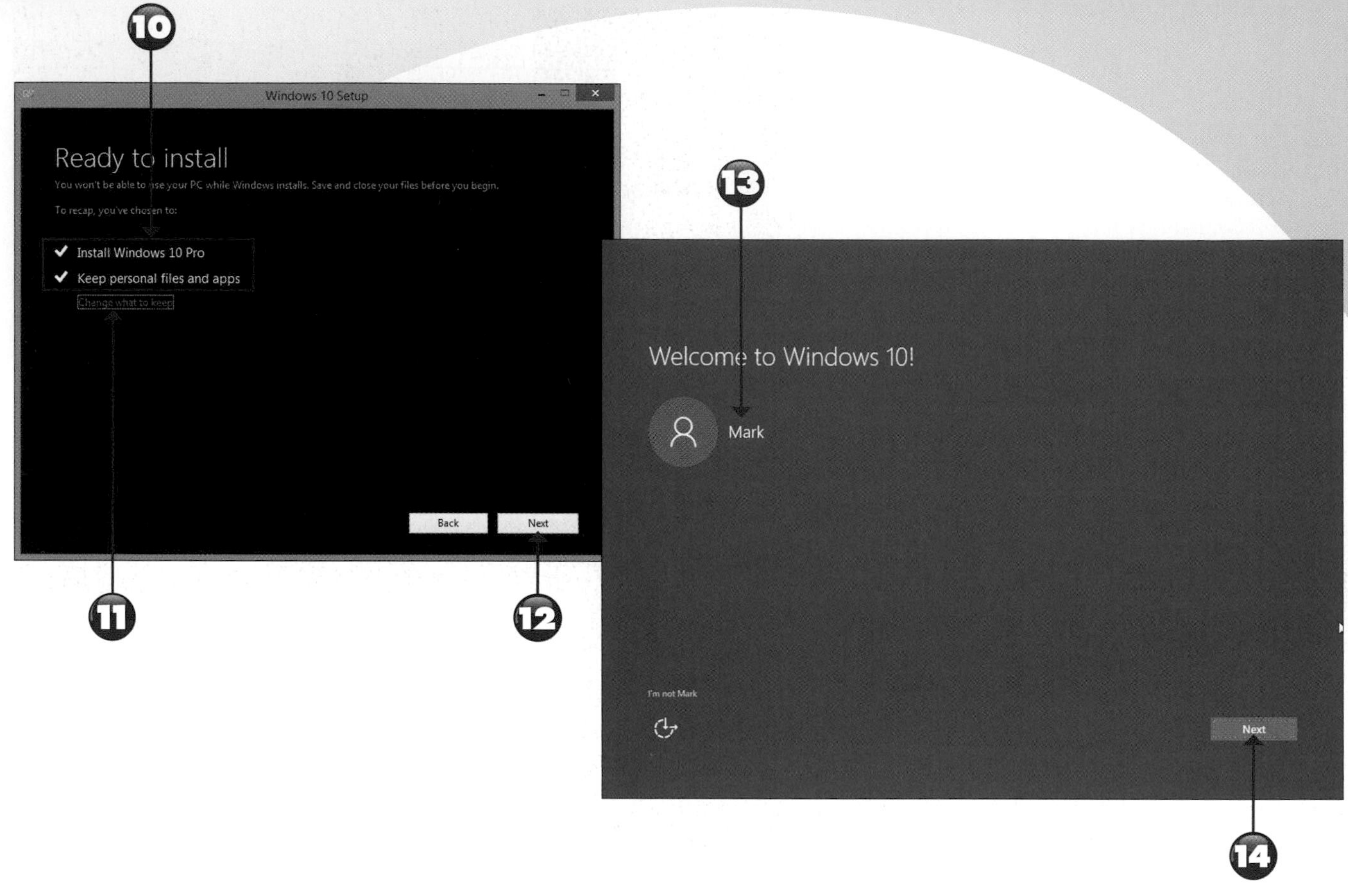

10 Default settings for the upgrade.

11 Click or tap here to change what to keep.

12 Click or tap **Next** to continue.

13 The welcome screen displays your user name.

14 Click or tap **Next** to continue.

Continued

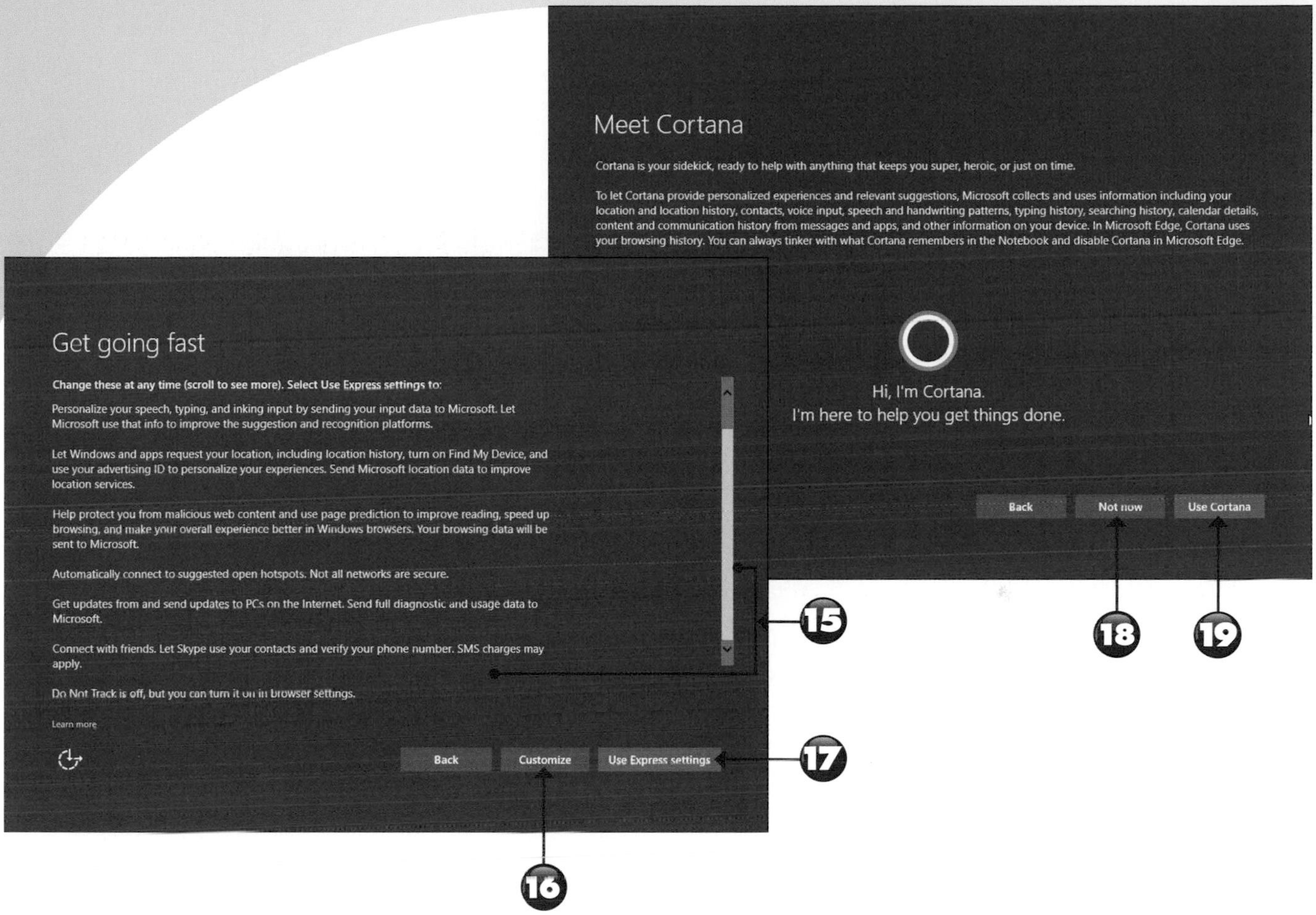

15 Review what Windows 10 AE's Express Settings do.

16 To change, click or tap **Customize**.

17 To use default settings, click or tap **Use Express settings**.

18 To skip setting up Cortana now, click or tap **Not now**.

19 To use Cortana, click or tap **Use Cortana**.

Continued

NOTE

Cortana Now or Later? If you don't set up Cortana when you install Windows 10, some search features are limited. We recommend enabling it during installation.

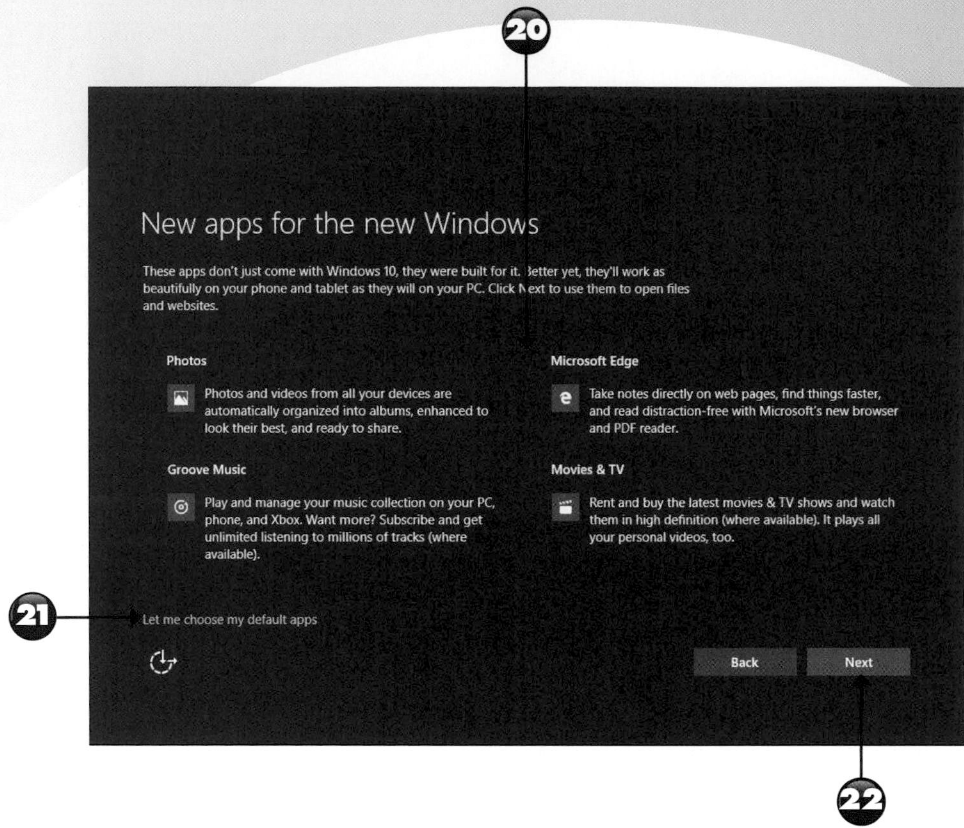

20 The default Windows 10 AE apps for photos, web browsing, music, and movies & TV are listed here.

21 If you want to choose your own default apps, click or tap **Let me choose my default apps**.

22 To use the default apps, click or tap **Next**.

Continued

23 The Windows 10 AE lock screen. Begin the login process here.

End

NOTE

Logging in with a Touchscreen If your device uses a touchscreen, go to Chapter 3, "Logging In, Starting Up, and Shutting Down Windows 10 Anniversary Edition with a Touchscreen." ■

NOTE

Logging in with a Mouse and Keyboard If your device uses a mouse and keyboard, go to Chapter 4, "Logging In to Windows 10 Anniversary Edition and Customizing the Start Menu." ■

LOGGING IN, STARTING UP, AND SHUTTING DOWN WINDOWS 10 ANNIVERSARY EDITION WITH A TOUCHSCREEN

Whether you're upgrading from Windows 7, switching to a new PC after running older versions of Windows, or upgrading from Windows 8/8.1, Windows 10 Anniversary Edition is designed to work the way you're accustomed to working. In this chapter, you find out how to use a touchscreen (such as those found on tablets, convertible 2-in-1 devices, or some all-in-one desktops) to log in to Windows, move around the Windows menus, and lock, sleep, or shut down your system. If you use a mouse and keyboard instead of a touchscreen, skip ahead to Chapter 4, "Logging In to Windows 10 Anniversary Edition and Customizing the Start Menu."

Closing a Modern UI/Universal app by dragging it downward
All Apps, Most Used, and Recently Added apps menus in Tablet Mode
Logging in with the touch keyboard
Expanded Start menu
Handwriting recognition
Click or tap to enable Tablet mode
Mark Soper
Recently added
Feedback Hub
Most used
ScreenHunter 6.0 Free
Alarms & Clock
Suggested
Dictionary.
Free*
3D Builder
Acrobat Reader DC
Mark Soper
File Explorer
Settings
Power
Tablet mode
Not connected
Note
10:57 AM
8/30/2016
mark
marks
Mark
Marks
Maris
Marie
Marin
Mark

LOGGING IN WITH A TOUCHSCREEN

To log in to Windows 10 Anniversary Edition, you must know the username and password (if any) set up for your account. If you installed Windows 10 AE yourself, be sure to make note of this information when you are prompted to provide it during the installation process. You also log in to Windows 10 AE when you are waking up the computer from sleep, unlocking it, or restarting it.

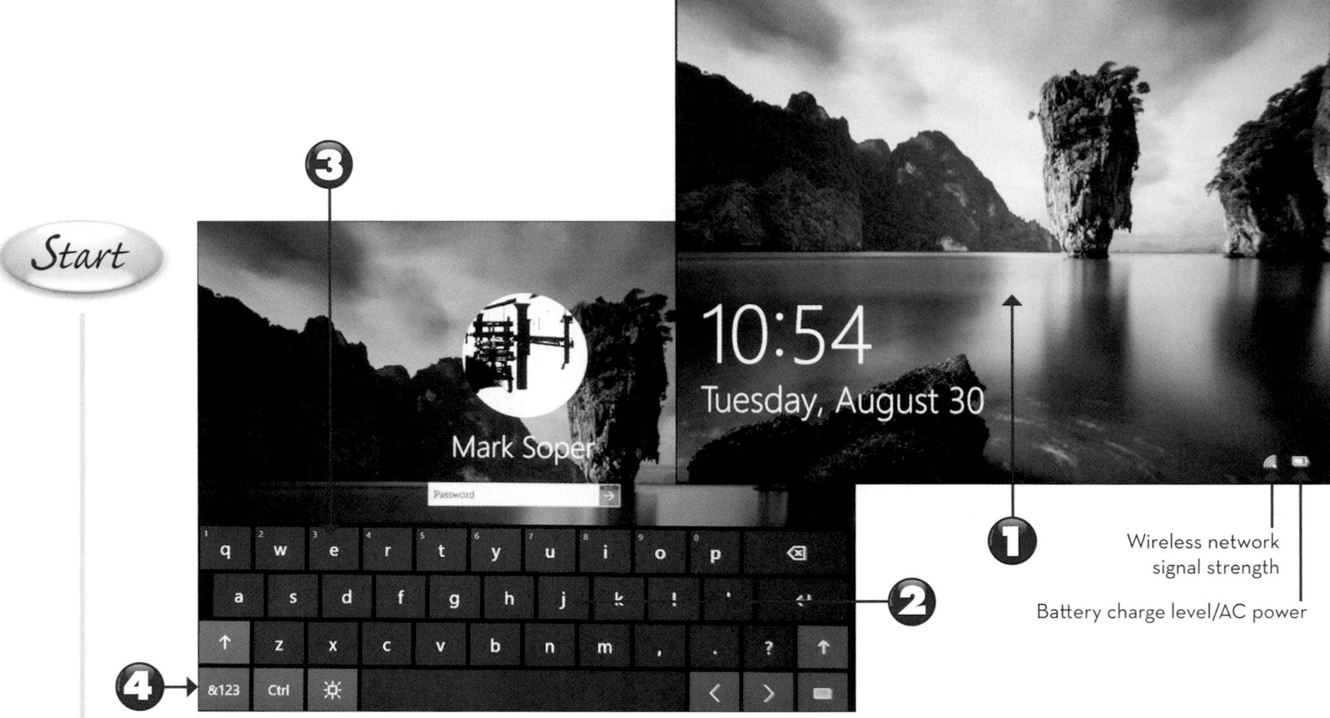

1. Tap your touchscreen and drag it upward when the Lock screen appears.
2. The alphabetic keyboard appears first.
3. Tap each letter in your password.
4. Tap to switch to the symbols and numbers keyboard.

Continued

5 Tap symbols and numbers in your password.

6 To see your password as you enter it, hold down the eye symbol (visible after you enter at least one character of your password).

7 Tap twice to start Windows.

End

NOTE

Touch Keyboards and Handwriting Recognition The touch keyboard works with any app that uses the keyboard and is also used to start the handwriting recognition feature. See "Using Handwriting Recognition," p. 38, this chapter, for details.

NOTE

Logins for Multiple Users If you have more than one user set up on your computer, there are additional steps to follow. See the section "Selecting an Account to Log In To," in Chapter 22, "Adding and Managing Users," for details.

THE START AND ALL APPS MENUS IN TABLET MODE

Devices that do not have a physical keyboard (or have the keyboard detached or folded away) typically start Windows 10 Anniversary Edition in Tablet Mode. In this lesson, you learn the major features of Tablet Mode.

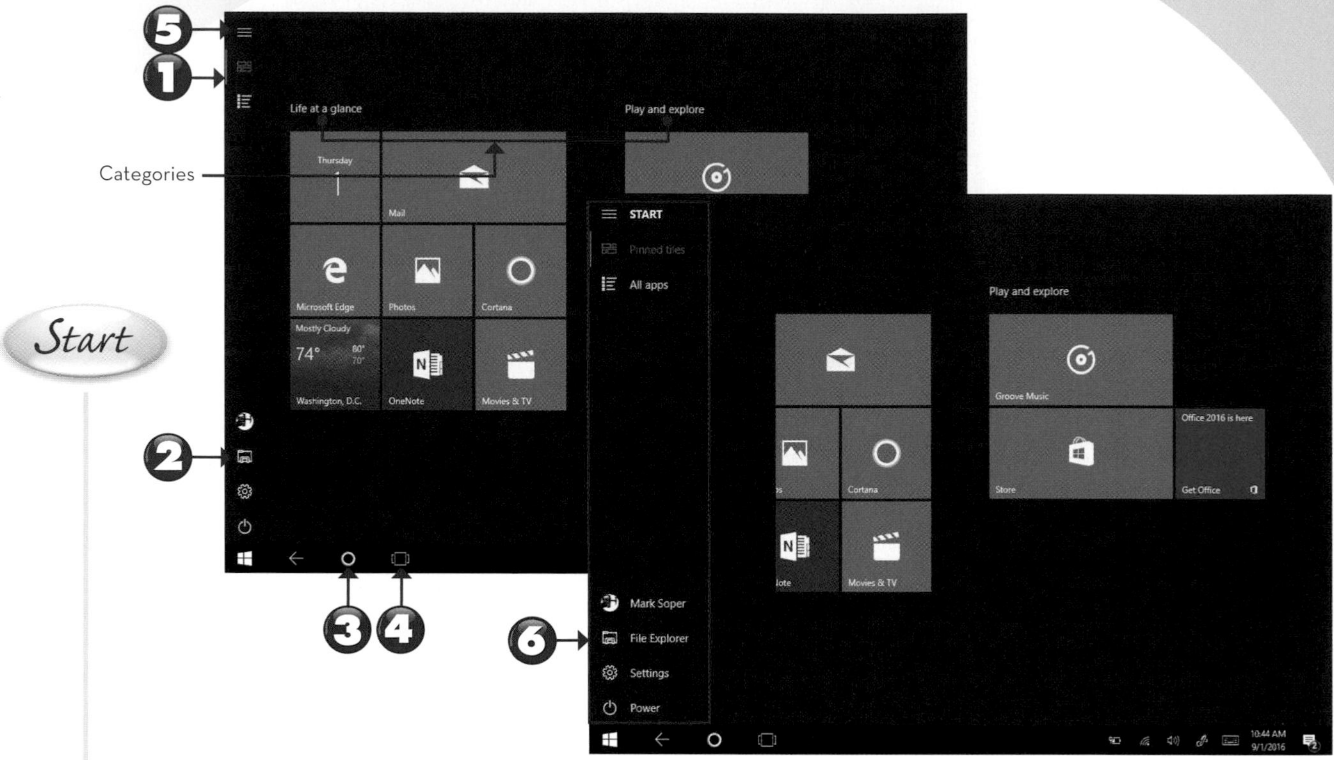

1. The Pinned Tiles menu opens by default.
2. Tap to open File Manager.
3. Tap to open the Cortana Search box.
4. Tap to open Task Switcher.
5. Tap to expand the Start menu.
6. Expanded Start menu.

Continued

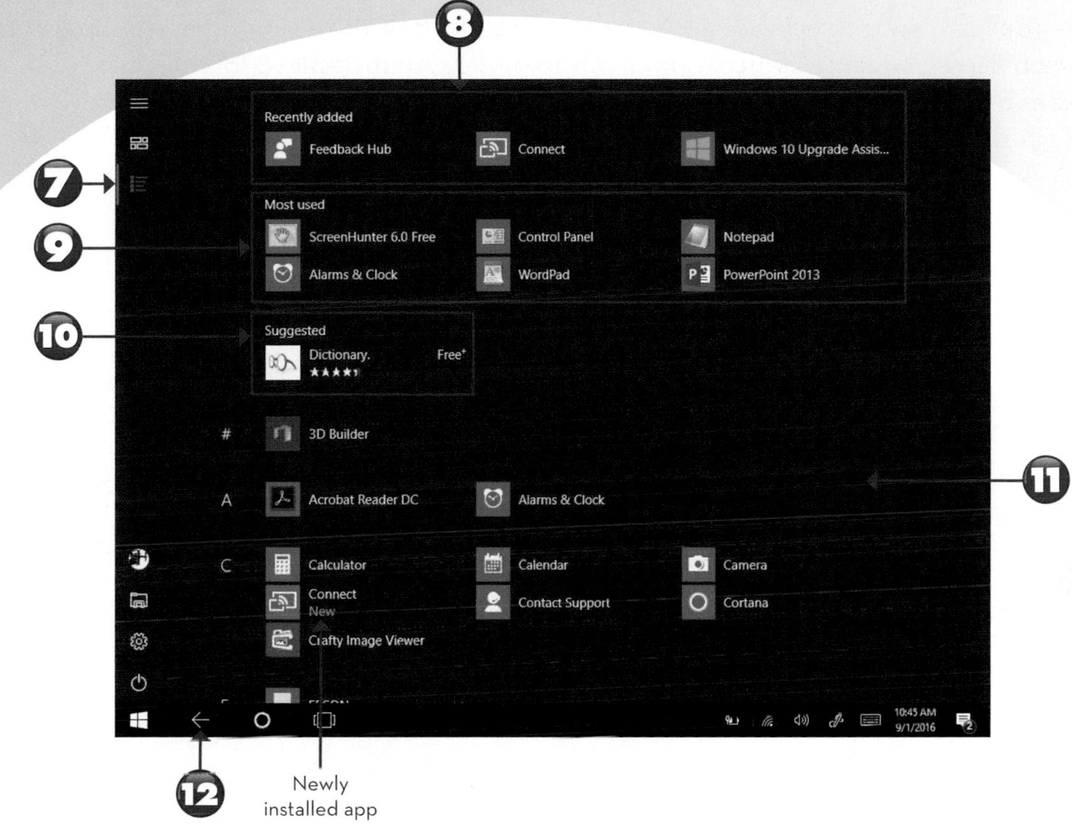

7. Tap to open the All apps menu.

8. Recently added apps.

9. Most-used apps.

10. Tap to install a suggested app.

11. Scroll down to see apps in alphanumeric order.

12. Click or tap to return to the previous view.

End

ENABLING TABLET MODE

As you have seen in the previous lessons, Tablet Mode is designed to be touch-friendly. If you use a convertible or two-in-one (tablet plus laptop) device, Tablet Mode might not be configured to start automatically. If Tablet Mode did not start automatically when you started Windows, you can start it from the Notifications menu. Here's how.

Start

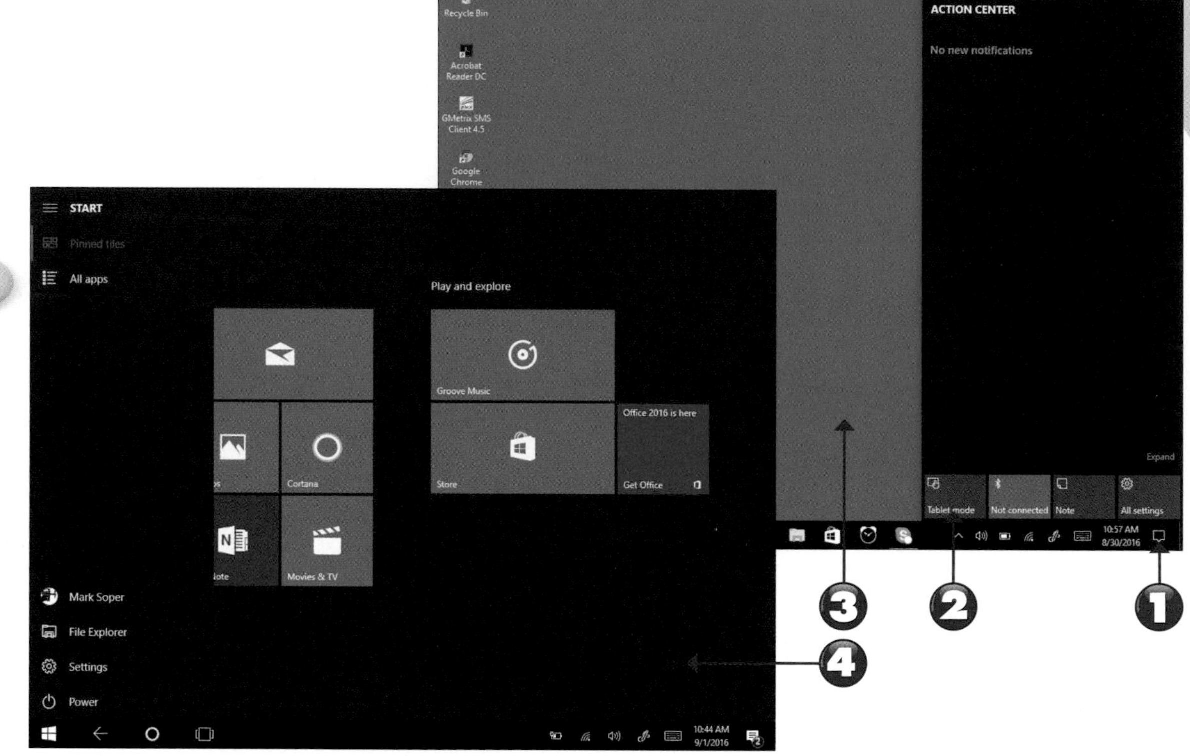

1. Click or tap the **Notifications/Quick actions** button.

2. Tap to toggle **Tablet Mode** off or on. (Off has a darker button.)

3. Tap an empty area of the screen to close Notifications.

4. The system has switched to Tablet Mode.

End

NOTE

Learning More about Tablet Mode You can configure Tablet Mode by using the Tablet Mode menu in the Settings dialog box's System menu. See Chapter 19, "Managing Windows 10 AE," for details. ■

STARTING AND CLOSING A UNIVERSAL OR MODERN UI APP

Modern UI apps and Universal apps (which work on any Windows device, including Windows 10 Mobile) are optimized for touchscreens. Although they are started the same way in either regular or Tablet Mode, Tablet Mode uses a different way to close them. In this example, I start and close Calculator from the All Apps menu.

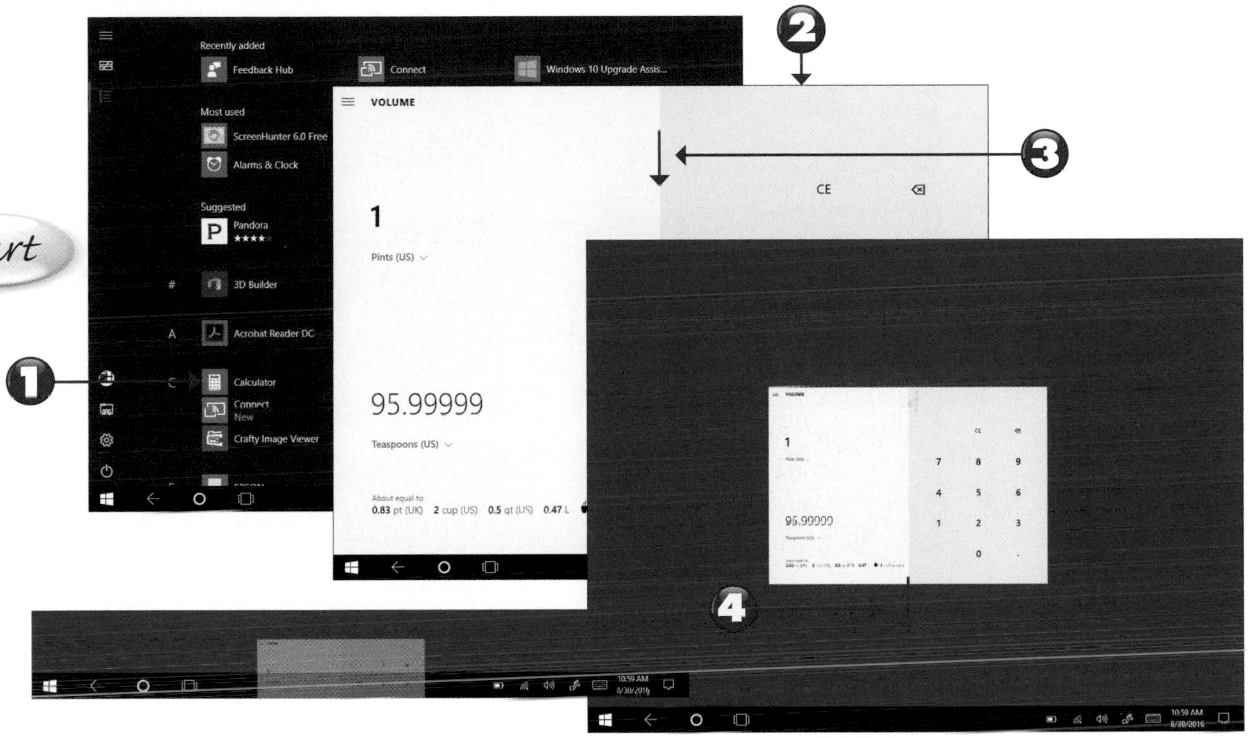

1. Tap a Modern UI or Universal app to start it.
2. When you are finished using the app, press and hold the top edge of the screen.
3. Drag the app downward.
4. Continue to drag the app window down until it disappears. The Tablet Mode Start menu appears immediately afterward.

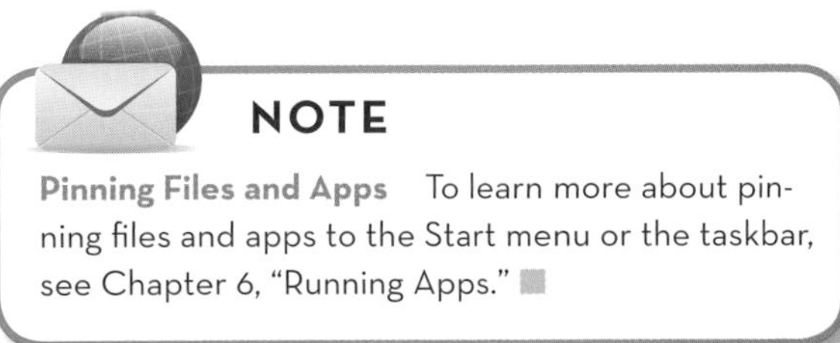

NOTE

Pinning Files and Apps To learn more about pinning files and apps to the Start menu or the taskbar, see Chapter 6, "Running Apps."

LOCKING YOUR PC

If you have a password on your account, you can lock your PC when you leave it and unlock it when you return. On laptop and desktop computers, you typically lock your system with the Windows key+L combination. However, you can also lock it with a touchscreen. Here's how.

Start

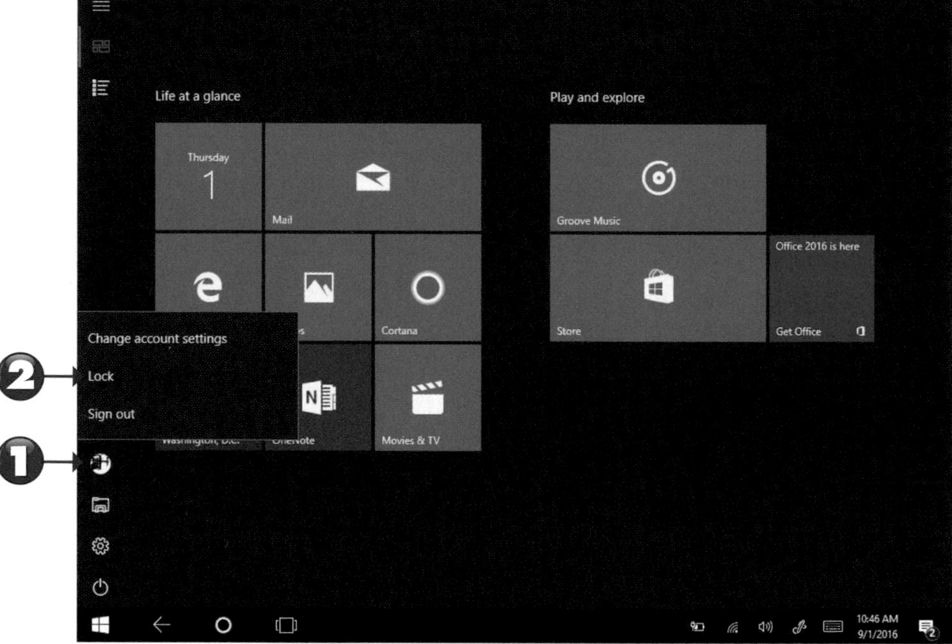

1. Tap your icon or username.
2. Tap **Lock**.

End

NOTE

Logging Back In to Your System To log back in to your system, follow the procedure given earlier in this chapter in "Logging In with a Touchscreen."

NOTE

Other Options To sign out, tap **Sign out** from the menu. To view and change account settings, tap **Change account settings**. For details about account settings, see Chapter 22, "Adding and Managing Users."

CHOOSING SLEEP, SHUT DOWN, OR RESTART

When it's time to put away the computer, Windows 10 Anniversary Edition makes it easy. Want to go back to work (or play) right where you left off? Choose Sleep. Want to "put away" your PC and start fresh next time? Choose Shut Down. In this lesson, you learn how to perform these tasks using the Start menu's Power button. These same tasks can also be performed from the login screen shown earlier in this chapter.

Start

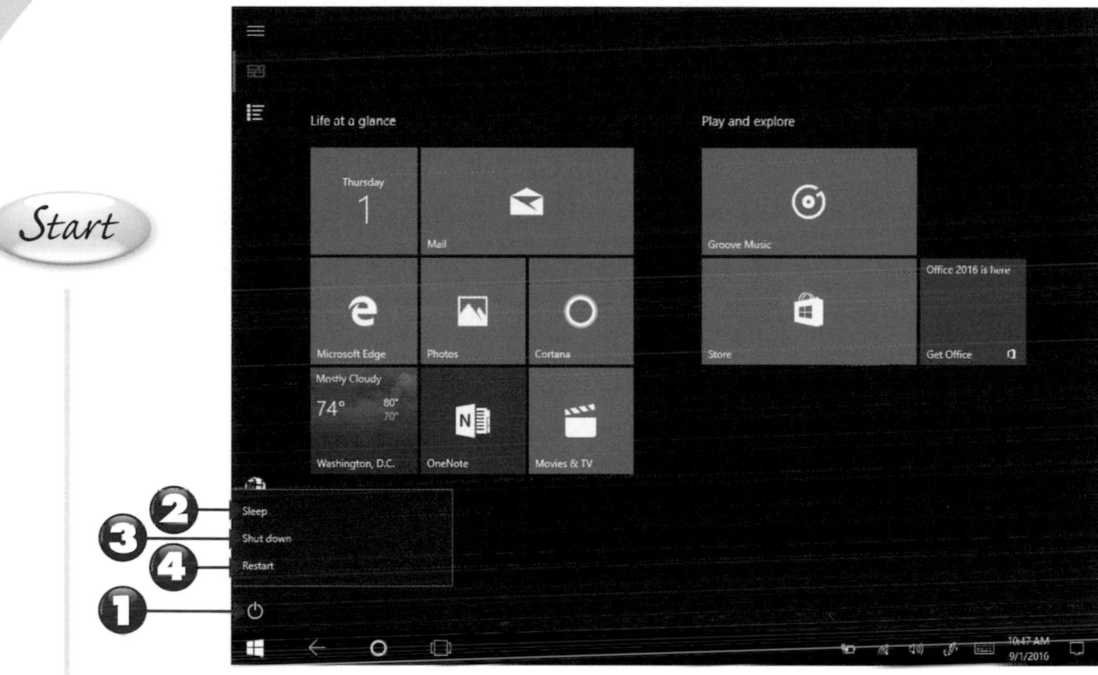

1. Tap the **Power** button.

2. Tap **Sleep** to put the device into low-power mode.

3. Tap **Shut down** to shut down the device.

4. Tap **Restart** to close Windows AE and restart it.

End

CAUTION

Power Options from the Login Screen The Power button is also available from the login screen and works the same way as from the Start menu. However, if you select **Shut down** or **Restart** when you or other users are logged in to the system, you are warned that shutting down or restarting can cause data loss. Be sure that any logged-in users have saved their work and closed their apps before you shut down or restart Windows AE. ■

USING HANDWRITING RECOGNITION

On tablets and laptops with touchscreens, the touch keyboard can also be used for text input using handwriting recognition. And if you have a touchpad with a stylus, you can also use this feature. Here's how to switch to and use handwriting recognition from the touch keyboard, using WordPad (found in the Windows Accessory folder in All Apps) as the app in this example.

Start

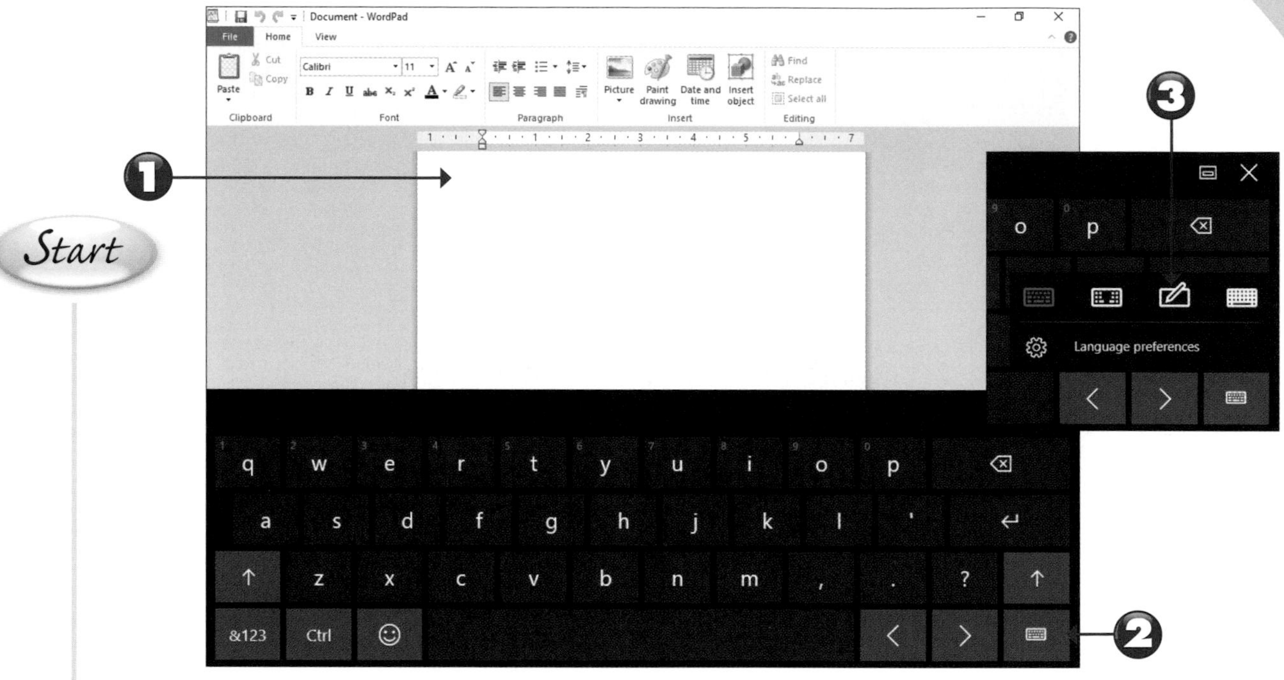

1. Tap the text input window or screen.
2. When the touch keyboard appears, tap the keyboard button.
3. Tap the **stylus** button.

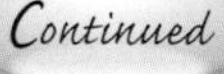

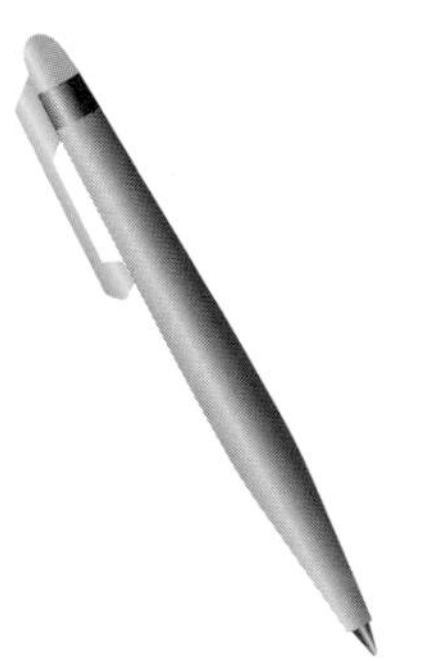

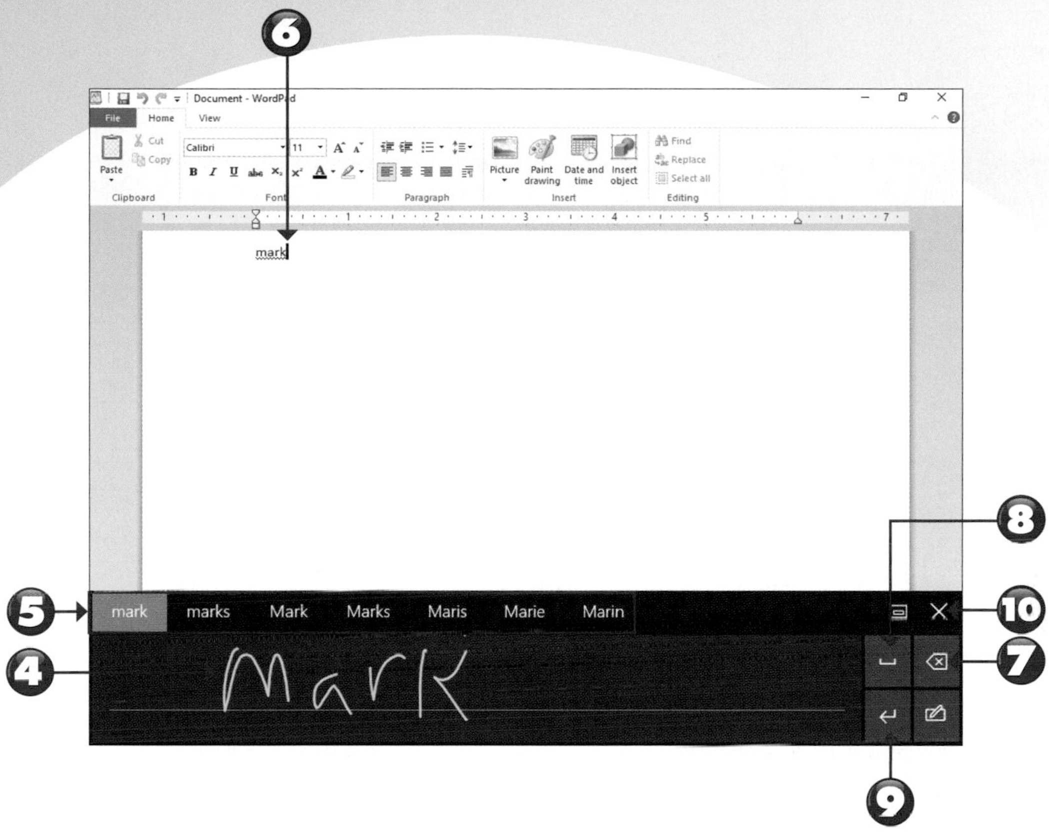

4 Print the text you want to insert with your finger or stylus.

5 If your printing is misrecognized, tap the correct word from the list (if present).

6 The text is automatically inserted into your text input area as it is recognized.

7 Tap the backspace button to remove any erroneous printing.

8 Tap the spacebar button to add a space.

9 Tap the Enter (Return) button to start a new paragraph.

10 Tap to close the keyboard.

End

LOGGING IN TO WINDOWS 10 ANNIVERSARY EDITION AND CUSTOMIZING THE START MENU

This chapter shows you how to log in to Windows 10 AE and navigate the standard Windows desktop and Start menu with a mouse and a keyboard. Whether you use a mouse/keyboard or touchscreen, you find out how to customize the Start menu's contents.

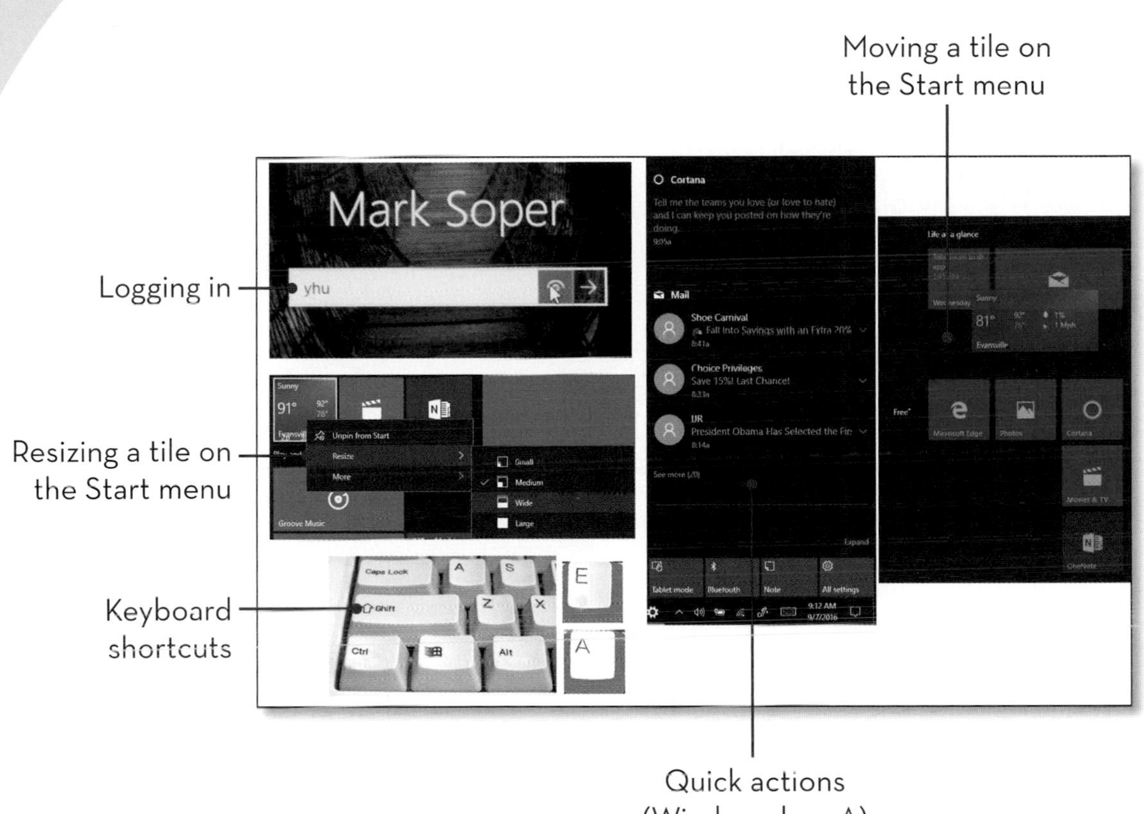

Moving a tile on the Start menu
Logging in
Resizing a tile on the Start menu
Keyboard shortcuts
Quick actions (Windows key+A)
Mark Soper

LOGGING IN TO WINDOWS 10 AE

To log in to Windows 10 AE, you must know the password (if any) to the account you want to log in to. If you installed Windows 10 AE yourself, be sure to make note of this information when you are prompted to provide it during the installation process. You also log in to Windows 10 AE when you are waking up the computer from sleep, unlocking it, or restarting it.

Start

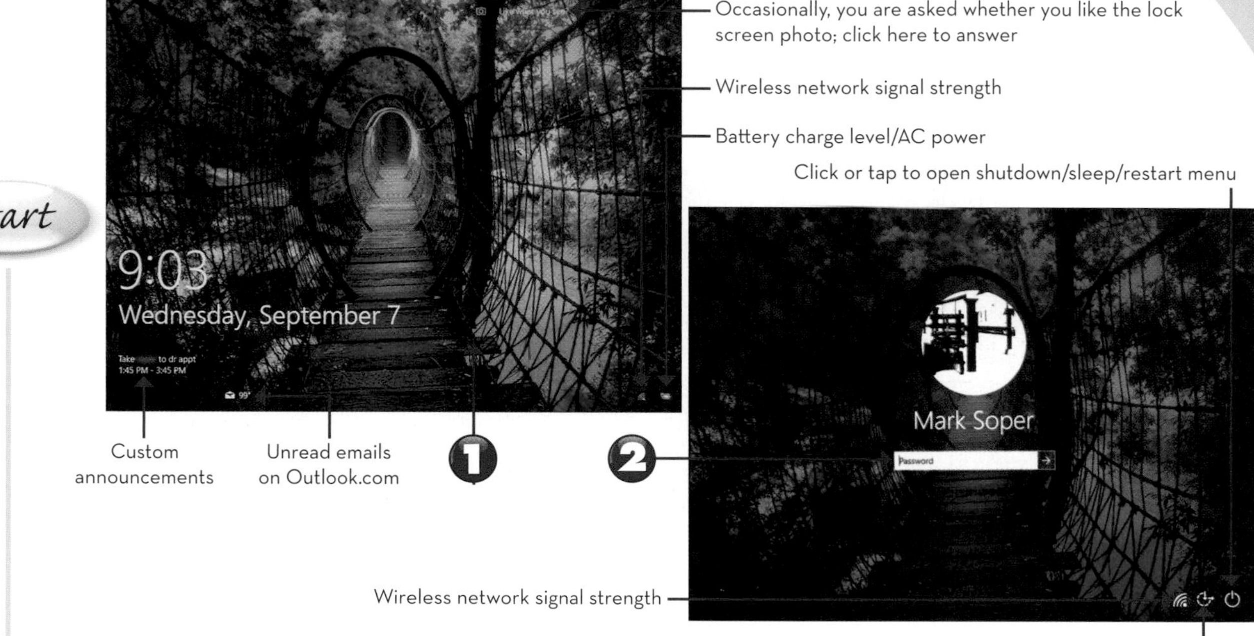

1. Press the spacebar, click your mouse, or tap your touchpad when the Lock screen appears.
2. Type your password.

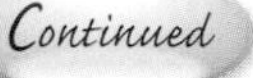

3 To see your password as you enter it, click or press and hold the eye icon. (You must type at least one character to see this icon.)

4 Password characters are visible when you click or press the eye icon.

5 Press **Enter** or click the arrow. The Windows desktop appears.

End

NOTE

Logins for Multiple Users If you have more than one user set up on your computer, there are additional steps to follow. See the section "Selecting an Account to Log In To," in Chapter 22, "Adding and Managing Users," for details.

USING THE START MENU

Laptop and desktop computers running Windows 10 AE typically display the Windows desktop after login. In this exercise, you learn how to open the Start menu. You use the left button on your mouse, the lower-left corner of your device's integrated touchpad, or the Windows key on the keyboard or tablet.

Start

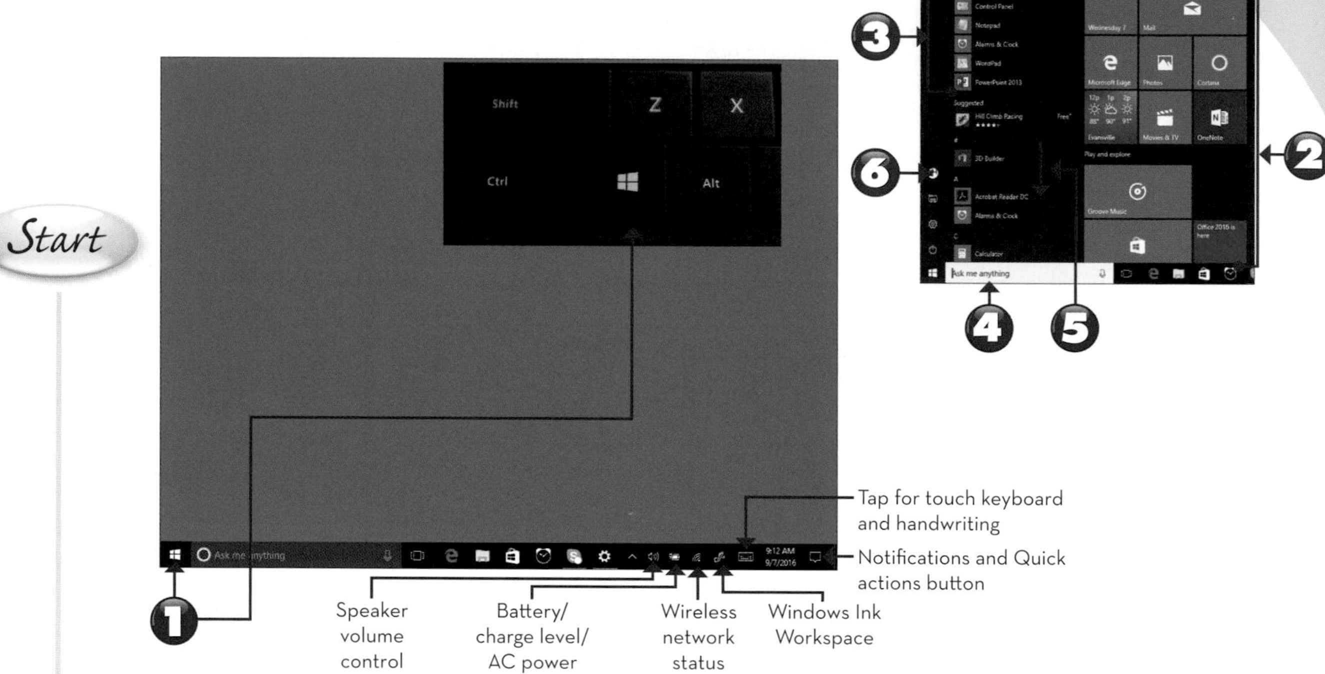

1. Click or tap the **Start** button in the lower-left corner of the desktop, or press the Windows key on the keyboard.
2. Links to Universal and Modern UI apps appear on the right side of the Start menu.
3. Shortcuts to frequently used apps are grouped here.
4. Use the Cortana Search window to find what you're looking for.
5. Scroll down to see all apps.
6. Click or tap to change account settings, log out, or lock the system.

End

USING KEYBOARD SHORTCUTS

This lesson illustrates a few of the dozens of Windows 10 AE shortcuts that use the Windows key.

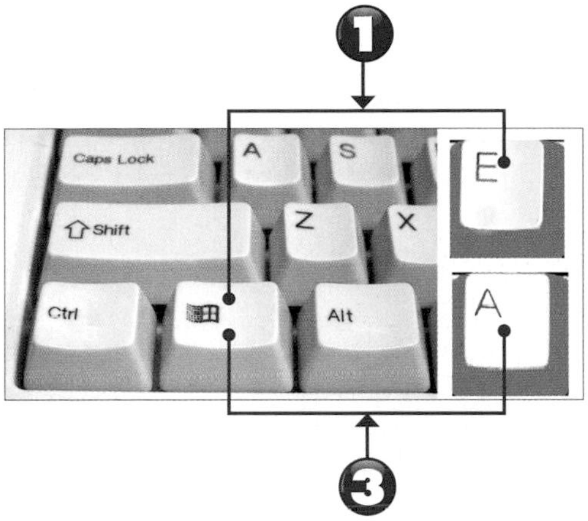

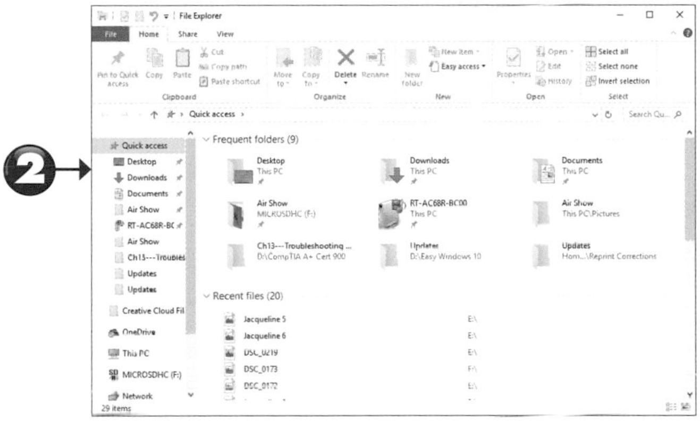

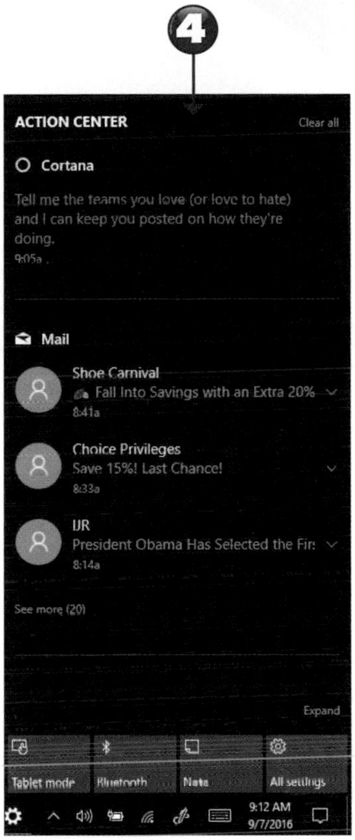

Start

1. Press **Windows key+E**.

2. The Quick access view of File Explorer opens on the Windows desktop.

3. Press **Windows key+A**.

4. The Notifications pane (Action Center and Quick actions) is displayed at the right of the Windows desktop.

End

NOTE

More Keyboard Shortcuts Some keyboard shortcuts used in Windows 7 and 8.1 also work in Windows 10 AE. For Microsoft's official list of keyboard shortcuts for Windows and apps, go to http://windows.microsoft.com/en-us/windows/keyboard-shortcuts and select the version of Windows you use.

RESIZING TILES ON THE START MENU

You can change the size of app tiles on the Start menu to help make them easier to use, smaller, or larger. In the example shown here, the Weather app is resized, showing how it can display more or less information as its size changes.

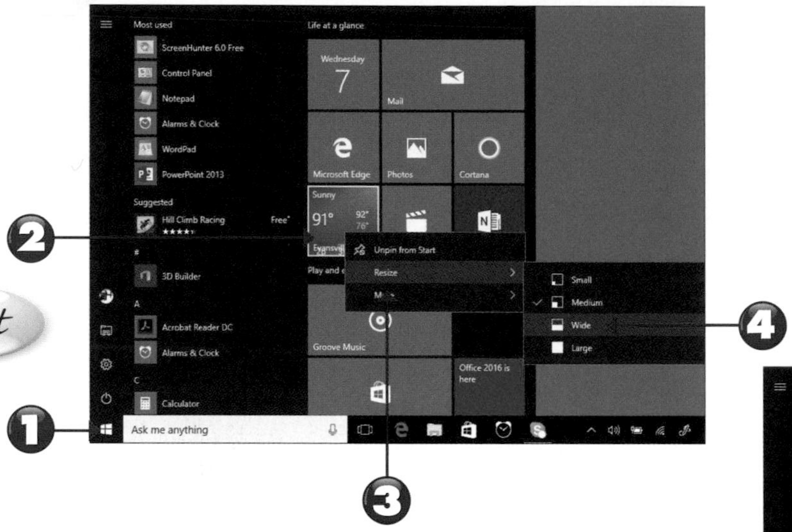

1. Click or tap **Start**.
2. Right-click the tile to resize.
3. Select **Resize**.
4. Select the size desired (Wide in this example.)
5. The tile is resized to occupy the space of two medium (the default size for most) tiles.

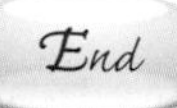

TIP

Removing Tiles or Changing Tile Sizes with a Touchscreen If you press and hold a Start menu icon, a thumbtack icon appears at the upper-right corner of the icon. Tap it to remove the app from the Start menu. In the lower-right corner, a three-dot button appears. Tap it to choose the icon size desired.

CHANGING TILE POSITIONS ON THE START MENU

Moving a tile to a new location is a simple drag-and-drop process, as this tutorial demonstrates.

Start

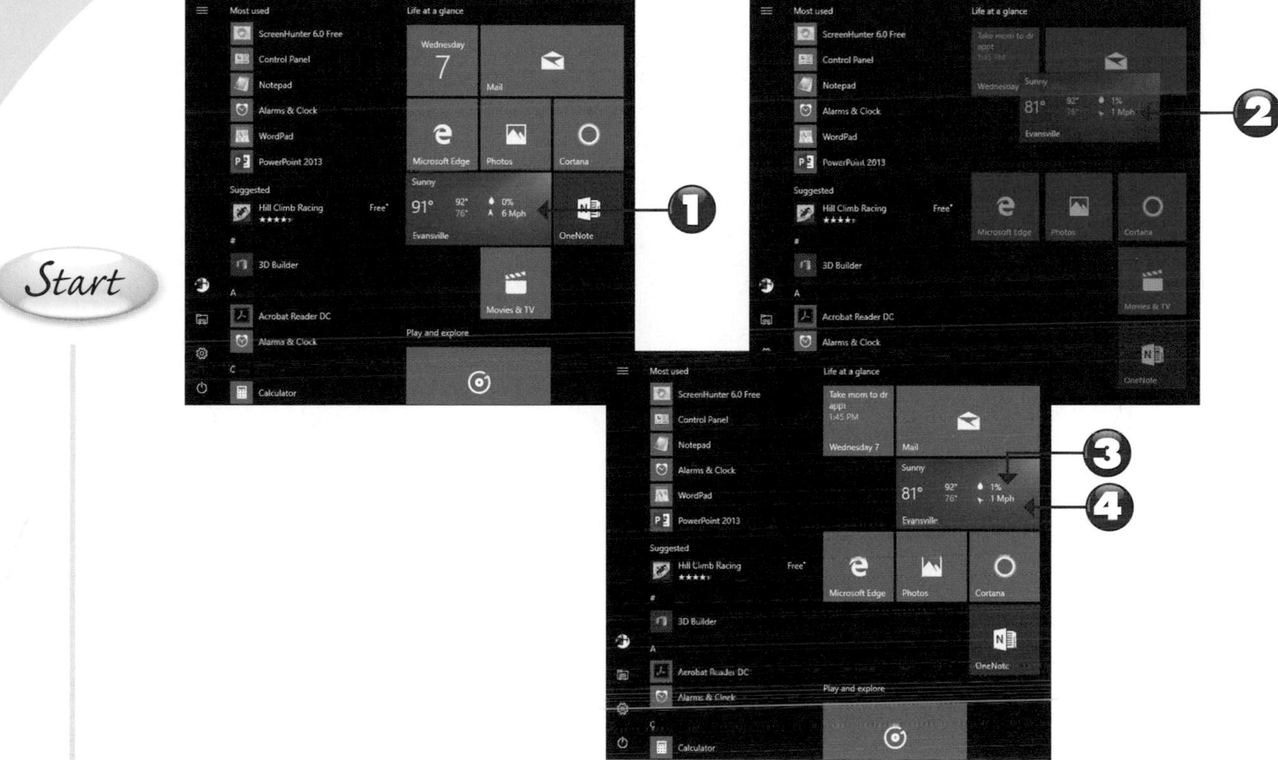

1. Click and hold or press and hold the tile to move it.
2. Drag it to the new location.
3. Release the tile when it is in the correct position.
4. The tile is in its new position.

End

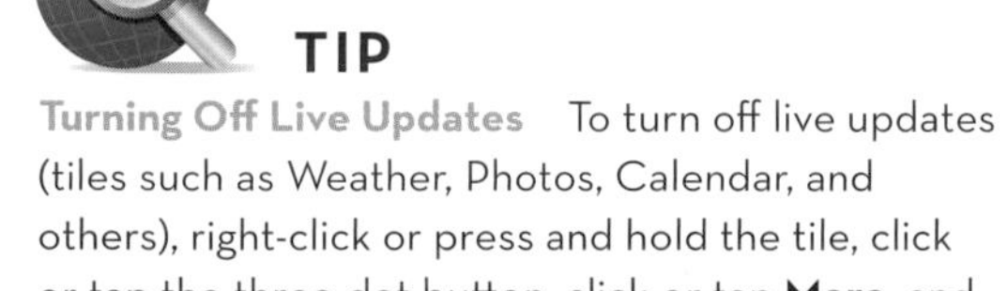

TIP

Turning Off Live Updates To turn off live updates (tiles such as Weather, Photos, Calendar, and others), right-click or press and hold the tile, click or tap the three-dot button, click or tap **More**, and click or tap **Turn live tile off**.

REMOVING AN APP FROM THE START MENU

You can remove an app from the Most used list on the left side of the Start menu or pinned app tiles from the right side of the Start menu. You can still run an app from All Apps, so use these methods for apps you don't use frequently.

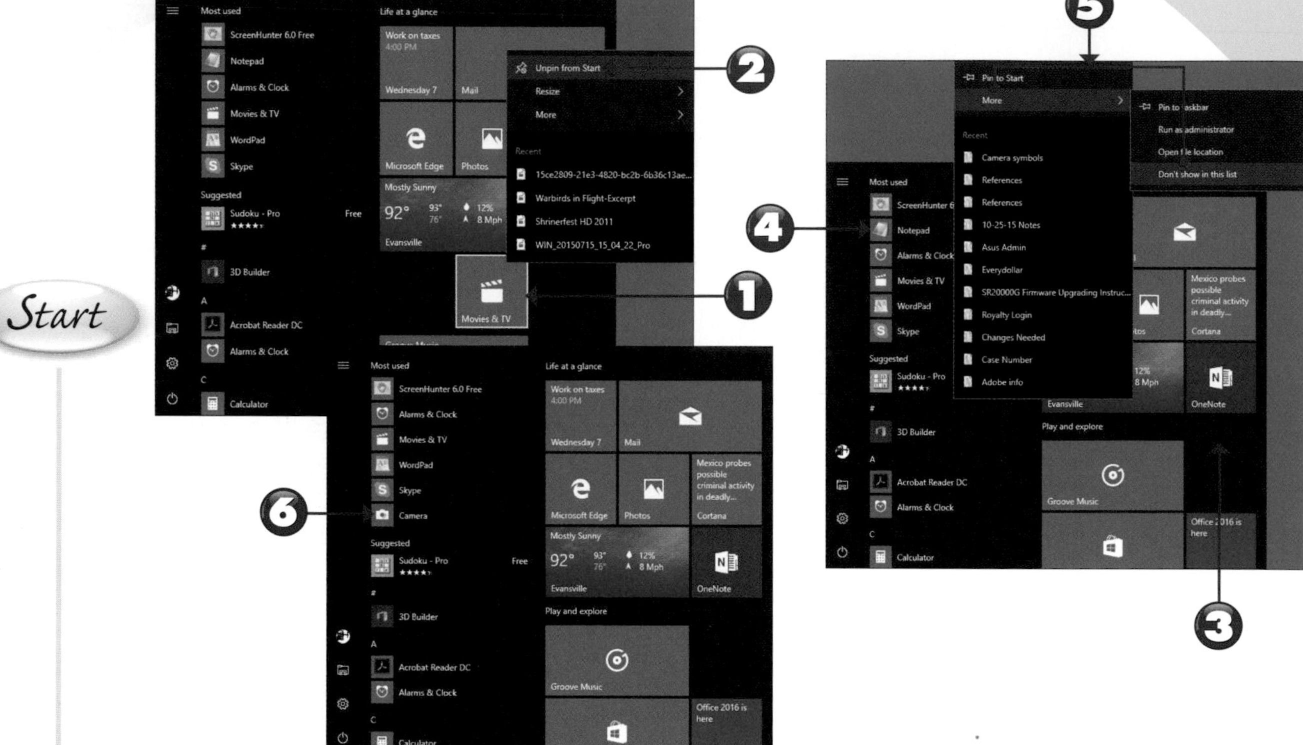

1. Right-click the tile you want to remove.

2. Click or tap **Unpin from Start**.

3. The tile is removed from the Start menu.

4. Right-click an app you want to remove from the Most used list.

5. Select **More**, and then click or tap **Don't show in this list**.

6. Another most-used app takes the place of the one you removed in step 5.

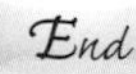

TIP

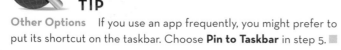

Other Options If you use an app frequently, you might prefer to put its shortcut on the taskbar. Choose **Pin to Taskbar** in step 5.

LOCKING YOUR SYSTEM

You can lock your system by clicking your name/icon in the Start menu. (For details, see Chapter 3, "Logging In, Starting Up, and Shutting Down Windows 10 Anniversary Edition with a Touchscreen.") However, you might prefer to use the keyboard, as shown in this lesson.

Start

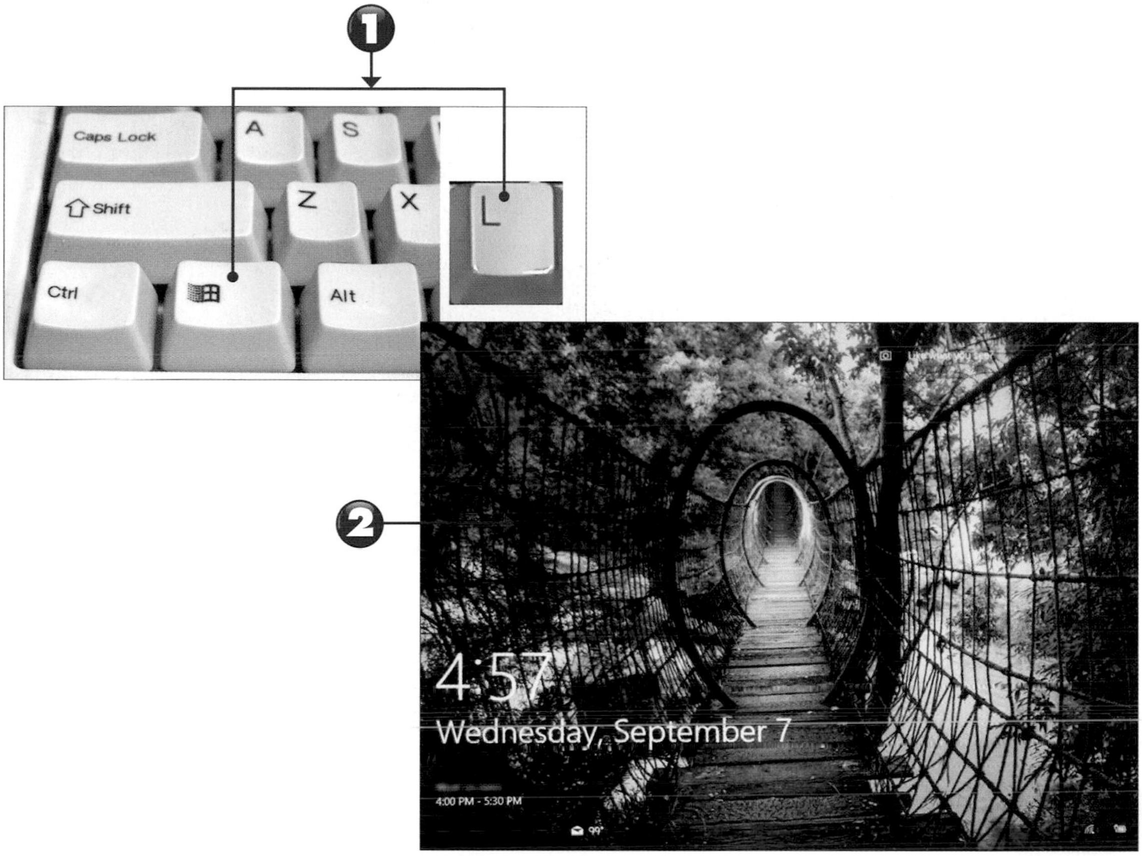

1. Press the **Windows key+L** key on your keyboard.

2. The Lock screen appears.

End

NOTE

Logging Back In To log back in, see "Logging In to Windows 10 AE," this chapter, p. 42.

CHOOSING SLEEP, SHUT DOWN, OR RESTART

When it's time to put away the computer, Windows 10 AE makes it easy. Want to go back to work (or play) right where you left off? Choose Sleep. Want to start from scratch the next time you start up Windows, or need to put away your PC for more than a few hours? Choose Shut Down. Need to restart the computer? Choose Restart. In this lesson, you learn how to perform these tasks using the Start menu's Power button. These same tasks can also be performed from the login screen shown earlier in this chapter.

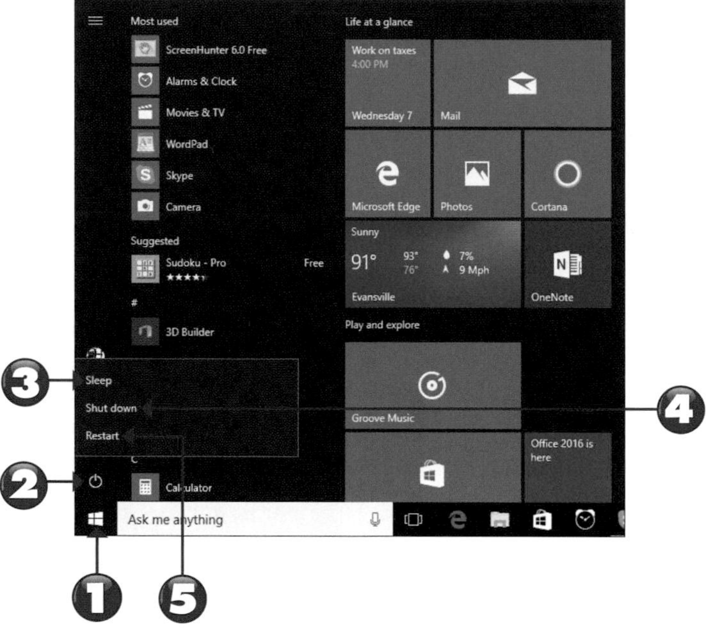

1. Click or tap the **Start** button or press the **Windows key** on your keyboard.
2. Click or tap the **Power** button.
3. Tap **Sleep** to put the device into low-power mode.
4. Tap **Shut down** to shut down the device.
5. Tap **Restart** to close Windows and restart it.

End

CAUTION

Power Options from the Login Screen The Power button is also available from the login screen and works the same way as from the Start menu. However, if you select **Shut down** or **Restart** when you or other users are logged in to the system, you are warned that shutting down or restarting can cause data loss. Be sure that any logged-in users have saved their work and closed their apps before you shut down or restart Windows.

USING CORTANA SEARCH

Windows 10 Anniversary Edition's Search is powered by Cortana. For any user with a Microsoft account, Cortana provides voice-activated or text search of both the Web and your device. Cortana can send you reminders and works hard to discover what you like so you get better search results. If you sign out of Cortana or use a local account, basic search is still available. Whichever you prefer, this chapter shows you how to get the most from the enhanced search tools in Windows 10 AE.

Using Cortana's speech recognition to create a reminder
Cortana provides a local digest of news, weather, and events
An event reminder
Search results can include Windows settings, Microsoft Store matches, and more
You can set recurring reminders using additional options
Evansville, Indiana 47712
89 °F
Sunny
Precipitation 0%
Get Cortana on your phone.
Then she can give you reminders and traffic info when you're away from your PC.
Android
WindowsPhone
iPhone
Not now
Get traffic updates for your commute?
Ask me anything
"create a to-do list."
remind me of the book study tonight at 6:30 PM
Remember to...
Car wash
Today at 2:50 PM
Snooze for
5 minutes
Snooze
Complete
Remind you about this?
Reminder
Book study
6:30 PM
Every Wednesday
Add a photo
Remind
Cancel
Search for "Remind me of the book study tonight at 6:30 PM."
you can say Yes, No, or Cancel
More
Best match
Change Wi-Fi settings
System settings
Turn wireless devices on or off
System settings
Settings
Turn airplane mode on or off
Connect wireless Xbox One controllers
Display settings
Store
Microsoft Wireless Display Adapter
Best Wireless Gadgets
Web
wireless
Documents
wireless

CONFIGURING CORTANA VOICE SEARCH

Cortana is ready to use for text searches as soon as you start Windows with a Microsoft account. If you prefer to speak your searches, setting up Cortana for voice interaction doesn't take long. Here's how to do it.

Start

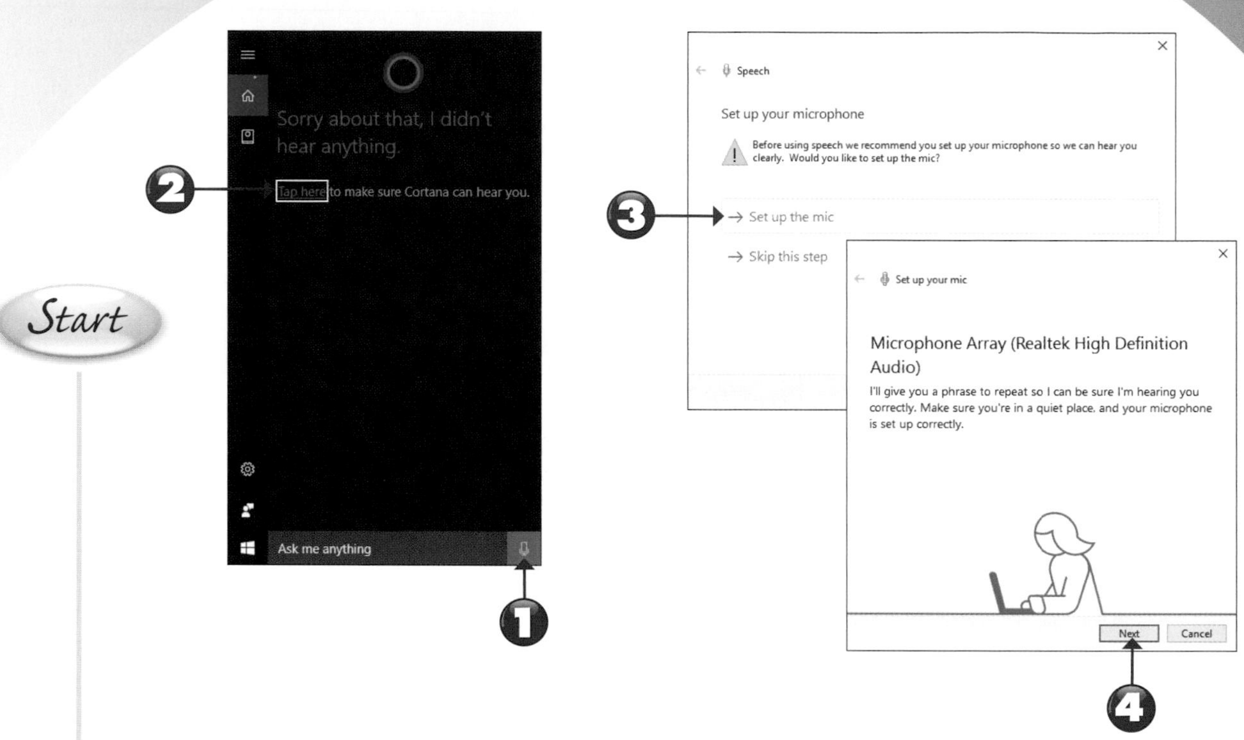

1. Click or tap the microphone icon in the Search box, and begin speaking your search terms or phrase.
2. If you see a "Sorry about that. I didn't hear anything" dialog box, click or tap **Tap here** to continue.
3. Click or tap **Set up the mic**.
4. Click or tap **Next** to start the process.

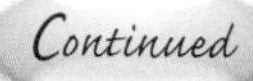

Set up your mic

Read the following sentences to complete setting up the microphone:

"Peter talks to his computer. He prefers it to typing, and particularly prefers it to pen and paper."

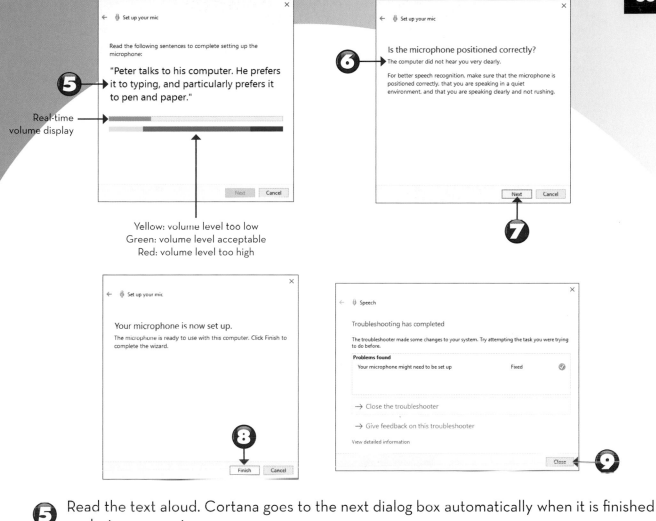

Real-time volume display

Yellow: volume level too low
Green: volume level acceptable
Red: volume level too high

Set up your mic

Is the microphone positioned correctly?

The computer did not hear you very clearly.

For better speech recognition, make sure that the microphone is positioned correctly, that you are speaking in a quiet environment, and that you are speaking clearly and not rushing.

Next Cancel

Set up your mic

Your microphone is now set up.

The microphone is ready to use with this computer. Click Finish to complete the wizard.

Finish Cancel

Speech

Troubleshooting has completed

The troubleshooter made some changes to your system. Try attempting the task you were trying to do before.

Problems found

Your microphone might need to be set up — Fixed

→ Close the troubleshooter

→ Give feedback on this troubleshooter

View detailed information

Close

5. Read the text aloud. Cortana goes to the next dialog box automatically when it is finished analyzing your voice.
6. If you see the "Is the microphone positioned correctly?" dialog box, you need to adjust the volume or position of your microphone (see NOTE).
7. Click or tap **Next** to continue.
8. Click or tap **Finish**.
9. Click or tap **Close**.

End

NOTE

Troubleshooting Cortana Voice Setup If Cortana cannot detect your speech in step 2, make sure your built-in microphone is enabled and not muted, or that your plug-in microphone is plugged in and not muted. To learn more about this process or to fine-tune microphone volume, see "Adjusting Microphone Volume" in Chapter 19, "Managing Windows 10 AE." ■

SEARCHING WITH CORTANA

Cortana enables you to search by typing or by using your voice. Here's how to search for online information by typing.

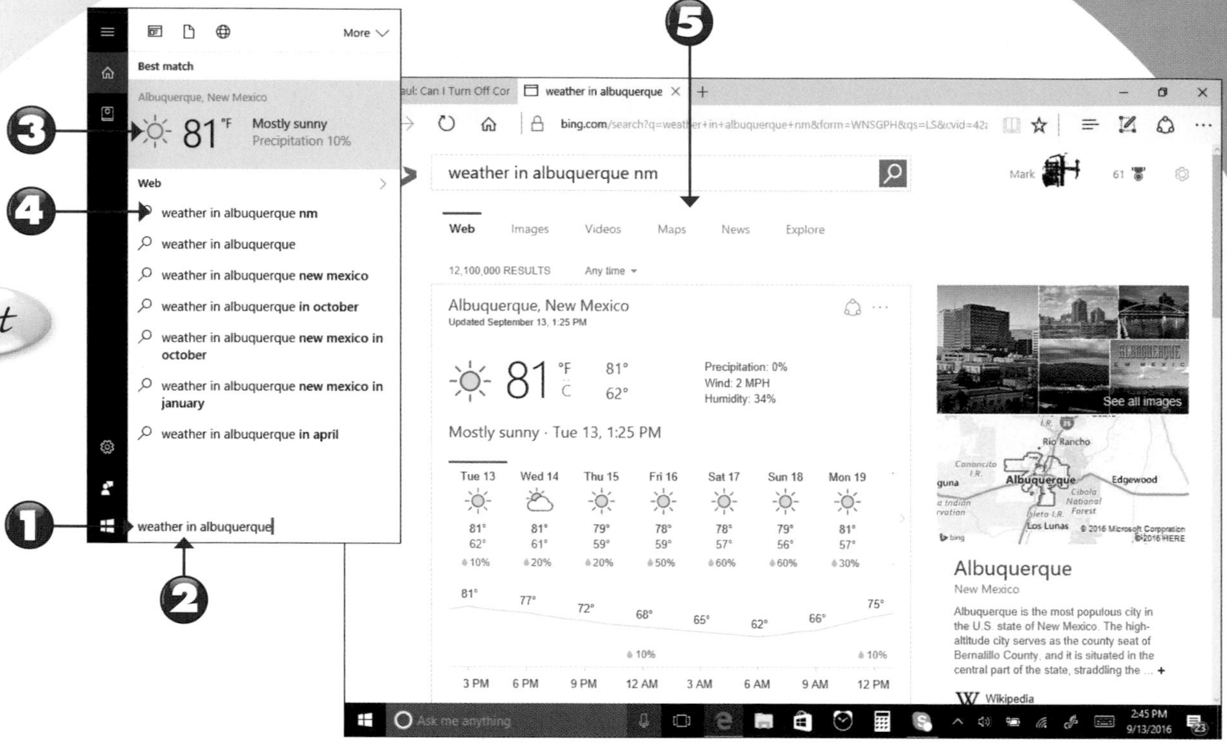

Start

1. Click or tap the **Search** box.
2. Type your search terms.
3. Cortana displays the search results.
4. Click or tap a link for more information.
5. A window with detailed information opens.

VOICE SEARCHES WITH CORTANA

Have a Windows tablet? Want to give your keyboard a rest? Here's how to perform a voice-driven web search using Cortana.

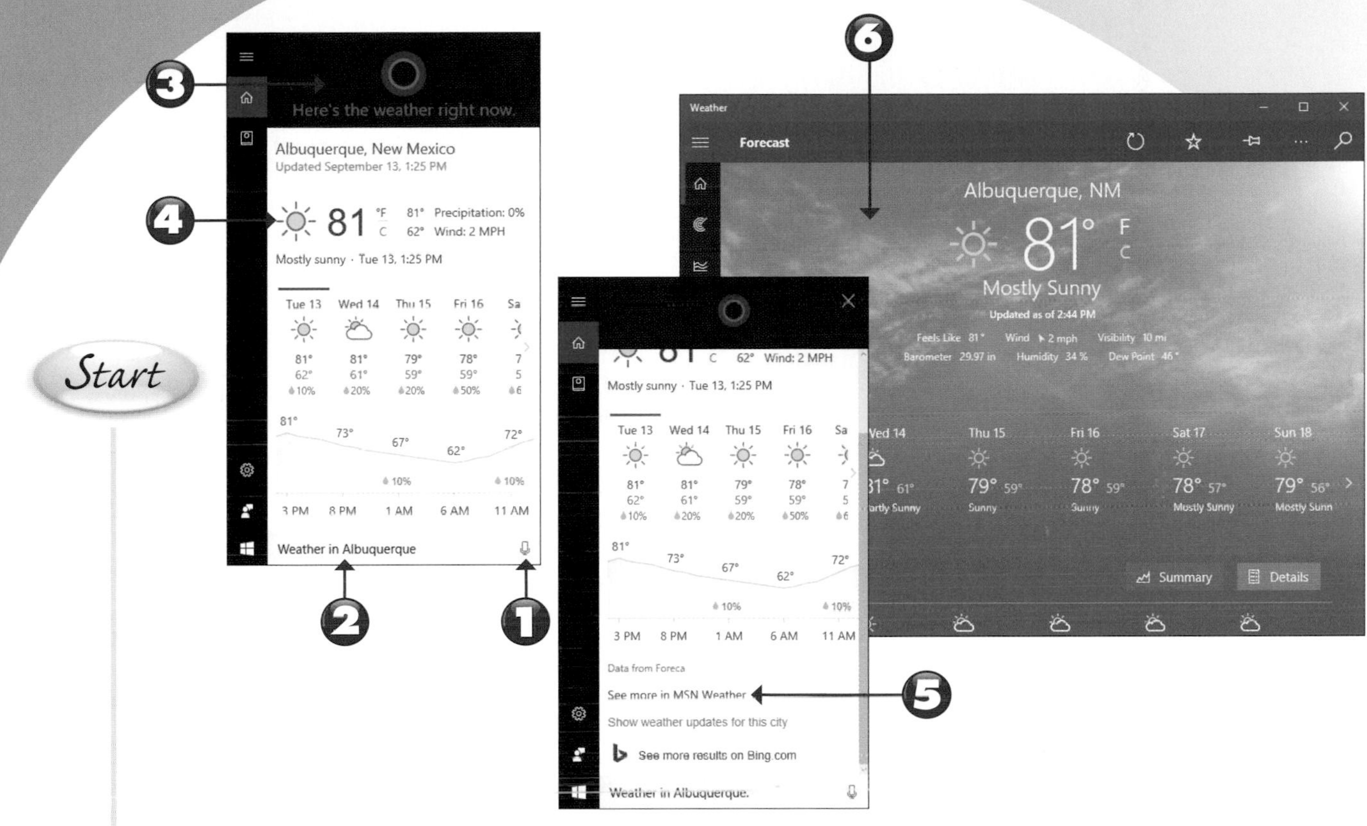

Start

1. To search by voice, click or tap the microphone.
2. Speak your search terms.
3. Cortana speaks the search results.
4. Cortana displays the search results in its window (if possible).
5. Click or tap a link for more information. (You might need to scroll down.)
6. If Windows 10 AE can display the information in an installed app, it will do so; otherwise, a browser window with detailed information opens.

End

STARTING APPS WITH CORTANA

Cortana can also start installed apps for you. Here's how.

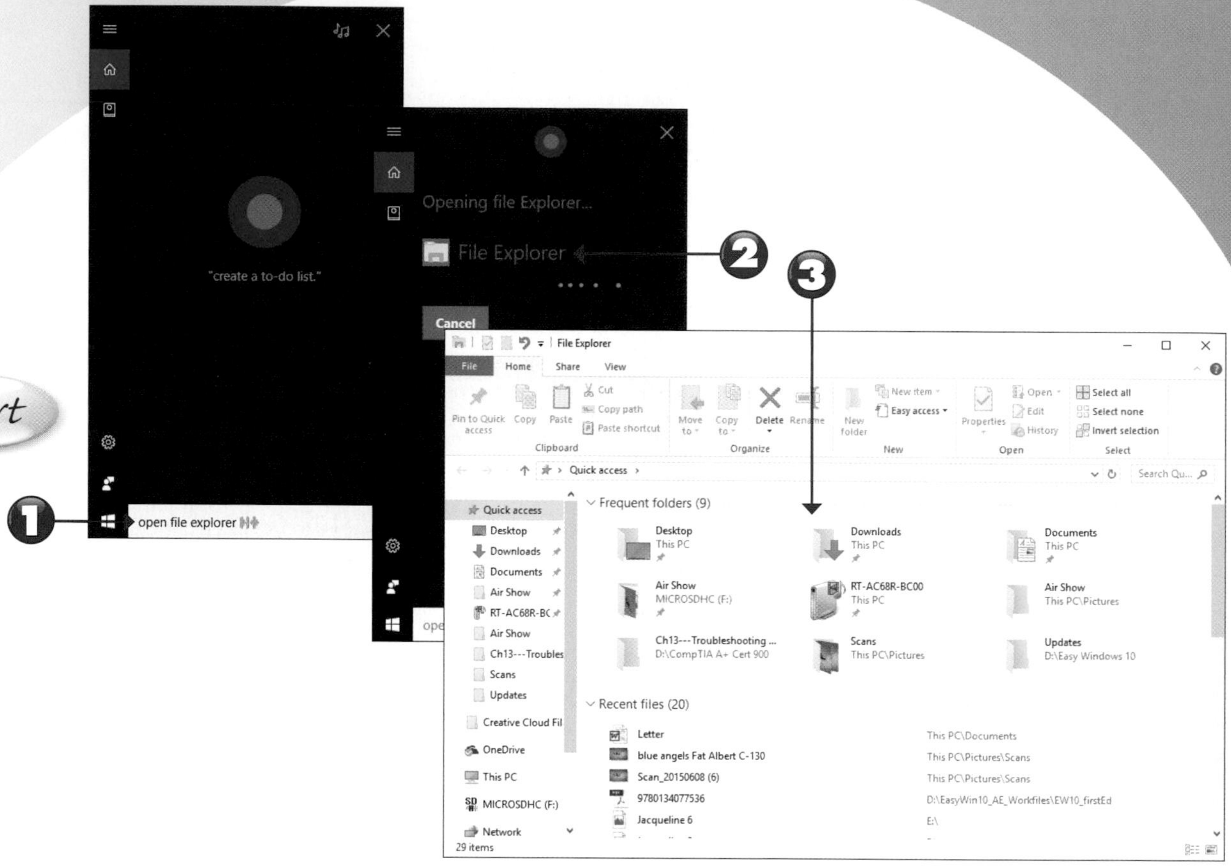

Start

1. Click or tap the microphone or search box and speak or type **open *name of app***.

2. Cortana checks the names of installed apps and selects the matching app.

3. The app opens.

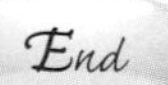

NOTE

Start Any App with Cortana You can start built-in apps, apps from the Windows Store, or apps you install yourself from downloads, USB drives, or optical drives using Cortana. ■

USING CORTANA IN TABLET MODE

Most of Cortana's features work the same in Desktop or Tablet mode, but the way you start Cortana in Tablet mode is different. Here's what to expect.

Start

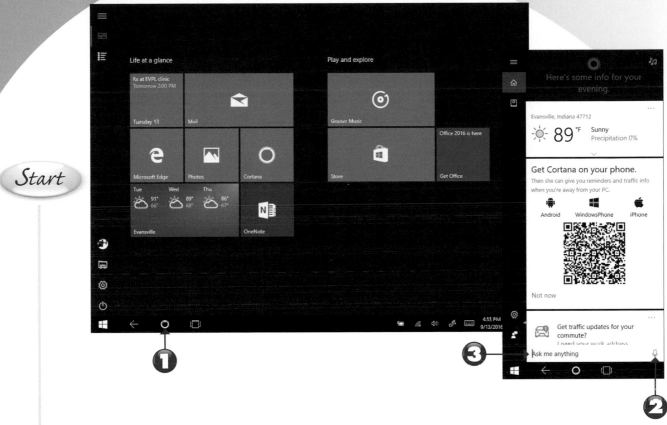

1. Click or tap the circle icon between the back arrow and app switcher icons.
2. Click the microphone to perform a voice search.
3. Click the box to type your search.

End

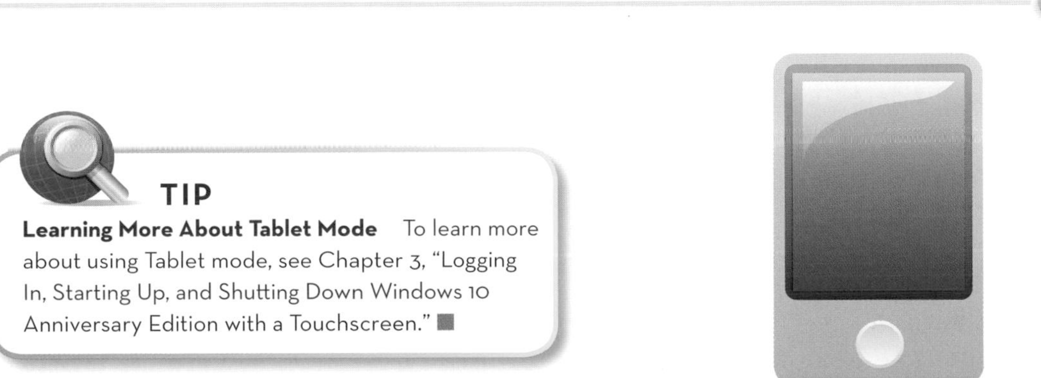

TIP

Learning More About Tablet Mode To learn more about using Tablet mode, see Chapter 3, "Logging In, Starting Up, and Shutting Down Windows 10 Anniversary Edition with a Touchscreen." ■

DISCOVERING CORTANA FEATURES

In addition to searching tasks, Cortana has many features to help keep your life organized. Here's an overview. Specific features are covered later in this chapter.

Start

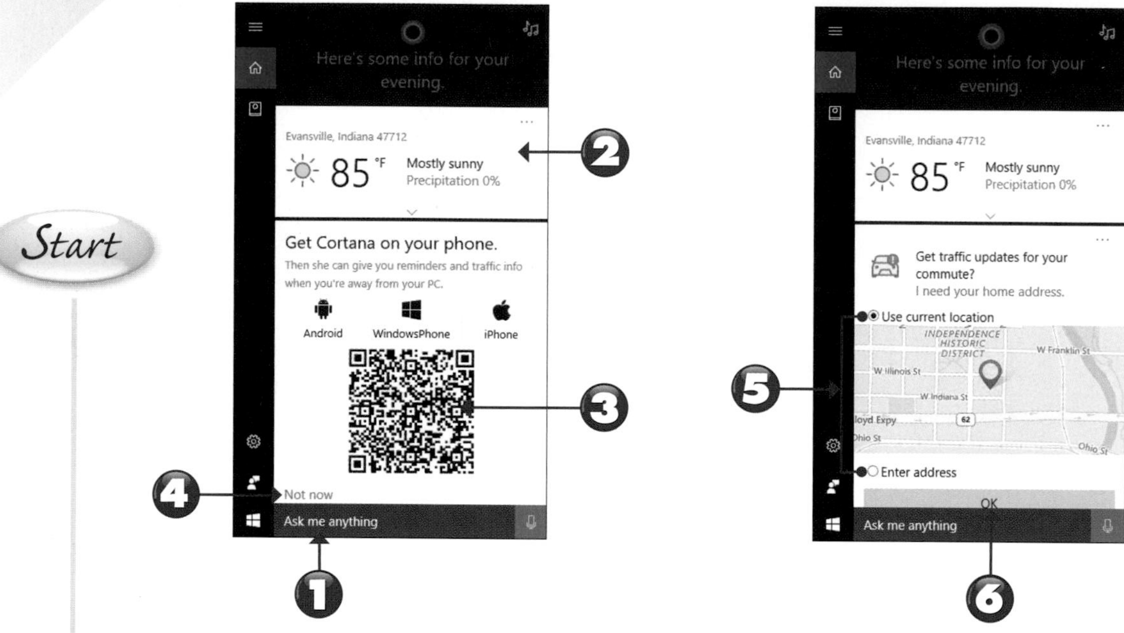

1. Click or tap the **Cortana/Search** box, and Cortana opens its Home tab.
2. Cortana displays the current weather for your location.
3. To add Cortana to your Android, Windows Phone, or iPhone, use your phone's QR Code reader to read the QR code displayed onscreen. Your phone will go to its app store's Cortana page.
4. To close the Get Cortana on Your Phone section, click or tap the **Not now** link.
5. To get traffic updates, choose from **Use current location** (verify your location on the map) or **Enter address** (enter address if prompted).
6. Click **OK** to use this feature.

Continued

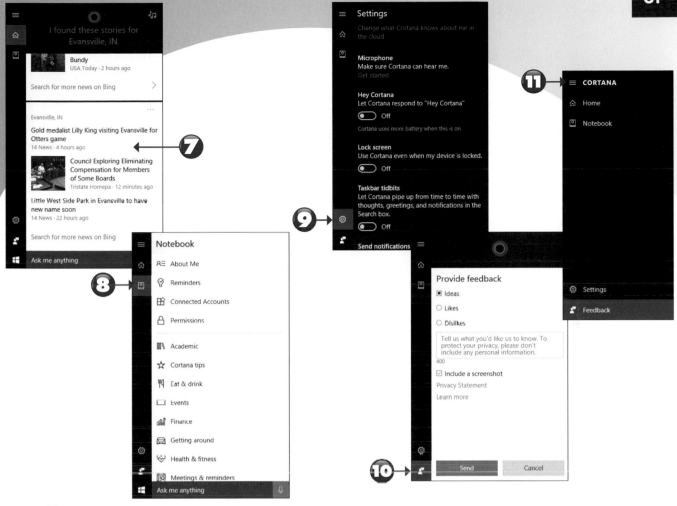

7 Scroll down to see national and local news.

8 Click or tap the **Notebook** button to set up reminders and provide Cortana with more information about your preferences.

9 Click or tap the **Settings** button to configure Cortana/Search functions.

10 Click or tap the **Feedback** button if you want to suggest improvements.

11 Click or tap the **Menu** button to expand the Cortana menu.

End

SEARCHING FOR FILES, APPS, AND SETTINGS

When you search (with or without Cortana running), you can specify what to search for. In this exercise, you learn how this feature provides a wider variety of search results.

Start

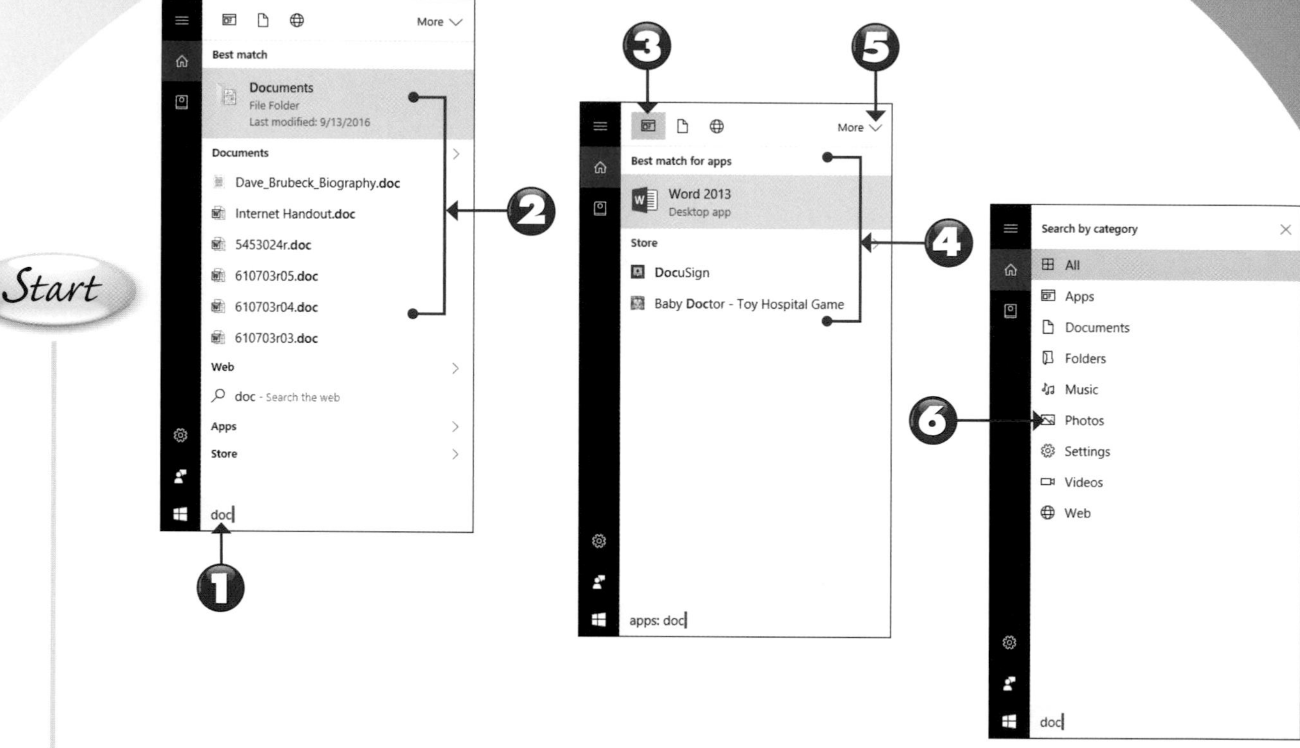

1. Click or tap the **Cortana/Search** window and type your search word or phrase.
2. The best matches on your system are shown.
3. Click or tap the **Apps** icon.
4. Matching apps installed on your system and Windows Store matches are shown.
5. Click or tap the down arrow for **More**.
6. Choose the search category desired.

Continued

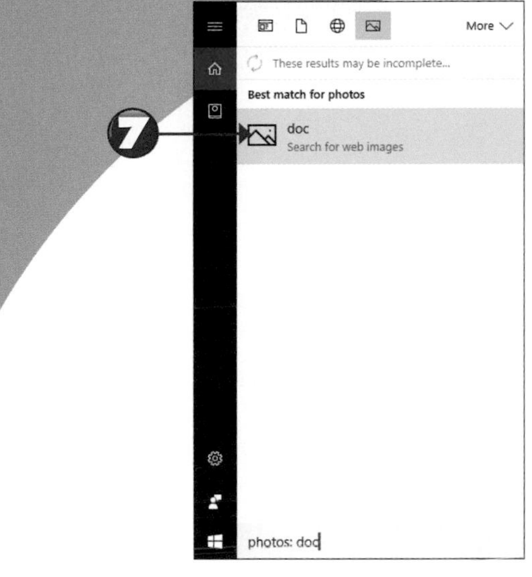

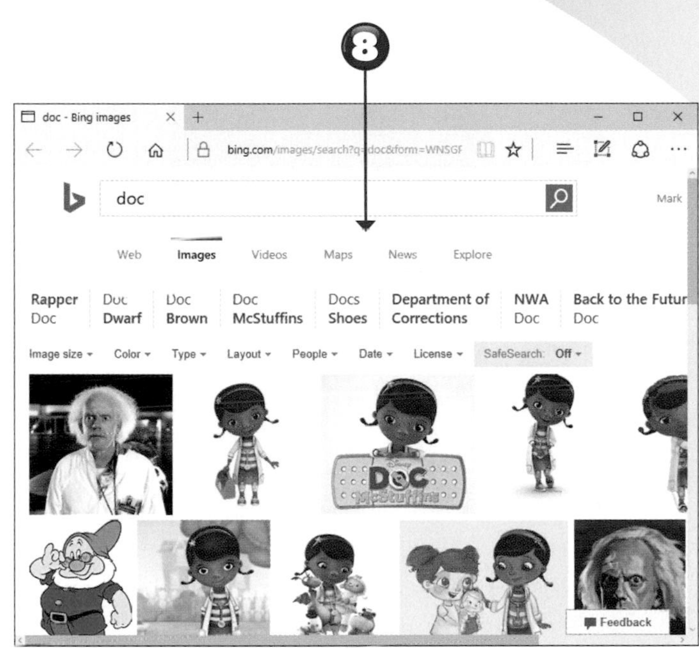

7 Click or tap to perform search.

8 If there are no local results, search results appear in a browser window.

End

TIP

Use Notebook to Improve Cortana's Results To improve Cortana's search results, use the Notebook feature to designate which topics appear as part of the results. Click or tap the **Notebook** button, click or tap topics (events, activities, recommendations) to turn them on or off, and then click or tap **Save**. ■

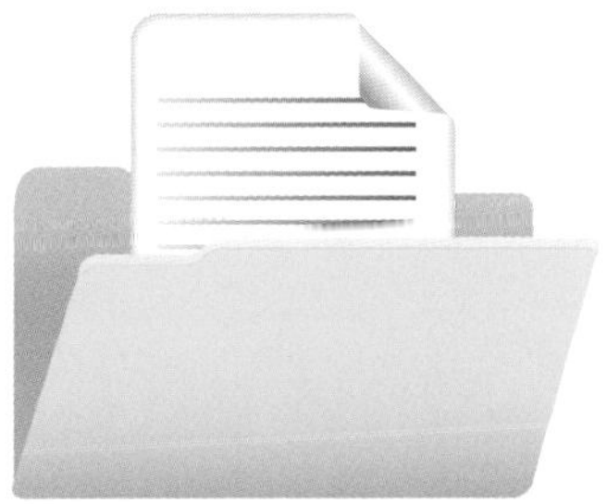

TEACHING CORTANA TO RECOGNIZE YOUR VOICE

You can make voice searches easier by using Cortana's Settings feature to turn on "Hey Cortana," which enables you to use Cortana as a voice-activated personal assistant.

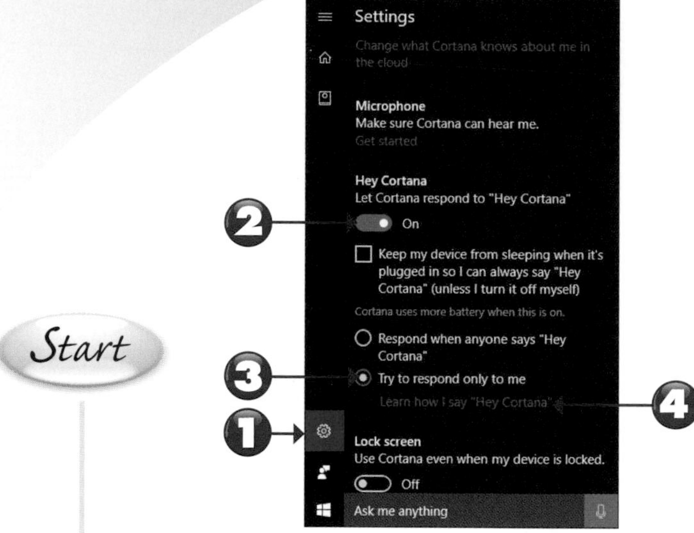

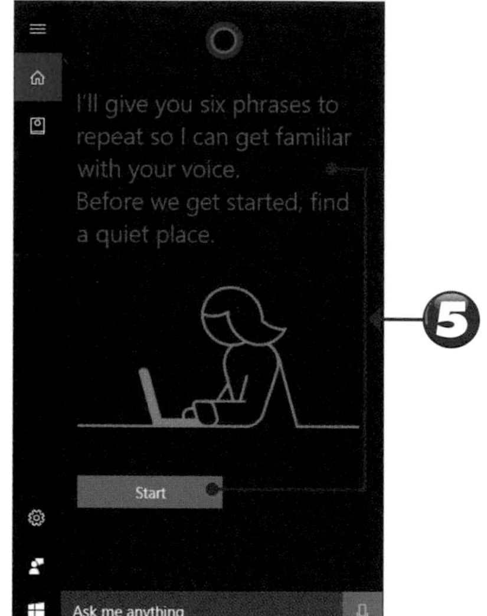

Start

1. Click or tap **Settings**.
2. Click or press and drag the toggle to **On** to enable you to say, "Hey Cortana" to start voice searches.
3. The default is for Cortana to respond to anyone. To change this, click or tap **Try to respond only to me**.
4. To optimize Cortana to respond to your voice, click or tap **Learn how I say "Hey Cortana"**.
5. Read the instructions, and then click or tap **Start**.

Continued

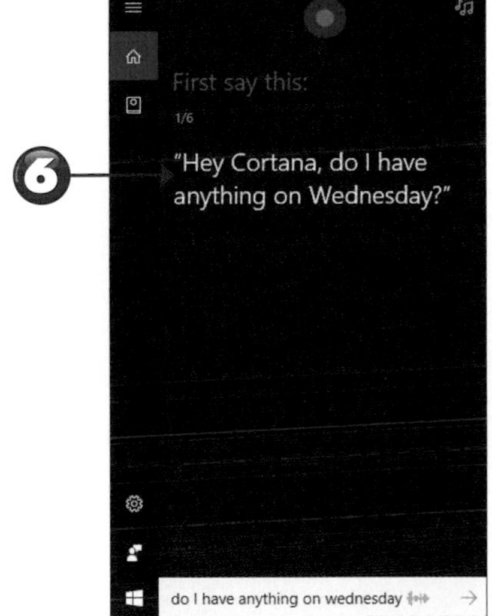

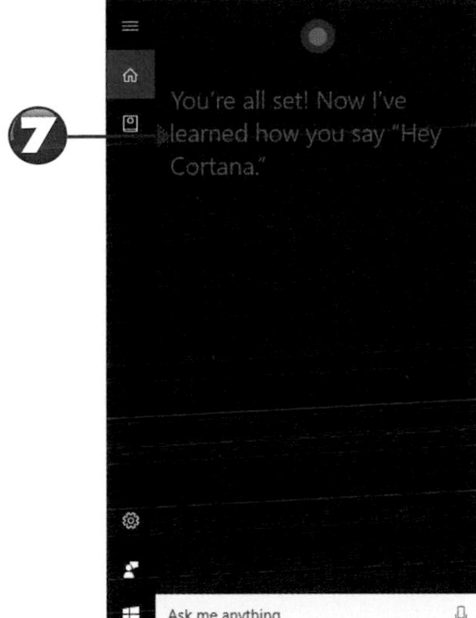

6. Speak each phrase Cortana displays. Cortana displays the next one after it recognizes the current phrase.
7. When you see this, Cortana has learned your voice. Say, "Hey Cortana," followed by your search or command.

End

TIP

Separate Accounts Help Optimize Cortana's Operation Want Cortana to provide you with really helpful search results and to understand how you say "Hey Cortana?" Don't share a single Windows 10 AE user account with multiple users. Each user needs an account, and that way Cortana will provide the best results for each user. ■

CREATING A REMINDER

You can create a reminder by using the Notebook's Reminder's button or by voice. Here's how to use your mouse and keyboard to have Cortana remind you of a task or event.

Start

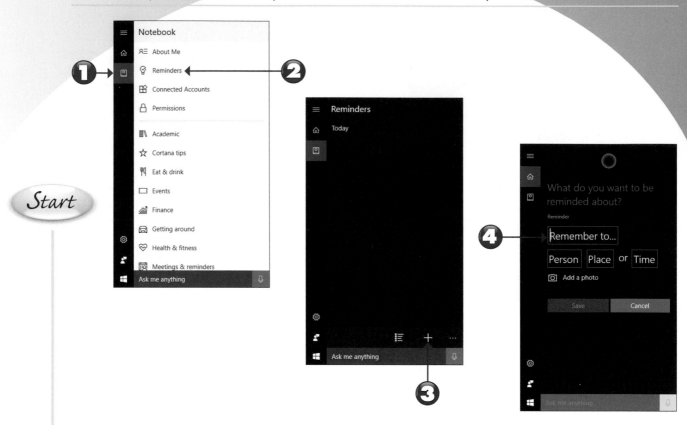

1. Click or tap **Notebook**.
2. Click or tap **Reminders**.
3. Click or tap the plus (+) sign to add a new reminder.
4. Enter what you want to be reminded about.

Continued

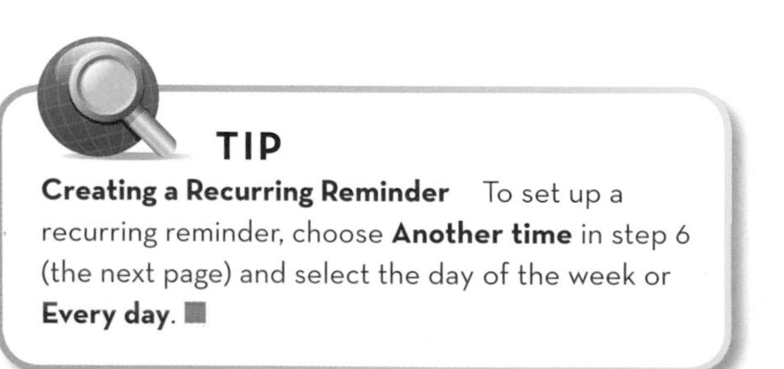

TIP

Creating a Recurring Reminder To set up a recurring reminder, choose **Another time** in step 6 (the next page) and select the day of the week or **Every day**. ■

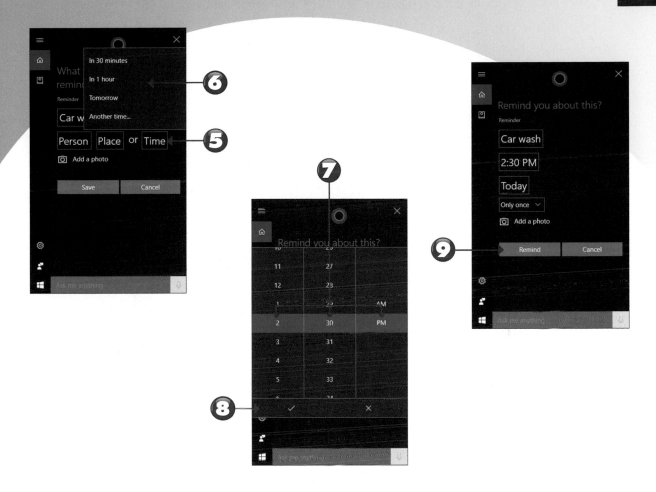

5. Click or tap **Time** to select when you want to be reminded.

6. Choose a time.

7. Scroll to select hour, minute, AM, or PM.

8. Click or tap the check box when finished.

9. Click or tap **Remind** to complete the reminder.

End

CREATING REMINDERS WITH "HEY CORTANA"

You can also use "Hey Cortana" to create a reminder. Here's how easy it is.

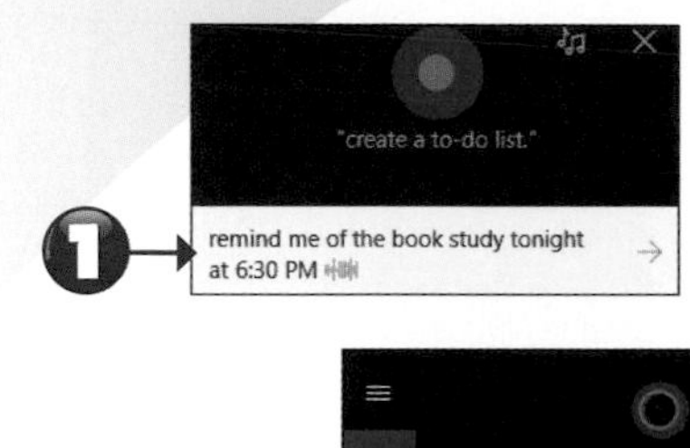

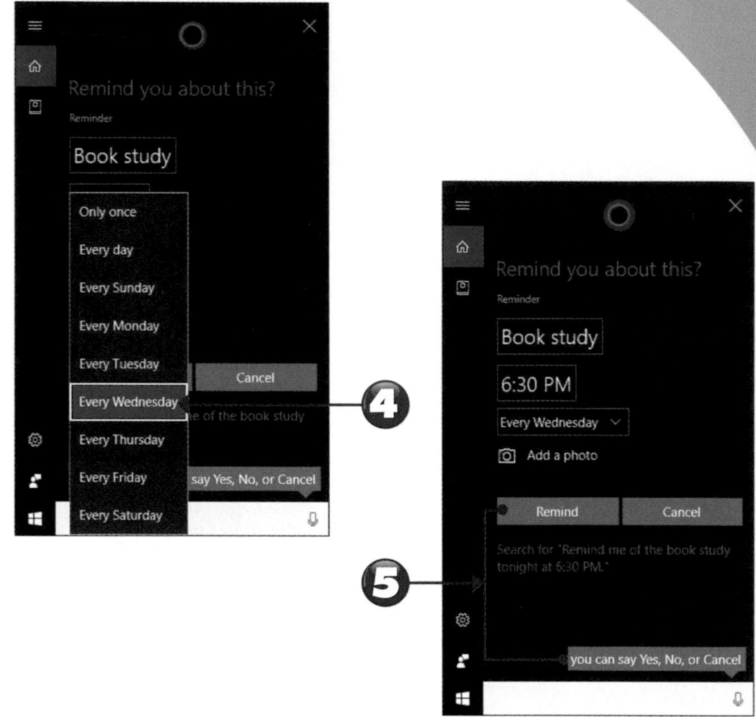

1. Say "Hey Cortana" and speak the reminder text.
2. Cortana fills in the reminder information.
3. To edit a field, click it.
4. Select the detail desired.
5. Say "Yes" to confirm your reminder, or click or tap **Remind**.

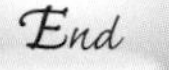

VIEWING REMINDERS

When you set a reminder, Cortana uses the Notification center to display it. Here's a typical example of how the reminder appears when it is triggered.

Start

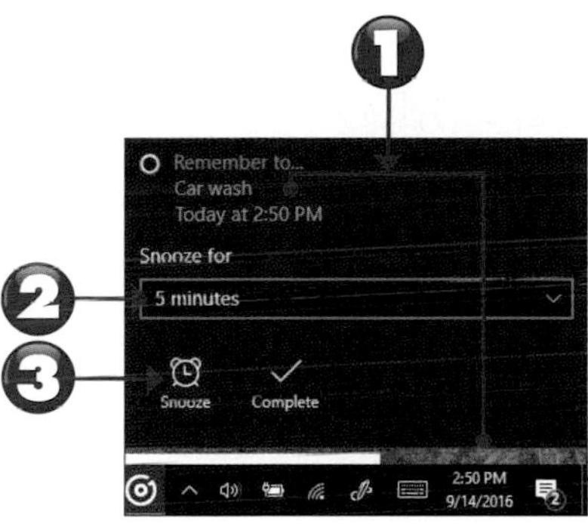

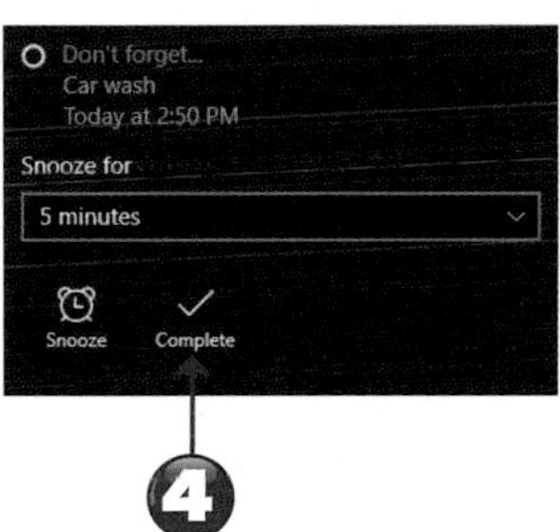

1. The reminder appears at the specified time.
2. Click or tap to select a different amount of time to snooze the reminder.
3. Click or tap **Snooze** to temporarily close the reminder.
4. Click or tap **Complete** when you are finished with the reminder.

End

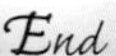

TIP

Reviewing Reminders Before They Are Triggered To see upcoming reminders, click or tap the **Cortana/Search** box or icon, click or tap **Notebook**, and then click or tap **Reminders**.

DISABLING CORTANA'S DIGITAL ASSISTANT FEATURES

In Windows 10 AE, you can't turn off Cortana completely. However, by signing out of Cortana, you can disable voice-enabled digital assistant features, online storage of your search history, and reminders and appointments. If you prefer to use Cortana mainly for searching and launching apps, here's what to do.

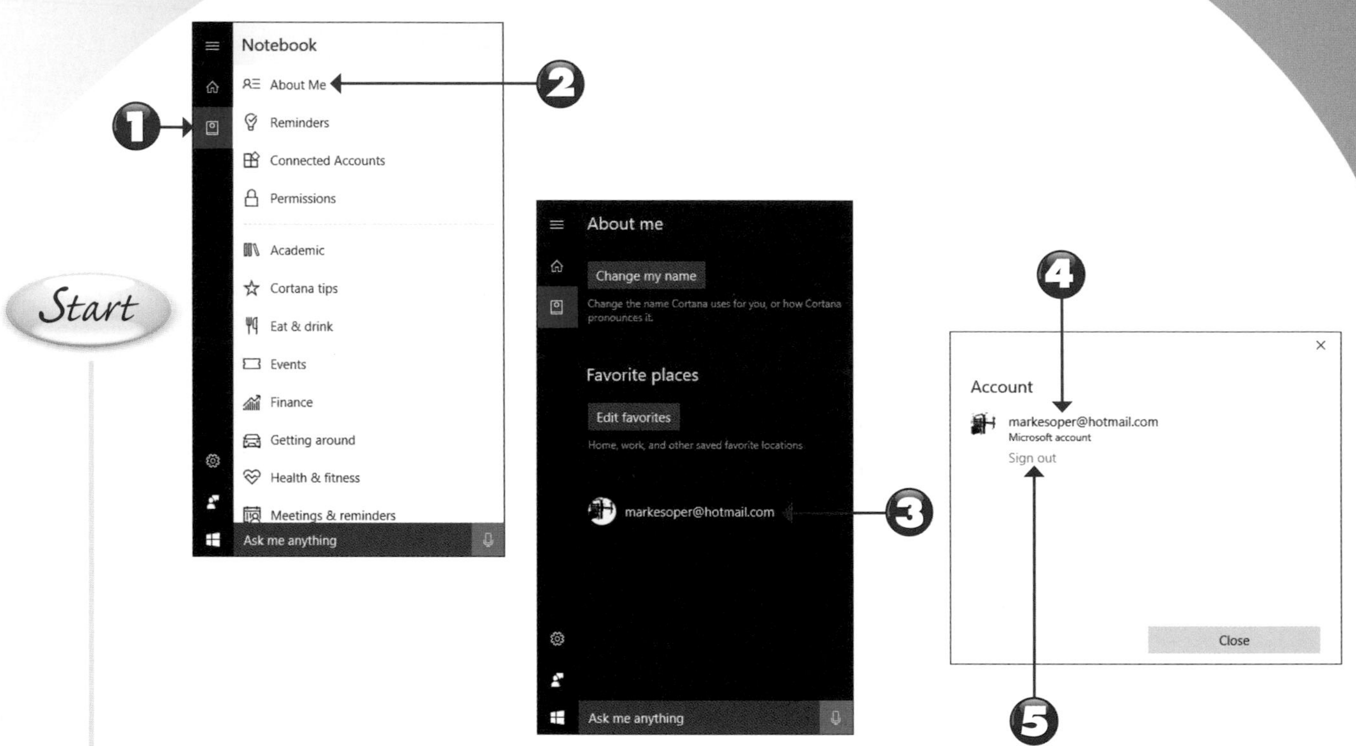

Start

1. Click or tap **Notebook**.
2. Click or tap **About Me**.
3. Click or tap your user name.
4. Click or tap your account.
5. Click or tap **Sign out**.

End

SEARCH AFTER SIGNING OUT OF CORTANA

If you sign out of Cortana, the Search feature works a little differently (and Cortana keeps reminding you it would like to do more for you). Here's what to expect.

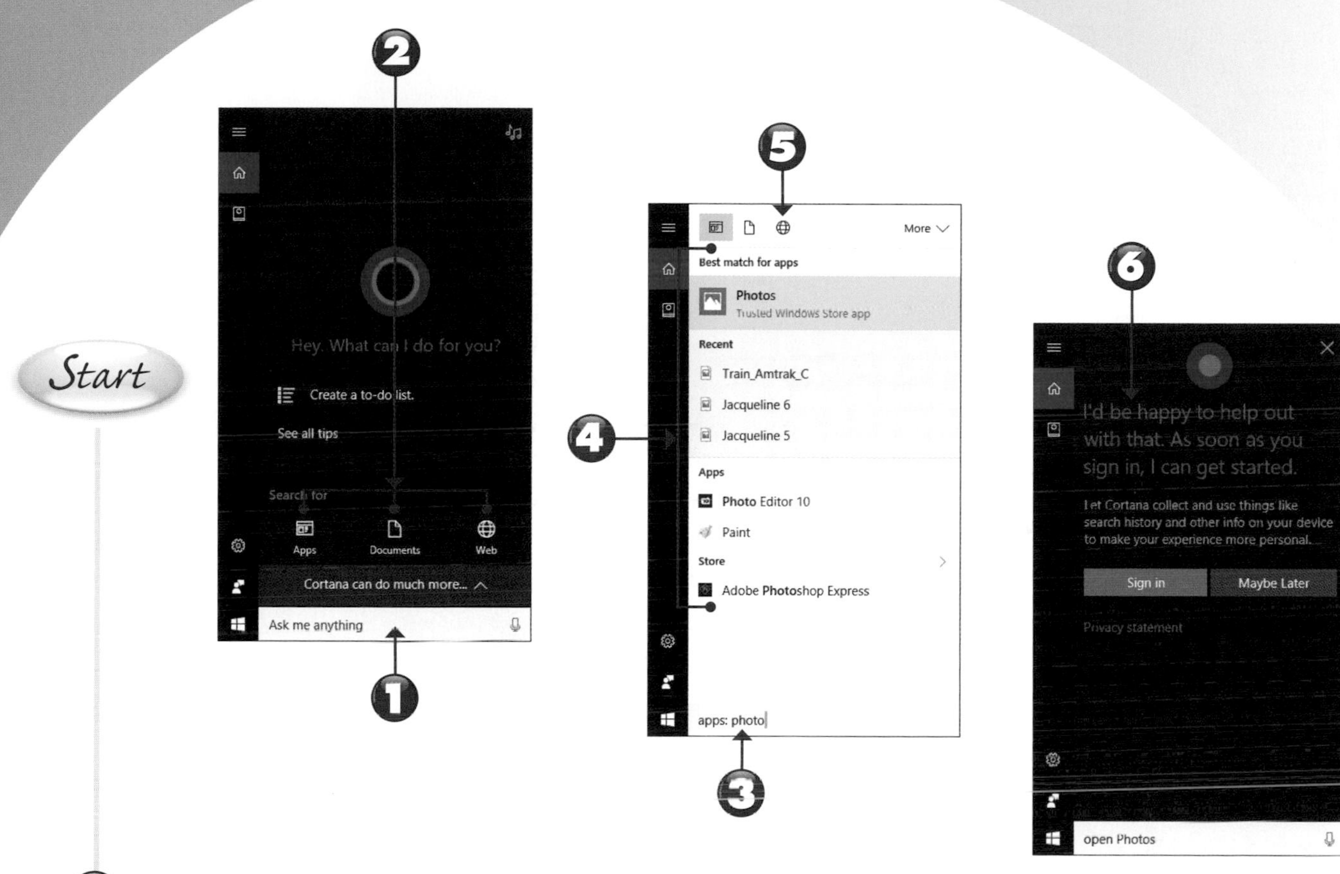

Start

1. Click or tap the **Cortana/Search** window or icon.
2. Click or tap **Apps** to focus your search. (Skip this step to search apps, documents, and the Web.)
3. Enter your search term.
4. Search finds matches.
5. To search for matches in other categories, click the appropriate icon.
6. If you try to use a feature that requires you to sign in, Cortana asks you to sign in with your Windows account.

End

RUNNING APPS

Windows 10 AE includes both desktop apps (the same types of apps found in Windows 8.1 and earlier versions that run from the Windows desktop) and Universal apps, which are optimized for touchscreens. Both types of apps are run from the Start menu. This chapter shows you how to locate the app you want and how to switch between running apps. You also learn how to run apps in full-screen or windowed modes, how to adjust the window size, how to add apps to the taskbar, and how to close an app when you're finished.

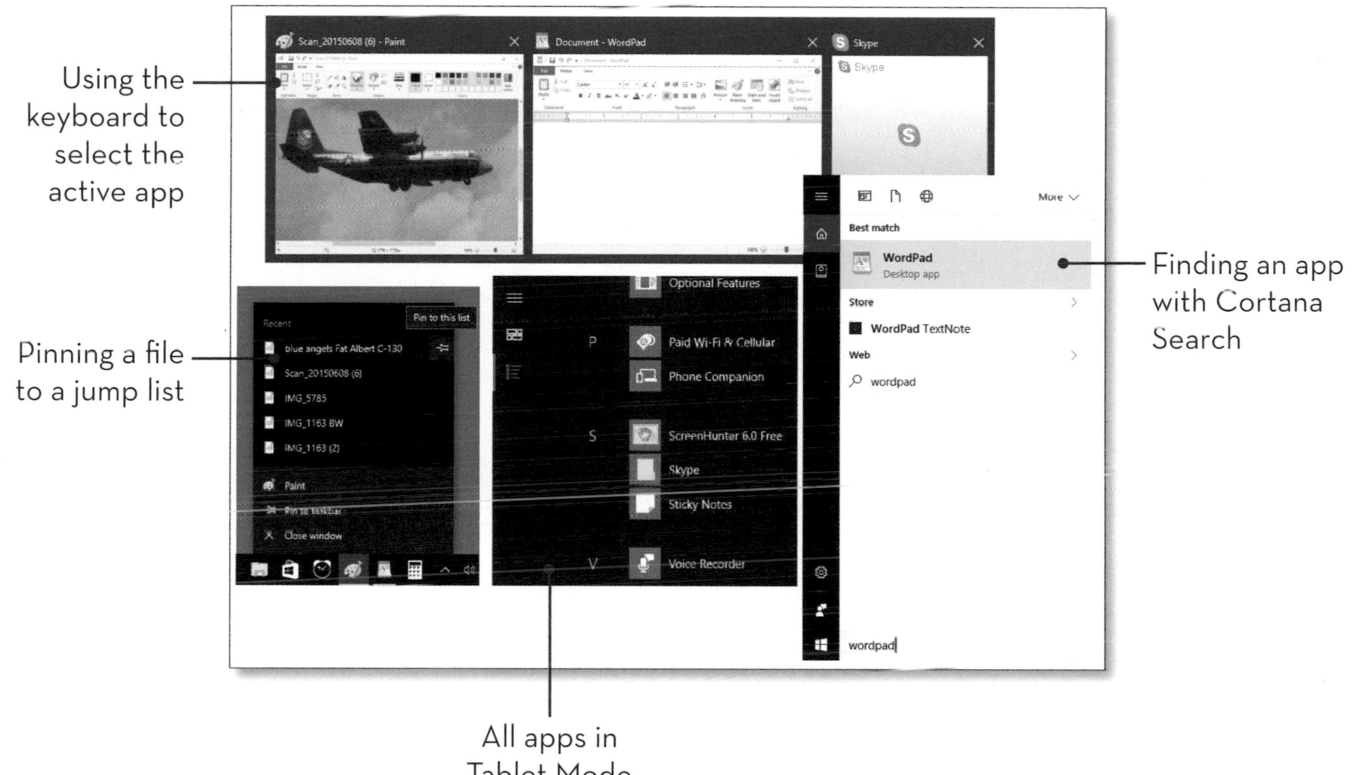
Using the keyboard to select the active app
Pinning a file to a jump list
Finding an app with Cortana Search
All apps in Tablet Mode
Scan_20150608 (6) - Paint
Document - WordPad
Skype
Best match
WordPad
Desktop app
Store
WordPad TextNote
Web
wordpad
More
Optional Features
Paid Wi-Fi & Cellular
Phone Companion
ScreenHunter 6.0 Free
Skype
Sticky Notes
Voice Recorder
Recent
Pin to this list
blue angels Fat Albert C-130
Scan_20150608 (6)
IMG_5785
IMG_1163 BW
IMG_1163 (2)
Paint
Pin to taskbar
Close window

FINDING APPS ON THE START MENU

Windows 10 AE makes it easier than ever to find the app you need. The Start menu includes an automatically generated list called Most Used. You can also find many Universal apps on the right side of the menu. Scroll down to find both Universal/Modern UI and Win32 (classic Windows) apps. Whether they are installed as part of Windows, installed from the Windows Store (app store), downloaded by the user, or installed from media, they are listed alphabetically. Here's how to locate an app.

Start

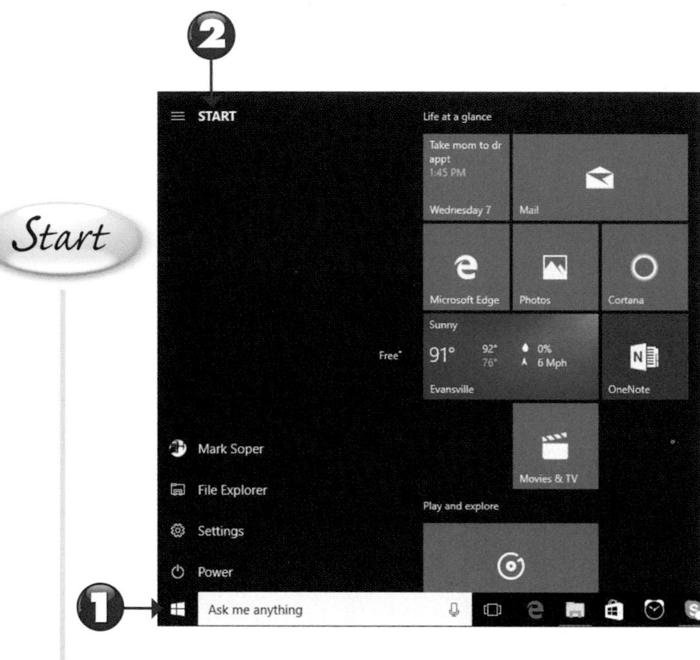

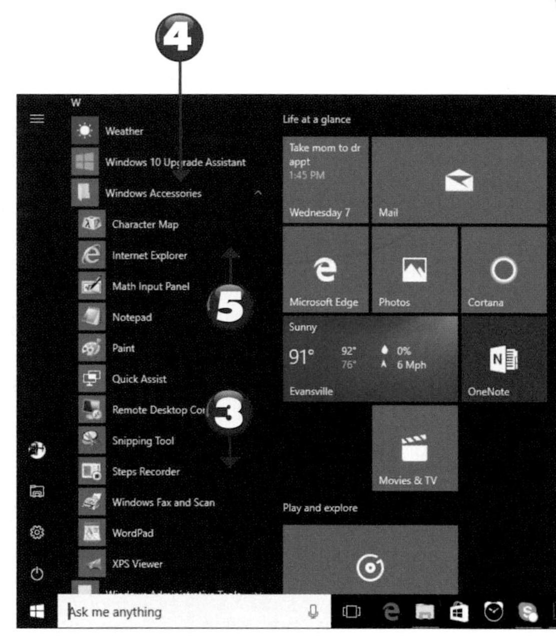

1. Click or tap **Start**.
2. If the Start menu is expanded, click or tap the **Start** icon at the top of the page to shrink it.
3. Scroll down the list of apps.
4. To view the contents of a folder, click or tap it.
5. To return to the original Start menu view, scroll back to the top.

End

TIP

All Apps in Tablet Mode If you are using Windows 10 Anniversary Edition in Tablet Mode, All Apps is a separate menu. See Chapter 3, "Logging In, Starting Up, and Shutting Down Windows 10 Anniversary Edition with a Touchscreen" for details.

[...]NG AN APP IN TABLET MODE

[...]Tablet Mode, the process of starting an app and the app window appearance are [...]n this example, we will open the same apps (Alarms & Clock and Notepad) as in [...]ous lesson.

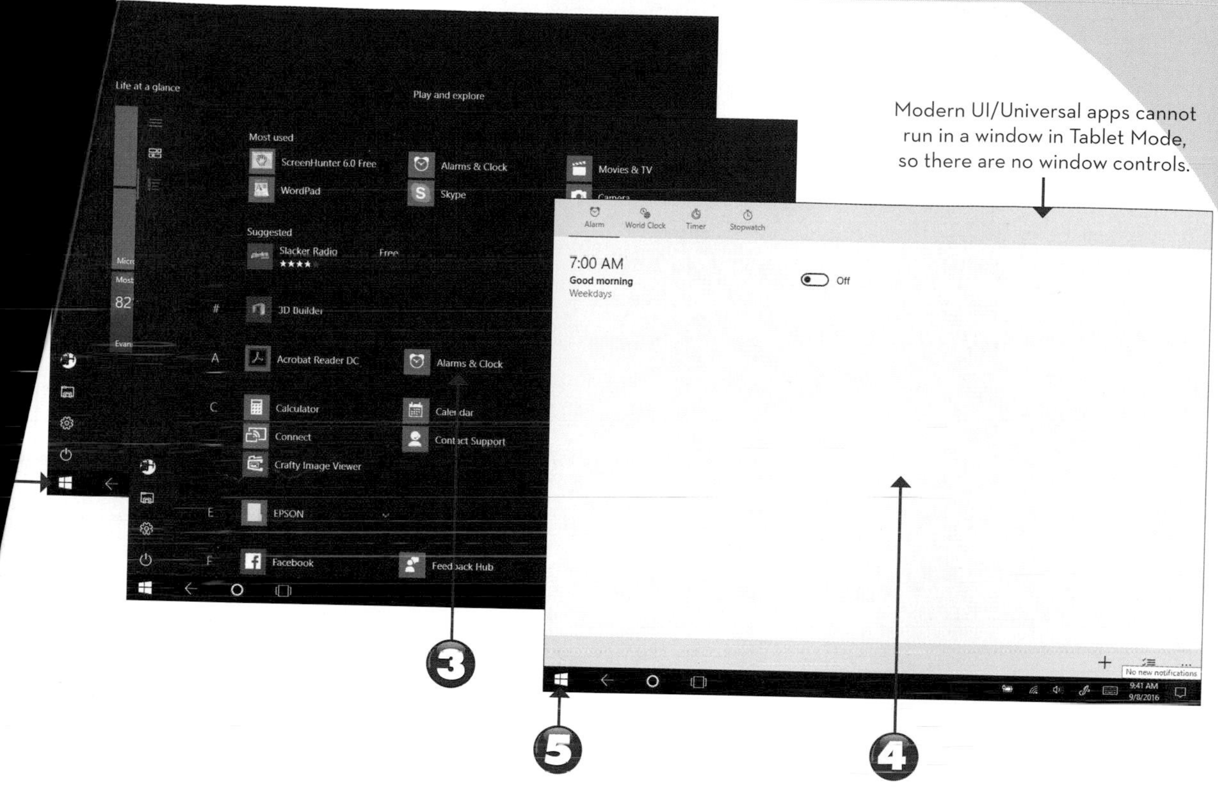

Modern UI/Universal apps cannot run in a window in Tablet Mode, so there are no window controls.
3
5
4

1. Tap the **Start** button.
2. If the app you want isn't visible, tap **All apps**.
3. Tap **Alarms & Clock**.
4. Modern UI/Universal apps run full-screen.
5. Tap **Start**.

Max[...] for the[...] taskbar[...] display o[...]

STARTING APPS

Starting apps from the Start menu is simple. Here's h
Clock and Notepad) as examples.

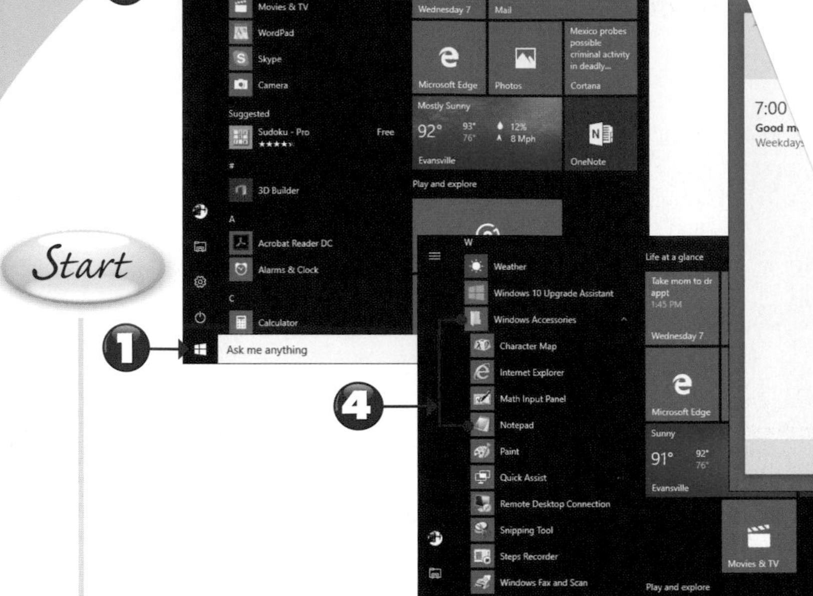

Start

1. Click or tap **Start**.
2. Click or tap **Alarms & Clock**.
3. Click or tap **Start**.
4. Click or tap **Windows Accessories**, then **Notepad**.
5. Alarms & Clock is a Modern UI/Universal app. It features large menu icons an friendly options, such as slider controls.
6. Notepad is a Win32 app. It uses a text-based menu (some apps also use icons) th designed for use with a mouse.

End

NOTE

mizing, Minimizing, and Windowed Modes A maximized app uses the entire active display (except taskbar). A minimized app does not have a visible window but is still running. Its icon is visible on the A windowed app runs in a window that occupies part of the display and can be dragged around that to a different display. See "Maximizing an App Window," this chapter, p. 79, for more information.

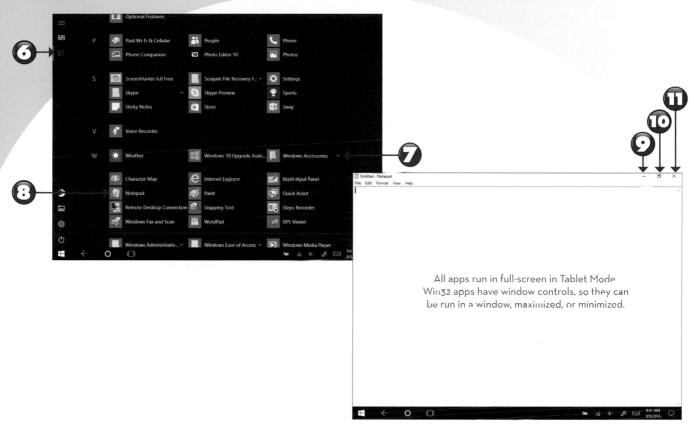

All apps run in full-screen in Tablet Mode Win32 apps have window controls, so they can be run in a window, maximized, or minimized.

6. Tap **All apps**.
7. Scroll to **Windows Accessories** and tap it.
8. Tap **Notepad**.
9. Tap to minimize the app to the taskbar.
10. Tap to run the app in a window.
11. Tap to close the app.

End

NOTE

Switching Apps Between Full-Screen and Window Modes To switch between these modes, see "Maximizing an App Window," p. 79, this chapter.

OPENING A FILE FROM WITHIN AN APP

This exercise explains how to open a file after starting an app using the Paint app as an illustration. The Paint app is a typical example of a traditional desktop app (also called a Win32 app), which is how Microsoft refers to apps that work the same way as in Windows 7 and earlier versions. The File menu works in a similar fashion in other desktop apps in Windows, such as WordPad and Notepad.

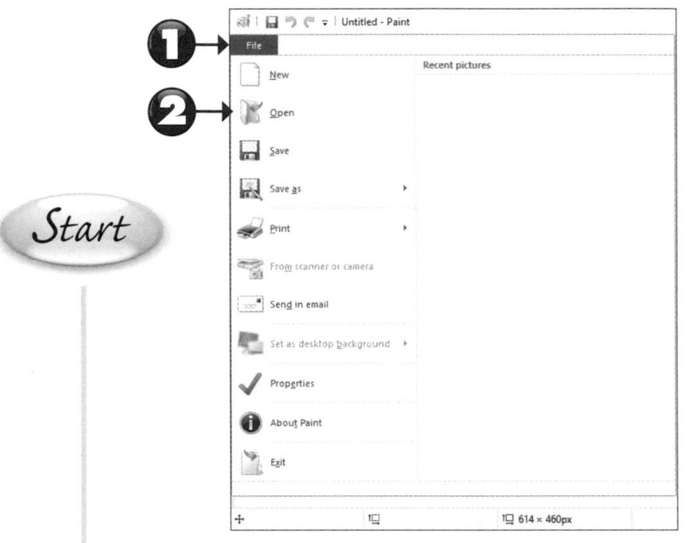

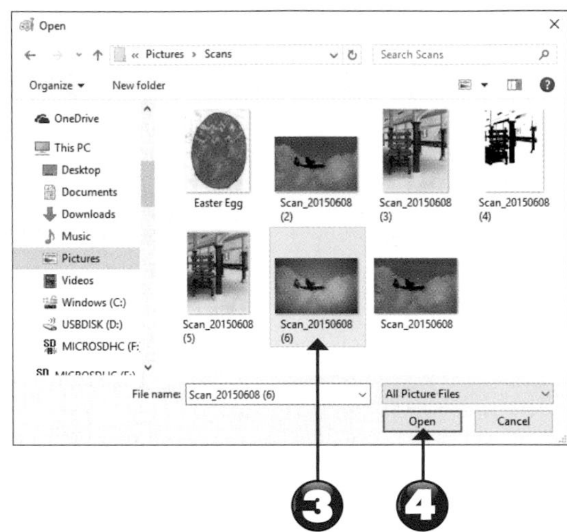

Start

1. Click or tap the **File** tab.
2. Click or tap **Open**.
3. Click or tap a picture.
4. Click or tap **Open**.

End

NOTE

Supported File Format Paint can work with .bmp, .tif, .jpg, .gif, .dib, .ico, and .png files. If you want to use Paint with digital camera RAW files or other types of unsupported image files, convert them into maximum-quality JPEG (.jpg) or TIFF (.tif) files first, using other software such as the Photos app.

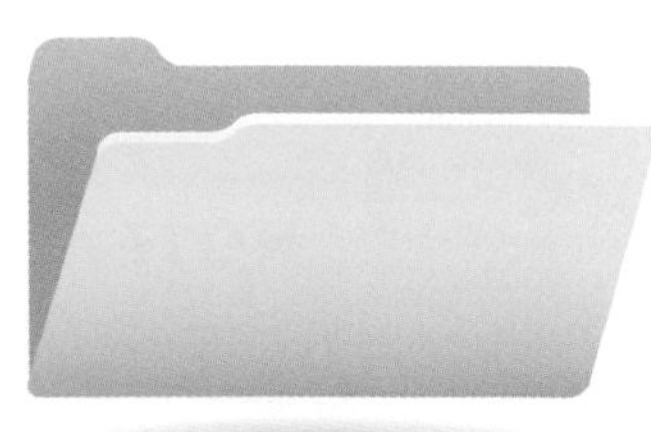

MAXIMIZING AN APP WINDOW

Some apps start in full-screen view (maximized), whereas others start in a window. If you prefer to have an app use the entire screen, you can maximize it. Here's how.

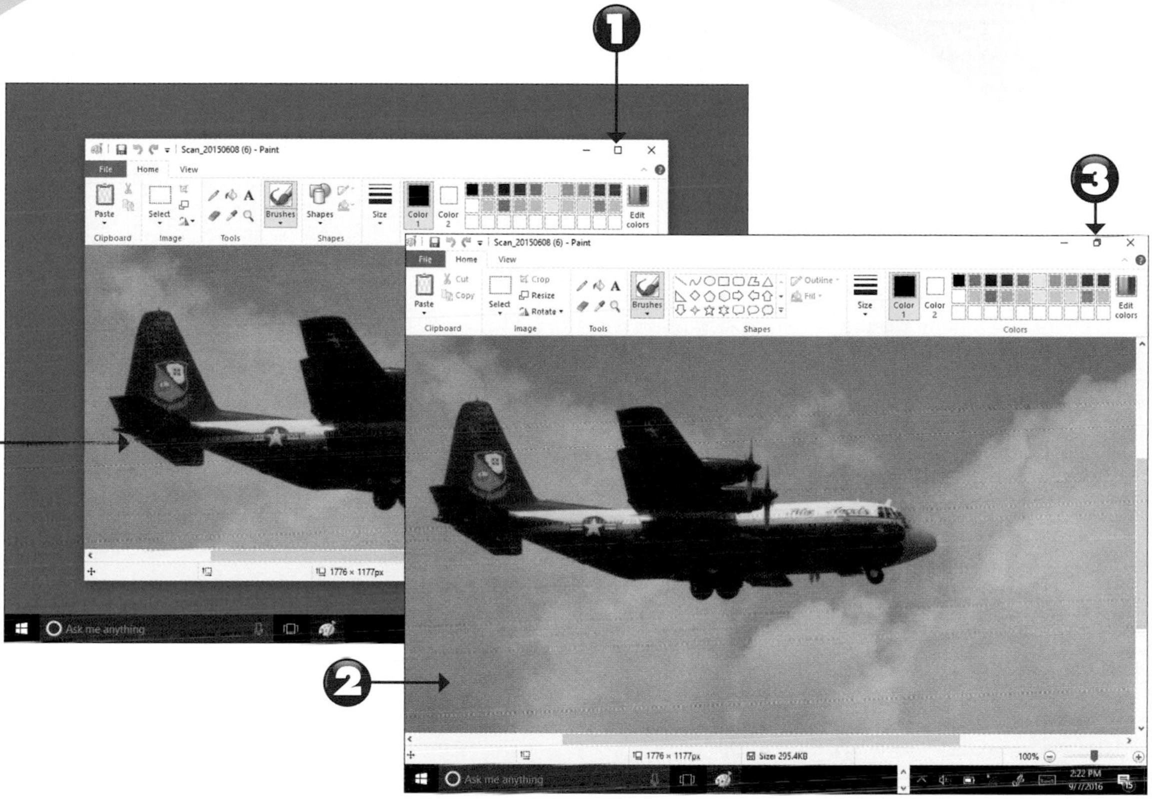

Start

1. Click or tap the **Maximize** (box) button.
2. The app window expands to fill the screen.
3. Click or tap the **Restore** (double-box) button.
4. The app returns to a window.

End

NOTE

Minimized Apps Are Still Running A minimized app does not have a visible window but is still running. Its icon is visible on the taskbar. To interact with a minimized app, click or tap its taskbar icon. It returns to the desktop.

STARTING AN APP FROM SEARCH

As an alternative to scrolling through the Start menu for an app you use occasionally, you can search for the app. This example demonstrates how to search for Windows 10 AE's simple word processing program, WordPad.

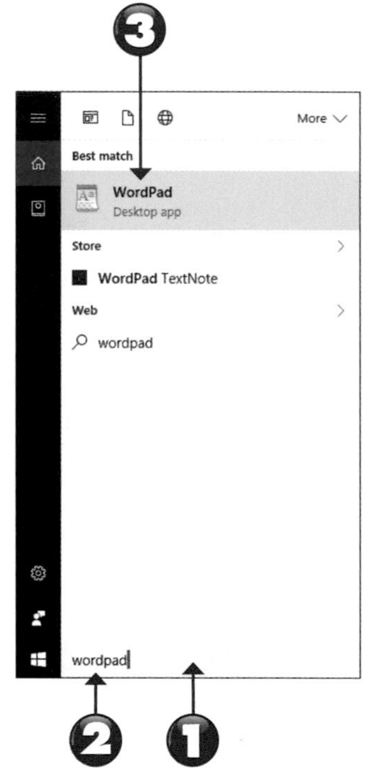

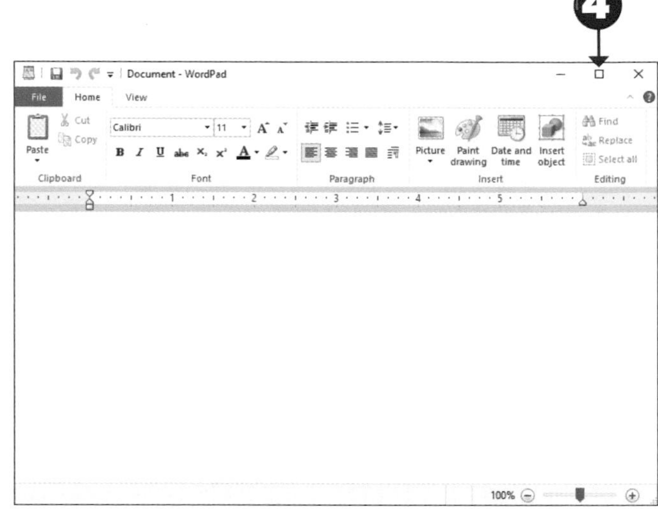

Start

1. Click or tap the **Search/Cortana** window.
2. Type **WordPad**.
3. Click or tap **WordPad**.
4. The WordPad window opens. Note the controls for maximizing and minimizing the app.

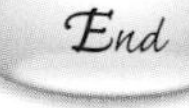

SWITCHING BETWEEN APPS WITH THE TASKBAR

Windows 10 AE can run two or more apps at the same time. In this lesson, you learn how to switch between apps by using the taskbar.

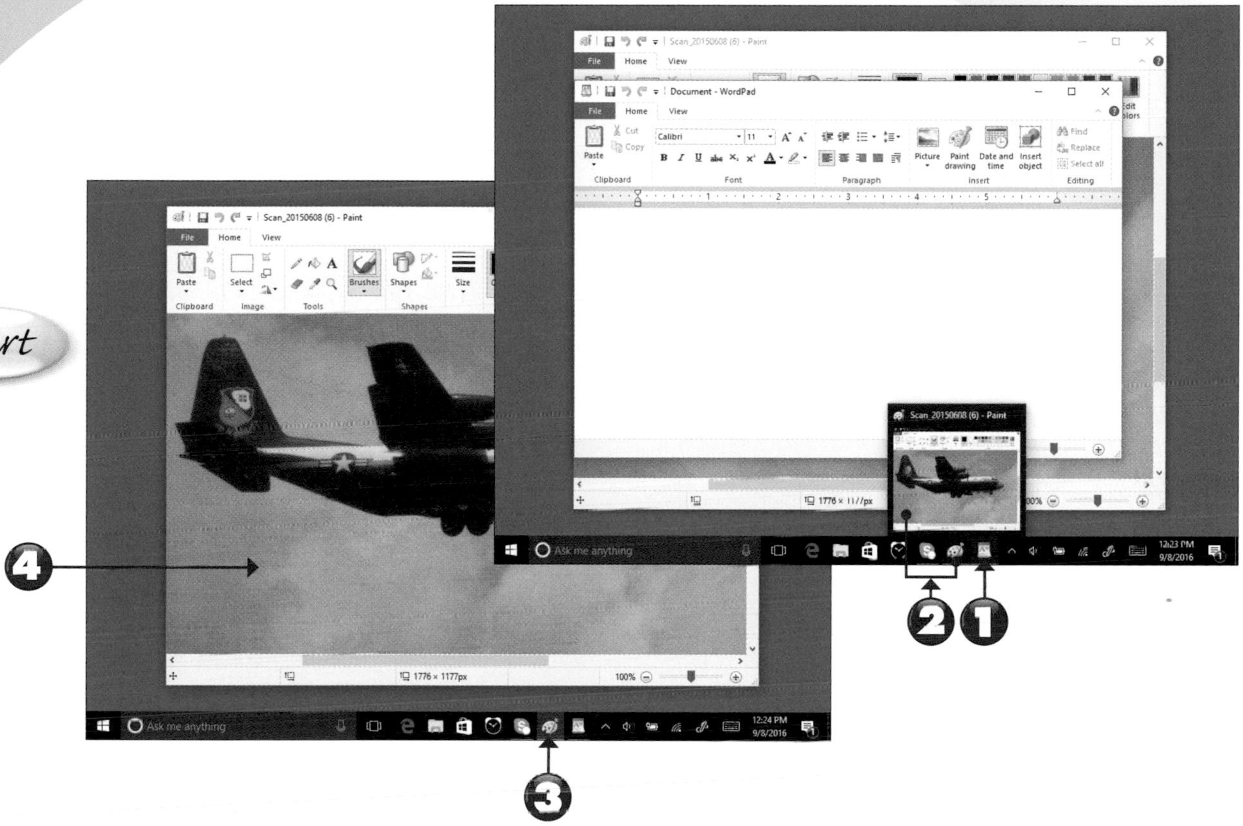

Start

1. WordPad is the active app.
2. Float the mouse over the Paint icon. A live preview appears.
3. Click the Paint icon in the taskbar.
4. Now Paint is the active app.

End

NOTE

What's the Active App? Running apps have a colored line below the taskbar app icon; however, the active app is the app you are working with (entering text, drawing, painting, entering numbers, and so on). When you see multiple windows onscreen, the active app is the one with the highlighted taskbar icon. (Compare WordPad in step 1 to Paint in step 4.)

SWITCHING BETWEEN APPS WITH A TOUCHSCREEN

If you use a touchscreen device, you can swipe in from the left to switch between apps. Here's how to use this feature.

Start

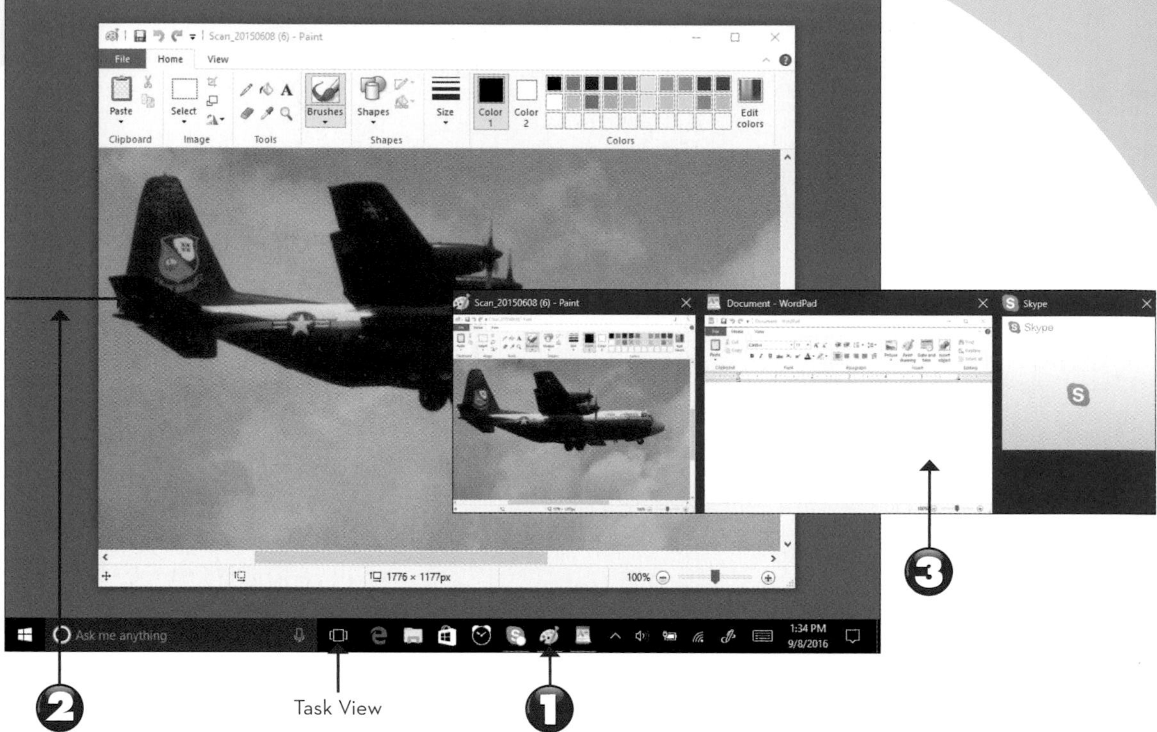

1. Paint is the active app.
2. Swipe from the left.
3. Tap an app preview to make it active.

End

NOTE

Using the Task View Button Instead of swiping, you can click or tap the Task View button on the taskbar to display active apps to choose from.

NOTE

Swiping in Tablet Mode The app previews appear larger if you are using Tablet Mode.

SWITCHING BETWEEN APPS WITH THE KEYBOARD

If you'd rather use the keyboard to switch between apps, you can do it with Windows 10 AE. Here's how.

Start

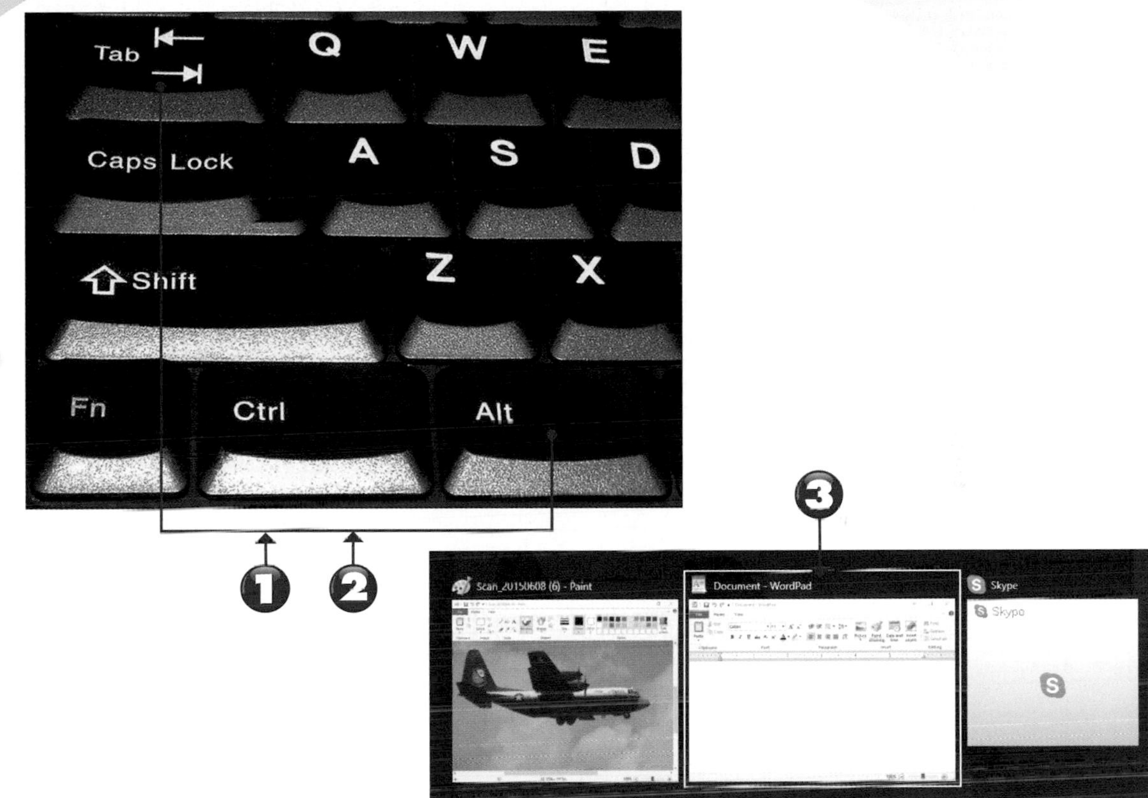

1. Press **Alt+Tab** on the keyboard.
2. Repeat step 1 until the app you want is highlighted.
3. Release the keys to make this app active.

End

NOTE

Windows+Tab and Arrow Keys You can also use Windows+Tab to see currently open apps. Use the left- and right-arrow keys to highlight the app you want to use.

SAVING YOUR FILE

After you change a file, or if you want to save a file as a different type, you must save the new file. This lesson explains how to save a file with a new name. If you are saving a new version of an existing file, this keeps the original version intact.

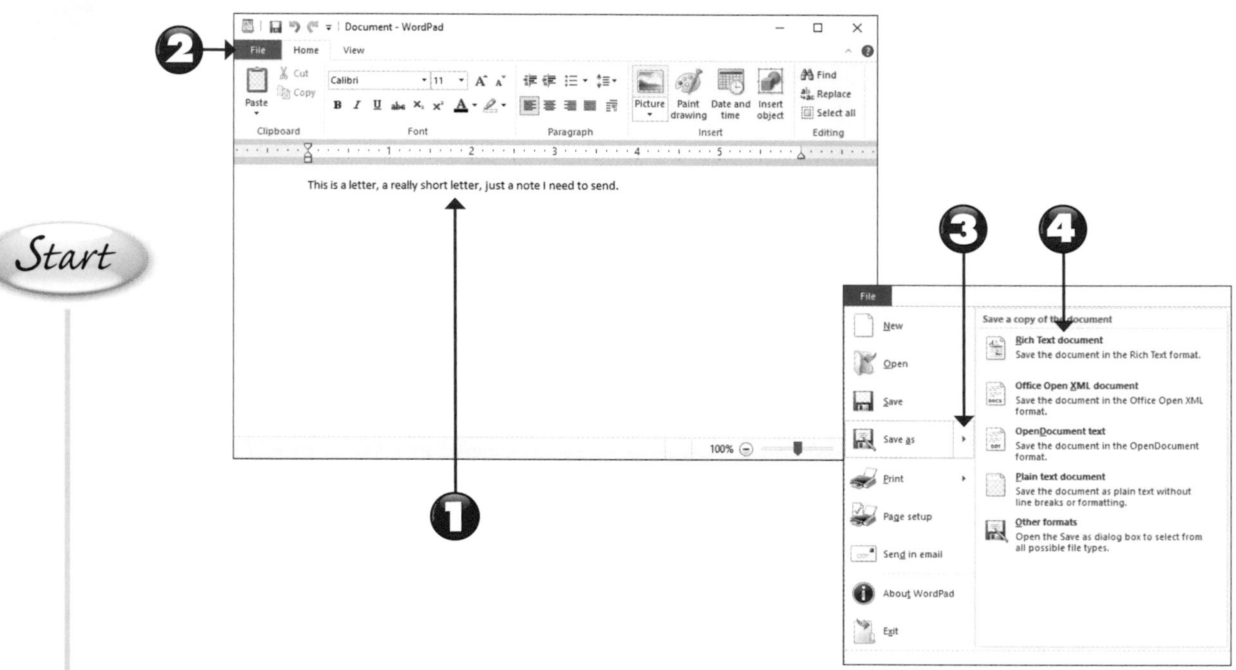

Start

1. Select WordPad as the active app and write some text.
2. Click or tap **File**.
3. Click or tap to open the **Save as** menu.
4. Choose the desired file type (Rich Text document in this example).

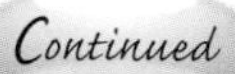

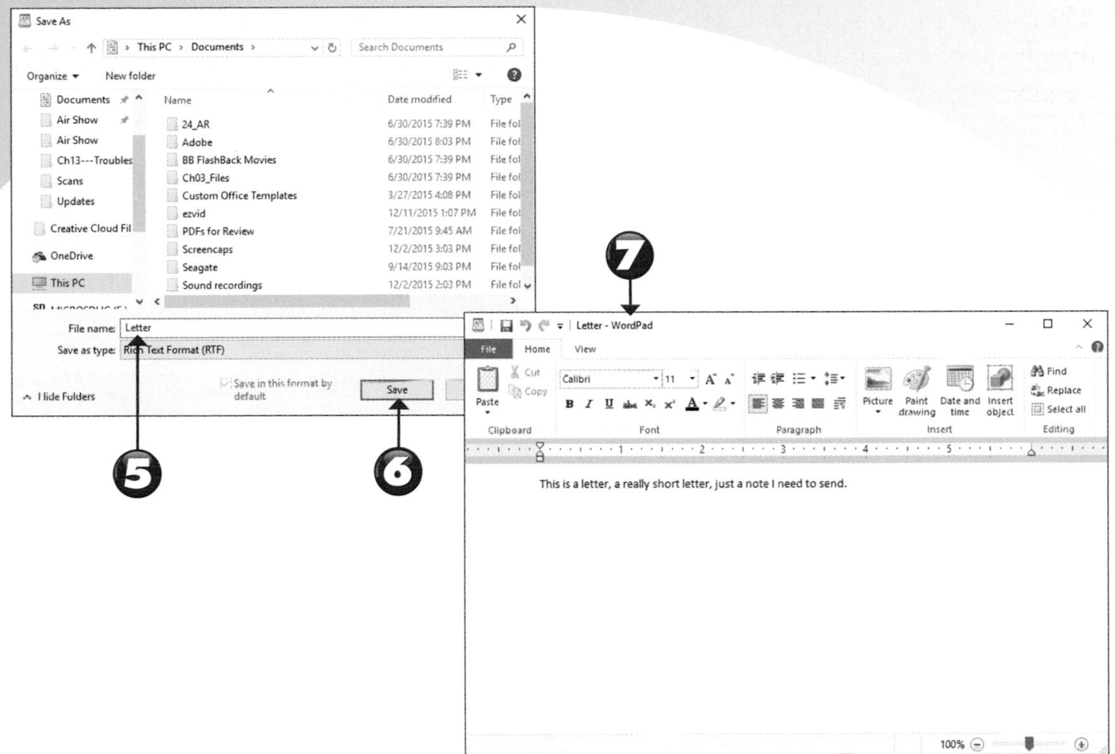

5 Enter a new name.

6 Click or tap **Save** to save the edited document.

7 The app window shows the new filename.

End

NOTE

Save As Versus Save If you use Save (step 3), you replace your original version with the changed version.

RESIZING AN APP WINDOW

When you run an app in a window, the normal window size might not be what you want. You can easily resize it. If you use a mouse on a laptop or desktop PC that does not have a touchscreen, use this method to resize the window of a desktop app.

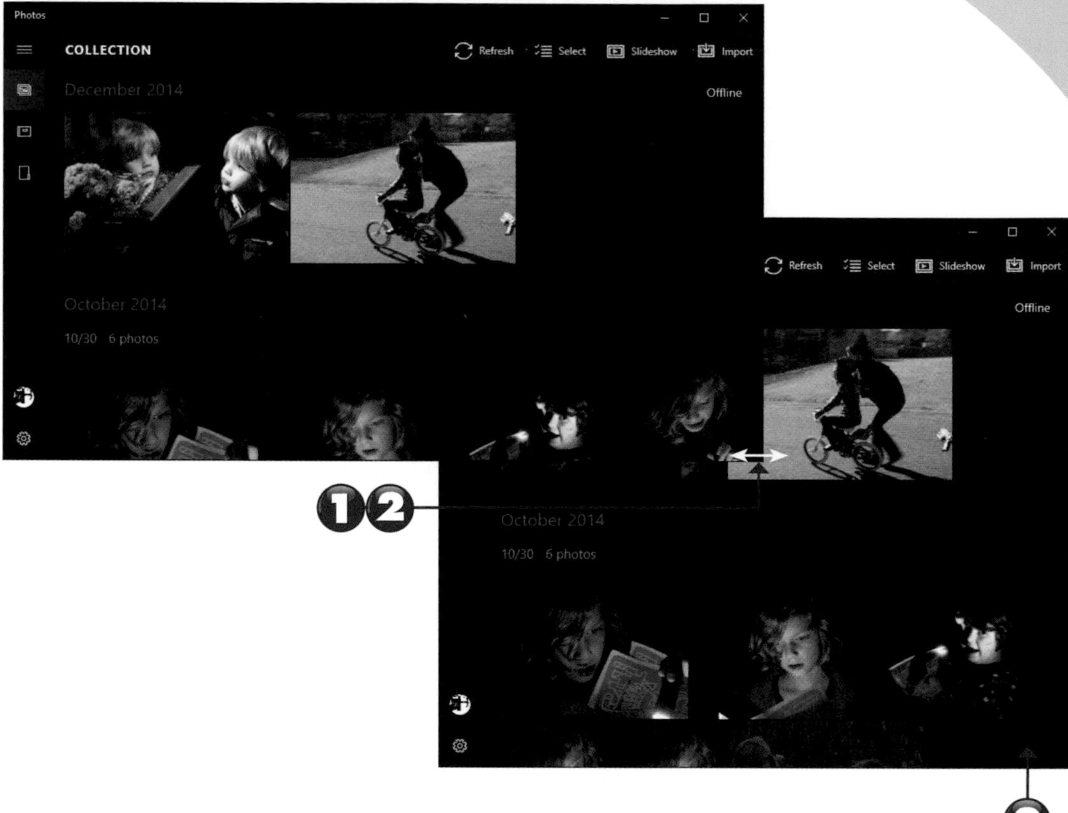

Start

1. Move the mouse over a corner or edge of a window.
2. When the mouse pointer changes to a double-headed arrow, click and drag the window corner or edge.
3. Drag the window to the size and shape you want, and release it.

End

NOTE

Note To resize a window using a touchscreen, touch and hold on the corner of a window and drag it to the position you want. ■

MAKING THE DESKTOP VISIBLE

Many apps offer to create a desktop icon, also called a shortcut, during installation. If you prefer to open apps from the desktop, you might need an easy way to make open windows and maximized apps “disappear” from view without actually closing them so you can easily activate a desktop icon. Windows 10 AE makes it easy to hide open apps when needed.

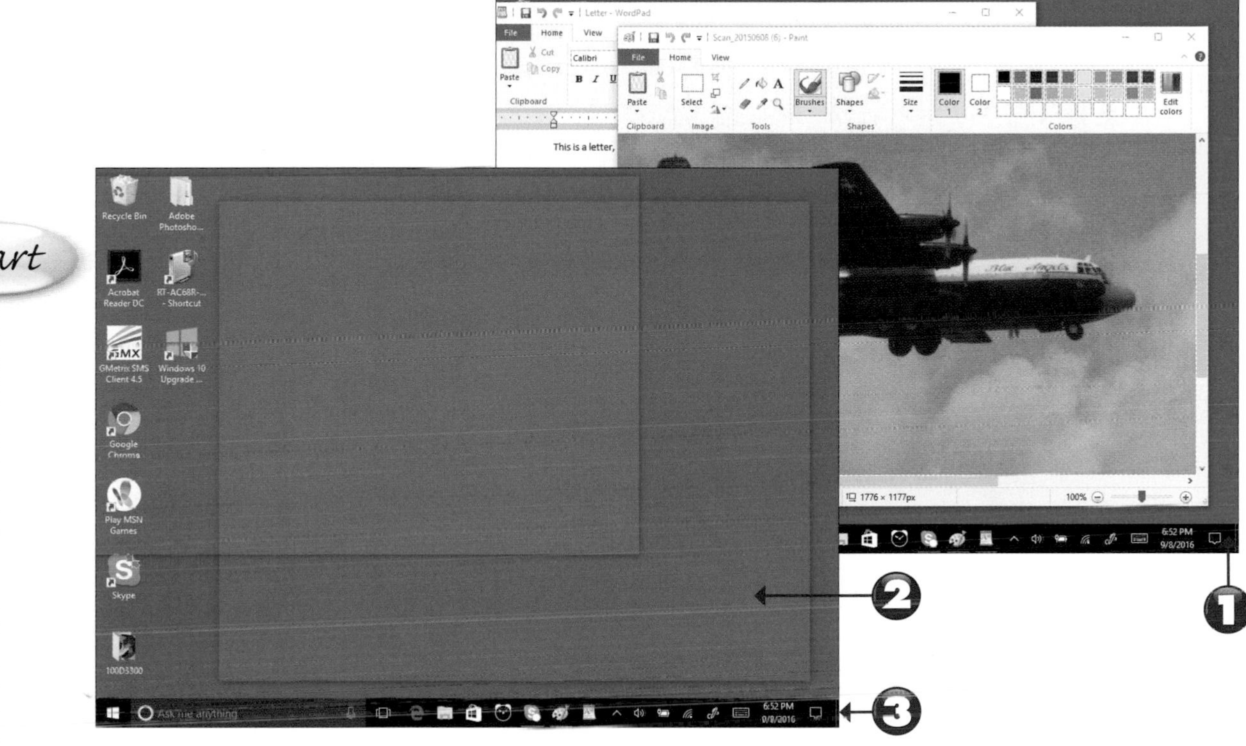

1. Move your mouse to the bottom-right corner of the taskbar.
2. All apps are hidden from the desktop (but continue to run).
3. Click or tap the bottom-right corner again to make all app windows visible.

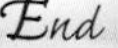

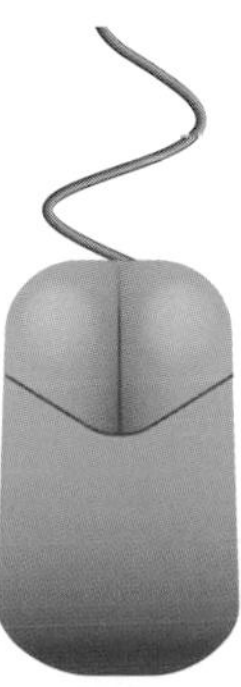

USING DESKTOP SHORTCUTS

Most Windows desktops include shortcuts (icons) for some installed apps. If these shortcuts are not visible, here's how to make them visible and use them to open apps.

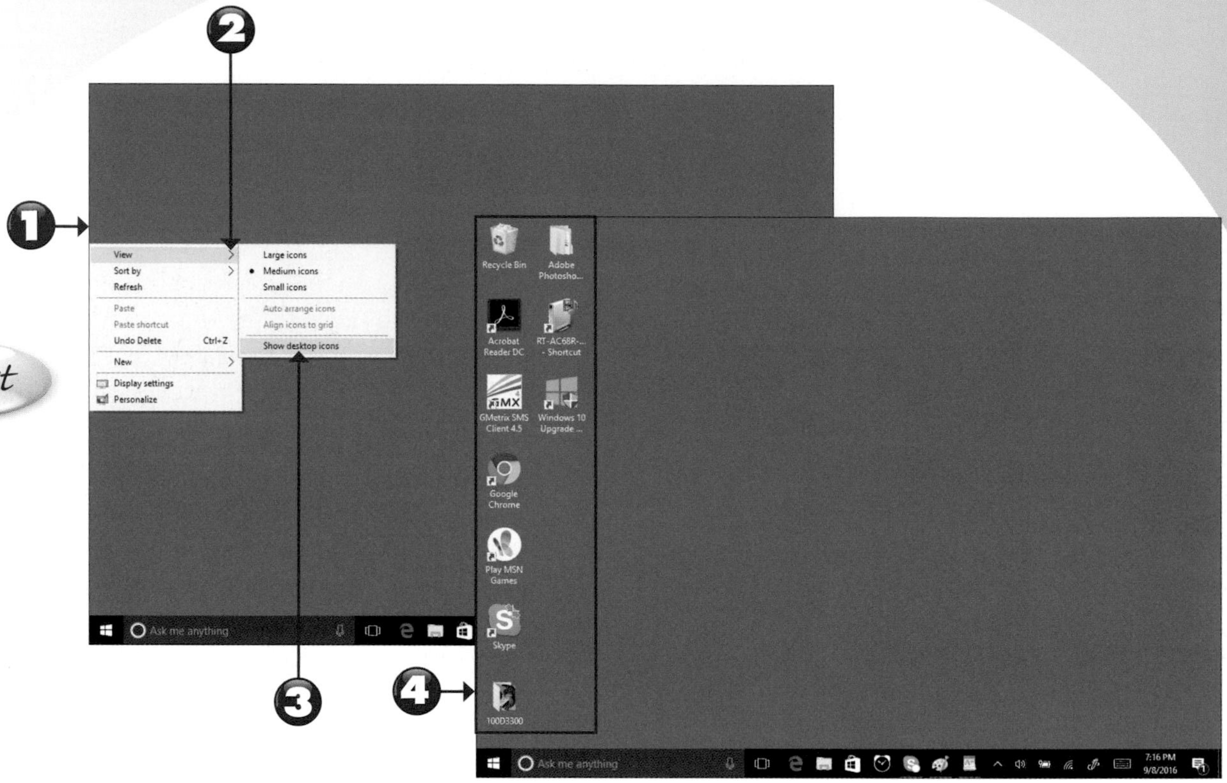

Start

1. Right-click or press and hold an empty spot on the desktop.
2. Click or tap **View**.
3. Click or tap **Show desktop icons**.
4. Double-click an icon to start the app.

End

NOTE

Changing Icon Sizes Windows 10 AE normally uses medium desktop icons. To use larger or smaller icons, select the size desired in step 3.

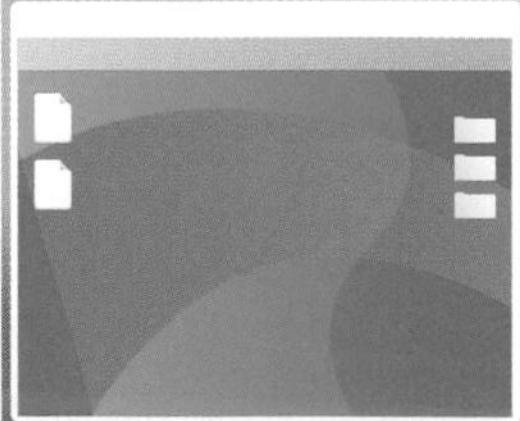

ADDING AN APP TO THE TASKBAR

The Windows AE taskbar is a fast way to start an app. Here's how to add your favorite app to the taskbar. With this example, you pin the Calculator app to the taskbar.

Start

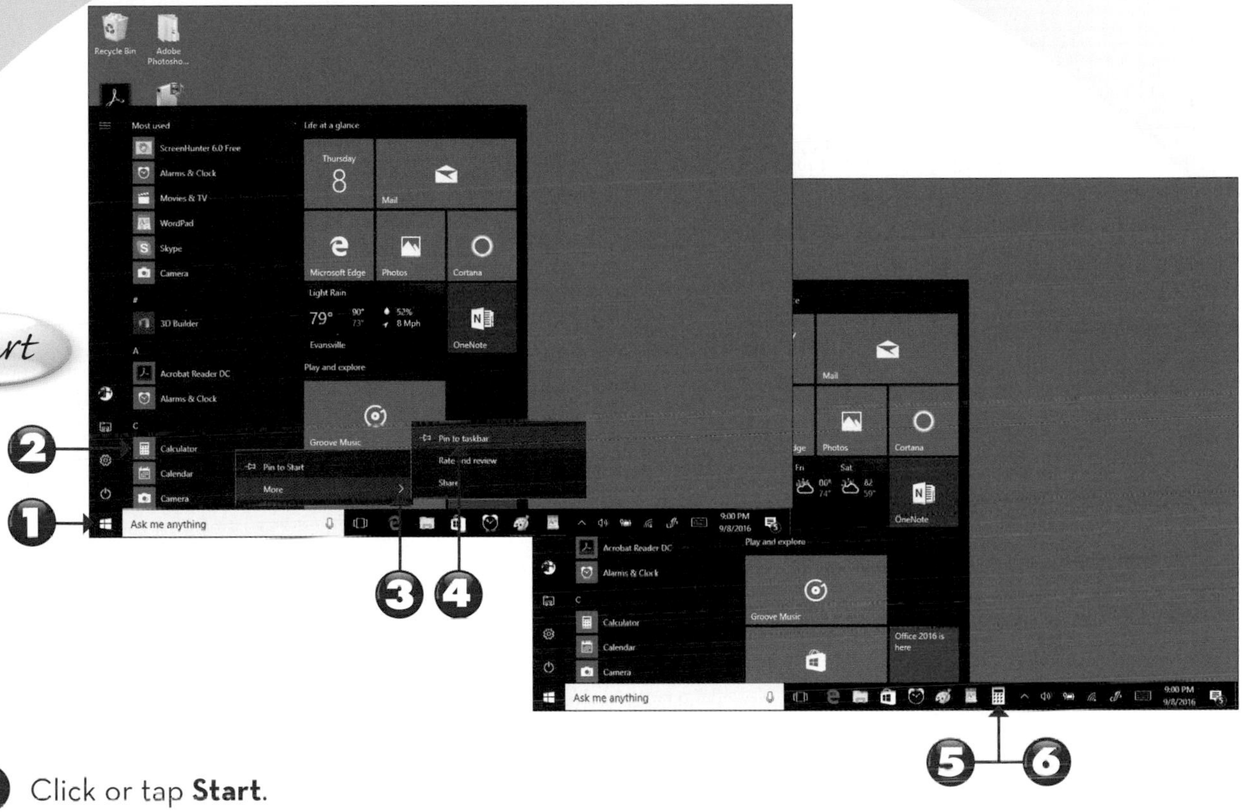

1. Click or tap **Start**.
2. Right-click or press and hold the Calculator app's icon.
3. Click or tap **More**.
4. Click or tap **Pin to taskbar**.
5. The app is added to the taskbar.
6. To start the app, click or tap the icon on the taskbar.

End

TIP

Pinning a Running App to the Taskbar To pin an app that is already running to the taskbar, right-click or press and hold the app's icon and select **Pin this program to taskbar**. See "Working with Taskbar Jump Lists" for an illustration.

WORKING WITH TASKBAR JUMP LISTS

Most icons on the taskbar also include a jump list, including recent files or common actions. Here's how to use the jump list for easier access to files you want to use again and again and to open your app with your favorite files.

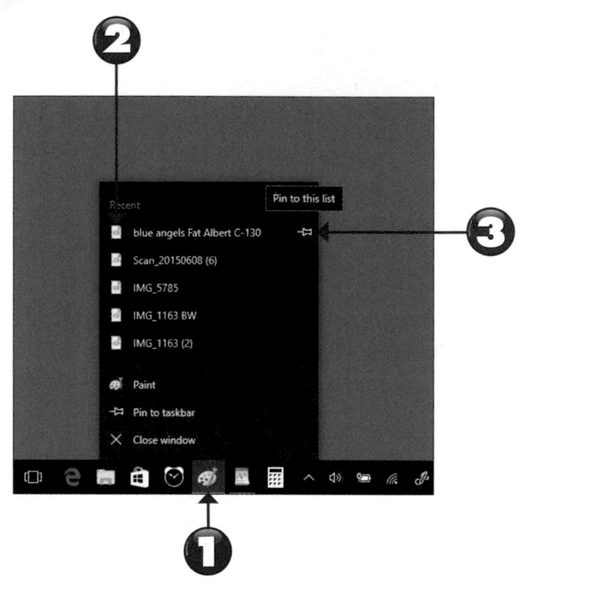

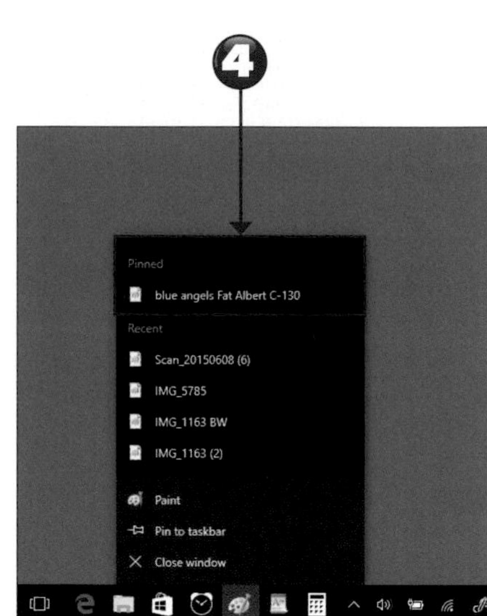

1. Right-click or press and hold the **Paint** icon in the taskbar.
2. Hover your mouse over a file you want to pin. With a touchscreen, press and hold the filename.
3. When the pushpin appears, click or tap it.
4. The file is pinned to the jump list.

TIP

Opening and Unpinning a File You can open any file on the jump list. More recently opened files replace older files on the jump list. To remove a file from the jump list, right-click or press and hold the file, and then click or tap **Remove from this list**.

Pin files you want to use frequently, because pinned files stay on the list until you remove them. To unpin a file, right-click or press and hold the file, and then click or tap **Unpin from this list**.

SNAPPING AND CLOSING AN APP WINDOW

You can change the position and size of the active app window directly from the keyboard by using a Windows 10 AE feature called *snapping*. This example uses the Microsoft Edge browser app included in Windows 10 Anniversary Edition.

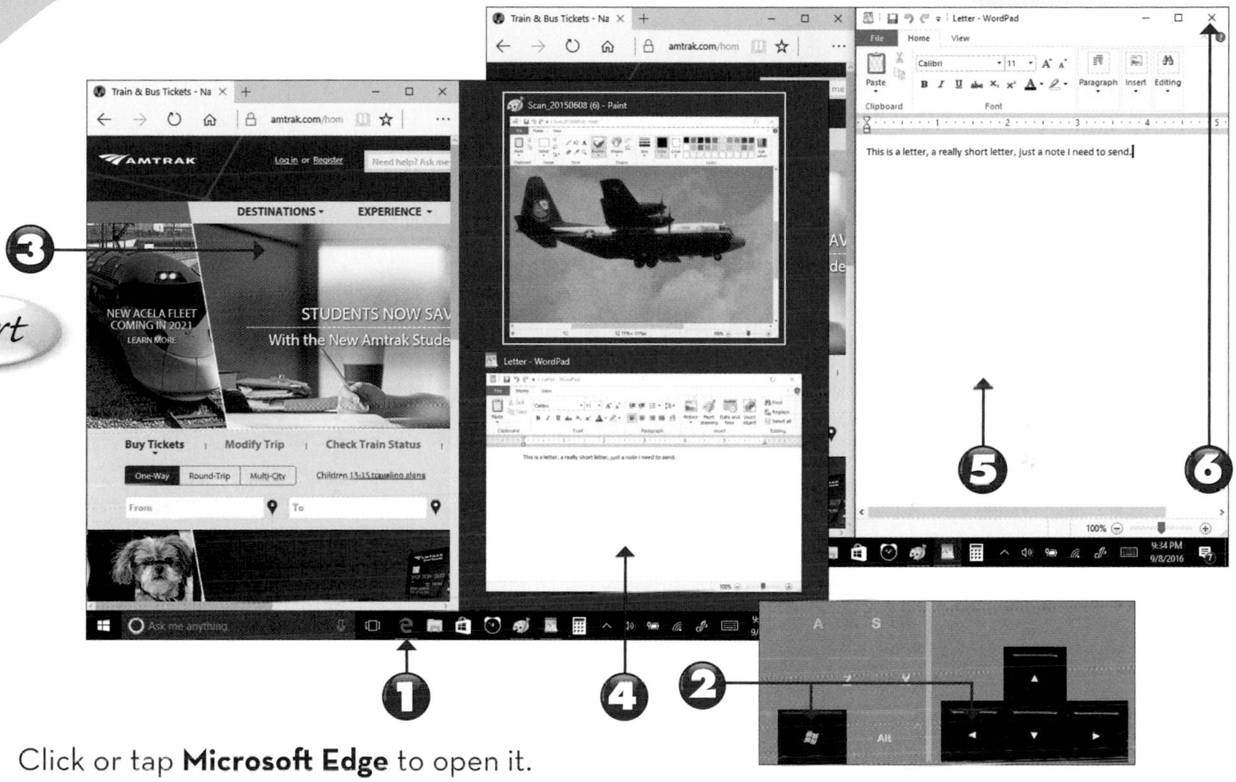

Start

1. Click or tap **Microsoft Edge** to open it.
2. Press **Windows key+left arrow**.
3. The active app (Microsoft Edge) snaps to the left edge of the current display.
4. To snap an open app into the other half of the desktop, click or tap it.
5. The selected app snaps into the right half of the desktop.
6. Click or tap to close the app.

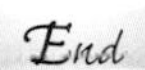

TIP

More Snapping Tips Press Windows key+right arrow to snap the active app to the right side of the screen. Press Windows key+up arrow to maximize the active app. If you drag a program window to the top of the screen, it snaps to full screen. Press Windows key+down arrow to minimize the active app. To remove the other app windows from the left or right side of the desktop, press the Esc (Escape) key on the keyboard.

WEB BROWSING WITH MICROSOFT EDGE

Windows 10 AE uses Microsoft Edge as its default browser. Edge is faster and easier to use than the older Internet Explorer browser—and more compatible with today's state-of-the-art websites, too. Designed for both touch and mouse/keyboard users, Edge has many new features and new takes on familiar functions. In AE, Edge now adds support for extensions, so you can add more features whenever you need to. In this chapter, you learn how to use Microsoft Edge for all your web browsing.

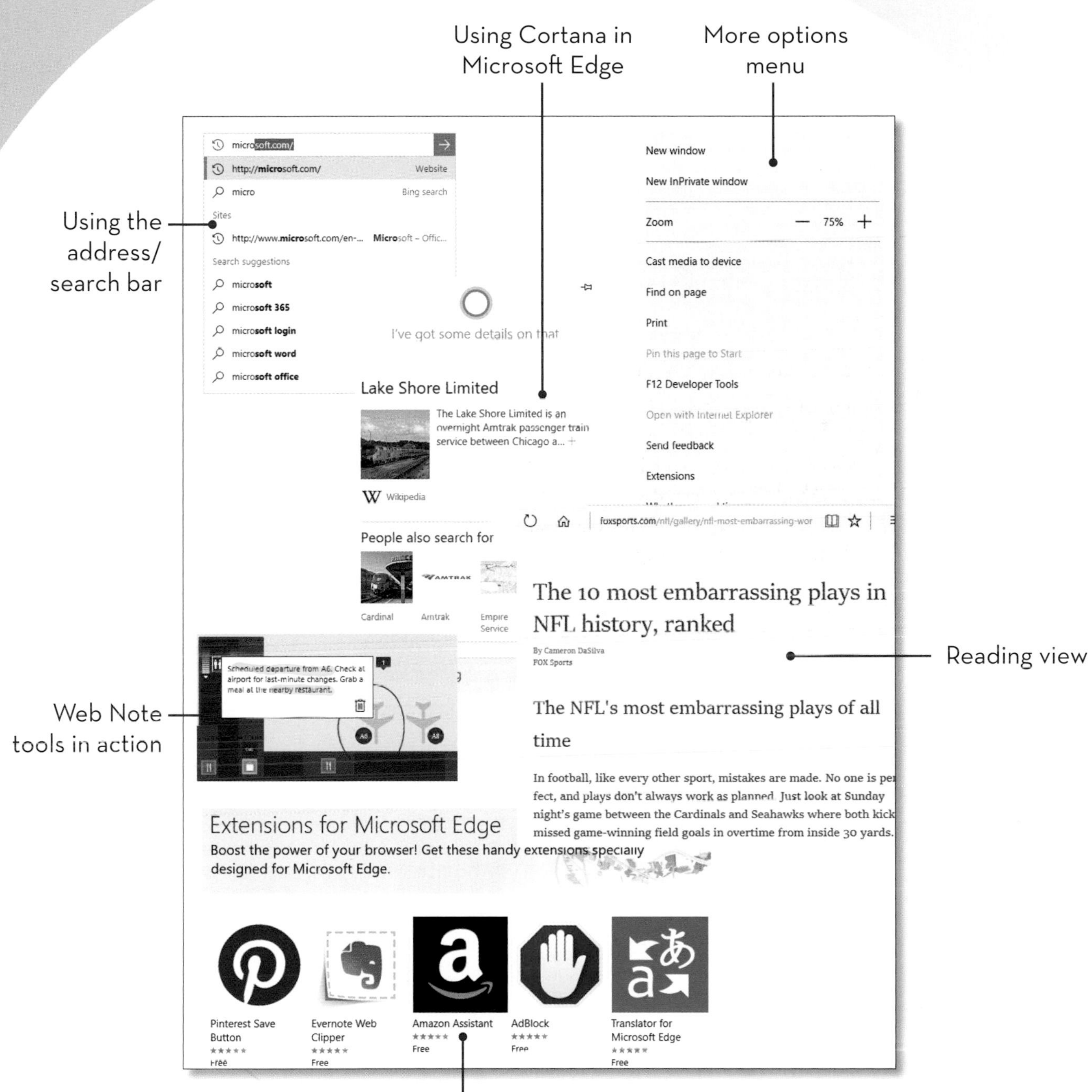

Using Cortana in Microsoft Edge
More options menu
Using the address/ search bar
Web Note tools in action
Reading view
Shopping for extensions in the Microsoft Store
New window
New InPrivate window
Zoom
Cast media to device
Find on page
Print
Pin this page to Start
F12 Developer Tools
Open with Internet Explorer
Send feedback
Extensions
I've got some details on that
Lake Shore Limited
The Lake Shore Limited is an overnight Amtrak passenger train service between Chicago a...
People also search for
The 10 most embarrassing plays in NFL history, ranked
By Cameron DaSilva
FOX Sports
The NFL's most embarrassing plays of all time
Extensions for Microsoft Edge
Boost the power of your browser! Get these handy extensions specially designed for Microsoft Edge.
Pinterest Save Button
Evernote Web Clipper
Amazon Assistant
AdBlock
Translator for Microsoft Edge

STARTING MICROSOFT EDGE

Microsoft Edge might be on your system's taskbar. If not, you can launch it from the Start menu. Here's how.

1. Click or tap **Start**.

2. Click or tap **Microsoft Edge**.

3. Use the Microsoft Edge address bar or search box to enter web addresses to visit.

4. Click or tap the **+** to create a new tab.

5. Click the **Make a Web Note** (annotation) button; for more information, see the sections later in this chapter about using the Web Notes feature.

6. Click or tap to see additional menu items.

End

ENTERING A WEBSITE ADDRESS (URL)

You can enter a web address, or URL, in the browser's search box. Edge displays more than just the address when you type in a site you've previously visited. This feature makes it easier to go back to an address you've previously visited, even if you have visited several pages in the same domain.

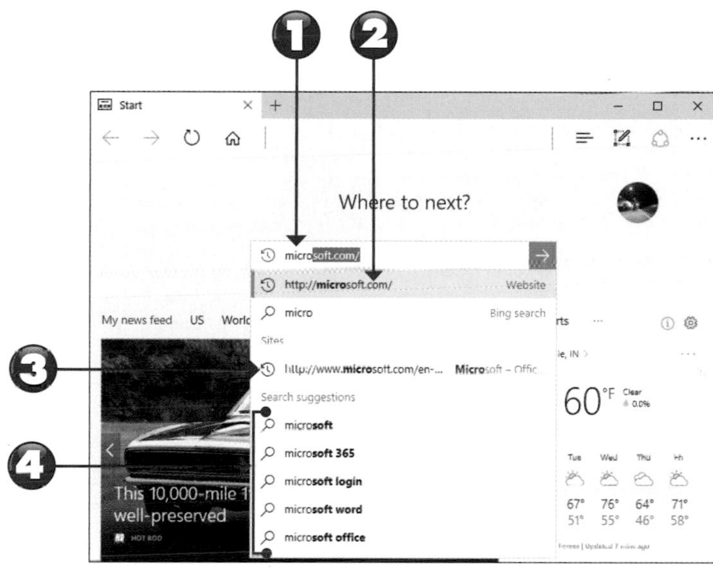

1. With Microsoft Edge open, begin typing the name of a website in the search box. You do not need to add the "www."
2. Potential matches are listed with the closest site match at the top of the list.
3. If you have already visited a web page with the text in either the website name (URL) or the web page title, this appears in the Sites list.
4. Search suggestions are listed at the bottom.

TIP

Selecting a Website or Search Use your mouse, touchpad, or touchscreen to select the website or search suggestion you want to open. You can also use the down arrow to highlight the page you want to load and then press **Enter**.

CAUTION

Making Sure Edge Has You Protected Before going to unfamiliar websites, make sure Edge's SmartScreen Filter is enabled. Learn more in "Setting Browser Privacy, Services, and Platform Controls," this chapter, p. 116.

WORKING WITH TABS

Microsoft Edge includes tabbed browsing, which lets you browse multiple pages in a single window. In this tutorial, you learn how to open and work with new tabs in Microsoft Edge.

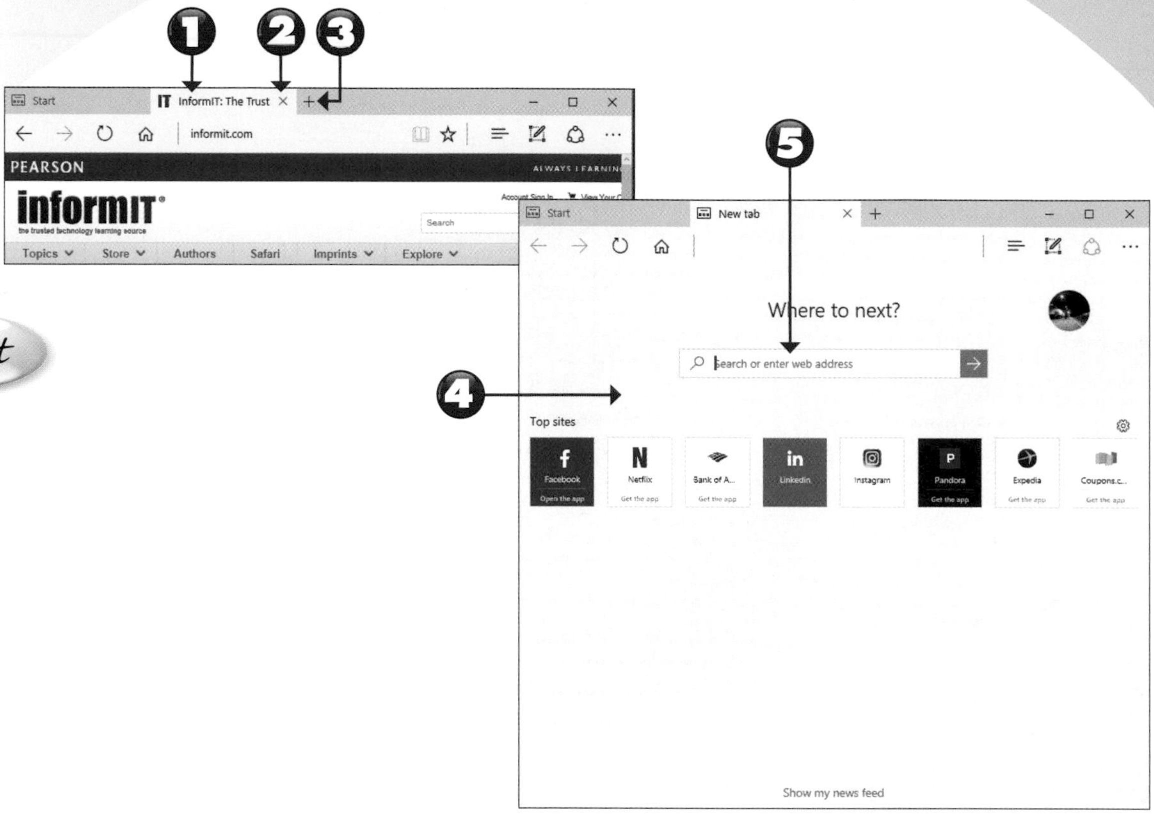

Start

1. Click or tap a tab to switch to that tab.
2. Click the X to close a tab.
3. Click or tap to open a new tab.
4. A New tab page lists top websites here for easy access.
5. Click or tap to enter a new URL.

End

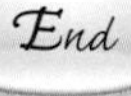

TIP

Changing New Tab Contents If you prefer other content displayed when you open a new tab, change your browser settings. To learn more, see "Configuring Your New Tab Page," this chapter, p. 99.

OPENING A LINK

Because Microsoft Edge supports tabbed browsing, you can open a link to another website in one of three ways: as a replacement for the current page (default), as a new tab in the same window, or in a new window. When you click or tap on a link, the link could open in the same window or in a new window. To specifically open the link in a new tab or window, use the method shown in this tutorial.

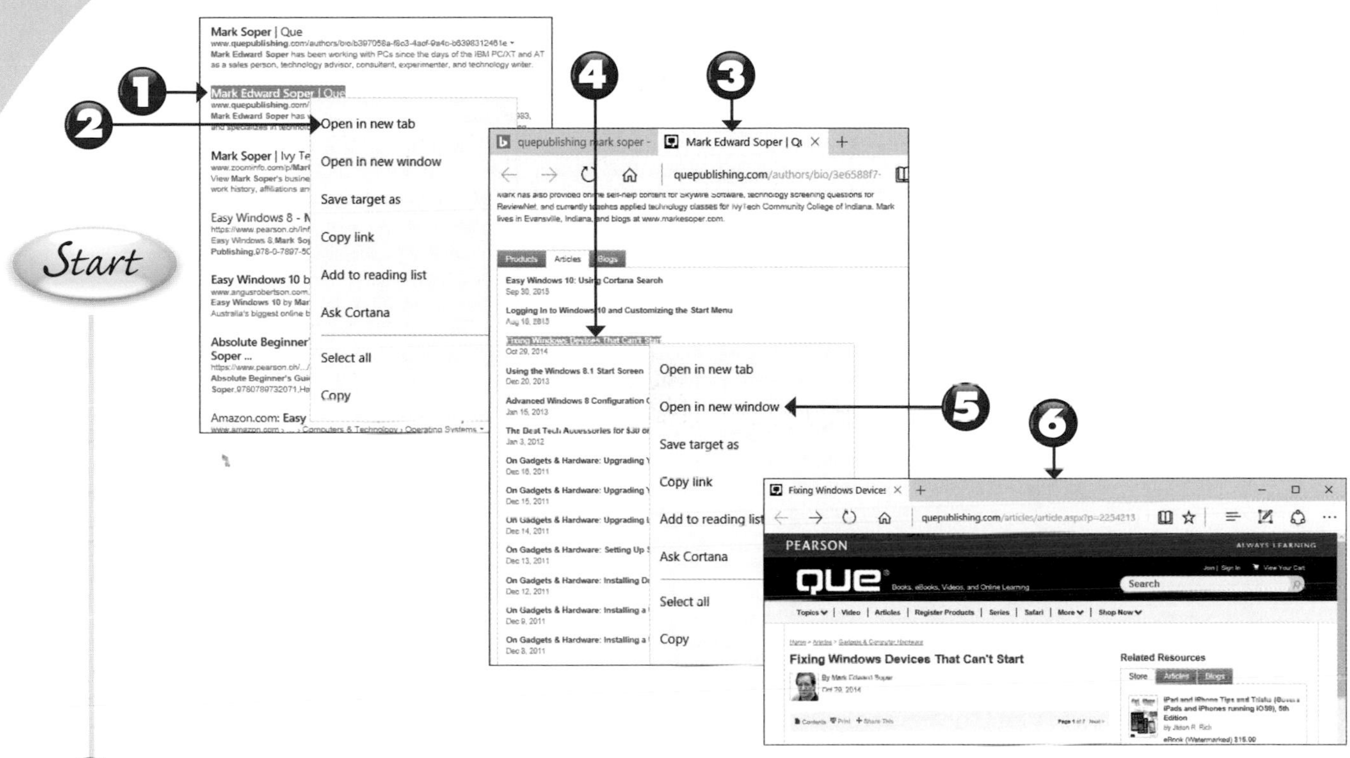

1. Right-click, or press and hold the link to display the options menu.
2. Click or tap **Open in new tab**.
3. Click or tap the new tab.
4. Right-click, or press and hold a link.
5. Select **Open in new window**.
6. A new window opens to display the link.

End

SETTING YOUR HOME PAGE

You can change your Microsoft Edge home page (also known as a Start page) whenever you want. Edge provides you with several options. Here's how to open Edge (or a new tab) with the options you prefer.

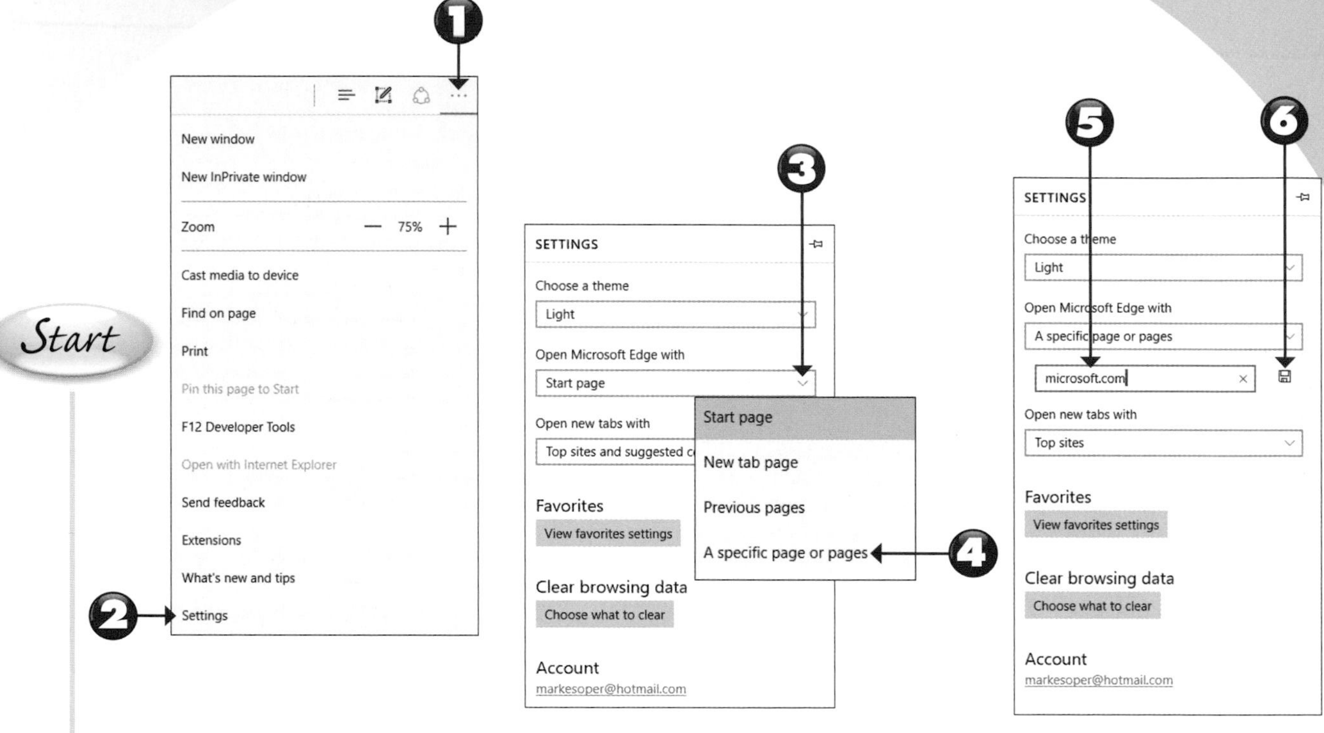

1. Open the **More** (three-dot) menu.
2. Click or tap **Settings**.
3. Click or tap **Open Microsoft Edge with**.
4. Click or tap **A specific page or pages**.
5. Enter the URL of the page you want as your home page into the **Enter a web address** box.
6. Click the **Save** button to save your changes.

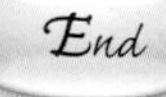

NOTE

Default Start Page The default Start page displays a list of the most commonly used websites ("top sites"). The New tab page can also display your news feed. To see how to change these options, see the next task, "Configuring Your New Tab Page."

CONFIGURING YOUR NEW TAB PAGE

The New tab page is the page that appears whenever you open a new tab. In this lesson, you learn how to customize it to show the sites you want.

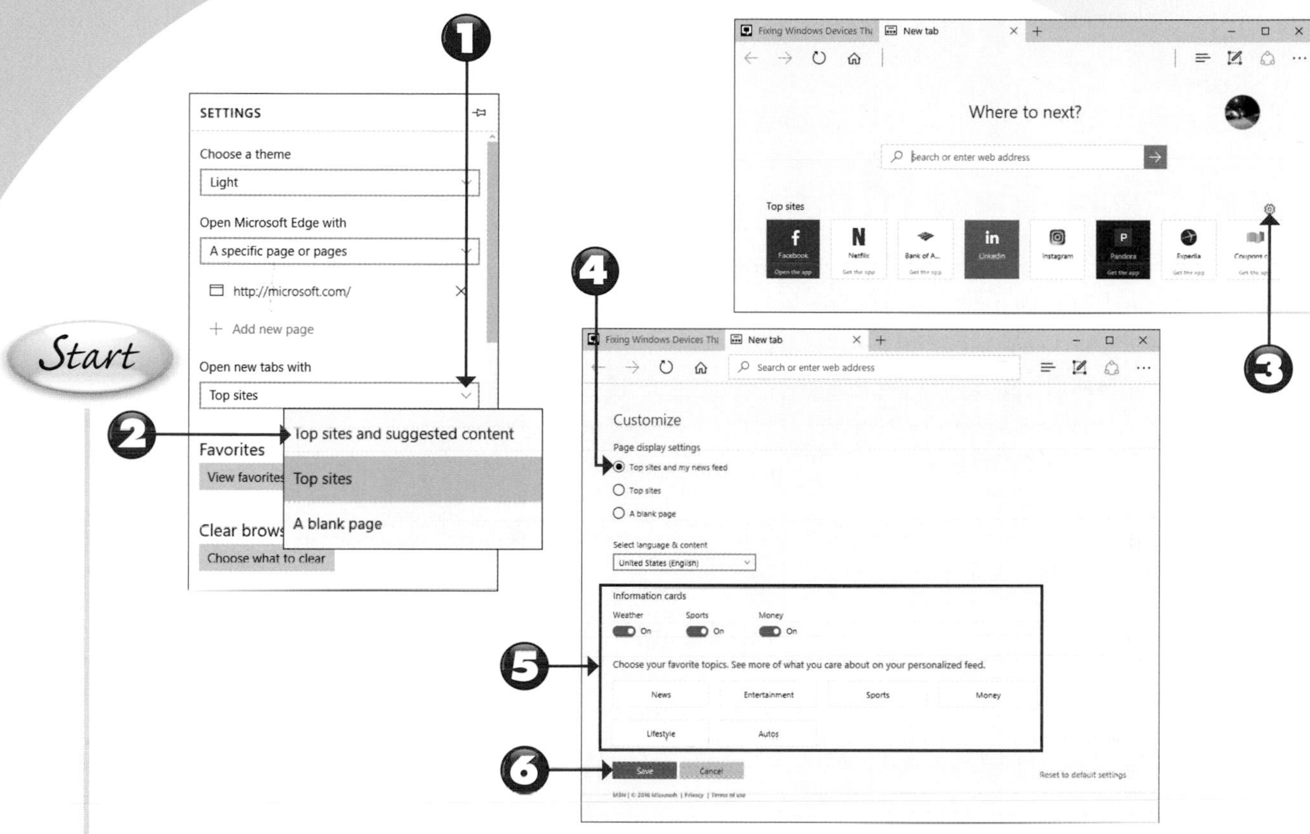

1. With the Settings menu displayed from the previous task, click or tap **Open new tabs with**.
2. Click or tap **Top sites and suggested content**.
3. Open a new tab and click or tap the **Settings** (gearbox) button.
4. Click or tap **Top sites and my news feed**.
5. Choose the information to display in your news feed.
6. Click the **Save** button to save your changes.

End

USING CORTANA IN MICROSOFT EDGE

Cortana is the powerful search and information technology included in Windows 10 AE. You can use Cortana in Microsoft Edge to get more information about a link, highlighted text, or a picture on a web page. Here's an example of how Cortana can help you learn more about what you see in a web page.

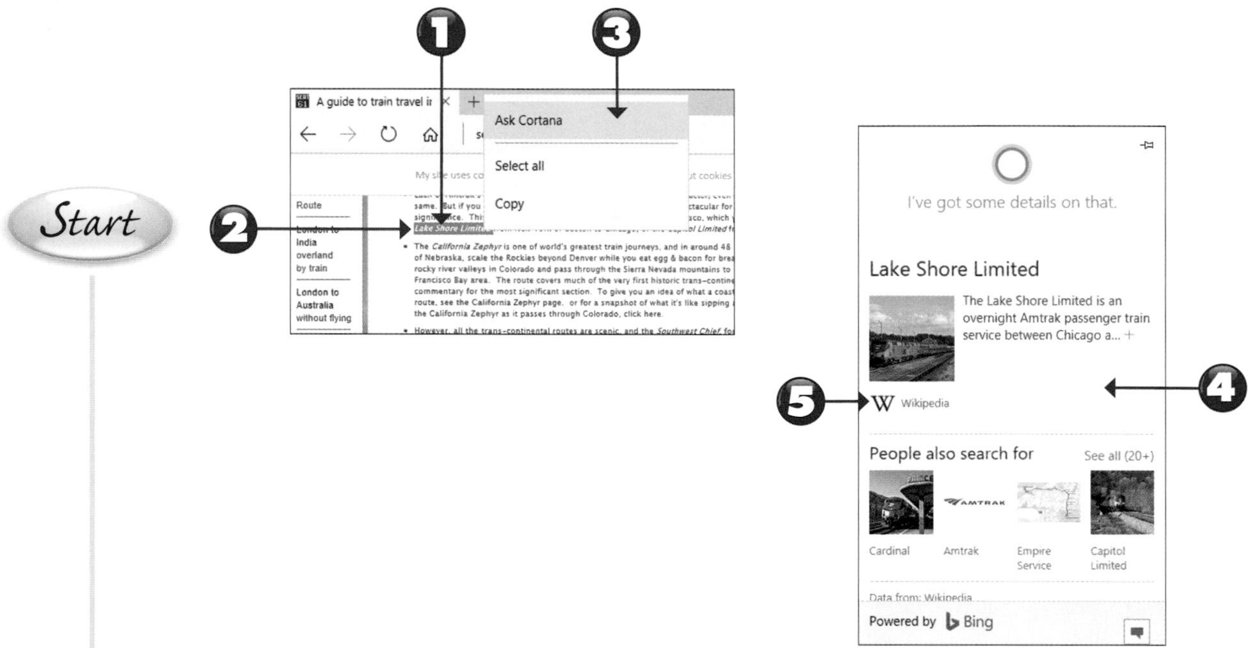

1. Highlight the text, or click a picture on a web page.
2. Right-click, or press and hold the highlighted text or picture.
3. Click or tap **Ask Cortana**.
4. Cortana opens a pane in your browser with the information requested. If you select a picture, Cortana tries to identify the subject and provides a link to a full-size version if available.
5. Click or tap a link to learn more, or click or tap an empty area of the browser window to close the Cortana pane.

End

NOTE

How to Highlight Text To highlight text with your mouse or touchpad, click and hold the beginning of the text, move to the right until the text is highlighted, and then release. To highlight text with your touchscreen, press and hold a word in the text until a highlight appears. Press and drag one of the circle markers at each end of the word until all the text desired is highlighted. ■

COPYING AND PASTING A LINK

The same right-click menu you use to open links or access Cortana can also be used to copy links that can be pasted into other apps. Here's how to use this feature with Windows 10 AE's built-in text editor, Notepad. You can also use this technique with Microsoft Word and other word-processing programs.

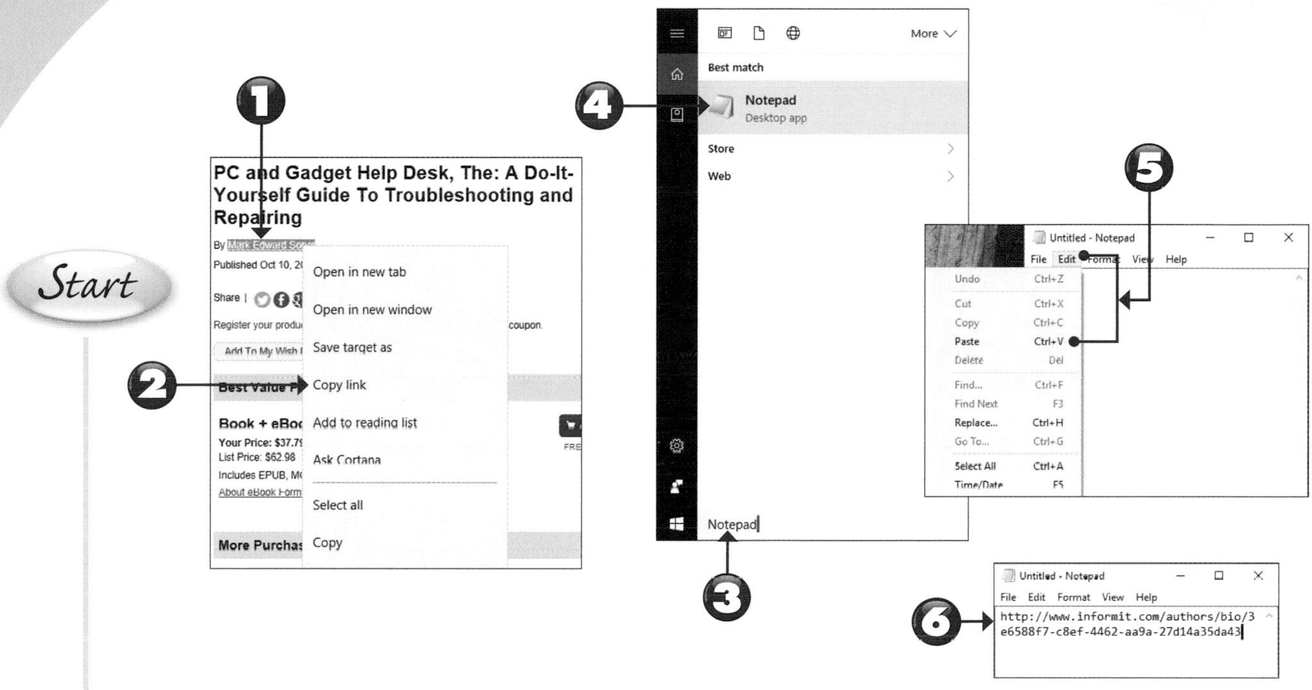

1. Right-click or press and hold a link.
2. Click or tap **Copy link**.
3. Click or tap the Cortana **Search** box and type **notepad**.
4. Click or tap **Notepad**.
5. Click or tap **Edit** and select **Paste**.
6. The link is pasted into Notepad.

End

USING ZOOM

Zoom enables you to increase or decrease the size of text and graphics on a web page. By increasing the size, you make pages easier to read, and by reducing the size, you enable page viewing without horizontal scrolling.

Start

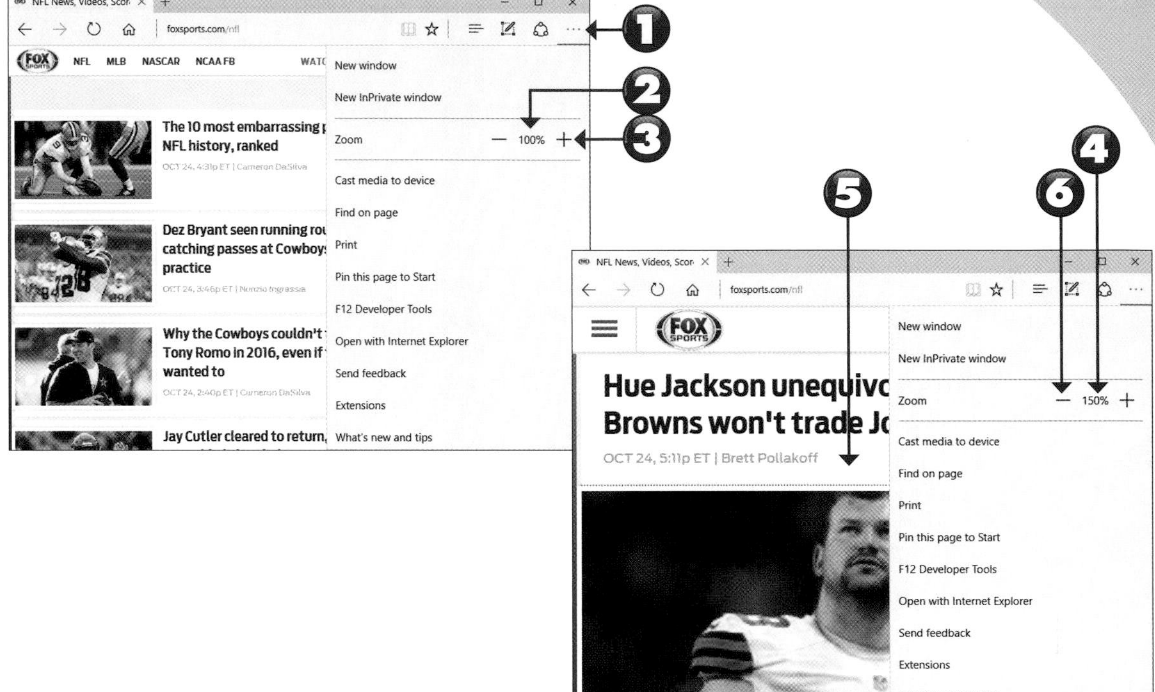

1. Click or tap the **More** (three-dot) menu.
2. The current zoom setting is listed here (the default is 100%).
3. Click or tap the plus (+) sign to increase the zoom level.
4. Page is zoomed to 150%.
5. Note the large text and graphics.
6. Click or tap the minus (-) sign to decrease the zoom level.

Continued

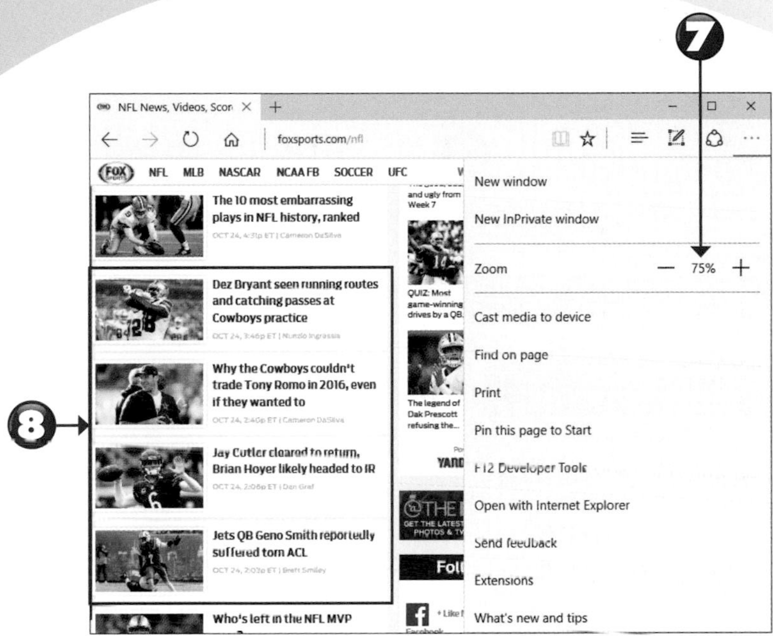

7 The page is zoomed to 75%.

8 More of the page is visible, but the text is smaller.

End

NOTE

When to Zoom The 150% view shown in step 5 makes the text and pictures on a web page easier to see, but you must scroll left and right as well as up and down to see the entire page. Use zoom settings smaller than 100% if you want to see more of the page without scrolling. These settings do not affect how the page prints.

USING READING VIEW

You can read a lot of terrific articles in your browser, but most commercial sites litter articles with ads and other visual distractions. The Reading view in Microsoft Edge shows you only the main contents of the current URL without the clutter. Although not all pages support it, here's how to use it when available.

Start

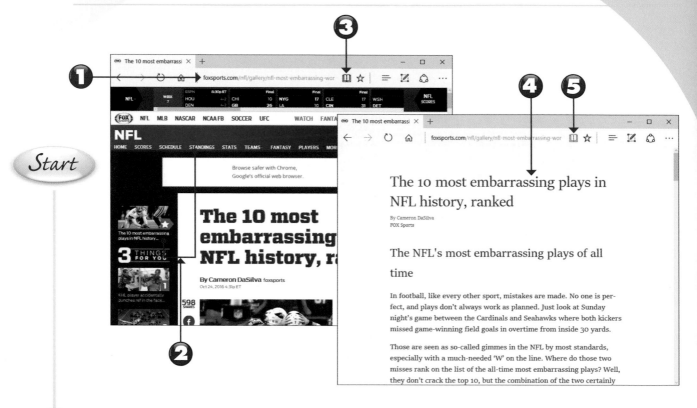

1. Open the web page you want to read.
2. Note the ads and other visual distractions.
3. Click or tap **Reading view**.
4. Microsoft Edge displays the web page without the clutter.
5. Click or tap to return to normal view.

End

NOTE

Changing Reading View Style and Font Size Open the **More** (three-dot) menu, click or tap **Settings**, and scroll to the Reading section. Styles include Default, Light, Medium, and Dark. Font sizes include Small, Medium, Large, and Extra Large.

PRINTING OR CREATING A PDF OF A WEB PAGE

Microsoft Edge enables you to preview and print web pages or turn them into PDFs. I recommend you switch to Reading view first (see the preceding exercise, "Using Reading View," for details) to avoid ads and other onscreen clutter, and then print your page as shown in this exercise.

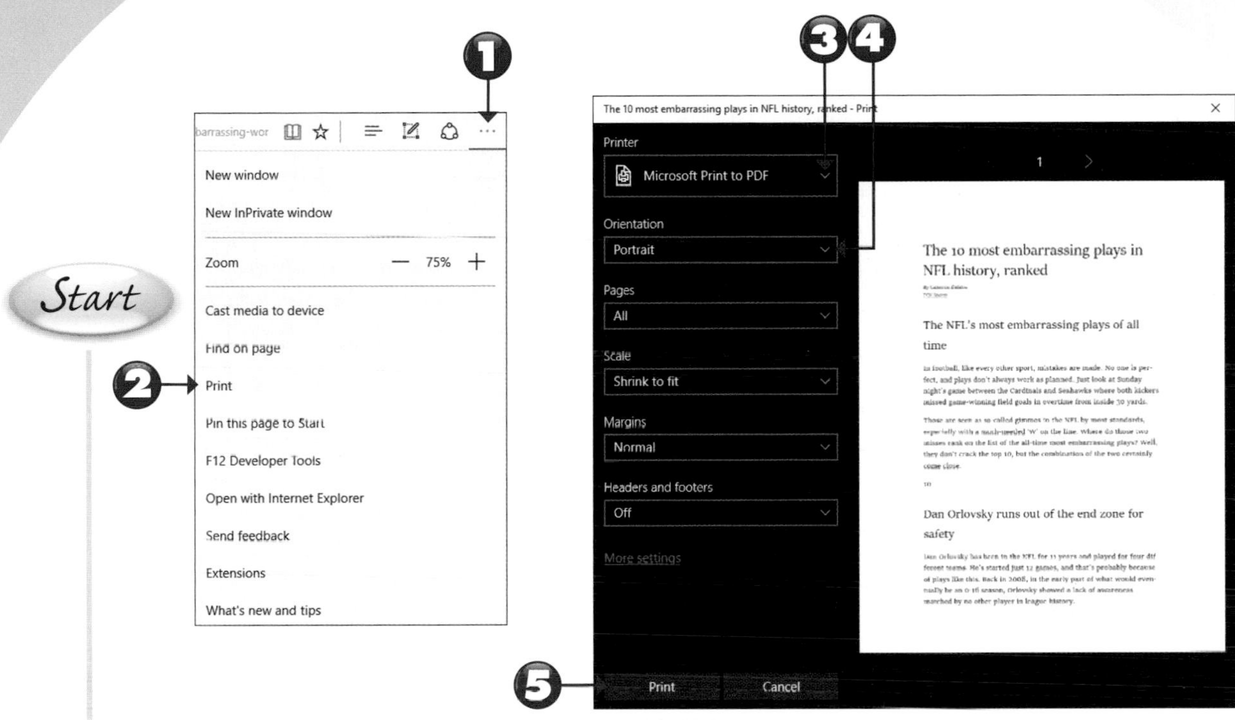

1. Click or tap the **More** (three-dot) menu.
2. Click or tap **Print**.
3. Click or tap if you need to change printers. (To create a PDF file, select **Microsoft Print to PDF** from the drop-down menu.)
4. Click or tap to change page orientation.
5. Click or tap to print the page.

End

NOTE

Changing Paper Size, Type, and Other Settings The default paper size is usually letter or A4. To change paper size, paper type (plain paper, photo paper, and so on), and other settings, click or tap **More settings**.

ADDING A WEB PAGE AS A FAVORITE

When you make a web page a favorite (also known as bookmarking a page), you can go to it quickly whenever you want. Microsoft Edge stores your favorites in the Favorites folder unless you specify otherwise. Here's how to store a favorite page.

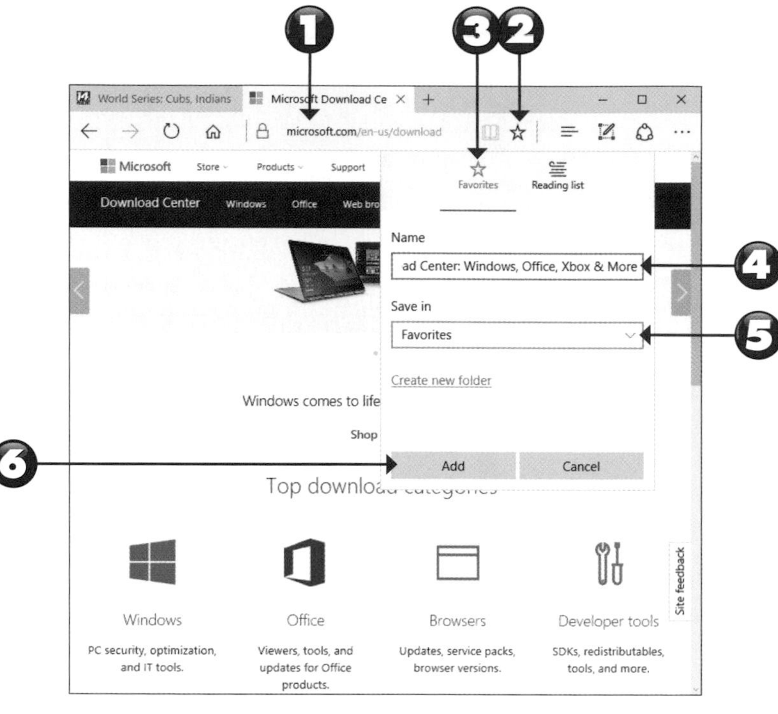

Start

1. Open a web page you want to save as a favorite.
2. Click or tap the **Add to Favorites or Reading List** (star) icon.
3. Click or tap **Favorites**.
4. Accept or edit the name of the page in the **Name** box.
5. If you want to store your pages in a folder other than Favorites, click or tap to open the **Save in** menu, and then select a folder.
6. Click or tap the **Add** button.

NOTE

Creating a New Folder If you don't see a suitable folder for your favorite in step 5, click or tap the **Create new folder** link, create a new folder, and then add your favorite to that folder.

NOTE

Confirming the Favorite Was Created The outline star icon you tap or click in step 2 turns a solid gold color after you add the page as a favorite.

VIEWING AND OPENING FAVORITES

You can reopen a favorite web page in just a few clicks or taps, as you learn in this exercise.

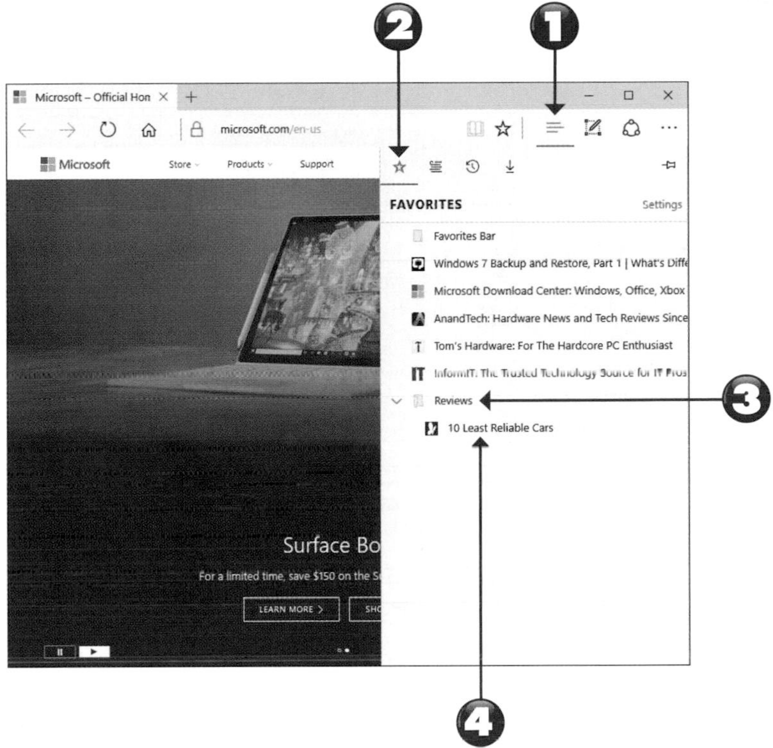

1. Click or tap the **Hub** icon.
2. Click or tap the **Favorites** (star) icon.
3. Click or tap a folder to view the website links it contains.
4. Click or tap a favorite to open it.

End

TIP

Removing Favorites If a favorite becomes outdated or no longer needed, you can discard it. From the Favorites list, right-click or press and hold the favorite. Click or tap **Delete** to remove it.

ADDING A WEB PAGE TO THE READING LIST

If you want to save a web page for reading later, use the Reading List feature built in to Microsoft Edge. Here's how.

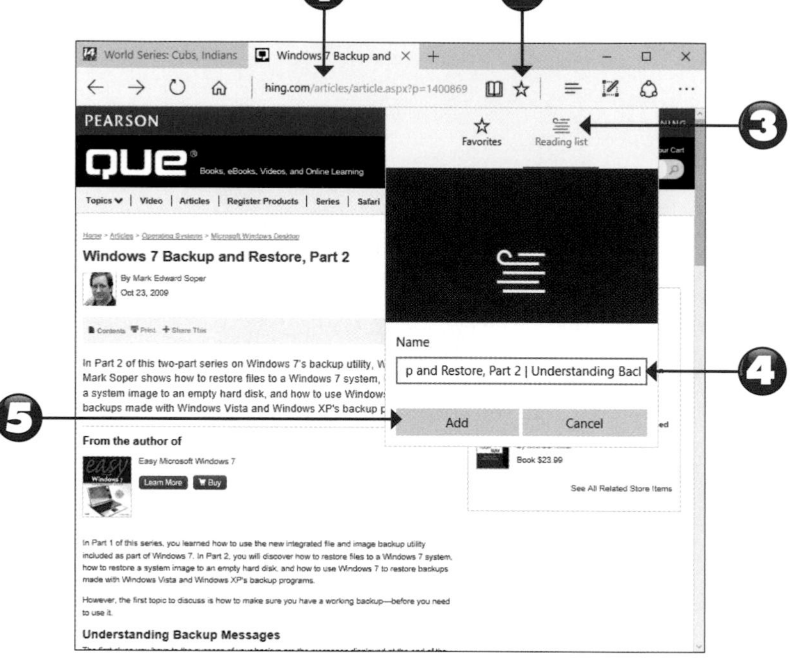

1. Open a web page you want to read later.
2. Click or tap the **Add to Favorites or Reading List** (star) icon.
3. Click or tap **Reading list**.
4. Review the name of the page. Change it if you'd like.
5. Click or tap **Add** to add the page to your reading list.

End

NOTE

Favorite or Reading List? If the page changes frequently (such as a news or information page), add it as a favorite. If the page is an article or essay, add it to your reading list.

USING READING LIST

Microsoft Edge provides fast access to the web pages on your reading list. In this exercise, you learn how this feature works.

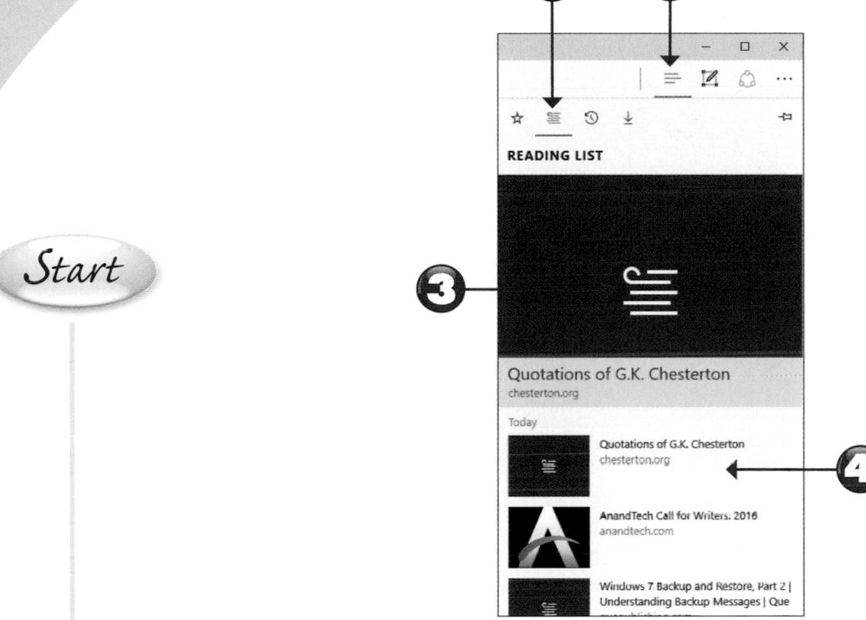

1. Click or tap the **Hub** icon.
2. Click or tap the **Reading List** icon.
3. The last-opened page in Reading List is at the top of the list and has a larger icon.
4. Click or tap an item to open it with Microsoft Edge.

End

NOTE

Reading List Entries Can Become Outdated The Reading List feature stores the URL of each web page you add to it and opens the page when you click its entry. If the website is offline or the URL is no longer valid, you will not be able to view the page. If you want a permanent copy of the page, create a PDF as described in "Printing or Creating a PDF of a Web Page," p. 105.

USING DOWNLOADS

Although Windows 10 AE encourages users to get apps from the Windows Store, there are still many types of apps, utilities, and driver files that must be downloaded from vendor websites. Microsoft Edge makes it easy to see what you've downloaded and to get to your downloads. Here's how to use this feature (be sure to download at least one file first).

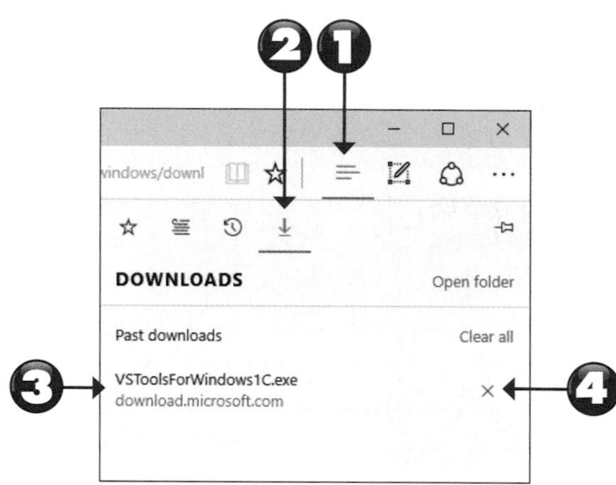

1. Click or tap the **Hub** icon.
2. Click or tap the **Downloads** icon.
3. Click or tap to open your download.
4. Click or tap to clear the download from the list.

End

TIP

Downloads Not Listed Aren't Gone Clearing the Downloads list with **Clear all** or removing an individual download from the list (step 4) does not remove the downloaded files from your device. If you want to remove a downloaded file, click the **Open folder** link to open the Downloads folder in File Explorer, and then delete it there.

TIP

Changing the Default Downloads Folder To change the default downloads folder, open the **More** (three-dot) menu, click or tap **Settings**, click or tap **View advanced settings**, and click or tap the **Change** button in the Downloads section.

USING THE WEB NOTES PEN TOOL

Microsoft Edge's Web Notes features makes it easy to grab a web page, annotate it, and share it with other users. In this exercise, you learn how to use the Web Notes Pen tool to make web page notes.

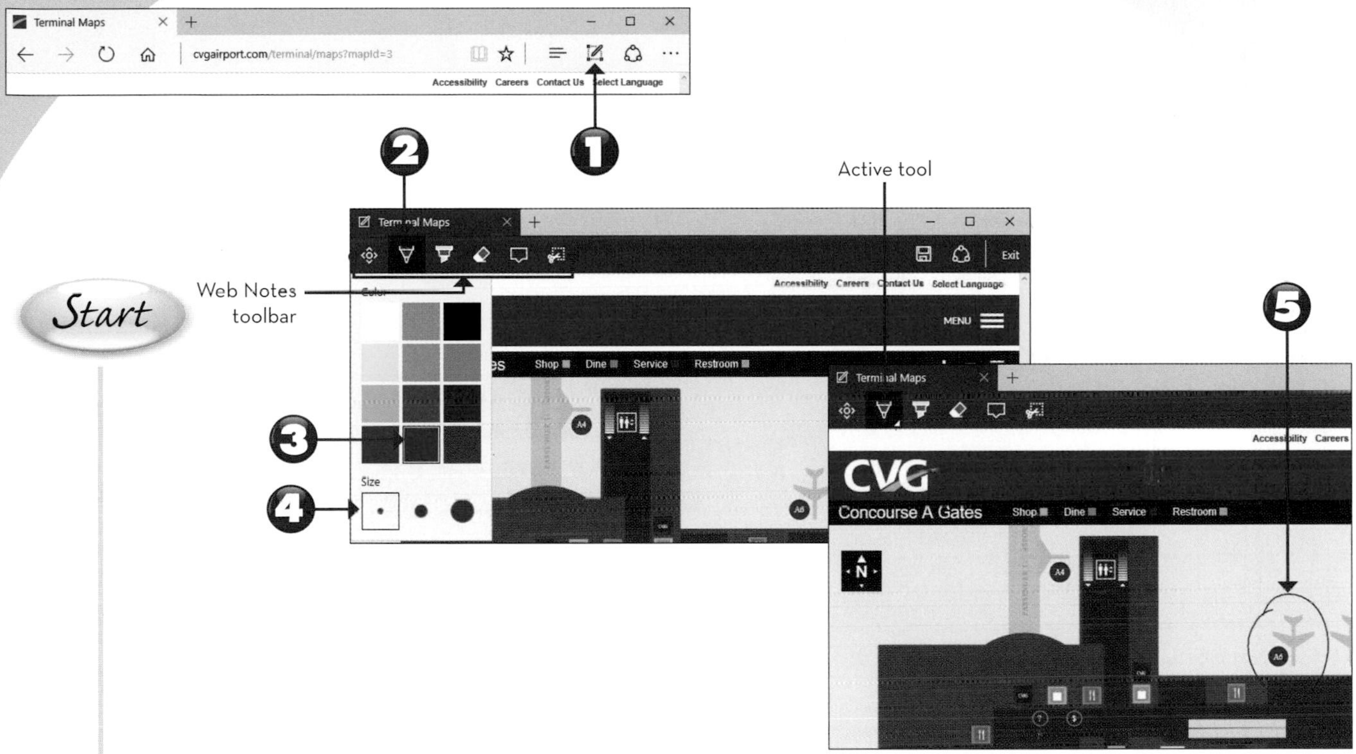

Active tool

Web Notes toolbar

Start

1. Click or tap **Make a Web Note**.
2. Double-click or double-tap the **Pen** tool.
3. Click or tap the desired color.
4. Click or tap the desired pen size.
5. Click or press and drag around an area of the page to mark it.

End

TIP

Changing Colors, Tip Sizes If you want to mark up several areas on a web page, you can open the Pen tool and select different colors and tip sizes to make each area distinctive.

USING THE WEB NOTES TEXT TOOL

In this exercise, you learn how to use the Web Notes Text tool to add notes to your web page.

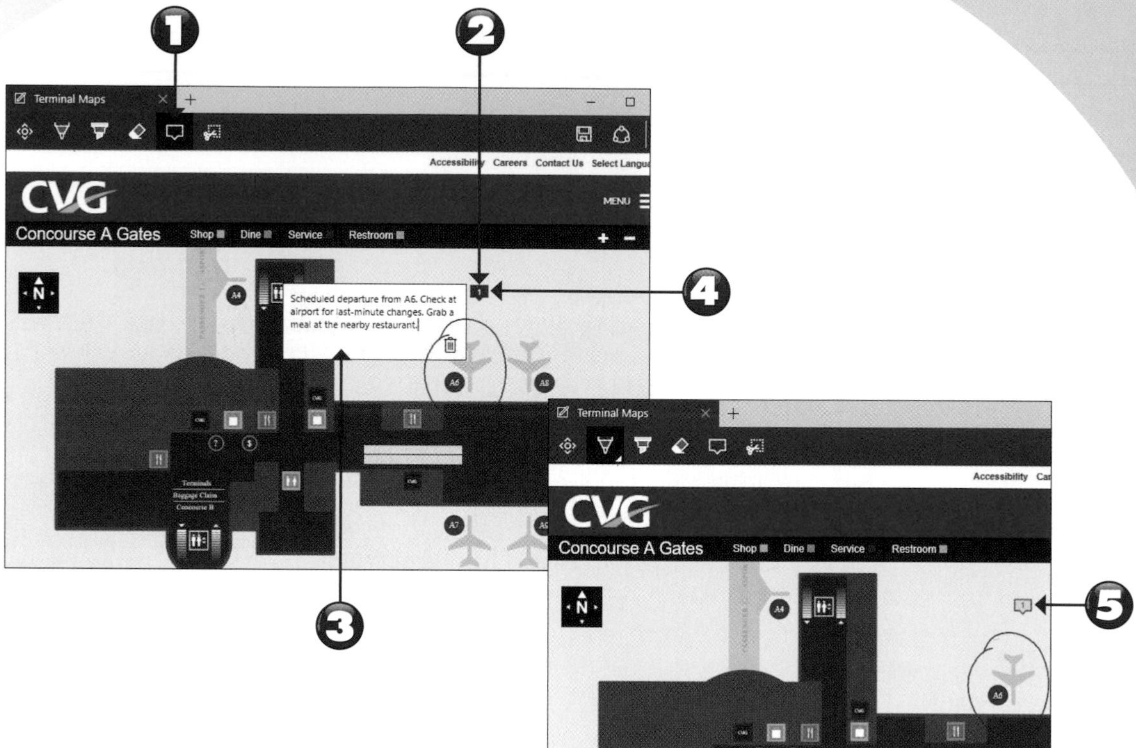

1. With Web Notes open, click or tap **Add a Typed Note**.
2. Click or tap the location where you want to place the note.
3. Enter the note text.
4. Click or tap the note number to close the text window.
5. A note number is placed on the web page. Click or tap the note number to display the note window.

End

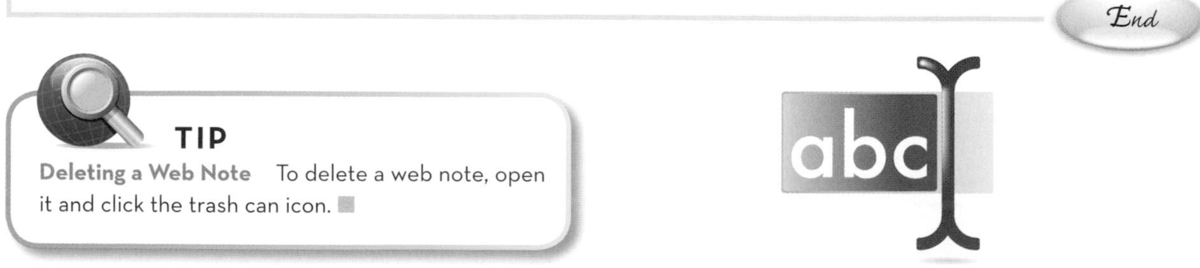

TIP

Deleting a Web Note To delete a web note, open it and click the trash can icon.

USING THE WEB NOTES HIGHLIGHTER TOOL

In this exercise, you learn how to use the Web Notes Highlighter tool to highlight text in a web page or a web note.

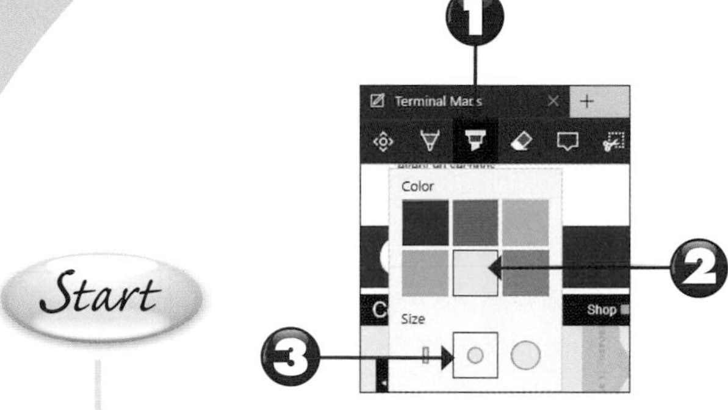

Start

1. With Web Notes open, double-click or double-tap **Highlighter**.
2. Click or tap the desired color.
3. Click or tap the desired pen size.
4. Click or press and drag across text to highlight it.

End

TIP

Changing Colors, Tip Style If you want to highlight several areas on a web page, you can open the Highlighter tool and select different colors and tip styles to make each highlight distinctive.

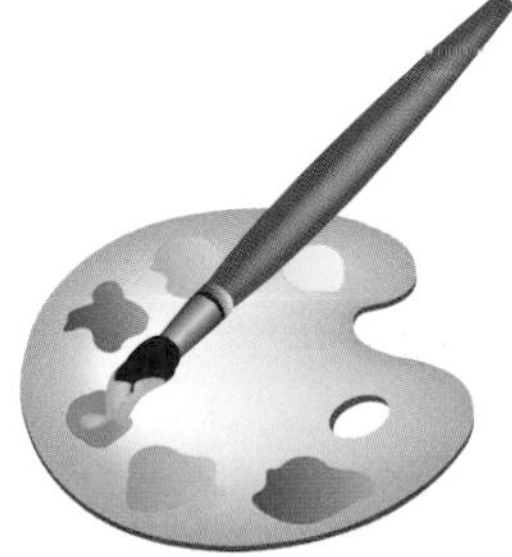

USING THE WEB NOTES CLIP TOOL

You can also use Web Notes to select a section of a web page and paste it into a document or graphics program. This example uses the Windows 10 AE WordPad word processor, but you could also use Paint or a commercial app such as Adobe Photoshop or Microsoft Word.

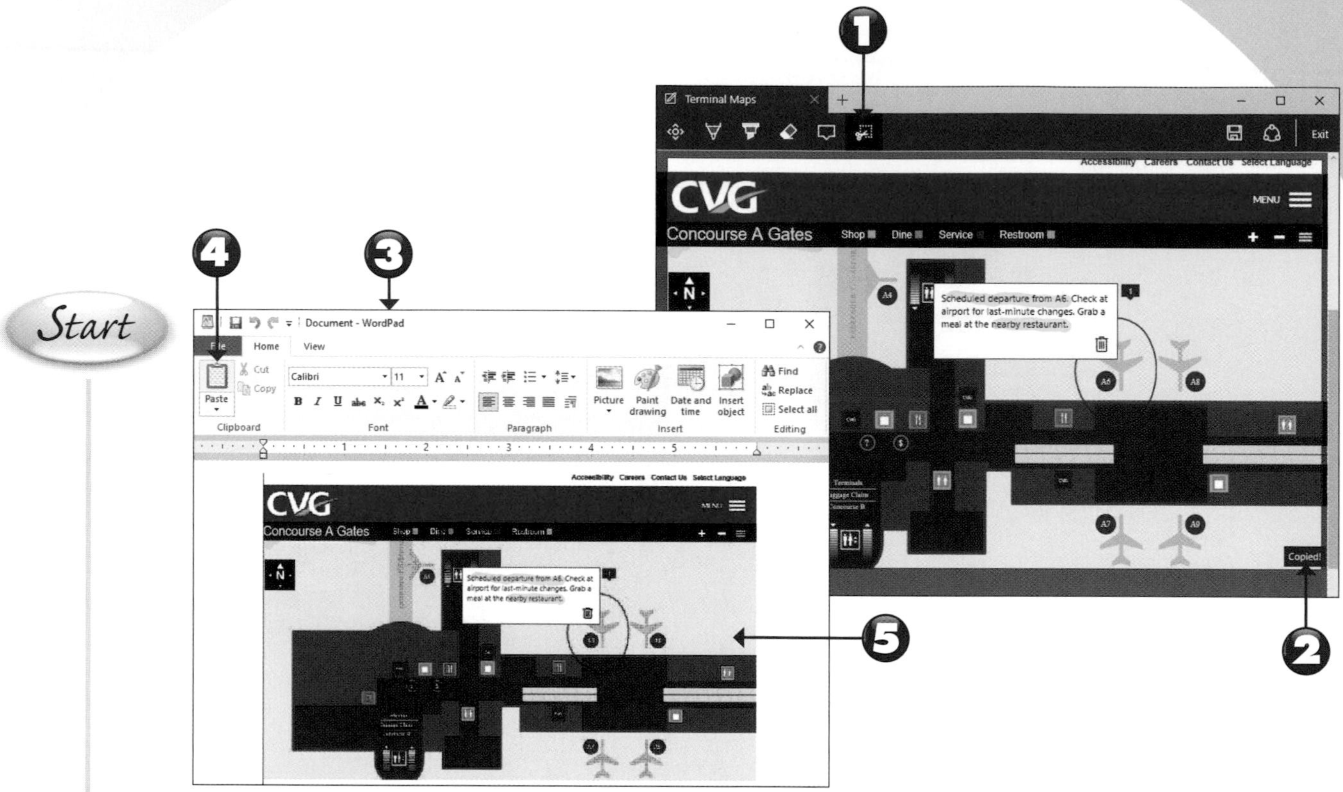

Start

1. With Web Notes open, click or tap the **Clip** tool.
2. Click or press and drag around the area to clip.
3. Open the other app where you want to paste the clipping.
4. Click or tap **Paste**.
5. The clipped area is pasted into the other app.

End

SAVING A WEB NOTE

There are two ways to make web notes available after you create them: saving them and sharing them. In this exercise, you learn how to save a web note.

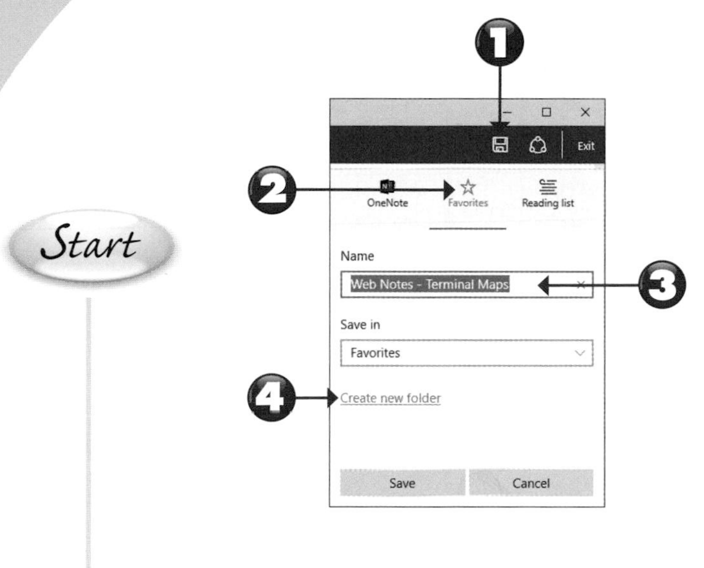

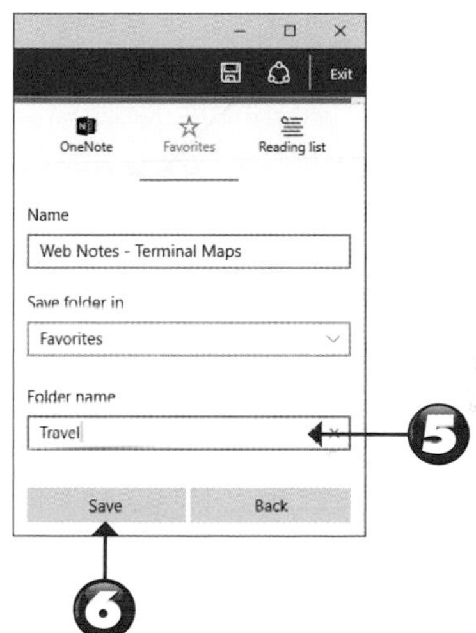

Start

1. With Web Notes open, click or tap **Save**.
2. Click or tap **Favorites**.
3. Enter the name to use for the note, or use the default name (shown).
4. The note is saved in Favorites by default; to select a different folder, click or tap to open the **Create new folder** link.
5. Enter a new folder name to save the note.
6. Click or tap **Save**.

End

TIP

Sharing a Web Note To share a web note, tap or click the **Share** icon (next to the Save icon) and select the app you want to use to share the note. Choose from apps such as OneNote, Mail, Cortana Reminders, and social media apps such as Facebook.

SETTING BROWSER PRIVACY, SERVICES, AND PLATFORM CONTROLS

The browser Settings, accessed from the bottom of the More (three-dot) menu, also enables you to configure privacy settings, protect your browser, and make it more efficient in page handling. Here are the options you can configure.

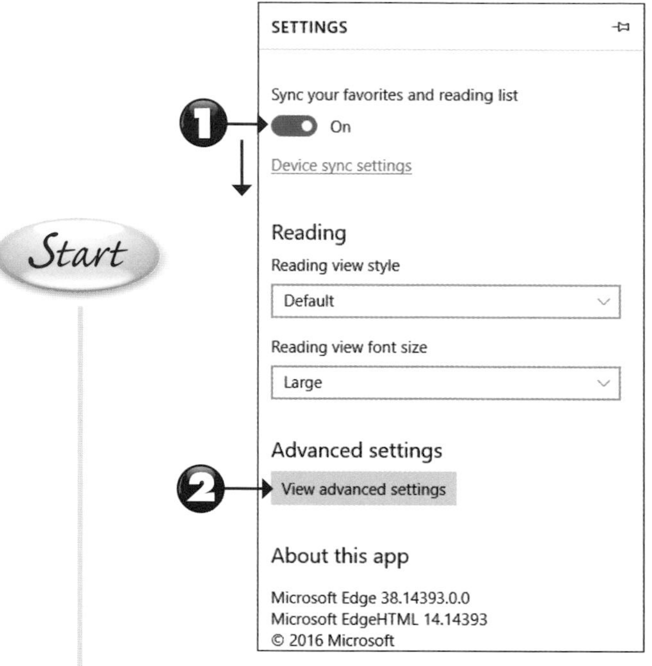

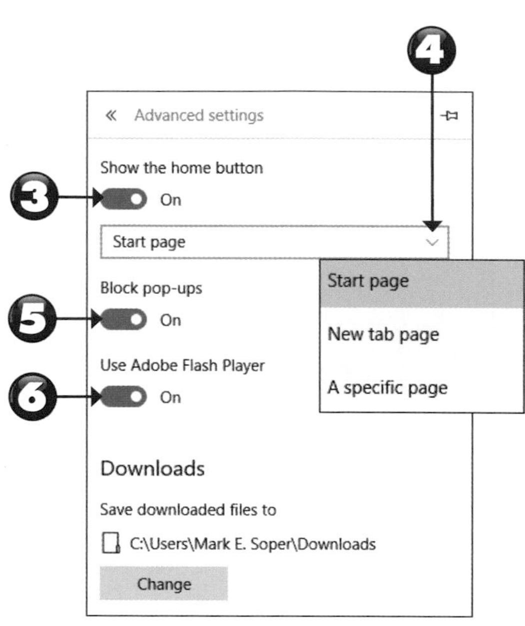

1. With browser Settings open, scroll down and turn on **Sync your favorites and reading list** to have the same information on all devices. This is handy if you use Windows 10 AE on more than one device.
2. Scroll to the bottom of Settings and click or tap **View advanced settings**.
3. To display a Home button next to the Address box, click or press and drag to **On**.
4. Select what should be displayed when you click or tap the **Home** button.
5. Pop-ups are blocked by default; to permit them, click or press and drag to **Off**.
6. The **Use Adobe Flash Player** setting should be turned on unless Flash causes problems for your system.

Continued

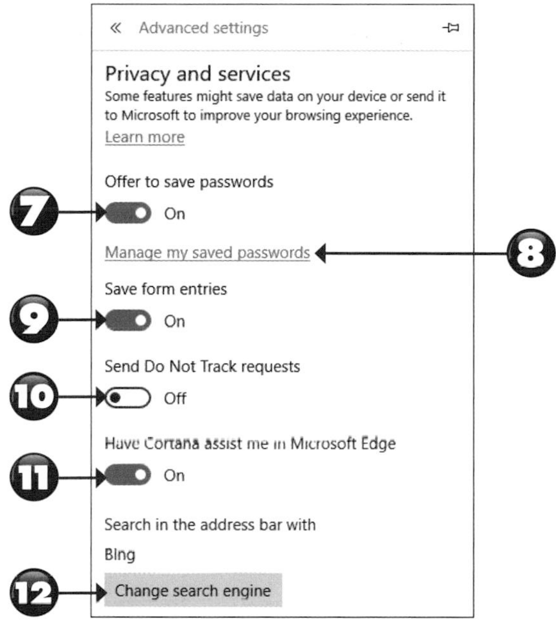

7 In the Privacy and Services section (scroll down to locate), if you do not want Edge to save passwords you enter, click or press and drag the **Offer to save passwords** control to **Off**.

8 If you have Edge save passwords for you, click or tap to manage them (remove outdated passwords, and so on).

9 If you do not want Edge to save form entries, click or press and drag to **Off**.

10 To send Do Not Track requests to websites, click or press and drag to **On**.

11 To disable Cortana when using Edge, click or press and drag to **Off**.

12 Edge uses the Microsoft Bing search engine in the address bar. If you prefer a different search engine, click or tap **Change search engine** and choose your favorite.

Continued

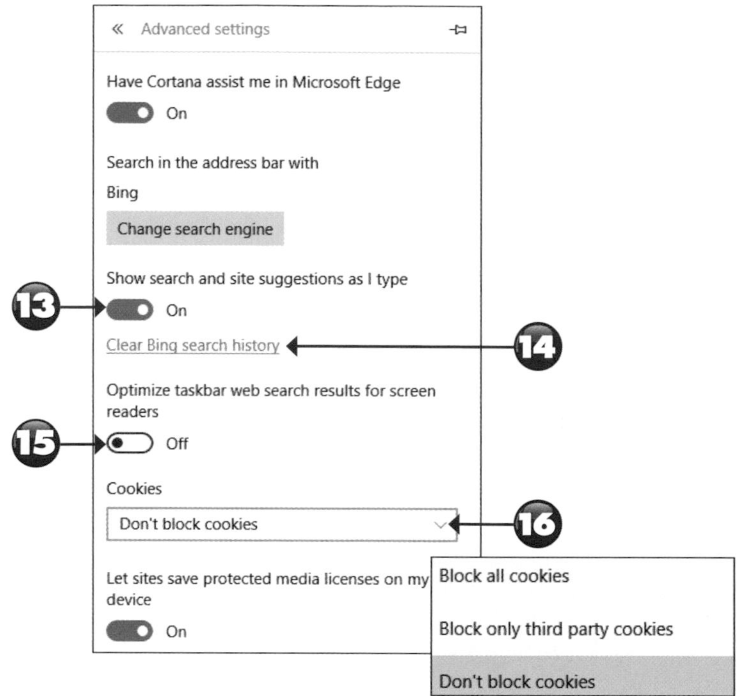

13 Scrolling down, leave this option enabled to make your searches easier.

14 Click or tap to clear Bing search history.

15 Enable this if you use a screen reader.

16 Open the Cookies menu if you want to block third-party cookies or all cookies.

Continued

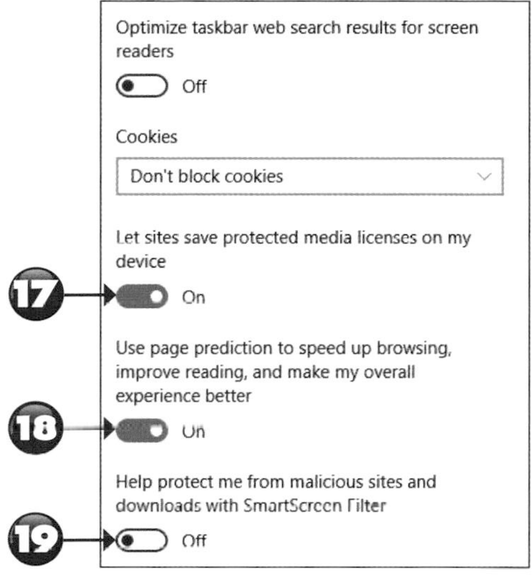

17 If you download protected media (TV, movies, music), leave this **On** so you can play it back on this computer.

18 Page prediction preloads pages to speed up browsing; leave this **On**.

19 SmartScreen Filter helps protect your browser from malicious sites; make sure this is turned **On** (may default to Off for some users).

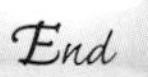

NOTE

What the Privacy Settings Do If you block third-party cookies (step 16), you reduce the number of ads you see based on your recent search history. If you block all cookies (step 16), many e-commerce and e-banking websites won't work properly. If you turn on Do Not Track (step 10), you are requesting that websites and web apps do not track your activity. This setting also reduces the number of ads you see based on your recent search history. However, some websites disregard Do Not Track requests, so this setting is not a substitute for browser cookie management.

INSTALLING BROWSER EXTENSIONS IN EDGE

In Windows 10 AE, Edge gains the capability to use browser extensions. A browser extension adds new features to a browser. For example, browser extensions for Edge can manage passwords, clip web content for use with Evernote and One Note information managers, block ads, translate web pages, and more. Extensions for Edge are available from the Windows Store, and this tutorial shows you how to find and install the ones you need.

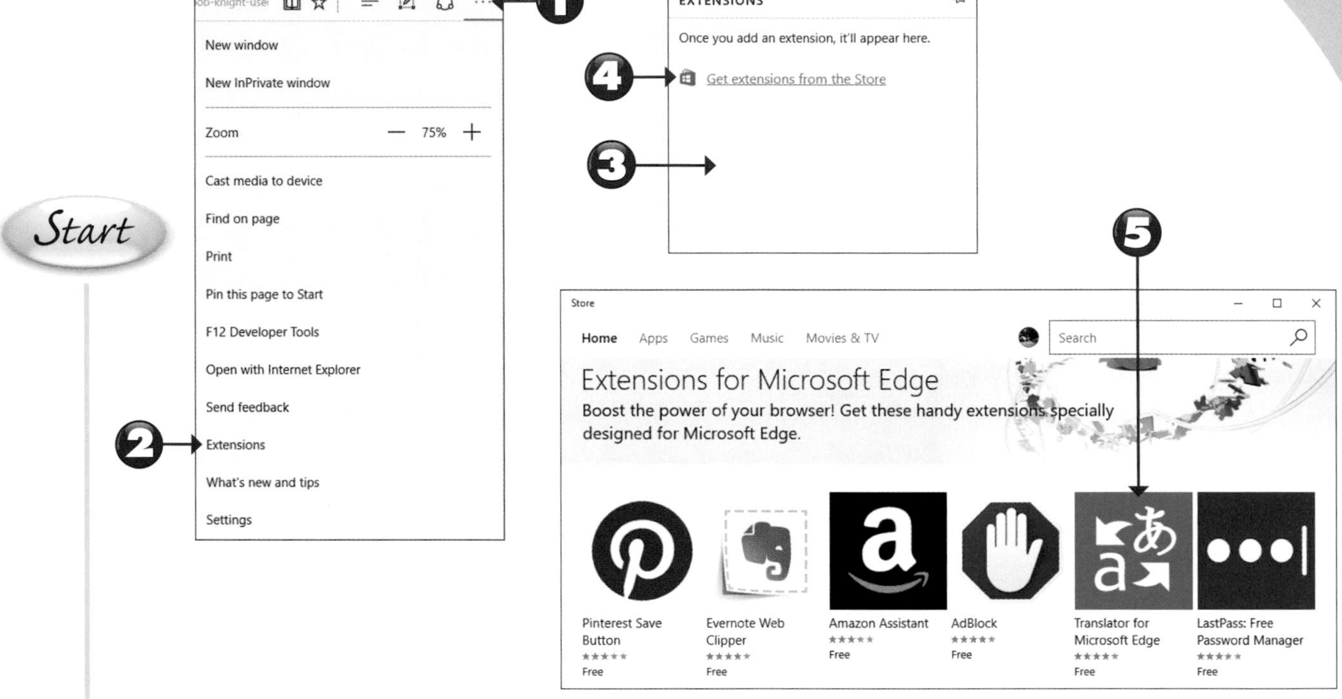

Start

1. Click or tap the **More** (three-dot) menu.
2. Click or tap **Extensions**.
3. If you have any installed extensions, they are listed here.
4. Click or tap to install new extensions.
5. Each extension is rated in the Windows Store, and its price (or Free) is listed. Tap an extension to learn more.

Continued

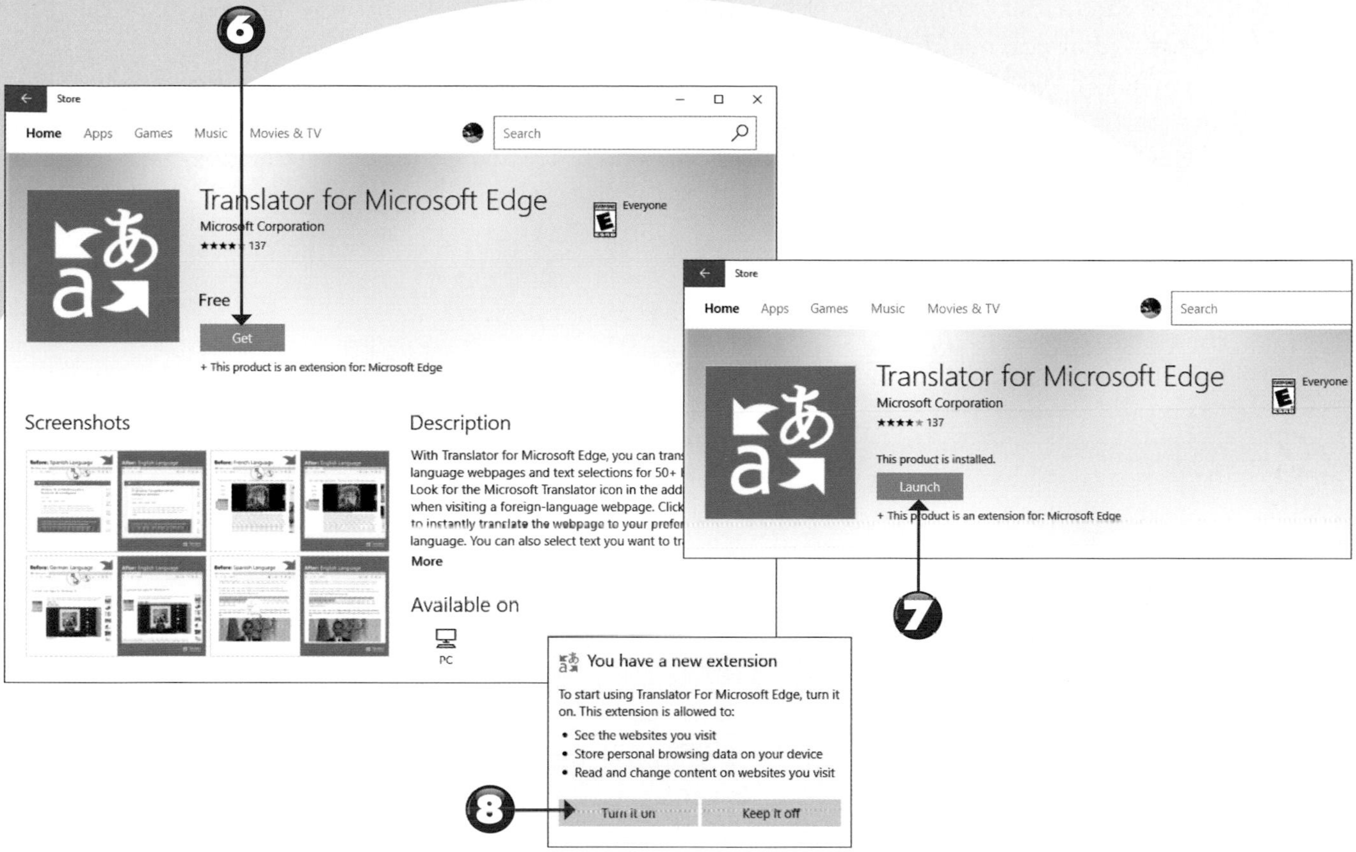

6. Click or tap **Get** to start the installation process.

7. Click or tap **Launch** to return to Edge.

8. Click or tap **Turn it on** to start using the extension.

End

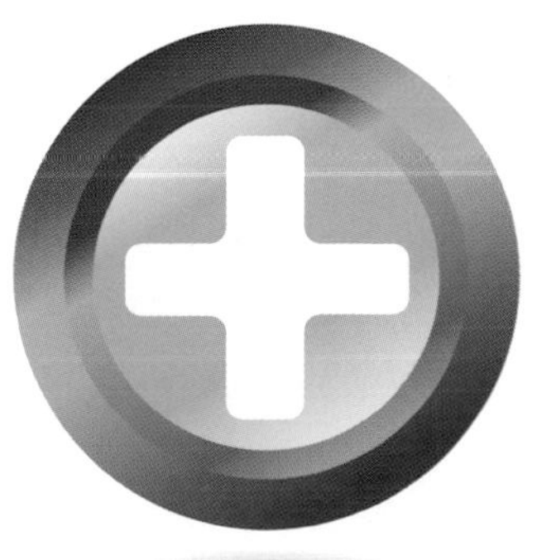

MANAGING BROWSER EXTENSIONS IN EDGE

After you install one or more extensions in Edge, use the Extensions panel to manage them. Here's what you can do.

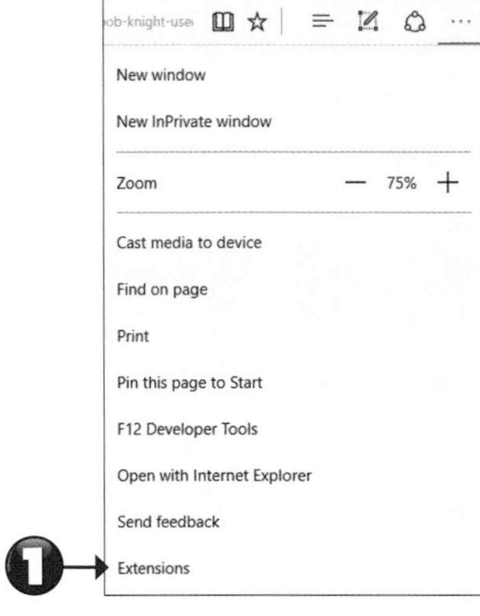

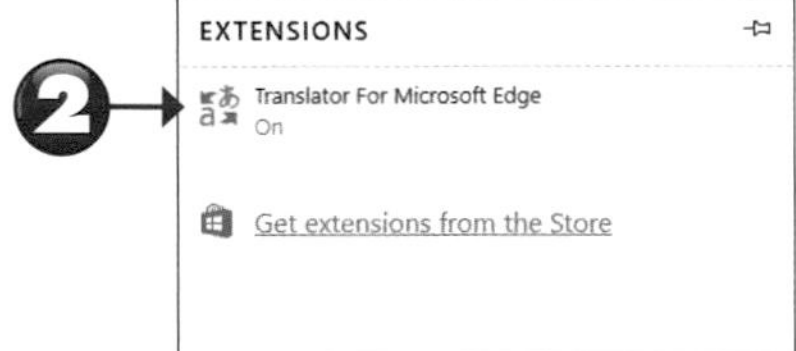

1. To view or manage extensions, click or tap **Extensions** from the More (three-dot) menu.
2. Click or tap an installed extension.

Continued

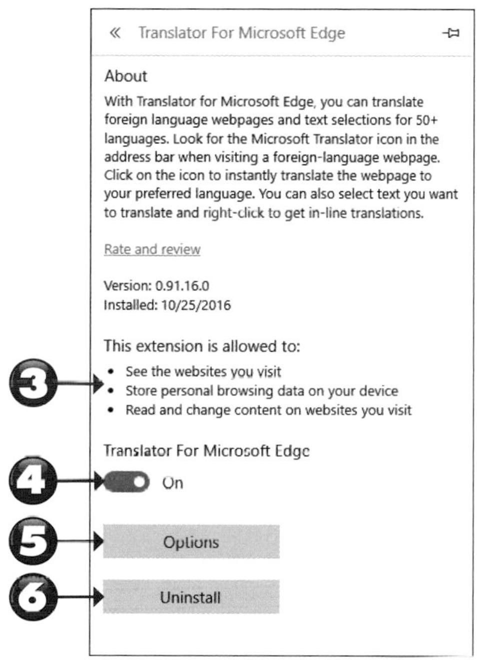

3. Extension permissions are listed here.
4. Extension enabled; turn to **Off** to disable it.
5. Click or tap to configure options.
6. Click or tap to uninstall this extension.

End

PLAYING AND CREATING MUSIC AND AUDIO

Windows 10 AE makes it easy to enjoy and build your audio collection with Groove Music and provides easy voice recording and editing with Voice Recorder. This chapter shows you how to use the most important features of both apps.

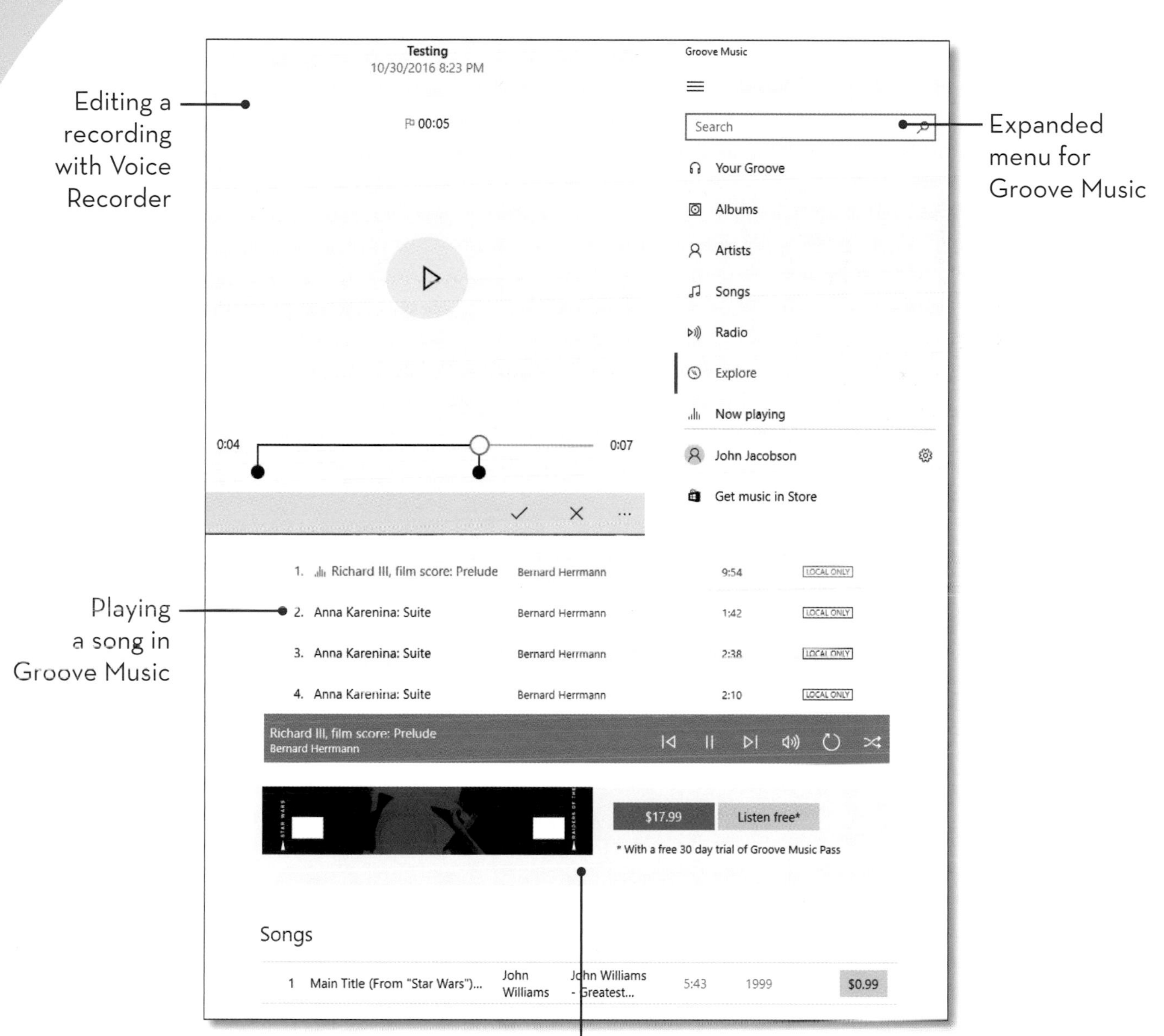
Editing a recording with Voice Recorder
Expanded menu for Groove Music
Playing a song in Groove Music
Preparing to buy an album or song from the Windows Store
Testing
10/30/2016 8:23 PM
00:05
0:04
0:07
Groove Music
Search
Your Groove
Albums
Artists
Songs
Radio
Explore
Now playing
John Jacobson
Get music in Store
1. Richard III, film score: Prelude Bernard Herrmann 9:54 LOCAL ONLY
2. Anna Karenina: Suite Bernard Herrmann 1:42 LOCAL ONLY
3. Anna Karenina: Suite Bernard Herrmann 2:38 LOCAL ONLY
4. Anna Karenina: Suite Bernard Herrmann 2:10 LOCAL ONLY
Richard III, film score: Prelude
Bernard Herrmann
$17.99
Listen free*
* With a free 30 day trial of Groove Music Pass
Songs
1 Main Title (From "Star Wars")... John Williams John Williams - Greatest... 5:43 1999 $0.99

STARTING THE GROOVE MUSIC APP

The Groove Music app in Windows 10 AE acts as a one-stop shop for your computer music needs. Whether you want to organize music files on your computer or tablet, listen to songs across devices, or purchase more music online, the Groove Music app is the place to start. First, let's learn how to open the app and see its major features.

Start

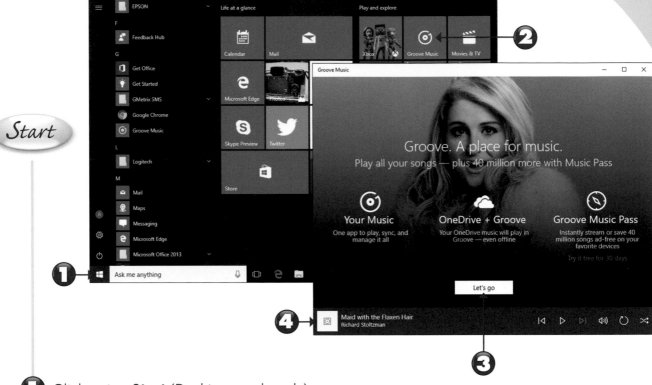

1. Click or tap **Start** (Desktop mode only).
2. Click or tap **Groove Music** (Desktop or Tablet mode).
3. The first time you open Groove Music, click or tap **Let's go**.
4. If a track is currently playing, you can find it listed here.

Continued

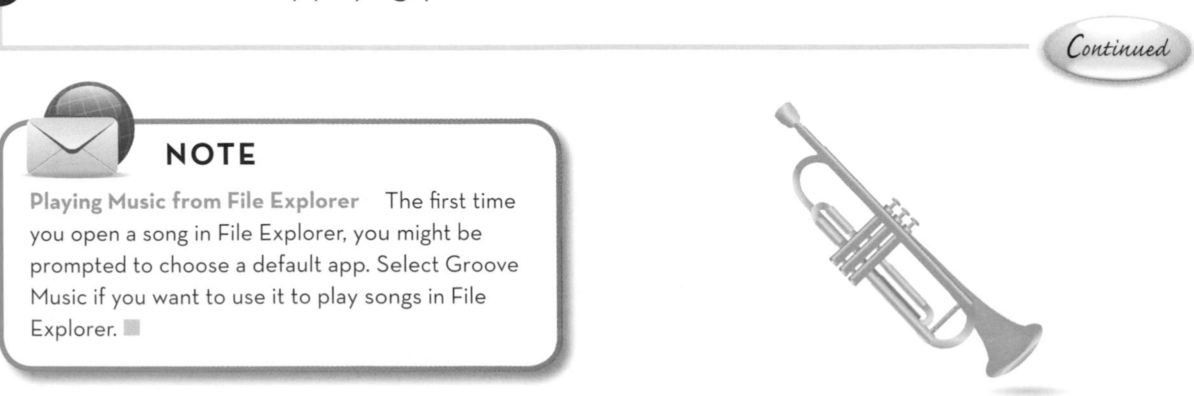

NOTE

Playing Music from File Explorer The first time you open a song in File Explorer, you might be prompted to choose a default app. Select Groove Music if you want to use it to play songs in File Explorer.

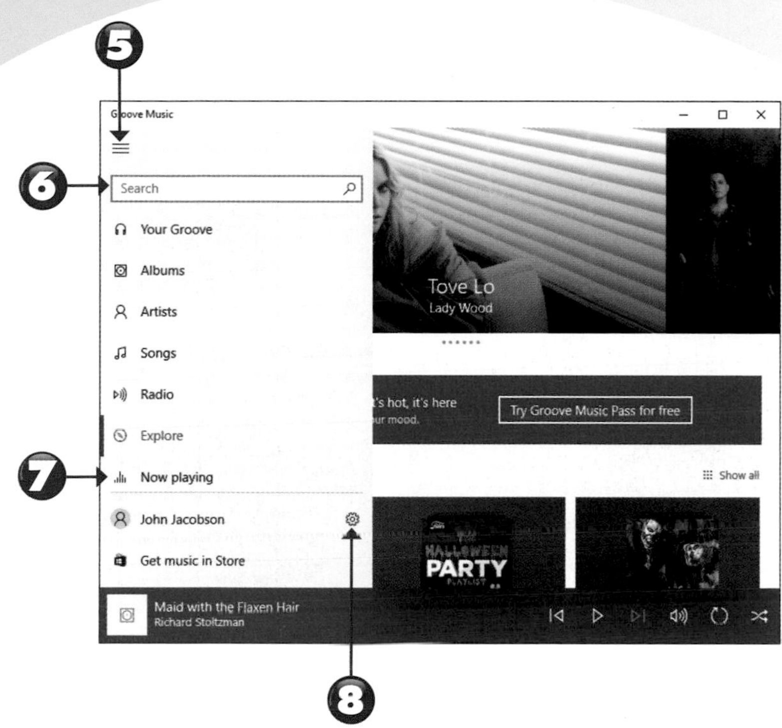

5 Click or tap to expand the menu.

6 Click or tap to search for music.

7 Click or tap to see what's playing.

8 Click or tap to configure Groove Music settings.

End

NOTE

Groove Music Settings Use the app's Settings dialog box to get a Groove Music Pass for audio streaming of millions of songs via subscription, check Microsoft account information, select music locations on your PC or network, import your iTunes playlists, update media artwork and metadata automatically, configure OneDrive music handling, delete playlists and music from the Groove catalog, and choose a visual theme. ■

VIEWING OPTIONS FOR YOUR MUSIC COLLECTION

The Groove Music app makes it easy to see the types of music in your collection and where it's located. Here's how to use these features.

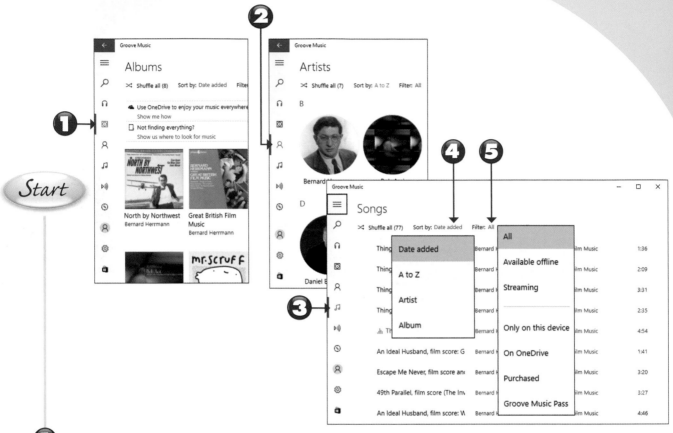

1. Click or tap to view your music by album.
2. Click or tap to view your music by artist.
3. Click or tap to view your music by song.
4. Click or tap to sort music.
5. Click or tap to filter music by location.

NOTE

Music Locations In step 5, choose **Available Offline** to see tracks that can be played back without an Internet connection. Choose **Streaming** to see tracks that require an Internet connection to play. Choose **Only on this device** to see tracks that are stored in the local Music folder. **On OneDrive** displays tracks that are stored in the OneDrive Music folder. **Purchased** displays tracks that were purchased from the Windows Store. **Groove Music Pass** displays tracks available via the Groove Music Service.

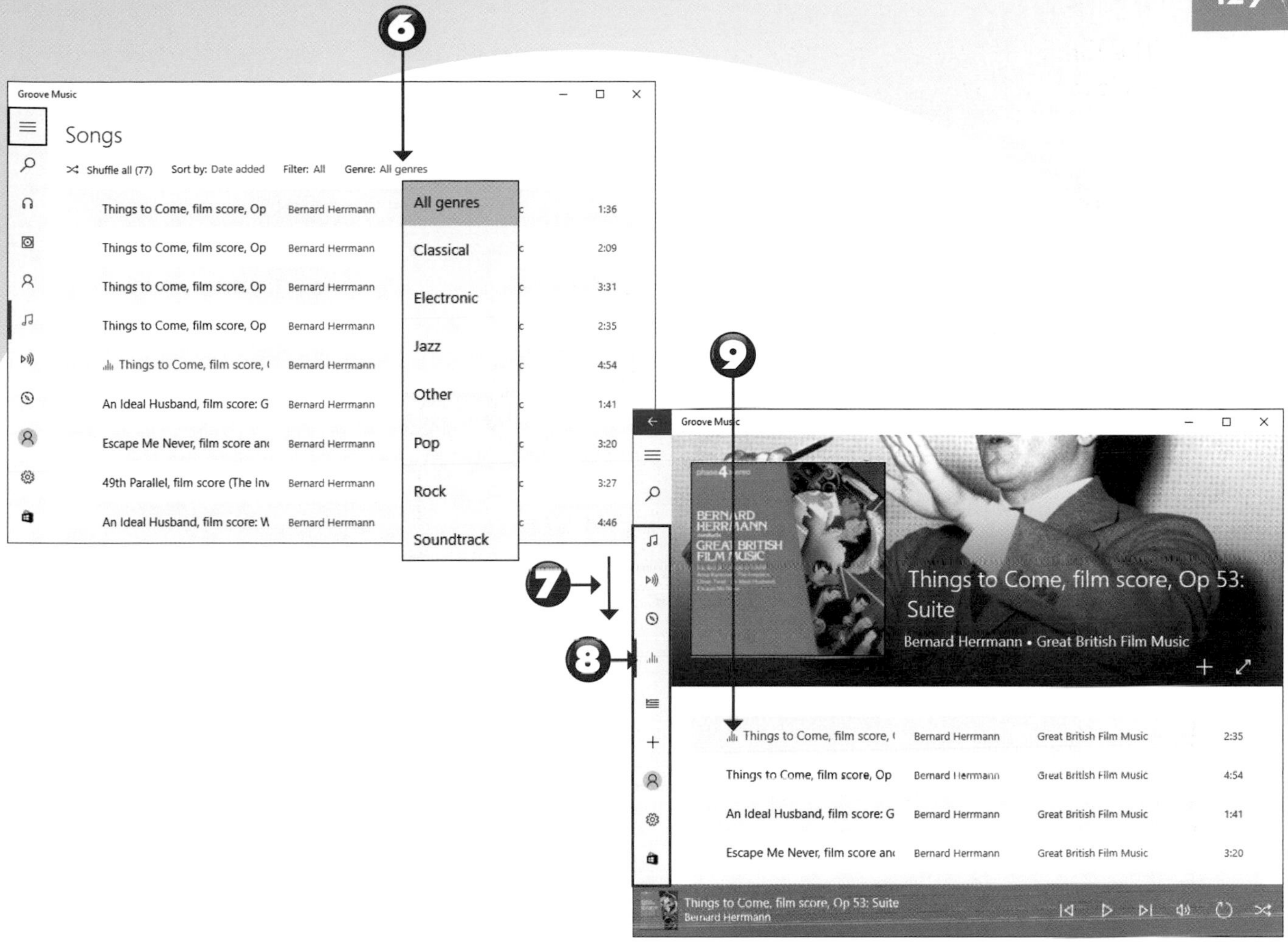

6. Click or tap to display music by genre.

7. Flick up or scroll down the menu until **Now playing** is visible.

8. Click or tap to view the currently playing track.

9. The currently playing track is highlighted.

End

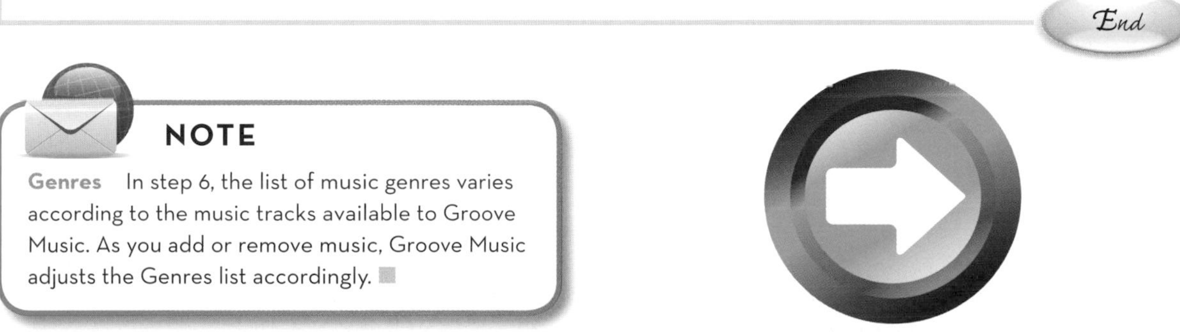

NOTE

Genres In step 6, the list of music genres varies according to the music tracks available to Groove Music. As you add or remove music, Groove Music adjusts the Genres list accordingly.

PLAYING YOUR MUSIC COLLECTION

By default, Groove Music displays your music collection by album. Here's how to play an album.

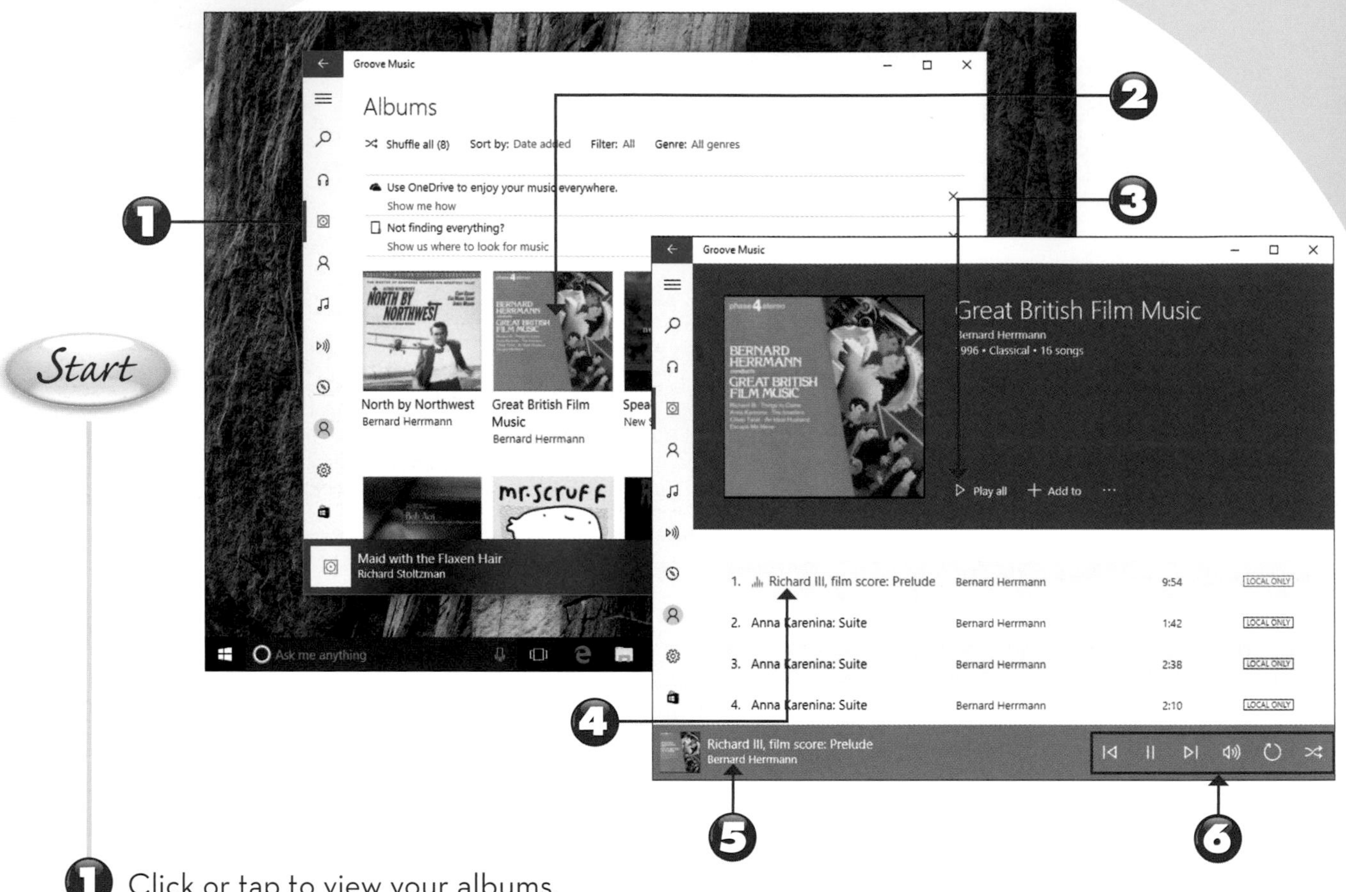

Start

1. Click or tap to view your albums.
2. Click or tap an album.
3. Click or tap to play all the tracks on the album.
4. Click or tap a track you want to play.
5. You can see the currently playing song in the bottom-left corner.
6. Use the playback controls to pause/play, switch tracks, adjust volume, repeat a track, or shuffle.

Continued

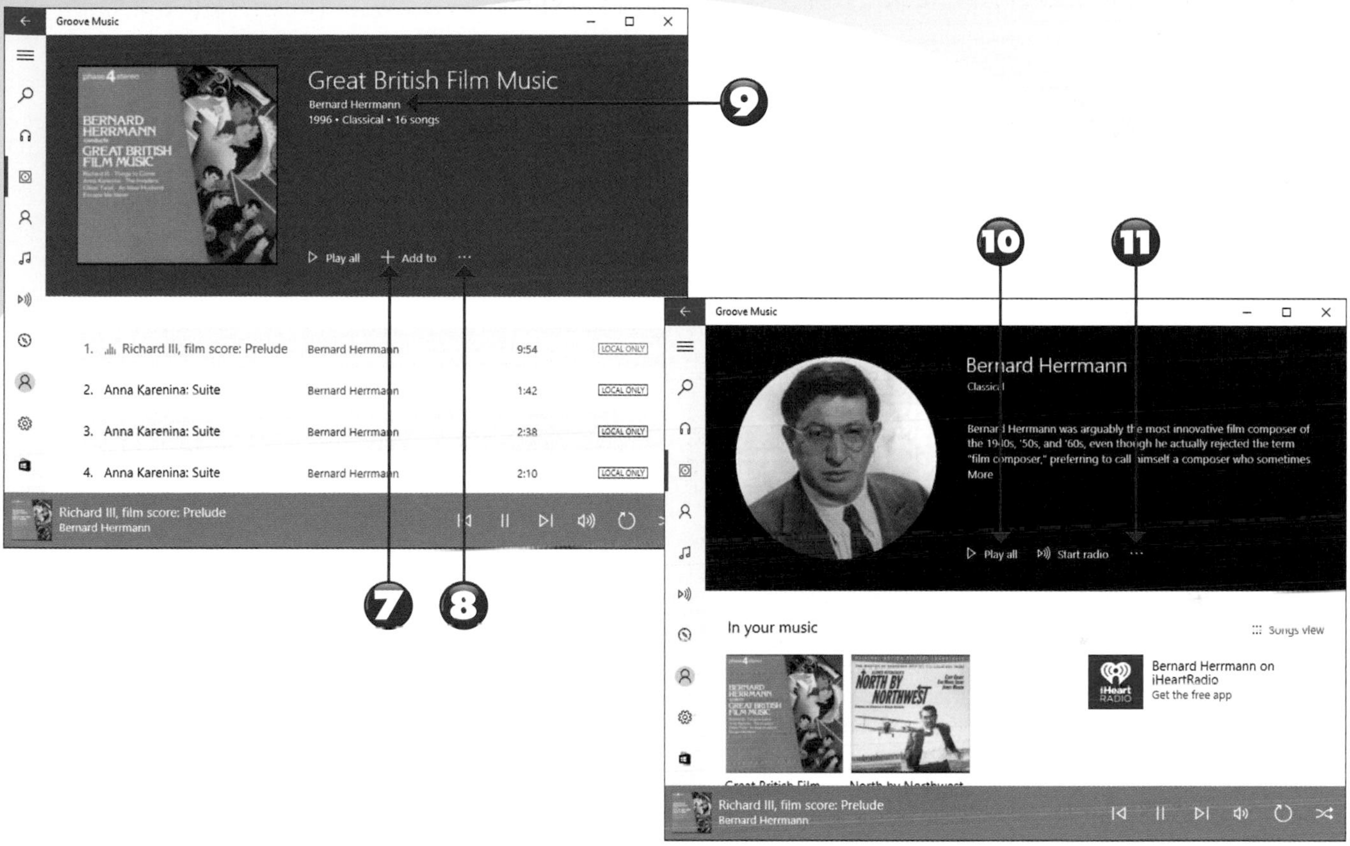

7 Click or tap to add the album to the Now playing list, an existing playlist, or a new playlist.

8 Click or tap to pin the album to the Start menu, delete the album, or find album information.

9 Click or tap to display more information about the artist.

10 Click or tap to play all albums by the artist.

11 Click or tap to add the artist's works to Now playing or a new or existing playlist, pin to Start, or share via email or social media.

End

NOTE

iHeart Radio The free iHeart Radio app (visible in steps 10–11) provides access to thousands of broadcast radio stations and lets you customize stations with the content you prefer. Click or tap to install the app from the Windows Store. ■

SEARCHING FOR YOUR FAVORITE MUSIC

When you have a large music library, it might be difficult to browse through all your albums and tracks. Instead, you can search your entire music library from the Groove Music app. Here's how.

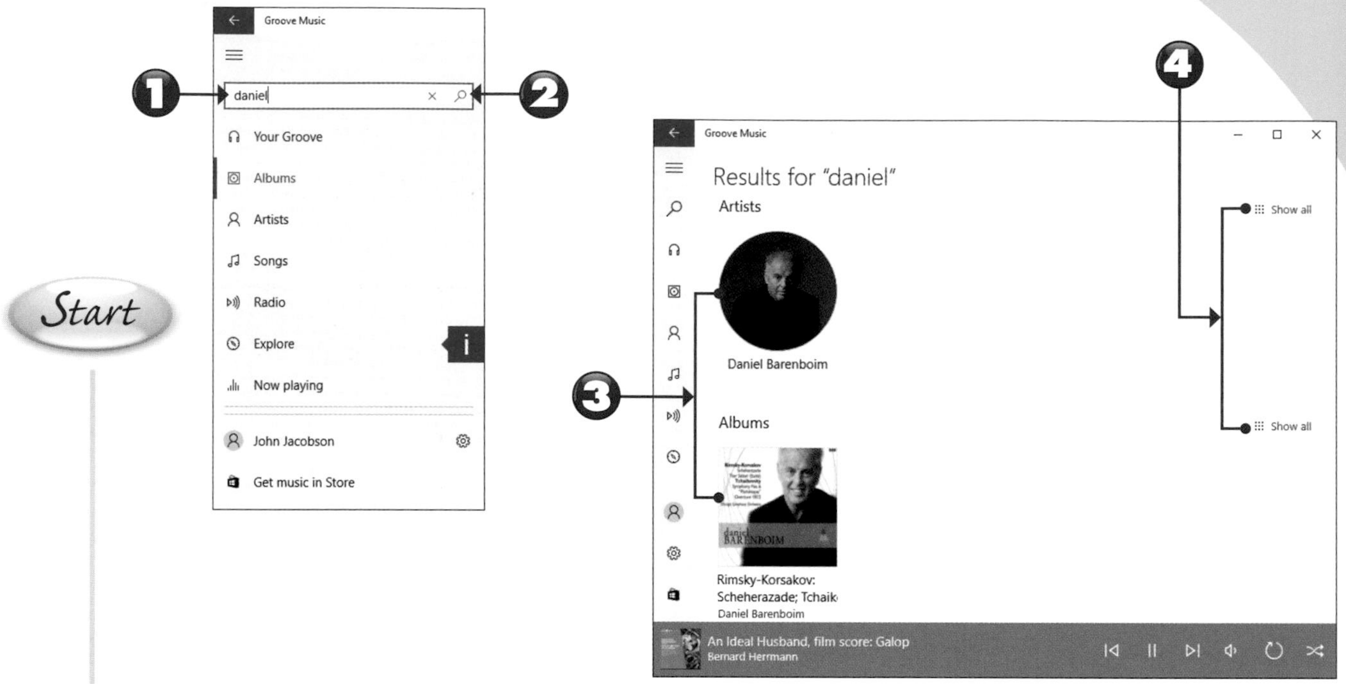

Start

1. Enter the music to search for (title, artist, or subject) into the Search box.
2. Tap the search icon or press the **Enter** key on the keyboard.
3. Click or tap to select the artist, album, or song you want.
4. If there are more results than are visible onscreen, click or tap **Show all** to see all results in any category.

End

NOTE

Groove Music Service Through the Groove Music app, Microsoft also offers the Groove Music streaming audio service. The Groove Music service offers more than 40 million tracks, ad-free, for listening on your Windows computer or mobile device. To sign up for the Groove Music service (a free trial is available), click the **Settings** button in the Groove Music app and click **Get a Groove Music Pass**. If you don't have payment information associated with your Microsoft account, you will be prompted to add it during the process.

CREATING A PLAYLIST

You can create a playlist from any selected tracks in your music collection. A playlist is simply a collection of songs. Here's how to make a playlist.

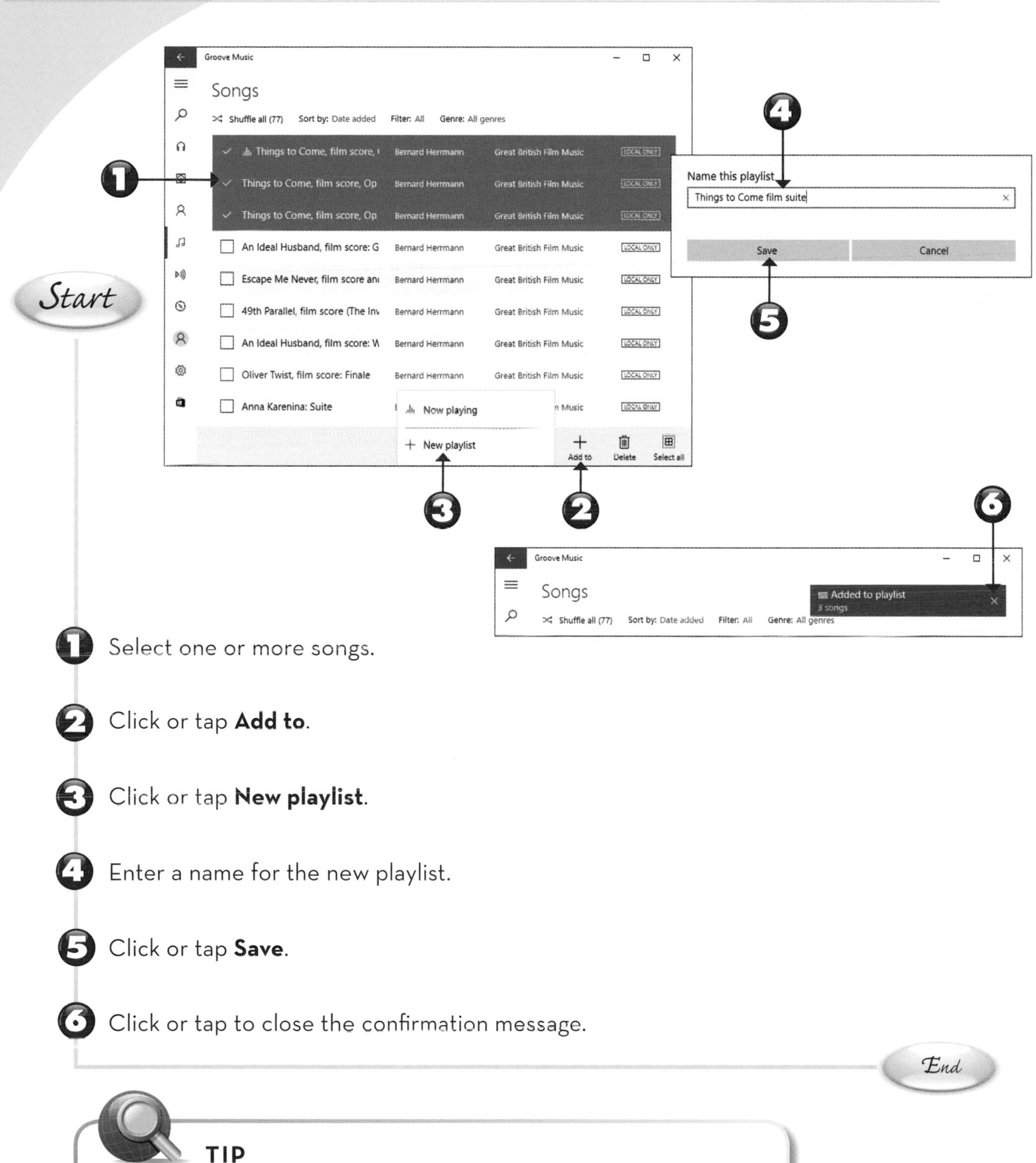

1. Select one or more songs.
2. Click or tap **Add to**.
3. Click or tap **New playlist**.
4. Enter a name for the new playlist.
5. Click or tap **Save**.
6. Click or tap to close the confirmation message.

End

TIP

One-click Playlist When you click or tap the New playlist button without tracks selected, you are prompted to select some as part of the playlist creation process.

PLAYING A PLAYLIST

Playing a playlist is as easy as playing an album or individual track.

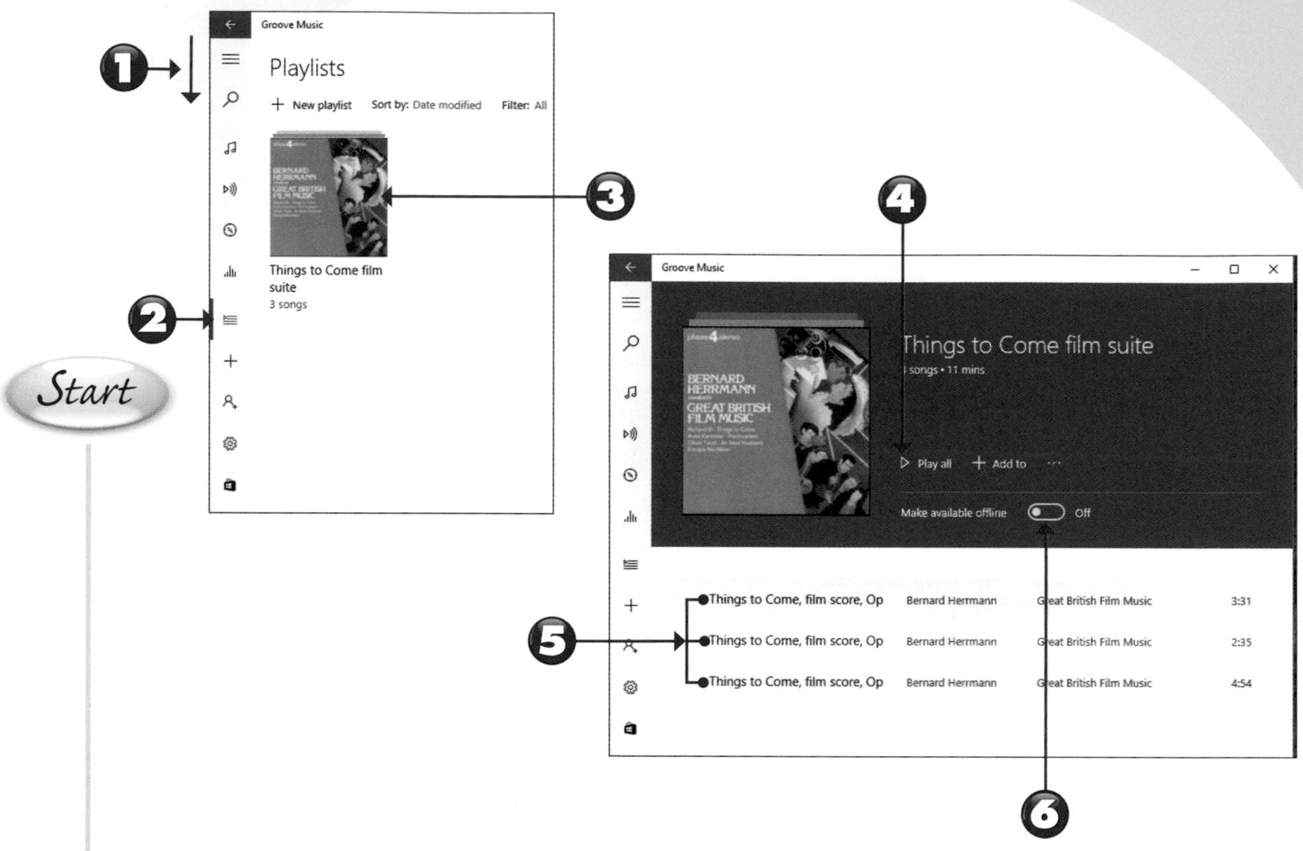

1. In the menu pane, scroll to the playlists section (just above the New playlist selection).
2. Click or tap to open playlists.
3. Click or tap to select a playlist.
4. Click or tap to play the entire playlist.
5. Click or tap a track to play it.
6. Click and drag to **On** to make the playlist available offline.

End

BUYING MUSIC

You can purchase and download music from Microsoft's Windows Store to play back in the Groove Music app.

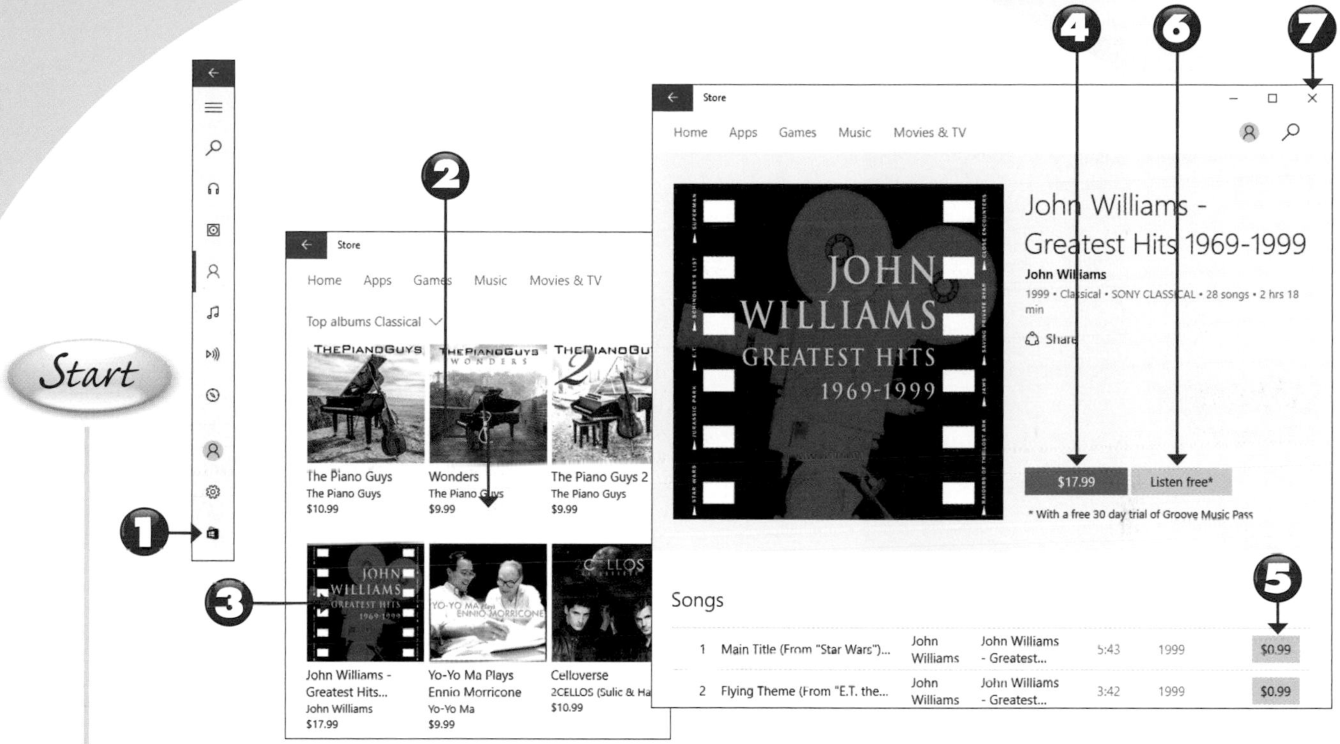

Start

1. From the Groove Music app, click or tap **Get music in Store** to open the Windows Store app.
2. Scroll down to display New albums, Top-selling songs, Top albums, Top artists, and Genres.
3. Click or tap to open an album.
4. Click or tap to purchase the album.
5. Click or tap to purchase a track.
6. Click or tap to set up a free trial of Groove Music Pass.
7. Click or tap to close the Store window.

End

NOTE

Adding Payment Information to Your Microsoft Account If you have not yet added payment information to your Microsoft account, you will be prompted to do so when you buy an album or a track.

RECORDING AUDIO WITH VOICE RECORDER

You can use your device's built-in or connected microphone to record sounds with Voice Recorder. Here's how to start Voice Recorder and make a recording.

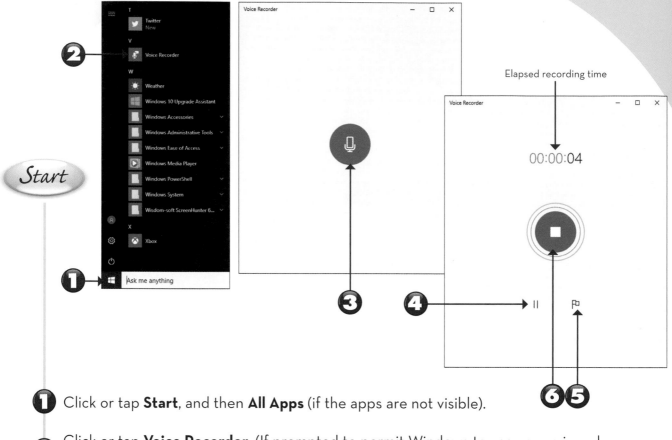

1. Click or tap **Start**, and then **All Apps** (if the apps are not visible).
2. Click or tap **Voice Recorder**. (If prompted to permit Windows to use your microphone, click **Allow**.)
3. Click or tap to begin recording.
4. Click or tap to pause/continue recording.
5. Click or tap to place a marker in the recording.
6. Click or tap to stop recording.

TIP

Adjusting Microphone Volume If you are not satisfied with the recording volume, adjust your microphone settings. See "Adjusting Microphone Volume" in Chapter 19, "Managing Windows 10 AE," to learn more.

PLAYING AND RENAMING A RECORDING

After you create a recording, you can play it back or change its name. You can perform these steps immediately after making a recording, or you can select a recording as described in the "Editing Recorded Audio" exercise.

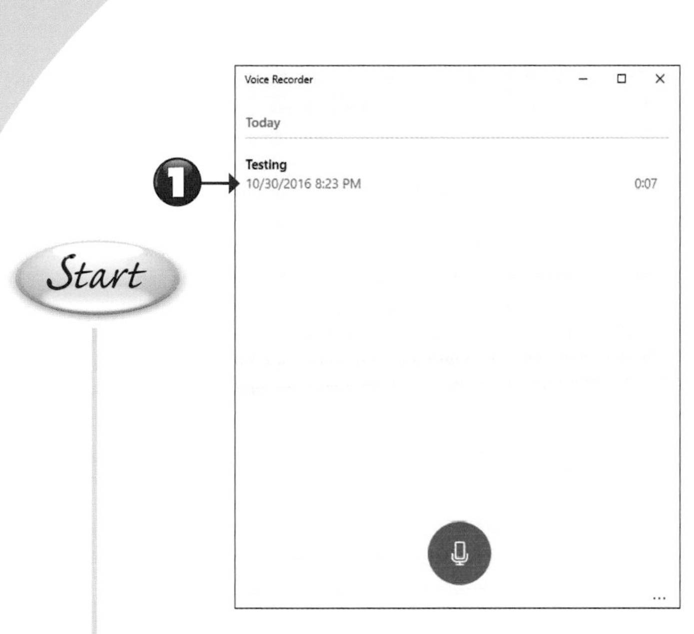

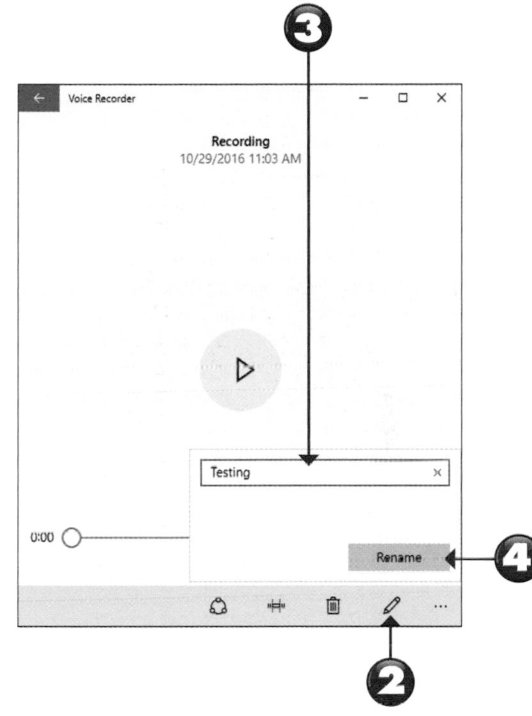

1. With Voice Recorder open, click or tap the recording you want to play.
2. Click or tap the **Rename** (pencil) icon to rename the recording.
3. Enter the new name.
4. Click or tap **Rename** to save the new name.

End

NOTE

Finding Your Recordings To play your recordings without restarting Voice Recorder, open File Explorer and go to the Sound Recordings folder in Documents. The default setting plays your recordings with Groove Music.

NOTE

More About File Explorer To learn more about using File Explorer, see Chapter 14, "Storing and Finding Your Files."

EDITING RECORDED AUDIO

You can cut out unwanted portions of a recording you make with Voice Recorder and save the remainder as a new file. In this example, we'll discard the part of the recording after the flag marker at 5 seconds (00:05).

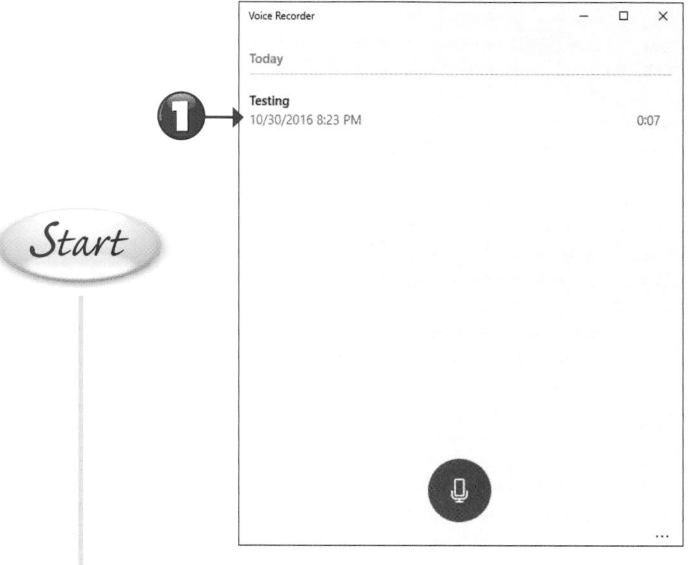

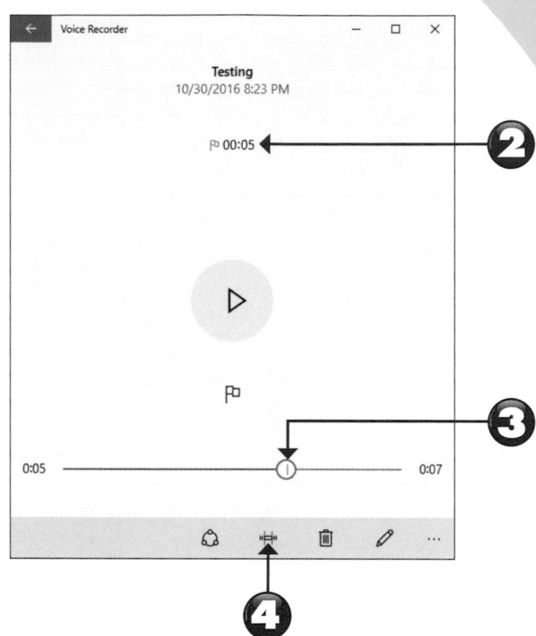

Start

1. With Voice Recorder open, select the recording you want to edit.
2. Click or tap the flag icon to move the playback slider to the position listed.
3. The playback slider at the 5-second position.
4. Click or tap **Trim**.

Continued

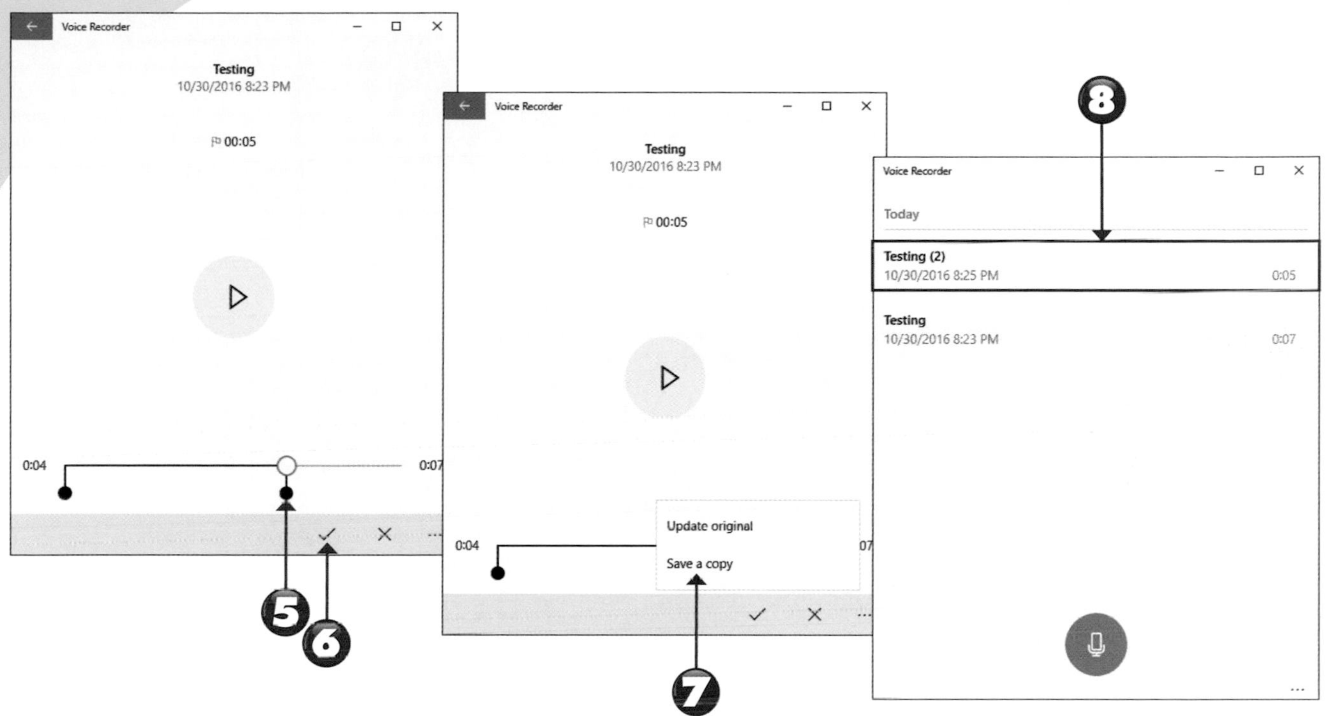

5 Move the slider to the end of the audio you want to keep.

6 Click or tap the check mark.

7 Click or tap **Save a copy**.

8 The edited copy of the recording now appears listed in Voice Recorder; click or tap to play the new recording.

End

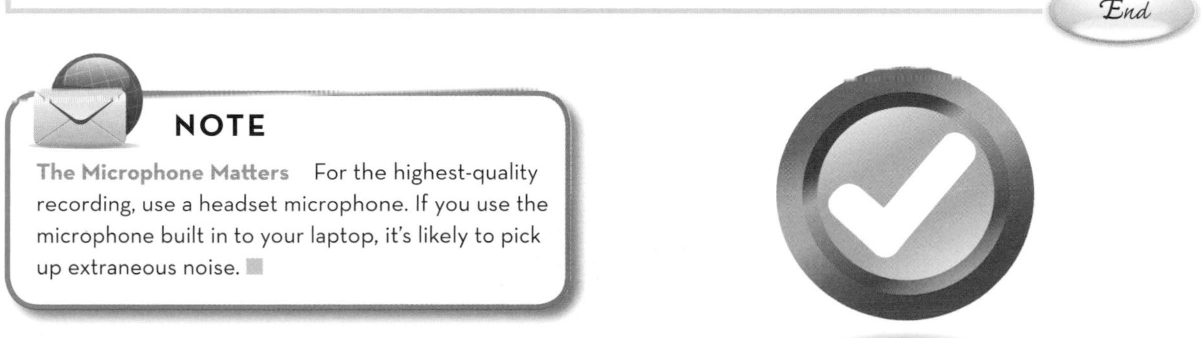

NOTE

The Microphone Matters For the highest-quality recording, use a headset microphone. If you use the microphone built in to your laptop, it's likely to pick up extraneous noise.

ENJOYING VIDEOS

Windows 10 AE includes the easy-to-use Movies & TV app, which helps you view both homemade and commercial video (TV, movie) content. In this chapter, you learn how to use Movies & TV to find and play your own video content and visit the Windows Store for TV and movie content. Movies & TV normally runs full-screen, but in this chapter we are running this app in a window to save space.

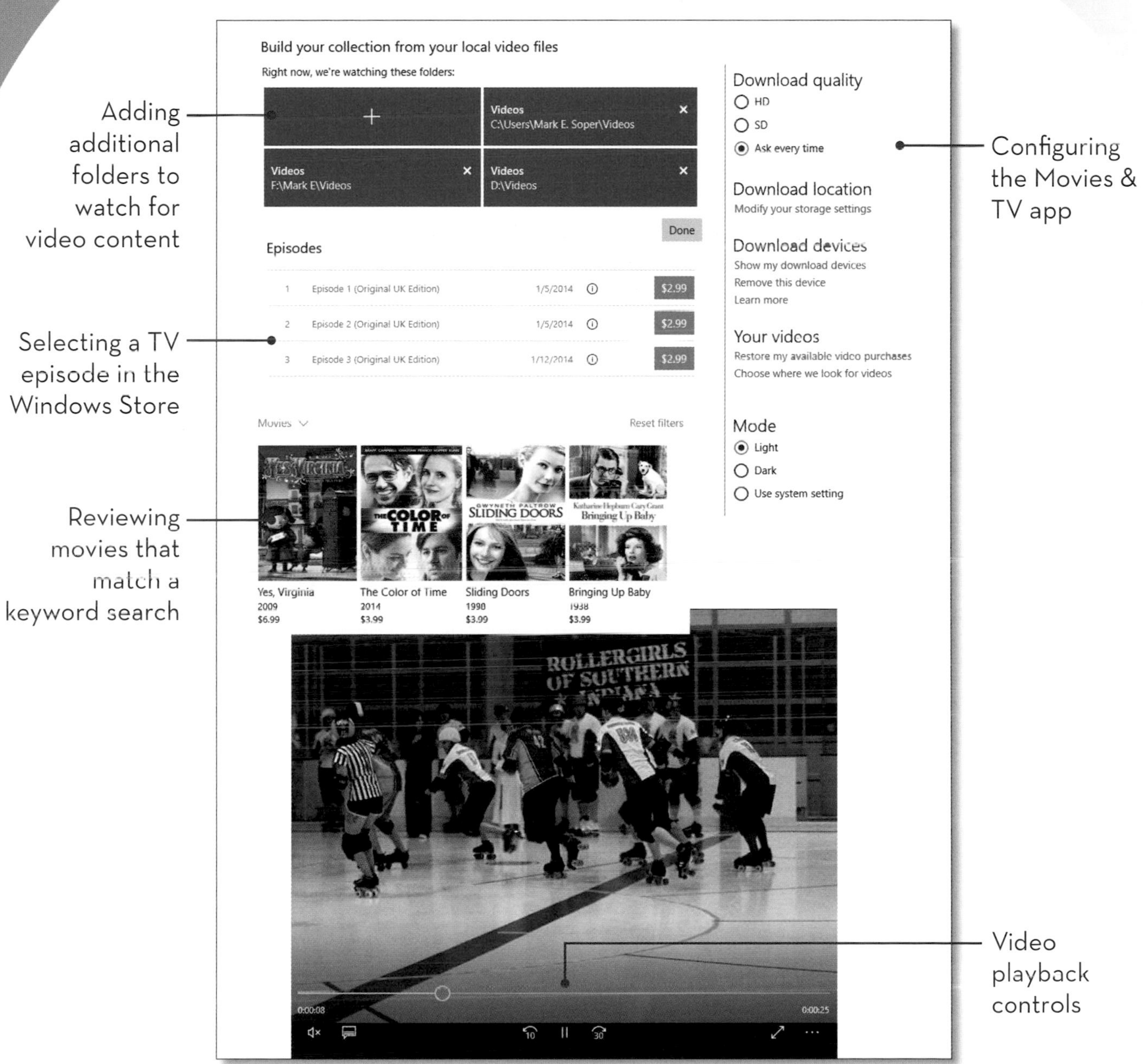

Adding additional folders to watch for video content
Selecting a TV episode in the Windows Store
Reviewing movies that match a keyword search
Configuring the Movies & TV app
Video playback controls
Build your collection from your local video files
Right now, we're watching these folders:
Videos
C:\Users\Mark E. Soper\Videos
Videos
F:\Mark E\Videos
Videos
D:\Videos
Done
Episodes
1 Episode 1 (Original UK Edition) 1/5/2014 $2.99
2 Episode 2 (Original UK Edition) 1/5/2014 $2.99
3 Episode 3 (Original UK Edition) 1/12/2014 $2.99
Movies
Reset filters
Yes, Virginia 2009 $6.99
The Color of Time 2014 $3.99
Sliding Doors 1998 $3.99
Bringing Up Baby 1938 $3.99
Download quality
HD
SD
Ask every time
Download location
Modify your storage settings
Download devices
Show my download devices
Remove this device
Learn more
Your videos
Restore my available video purchases
Choose where we look for videos
Mode
Light
Dark
Use system setting
ROLLERGIRLS OF SOUTHERN INDIANA
0:00:08
0:00:25

STARTING THE MOVIES & TV APP

You can use the Movies & TV app to preview, download, and buy video content from the Microsoft store as well as to view video content you create. The app groups your video content into several categories: Movies, TV, and Videos (your own video content). Here's how to get started using the app.

Start

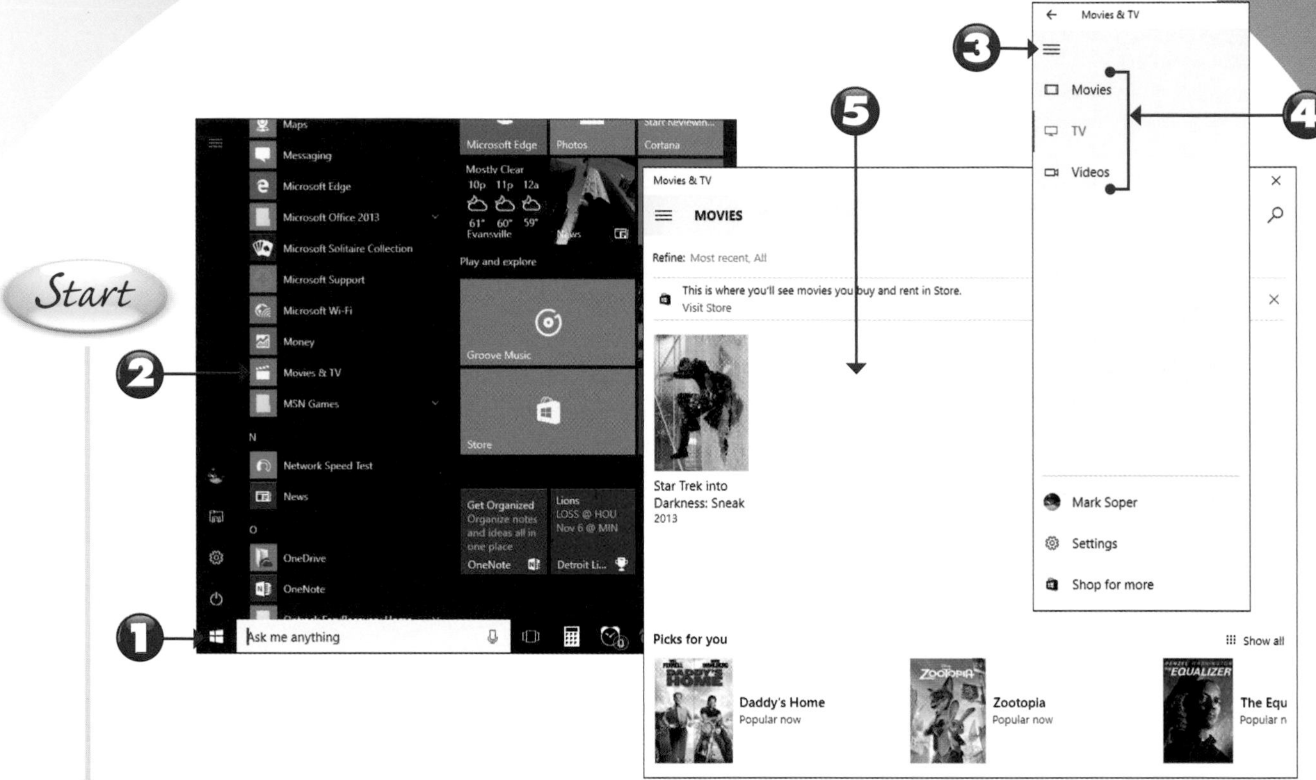

1. Click or tap **Start** in Desktop mode.
2. Click or tap **Movies & TV** (Desktop and Tablet modes).
3. Click or tap the **Menu** button to view categories.
4. Click or tap a category to view its contents.
5. The Movies category lists any movies you rent or purchase.

Continued

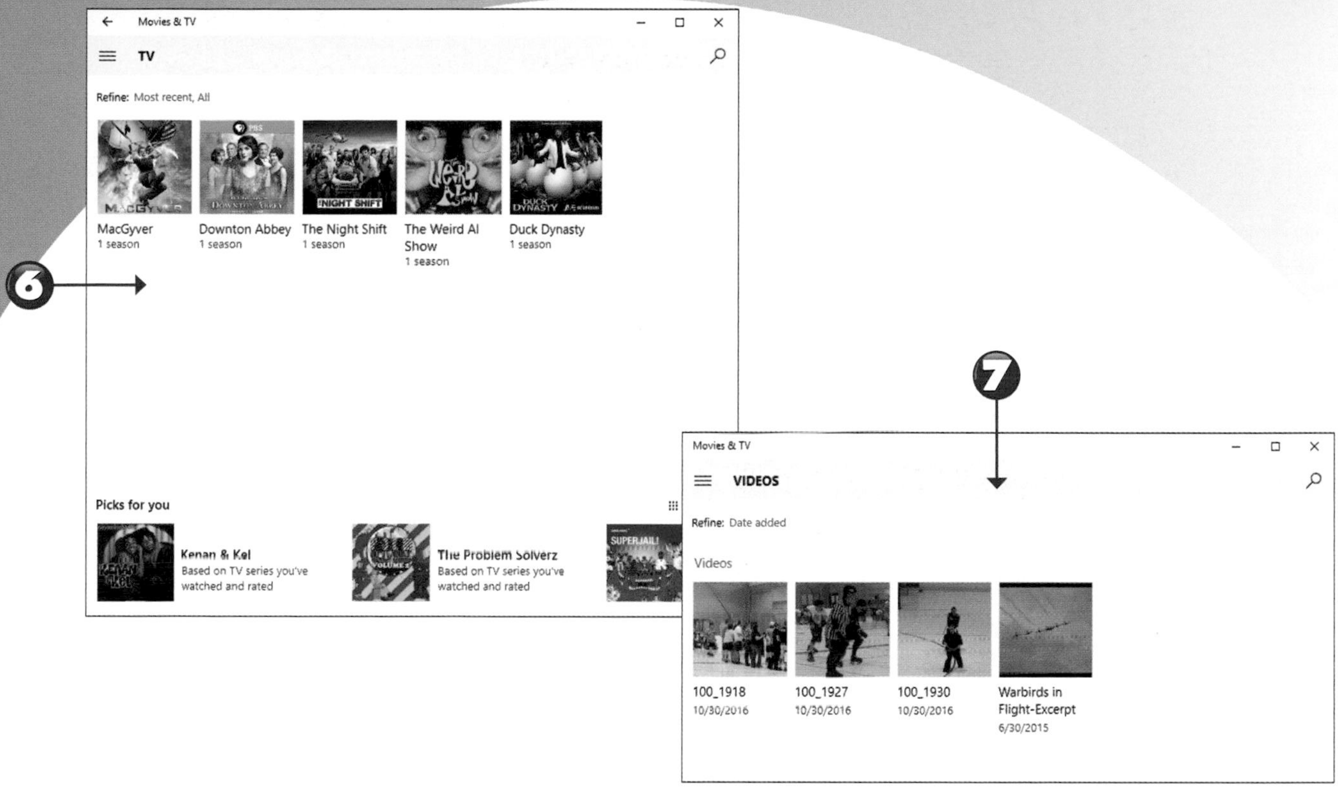

6. The TV category lists TV shows you have purchased.

7. The Videos category lists your video files and folders.

End

ADDING A LOCATION TO LOOK FOR VIDEOS

The Movies & TV app looks in the current user's Videos folder for videos. However, you can also check other folders, such as external drives, network locations, and Camera Roll (the folder used for storing photos and videos shot with your device's onboard camera). Here's how to configure Movies & TV to find videos in other folders.

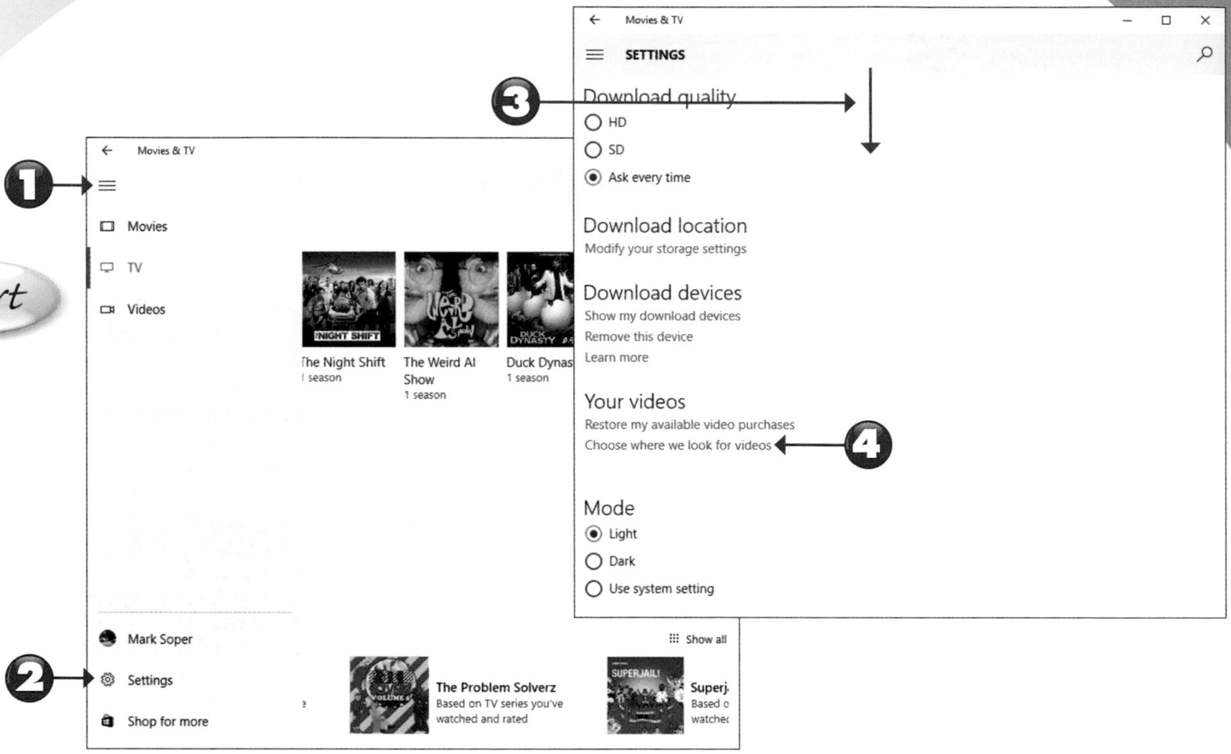

Start

1. With the Movies & TV app open, click or tap the **Menu** button.
2. Click or tap **Settings**.
3. Scroll to the **Your Videos** section.
4. Click or tap **Choose where we look for videos**.

Continued

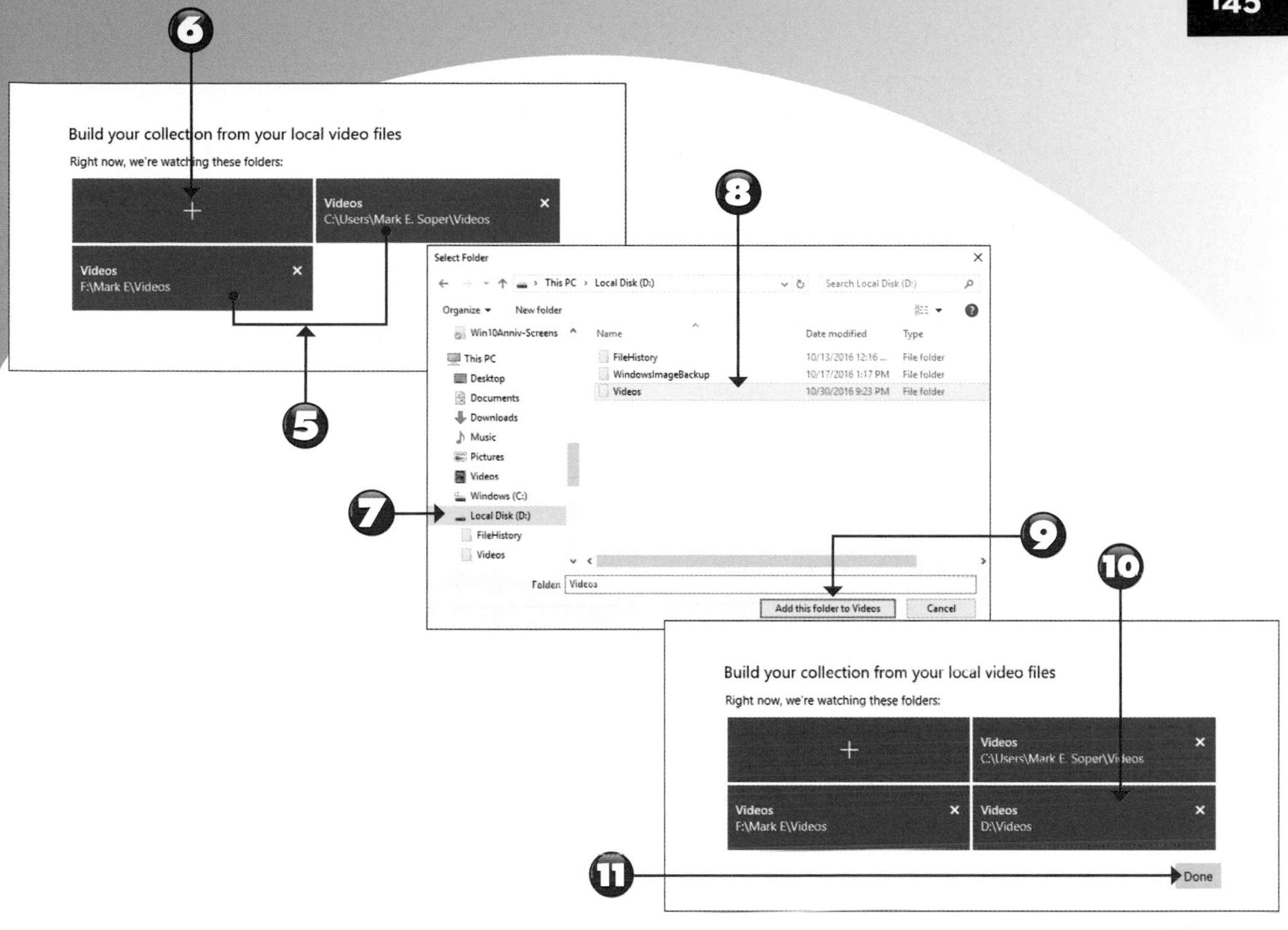

5. Current folders used by the Video app are listed here.
6. Click or tap to add a folder.
7. Navigate to the location containing the folder you want to add.
8. Click or tap the folder.
9. Click or tap **Add this folder to Videos**.
10. The new source is added to the list.
11. Click or tap **Done** when finished.

End

PLAYING A VIDEO, MOVIE, OR TV SHOW

You can play a video, movie, or TV show in a window or full screen using the Movies & TV app. You can quickly display playback controls to help you adjust the volume, change the aspect ratio, or pause the video. This example shows you how to play a video from the Videos collection.

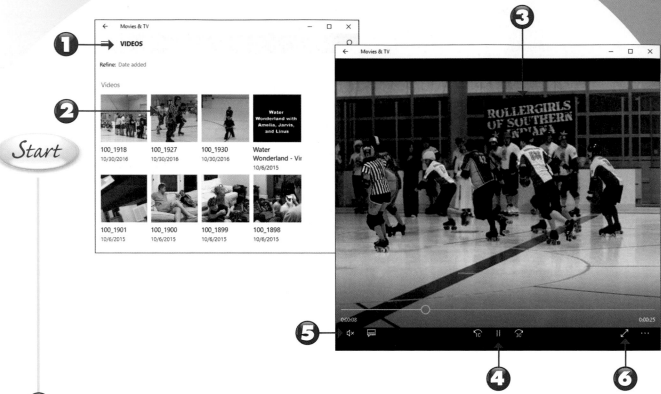

Start

1. With the Movies & TV app open, display the Videos category.
2. Click or tap a video to play.
3. Move the mouse or point anywhere in the playback window to display playback controls.
4. Click or tap here to pause/continue playback.
5. To adjust volume, click or tap here and drag the volume slider.
6. Click or tap to switch to full-screen playback.

NOTE

Viewing Closed Captioning If your video, movie, or TV show includes closed captioning, you see a CC button in the toolbar. Click or tap it to enable/disable closed captioning. ■

7. Full-screen view fills the entire screen.
8. You can click or press and drag to go to a particular moment in the video.
9. Click or tap to go back 10 seconds or go forward 30 seconds.
10. Click or tap for subtitles or audio options.
11. To view more playback options, click or tap the three-dot menu.
12. Click or tap to switch to windowed playback.

End

NOTE

Audio and Playback Options To display subtitles (step 10), click or tap a subtitle file (if available; embedded subtitles might not render properly). To play back (or cast) the video on a streaming video device (step 11), click or tap **Cast to device** and select the device to use. To remove black bars around the image, click or tap **Zoom to fill**. To play the video again, click or tap **Repeat**. ■

USING SEARCH TO FIND LOCAL AND WINDOWS STORE MEDIA

The Movies & TV app's powerful search feature can look for matches within your existing collection of videos, movies, or TV shows as well as matches in the Windows Store. In this example, you learn how this feature makes finding your favorite content easier.

Start

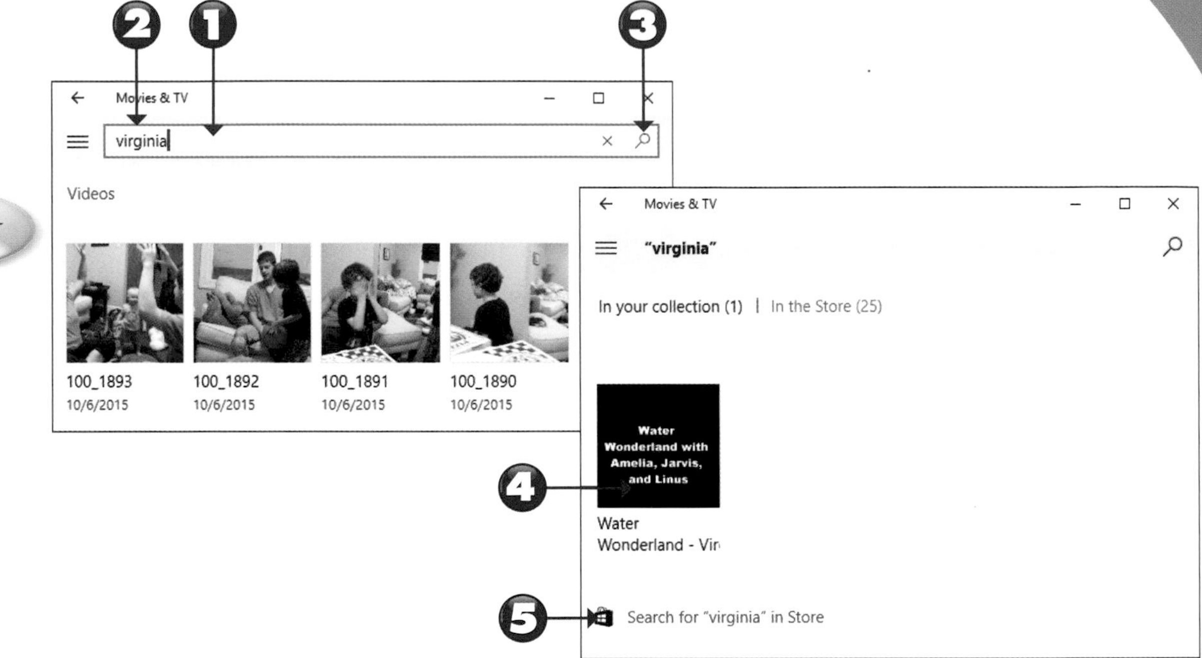

1. With the Movies & TV app open, click or tap **Search**.
2. Enter a search term or phrase.
3. Press **Enter/Return** or click or tap the **Search** icon.
4. The app lists matches from your own content; you can click or tap to choose a video to play.
5. To look for more matches from the Windows Store, click or tap the search link.

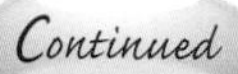

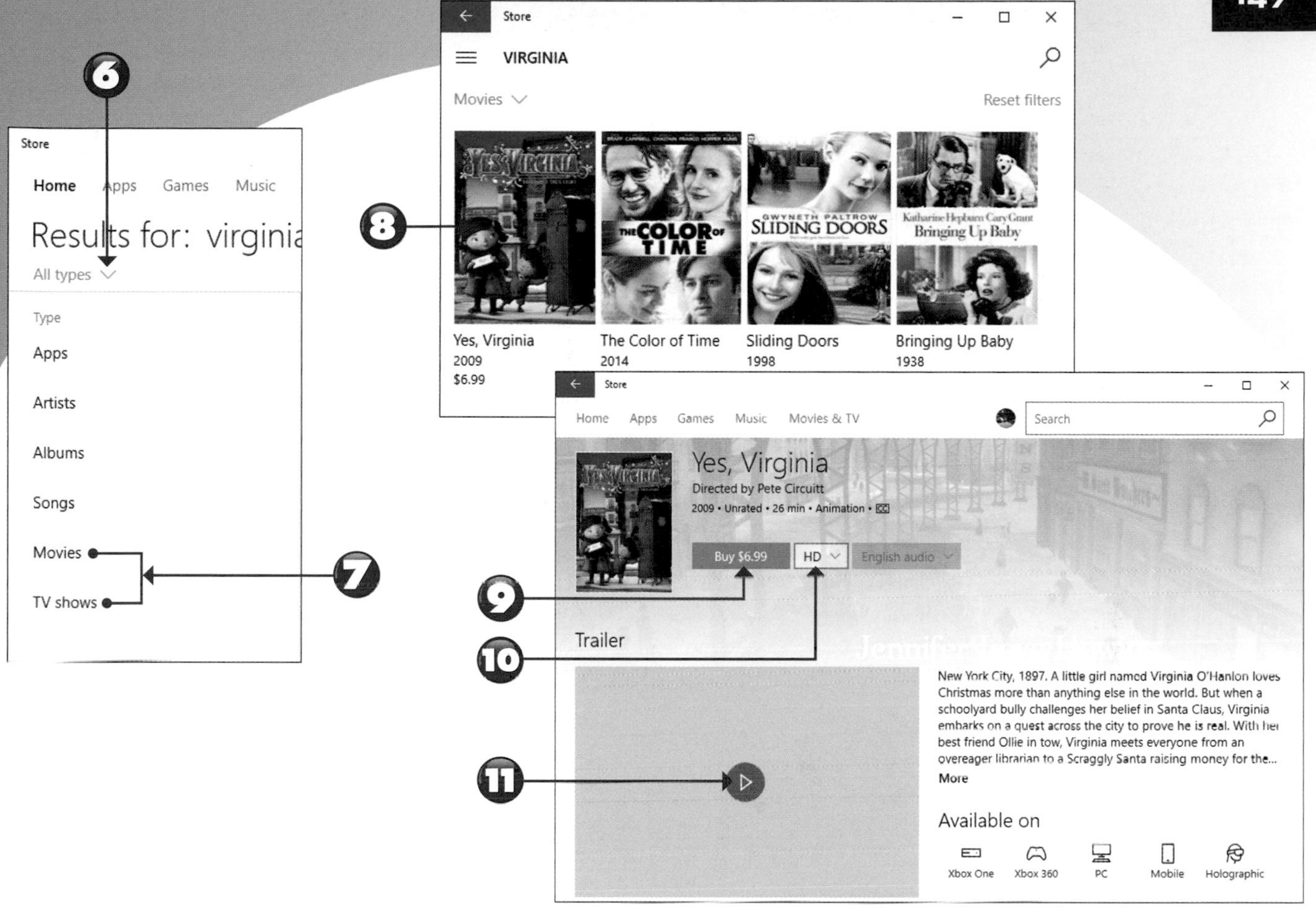

6. From the Windows Store, click or tap **All types** to select the content you want.
7. Click or tap **Movies** or **TV Shows** to filter results to video content.
8. Click or tap to select a movie or TV show.
9. Click or tap to select high-definition (HD) pricing.
10. Click or tap here to see pricing for other formats.
11. Click or tap to preview the selected movie or show.

End

BUYING OR RENTING A MOVIE OR TV SHOW

You can shop for music and videos online from within the Movies & TV app. Using your Microsoft account, you can purchase items for downloading or streaming. This example demonstrates buying an episode of a TV series.

Start

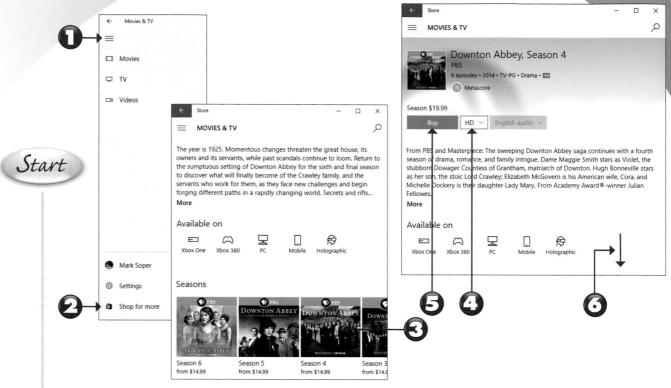

1. From the Movies & TV app, click or tap the **Menu** button.
2. Click or tap **Shop for more**.
3. From the Store, select the item you want to buy or rent.
4. Select the format desired.
5. To buy the show or season, you can click or tap here.
6. To view individual episodes to purchase, scroll down or flick up.

Continued

NOTE

Microsoft Account and Your Payment Information If you did not set up payment information when you set up your Microsoft account, you are prompted to provide a form of payment before you can complete your purchase. Follow the prompts to set up payment options.

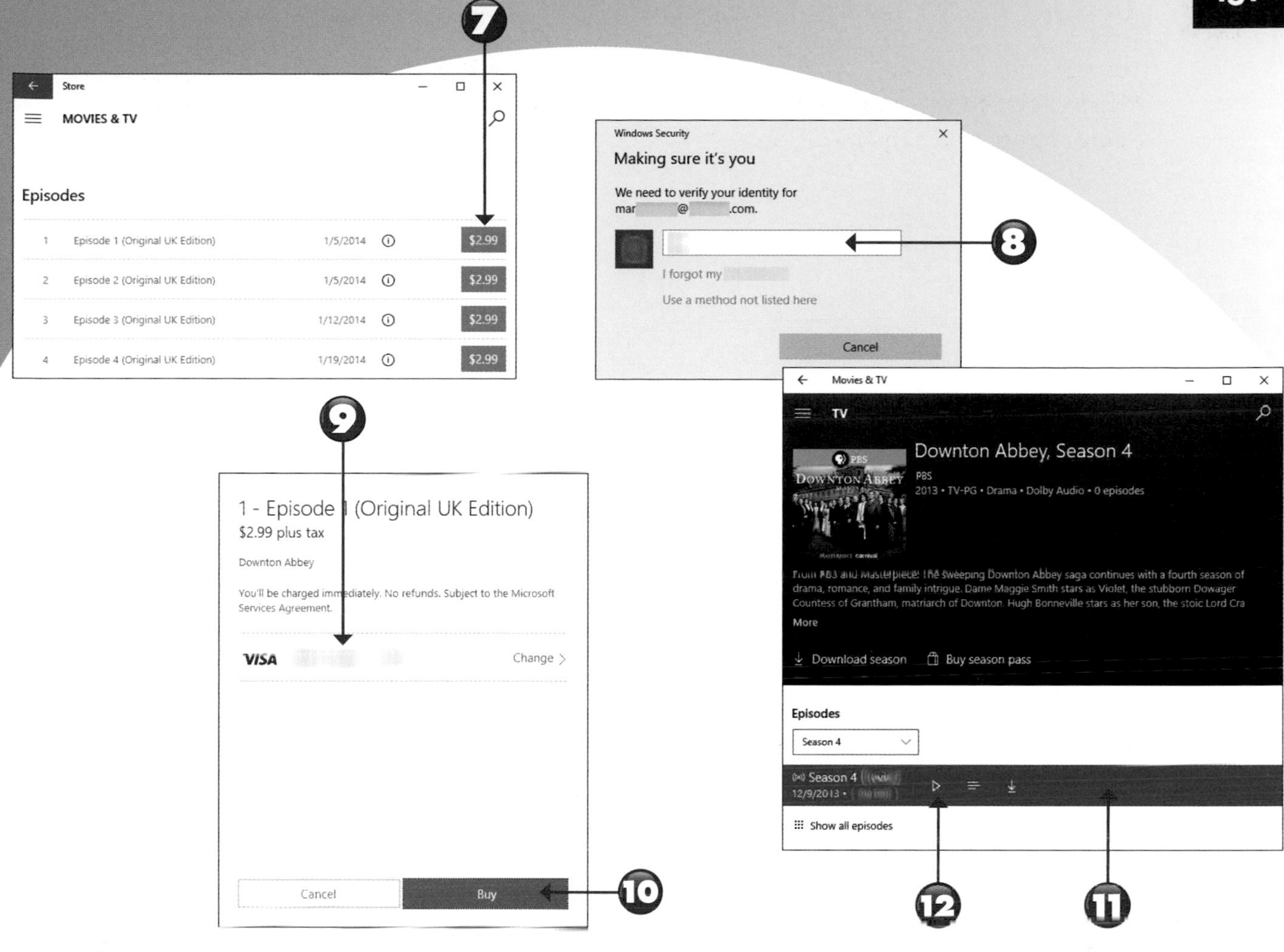

7. Click or tap the price button for the episode you want to buy or rent.

8. Sign in to your Microsoft account as prompted.

9. Review purchase details.

10. Click **Buy**.

11. Click or tap to display playback controls.

12. Click or tap **Play** to start watching the video.

End

USING SETTINGS TO REVIEW BILLING

The Settings menu in Movies & TV can help you with account information and issues. You can review media content you've purchased, change billing information, and more.

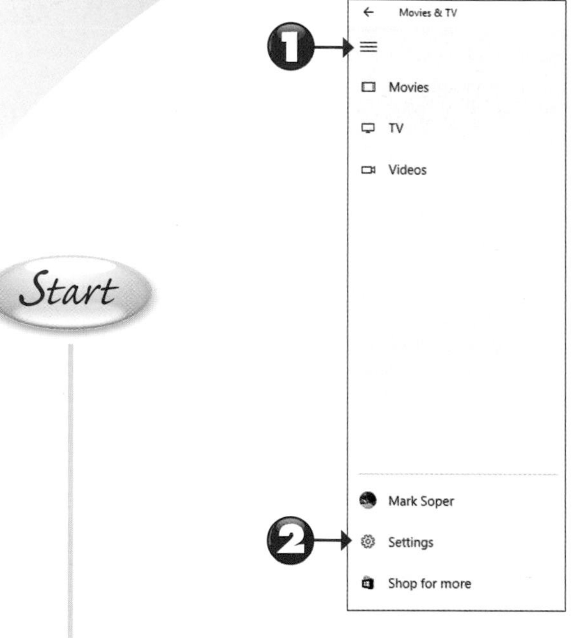

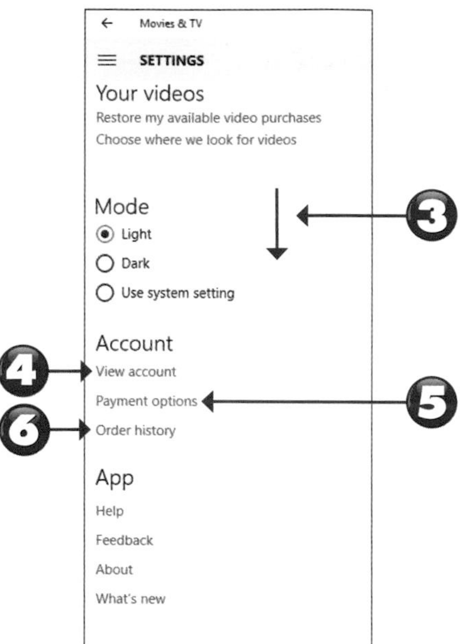

Start

1. Click or tap the **Menu** button.
2. Click or tap **Settings**.
3. Scroll down to view account options.
4. To view or change account information, click or tap **View account**.
5. To view or change the method of payment, click or tap **Payment options**.
6. To see previous purchases from the Windows Store, click or tap **Order history**.

Continued

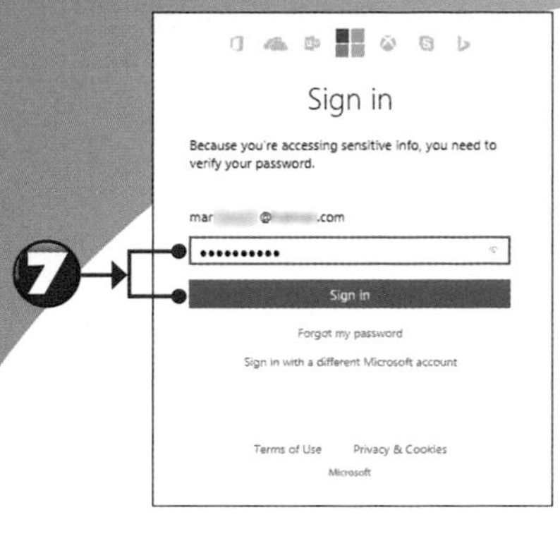

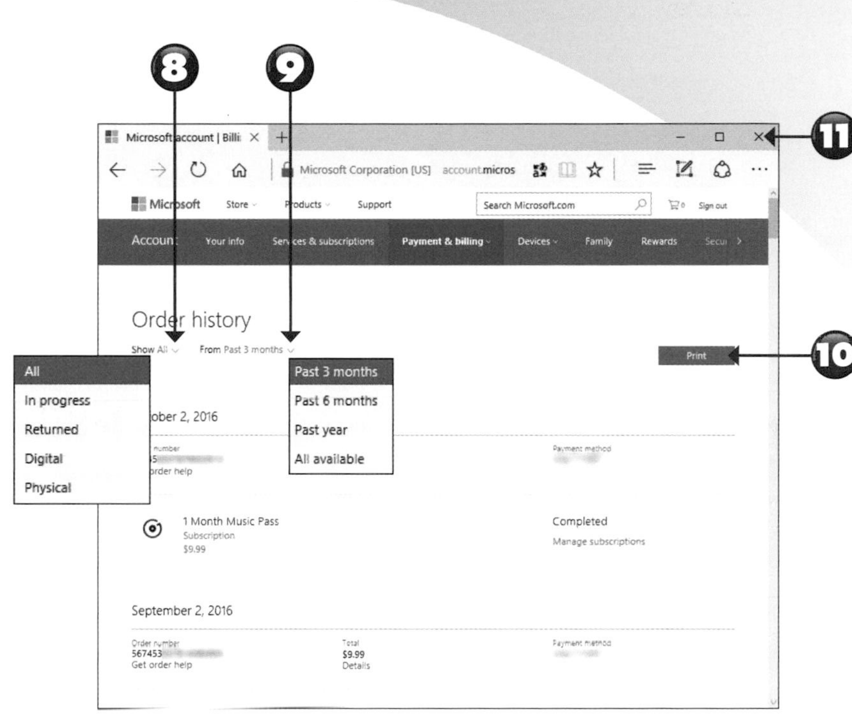

7 The browser window opens to your Microsoft account's Sign In page. Sign in to your account as directed.

8 Click or tap to filter orders by category.

9 Click or tap to view order by time period.

10 Click or tap to print order history.

11 Click or tap to close the browser window and return to the Movies & TV app.

End

VIEWING AND TAKING PHOTOS WITH CAMERA

Windows 10 AE includes the Camera app so you can take digital photos and videos with your device's webcam, front-facing camera, or rear-facing camera. Once the photos or videos have been taken or recorded, you can view and edit them using the Photos app. In this chapter, you learn how to use the Camera and Photos apps. The instructions in this chapter are written for Tablet mode, but Camera and Photos work in either Desktop or Tablet modes.

Exposure adjustment menu in Camera
Editing options in Photos
Photo and video settings in Camera
Collection view (Photos)
Basic fixes
Filters
Light
Color
Effects
1.0
SETTINGS
Press and hold camera button
Disabled
Photos
Aspect ratio
16:9
Framing grid
Off
Videos
Video recording
Flicker reduction
60 Hz
COLLECTION
Refresh
Select
Slideshow
Import
November, 2013
October, 2013

STARTING THE CAMERA APP

The Camera app is a default app that installs with Windows 10 AE. Camera is usually available from the Start menu. If it is not located there, it can be opened from All Apps.

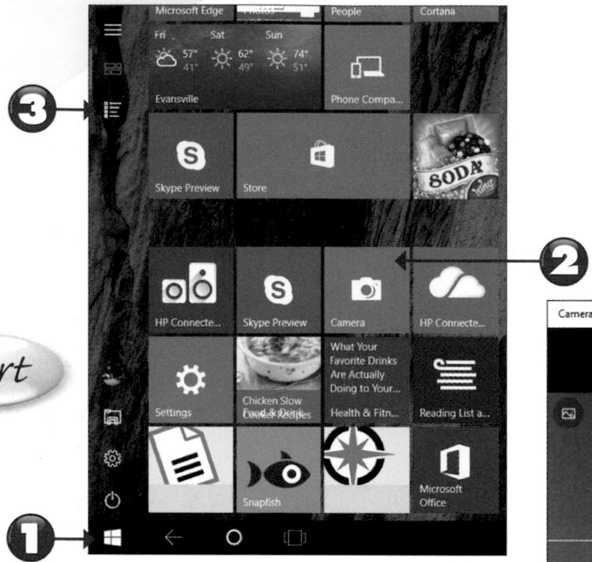

16×9 widescreen is the default setting for photos and videos.

Start

1. If the Start menu is not visible, tap or click **Start**.

2. Tap or click **Camera**.

3. If the Camera app is not visible, you can tap or click **All apps** and scroll to the app.

4. Tap or click the camera/arrow icon to switch between main camera (default) and rear-facing camera.

End

NOTE

First-time Only Setting The first time you start Camera on a new system, you are asked whether you want to allow the app to use location features. Camera remembers your choice and won't ask you again. You can change this setting through the Privacy settings available in the Windows Settings dialog box. (See Chapter 19 to learn more about viewing and changing settings.)

NOTE

The "Missing" Camera Switching Icon If your device doesn't have a rear-facing camera, the camera switch icon in step 4 isn't present.

SELECTING CAMERA SETTINGS

Some tablets have cameras that include advanced exposure and color settings. Some tablets offer more options in Camera mode than in Video mode. Here's how to open the advanced menu and use typical options.

After tapping a control, use the adjustment wheel to select the setting you want. EV+1 doubles the exposure, making it easier to see the flowers against a bright background.
Camera
Camera
WB
ISO
auto
auto
auto
1.0
1.0
Start
1
2
3
4
5
6

1. Tap or click the right arrow next to the camera selection button.
2. **White balance**—Tap or click to select the appropriate setting for the light used in the photo.
3. **ISO**—Tap or click to change the camera's sensitivity to light.
4. **Shutter speed**—Tap or click to change how quickly the shutter opens and closes.
5. **EV adjustment**—Tap or click to adjust exposure.
6. Tap or click to close the advanced menu and return to normal settings.

End

NOTE

Adjustments Vary by Camera Some built-in cameras don't have adjustments. If no right arrow is visible next to the camera switch button, the camera doesn't have any adjustable features. ■

NOTE

Learn More About Camera Controls To learn more about how white balance, ISO, shutter speed, and EV adjustments can improve your pictures with any type of device, see my book *The Shot Doctor: The Amateur's Guide to Taking Great Digital Photos*, Que Publishing, 2009. ■

USING VIDEO MODE

When you select Video mode in the Camera app, you can shoot MPEG4 video files with your device. Here's how to use this feature.

Start

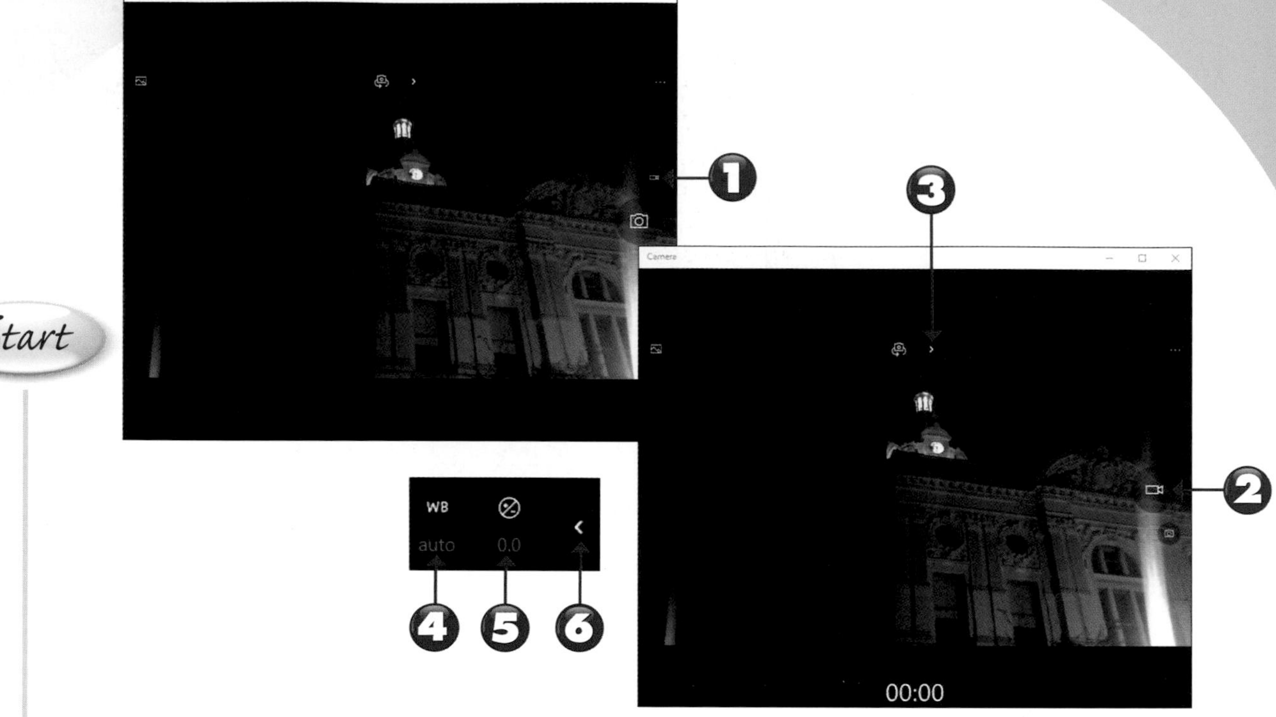

1. Tap or click to switch to Video mode.
2. Tap or click to start recording.
3. Tap to change video camera settings.
4. Tap to change white balance settings.
5. Tap to change EV adjustment (exposure) settings.
6. Tap to close the adjustments menu.

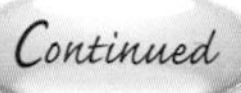
Continued

NOTE

Pinch to Zoom In either Camera or Video mode, you can use the touchscreen to zoom: Touch the screen with two fingers and move them apart to zoom in (larger image). To zoom back, move the fingers closer together. Note that this is a digital zoom (enlarges pixels), so image quality declines as you zoom in. ■

7 Tap or click to pause recording at any time.

8 The elapsed recording time is shown here.

9 Tap or click to stop recording.

End

CHANGING CAMERA APP SETTINGS

You can change the proportions (widescreen or standard), recording quality, and other settings with the Camera app's Settings menu. Here's how.

Start

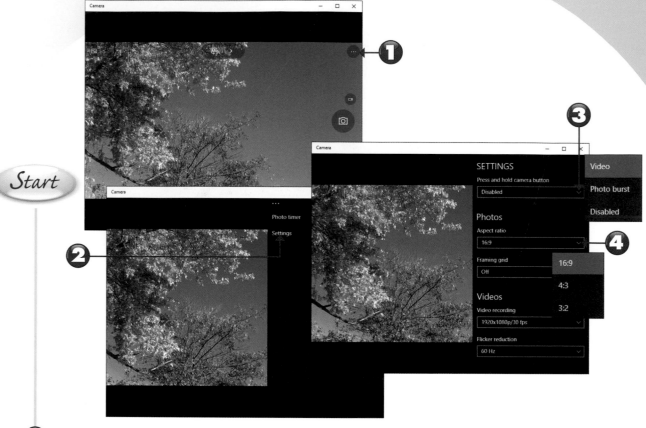

1. Tap or click the **More** (three-dot) button.
2. Tap or click **Settings**.
3. Tap or click to select how to use a long press on the shooting key.
4. Tap or click to adjust the proportions of your photos and videos.

Continued

NOTE

Photo Timer The photo timer option (available on some tablets in step 2) can be used to delay taking a photo or to take photos at intervals. Intervals include 2, 5, 10, and 30 seconds. ■

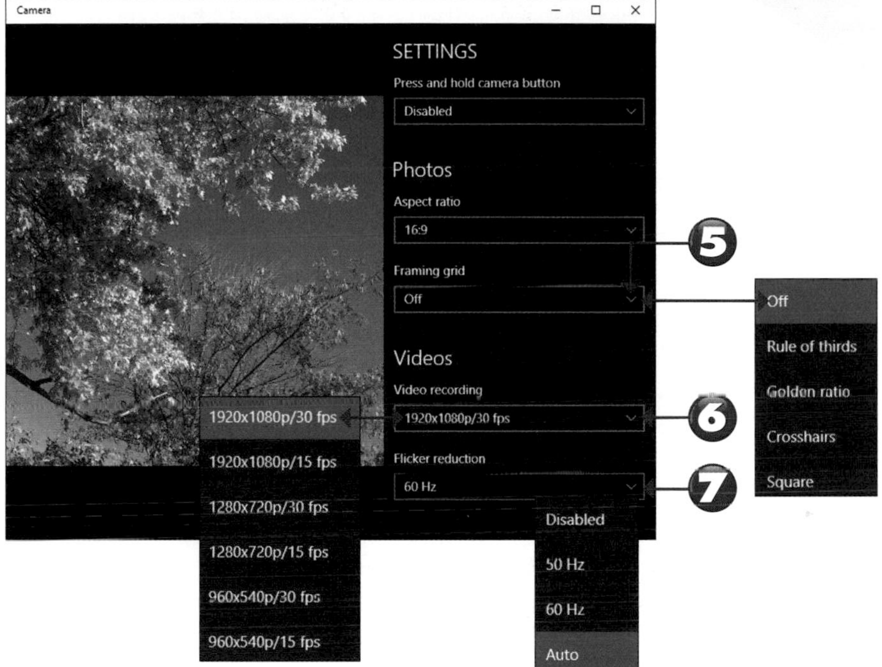

5. Tap or click to select a framing grid type.

6. Tap or click to select the video size and frames per second shooting rate.

7. Tap or click to select a flicker reduction rate (if needed).

End

NOTE

Why Available Resolutions Vary The options shown in this exercise are based on the Microsoft Surface Pro 3 Windows tablet using its main (rear-facing) camera. Other tablets, laptops, and webcams might have different settings, and available resolution settings might vary depending on whether you have selected the main or rear-facing camera.

OPENING THE PHOTOS APP FROM CAMERA

Windows 10 AE uses the Photos app to display your photos and videos, and you can start it from within the Camera app. Here's how.

Start

1. Tap or click the **Photos** button.
2. The most recent photo or video is shown first.
3. Swipe right to see the previous photo or video.
4. Tap or click **View all photos** to see all older photos and videos in order, newest to oldest.

End

TIP

Other Ways to Launch Photos If Photos is available from the Start, tap or click it to start it. In Desktop mode, you can also scroll down the left-hand Start menu to locate it. In Tablet mode, tap or click **All apps** and the scroll to locate it. In either mode, you can search for Photos and tap or click it in search results. ■

VIEWING YOUR PHOTO AND VIDEO COLLECTION

When viewing photos in the Photos app, you have a variety of ways to move through your photos and videos and add more from other devices. Here's an overview.

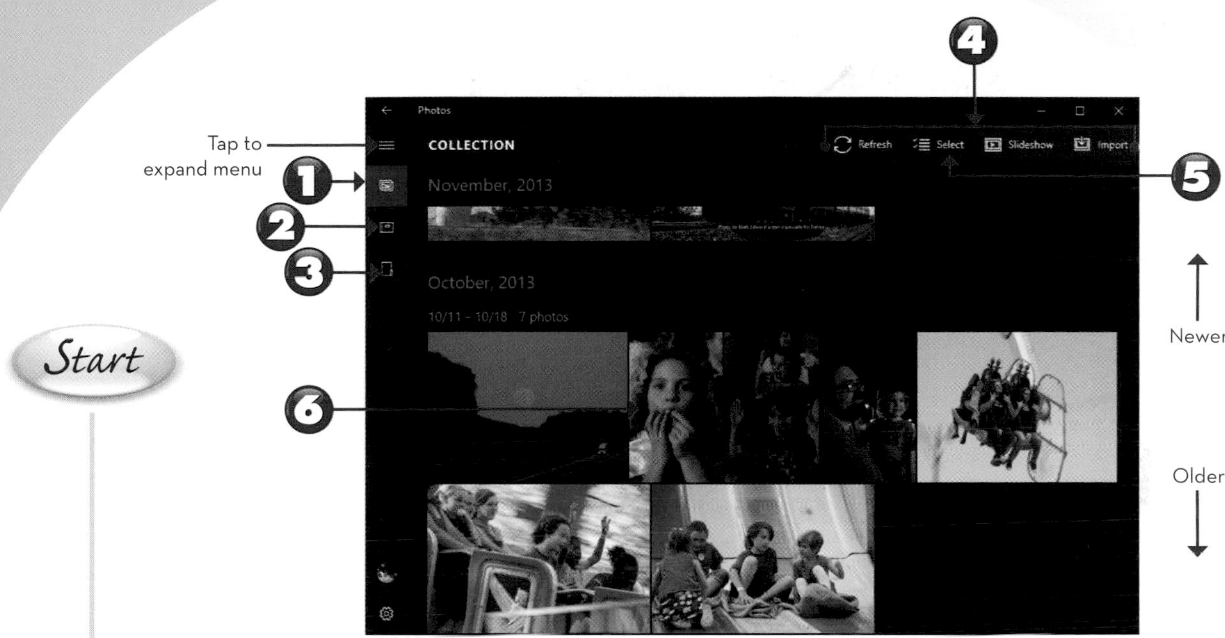

1. Default view displays Collection (newest to oldest).
2. Tap or click to view Albums, including Camera Roll and Screenshots folders.
3. Tap or click to select folders to view with the Photos app.
4. You can use these options to refresh, select, play slide show, or import photos.
5. Tap or click **Select** and choose photos you want to share, add to an album, copy, or delete.
6. You can tap or click a photo you want to edit.

End

TIP

Importing Photos To import photos from a storage device (USB, flash memory card, or optical drive), insert the device, click **Import**, select the device, and tap or click **Continue** to import all selected photos. If you don't want to import a photo, tap or click it to remove the checkmark before continuing. Select whether to import photos by month or day, and then click **Import**.

BASIC OPTIONS FOR YOUR PHOTOS

After you select a photo in the Photos app, you can print it, view camera information, rotate it, or use it in various places on your device. Here's an overview of several basic options you can apply.

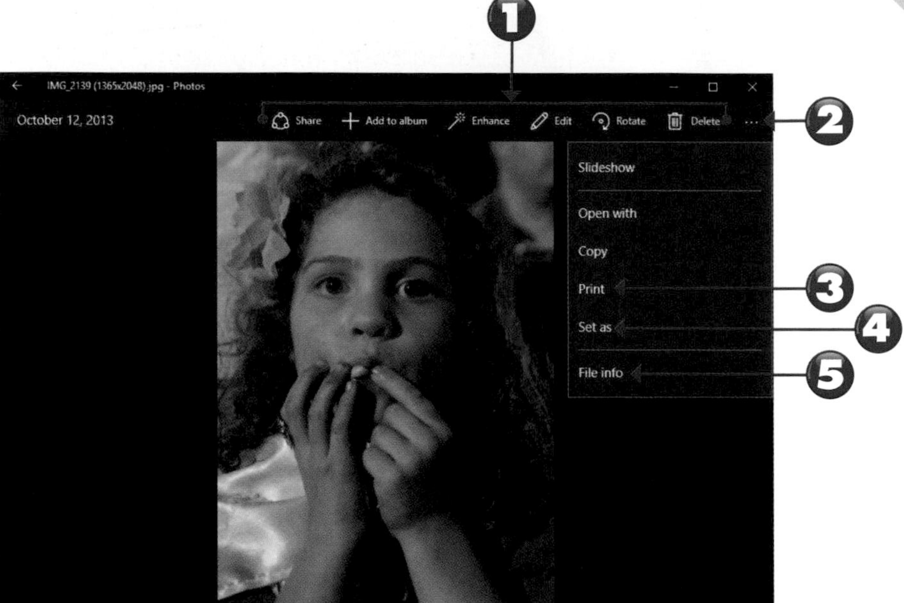

Start

1. With a photo selected, use these controls to share the photo, add it to an album, enhance it, edit it, rotate it 90 degrees, or delete it.
2. Tap or click the **More** (three-dot menu) button for additional options.
3. Tap or click **Print** to print the photo.
4. Tap or click here to use the photo on the lock screen, background, or Photos tile.
5. Tap or click **File info** to open file information about the photo.

Continued

TIP

Rotating Photos Do you have an image that was taken at an angle? Tap or click the Rotate tool; each tap or click rotates the image 90 degrees clockwise.

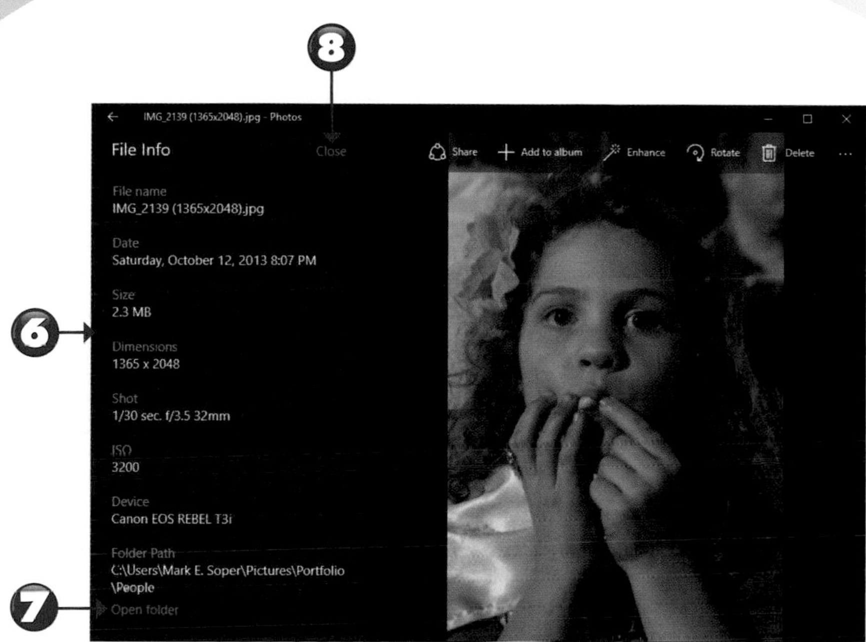

6. The File Info pane lets you review the exposure, camera, and file information.
7. Tap or click here to open the folder containing this photo.
8. Tap or click to close File Info.

End

NOTE

Keyboard Shortcuts for Photos You can perform many of the tasks in this chapter with your keyboard. For a complete list of keyboard shortcuts for various Windows 10 AE apps, including Photos, go to https://support.microsoft.com/en-us/help/13805/windows-keyboard-shortcuts-in-apps.

VIEWING YOUR VIDEOS WITH PHOTOS

When you view a video with the Photos app, you can select how much to play back and whether to trim the length of your video. Here's what the menus look like.

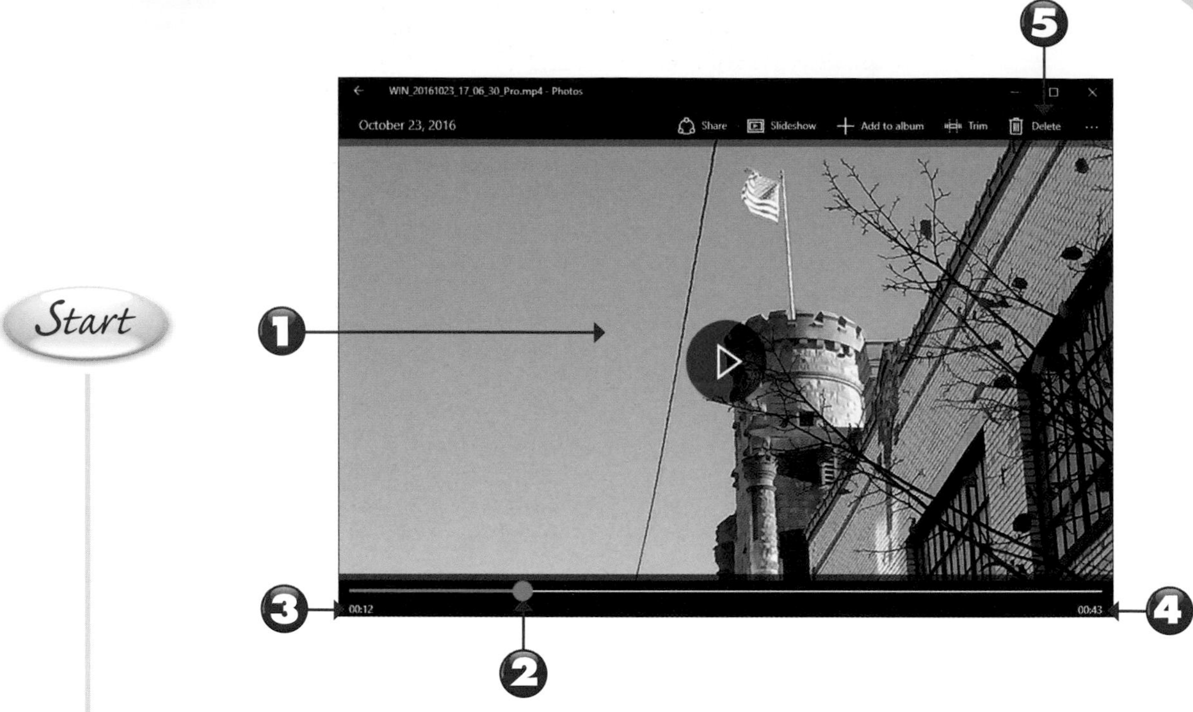

1. When you tap or click a video in Photos, the video plays automatically when opened. Tap the screen to pause/play it.
2. Press and drag the slider to go to a particular place in the video.
3. The current position in the video appears here.
4. The length of the video appears here.
5. Tap or click **Delete** to discard the video.

Continued

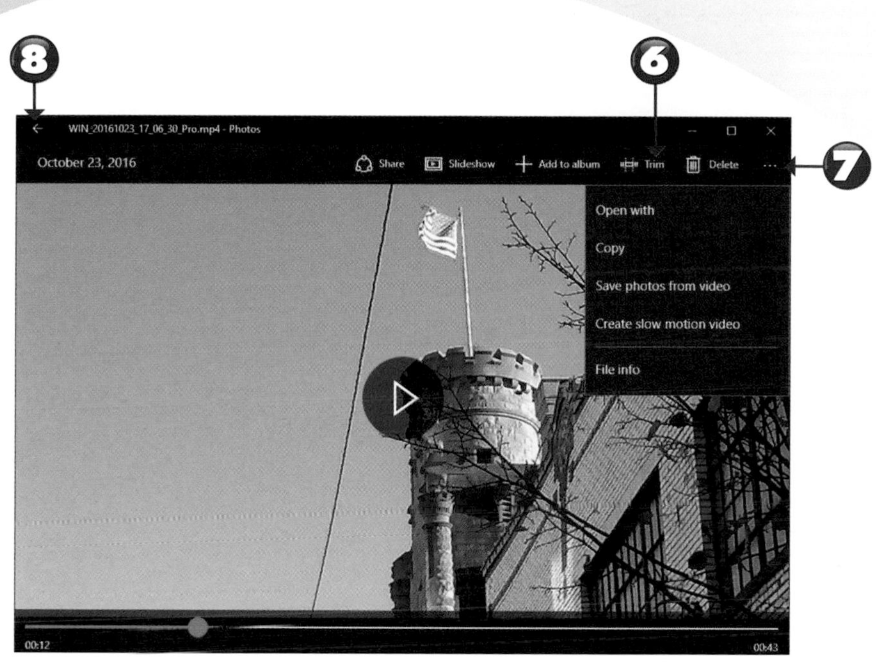

6 Tap or click **Trim** to edit the video length.

7 Tap or click **Menu** (three-dot menu) to see additional options.

8 Tap or click to return to all photos and videos.

End

CROPPING A PICTURE WITH PHOTOS

Photos offers tools you can use to crop, change colors, adjust brightness, and add effects to your photos. Here's how to crop a photo to the size you want.

Start

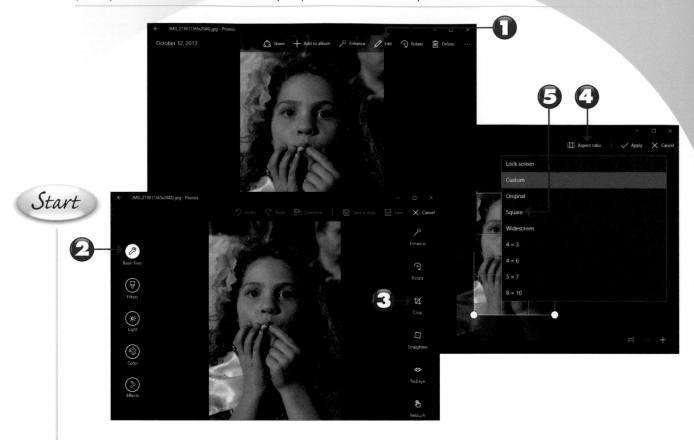

1. With the photo you want to edit opened in the Photos app window, tap or click the **Pencil** icon (**Edit**) to open the editing tools.
2. Tap or click **Basic fixes**.
3. Tap or click **Crop**.
4. Tap or click **Aspect Ratio** (proportions).
5. Tap or click the aspect ratio you want.

Continued

NOTE

Resize to View Missing Menu Items If the Photos window is too narrow, some tools won't be visible. You can drag the right edge of the window or click the **Maximize** icon in the top-right corner of the window to make all menu items visible.

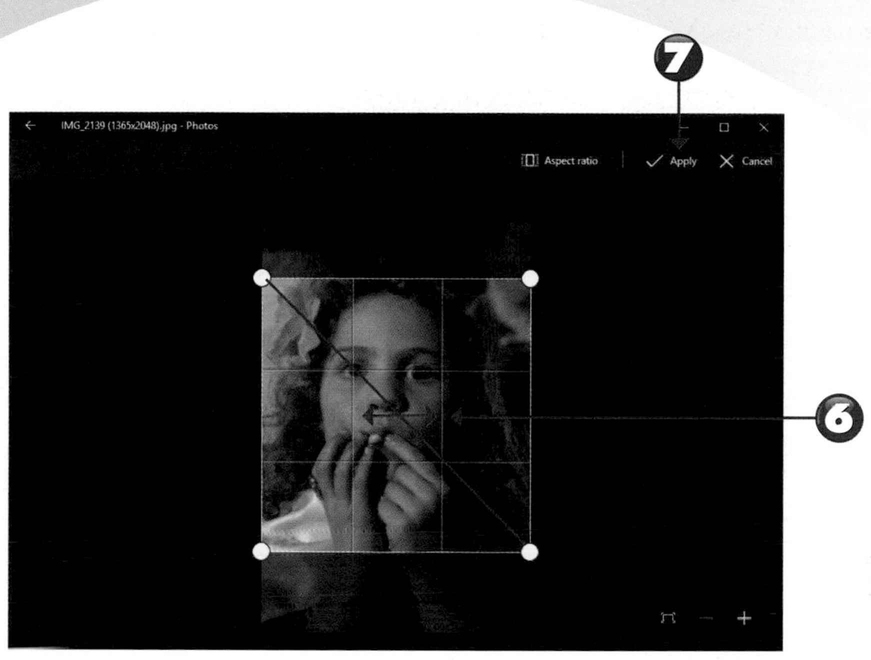

6 Press and drag the window and corners to adjust the crop.

7 Tap or click to complete the crop.

End

NOTE

Other Basic Edits You Can Make Use **Enhance** to automatically fix a bad picture. Use **Rotate** to turn a picture 90 degrees at a time. Use **Straighten** to fix a crooked photo. Fix red eye in people (but not pets) with **Red eye**. Use **Retouch** to fix surface imperfections.

IMPROVING BRIGHTNESS AND ADDING EFFECTS WITH PHOTOS

Photos also includes tools to help you brighten or darken a photo and add effects such as vignette (brightens or darkens corners of the photo) or selective focus (blurs part of the photo). Here's an example of what you can do.

Start

1. With the editing tools displayed, tap or click **Light**.
2. Tap or click **Brightness**.
3. Press and drag the brightness control clockwise to make the photo brighter (shown) or counterclockwise to make it darker.
4. To display the zoom control (and zoom in photo), press Ctrl-+ (plus sign) on the keyboard.

Continued

TIP

Pinch to Zoom, Click to Zoom To zoom in with a touchscreen, press both fingers to the screen and pinch them together. To zoom out, move both fingers apart. When the zoom control is visible (step 4), click or tap the plus (+) sign to zoom in, the minus (-) sign to zoom out, and the box icon on the left side to switch between minimum and maximum zoom. ■

NOTE

Additional Editing Options Use **Contrast** to increase or decrease the differences between light and dark areas in your photo. Use **Highlights** to lighten or darken bright areas in your photo. Use **Shadows** to lighten or darken dark areas in your photo. ■

5. Tap or click **Effects**.

6. Tap or click **Vignette**.

7. Press and drag the Vignette control clockwise to darken the corners of the photo, or counterclockwise to brighten the corners (as shown here).

End

NOTE

Undo/Redo Each time you tap **Undo**, an edit to your photo is reversed. After you undo at least one edit, you can tap **Redo** to redo an edit. You can undo/redo multiple changes.

COMPARING EDITED AND ORIGINAL VERSIONS

Before you save your changes, you can quickly compare your edited photo to the original. Here's how.

Start

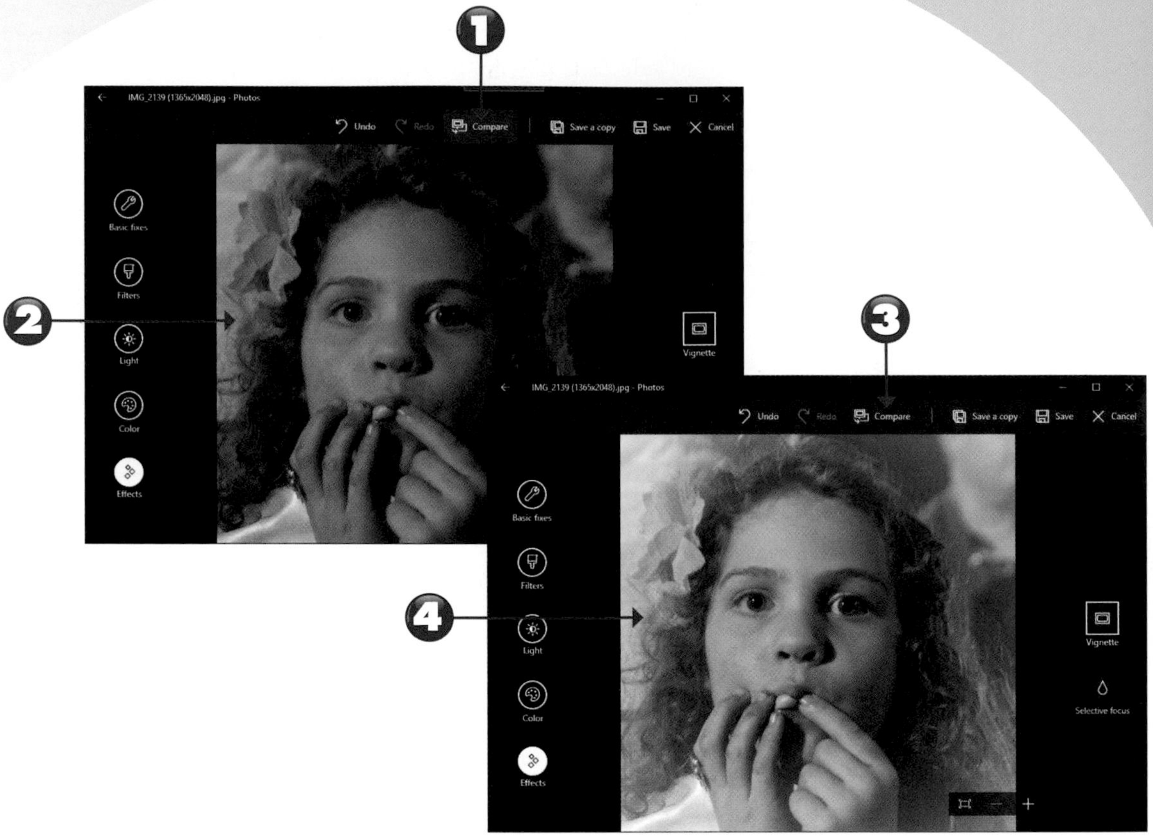

1. With the editing tools displayed, press and hold **Compare**.
2. The photo appears as it did before you made changes.
3. Release the **Compare** button.
4. The edited version of the photo appears again.

End

NOTE

Color and Effects Menu Options Tap or click the **Color** tool to view color options; use **Temperature** to fix problems with a photo being too warm (yellow) or too cool (blue); use **Tint** to tweak color balance; use **Saturation** to make all colors more or less intense; use **Color boost** to increase or reduce the intensity of the selected color. Tap or click the **Effects** tool to use **Selective focus** to blur less-important parts of the photo. ■

SAVING CHANGES

Do you like the improvements you made in your photo? Save your changes. Here's how.

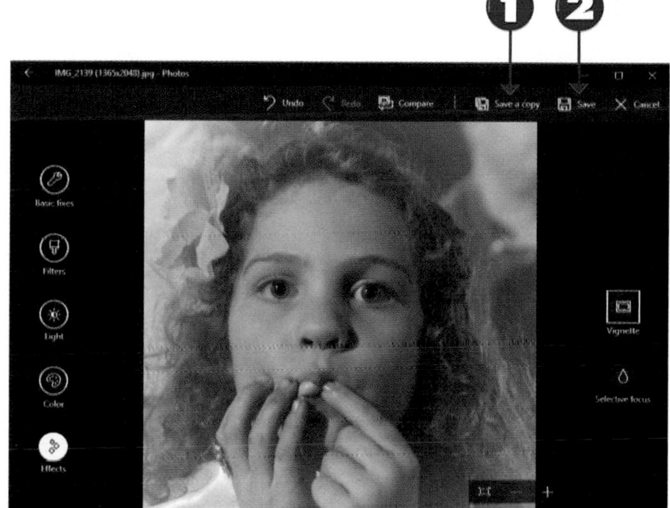

Start

1. Tap or click **Save a copy**. A copy is saved in the same location as your original, but the original name has a number added to it. Your original photo file is not changed.
2. Tap or click **Save** if you want to replace your old version.

End

CAUTION

Save a Copy Is Safer Than Save Even if you're certain that your changes have improved a photo, I recommend using **Save a copy** so that you don't lose your original. After all, you might have even better ideas for changing it later!

CONNECTING WITH FRIENDS

Windows 10 AE offers a variety of ways you can connect with people, ranging from email to social media to face-to-face connections over your computer. In this chapter, you learn how to use several of the key communications apps and features.

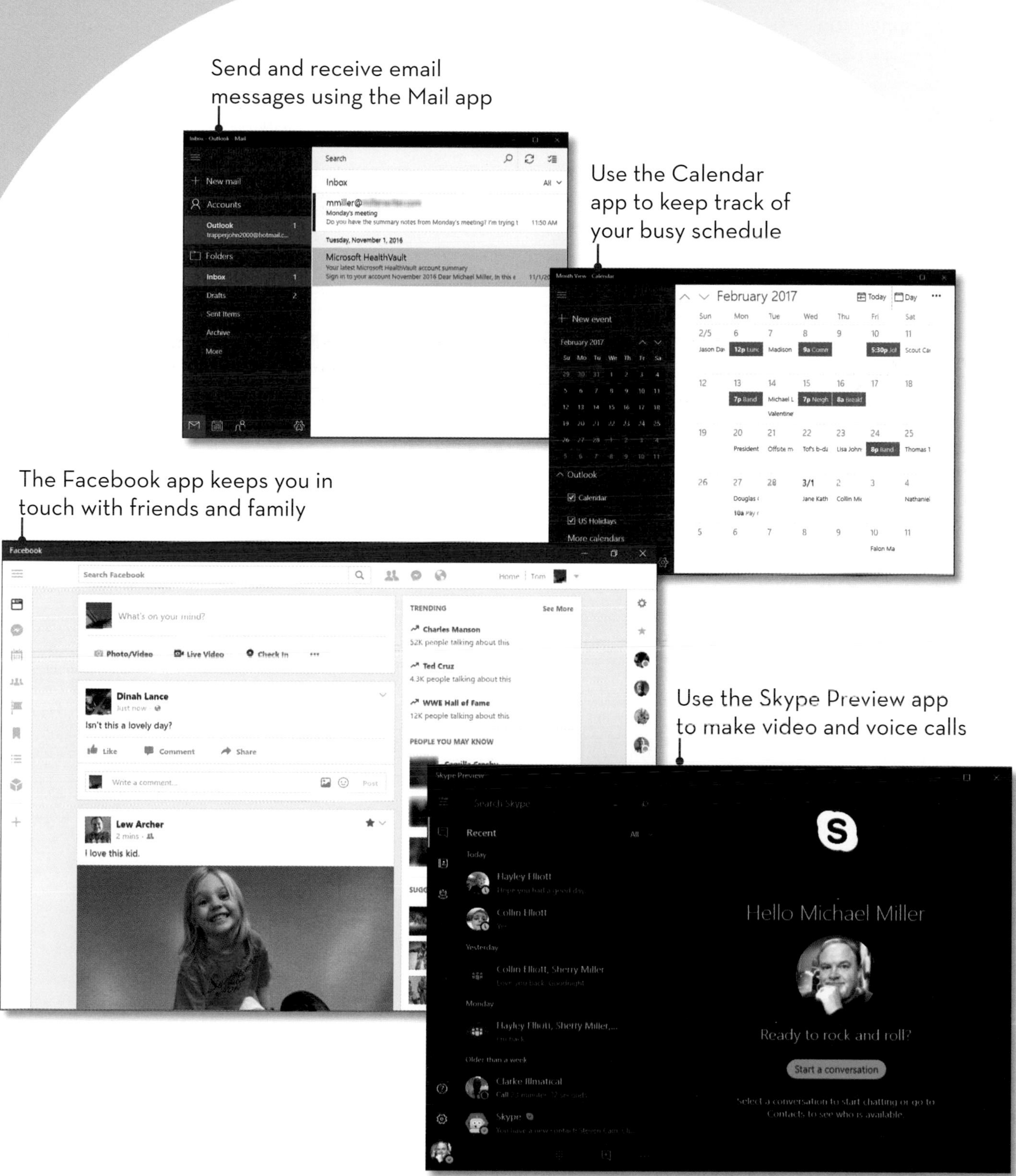
Send and receive email messages using the Mail app
Use the Calendar app to keep track of your busy schedule
The Facebook app keeps you in touch with friends and family
Use the Skype Preview app to make video and voice calls

USING THE PEOPLE APP

You can use the People app to compile and maintain a list of contacts. Behaving like a digital address book, the People app keeps a list of people you contact the most, including email contacts. You can add as many contacts as you like and view each with just a click.

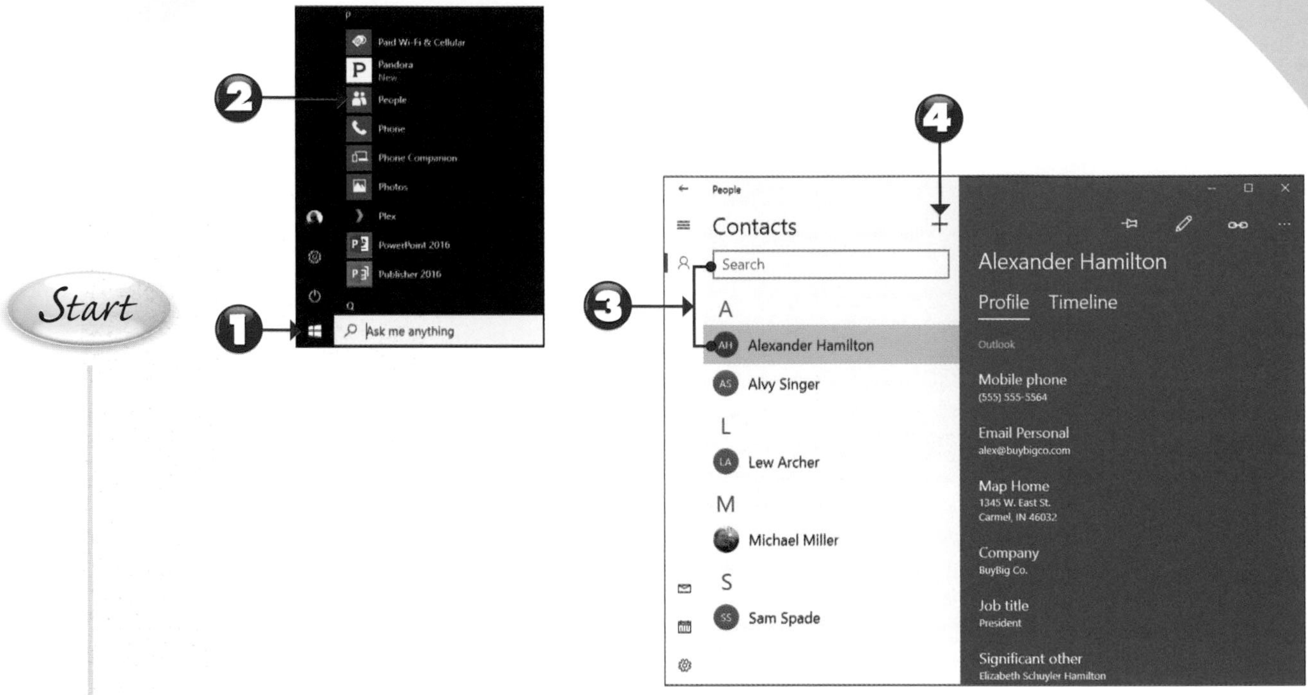

1. Click or tap **Start**. (If you're using a Windows tablet, you also need to tap the **All Apps** button.)
2. Click or tap **People**.
3. The People app opens with your contacts displayed in the left column. Click or tap a contact name to view that contact's information, or use the **Search** box to search for a specific contact.
4. Click or tap the **+** to start a new contact.

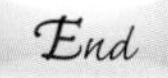

TIP

Associate an Account The first time you use the People app, you are prompted to associate an account. Click or tap the account you want to use.

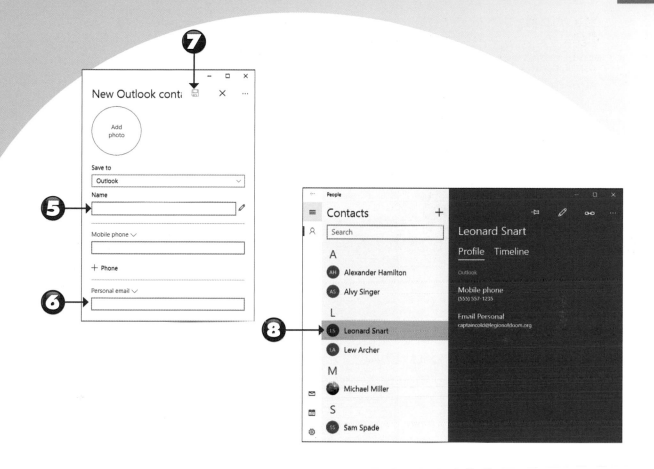

5. Fill out the contact form; click or tap a text box or field and enter the contact information.

6. Scroll down the form to view more fields.

7. Click or tap **Save** when you finish entering contact information.

8. The contact is added to your digital address book.

End

NOTE

Save to a Different Account By default, new contacts are saved to your currently active account. You can save a contact to a different account by clicking or tapping the **Save to** drop-down arrow and choosing an account from the list.

TIP

Edit Contacts To make changes to a contact's information, click or tap the contact, and then click or tap the **Edit** icon (looks like a pencil). Make your changes to the form fields, and click or tap **Save**.

CONNECTING TO FACEBOOK WITH THE FACEBOOK APP

You can use the free Facebook app in the Windows Store to keep up with the latest Facebook postings, add status updates, and upload photos to your profile page. If you don't already have the Facebook app, you must install it first.

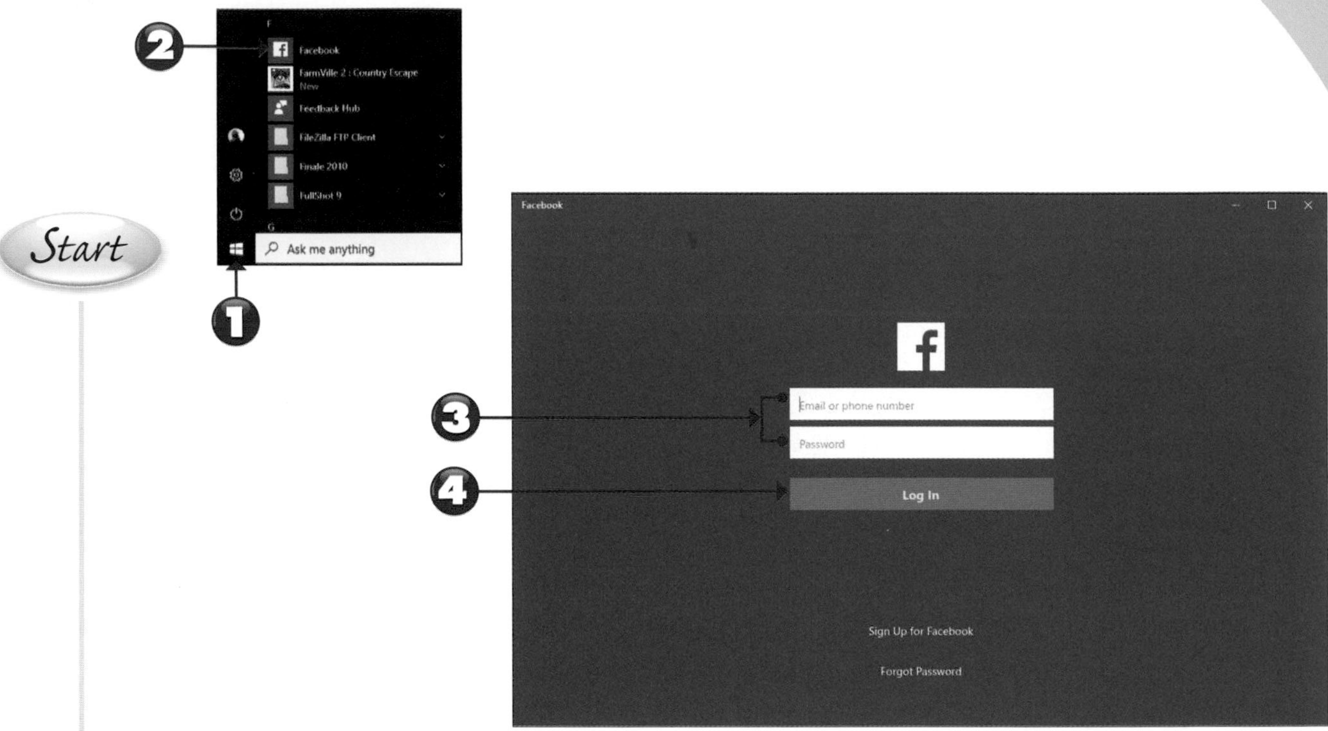

1. Click or tap **Start**.
2. Click or tap **Facebook**.
3. Click or tap the **Email** box and enter your email login, and then enter your password in the **Password** box.
4. Click or tap **Log In**. You might be prompted to connect with nearby places, friends, and more; access your current location; or sync your profile picture and cover photo to your Windows account and lock screen. Click or tap **Yes** or **OK** to do any of these.

Continued

NOTE

Download the Facebook App To find the Facebook app, open the Store app and search for Facebook. Most likely, you'll find it listed among the top free apps. Select the app and click or tap **Install**. The app downloads, and when it finishes it appears listed among your apps ready to go.

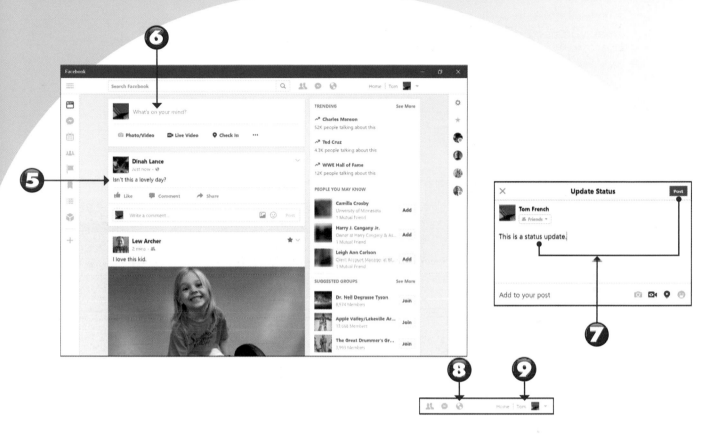

5 By default, the app shows your News Feed. Scroll to view more posts from your friends and favorite pages.

6 To post a status update, click or tap in the Publisher box ("What's on your mind?").

7 Type your status update, and then click or tap **Post**.

8 To view notifications from Facebook and other users, click or tap the **Notifications** icon.

9 Click or tap your name or profile picture to view your Timeline (profile) page.

End

TIP

App Screen Size Depending on how your app screen is sized, you might be able to view all the Facebook features without having to open hidden items. You can click and drag a border or press and hold a border to resize a window.

NOTE

Find More Settings If you're looking for the logout option or other Facebook settings, click or tap the down arrow located in the top-right corner of the app window, next to your name.

STARTING MAIL

Windows Mail works with Microsoft's web-based Outlook.com email service and many other email services, including Gmail, Yahoo! Mail, and Exchange. Mail automatically detects the email you used to create your Microsoft account and adds it as your first account. In this task, you learn how to navigate the Mail app.

Start

1. Click or tap **Start** to open the Start menu.
2. Click or tap **Mail**.
3. Click or tap the **Maximize** button to view the Mail app full screen. (This enables you to view the content of messages in a separate pane than the list of messages in your Inbox.)
4. Mail opens with the default account selected. If you have additional accounts added, click or tap to select any account.
5. To view any message in the Inbox, click or tap the message.

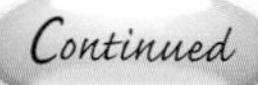

Continued

NOTE

First-Time Use When you first start Mail, a Welcome window might appear; click or tap **Get Started**. You'll then see another first-time use window that lists your default account (or accounts), along with an option to add more accounts; click or tap **Ready to go** to begin.

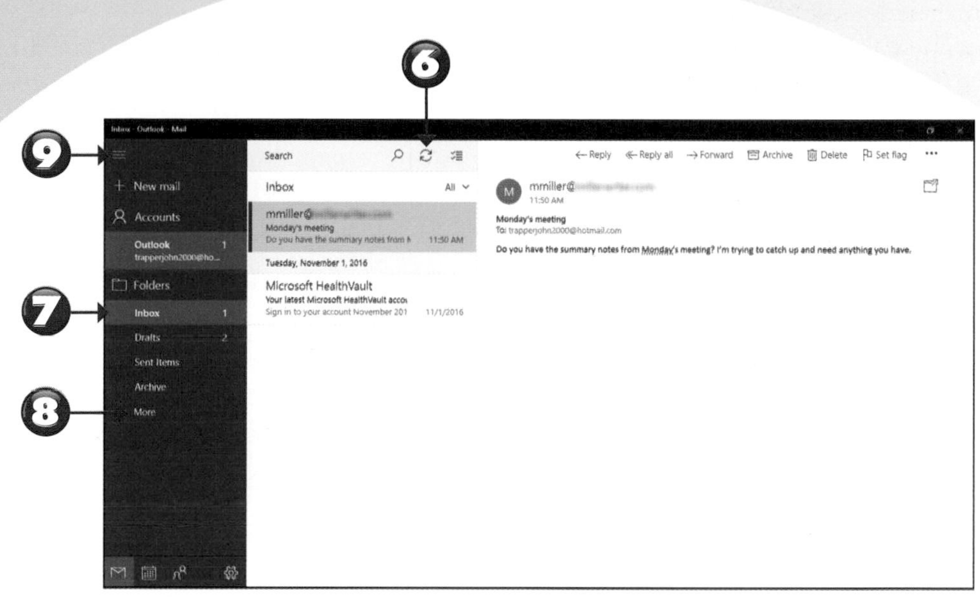

6. Click or tap **Sync** to download new messages.

7. Click or tap a folder name, such as **Inbox**, to view the folder's contents.

8. Click or tap **More** to view additional Mail folders.

9. Click or tap **Menu** to hide or display the left pane listing the main Mail components.

Continued

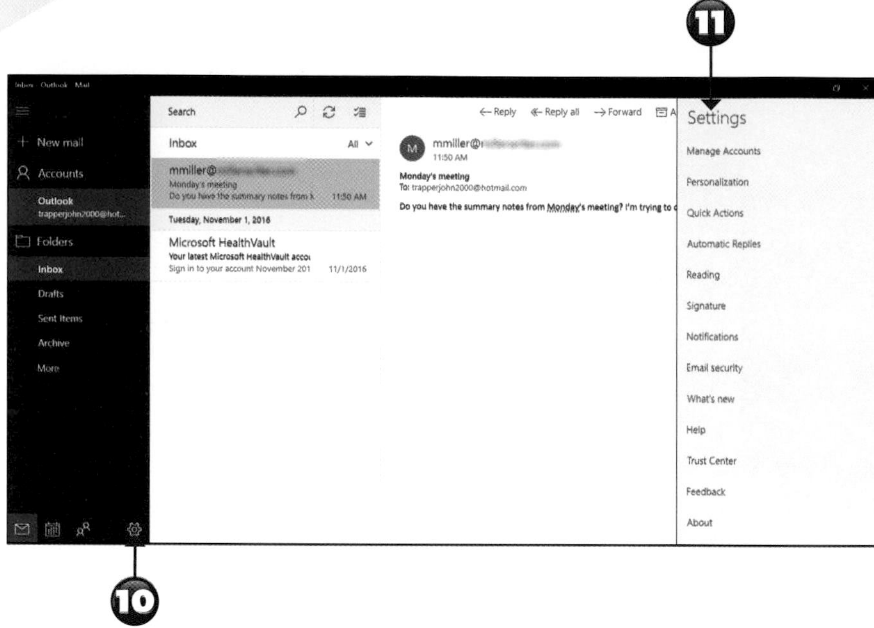

10 Click or tap **Settings**.

11 The Settings panel opens; use this panel to find settings for controlling accounts, adding a signature, specifying how email is marked, and more.

End

TIP

Using Another Email Client? If you're using a web-based email client, such as Yahoo! or Google, you can use your web browser to access messages rather than using the Mail app.

NOTE

Setup Help If you're using an Outlook email account, one of the easiest ways to start setting up your email is to utilize the links found in the Outlook.com team's introductory email. Just click or tap the message to open it, and then follow the instructions and links provided.

ADDING AN EMAIL ACCOUNT

You can add other email providers to the Windows 10 AE Mail app and check your messages in one convenient spot. You might have a work email and a home email account, for example, or a Google and a Yahoo! Mail account. You can add them to Mail.

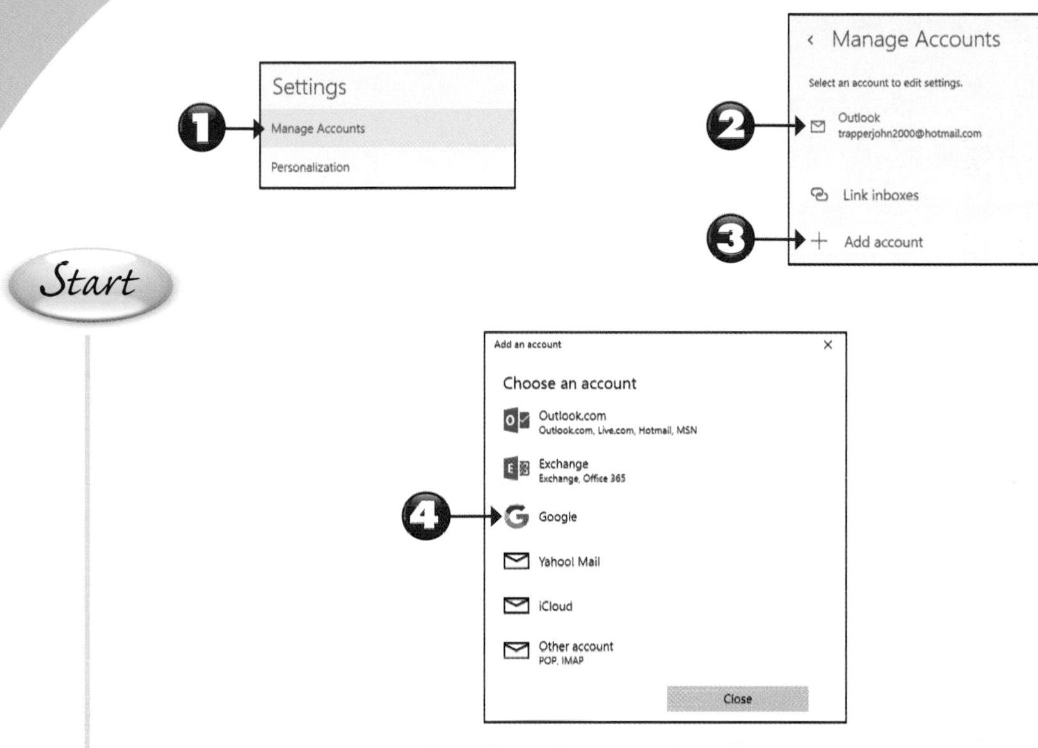

1. With the Mail app open, click or tap **Settings**, and then tap **Manage Accounts**.
2. Click or tap an account to make changes to its settings.
3. To add an email account, click or tap **Add account**.
4. Click or tap an account type.

Continued

NOTE

Mail and Calendar The Windows 10 Mail and Calendar apps are designed to work together, making it easy to email a schedule, set up appointments with other users, and more. That's why there's a Calendar app icon at the bottom of the folder list in Mail. You can click the icon to open the Calendar app. You learn more about Calendar later in this chapter.

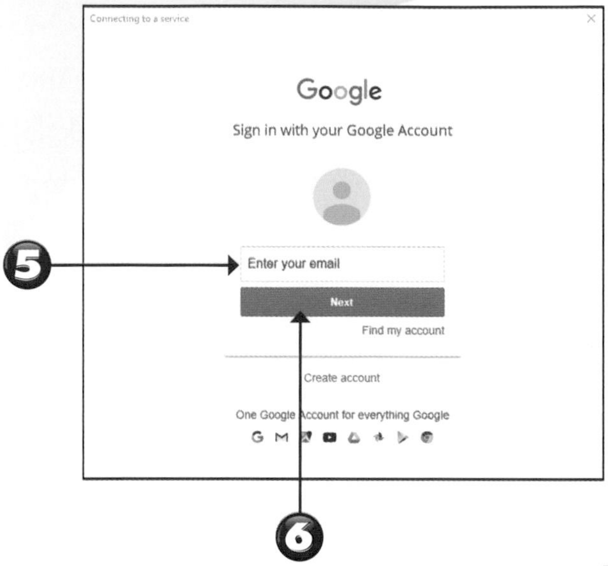

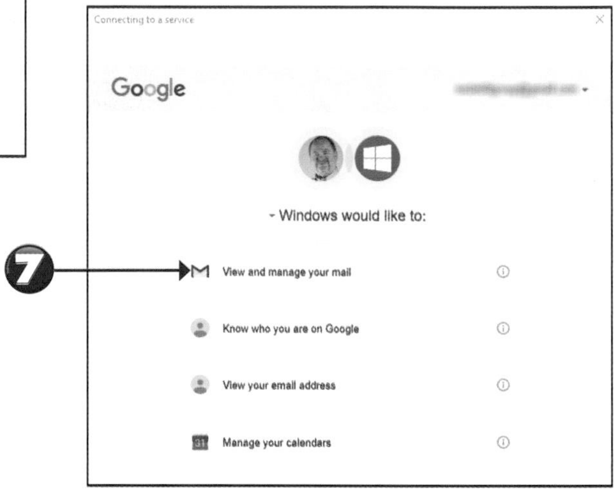

5. Fill out the form, as needed; for most types of email, you'll need to enter the account's email address and password.

6. Click or tap **Next**.

7. Depending on your email provider, you might encounter additional windows to finish the process; click or tap to fill in the appropriate information as prompted. Click or tap **Done** when the account is successfully added.

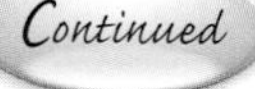

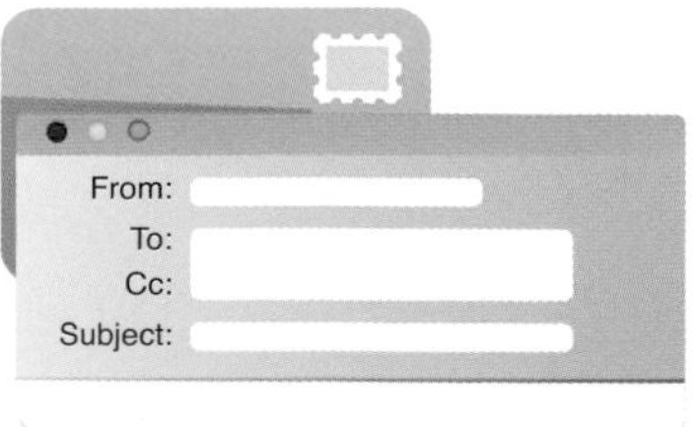

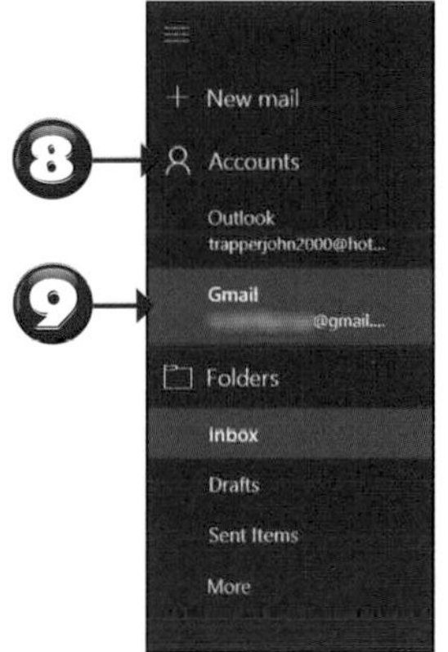

8 All the email accounts you've added are displayed in the Accounts section of the left pane.

9 Click or tap an account to use it.

End

NOTE

Edit an Account If you need to make changes to an account's settings or delete the account entirely, click or tap the account. This opens a window with the account's name, settings, and an option for removing the account from your Mail app. Simply make your changes and click or tap **Save** when finished.

COMPOSING AND SENDING A MESSAGE

You can easily compose a new email message and send it on its way. The Mail app lets you add simple formatting, insert pictures or links, attach files, and even check your spelling before you hit the Send button. In this task, you learn to quickly create a message and add a file attachment.

Start

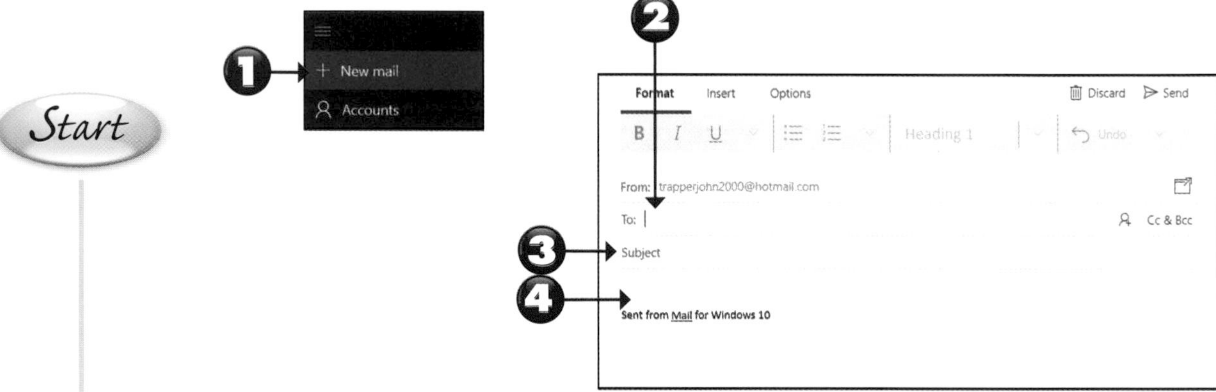

1. With the Mail app open, click or tap **New mail**.
2. Click or tap the **To** field and enter the email address for the person to whom you want to send a message. If you're sending the email to multiple people, include a semicolon between addresses.
3. Click or tap the **Subject** field and give your message a heading or title.
4. Click or tap the blank area below the Subject field and enter your message text.

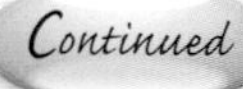

TIP

Use a Contact As you're typing an email address in the To field, a list of possible matches might appear courtesy of the People app (your digital address book of contacts). If the name matches a contact, you can click or tap it to finish the entry.

NOTE

Check Your Folders To see a list of sent emails for an account, click or tap the **Sent Items** folder in the Folder pane. Mail pins the Sent Items and Drafts folders to the Folders pane by default. To pin other folders, first click or tap the **More** button at the bottom of the account listed in the Folder pane. (You might need to scroll to view the option.) Next, right-click or press and hold a folder name and click or tap **Favorites**. You can also use the same technique to unpin folders from the pane, but you should choose **Remove from Favorites**.

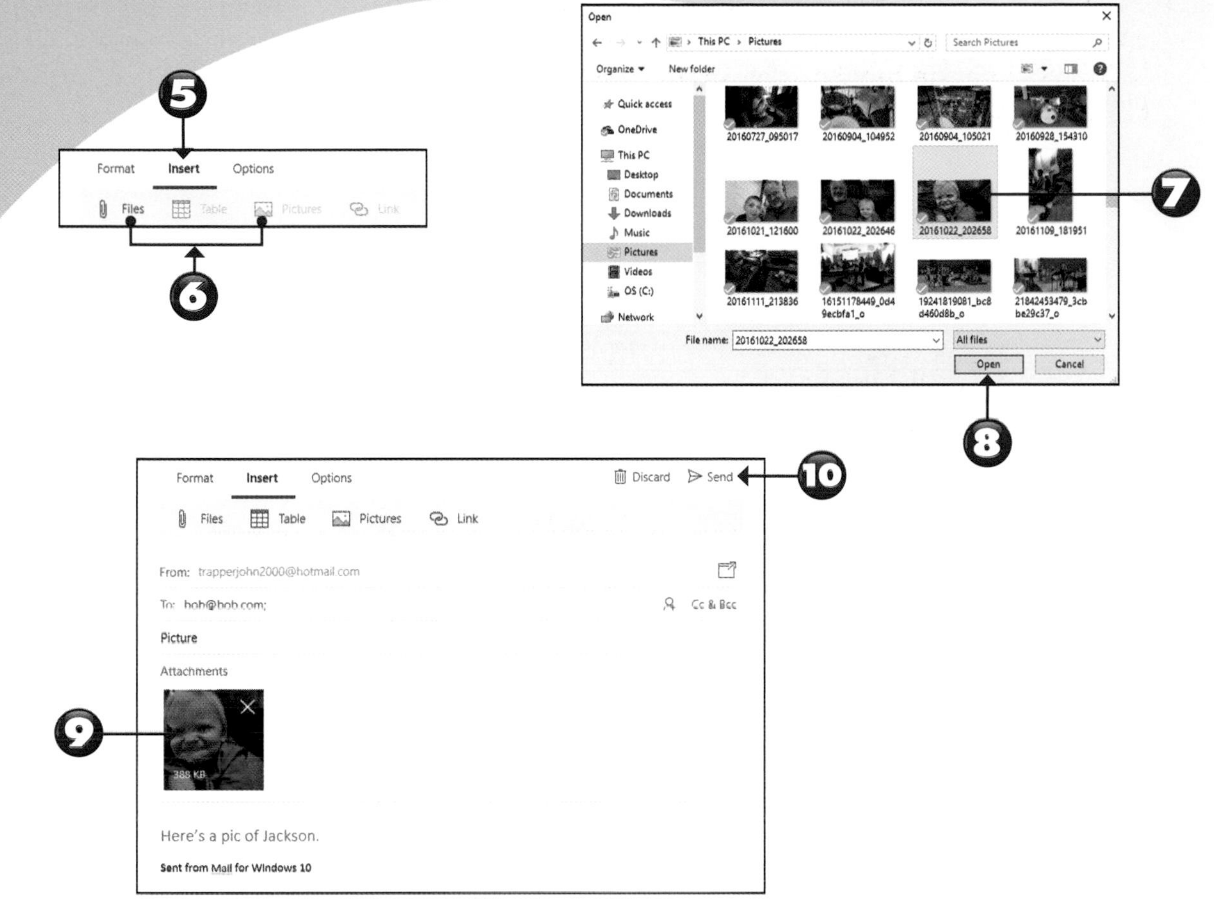

5. To add a file attachment, click or tap the **Insert** tab.

6. Click or tap **Files** to attach a file, or **Pictures** to attach a picture.

7. Navigate to the file you want to attach; click or tap the filename.

8. Click or tap **Open**.

9. Mail adds the file attachment.

10. Click **Send** when you're ready to send the file.

End

READING AND REPLYING TO MESSAGES

Mail lists the email messages for each account in the main window, along with a brief peek at the content of each. You can read individual messages in their entirety in a separate window. You can also reply to a message from within the message window.

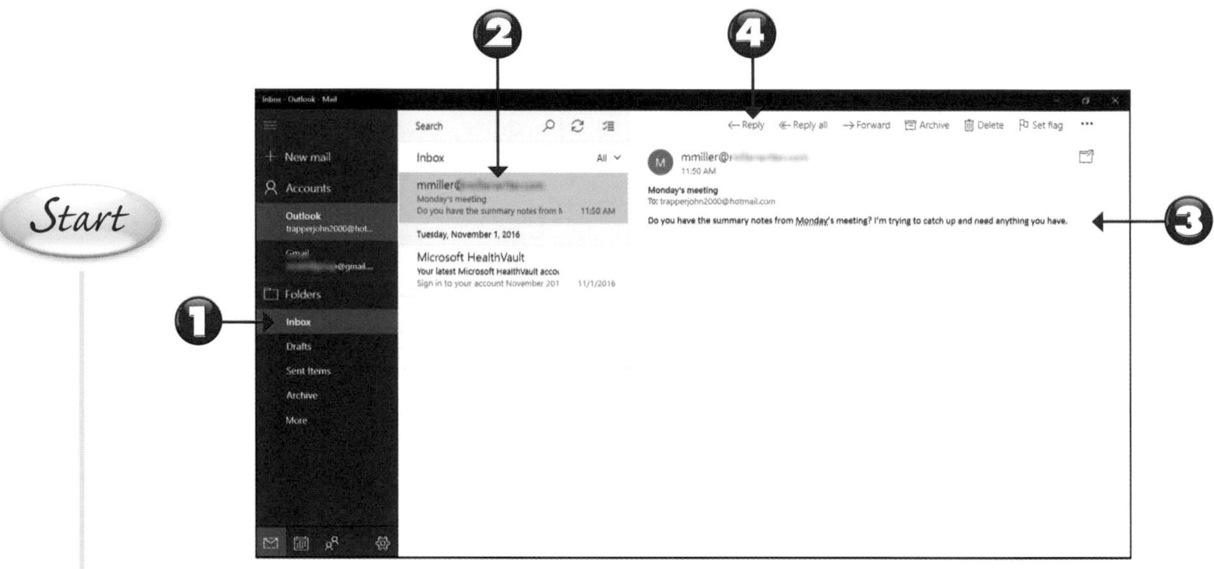

1. From Mail's navigation pane, click or tap the email account or Inbox you want to view.
2. Click or tap the message you want to read.
3. The message opens on the right side of the app window, along with a toolbar of commands.
4. To reply to a message, click or tap **Reply**. If the message went to multiple people, you can reply to all of them using **Reply All**.

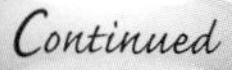

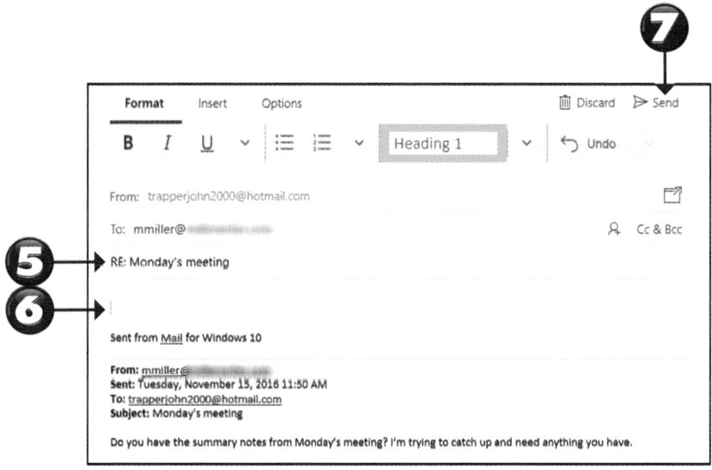

5. Mail automatically fills in the sender's email address and adds RE: to the subject line to indicate the message is a reply. Mail also includes the original message text.

6. Type your message reply here.

7. Click or tap **Send**.

End

NOTE

Reading Conversations If you're corresponding with the same person (or persons) with replies back and forth, you can click or tap the message in the main Mail window to view each reply as a submessage to the original message. This lets you see the conversation's progress as each person responds. ■

FORWARDING MESSAGES

It's easy to forward a message to another person. Mail automatically inserts FW: in the subject title to indicate a forwarded message.

Start

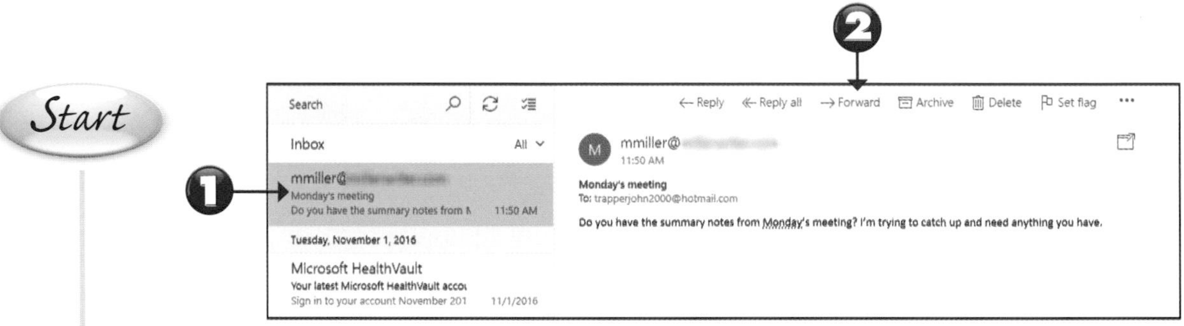

1. From your account's Inbox in Mail, click or tap the message you want to forward.
2. Click or tap **Forward**.

Continued

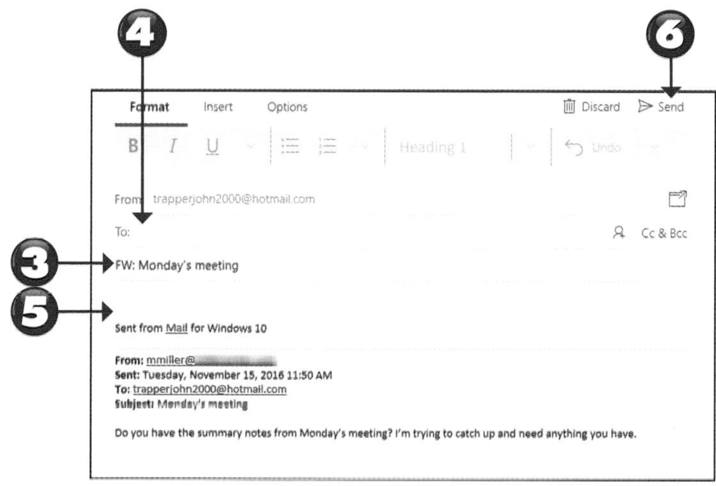

3 Mail automatically adds FW: to the subject line to indicate the email is a forwarded message.

4 Click or tap the **To** box and type in the email address you want to send to.

5 You can add any additional message text here.

6 Click or tap **Send**.

End

TIP

Adding Formatting You can use the Format tab to add simple formatting to your message text, such as bold and italics, or assign a preformatted style. Click or tap **Format** to view the formatting options.

FLAGGING MESSAGES

You can use Mail's flagging tool to flag a message. When you add a flag, it's easier to spot the message in the list later, such as flagging an important message you want to reread or respond to at a later time. Start by opening the email account you want to use.

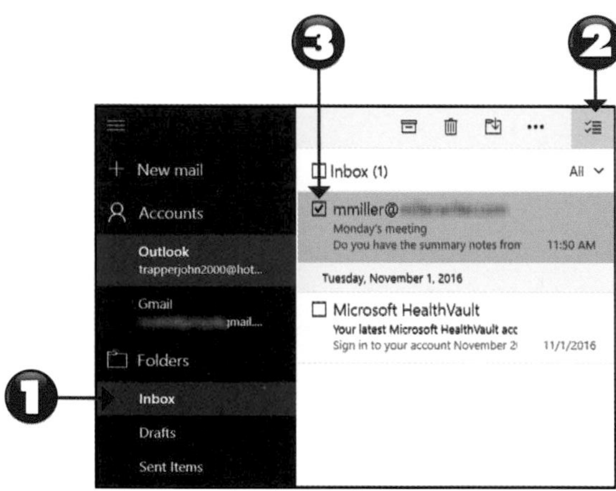

1. From your Mail account's Folders pane, click or tap the Inbox or folder you want to view.
2. Click or tap **Select**.
3. Click or tap the check box for the message you want to mark.

Continued

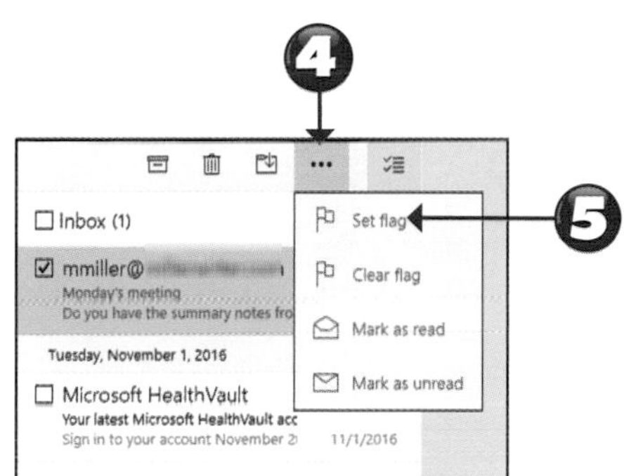

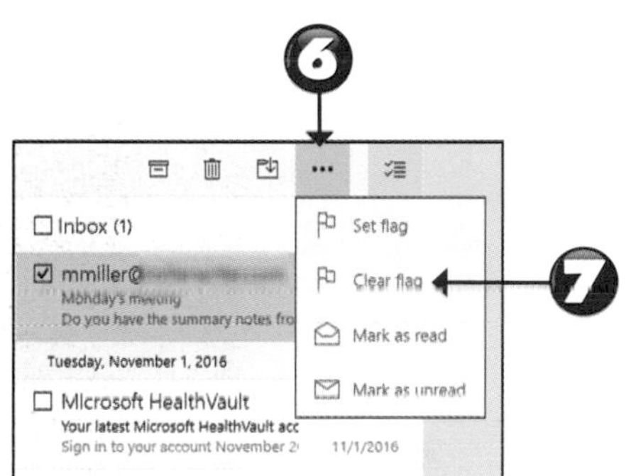

4. Click or tap **More Options**.

5. Click or tap **Set flag**. Mail adds a flag icon to the message.

6. To clear a flag, select the message and click or tap **More Options**. (You might need to click or tap **Select** again to display the More Options icon.)

7. Click or tap **Clear flag**.

End

TIP

Quick Flagging You can also hover the mouse pointer over or tap and hold an email message and select **Delete** or **Set flag** to delete or flag the selected message.

DELETING MESSAGES

To help keep your Inbox lean and clean, it's a good practice to delete messages you no longer want to keep. You can use the Select feature to check multiple messages for deletion.

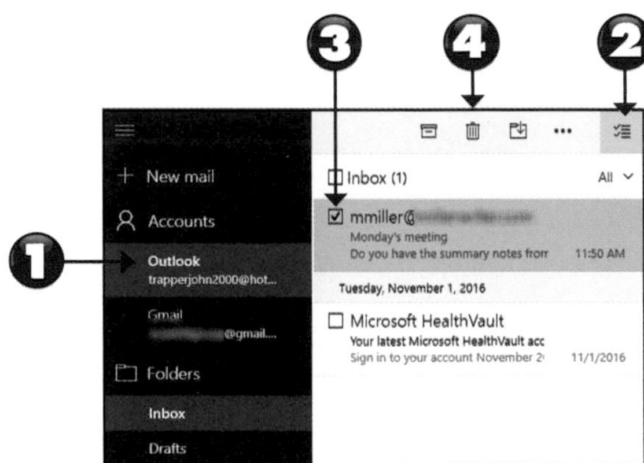

1. From Mail's navigation pane, click or tap the email account you want to view.
2. Click or tap **Select**.
3. Click or tap the check box for the message or messages you want to delete.
4. Click or tap **Delete**.

End

TIP

Quick Delete You can move the mouse pointer or your finger over an email message to reveal a Trash icon at the far right side of the highlighted message. Click or tap the **Delete** icon to delete the message.

CREATING AN EMAIL SIGNATURE

A signature is information, typically text, that appears appended to every email message you send, rather like a sign-off to your message. A signature can be as simple as your name and contact information, a website URL, your favorite quote, or your company name and number.

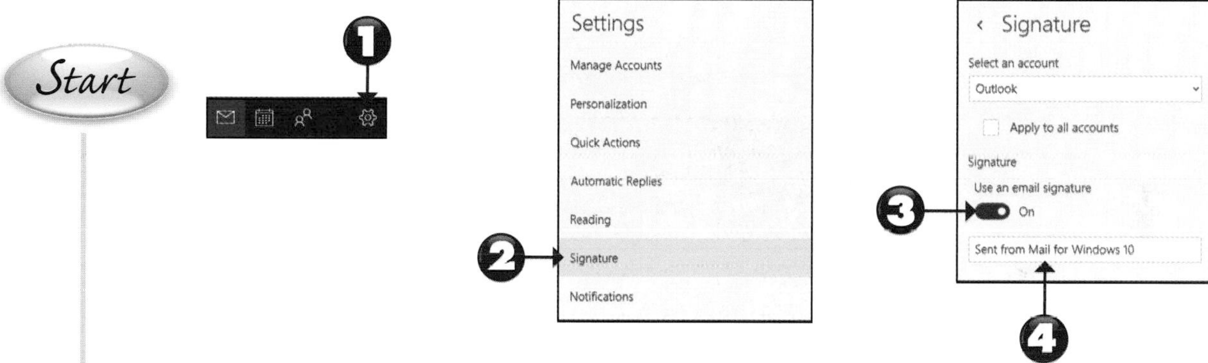

1. With the Mail app open, click or tap **Settings**.
2. Click or tap **Signature**.
3. If it is not currently selected, toggle the **Use an email signature** control to **On**.
4. Click or tap the signature box, and type in your own signature text.

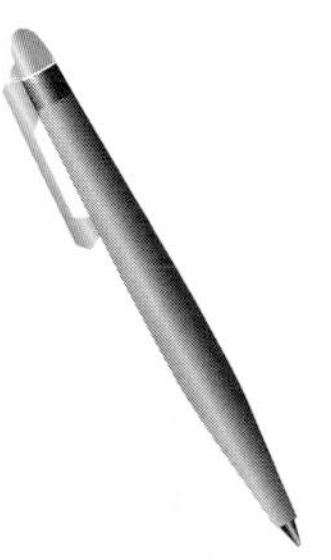

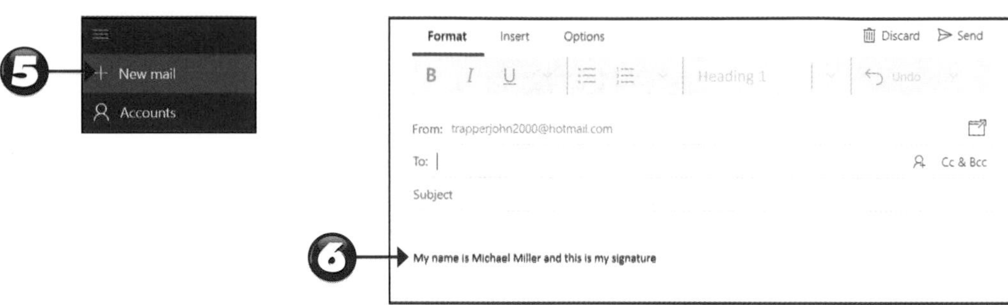

5. To view your new signature, click or tap **New mail**.

6. The signature automatically appears at the bottom of the new message.

End

NOTE

Turn Off Signatures If you don't want to include a signature with your emails, you can turn off the feature. Click or tap **Settings**, **Options**, and then scroll to the Signature feature. Click or tap the **On/Off** button to the **Off** position.

USING THE CALENDAR APP

You can use the Calendar app to keep track of appointments you make with friends, colleagues, and others. Calendar helps you remember important birthdays and special occasions, events, and other daily, weekly, or monthly activities you pursue. You can flip back and forth between daily, weekly, or monthly view and check out your work-week schedule, too.

Start

1. Click or tap **Start**.
2. Click or tap **Calendar**.
3. Click or tap the **Maximize** button to display the Calendar app full screen.

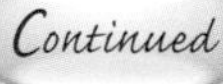

NOTE

First Time Use The first time you use Calendar, you might encounter one or two screens to help you get started. When you see the Welcome screen, click or tap **Get started**, and then follow the on-screen instructions to proceed.

NOTE

Associate Your Accounts Calendar pulls data from designated email accounts and social media associations (such as Facebook) to populate your main calendar display. Associating your email accounts with Calendar helps make scheduling meetings with others easy and fast because you can view your friends' calendar data as well.

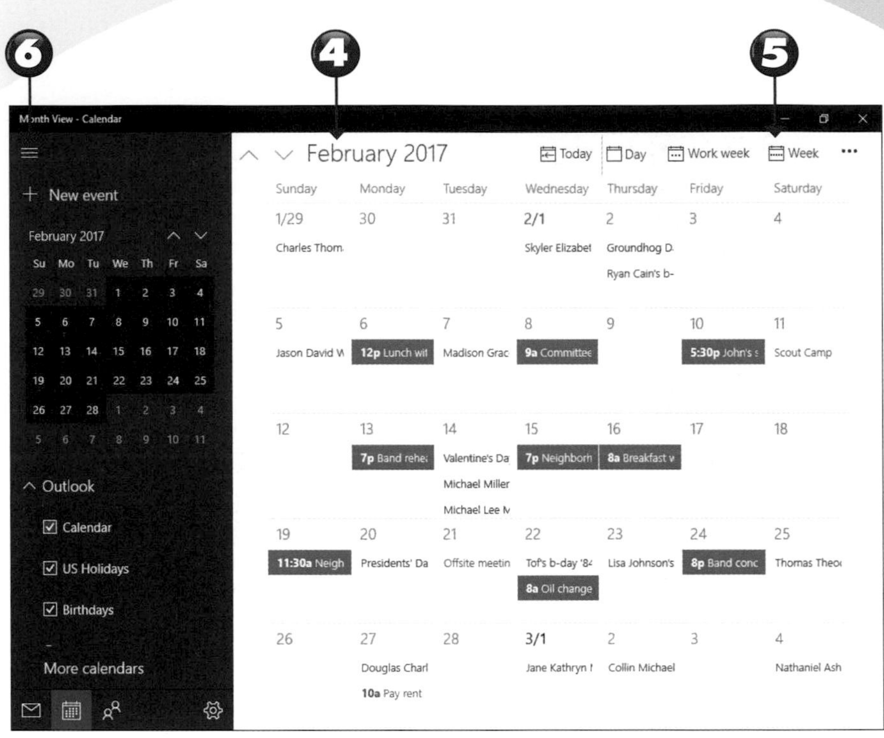

4 Calendar opens to the current date. If you're using several email and social media accounts, Calendar already inserts items such as birthdays and anniversaries for you.

5 To change views, click or tap a view: **Day**, **Work week**, **Week**, **Month**, or **Year**.

6 To view details on the navigation bar, click or tap the **Menu** button.

Continued

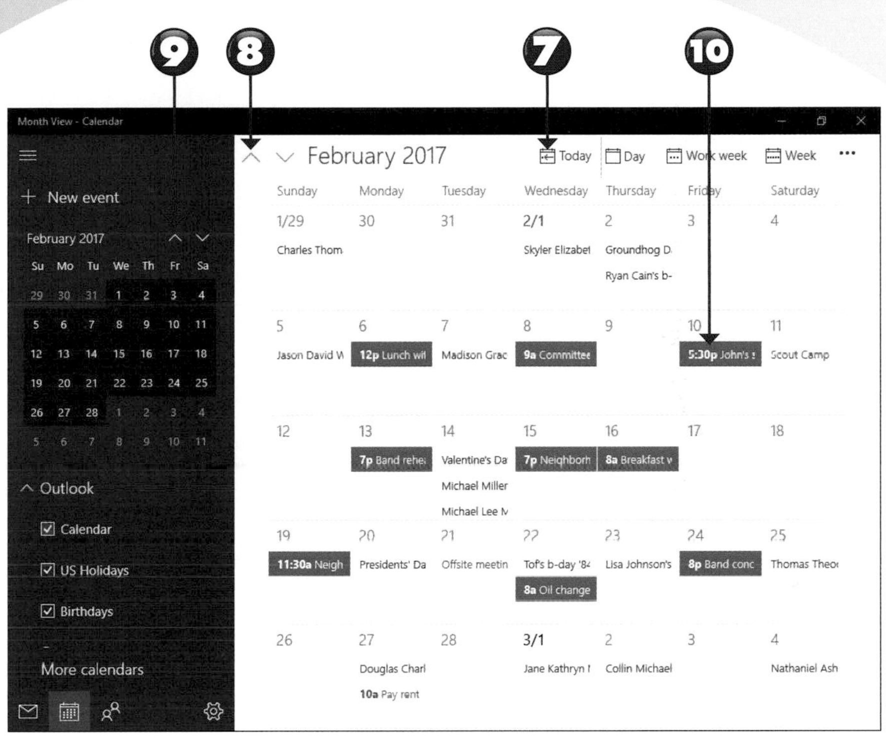

7 To display the current date, click or tap **Today**.

8 To move between days, weeks, or months, click or tap the up or down arrows at the top-left corner of the window.

9 Use the navigation calendar to view a particular date; click the up or down arrows above the navigation calendar to move to the next or previous month.

10 Click or tap the date you want to view.

End

NOTE

Turn Off Calendars Account calendars are listed below the navigation calendar, including the Birthday calendar with Facebook birthdays. You can uncheck a calendar to turn off its display as part of your main calendar. For example, if you uncheck the Birthday calendar, you no longer see your friends' birthdays listed in the calendar display.

SCHEDULING AN APPOINTMENT WITH CALENDAR

It's easy to set up an appointment using Calendar. Appointments are called *events* in Calendar's lingo. You can set up a quick event using the pop-up box, or you can fill out more details for an event using a form. In this task, you learn how to schedule a detailed appointment.

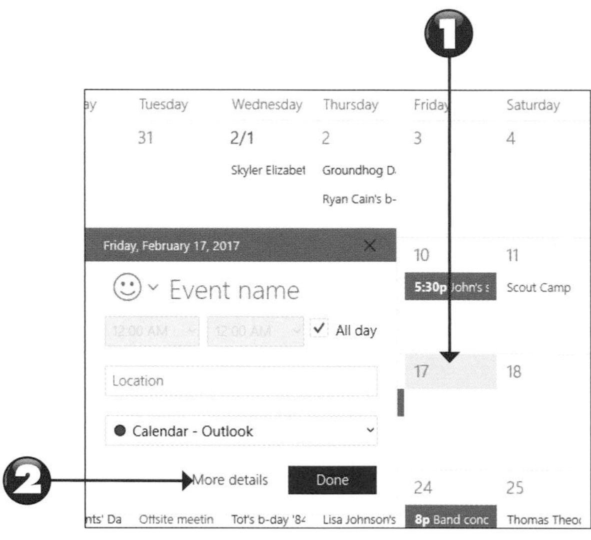

1. With Calendar open, navigate to the date to which you want to add an appointment, and click or tap the date. If you're in Day, Work week, or Week view, you can click or tap a specific time.
2. Click or tap **More details**.

Continued

NOTE

Set a Quick Appointment In Day, Work week, or Week view, you can set a quick appointment without having to open the Event form. Just fill out the start and end times for the appointment and a location, and then click or tap **Done**. Keep in mind, however, that the appointment won't have a title, so you won't know exactly what it's for when you glance at it on the calendar display.

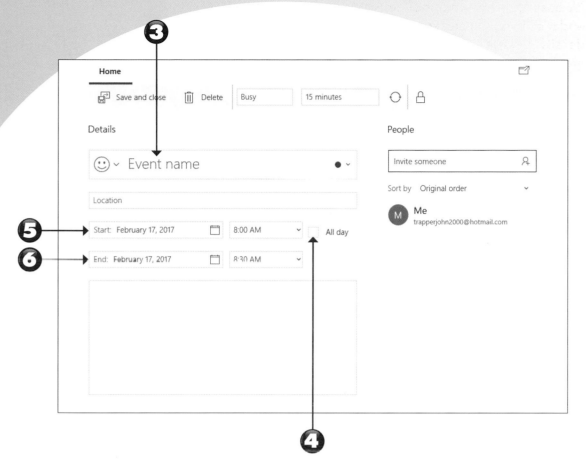

3. Calendar opens a form window for filling out more details. Click or tap the **Event name** box and enter a title for the appointment, such as Doctor Appointment or Staff Meeting.

4. If the event is *not* an all-day event, uncheck the **All day** box.

5. Click or tap the **Start** controls and choose a start time and date.

6. Click or tap the **End** controls and choose an end time and date.

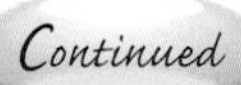

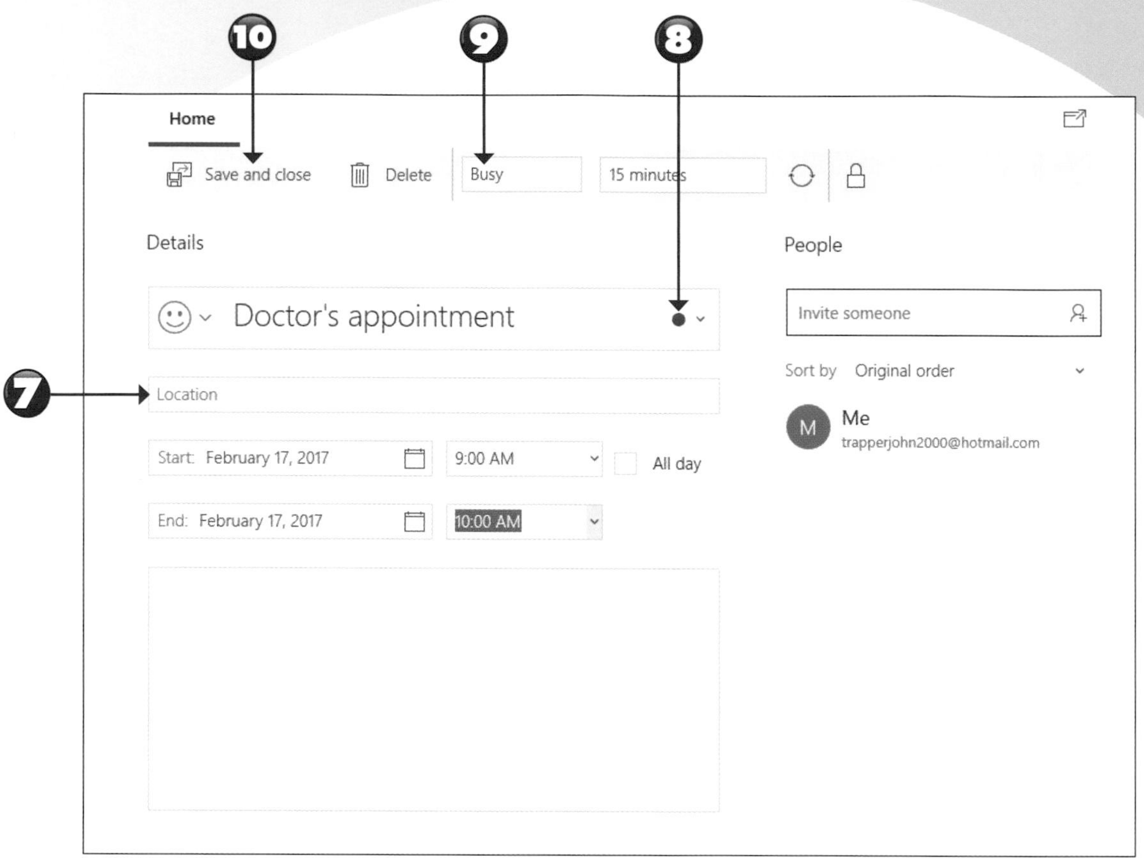

7 Optionally, click or tap the **Location** box to enter a place for the appointment.

8 Optionally, to choose a different calendar to post the event to, click or tap here and choose another calendar.

9 To change how the event appears on shared calendars, click or tap the **Show As** arrow and select **Free**, **Tentative**, **Busy**, or **Out of office**.

10 Click or tap **Save and close** to add the event to your schedule.

Continued

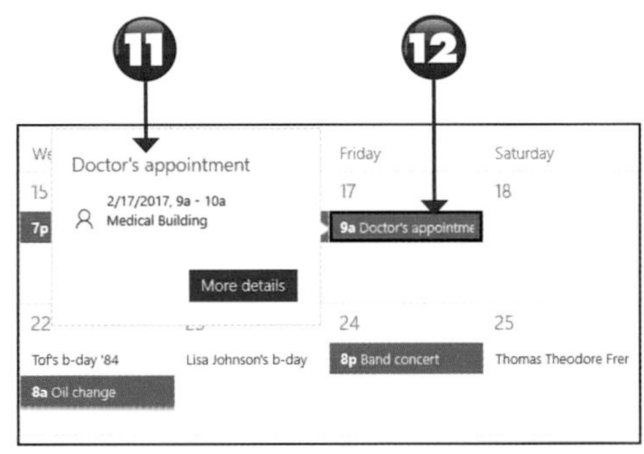

11 The appointment is added to your calendar. Mouse over the appointment to view more details.

12 To make changes to the appointment, simply click or tap it to reopen the form.

End

NOTE

Regular Events and All-Day Events Regular events are appointments you can assign with a block of time on your calendar. All-day events (such as birthdays, anniversaries, and conferences) last the entire day. Learn more about assigning an all-day event in the next task.

SCHEDULING AN ALL-DAY EVENT

An all-day event is anything that lasts for the entire day, such as a birthday or a conference you're attending. All-day events appear listed at the top of a date in Day, Week, or Work week view.

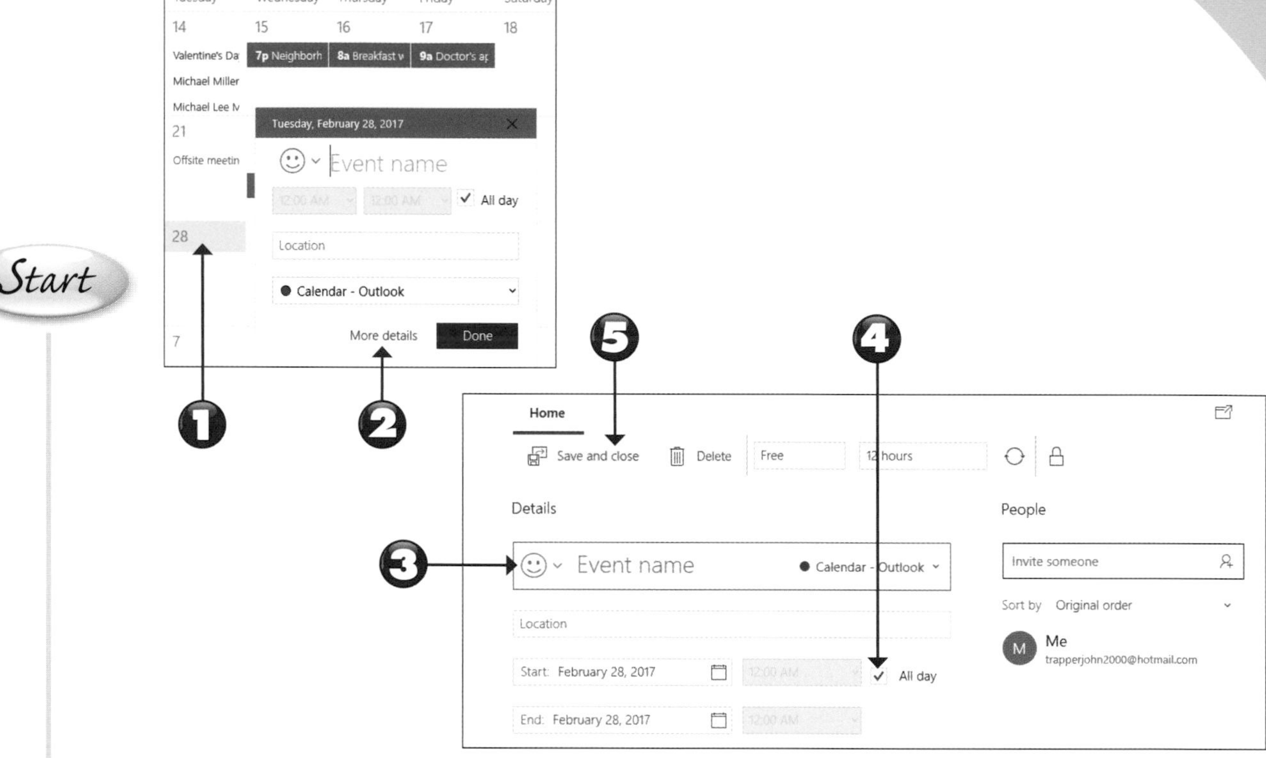

1. From Calendar, click or tap the date to which you want to add an appointment.
2. Click or tap **More details**.
3. Click or tap the **Event name** box and enter a name for the all-day event, such as Sales Conference.
4. If it is not already checked, click or tap the **All day** check box. The box must be checked to record the event as an all-day item.
5. Click **Save and close**.

End

TIP

Easy Edits You can always make changes to items on your schedule. Just click or tap the event on the calendar to open the form window and make your edits.

SCHEDULING A RECURRING APPOINTMENT

If your schedule involves regular appointments, such as a weekly staff meeting, you can set a recurring event. Using the Repeat feature, you can specify how often the event occurs and when it stops recurring.

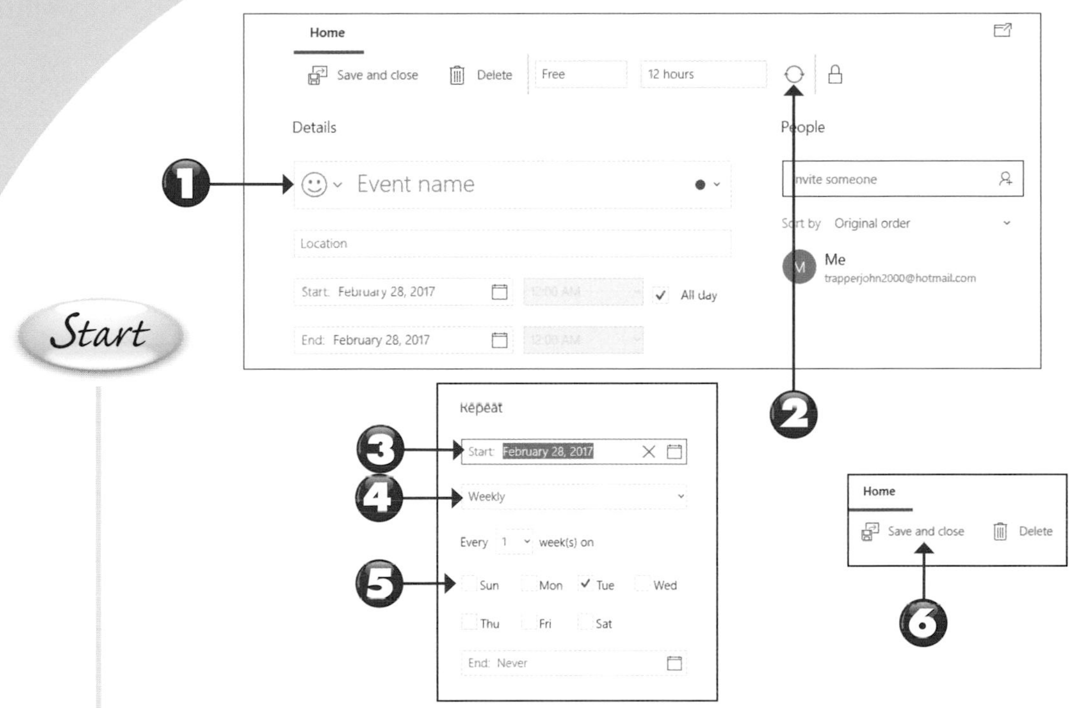

1. Open the Event form and fill out the appropriate appointment details.
2. Click or tap **Repeat**.
3. Click or tap **Start** to choose a date when the recurring event begins.
4. Click or tap the **Occurrence** arrow and choose how often the event repeats: Daily, Weekly, Monthly, or Yearly.
5. Set the end date and other relevant details for the recurring event. (These details differ by type of occurrence; an event recurring weekly has different details than one recurring monthly.)
6. Click or tap **Save and close**.

NOTE

Editing Recurrences You can make changes to a repeating appointment by clicking or tapping the event on the calendar. This opens the form where you can click or tap **Edit series** to change how often the appointment repeats. To remove the appointment entirely, click or tap **Delete**.

SETTING AN APPOINTMENT REMINDER

Calendar has a handy feature for helping you remember upcoming events on your calendar. The Reminder feature lets you set an alarm that notifies you with a prompt box when the appointment draws near.

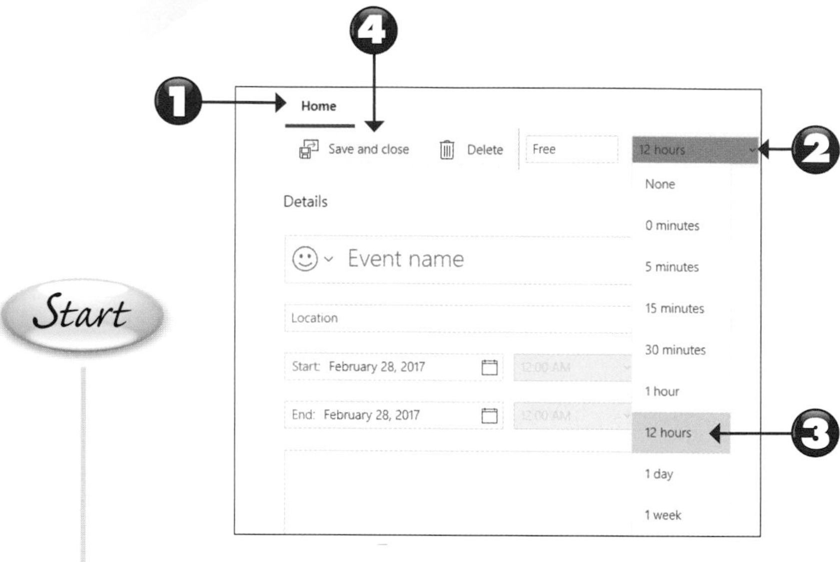

Start

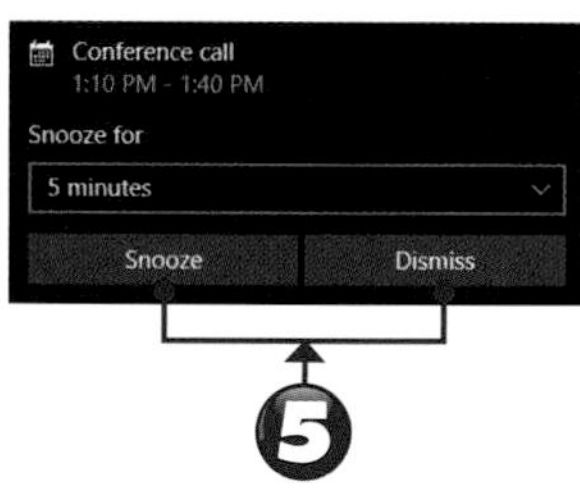

1. Open the event's form.
2. Click or tap the **Reminder** drop-down arrow.
3. Click or tap a reminder time.
4. Click or tap **Save and close**.
5. When the specified reminder time arrives, a notification reminder box pops up onscreen; click or tap **Snooze** to ignore it for a few minutes, or click or tap **Dismiss** to close the reminder.

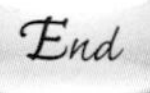

TIP

Removing a Reminder To remove a reminder, reopen the form, click or tap **Reminder**, and choose **None** from the drop-down menu.

HIDING AND DISPLAYING CALENDAR'S FOLDERS PANE

The left side of the Calendar app lists your folders, a navigation calendar, and icons for accessing Mail, Settings, and more. You can hide the pane to free up more viewing space for the calendar display.

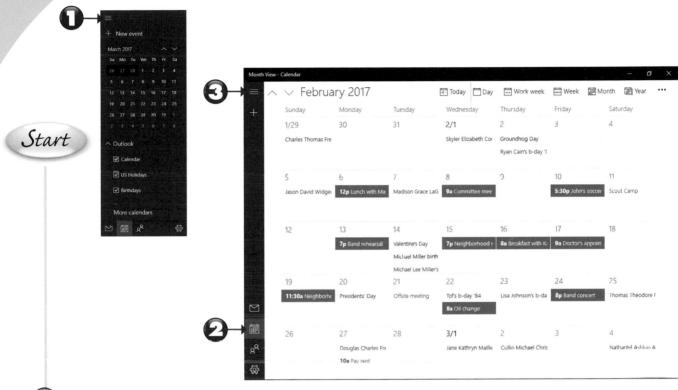

Start

1. With the Calendar app open, click or tap here to hide the pane.
2. Calendar hides the pane but still offers access to the icons.
3. Click or tap to display the pane again.

End

TIP

Switching You can switch back and forth between the Calendar app and the Mail app. Click or tap the **Mail** icon to view mail; click or tap the **Calendar** icon to view your schedule.

STARTING SKYPE PREVIEW

You can use the Skype Preview app, included free with Windows 10 AE, to make face-to-face video calls over the Internet. You can also use Skype Preview to send and receive text messages and voice calls around the world.

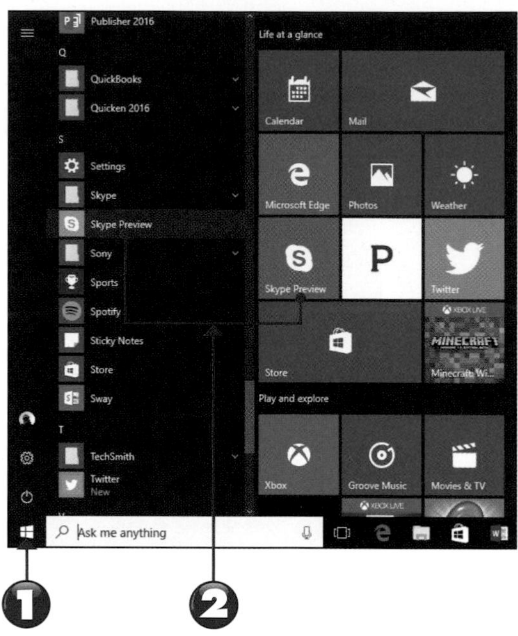

1. Click or tap **Start**.

2. Scroll down the All Apps list and click or tap **Skype Preview**, or tap or click the **Skype Preview** tile on the Start menu.

Continued

NOTE

Requirements You need a webcam and a microphone (which are built in to most laptop PCs) to use Skype Preview. If you're new to Skype, you must also create an account before you start using the service.

NOTE

Skype for Desktop Skype also offers a traditional desktop app, which offers similar functionality to the Windows app discussed here. You can download the desktop app for free at www.skype.com.

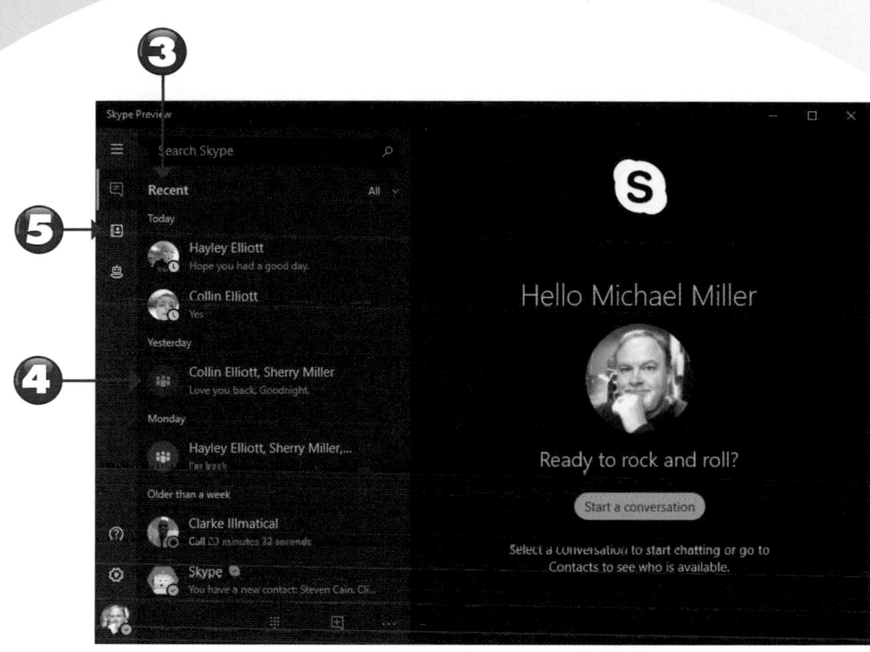

3 The Skype Preview app opens with the Recent Conversations panel displayed.

4 Click to reopen a recent conversation.

5 Click or tap **Contacts** to view your Skype contacts list.

Continued

TIP

Testing, Testing To quickly test your device's sound, click or tap **Echo/Sound Test Service** located under the Contacts category on the main Skype Preview window. Click or tap the **Call** button and follow the instructions to conduct a sound test.

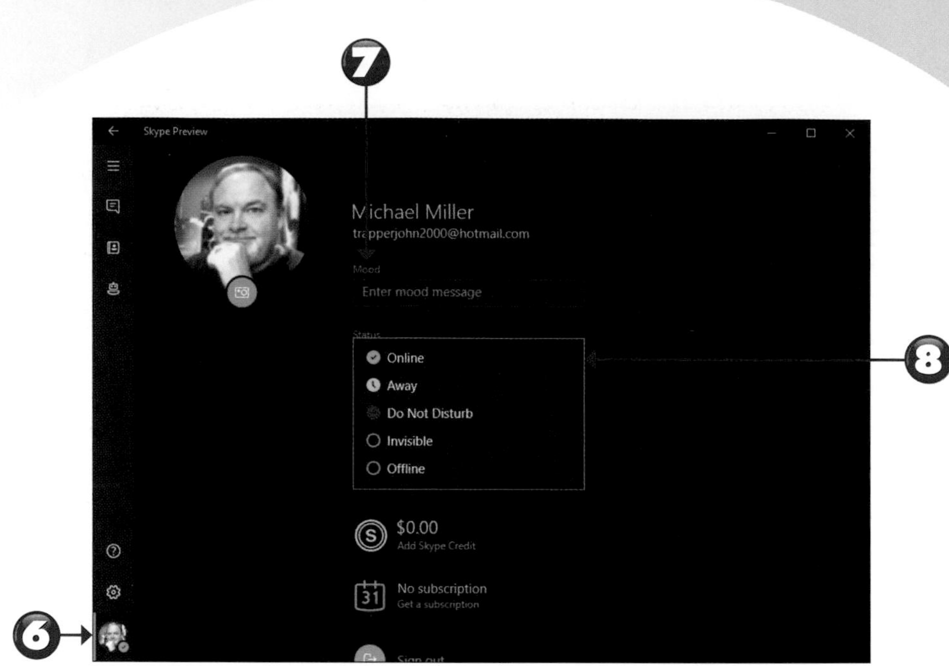

6 To change your online status, click or tap your name or picture at the bottom of the navigation pane.

7 Click or tap the **Status** box.

8 Click or tap a status: Online, Away, Do Not Disturb, Invisible, or Offline.

Continued

NOTE

No Skype Preview? If you can't find the Skype Preview app on your computer, tablet, or smartphone, you can download the app from the Store. Click or tap **Start**, and click or tap **Store**. Using the Search box, type **Skype** and locate the app. Select the app and click or tap the **Free** button to download and install it. During the installation, Skype Preview helps you get everything set up to use the app. After you have everything ready, you can open Skype Preview any time you want from the Start menu's apps list.

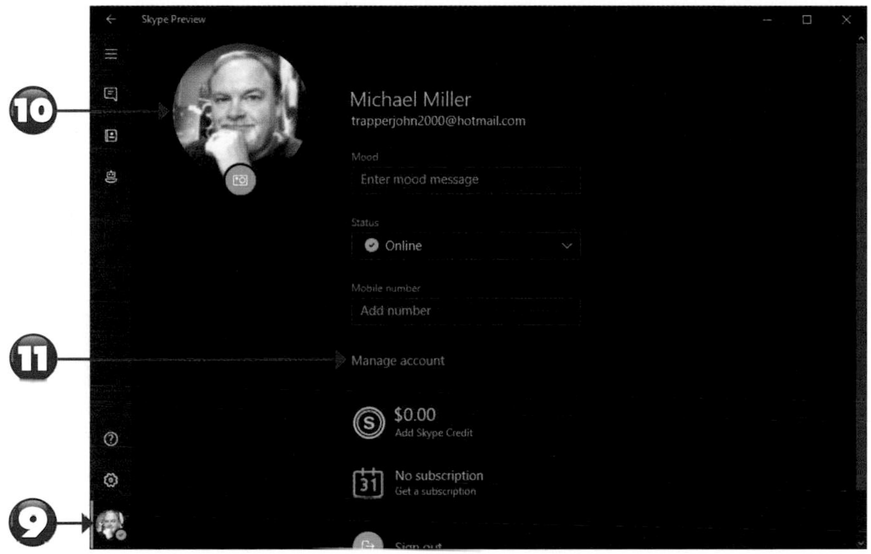

9. To edit your profile, such as change your profile picture or add contact numbers, click or tap your name or profile picture at the bottom of the navigation pane.

10. Click or tap your profile picture to change the picture.

11. Click or tap **Manage account** to open your Skype account page in your web browser. You can edit other account settings from there.

End

NOTE

Configure Settings To find settings for Skype Preview, click or tap the **Settings** icon in the navigation pane. The Settings page includes settings for audio, video, microphone, notifications, and more.

ADDING CONTACTS WITH SKYPE PREVIEW

You can add contacts to Skype Preview for people you communicate with the most. You add a contact when you send your first message to a given person, and that person accepts your message.

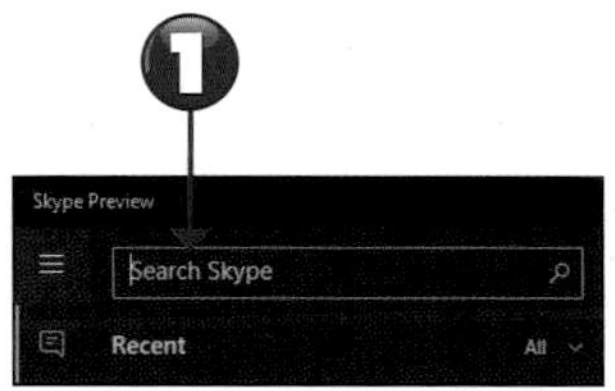

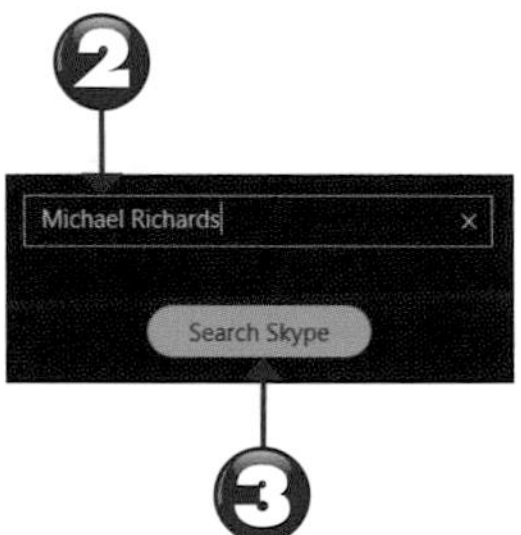

1. From either Skype's Recent conversations or the Contacts tab, click or tap in the **Search Skype** box.
2. Type in the name of the person you want to find and press Enter/Return.
3. Click or tap **Search Skype**.

Continued

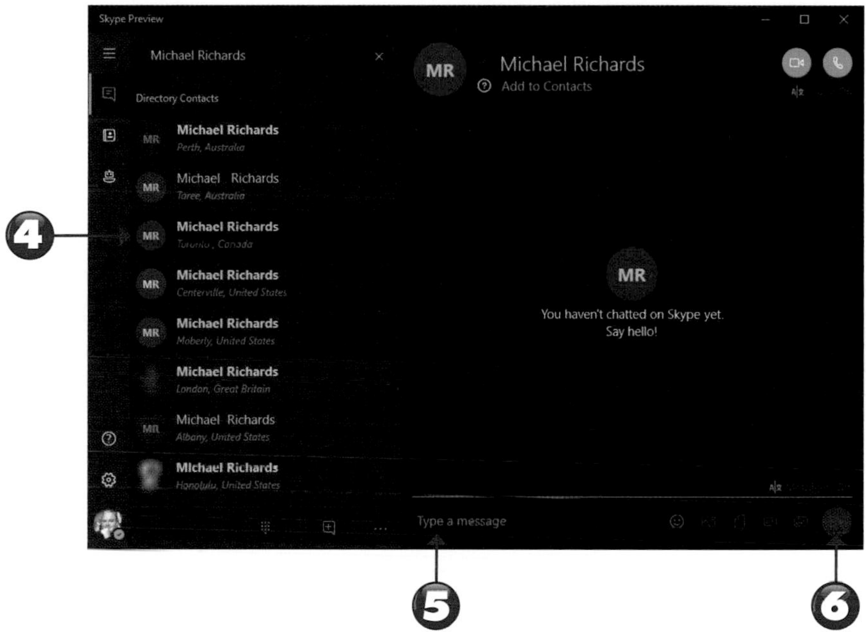

4. Click or tap the person you want to add.

5. Type a message to this person in the **Type a message** field.

6. Click or tap **Send**. The person is added to your contact list but appears as offline until he accepts your request. After your request is accepted, you can see when this person is online and conduct video calls with him or her.

End

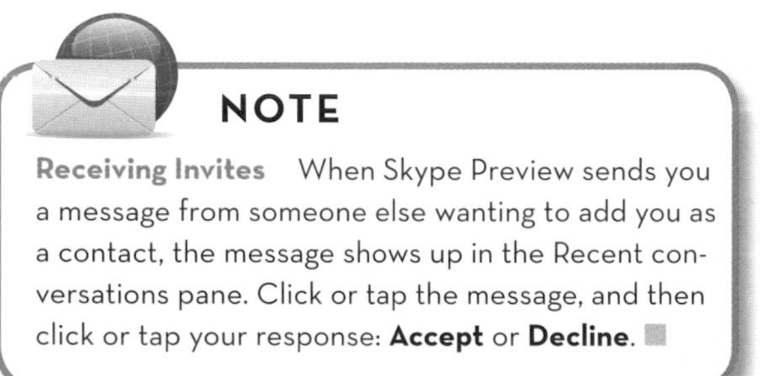

NOTE

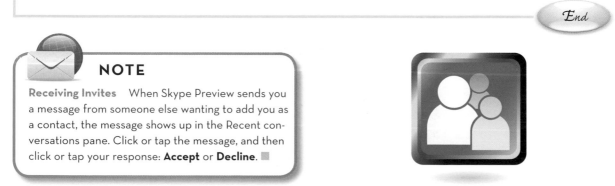

Receiving Invites When Skype Preview sends you a message from someone else wanting to add you as a contact, the message shows up in the Recent conversations pane. Click or tap the message, and then click or tap your response: **Accept** or **Decline**.

PLACING A VIDEO CALL WITH SKYPE PREVIEW

With your webcam, you can place a face-to-face video call. When making a video call, Skype Preview displays a few tools you can use, and it keeps track of the call duration.

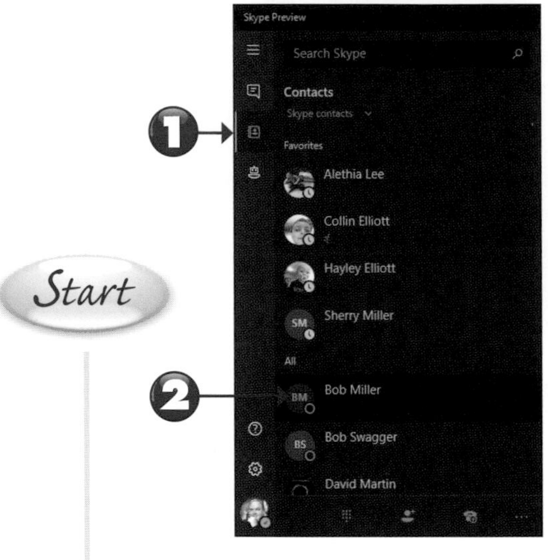

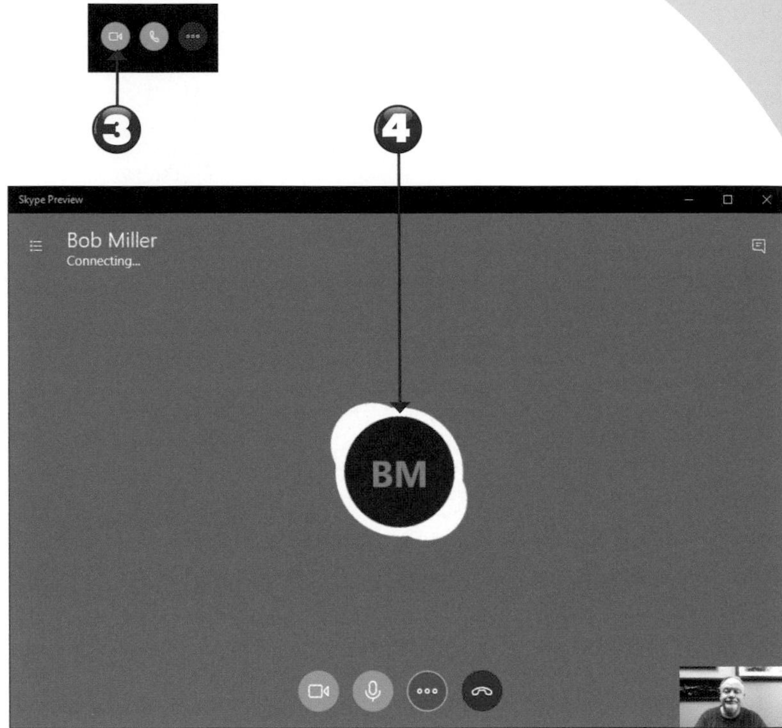

Start

1. With the Skype Preview app open, click or tap the **Contacts** icon to open the Contacts pane.
2. Click or tap the contact you want to call.
3. Click or tap the **Video Call** icon.
4. Skype Preview begins calling the other person for you.

Continued

NOTE

Voice Calls A voice call works the same way as a video call in Skype Preview. Click or tap the **Voice Call** icon instead of the **Video Call** icon to place your call. When you're connected, only the microphone works; the video feed is turned off.

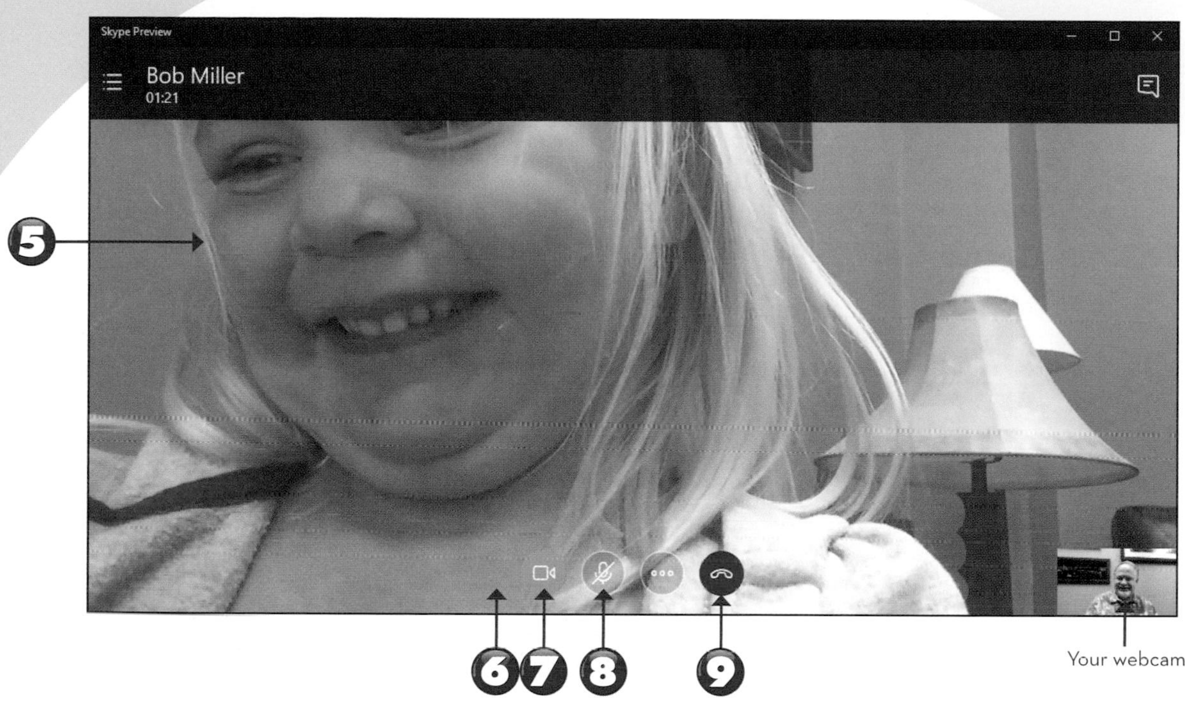

5. When the person accepts your call, the screen shows the view from their webcam, with the view from your webcam in the lower-right corner.

6. Mouse over or tap the screen to display Skype's call controls.

7. Click or tap the camera icon to turn off your video feed; the other user will see your profile picture instead.

8. Click or tap the microphone icon to mute the sound from your microphone.

9. Click or tap the hangup icon to end the call.

End

RECEIVING A CALL WITH SKYPE PREVIEW

When you receive a Skype Preview call, a notification box pops up, and you can choose to accept or decline the call. You can choose between taking a video call or a voice call.

Start

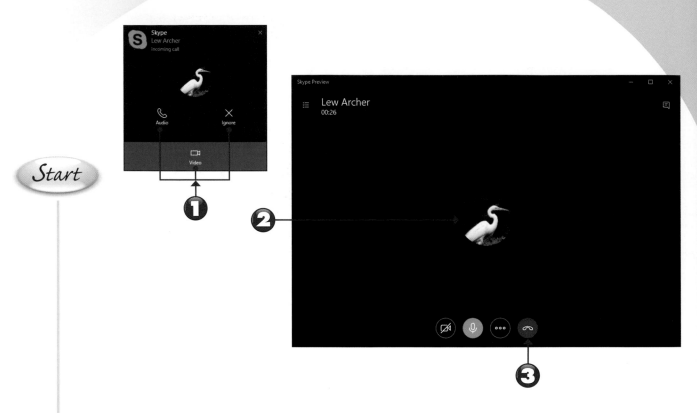

1. From the Skype Preview app, click or tap **Video** for a video call or **Audio** for a voice call, or click or tap **Ignore** to decline the call.
2. Skype Preview opens and starts the call.
3. To end the call, click or tap the hangup icon.

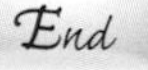

TEXT MESSAGING WITH SKYPE PREVIEW

You can also use Skype Preview to send instant messages to your friends and family. Text messages appear as a conversation in the contact window.

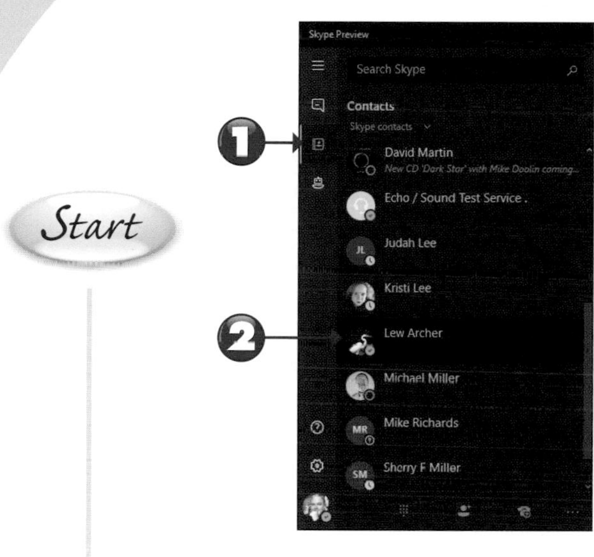

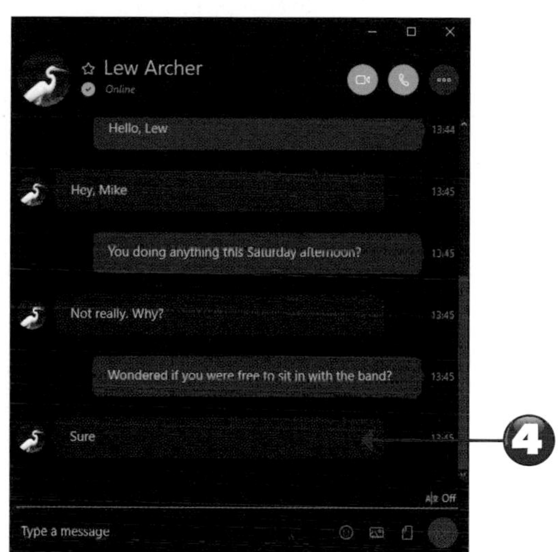

1. With Skype Preview open, click or tap the **Contacts** icon to open the Contacts pane.

2. Click or tap the contact you want to message.

3. Click or tap the **Type a message** box, type your message text, then press Enter/Return.

4. When the other person responds, the conversation scrolls up the window, with the latest message appearing at the bottom.

End

TIP

Add an Emoji You can include emoji, those cute smiley faces and other images, in your Skype text messages. Just click the **Insert emoticon or Moji** (smiley face) icon and choose from a variety of graphics images.

CONTROLLING NOTIFICATIONS

By default, notifications are turned on for all the communication apps you use, such as People, Facebook, Mail, and Skype Preview. You might prefer not to see so many notifications from these apps. You can control notifications through the Notifications & Actions settings.

Start

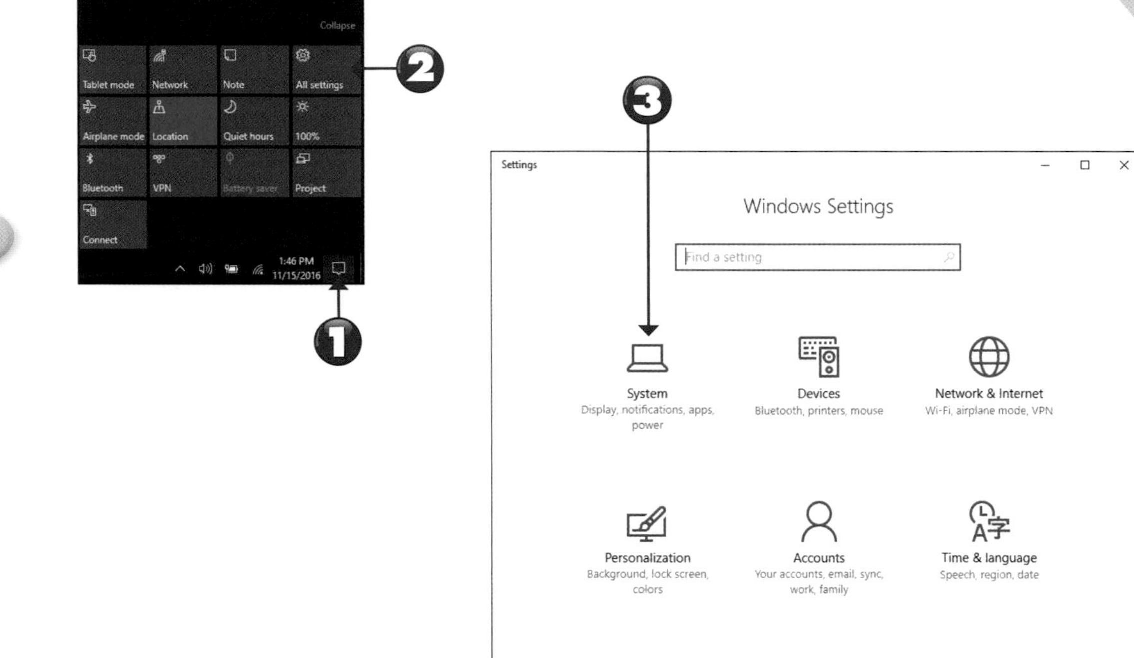

1. Click or tap **Notifications** in the taskbar.
2. In the Action Center pane, click or tap **All settings**.
3. Click or tap **System**.

Continued

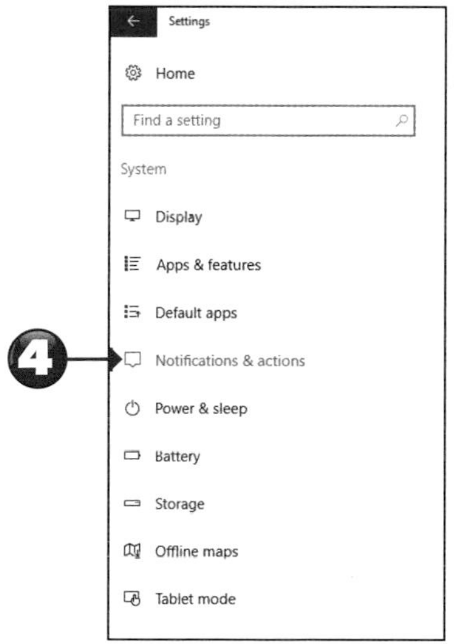

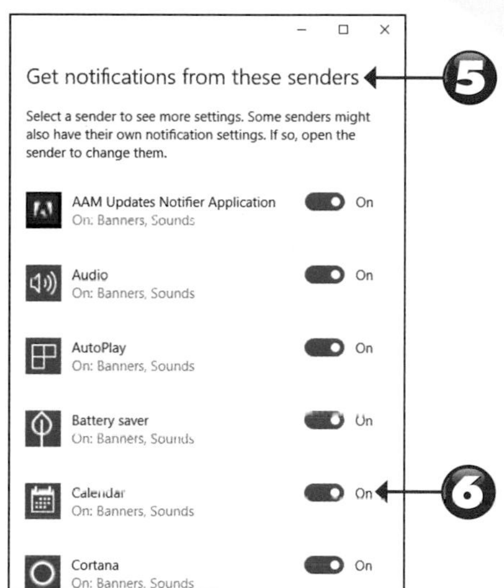

4. Click or tap **Notifications & actions**.

5. Scroll down the window to view the Get notifications from these senders settings.

6. Click or tap the toggle to turn an app's notifications on or off.

End

TIP

Turn Them All Off To turn off all notifications from all apps, click or tap the Get notifications from apps and other senders toggle.

NEWS, WEATHER, SPORTS, AND MONEY

You can use Windows 10 AE to keep abreast of the latest news and information the Internet has to offer. This chapter shows you how to use the Windows 10 AE apps to access headlines, local news, maps, weather, sports, and financial news.

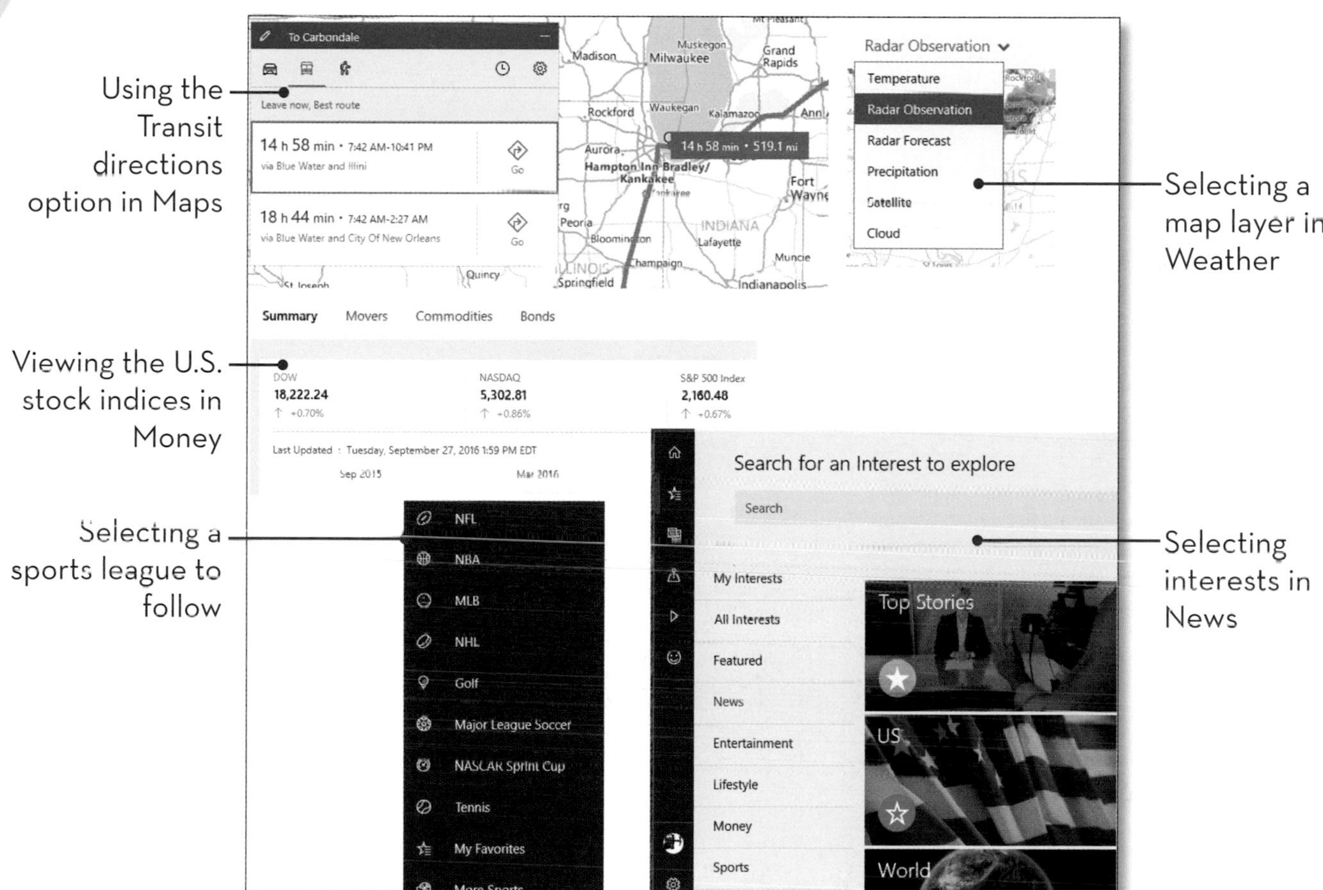
Using the Transit directions option in Maps
Selecting a map layer in Weather
Viewing the U.S. stock indices in Money
Selecting a sports league to follow
Selecting interests in News
To Carbondale
Leave now, Best route
14 h 58 min • 7:42 AM-10:41 PM
via Blue Water and Illini
Go
18 h 44 min • 7:42 AM-2:27 AM
via Blue Water and City Of New Orleans
Go
14 h 58 min • 519.1 mi
Radar Observation
Temperature
Radar Observation
Radar Forecast
Precipitation
Satellite
Cloud
Summary
Movers
Commodities
Bonds
DOW
18,222.24
+0.70%
NASDAQ
5,302.81
+0.86%
S&P 500 Index
2,160.48
+0.67%
Last Updated : Tuesday, September 27, 2016 1:59 PM EDT
Sep 2015
Mar 2016
NFL
NBA
MLB
NHL
Golf
Major League Soccer
NASCAR Sprint Cup
Tennis
My Favorites
More Sports
Search for an Interest to explore
Search
My Interests
All Interests
Featured
News
Entertainment
Lifestyle
Money
Sports
Top Stories
US
World

STARTING THE NEWS APP

Here's how to start up the Windows 10 AR News app (also known as MSN News).

Start

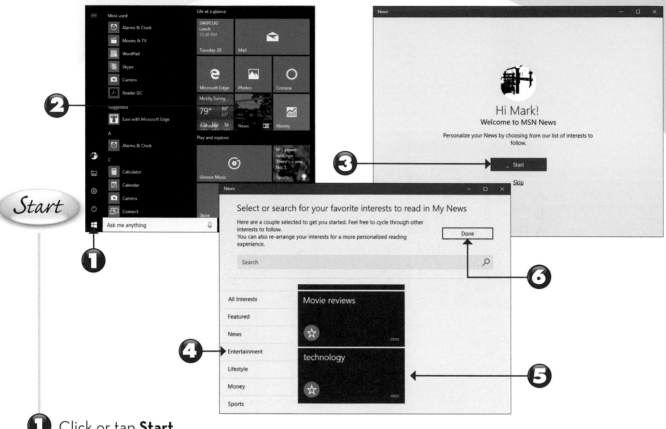

1. Click or tap **Start**.
2. Click or tap **News**.
3. Click or tap **Start**.
4. Click or tap a category or search for an interest.
5. Click or tap each interest you want to follow. Green stars indicate the ones you have selected.
6. When you are finished, click or tap **Done** to open the News app.

NOTE

Finding News, Weather, Map, Money, and Sports If these apps are not on the right pane of the Start menu on your device, scroll down or open All Apps to find them. For this chapter, we added them to the Start menu. See Chapter 4, "Logging In to Windows 10 Anniversary Edition and Customizing the Start Menu," to learn more about customizing the Start menu.

USING THE NEWS APP

The News app taps into the powerful Bing search engine to bring you the latest news and headlines from around the world or in your own locale.

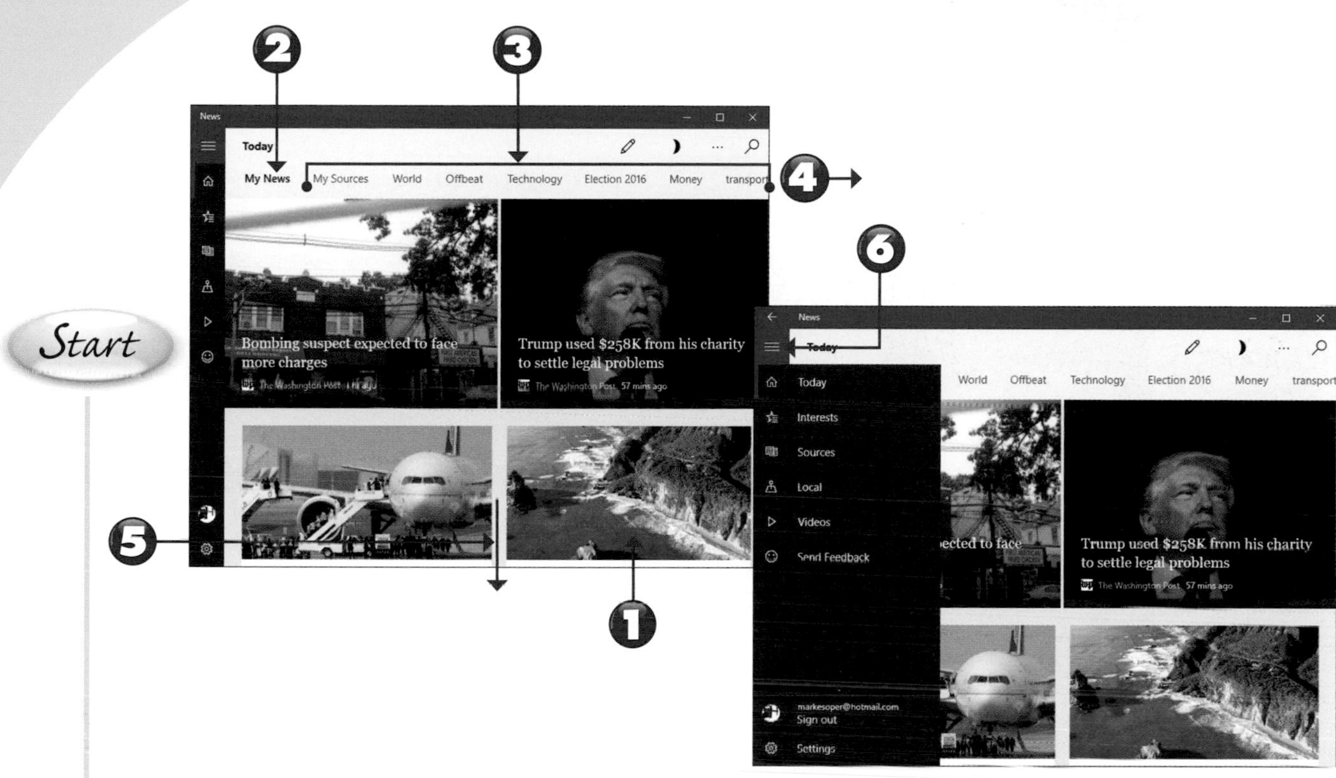

1. Click or tap a story to read more about it.
2. Click or tap **My News** to see stories matching the interests you set up.
3. Click or tap a category to view more news.
4. Scroll right to view more topic categories.
5. Scroll down to view more news in the current category.
6. Click or tap to expand the menu.

End

CUSTOMIZING NEWS

You can look up your favorite news sources and add them to the News app's Interests list. News stories from your favorite sites appear listed among the default content on the Home page. You can toggle the default topics on or off to control which news topics appear listed across the screen.

Start

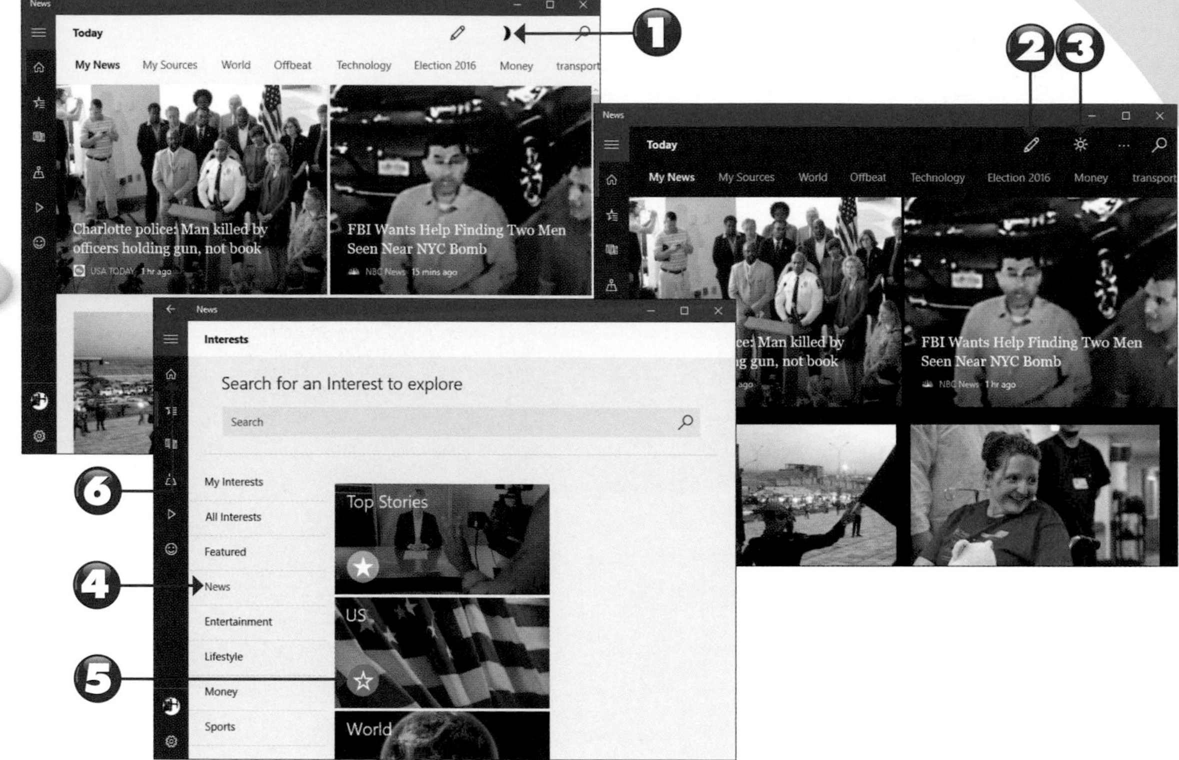

1. Click or tap to change to the dark theme.
2. Click or tap to change back to the default light theme.
3. Click or tap to add more interests.
4. Click or tap a category.
5. Click a star to add the interest to your news feed.
6. Click or tap anytime you want to return to the home screen.

Continued

7. Click or tap **Search**.

8. Enter a search term or phrase.

9. Click a search result to see matching stories.

10. Each news story lists the source and time of posting.

End

TIP

See Local News To see local news, click or tap the **Local** option in the main menu.

TIP

Removing Interests or Sources To remove an interest or source, go to the appropriate menu and click or tap the green star.

CHECKING WEATHER WITH THE WEATHER APP

You can use the Weather app to check your local weather report, view forecasts, and track the weather in your favorite locations.

Start

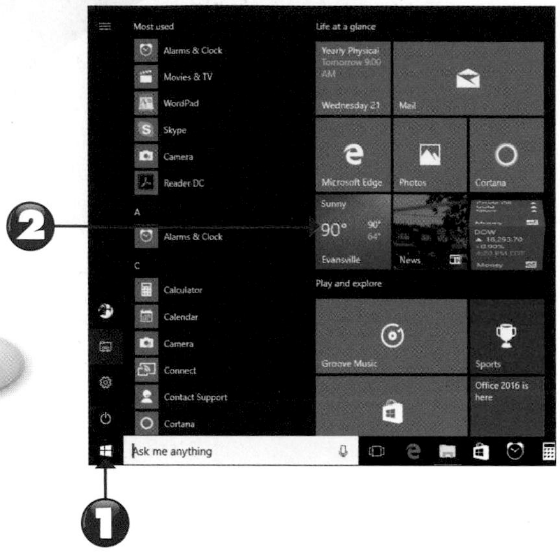

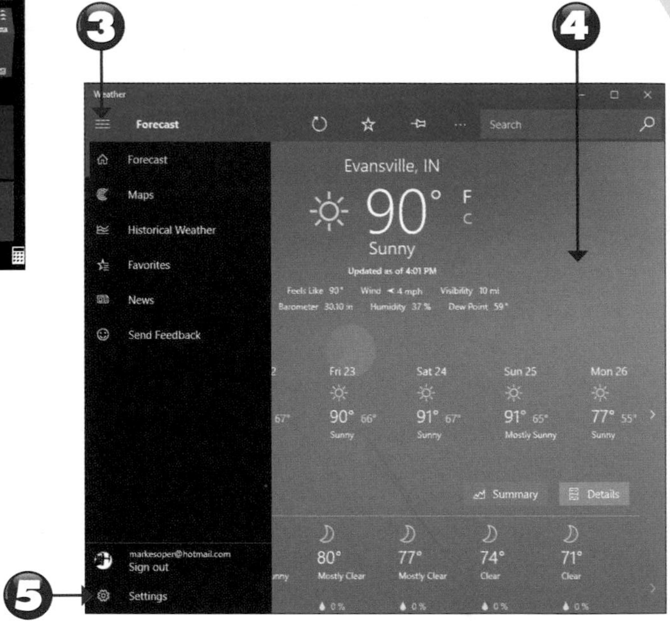

1. Click or tap **Start**.
2. Click or tap **Weather**.
3. Click or tap to expand the menu.
4. The Forecast shows the current conditions and forecast for your location; scroll down the window to view more details.
5. Click or tap **Settings** if you need to change the default location or temperature scale.

TIP

Celsius or Fahrenheit? To toggle your view of temperature in the Forecast window to Celsius or Fahrenheit, click or tap the appropriate symbol next to the current temperature.

6. Click or tap to see radar.
7. Select the weather data desired.
8. Click or tap to see historical weather.
9. Select the month.
10. Click or tap to see weather news.

End

TIP

Weather on Your Start Menu To display weather for your home location on the Start menu, right-click or press and hold the Weather tile. Select the three-dot button (touchscreen), **More**, **Turn live tile on**.

ADDING LOCATIONS TO WEATHER

Whether you're checking the weather before you travel or keeping an eye on the sky where friends or relatives live, Weather makes it easy to add more locations. Here's how.

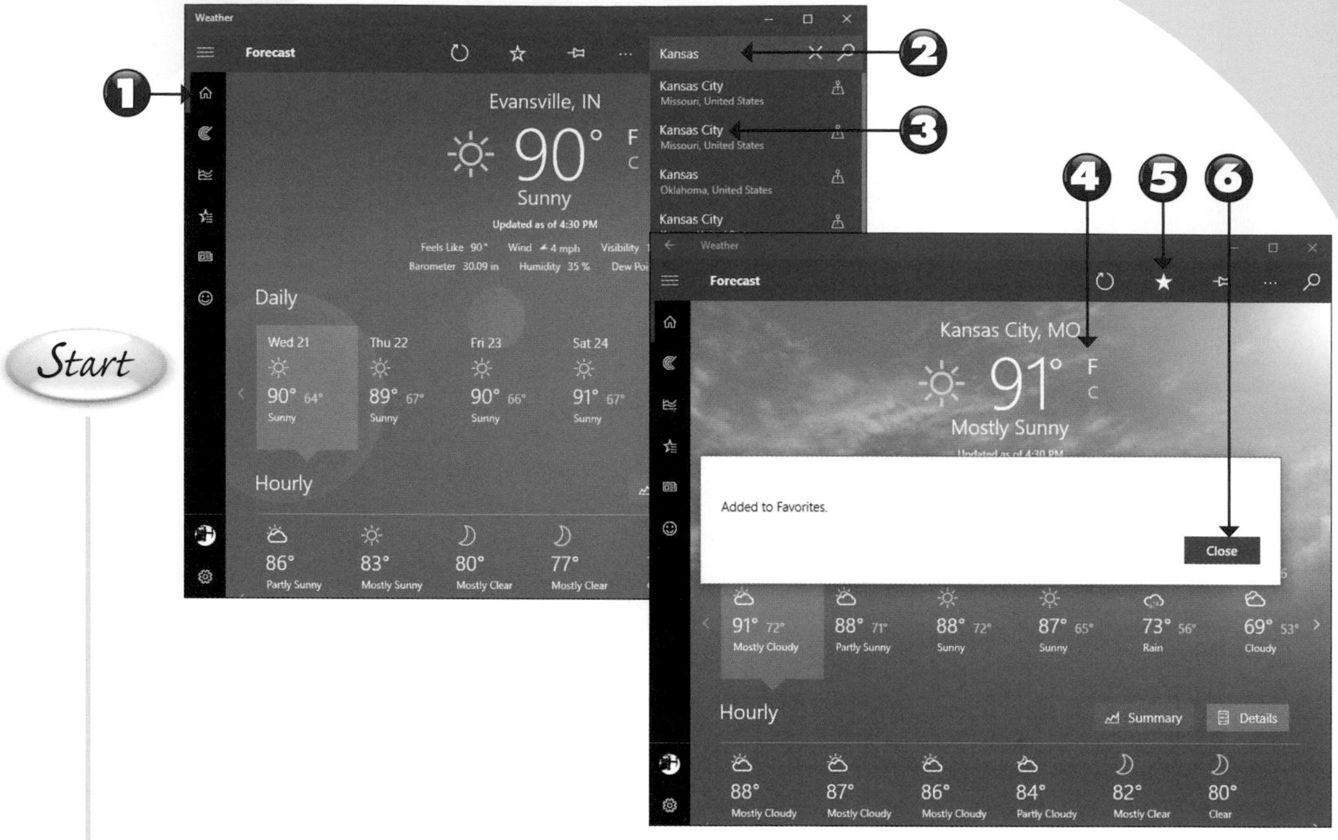

Start

1. To check weather for a specific location, tap the **Home** button.
2. Click or tap in the **City or ZIP Code** box and type the location.
3. Click or tap the location from the list, or click or tap the **Search** icon to conduct a search.
4. The Weather app window displays the current information and forecast for the designated place.
5. Click or tap the star to add this location to your favorites.
6. Click or tap **Close**.

Continued

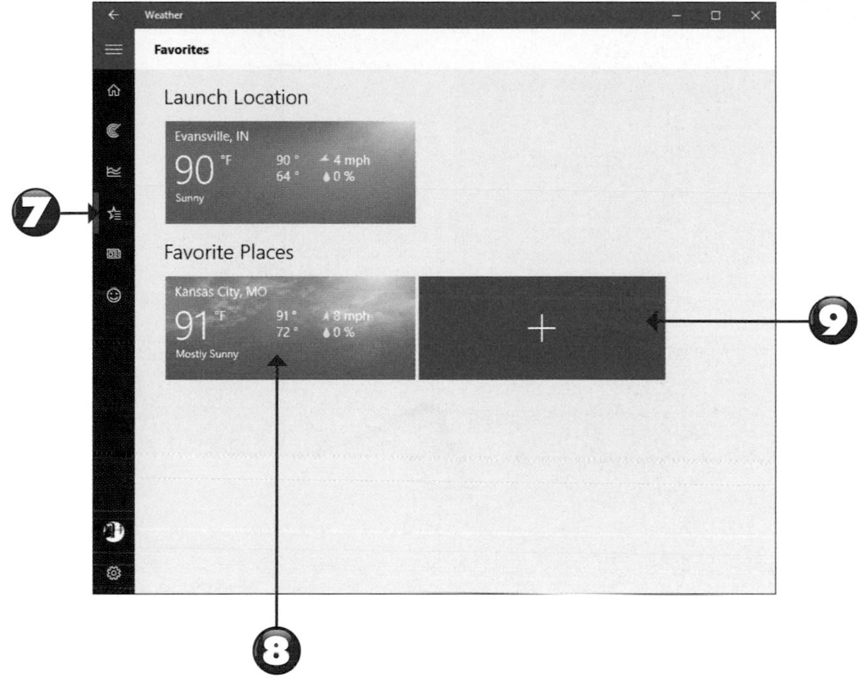

7 Click or tap **Favorites**.

8 Click or tap a location to see more weather details.

9 Click or tap to add another location.

End

TIP

Removing a Location from Weather Favorites To remove a location, right-click or press and hold it, and then click or tap **Remove from Favorites**.

STARTING MAPS

The Maps app (also known as MSN Maps) works with Microsoft's Bing search engine to help you find locations around the world or down the street. You can find directions, look up an address, or view your own current location using this app. In this task, you learn how to start the improved Maps app for the first time.

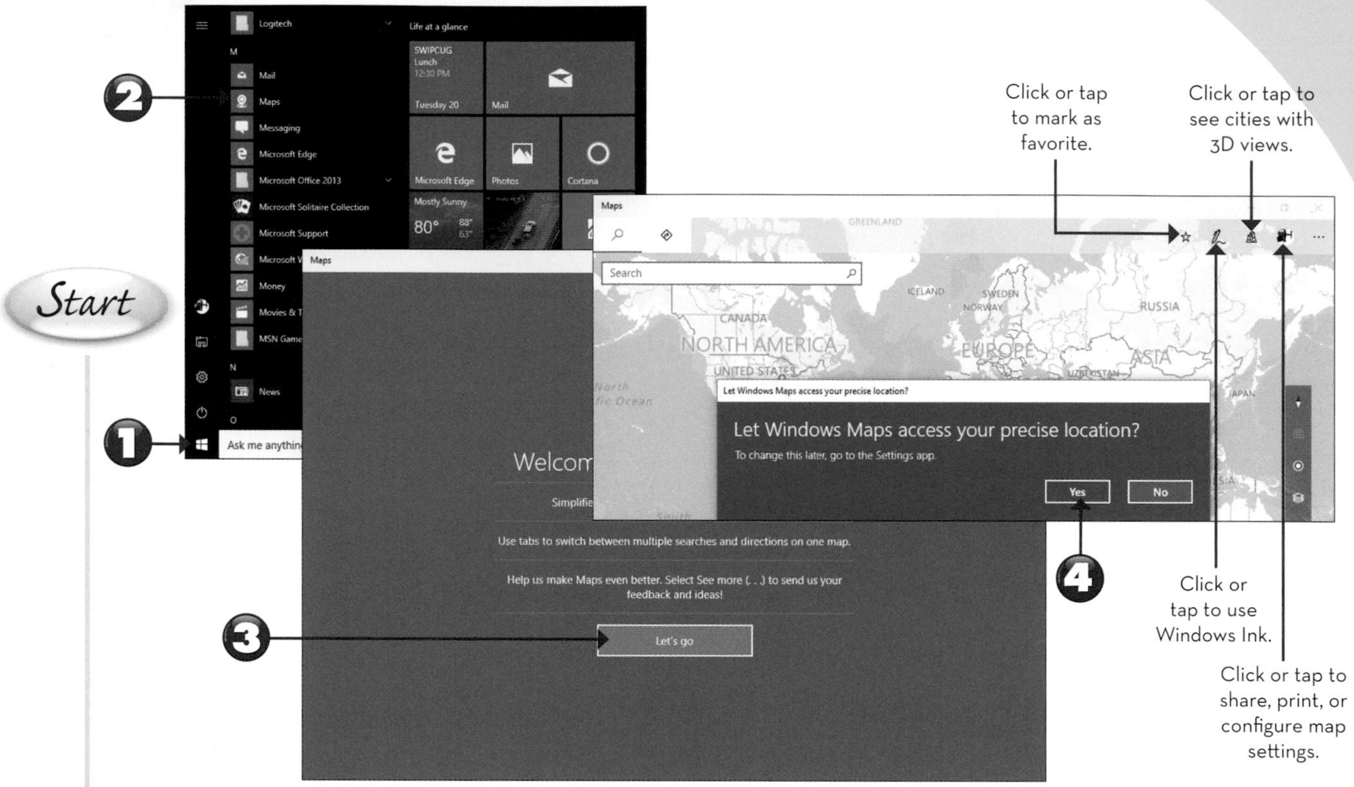

Click or tap to mark as favorite.

Click or tap to see cities with 3D views.

Click or tap to use Windows Ink.

Click or tap to share, print, or configure map settings.

Start

1. Click or tap **Start**.
2. Click or tap **Maps**.
3. The first time you run Maps, click or tap **Let's go** to continue.
4. The first time you run Maps, a prompt box appears asking whether Maps can use your precise location and location history; click or tap **Yes** (used in these lessons) or **No** to continue.

Continued

TIP

Easier Access Tablet Mode In Tablet mode, if Maps is not pinned to the Start menu, tap **All apps** to view it. You can pin the Maps app (or other apps) to the Start menu so it's easy to access. Click or tap the **Start** menu, click or tap **All Apps**, right-click the **Maps** app name, and choose **Pin to Start**.

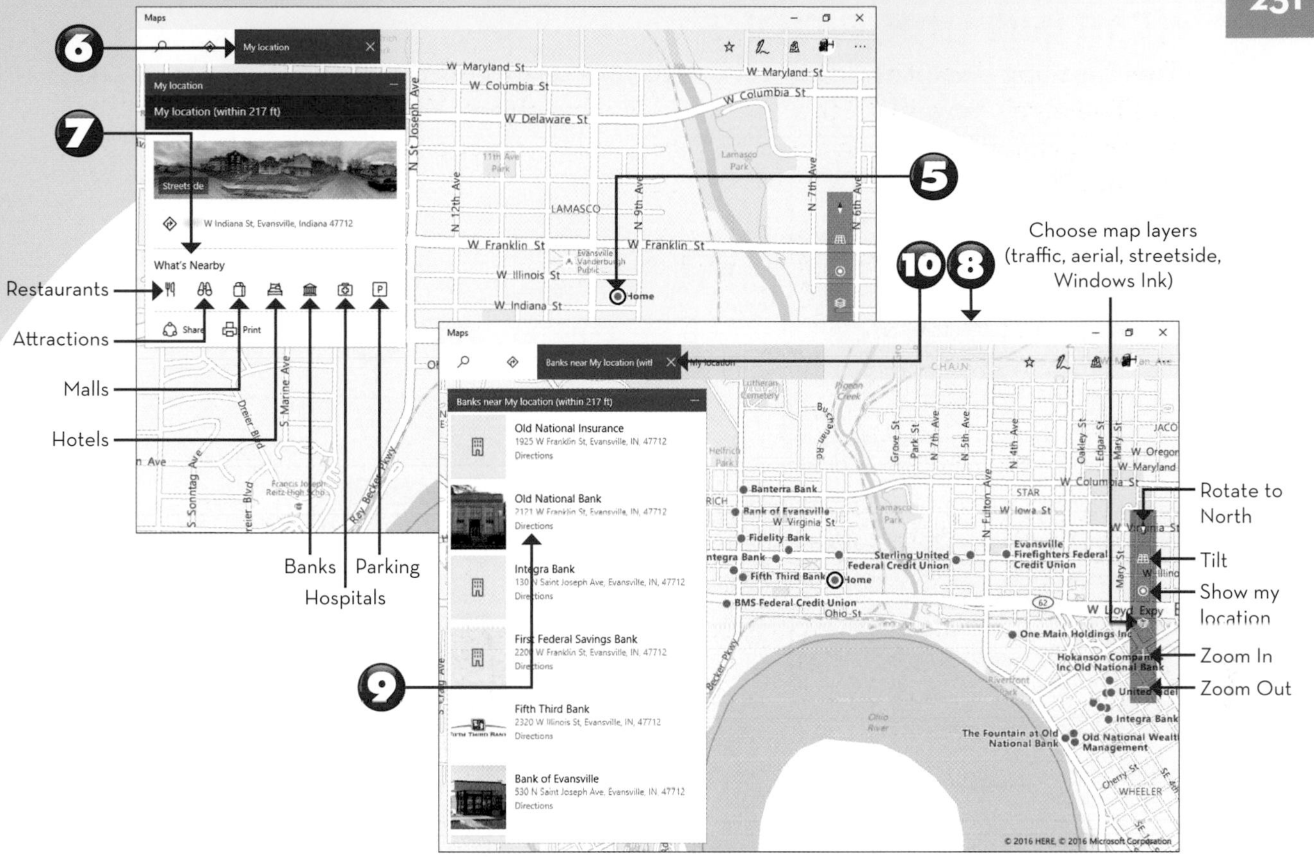

Restaurants
Attractions
Malls
Hotels
Banks
Hospitals
Parking
Choose map layers (traffic, aerial, streetside, Windows Ink)
Rotate to North
Tilt
Show my location
Zoom In
Zoom Out

5 If you answered Yes in step 4, your location is marked on the map. If you are at home, it is marked Home.

6 Click or tap **My location** to view nearby businesses.

7 Click or tap a business type to see what's nearby.

8 Maps displays a list of the nearest locations and shows them as well as mapping additional locations.

9 Click or tap to get directions.

10 Click or tap to close the listing.

End

TIP

Windows Ink and Maps If your computer has pen support, click the **Windows Ink** pen icon and use it to draw on the map. Point out landmarks not shown on the map, add your own take on directions, or point out hazards not listed in traffic reports. To learn more about Windows Ink, see Chapter 13, "Using Windows Ink."

GETTING DIRECTIONS

The Maps app also provides directions to your destination by car, transit (train/bus), or walking. Here's how.

Start

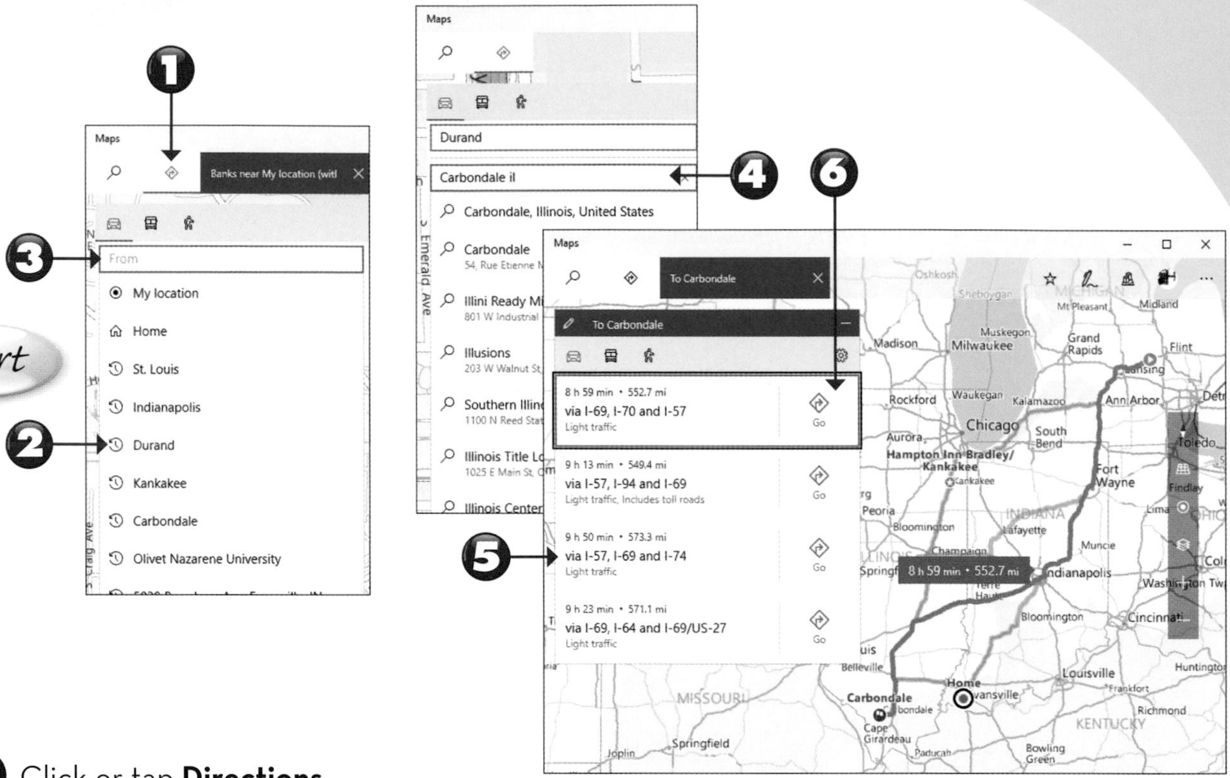

1. Click or tap **Directions**.
2. If the starting location is listed in your search history, click or tap it.
3. If the starting location is not listed, search for it.
4. Search for or click/tap the destination.
5. Each route lists estimated time, current traffic, mileage, and major highways.
6. The fastest route by car is listed first. Tap or click **Go** to start, or click the description for details.

Continued

TIP

Printing and Sharing Directions To print, share, or pin a particular route, press and hold it in step 6. Share (via email, Facebook, or other apps), Print, and Pin icons appear, followed by step-by-step directions. To print the map, open the three-dot menu at the top-right corner and click or tap **Print**.

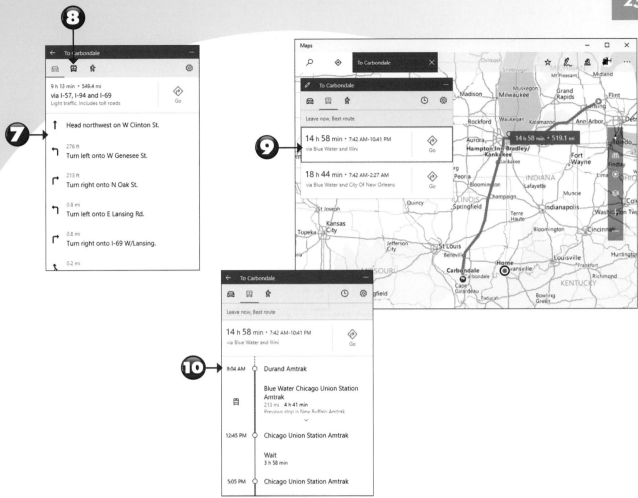

7 View details of the trip shown in step 6.

8 For transit directions, click the bus icon.

9 Transit directions (when available) list bus or train schedules and total time. Tap your preferred schedule for details.

10 View details of the trip shown in step 9.

End

STARTING THE MONEY APP

Whether you're browsing financial news or focusing on a single company, the Money app (also known as MSN Money) is ready to help. Here's how to get started.

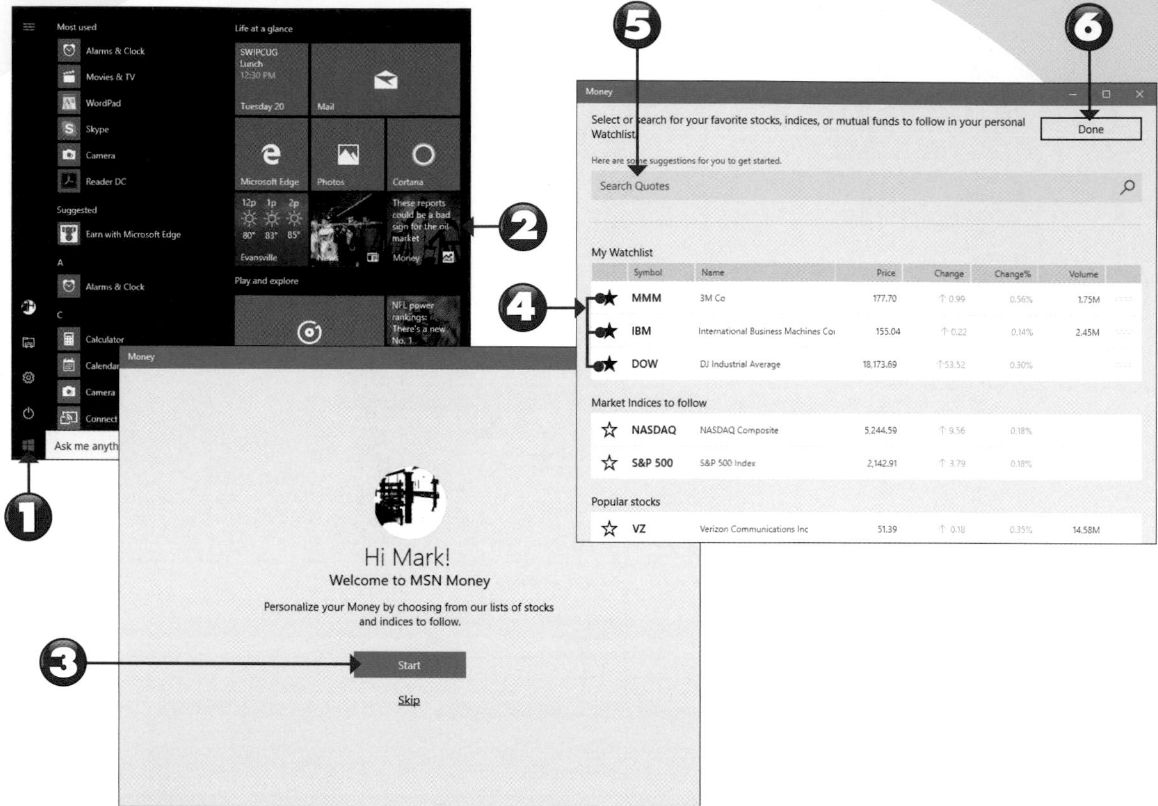

1. Click or tap **Start**.
2. Click or tap **Money**.
3. Click or tap **Start** to choose stocks and indices to follow.
4. Click or tap the stocks and indices you want to follow.
5. Use Search to quickly locate your favorites.
6. Click or tap **Done** to continue.

Continued

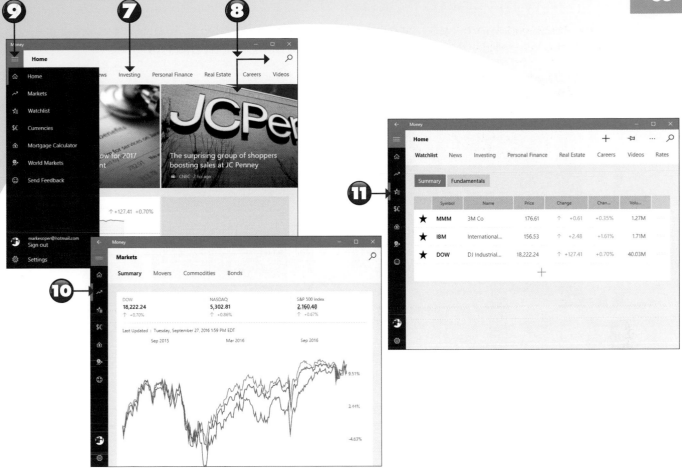

7 The Today page opens by default, displaying current stock information and news stories.

8 Scroll or flick down for more stories and to the right for more categories.

9 Click or tap to expand the menu.

10 Click or tap **Markets** to see a summary of the major stock indices.

11 Click or tap **Watchlist** for a summary of your stocks or indices.

End

TIP

Using Cortana If you've activated Cortana (the Windows 10 AE digital assistant), you can view news by clicking or tapping the **Ask me anything** box next to the Start menu. Cortana lists the day's top headlines, displays any stocks you're watching, and shows your local weather report, all in a scrollable pop-up menu.

USING THE SPORTS APP

You can use the Sports app to view the latest news and scores from athletic events around the world, including video clips and slideshows of the latest events.

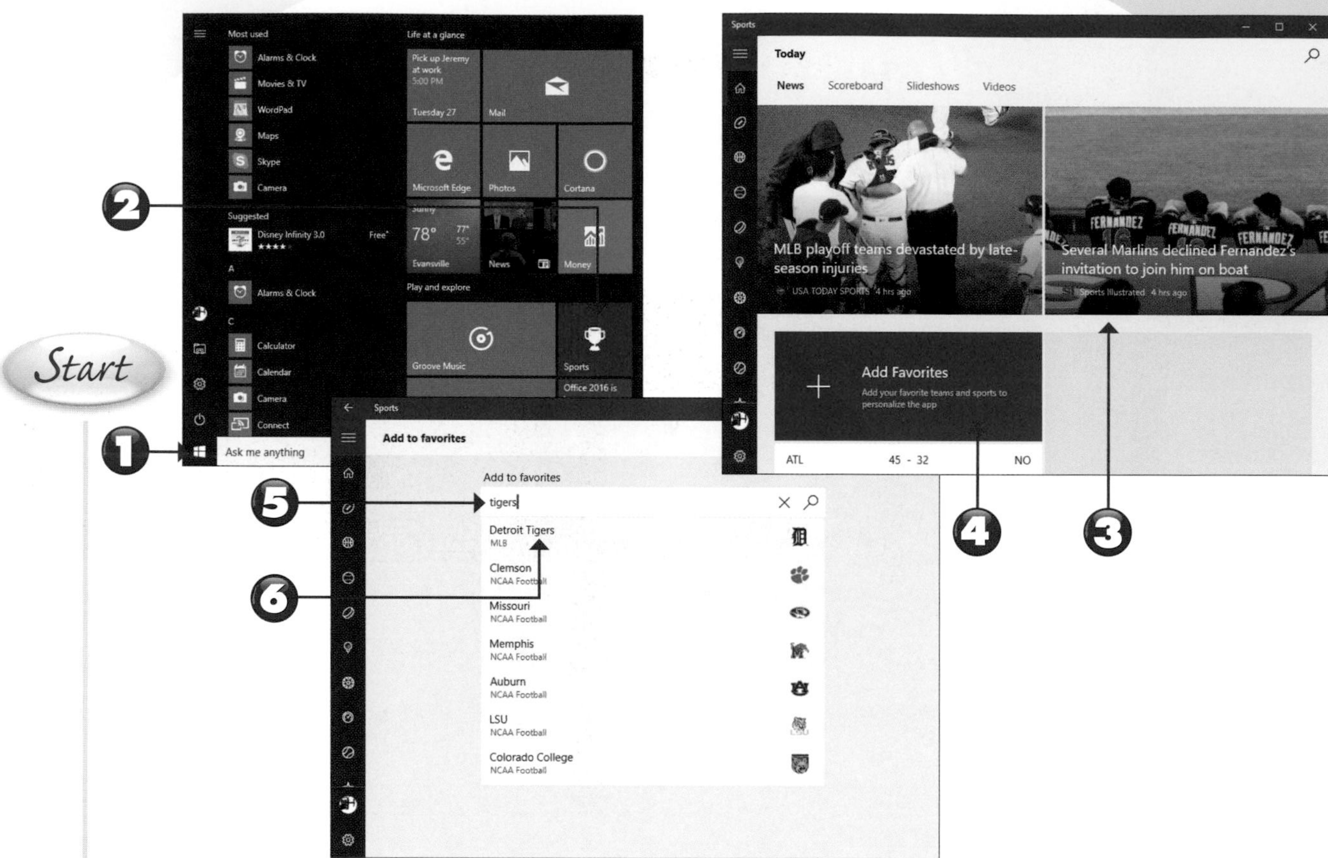

1. Click or tap **Start**.

2. Click or tap **Sports**.

3. The Sports app opens to the Today window, the app's home page. Click or tap a sport topic to view news, or scroll down the window to view other sports news stories.

4. To add your favorite teams to the front page, click or tap **Add Favorites**.

5. Type in all or part of the team name.

6. Click or tap your team.

Continued

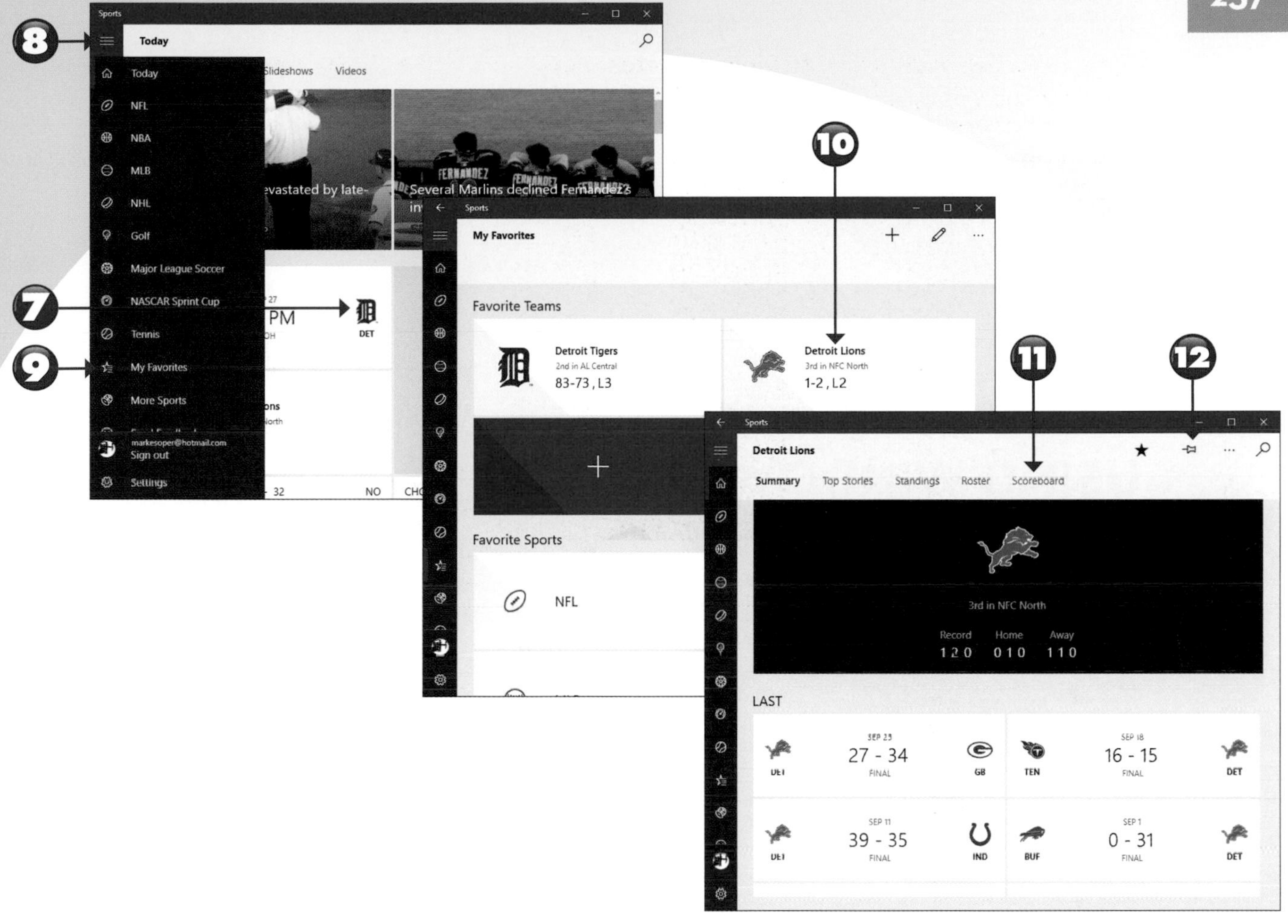

7. Your team(s) are listed on the Home page.

8. Click or tap to expand the menu.

9. Click or tap **My Favorites** to see more about your teams.

10. Click or tap your team.

11. After reviewing the summary, click or tap categories for more.

12. To pin a team to the Start menu, click or tap the pushpin.

End

USING WINDOWS INK

The new Windows Ink Workspace combines old and new pen-enabled apps to make your pen, touchscreen, or touchpad more powerful and easier to use for creating notes, reminders, and simple drawings. As you learn in this chapter, Windows Ink Workspace can also work with Cortana, Mail, and other apps.

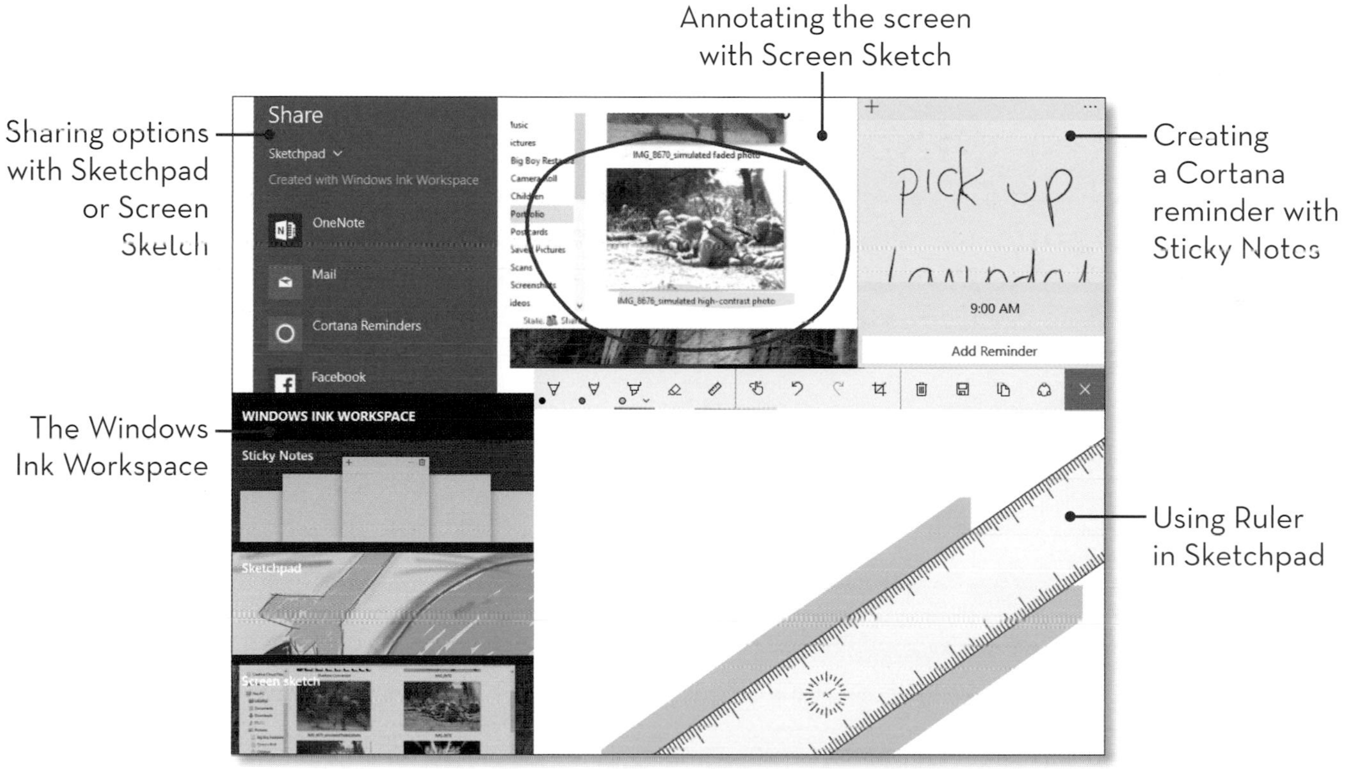
Annotating the screen with Screen Sketch
Sharing options with Sketchpad or Screen Sketch
Creating a Cortana reminder with Sticky Notes
The Windows Ink Workspace
Using Ruler in Sketchpad
Share
Sketchpad
Created with Windows Ink Workspace
OneNote
Mail
Cortana Reminders
Facebook
pick up
9:00 AM
Add Reminder
WINDOWS INK WORKSPACE
Sticky Notes
Sketchpad
Screen sketch

OPENING THE WINDOWS INK WORKSPACE

You launch the Windows Ink Workspace from the taskbar. Here's how to get started with it.

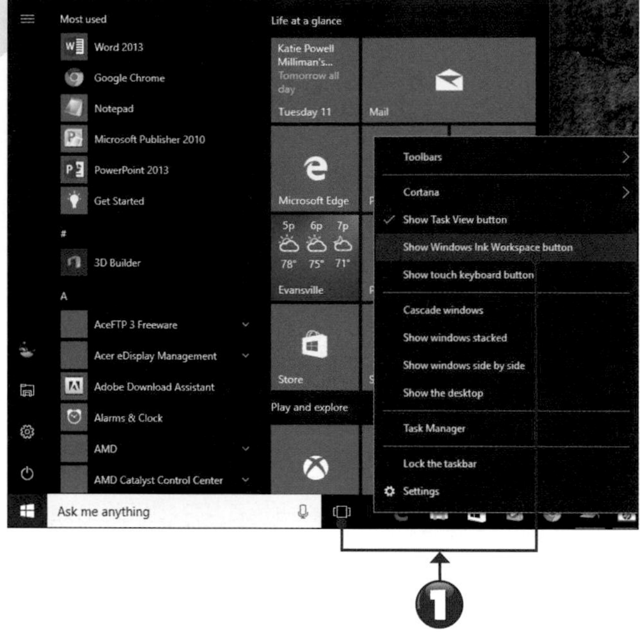

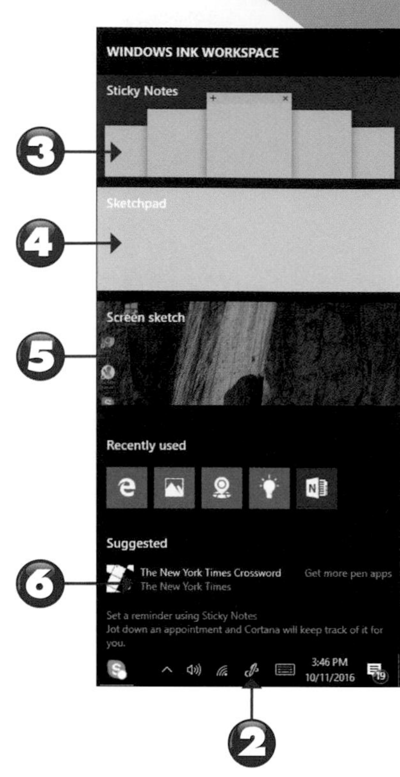

Start

1. If the Windows Ink Workspace icon is not visible, right-click the taskbar and click or tap **Show Windows Ink Workspace button**.
2. Click or tap the **Windows Ink Workspace** icon in the taskbar.
3. To create a sticky note, click or tap **Sticky Notes**.
4. To create a sketch you can save as an image file, click or tap **Sketchpad**.
5. To sketch over the current screen and save the result as an image file, click or tap **Screen sketch**.
6. Click or tap **Get more pen apps** from the Windows Store.

End

NOTE

Pen, Tablet, Touchpad, or Mouse Windows Ink Workspace works with any of these input devices. ■

CREATE A STICKY NOTE

Windows lets you place sticky notes anywhere on your desktop, gives you a choice of colors, and lets you resize them as needed. You can create sticky notes in either Desktop or Tablet mode, but you can see them only in Desktop mode.

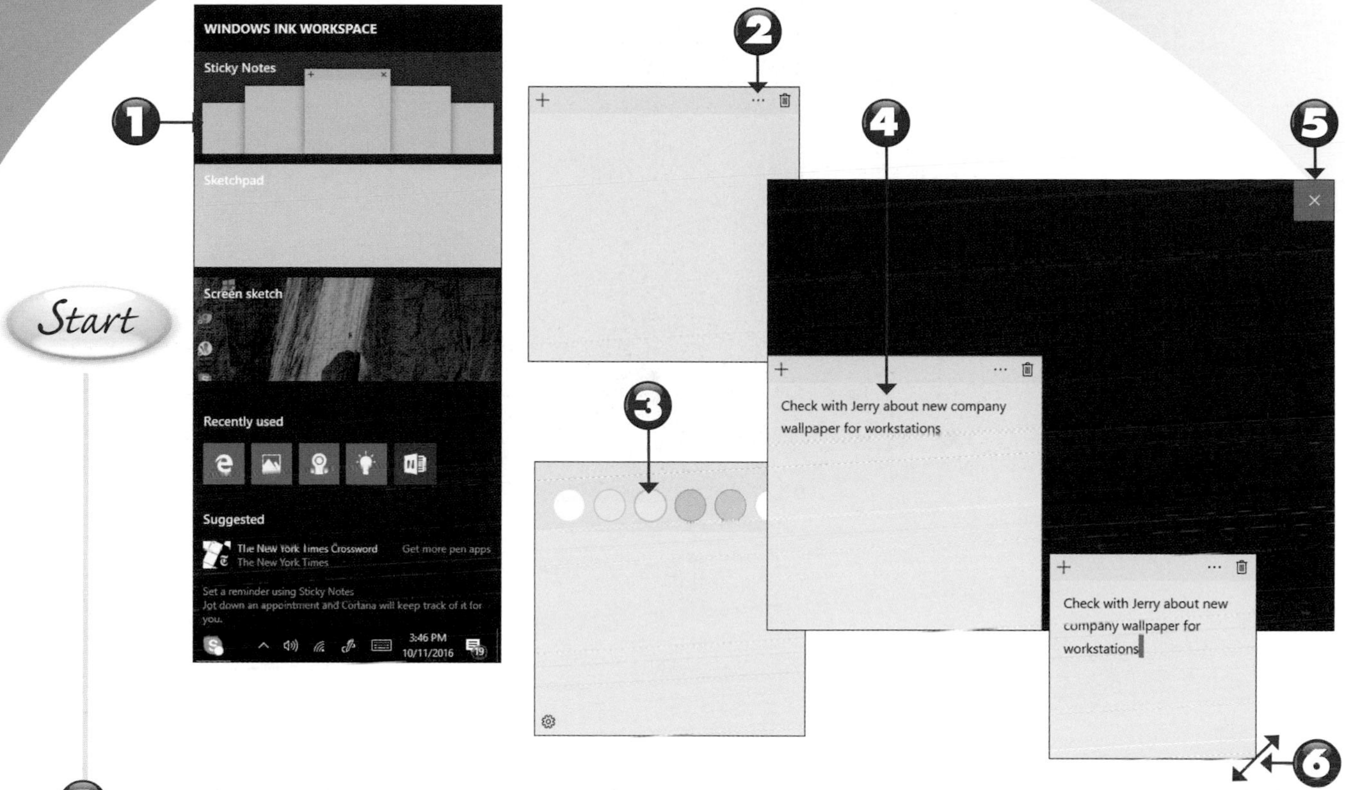

Start

1. From the Windows Ink Workspace, click or tap **Sticky notes**.
2. To change the note color, click or tap the three-dot menu button.
3. Click or tap your preferred note color.
4. Type or handwrite the note text.
5. Click or tap the **X** to return to the Windows desktop.
6. To resize the note, hover over a corner or side. When the cursor changes to a double-headed arrow, click or press and drag an edge or corner, and then release.

End

TIP

Drag It Anywhere To place the sticky note where you want it, click and hold the top border of the note with a mouse or touchpad, and then drag it into position. Release the mouse button to drop it. ■

CREATE A REMINDER USING STICKY NOTES

In Windows 10 AE, sticky notes are far more powerful than in earlier versions: they can be used to set up reminders that Cortana can use. Here's how it works.

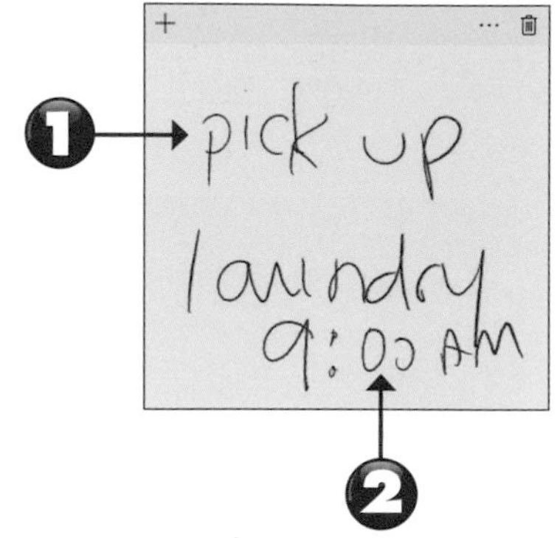

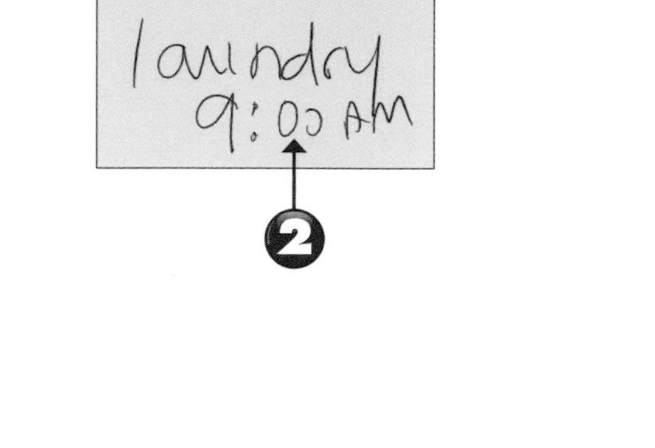

Start

1. Handwrite or type a note that includes a date or time.

2. The date or time portion of the note turns blue. Click or tap the blue text.

3. Click or tap **Add Reminder**.

Continued

NOTE

Enable Insights When you start Sticky Notes for the first time, you are prompted to enable Cortana's insights feature. This lets Cortana help you with reminders. ■

4. After Cortana finishes recognizing text, make any edits needed.

5. Click or tap **Remind**.

6. Look for the confirmation message from Cortana.

7. Click or tap to close the sticky note workspace.

End

CAUTION

Troubleshooting Reminders with Sticky Notes If Sticky Notes does not recognize dates or times (step 2), make sure you have signed in to Cortana, are not using a local account (Cortana cannot provide reminders for local accounts), and have enabled Cortana insights in Sticky Notes. (See "Configuring Sticky Notes," later in this chapter, to learn how.) ■

DELETE A STICKY NOTE

You can delete a sticky note you no longer need. Here's how.

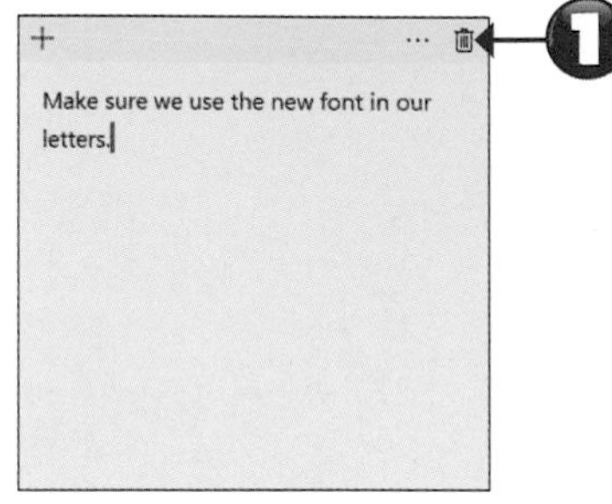

Start

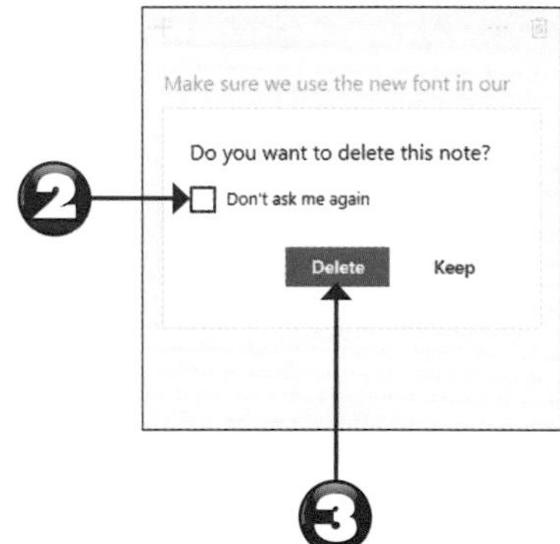

1. To start the deletion process, click or tap the note's trashcan icon.
2. If you don't want to confirm deletions in the future, enable this feature; click or tap the **Don't ask me again** checkbox.
3. Click or tap **Delete** to remove the sticky note from your screen.

End

TIP

Goodbye Sticky Note, Cortana's Got Your Back After you create a Cortana reminder with a sticky note, you can delete the sticky note. The reminder stays in Cortana. To learn more about Cortana, see Chapter 5, "Using Cortana Search." ■

CONFIGURING STICKY NOTES

In addition to changing the color of sticky notes, you can make other configuration changes. Here's what to do.

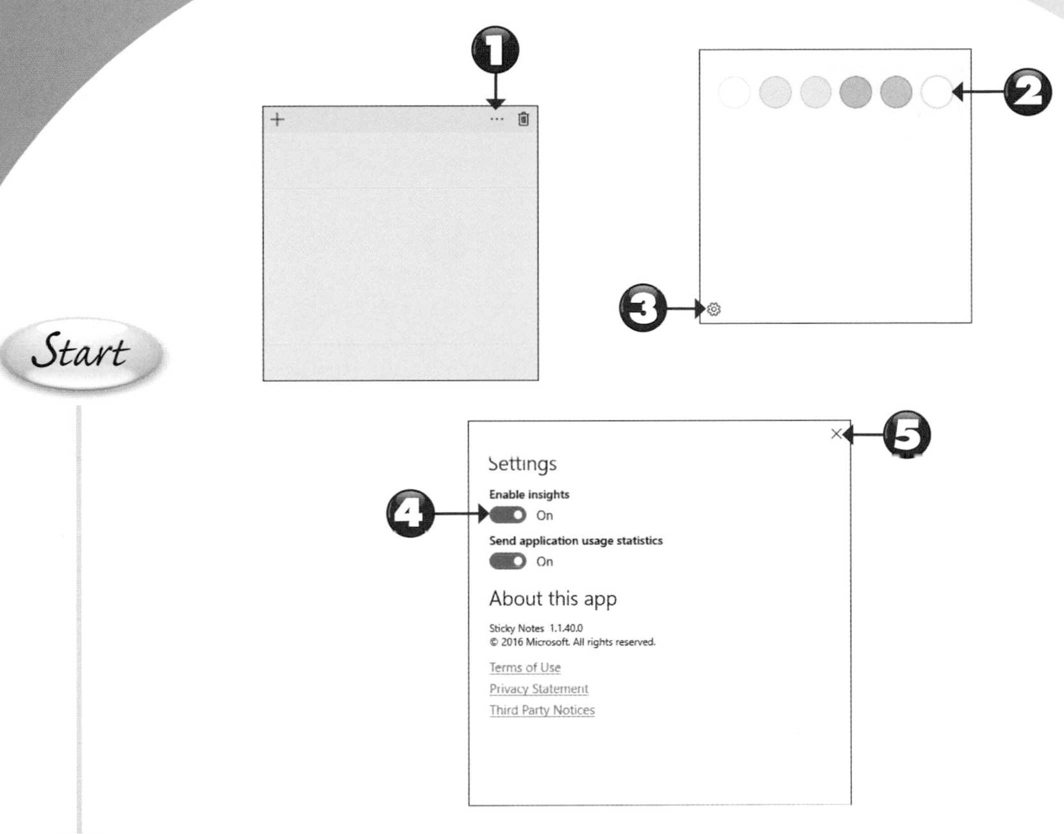

1. Click or tap the note's three-dot menu button.
2. Choose a new note color if desired.
3. Click or tap the **Settings** (gearbox) icon.
4. If you want to create Cortana reminders using sticky notes, make sure **Enable insights** is turned on; click or press and drag the control to **On**.
5. Click or tap to close Settings.

End

TIP

Bold, Italics, Underlining, and More To add bold text to your sticky note, type the text and highlight it; then press Ctrl+B. For italics, highlight the text and press Ctrl+I. For underlining, highlight the text and press Ctrl+U. You can also make highlighted text bigger with Ctrl+Shift+> and smaller with Ctrl+Shift+<. ■

GETTING STARTED WITH SKETCHPAD

Sketchpad is the second member of the Windows Ink Workspace team. It's designed to create simple sketches that you can save as PNG files for use with other apps. You can draw using ballpoint pen, pencil, or highlighter tools from the Sketchpad toolbar. The toolbar also offers features to help you as you draw and edit your sketches.

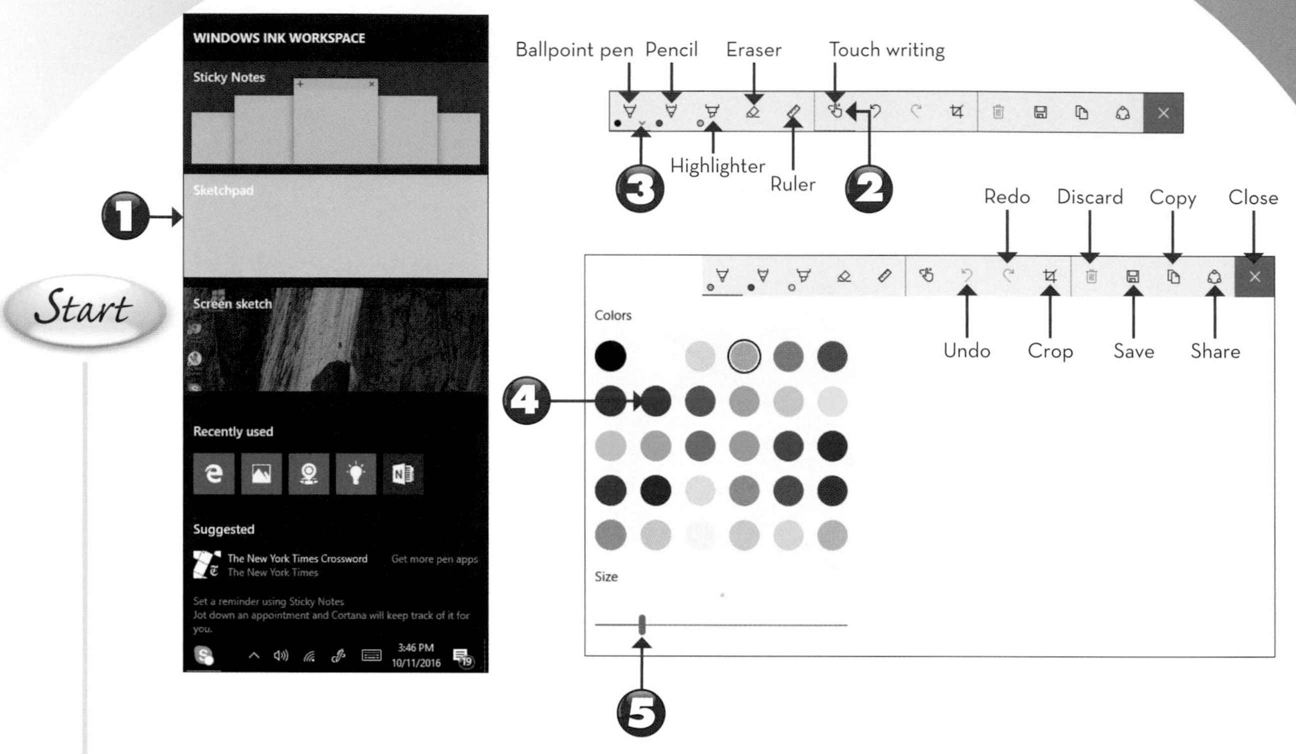

1. From the Windows Ink Workspace menu, click or tap **Sketchpad**.

2. Click or tap **Touch writing** to use your mouse, touch pad, touchscreen, or stylus to write on the screen.

3. Click or tap the down arrow to view colors and drawing tip size.

4. Click or tap to choose a drawing color.

5. Drag left to reduce drawing tip size; drag right to increase drawing tip size.

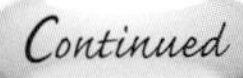

TIP

Clearing the Workspace If Sketchpad has an unneeded drawing in the workspace, click or tap **Discard**. It will be removed immediately. ■

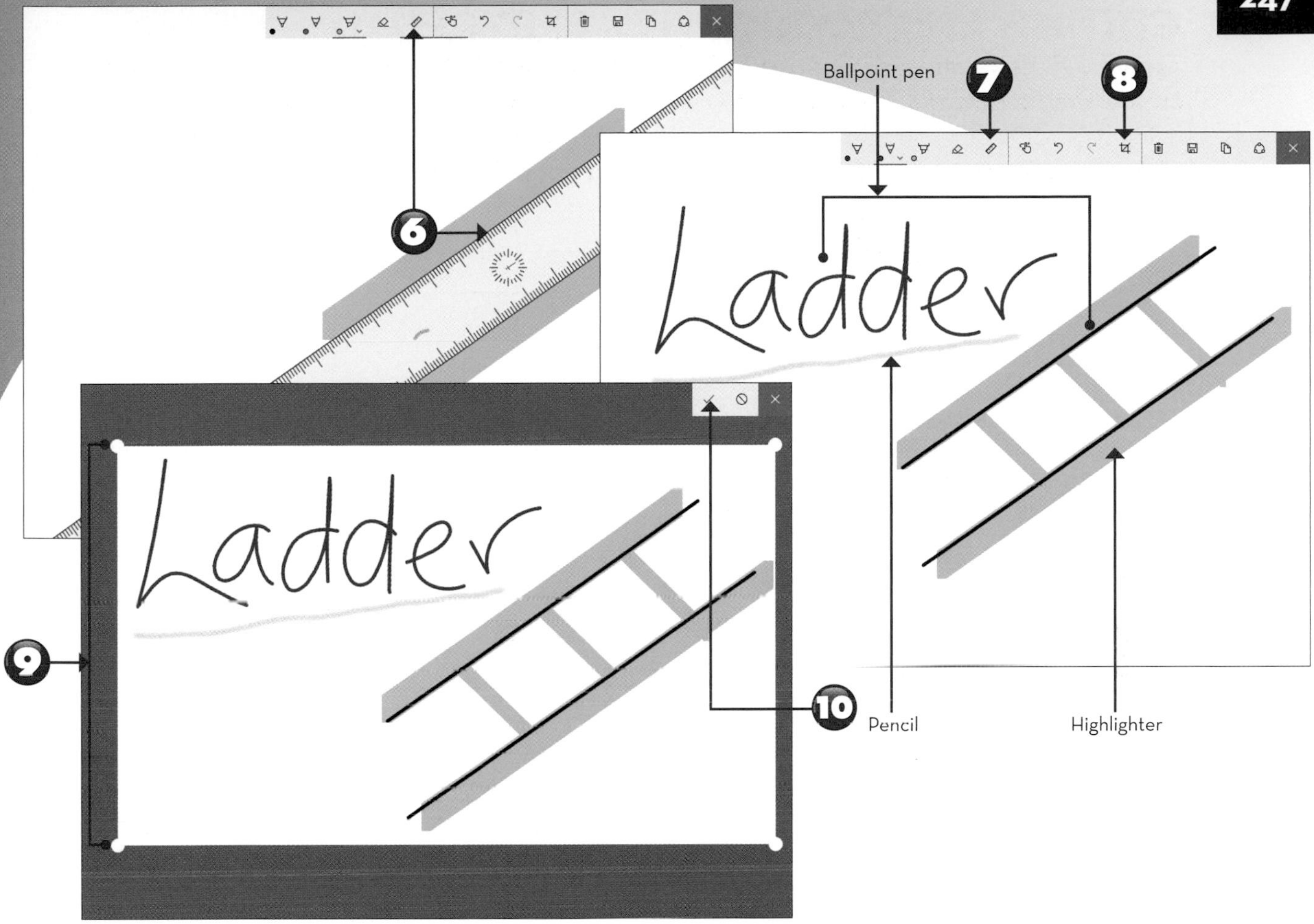

6 Click or tap the **Ruler** to help you draw straight lines. Use the touchscreen or touchpad to position and rotate the ruler to the desired angle.

7 When you are finished using the ruler, click or tap the **Ruler** icon again to remove it from the screen.

8 Click or tap the **Crop** tool to crop the picture.

9 Drag the corners to the desired crop size.

10 Click or tap the check mark to complete the crop.

End

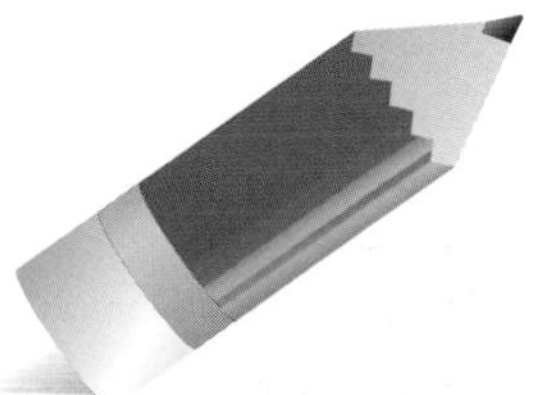

EDITING AND SAVING WITH SKETCHPAD

Sketchpad can be used to create drawings that work with many different apps. Here's how to make changes and save your work.

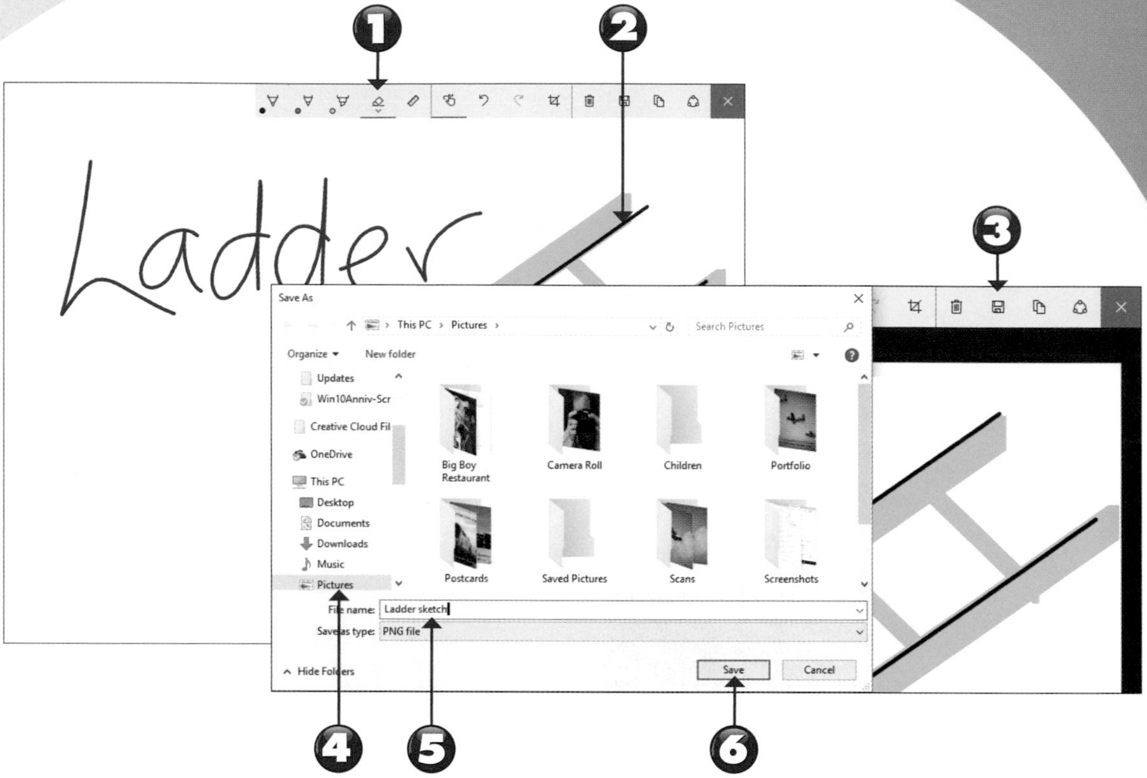

Start

1. To remove an unwanted shape or line, click or tap **Eraser**.
2. Click or tap a shape or line to remove it.
3. After making corrections, click or tap the **Save** button to save your sketch.
4. Sketches are saved to your Pictures folder by default; you can choose a different location if desired.
5. Enter the name for the file.
6. Click or tap **Save**.

End

TIP

Removing All Ink To remove all the shapes and lines in a sketch without closing Sketchpad, click or tap the **Eraser** tool, and then click or tap the down arrow and select **Erase All Ink**. ■

SHARING WITH SKETCHPAD

Sketchpad can also send sketches to other Windows 10 AE apps by using the Share option. In this example, we share a sketch with Mail.

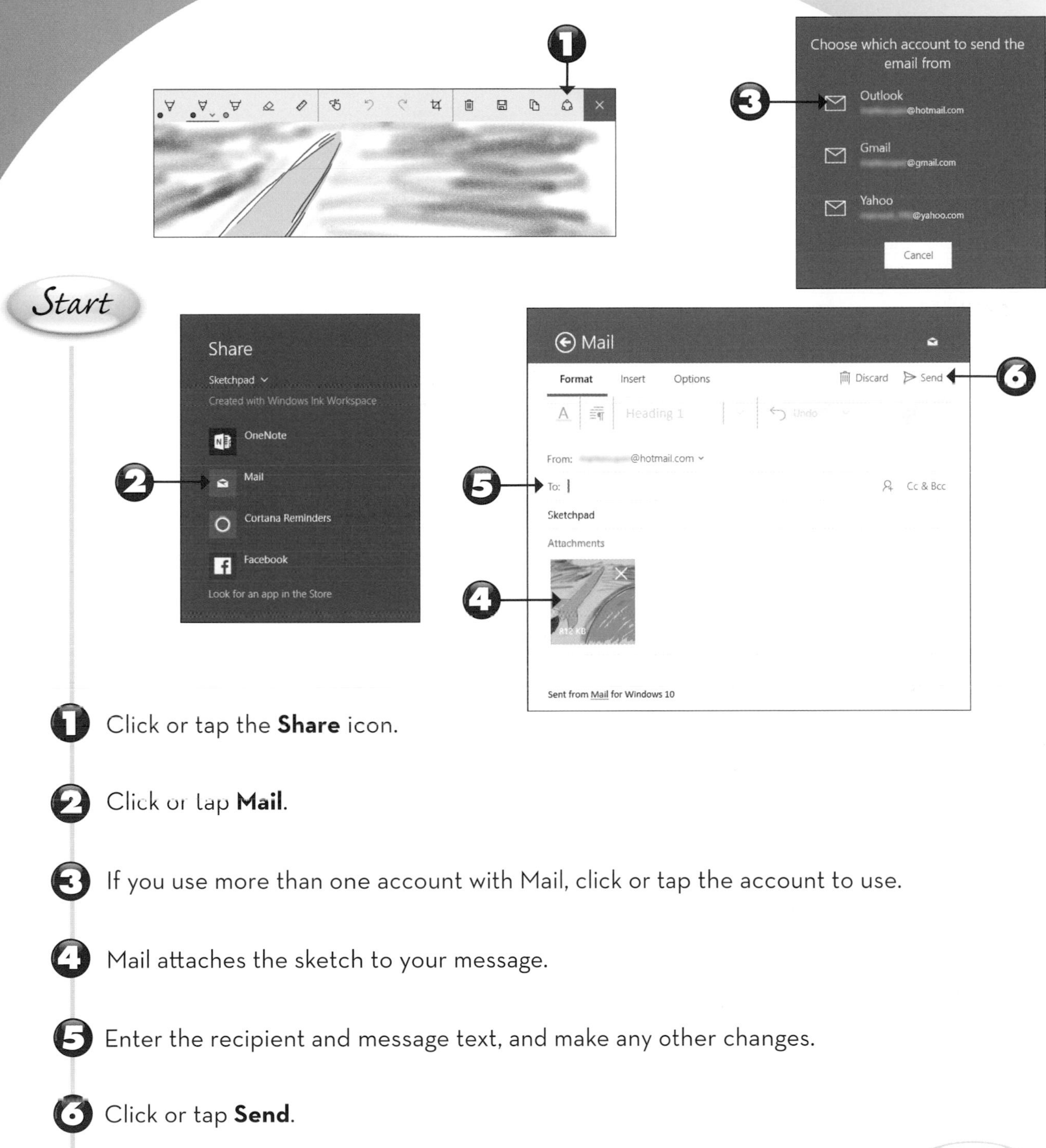

1. Click or tap the **Share** icon.
2. Click or tap **Mail**.
3. If you use more than one account with Mail, click or tap the account to use.
4. Mail attaches the sketch to your message.
5. Enter the recipient and message text, and make any other changes.
6. Click or tap **Send**.

End

USING SCREEN SKETCH

Screen Sketch combines the features of Sketchpad with screen capture. Use it to sketch or make quick notes about whatever you have onscreen. In this example, we capture a screen showing photos that might be used for a brochure and use the Screen Sketch feature to annotate the pictures.

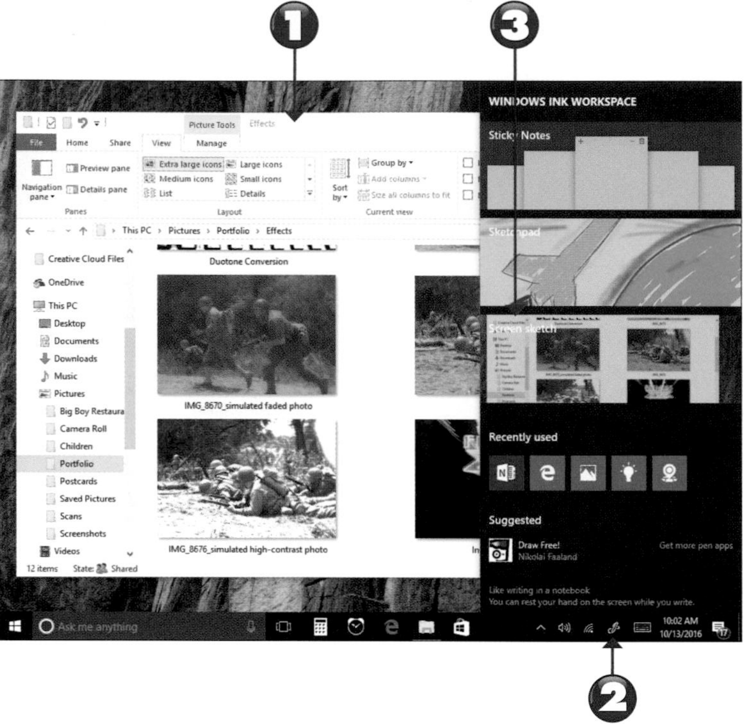

Start

1. Open the app or apps you want to use with Screen Sketch.
2. When you have everything onscreen that you want to capture, click or tap the **Windows Ink Workspace** icon in the taskbar.
3. Click or tap **Screen sketch**.

Continued

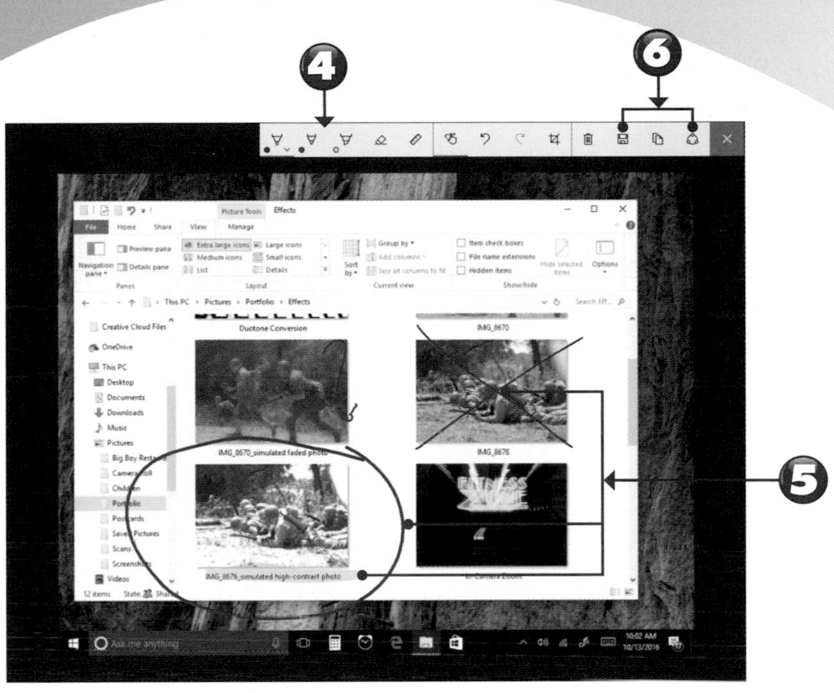

4. The same Sketchpad tools are available for marking up the screen.

5. Mark the screen as needed.

6. When you are finished, save or share the sketch using the same Save and Share tools as with Sketchpad.

End

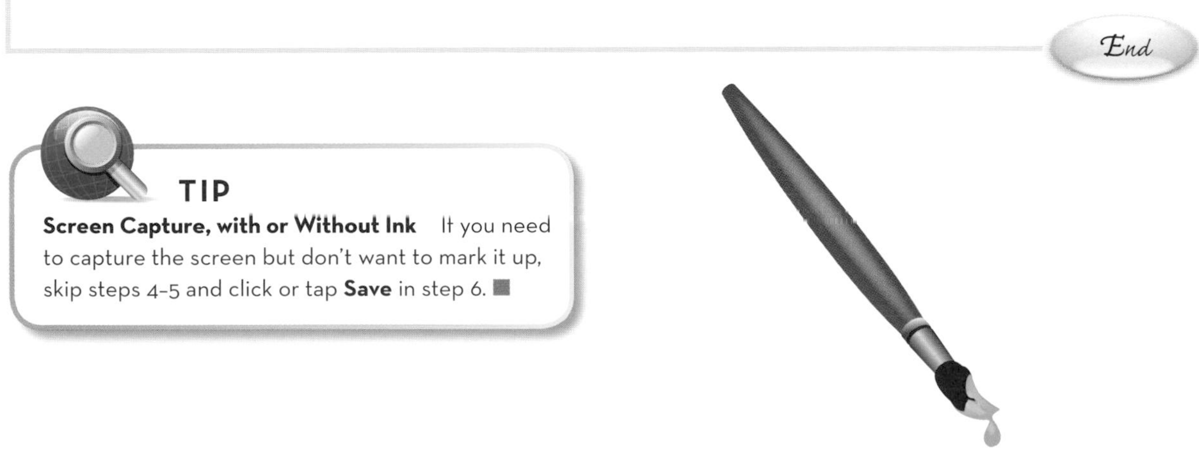

TIP

Screen Capture, with or Without Ink If you need to capture the screen but don't want to mark it up, skip steps 4–5 and click or tap **Save** in step 6. ■

STORING AND FINDING YOUR FILES

Windows 10 AE's File Explorer provides access to both local files and OneDrive cloud-based storage. File Explorer makes it easier than ever to locate folders and files and access recently used documents, photos, and other file types. In this chapter, you find out how to utilize File Explorer to learn more about your folders and files and find ways to make them more useful.

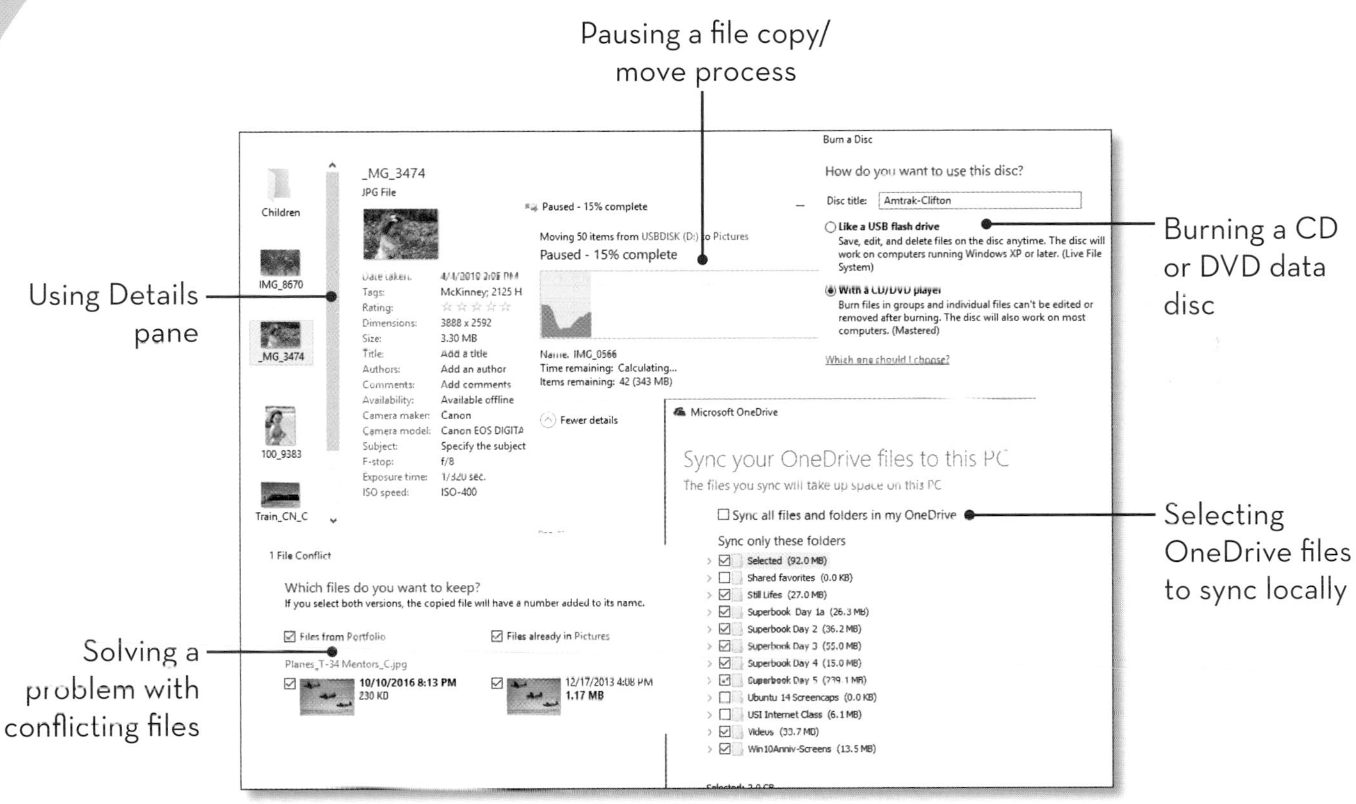
Pausing a file copy/ move process
Burning a CD or DVD data disc
Using Details pane
Selecting OneDrive files to sync locally
Solving a problem with conflicting files
Burn a Disc
How do you want to use this disc?
Disc title: Amtrak-Clifton
Like a USB flash drive
With a CD/DVD player
Which one should I choose?
_MG_3474
JPG File
Paused - 15% complete
Moving 50 items from USBDISK (D:) to Pictures
Fewer details
Microsoft OneDrive
Sync your OneDrive files to this PC
The files you sync will take up space on this PC
Sync all files and folders in my OneDrive
Sync only these folders
1 File Conflict
Which files do you want to keep?
If you select both versions, the copied file will have a number added to its name.
Files from Portfolio
Files already in Pictures

OPENING FILE EXPLORER

File Explorer is Windows 10 AE's version of the venerable Windows Explorer file and drive management interface. Follow these steps to open File Explorer and view some of its features.

Start

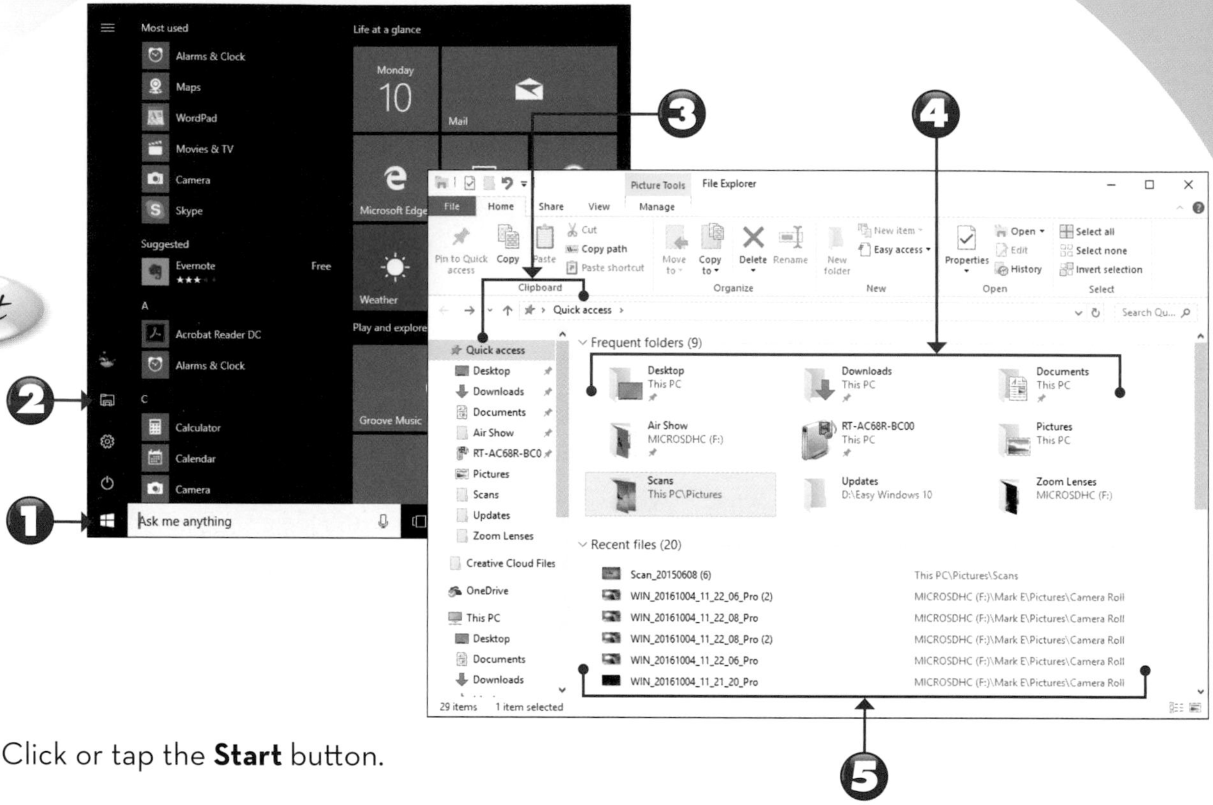

1. Click or tap the **Start** button.
2. Click or tap **File Explorer**.
3. File Explorer opens to the default Quick access view.
4. Folders you open most often (Frequent folders) are at the top of the pane.
5. Files you've opened most recently (Recent files) are at the bottom of the pane.

Continued

NOTE

Using the Home Tab Click or tap the **Home** tab to view sections of tools for working with folders and files. The Clipboard section enables you to cut, copy, and paste files and folders and their locations (paths) to different locations. Use the Organize section to move, copy, delete, or rename selected files or folders. The New section's Easy Access tool lets you map a location to a drive letter or add a folder to a library. Use the Open section to see file or folder properties and history. Use the Select section to select or deselect files and folders. ■

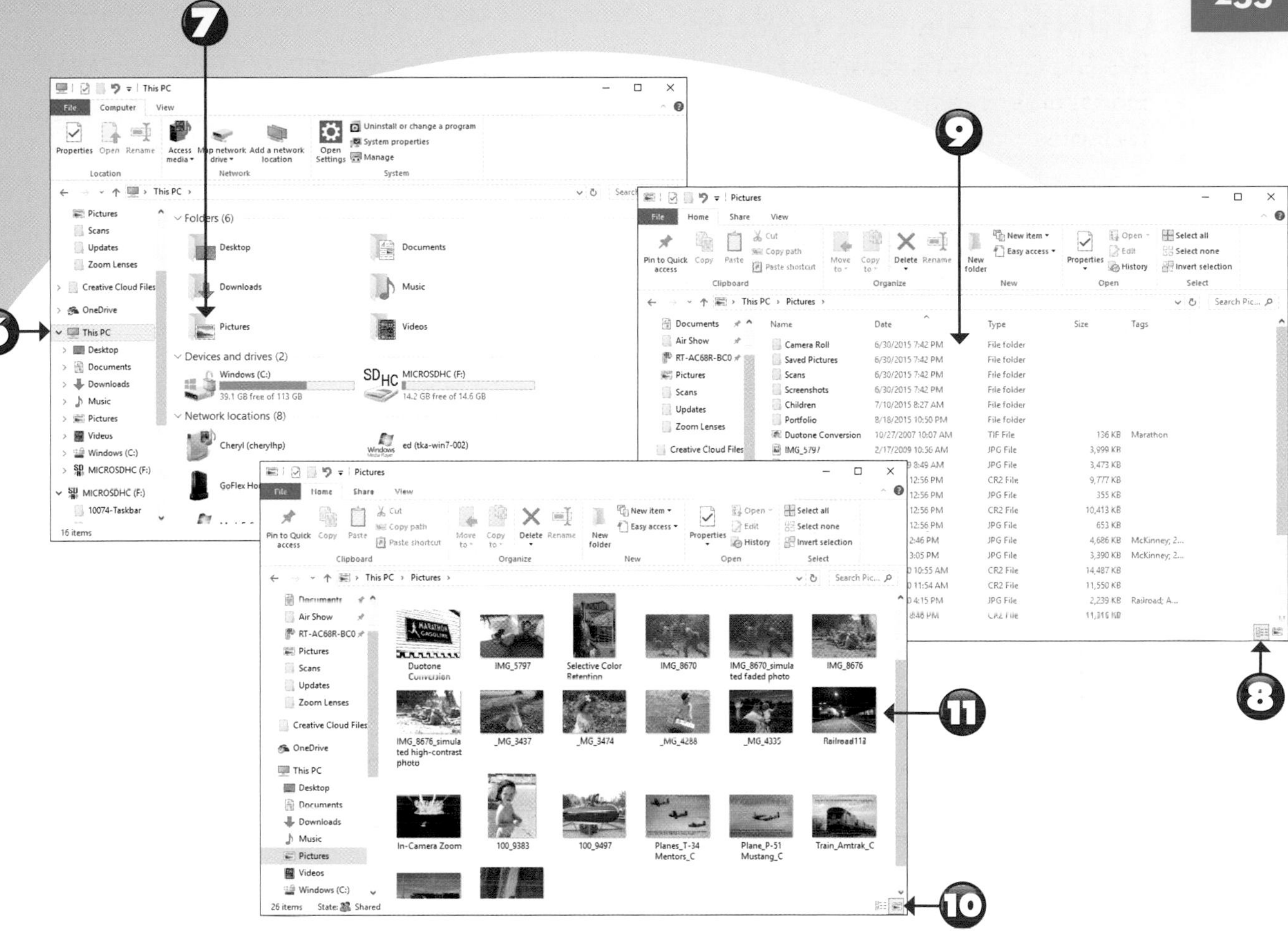

6. Click or tap **This PC** to see the folders and drives on your computer.

7. Click or tap the **Pictures** folder.

8. The Details view is active. (If not, click or tap to view Details.)

9. The Details view lists filenames, date created, size, type, and tags.

10. Click or tap to switch to the Large thumbnails view.

11. The Large thumbnails view shows a preview of each file.

End

TIP

Open File Explorer from the Keyboard To quickly open File Explorer from the keyboard, press the Windows key+E. ■

USING THE VIEW TAB

The File Explorer's View tab helps you select from a variety of settings so you can view drives, files, folders, and network locations in the most appropriate ways. Here are some examples of how to use the View tab.

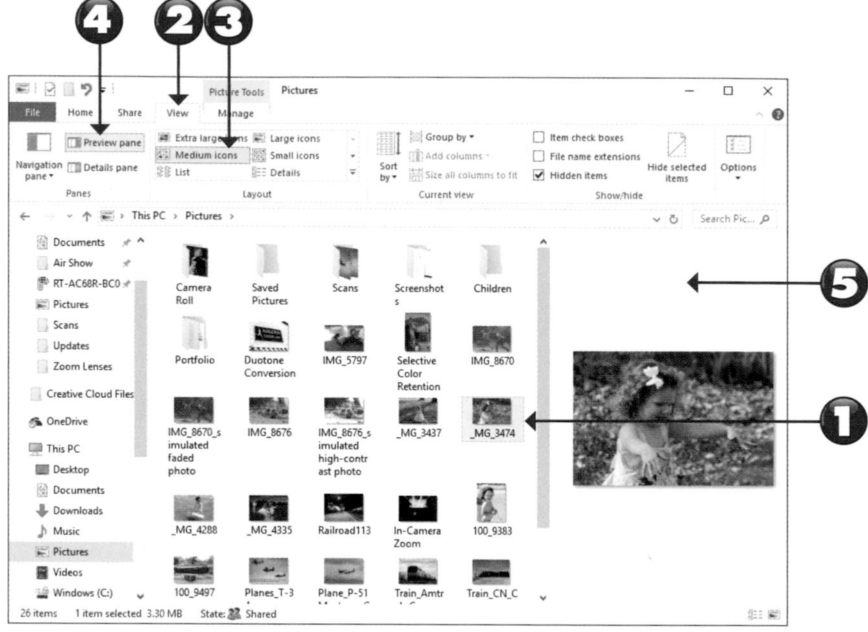

1. Click or tap a picture from your Pictures folder.
2. Click or tap the **View** tab.
3. Click or tap **Medium icons**.
4. Click or tap the **Preview pane** button.
5. A preview of the selected file.

Continued

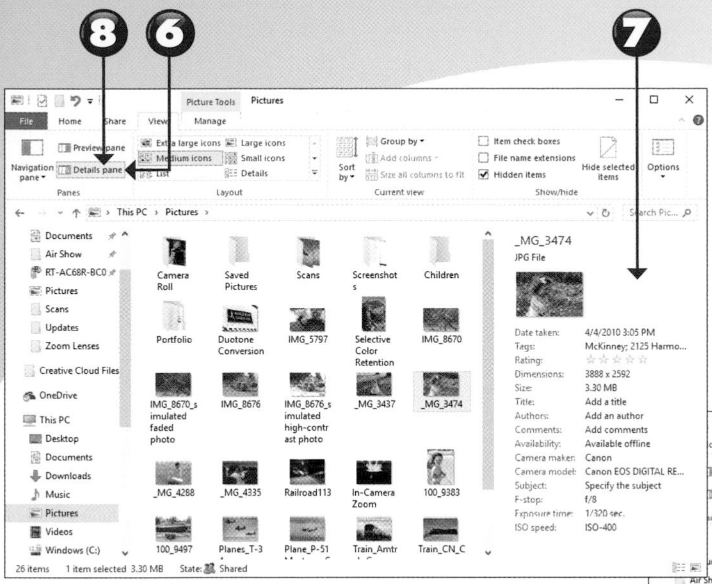

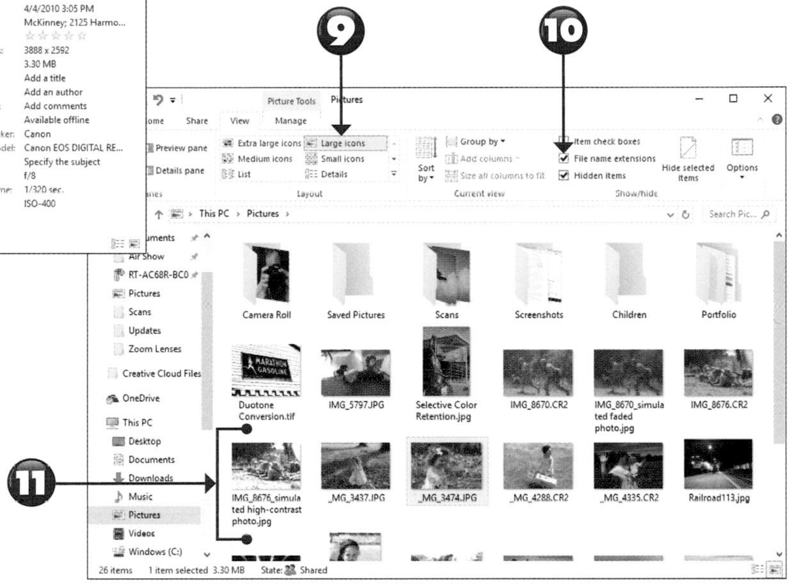

6. Click or tap the **Details pane** button.

7. View details about the selected file.

8. Click or tap the **Details pane** button again to close the pane.

9. Click or tap the **Large icons** button.

10. Click or tap the empty **File name extensions** check box.

11. View files with various file name extensions.

End

NOTE

File Name Extensions Displaying file name extensions is useful when you have similar-looking files or want to view file types. For example, CR2 and other RAW files created by high-end digital cameras are very large and need special software to be viewed, but JPG (JPEG) and PNG files use less disk space and can be viewed in web browsers and by email apps. TIF files are a good choice for publications. File extensions tell you what kind of file it is. To turn off file name extensions, simply uncheck the **File name extensions** check box.

USING COPY TO

In this exercise, you create a new folder in the Pictures folder and copy files to it. You can use these same steps to create other types of new folders in File Explorer and copy files.

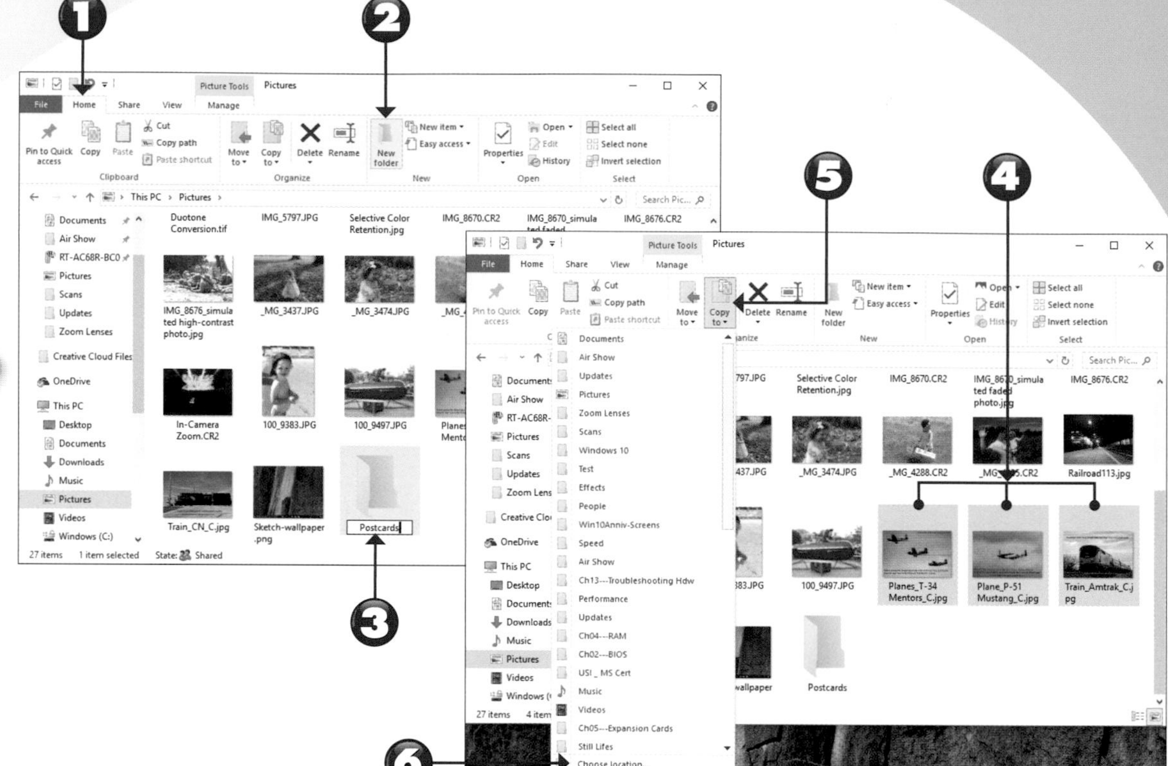

Start

1. Click or tap the **Home** tab.
2. Click or tap **New folder** to create a new folder.
3. Enter the name of the new folder. Press the **Enter** key or click outside the naming box when done.
4. Select the files you want to copy.
5. Click or tap **Copy to**.
6. Click or tap **Choose location**.

NOTE

Selecting Multiple Items To select more than one item, click the first item, and then hold down either the Ctrl key on the keyboard and click additional items or press and drag a box around items you want to select.

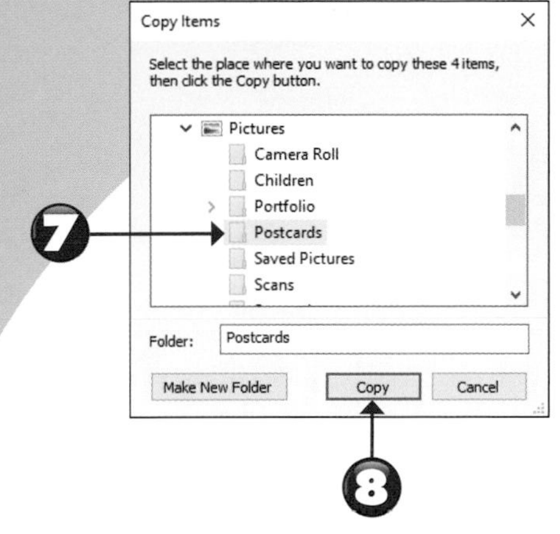

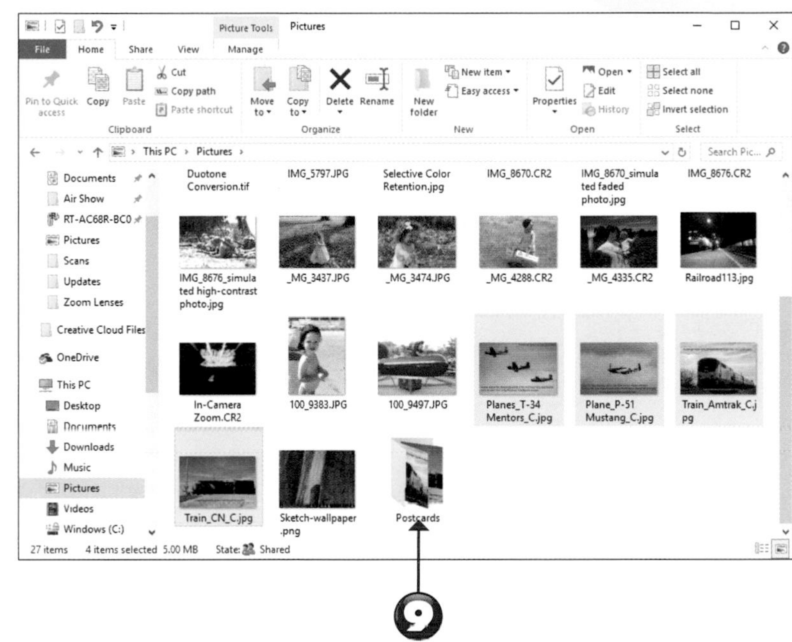

7. Navigate to and click or tap the folder you created in steps 2 and 3.

8. Click or tap **Copy**.

9. The files are copied into the folder; click or tap an empty section of the **File Explorer** window to unselect the highlighted files.

End

RENAMING FILES

You can easily rename files to better help you identify them and keep them organized. In this exercise, you rename a file you copied in the previous exercise.

Start

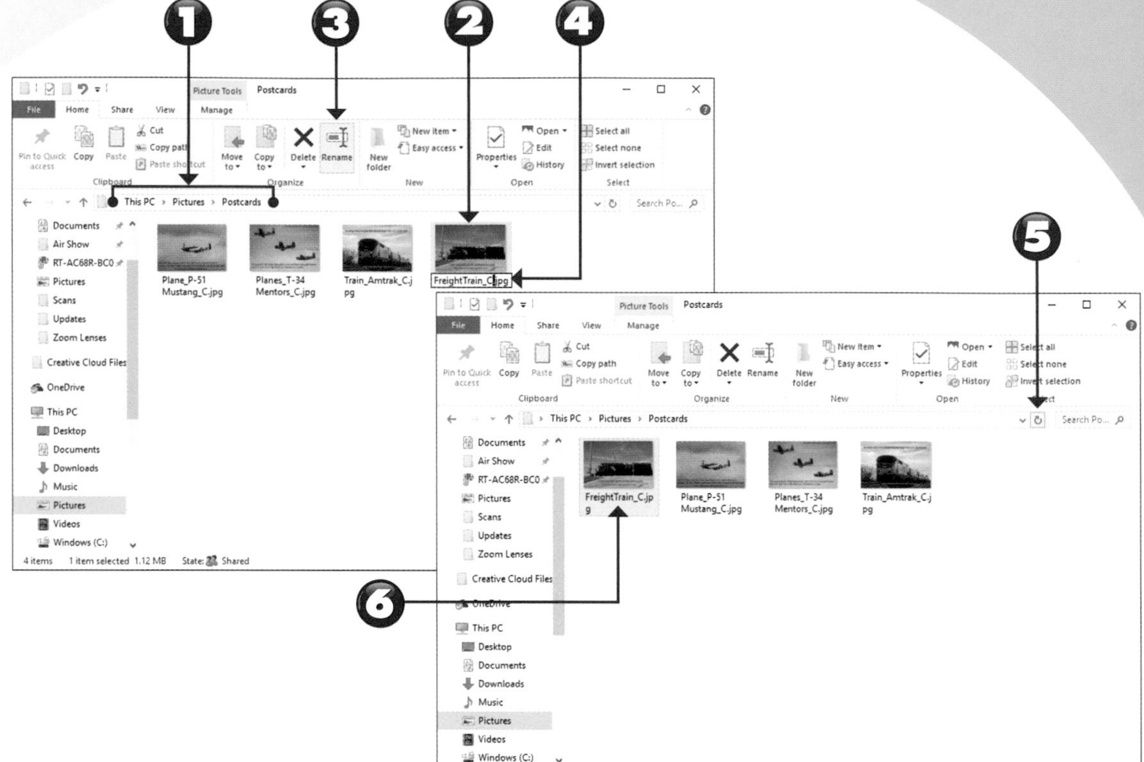

1. Open the folder where the file copies are located.

2. Click or tap a file.

3. Click or tap **Rename** on the Home tab.

4. Enter a new name for the file.

5. Press the **F5** key on your keyboard, or click or tap the **Refresh** button.

6. The file is renamed (and reordered alphabetically if appropriate).

End

NOTE

Renaming Multiple Files If you select more than one file in step 2, the files are renamed using the name you specified in step 4, followed by a sequential number (1, 2, 3, and so on).

SELECTING FILES

Although you can select a file simply by clicking or tapping its name, you can also activate other selection options in File Explorer. This exercise demonstrates how to select files using Invert Selection and deselect files.

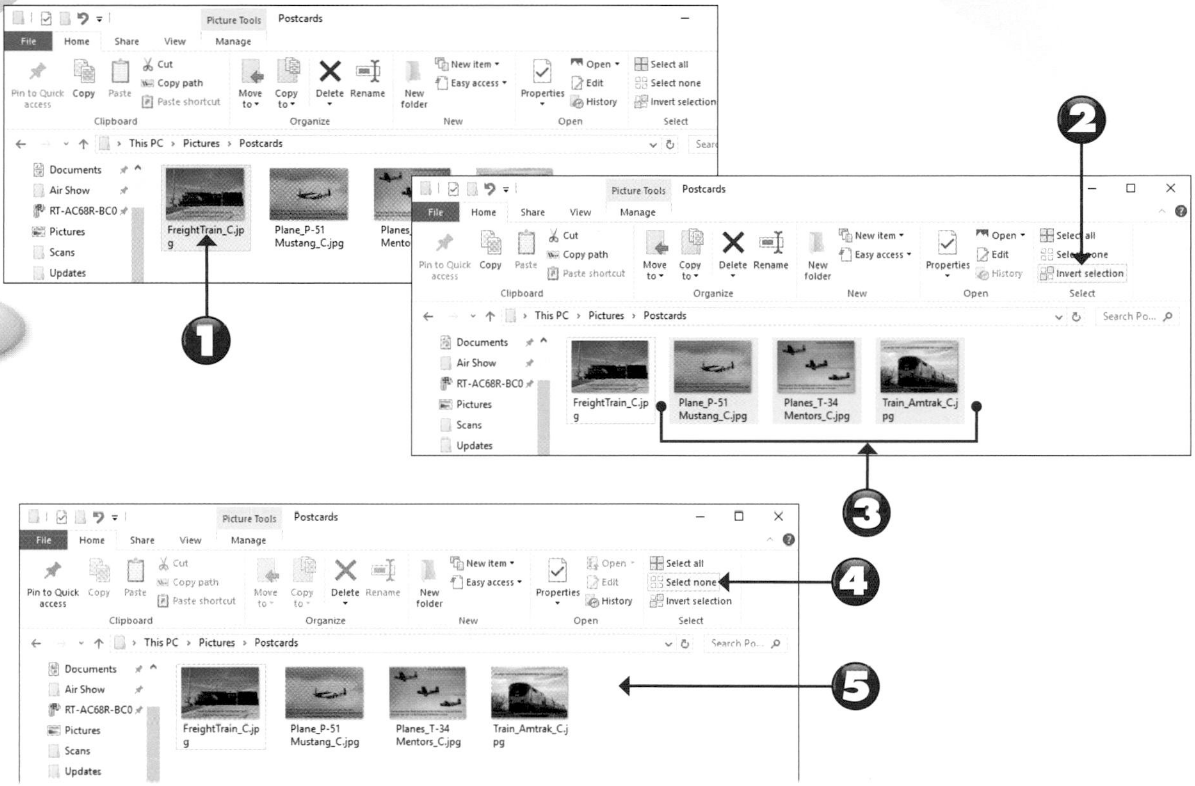

Start

1. Click or tap the file you renamed in the previous exercise.

2. From the Home tab, click or tap **Invert selection**.

3. All files in the folder except the one selected in step 1 are selected.

4. Click or tap **Select none** on the Home tab.

5. None of the files are selected.

End

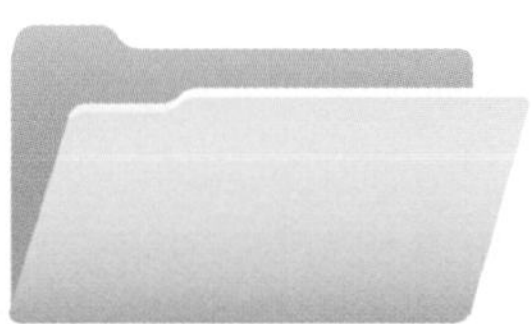

DELETING FILES

This exercise demonstrates how to select and delete all files in a location and remove them to the Recycle Bin.

Start

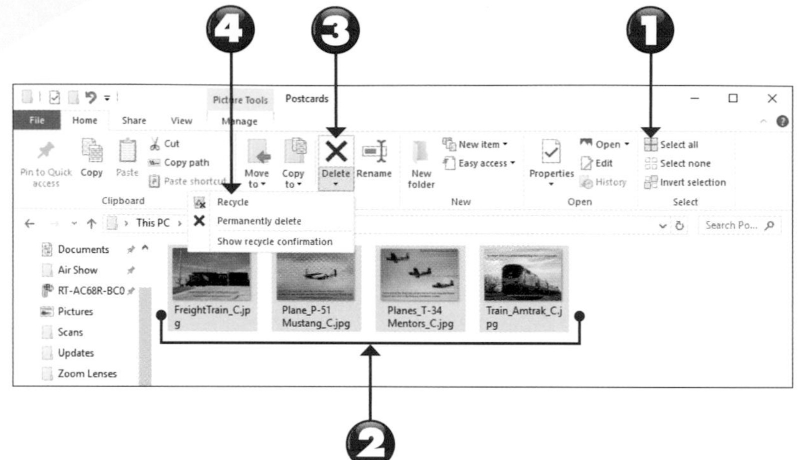

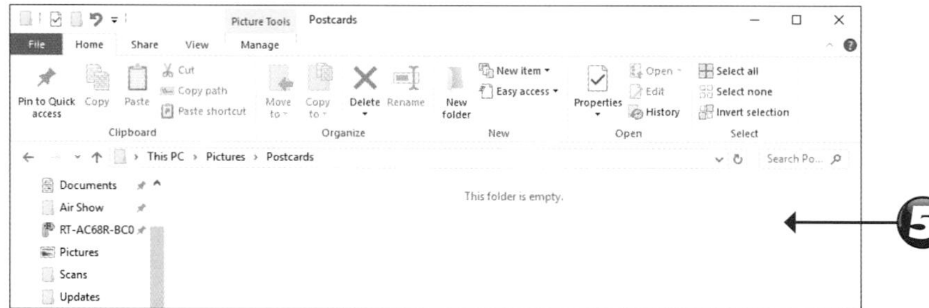

1. From the Home tab, click or tap **Select all**.
2. All the files are selected.
3. Open the **Delete** menu.
4. Click or tap **Recycle** to send files to the Recycle Bin.
5. The files are removed from the folder.

CAUTION

Permanently Delete Versus Recycle If you permanently delete files, the space they occupy on the drive can be reused by new files. If you decide you need to retrieve those files, you must use a third-party data-recovery utility.

RETRIEVING FILES FROM THE RECYCLE BIN

If you delete files you should have kept, the Recycle Bin is here to help. In this lesson, you learn how to restore files from the Recycle Bin to their original location.

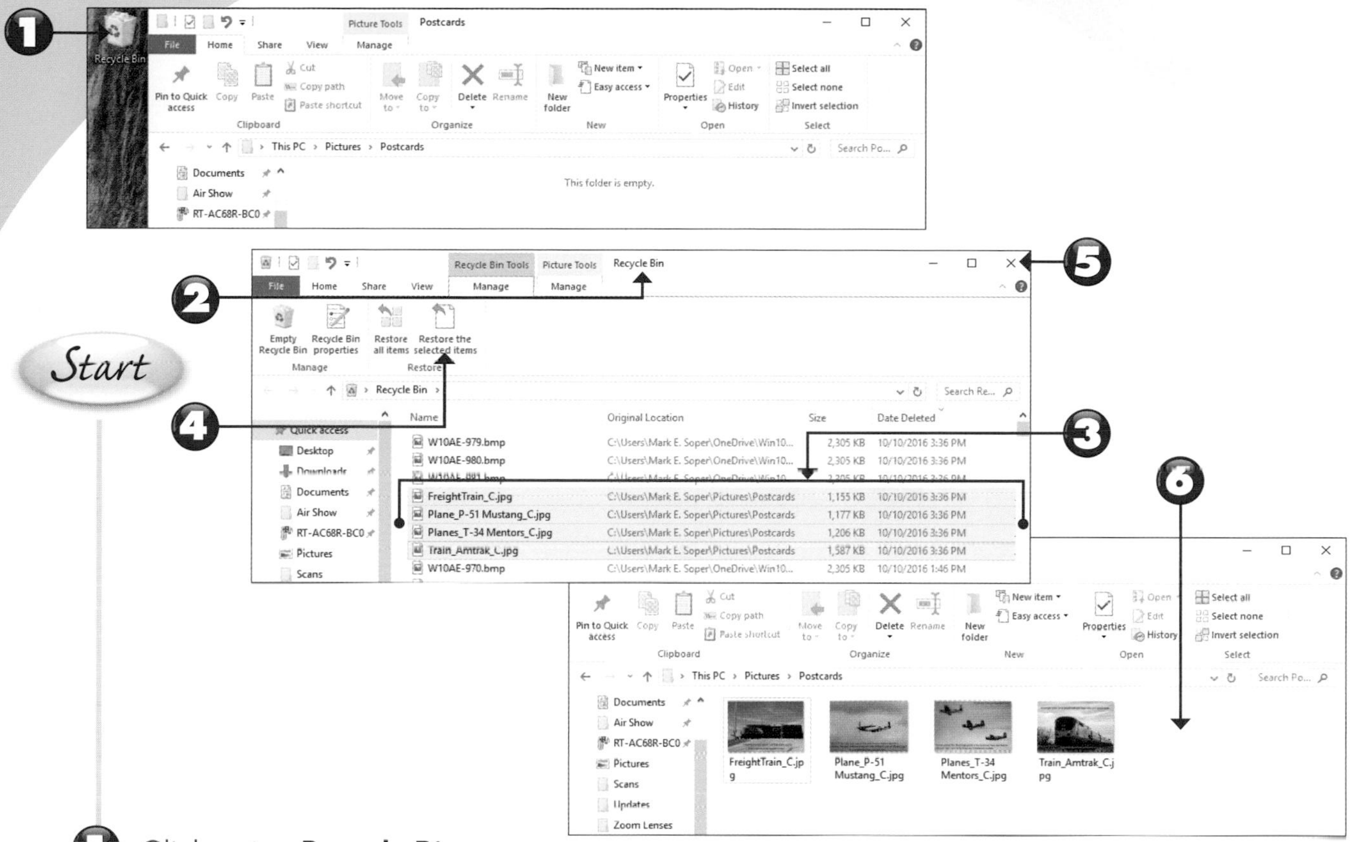

Start

1. Click or tap **Recycle Bin**.
2. Click or tap the **Recycle Bin** folder.
3. Select the files you want to restore.
4. Click or tap **Restore the selected items**.
5. Click or tap to close the Recycle Bin.
6. The files are restored to their original location(s).

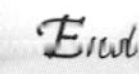

TIP

Recycle Bin Tips If you can't see the Recycle Bin on your desktop, right-click or press and hold an empty area on the desktop, select **View**, and click or tap **Show desktop icons**. To remove files you no longer need, click or tap Empty Recycle Bin. If you send more files to the Recycle Bin than it has room for, the oldest files in the bin are permanently deleted to make room for newer files.

MOVING FILES OR FOLDERS

The Move To command enables you to easily move files or folders to a different location. You can select from a listed destination (as in this example) or choose another location. With either Copy To or Move To, you might be able to pause and continue the process if the process takes more than a few seconds. In this example, you see how to move a folder containing many photos from an external drive to your Pictures folder.

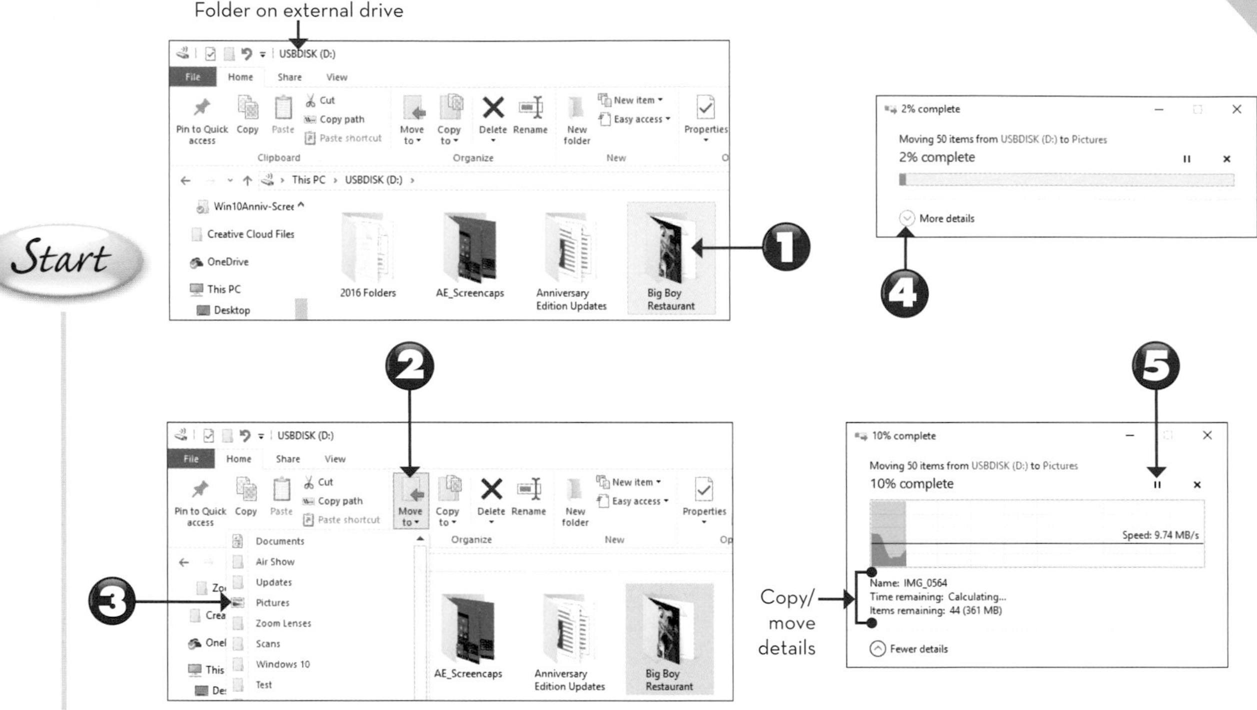

1. Select the folder you want to move.
2. On File Manager's Home tab, open the **Move to** menu.
3. Click or tap **Pictures**.
4. To see more information about the process, click or tap the down arrow next to **More details**.
5. To pause the process, click or tap the **Pause** button.

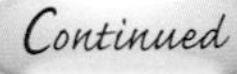

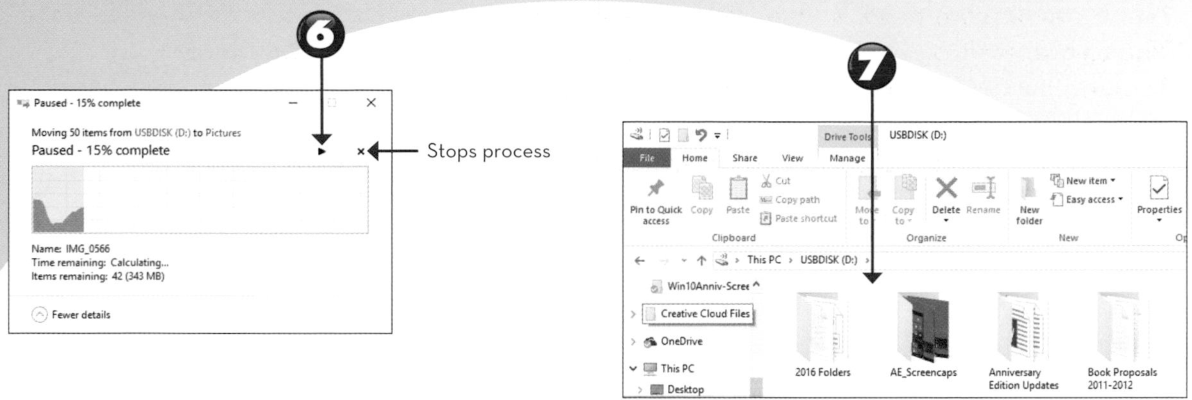

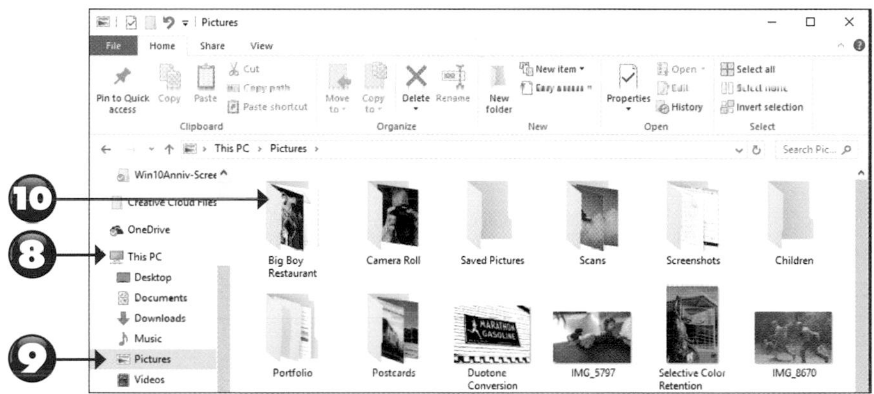

6. To continue the process, click the **Resume** button.

7. The folder has been moved from its original location.

8. Click or tap **This PC**.

9. Click or tap **Pictures**.

10. The folder is in its new location.

End

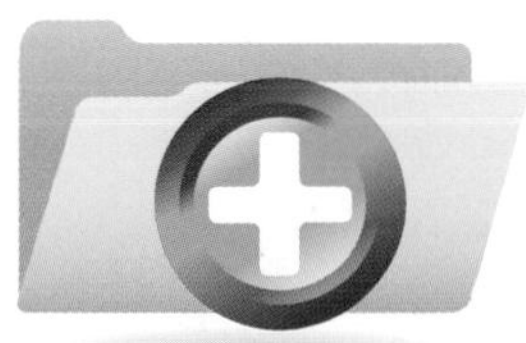

DEALING WITH FILE NAME CONFLICTS

When you copy or move files with File Explorer, you might discover that some files being copied or moved have the same names as files already in the destination location. File Explorer can help you resolve duplicate naming issues. Using a photo file as an example in this task, here's what to do.

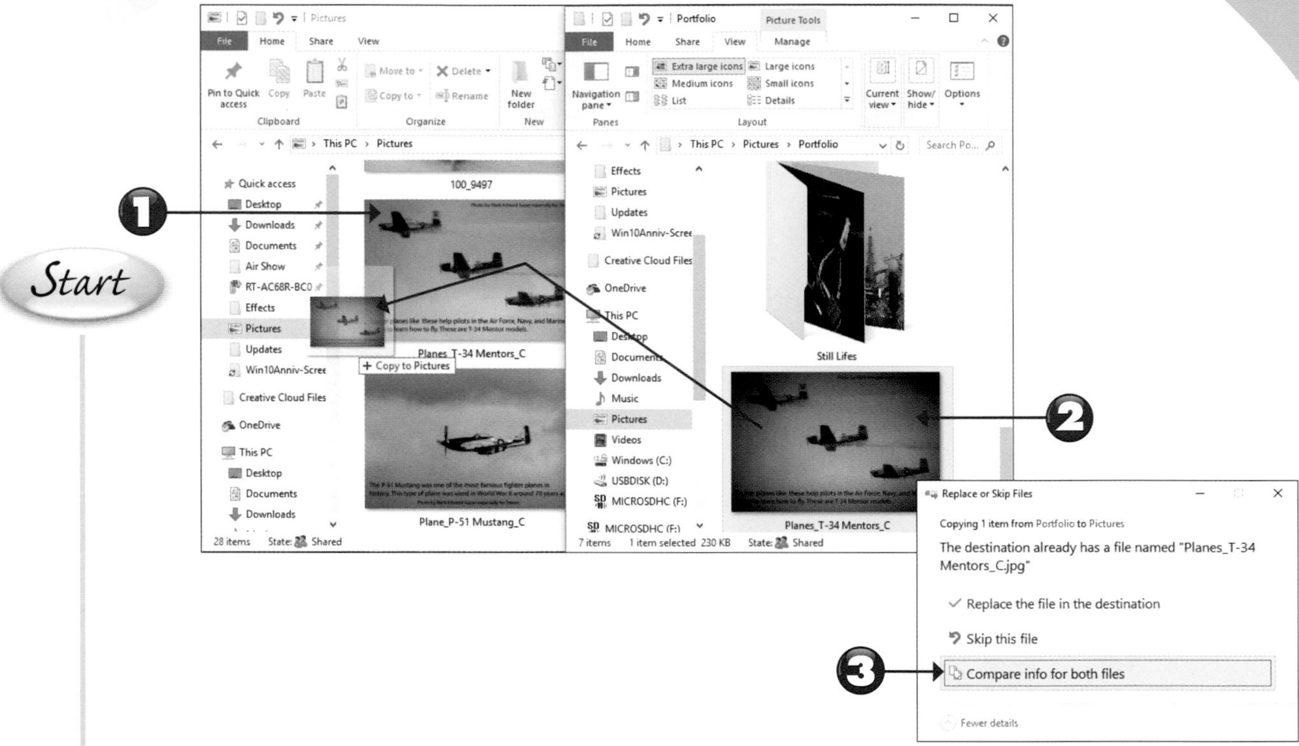

1. Note the photo in the Pictures folder.

2. Copy a different photo with the same name to that folder.

3. Click or tap **Compare info for both files**.

NOTE

Using Drag and Drop In step 2, the file is copied using drag and drop. (You can also use the Copy and Paste or Copy to commands.) If you use drag and drop with a file or folder on the same drive (as in step 2), the default is to move the file from the old to the new location. To copy the file instead, press and hold the **Ctrl** key while dragging the file. The text next to the file/folder thumbnail tells you whether you are copying or moving the file or folder.
If you use drag and drop with a file or folder from a different drive, the default is to copy the file. To move the file instead, press and hold the **Ctrl** key while dragging the file.

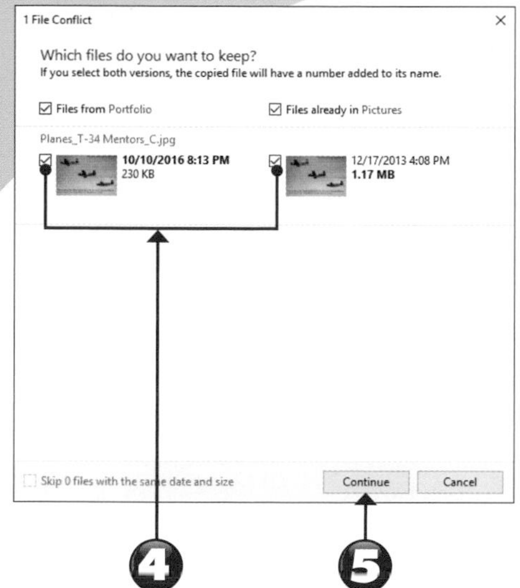

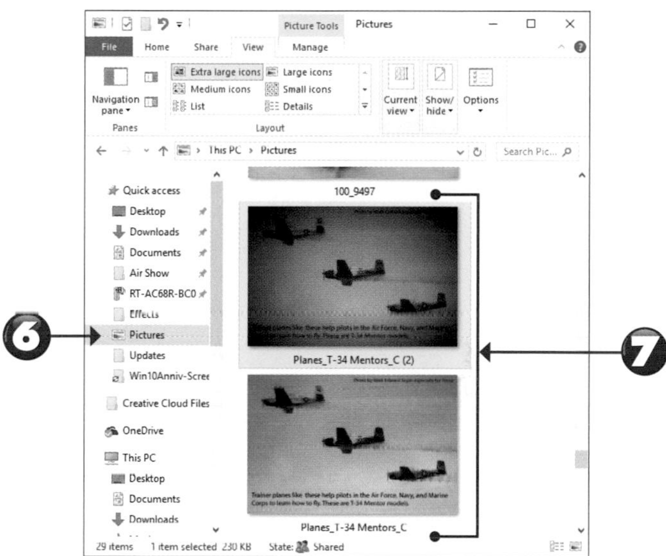

4 To keep both files, click or tap both check boxes.

5 Click or tap **Continue**.

6 Click or tap the destination folder.

7 The copied file with the name conflict is renamed to avoid replacing the original file.

End

NOTE

Dealing with Multiple File Name Conflicts If you copy or move more than one file or folder with a name conflict, choose **Let me decide for each** in step 3. You are then prompted to choose what to do with each file.

BURNING DATA DISCS

You can use options on the Share tab in File Explorer to easily burn CDs or DVDs of your favorite files. Here's how.

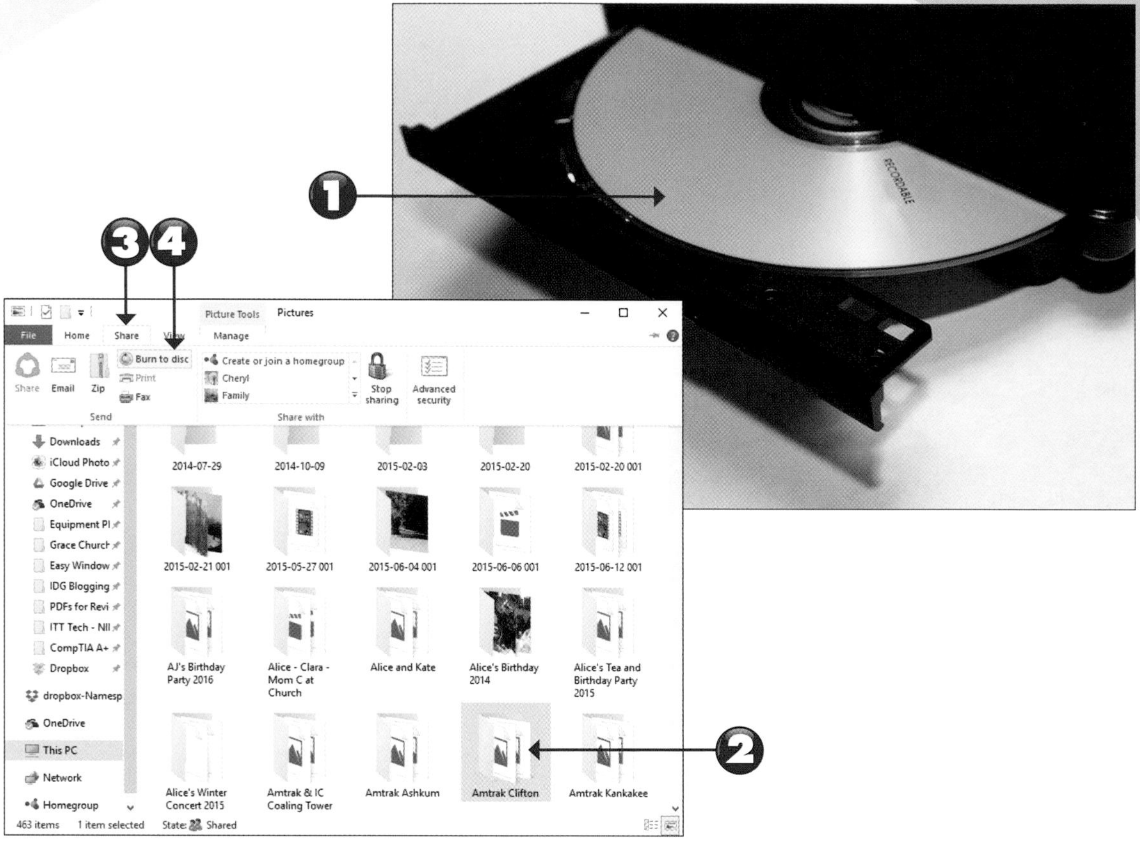

Start

1. Place a writeable disc in your optical drive and close the drive.
2. Select the files or folders you want to burn to an optical disc.
3. Click or tap the **Share** tab.
4. Click or tap **Burn to disc**.

Continued

NOTE

Disc-Formatting Options In step 6 on the next page, choose the **Like a USB flash drive** option if you are using rewriteable (erasable) media such as a CD-RW, DVD-RW, or DVD+RW disc, and you are sharing the disc with Windows XP systems or later versions. Choose the **With a CD/DVD player** option if you aren't sure what type of computer or device will be used with the media or if you are using recordable media (CD-R, DVD+R, or DVD-R).

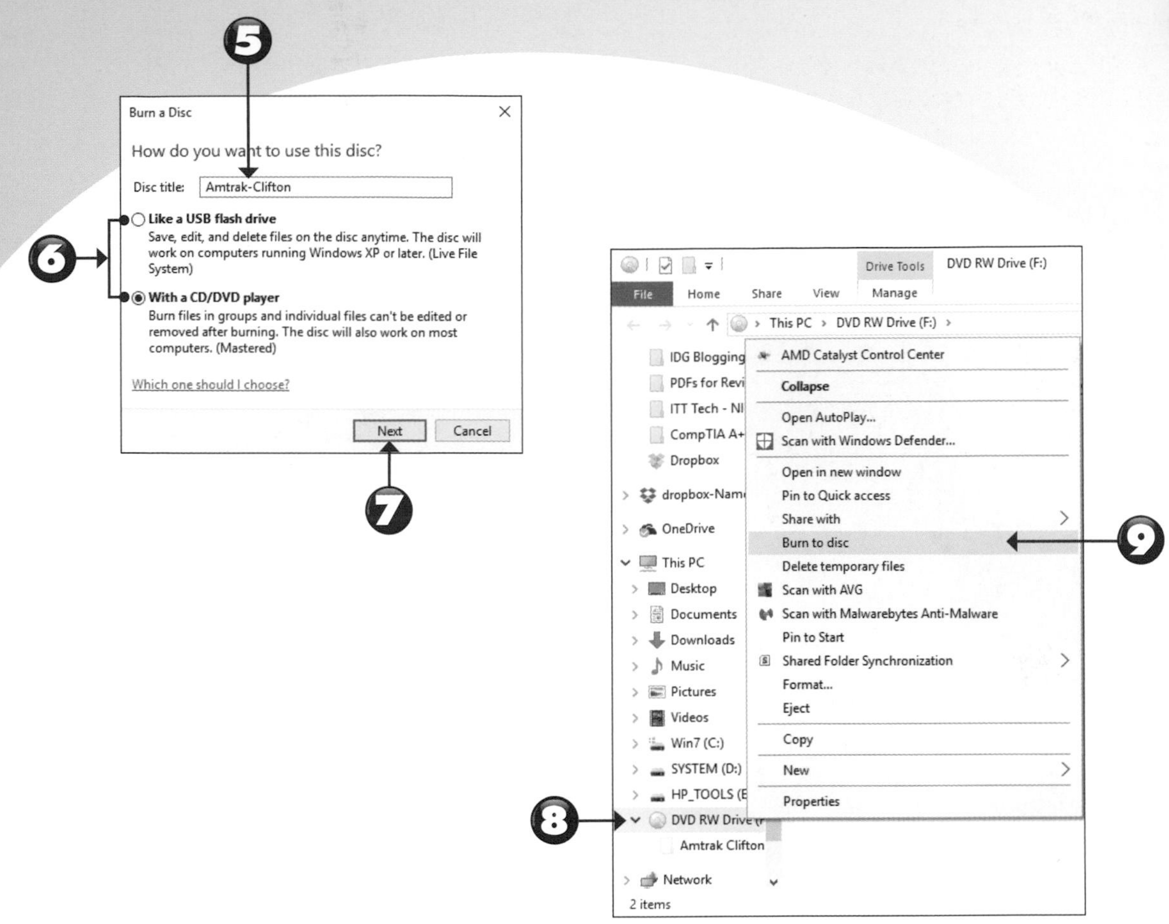

5. Enter a name for the disc.
6. Select the method to use.
7. Click or tap **Next**.
8. Right-click or press and hold the drive letter of your optical drive.
9. Click or tap **Burn to disc**.

Continued

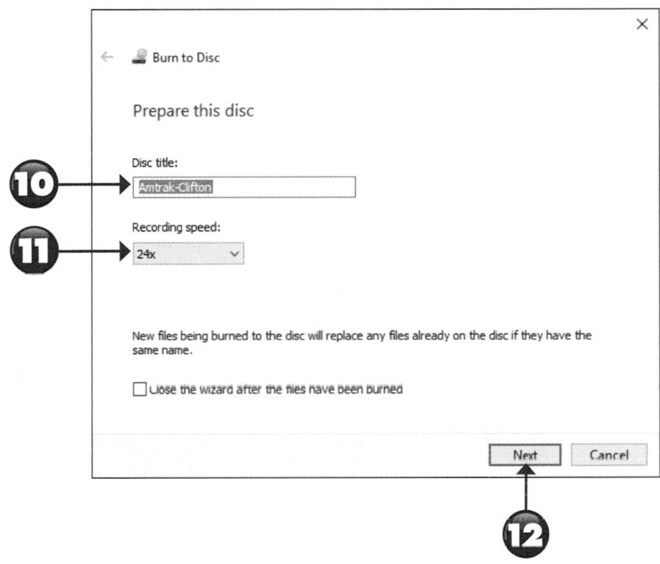

10 Confirm the disc name or type a new name.

11 Confirm or change the recording speed.

12 Click or tap **Next**.

Continued

NOTE

Burning One Disc Only If you don't need to burn additional discs from the files you selected, click or tap the **Close the wizard after the files have been burned** check box shown in steps 10–12 to opt out of additional disc burning steps.

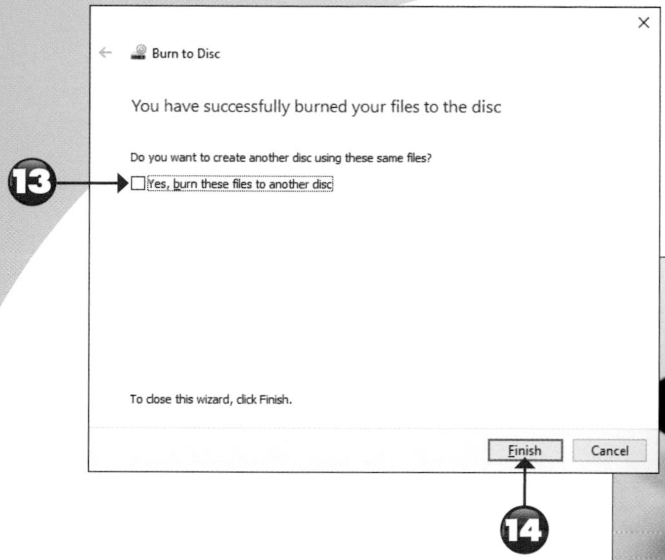

Burn to Disc

You have successfully burned your files to the disc

Do you want to create another disc using these same files?

13 Yes, burn these files to another disc

To close this wizard, click Finish.

Finish 14 Cancel

15

RECORDABLE

13 Click or tap the **Yes, burn these files to another disc** check box if you want to burn another copy of the disc.

14 Click or tap **Finish**.

15 Remove the disc from the drive.

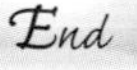

TIP

Recording Speeds Choose a slower recording speed in step 11 if you have had problems using recorded media from your computer on another device, such as a CD player. ■

SORTING AND GROUPING FILES

Windows 10 AE provides a variety of ways to sort and group files to make it easier to find the files you want. This lesson uses some folders containing photos. However, the methods described here can also be used with music files, videos, or other types of documents.

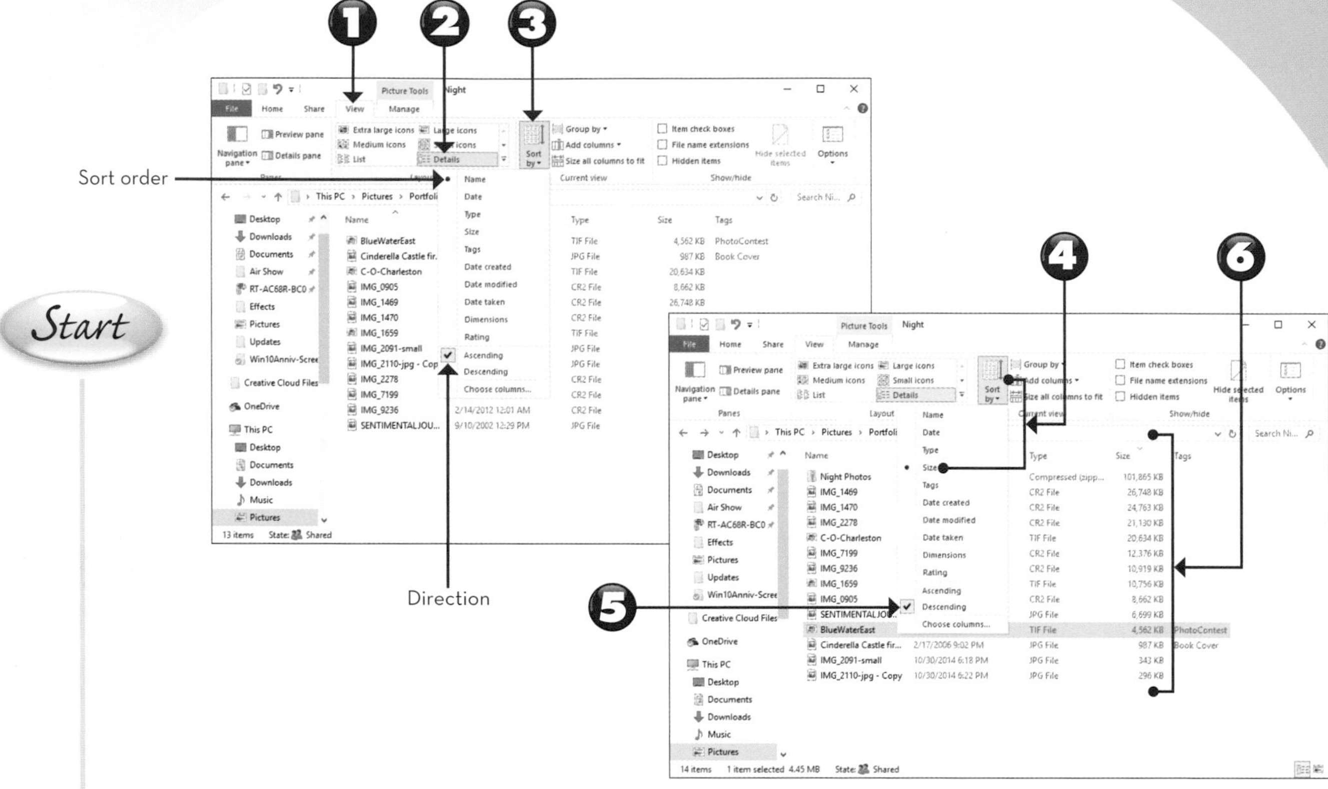

1. Click or tap the **View** tab.

2. Click or tap the **Details** button.

3. Open the **Sort by** menu to see the current sort option (Name, indicated by dot) and direction (Ascending indicated by check mark).

4. Open the **Sort by** menu again, and click or tap **Size** as the **Sort by** setting.

5. **Descending** is selected as the current sort direction.

6. Files are sorted largest to smallest.

Continued

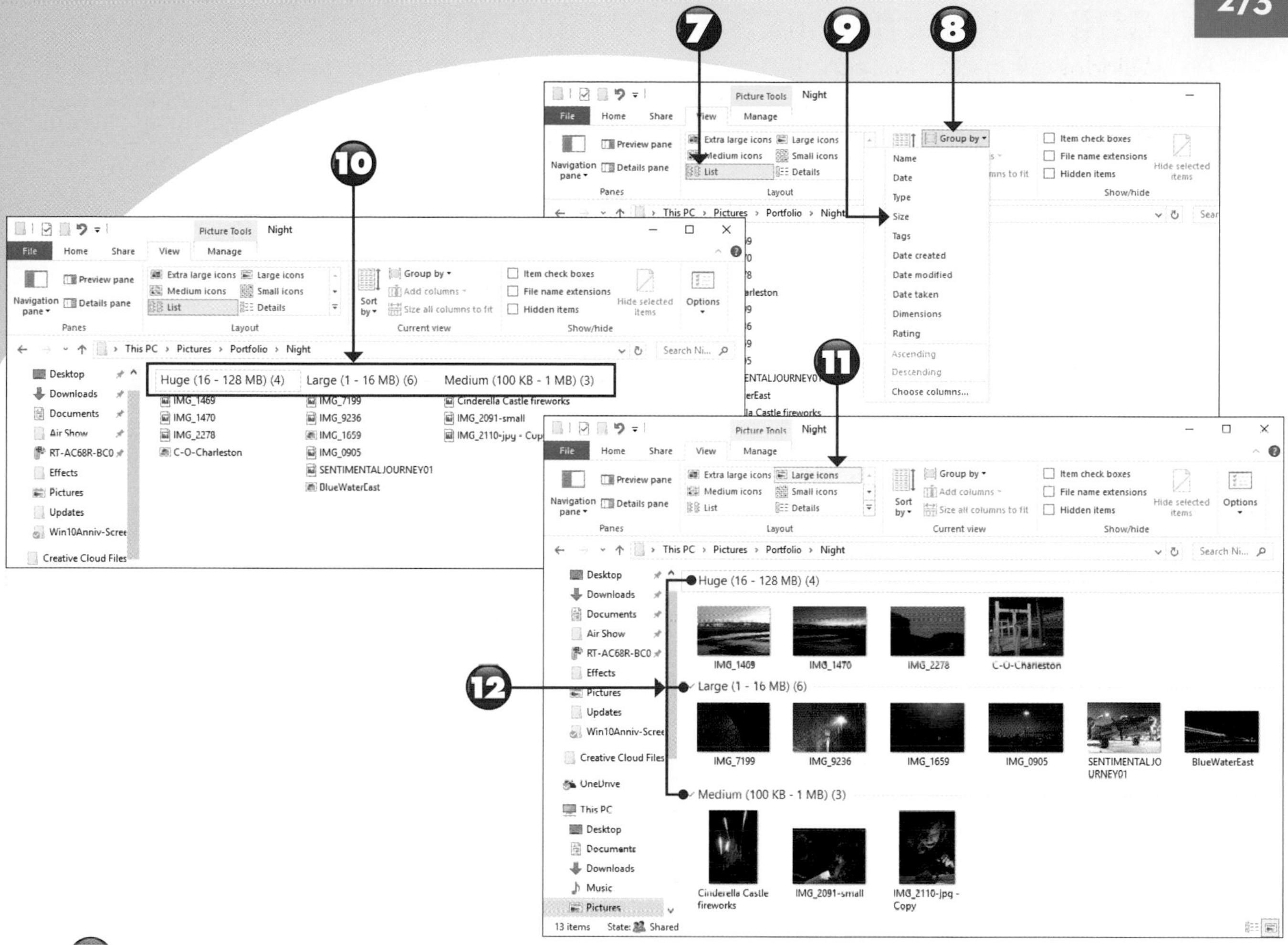

7 Select **List** as the view.

8 Open the **Group by** menu.

9 Click or tap **Size**.

10 Files are grouped by size.

11 Select **Large icons** as the view.

12 Files are grouped by size.

End

TIP

Adding Group Columns and Ungrouping Files To choose other items to group files by or to display in Details view, click or tap **Choose columns** in the Group menu. To stop grouping items, click or tap **(None)** in the Group menu.

CREATING ZIP FILES WITH THE SHARE TAB

Zip files are handy because you can store multiple files and folders into a single file that's usually smaller than the combined size of the original files. The resulting file is also easier to email or upload. Zip file creation is available from the Share tab in File Explorer.

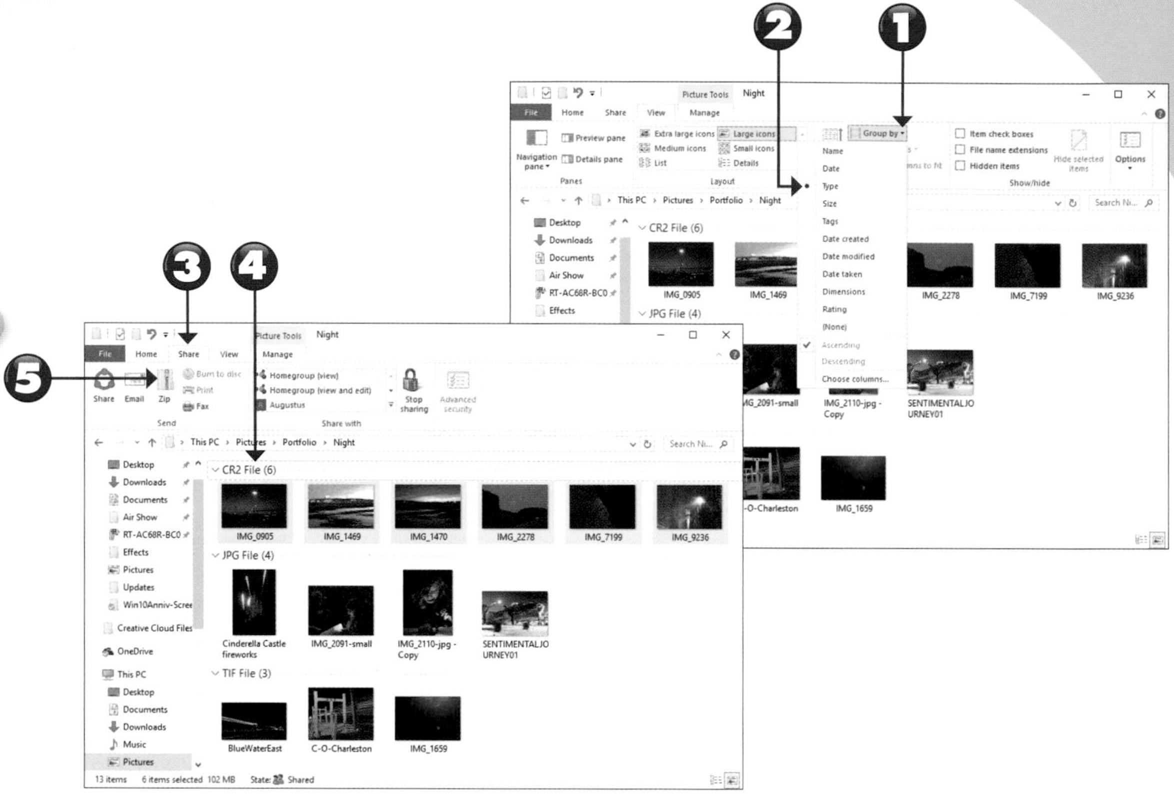

Start

1. From the View tab, open the **Group by** menu.
2. Click or tap **Type**.
3. Click or tap the **Share** tab.
4. Click or tap a group category to select all files.
5. Click or tap **Zip**.

Continued

NOTE

Easy File Selection with Grouped Files When files are grouped, you can select all the files in the group by clicking the group name, such as CR2 File (as in step 4).

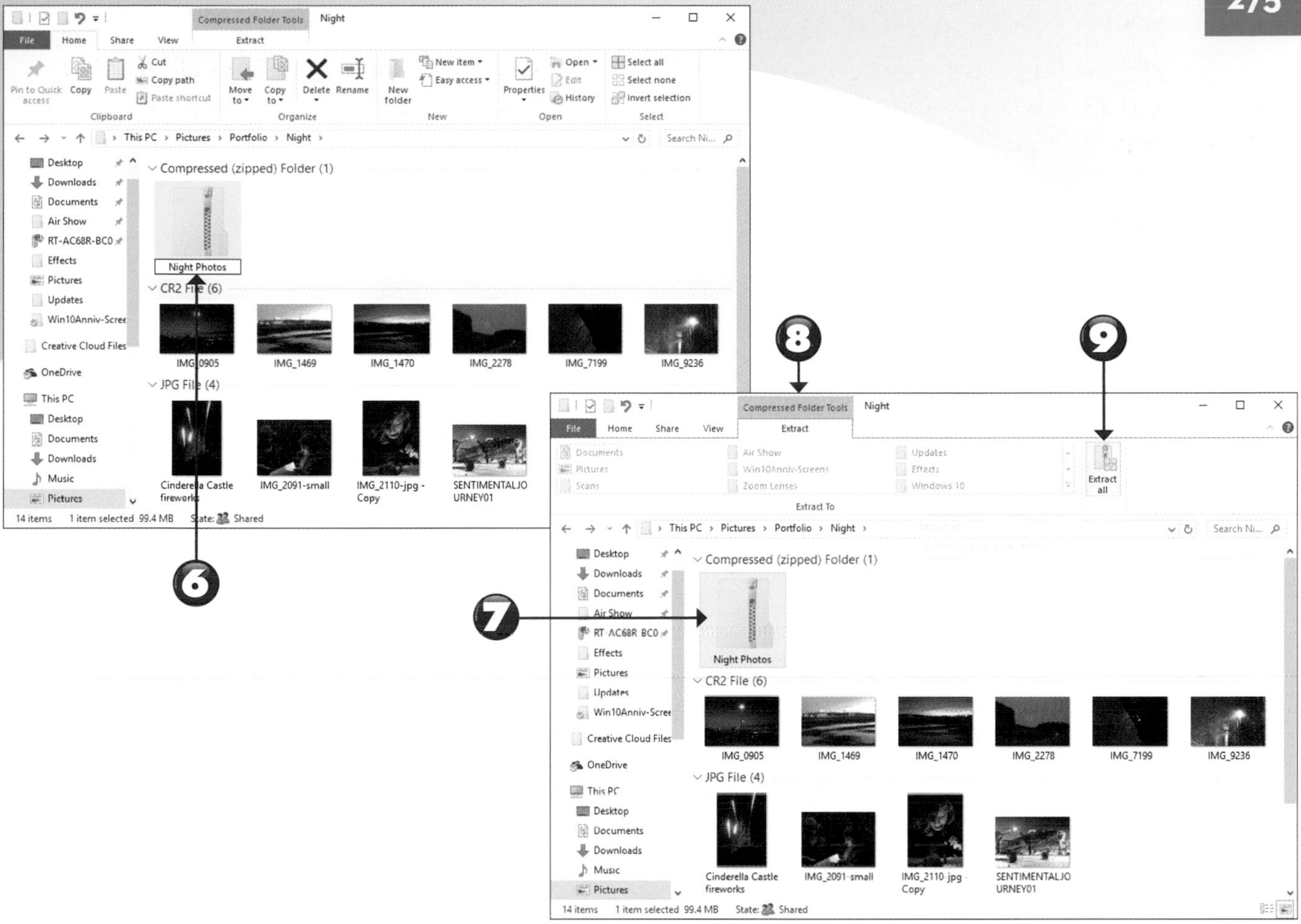

6. Enter a new name for the Zip file. Press **Enter** or click outside the name box when finished.

7. When you need to extract files from the Zip file, click or tap the Zip file.

8. Click or tap **Compressed Folder Tools**.

9. Click or tap the **Extract all** button.

End

NOTE

Extracting Files You can use the **Extract all** button to copy all files from the Zip file to a folder named after the Zip file in the current location. You can also specify a different destination.

NOTE

Renaming the Zip File You can rename a Zip file or any other type of file by using the **Rename** button on the **Home** tab.

SYNCING A FOLDER WITH ONEDRIVE

Microsoft provides OneDrive cloud-based storage to everyone with a Microsoft account and Internet access. You can synchronize local files and folders with OneDrive. You can use this feature to back up files to the cloud or to make sure that your files are available wherever you need them, on the go or at your desk. Here's how.

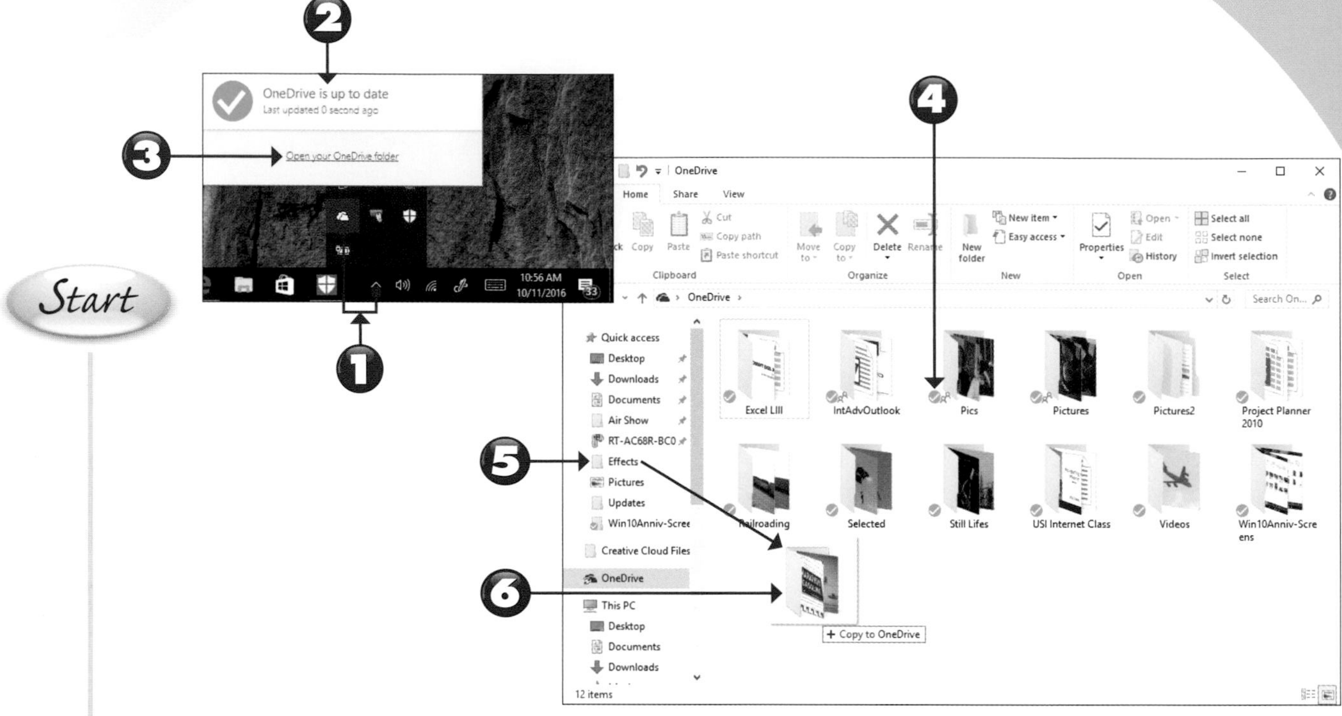

1. From the taskbar, click or tap the OneDrive icon. Click or tap the up arrow to display the OneDrive icon if necessary.
2. The current status is displayed.
3. Click or tap **Open your OneDrive folder**.
4. File Explorer opens and displays your OneDrive folders and files. Green check marks indicate files and folders synchronized with OneDrive.
5. Navigate to the folder you want to sync.
6. Drag and drop it to copy it to OneDrive.

Continued

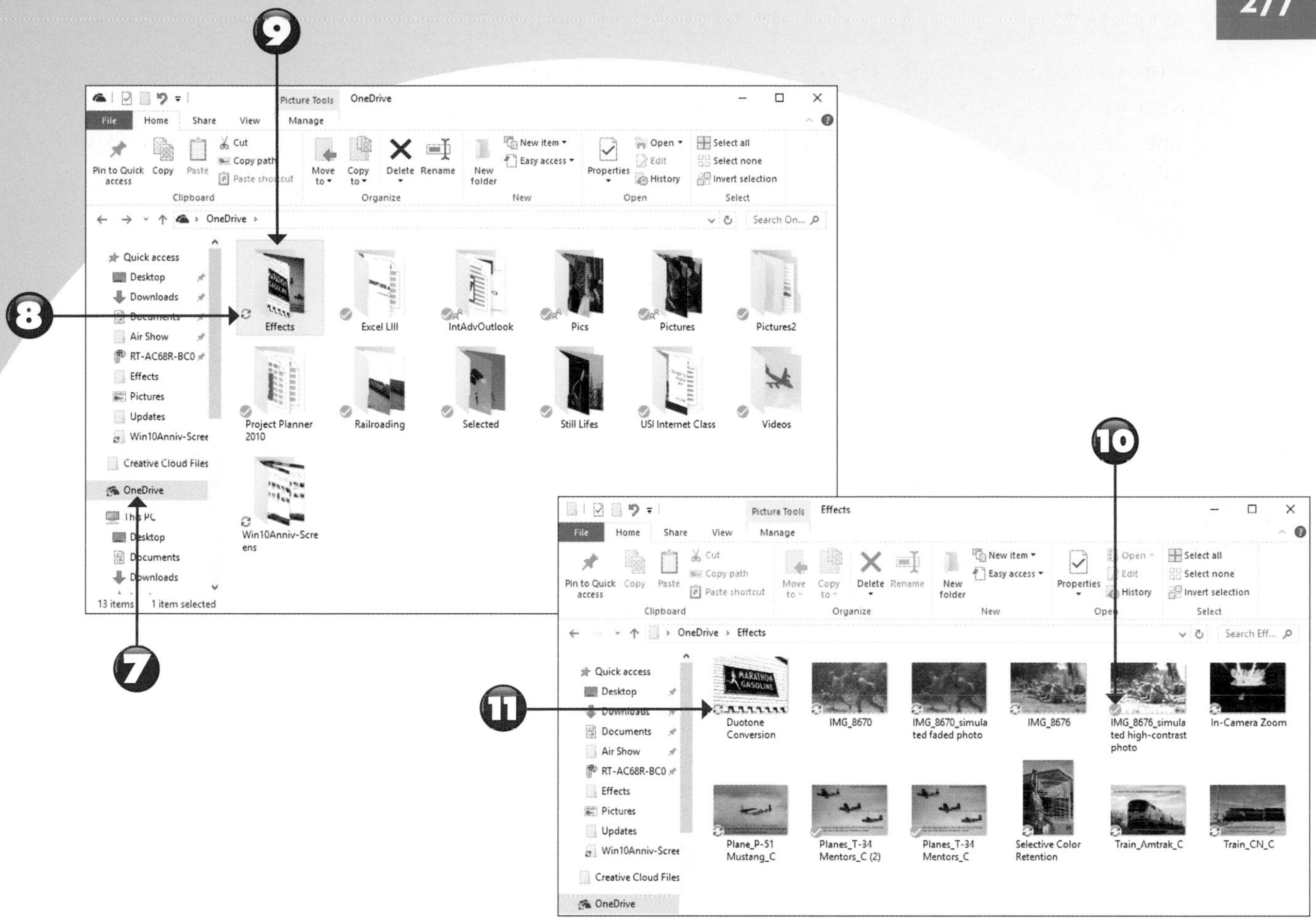

7. Click or tap **OneDrive** (if it is not already open).

8. Folders are being synced to OneDrive.

9. Click or tap the folder you copied in step 6 to see the files that are still syncing.

10. Files that have finished syncing to OneDrive have a green check mark.

11. Files are still in the process of syncing to OneDrive.

End

CONFIGURING ONEDRIVE

If you've already used OneDrive with a different computer, you can sync files and folders on OneDrive with the computer you're currently using. This section covers how to configure this and other options.

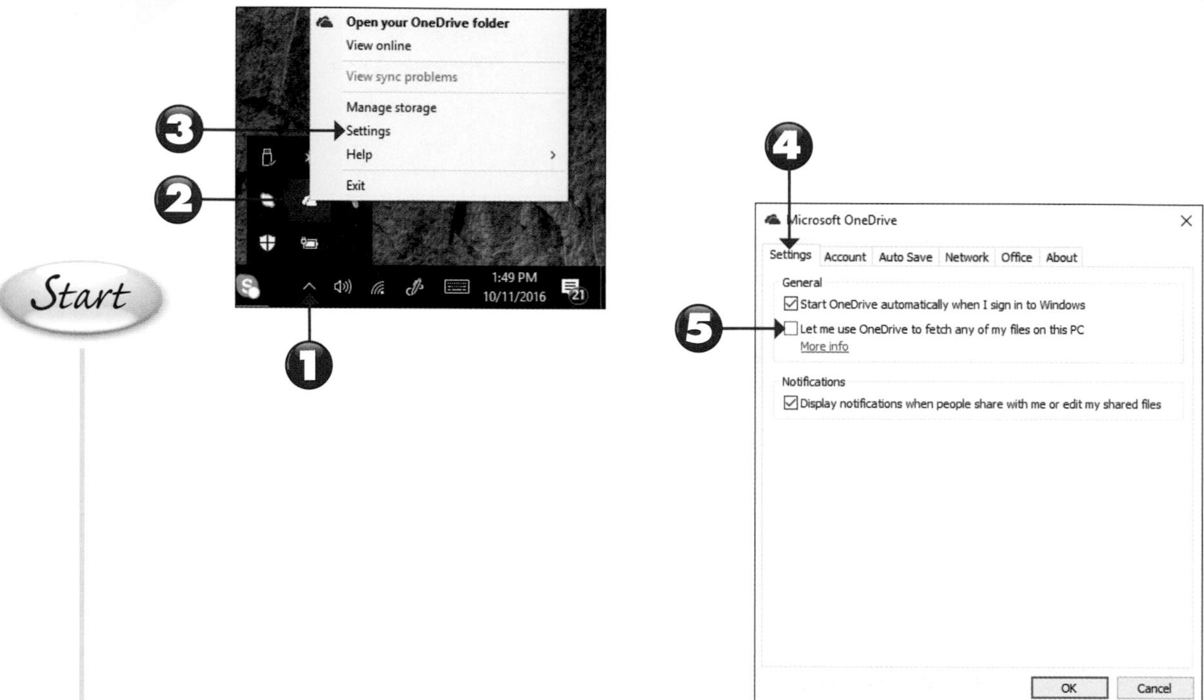

1. If the OneDrive icon is not visible in the taskbar, click or tap the up arrow to view hidden icons and display the OneDrive icon.
2. Right-click or press and hold the **OneDrive** icon.
3. Click or tap **Settings**.
4. Click or tap the **Settings** tab.
5. Click or tap the empty **Let me use OneDrive...** box if you want OneDrive to fetch files from this PC so you can use them on another PC.

Continued

NOTE

Learning More About OneDrive Options Click or tap the **More info** link whenever it's available to find out more about a OneDrive option.

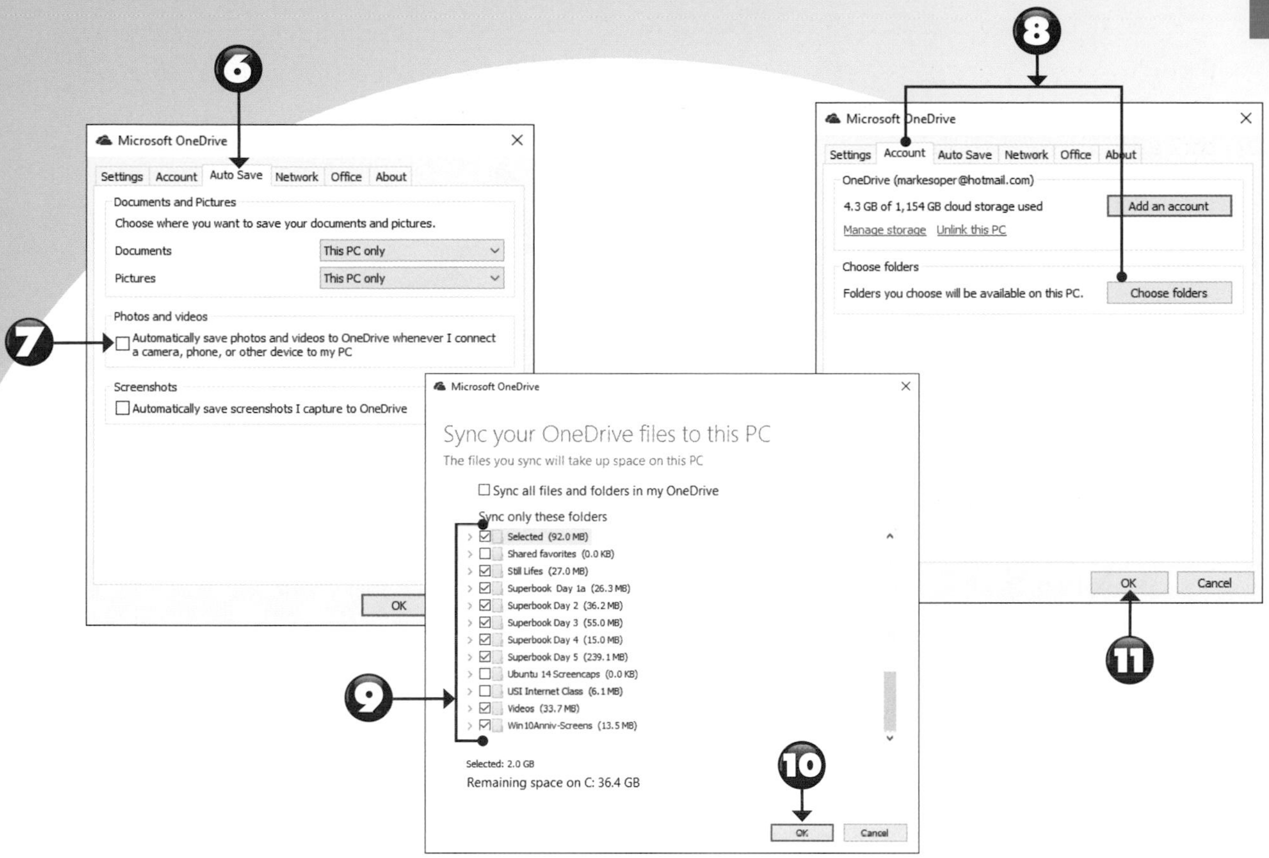

6. Click or tap the **Auto Save** tab.

7. Click or tap **Automatically save photos** if you want OneDrive to automatically save photos and videos whenever you connect a device containing photos and/or videos.

8. Click or tap the **Account** tab, and then the **Choose folders** button to view the folders stored in the cloud on OneDrive, and select the ones you want to sync to this computer.

9. Click or tap the empty check box for each OneDrive folder you want to sync to your device. Clear check boxes for folders you don't want to sync.

10. Click or tap **OK** when finished.

11. Click or tap **OK** when finished configuring OneDrive.

End

NOTE

Viewing OneDrive Folders and Files in Your Browser and on Your Device You can also use your web browser to view and download OneDrive files. Go to https://onedrive.live.com, log in if prompted, and your OneDrive folders and files appear in your browser window.

To install a OneDrive app for your device, log in to OneDrive from your browser and click or tap **Get the OneDrive apps**. You can also open the menu (three-line icon) and click or tap **Get the OneDrive apps** to learn more or start the process.

DISCOVERING AND USING WINDOWS 10 AE'S TOOLS AND ACCESSORIES

Windows 10 AE includes a variety of apps. Some apps, such as Money and Sports, are designed to perform a variety of tasks and are covered in other chapters. This chapter focuses on Windows accessories such as Notepad and the Character Map as well as Universal apps designed for specialized tasks, such as Calculator and Alarms & Clock. Although there are differences, most apps work similarly after you open them.

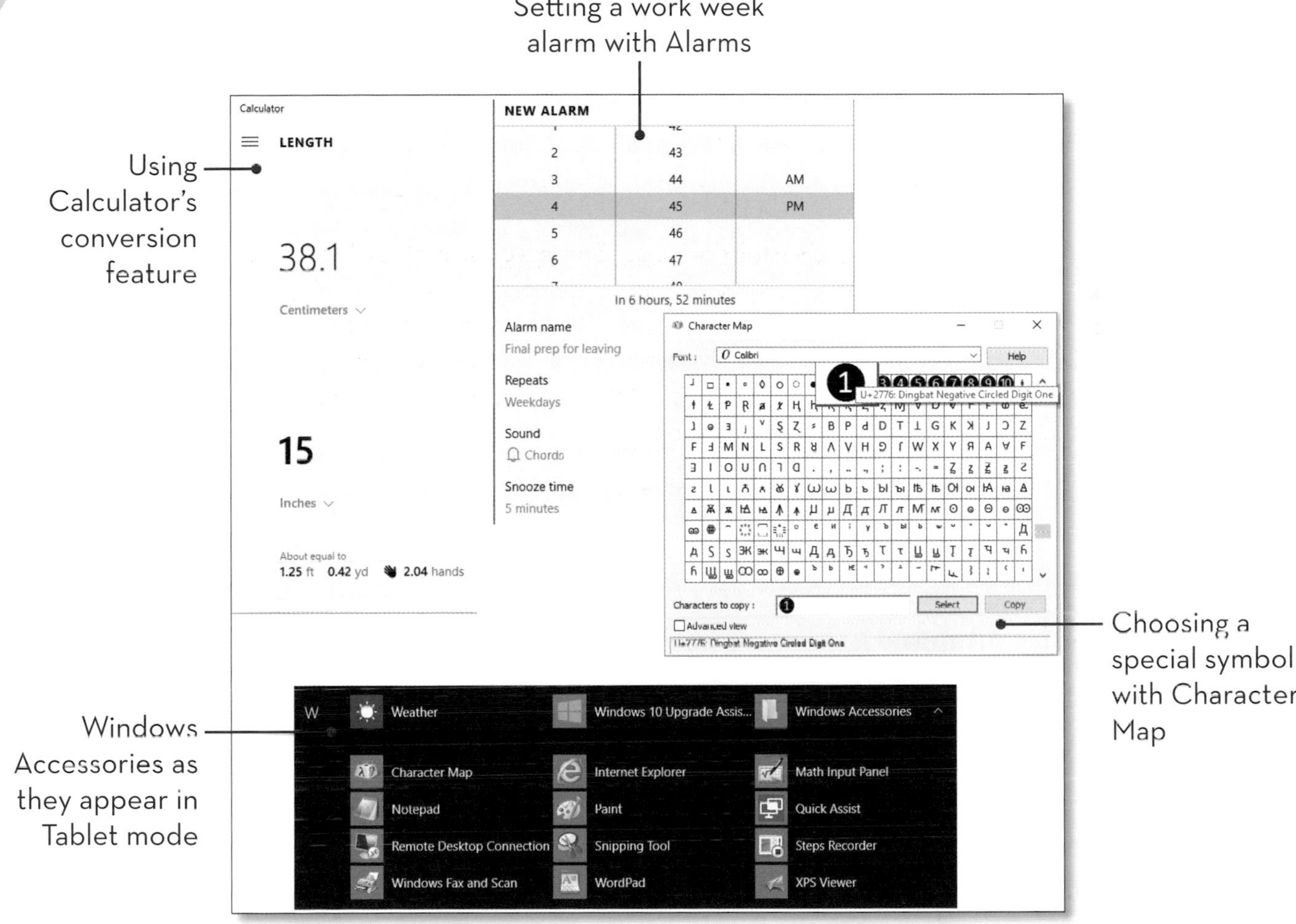

Setting a work week alarm with Alarms
Using Calculator's conversion feature
Choosing a special symbol with Character Map
Windows Accessories as they appear in Tablet mode
Calculator
LENGTH
38.1
Centimeters
15
Inches
About equal to
1.25 ft 0.42 yd 2.04 hands
NEW ALARM
2 43
3 44 AM
4 45 PM
5 46
6 47
In 6 hours, 52 minutes
Alarm name
Final prep for leaving
Repeats
Weekdays
Sound
Chords
Snooze time
5 minutes
Character Map
Font : Colbri
Help
U+2776: Dingbat Negative Circled Digit One
Characters to copy :
Select
Copy
Advanced view
Weather
Windows 10 Upgrade Assis...
Windows Accessories
Character Map
Internet Explorer
Math Input Panel
Notepad
Paint
Quick Assist
Remote Desktop Connection
Snipping Tool
Steps Recorder
Windows Fax and Scan
WordPad
XPS Viewer

FINDING ACCESSORIES AND TOOLS IN TABLET MODE

To find Windows tools from the Start menu in Tablet mode, you must dig in to the All Apps menu. Here's what you'll find.

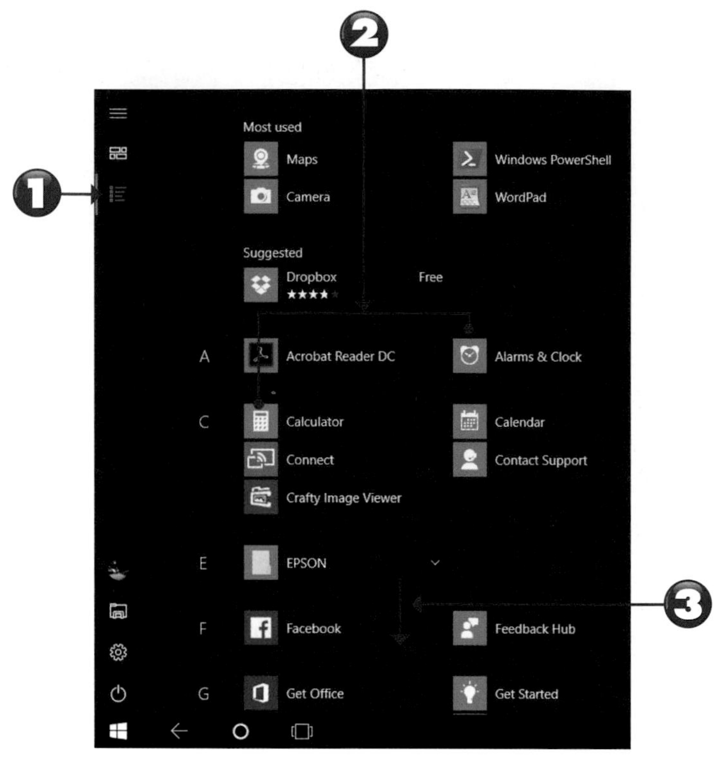

1. Click or tap **All apps**.

2. Alarms & Clock and Calendar apps.

3. Flick up or scroll down to see additional Windows apps covered in this chapter.

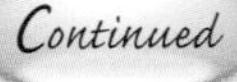

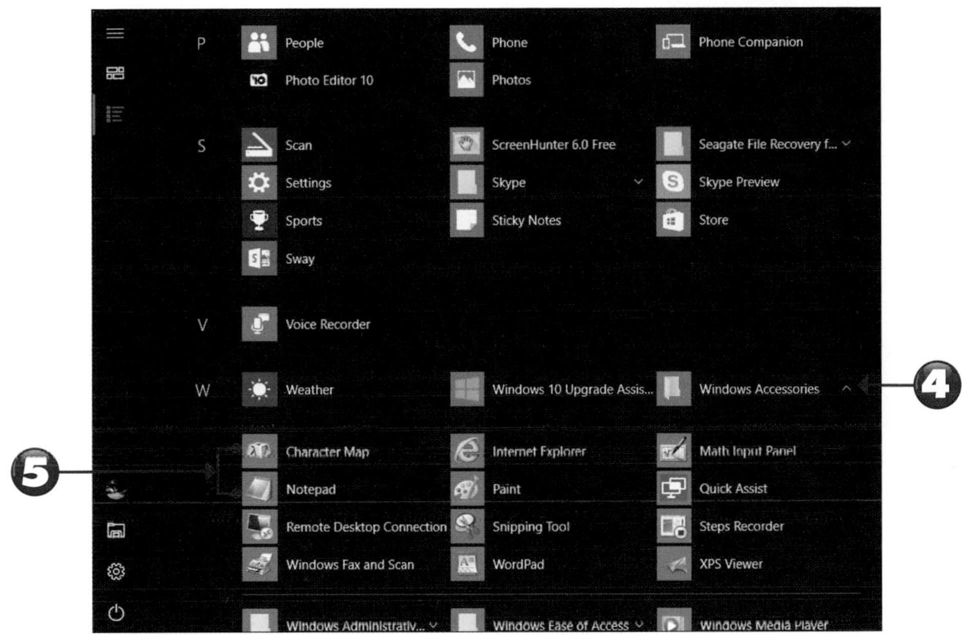

4. Click or tap the arrow for the **Windows Accessories** folder to see more Windows tools.

5. Note the Character Map and Notepad.

End

NOTE

Finding Windows Tools in Desktop Mode Click or tap the **Start** button, and then scroll down to find Alarms, Clock, and Calculator. Click or tap the **Windows Accessories** folder to find Notepad, Character Map, and other accessories.

SETTING ALARMS WITH THE ALARMS & CLOCK APP

You can use the Modern UI Alarms & Clock app as a stopwatch, an alarm clock, or a timer. Here's how to use it as an alarm clock to leave for work Monday through Friday.

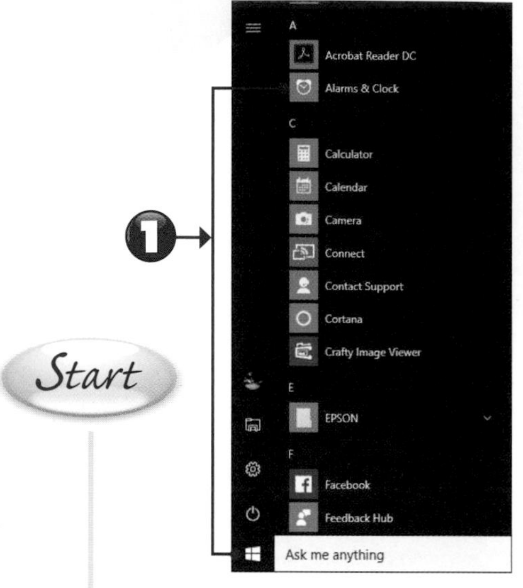

Start

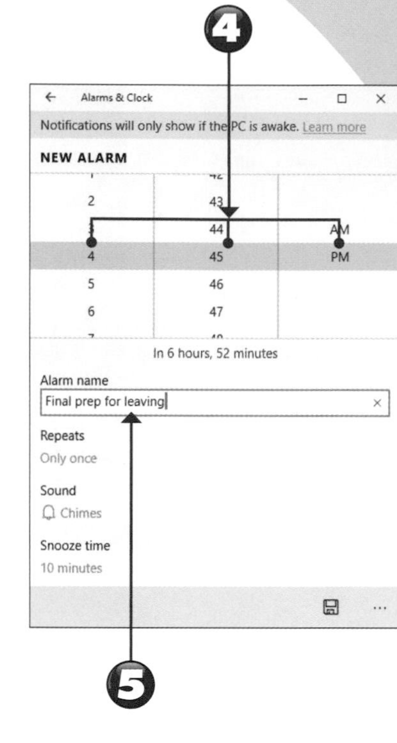

1. Click or tap **Start** (Desktop mode, shown) or **All apps** (Tablet mode), and then **Alarms & Clock**.
2. The Good Morning alarm is automatically set up. Click or press and drag the button to turn it on.
3. Click or tap the plus (+) sign to set up a new alarm.
4. Click or tap each column, and scroll with your finger or mouse to select hour, minute, and AM/PM settings.
5. Type in a unique name for the alarm.

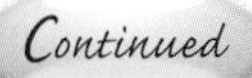
Continued

NOTE

Modern/Universal UI Appearance Modern UI and Universal UI apps (apps that also run on Windows 10 Mobile) run full screen in Tablet mode. Illustrations in this chapter use desktop mode to save space.

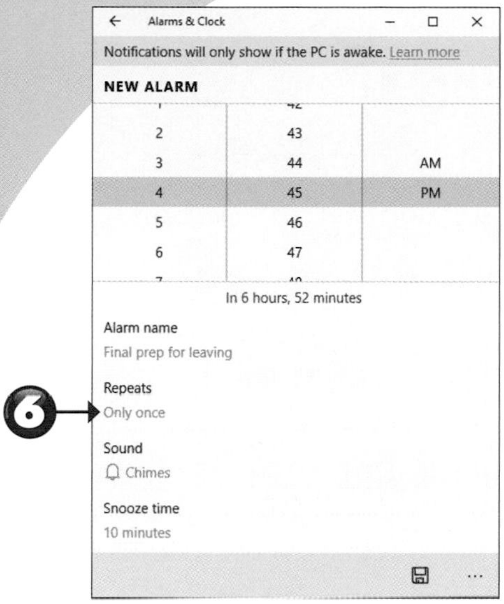

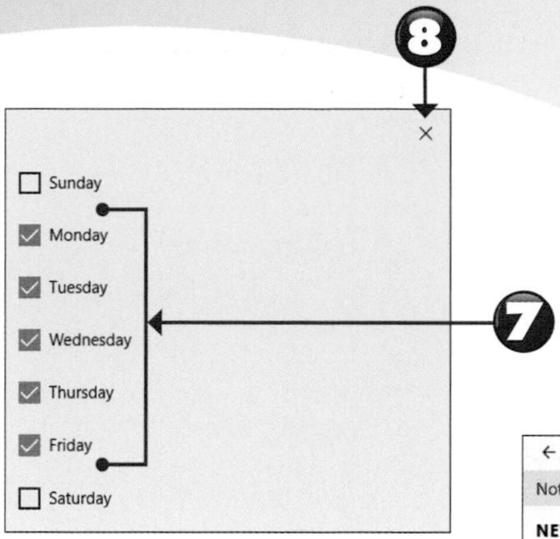

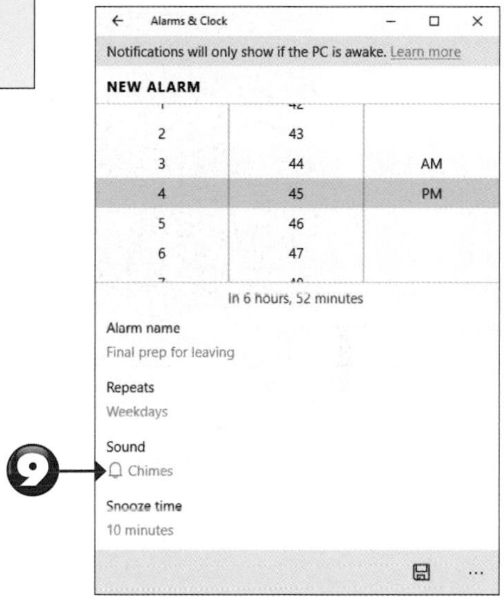

6. Click or tap to select which day(s) of the week the alarm repeats.

7. Click or tap the check box for each day of the week.

8. Click or tap the **X** (Close) button to continue.

9. Click or tap to select a different alarm sound.

Continued

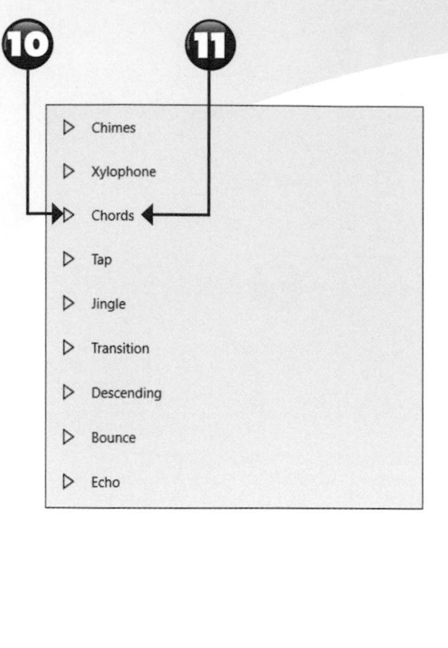

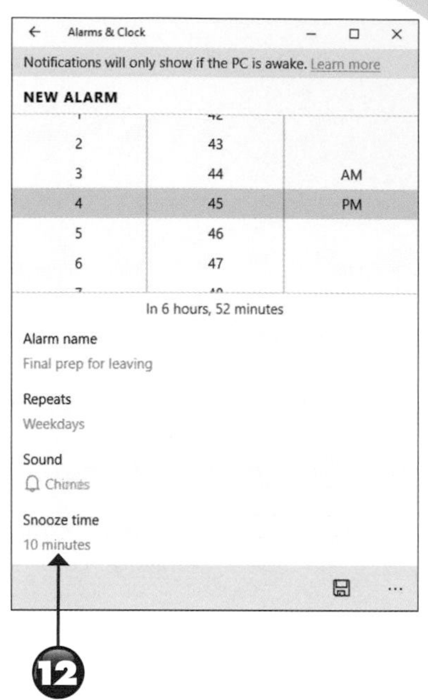

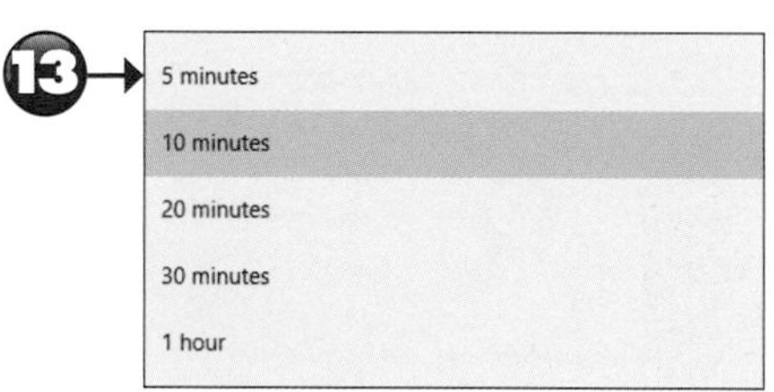

10. Click or tap to preview a sound.
11. Click or tap a sound to select it.
12. Click or tap to select a different snooze interval.
13. Tap the snooze interval desired.

Continued

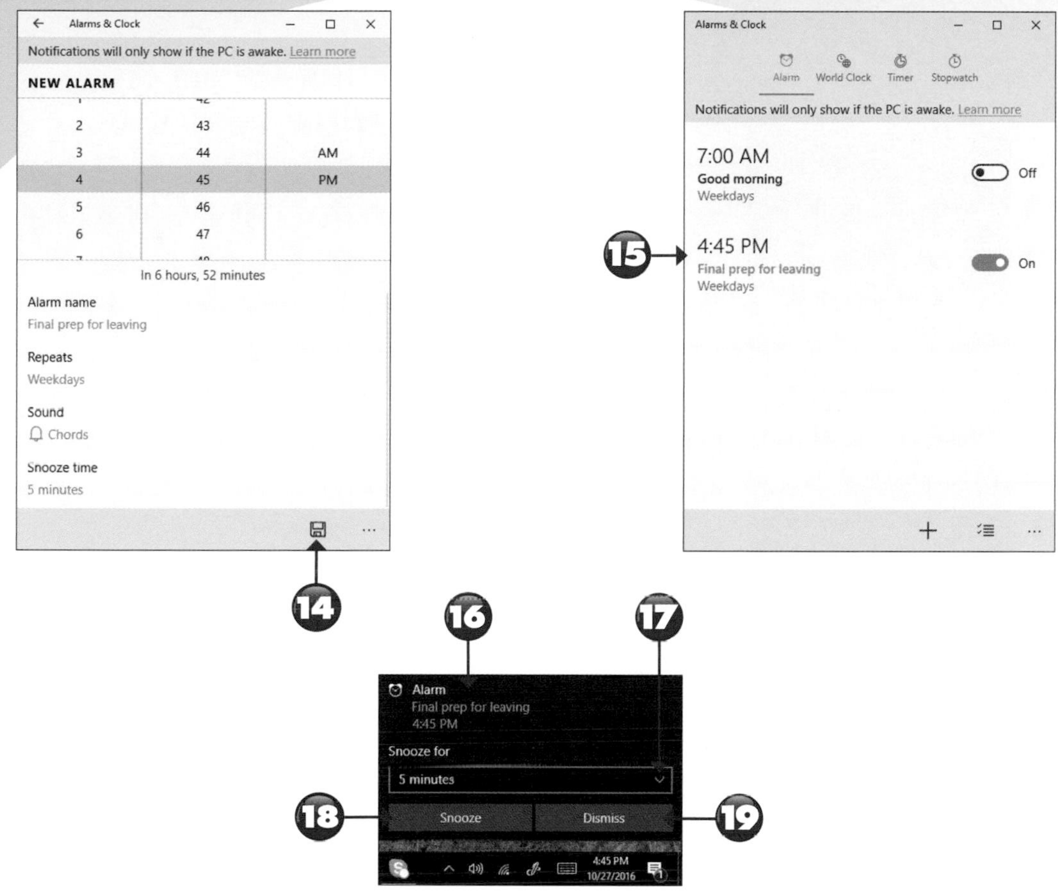

14 Click the **Save** icon to save the alarm.

15 The new alarm is added to the Alarms & Clock app screen.

16 The alarm is displayed in the Notification area when triggered.

17 Click or tap to change the snooze interval.

18 Click or tap to snooze the alarm.

19 Click or tap to shut off the alarm.

End

CONVERTING NUMBER VALUES WITH CALCULATOR

Windows 10 AE's Calculator includes a powerful conversion feature as well as standard and scientific calculations. Here's how to use it.

Start

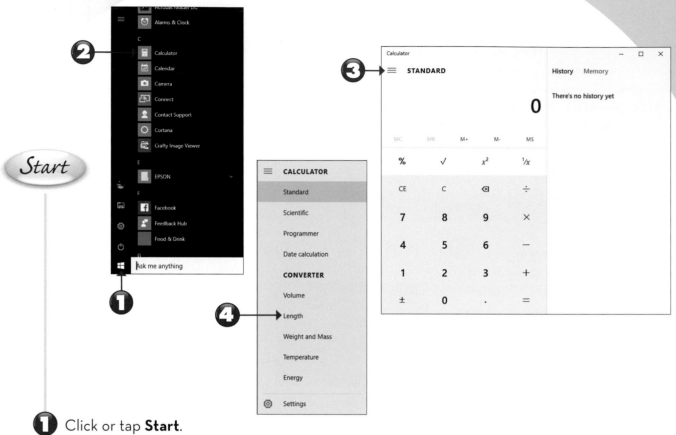

1. Click or tap **Start**.
2. Click or tap **Calculator**.
3. Click or tap the **Menu** button.
4. Select the type of conversion to perform.

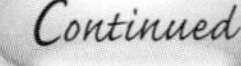

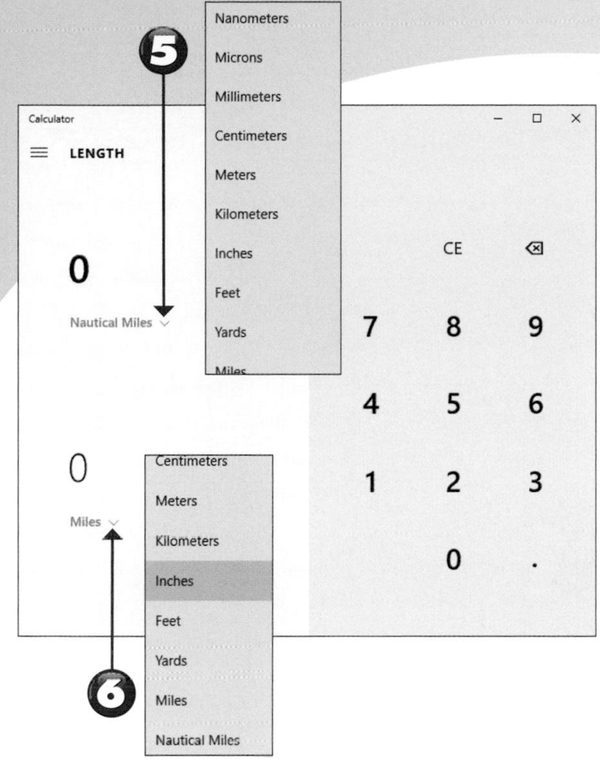

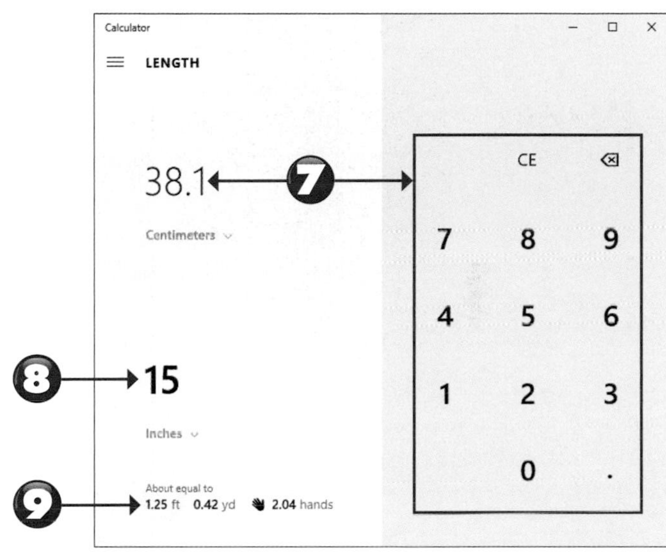

5. Select the units to convert from.
6. Select the units to convert to.
7. Enter the value.
8. The answer appears.
9. Other common measurements for the value are listed here.

End

ENABLING WORD WRAP IN NOTEPAD

Notepad is a simple text editor included in Windows 10 AE. You can use it for note taking and for creating lists of items. When you type a long line of text into Notepad, the text might extend past the right edge of the window. Here's how to search for the app and set Notepad so you can see all of the text.

Start

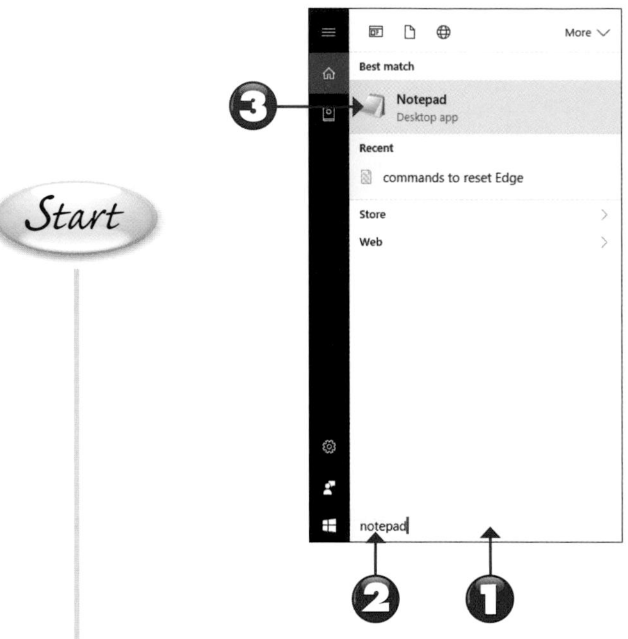

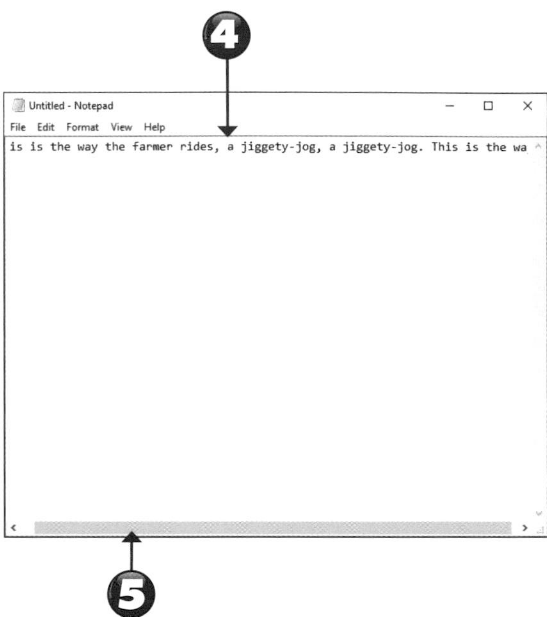

1. Click or tap the **Cortana/Search** window.
2. Type **Notepad**.
3. Click or tap **Notepad**.
4. Type some text (do *not* press the Enter key).
5. Type text until the scrollbar appears.

Continued

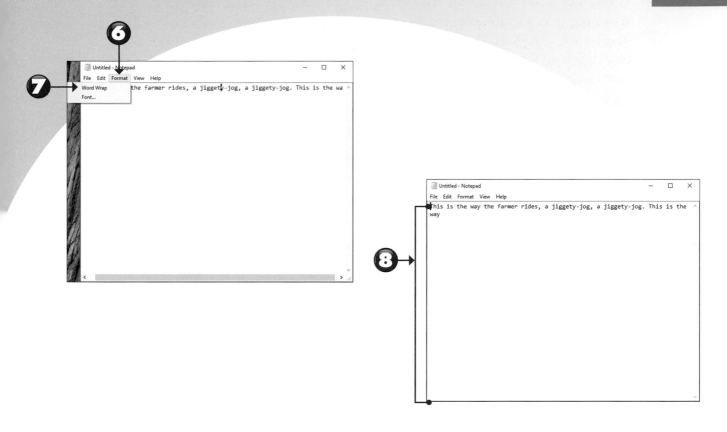

6 Tap or click **Format**.

7 Tap or click **Word Wrap**.

8 The scrollbar vanishes because all text is now visible.

End

NOTE

Word Wrap Benefits and Drawbacks Enable Word Wrap to see an entire paragraph without scrolling or if you want to print your Notepad text. However, if you are using Notepad along with another app, such as WordPad, Word, or a web browser, be sure to disable Word Wrap before copying and pasting text. If you leave Word Wrap enabled, the line breaks you see onscreen will also be used when the text is pasted.

USING CHARACTER MAP WITH WORDPAD

If you need to add special characters or icons to a document, you can use the Character Map app in the Windows Accessories folder to copy the character you want to use. This example uses Character Map with WordPad, but you can use Character Map with any app that supports text.

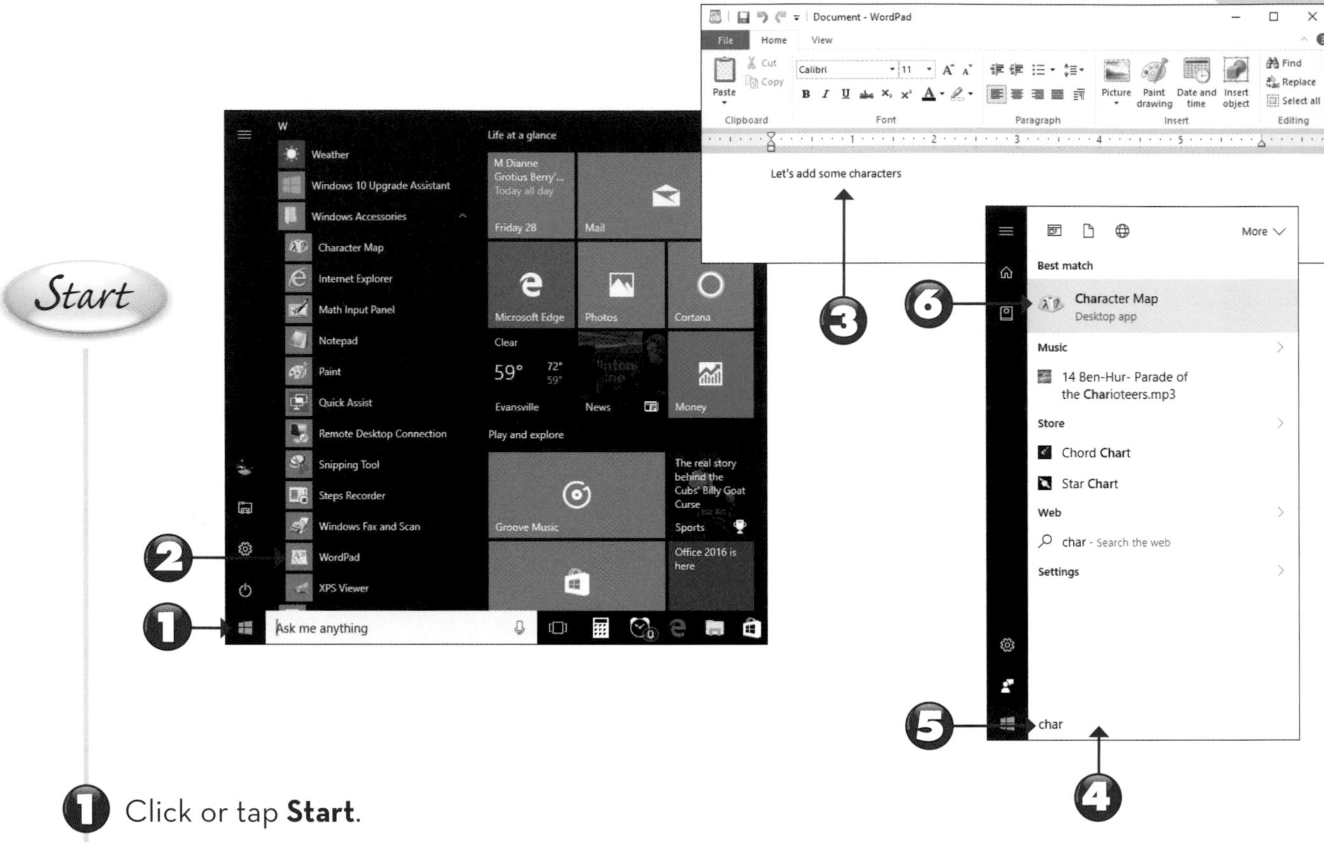

1. Click or tap **Start**.
2. From the Apps (shown) or All Apps menu, click or tap **WordPad**.
3. Add text.
4. Click or tap the **Cortana/Search** box.
5. Type **char**.
6. Click or tap **Character Map** in the search results.

Continued

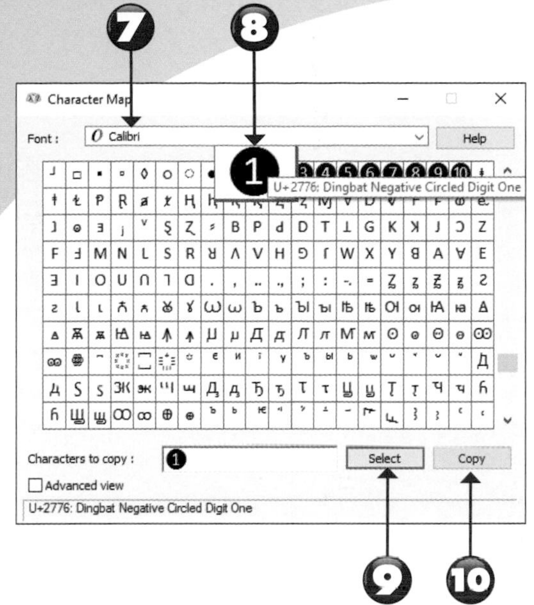

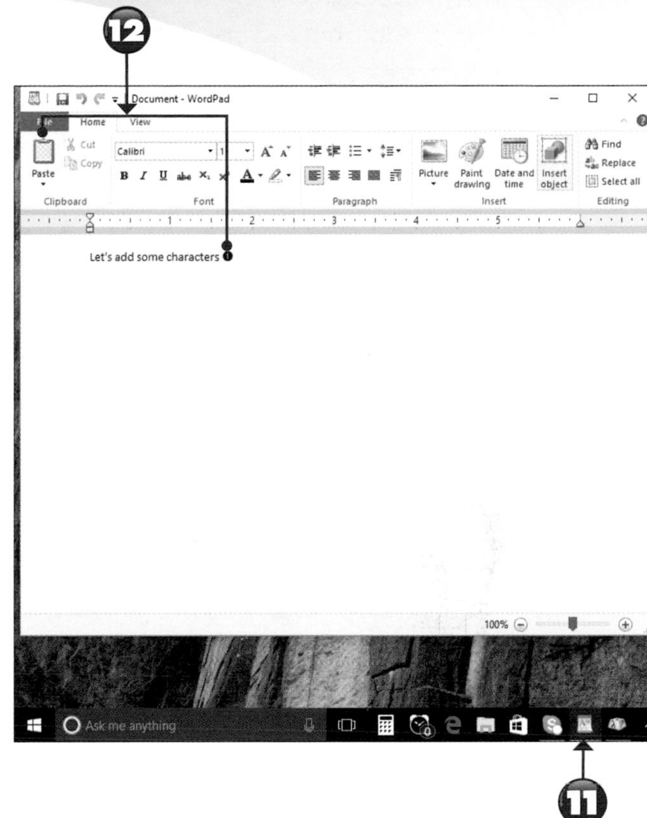

7. Select a font that has the character you need.

8. Click or tap the character needed.

9. Click or tap **Select**.

10. Click or tap **Copy**.

11. Click or tap the WordPad icon in the taskbar.

12. Click or tap **Paste** to add the character to the document at the current cursor position.

End

TIP

Finding the Font with the Characters You Need For characters such as copyright and math symbols, select the same font in Character Map as you used in WordPad. If you need specialized characters (such as icons, circled numbers, and so on), select the Wingdings or Webdings fonts in Character Map.

USING THE WINDOWS STORE

You can use the Windows Store app to shop online for more apps, music, and TV shows and movies. The Windows Store features a variety of apps and media content for a variety of uses. You can find plenty of free apps, paid apps, and trial versions in the Store using the Search or Categories view. In this chapter, you learn how to navigate the Store to find just the right apps for you and your device.

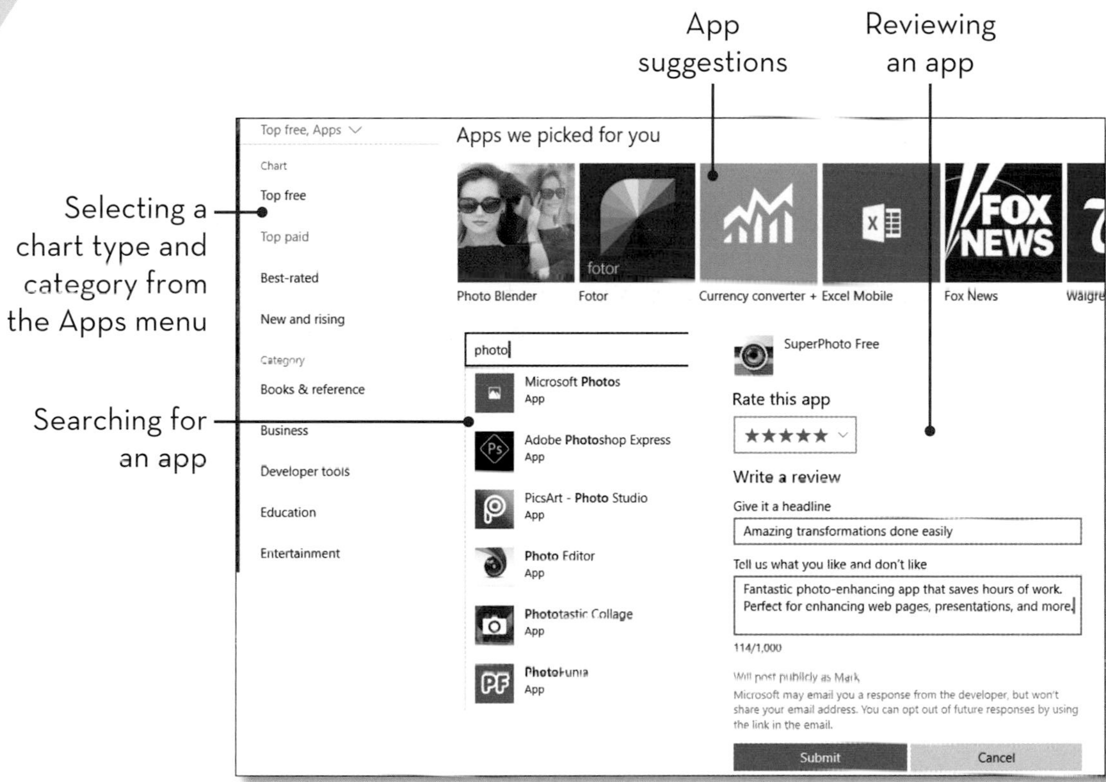

App suggestions
Reviewing an app
Selecting a chart type and category from the Apps menu
Searching for an app
Top free, Apps
Chart
Top free
Top paid
Best-rated
New and rising
Category
Books & reference
Business
Developer tools
Education
Entertainment
Apps we picked for you
Photo Blender
Fotor
Currency converter + Excel Mobile
Fox News
photo
Microsoft Photos
App
Adobe Photoshop Express
App
PicsArt - Photo Studio
App
Photo Editor
App
Phototastic Collage
App
PhotoFunia
App
SuperPhoto Free
Rate this app
Write a review
Give it a headline
Amazing transformations done easily
Tell us what you like and don't like
Fantastic photo-enhancing app that saves hours of work. Perfect for enhancing web pages, presentations, and more.
114/1,000
Will post publicly as Mark
Microsoft may email you a response from the developer, but won't share your email address. You can opt out of future responses by using the link in the email.
Submit
Cancel

GOING TO THE STORE

When you initially open the Windows Store app, the first screen displays the currently featured app and links to the most popular apps and new releases. As you scroll through the Store, you can find new apps and the most popular paid and free apps.

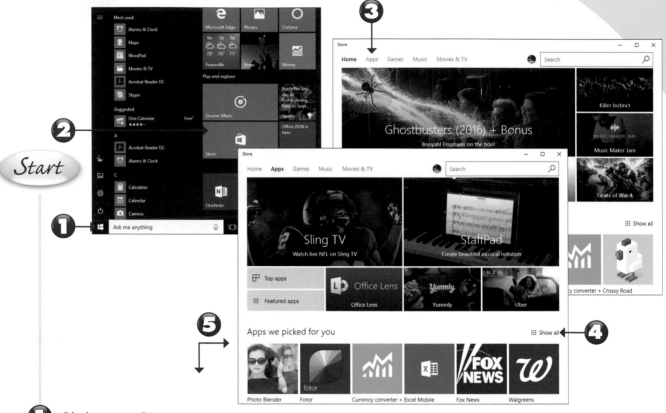

1. Click or tap **Start**.
2. Click or tap **Store**.
3. Click or tap to go to a category.
4. Click or tap to see all items in the category.
5. Scroll or flick right or down to see more apps.

NOTE

Picks for You After you visit the Store and download or purchase content, the next time you open the Store, you see a "Picks for You" category when you scroll down. These choices are based on the apps you have downloaded or what people with similar interests are downloading or purchasing.

SEARCHING FOR APPS BY NAME

You can use the Windows Store Search window to search the Store for a specific app or type of app. Here's how to search for your favorite app.

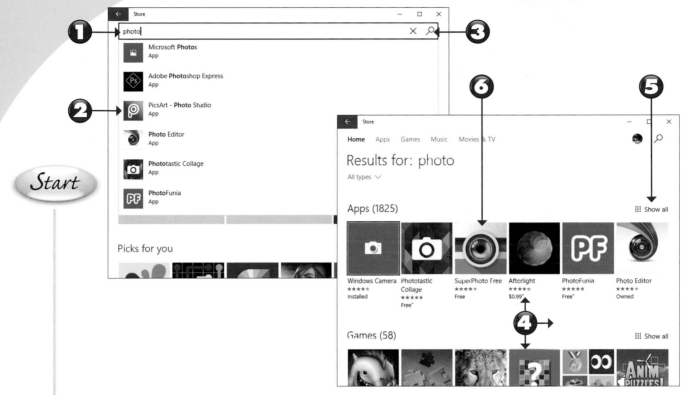

Start

1. From the Windows Store, click or tap the **Search** icon and type the search text.
2. Matches appear as you start typing the search text.
3. Press **Enter**/**Return** or click or tap the **Search** icon.
4. You can scroll or flick through results.
5. Click or tap to see all the matches in a category.
6. Click or tap an app you want to check out.

End

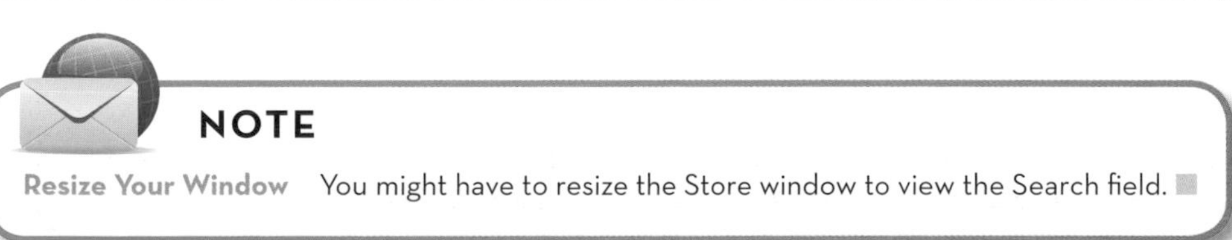

NOTE

Resize Your Window You might have to resize the Store window to view the Search field.

DECIDING ON AN APP

When you go to an app's details page, here's what to look for as you decide whether to download or buy the app.

Start

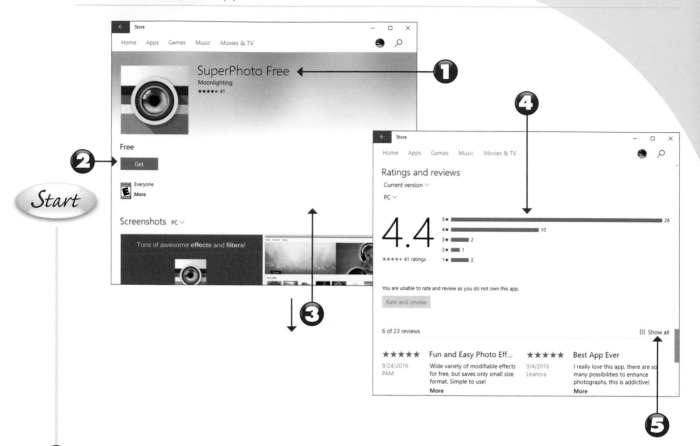

1. The app name and overall rating appear here.
2. A **Get** button is used to download and install free apps. The app price and a **Buy** (and sometimes a **Free** trial) button are displayed with purchased apps.
3. Scroll down or flick up for more information.
4. Scroll/flick to the Ratings and reviews section for a review digest.
5. Click or tap to see all reviews.

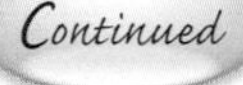

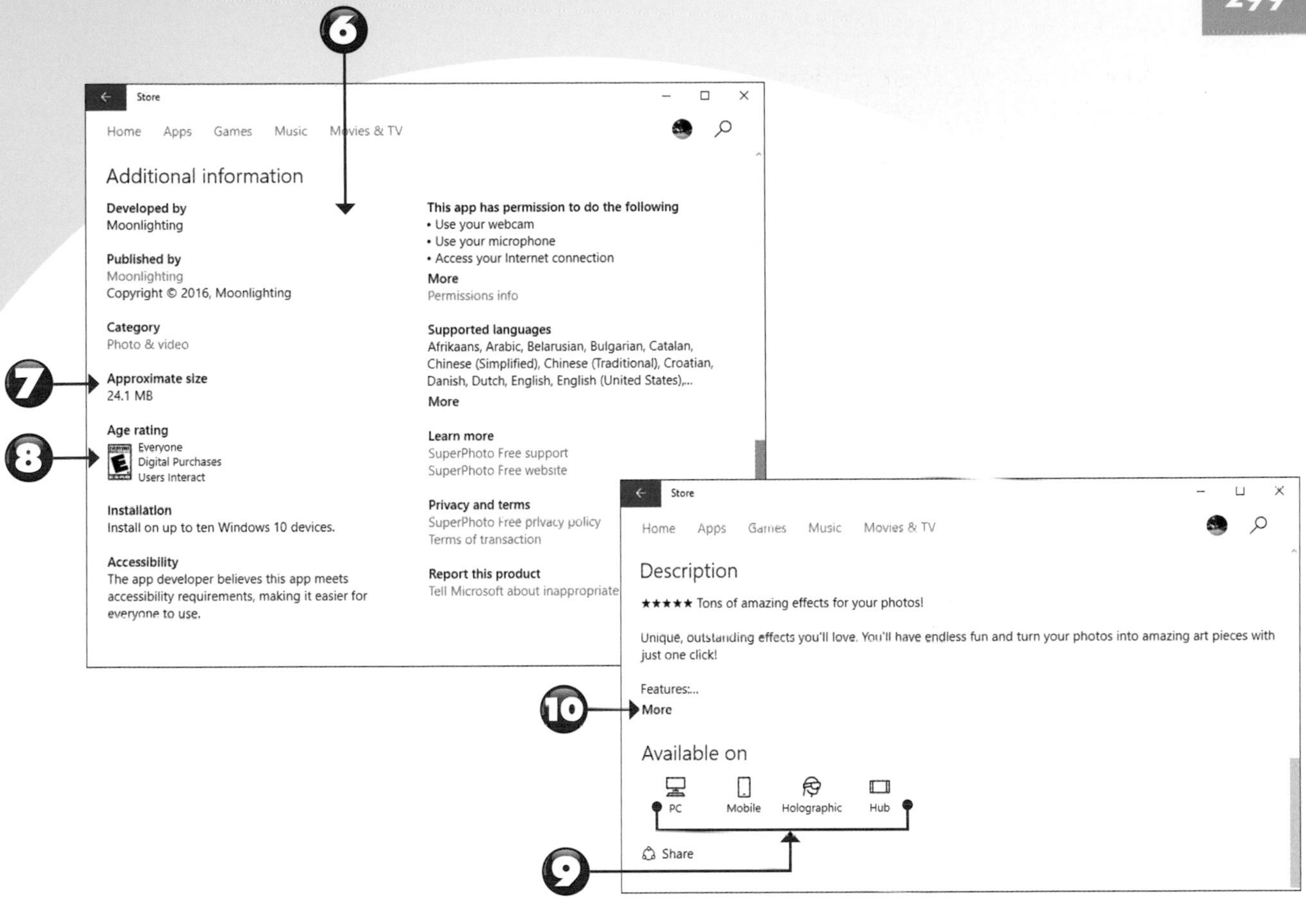

6. Scroll/flick to the Additional information section for age rating, app size, permissions, and developer website.

7. The app size is listed here.

8. View the app's age rating here.

9. Scroll/flick to the Available on section to see which types of devices are supported.

10. Click to see more features.

End

NOTE

Supported Processors and Devices PC works on PCs and devices with 32-bit or 64-bit Intel or AMD processors. ARM works on Windows RT devices, such as Microsoft Surface and Surface 2. Mobile works with Windows Phones. Holographic works with Microsoft HoloLens and other Windows 10-class holographic devices. Hub works with the Microsoft Surface Hub multitouch and ink collaborative platform.

BROWSING FOR APPS BY CATEGORY

The Windows Store also enables you to browse by category or by collection. Here's how to open the category view from the Home page.

Start

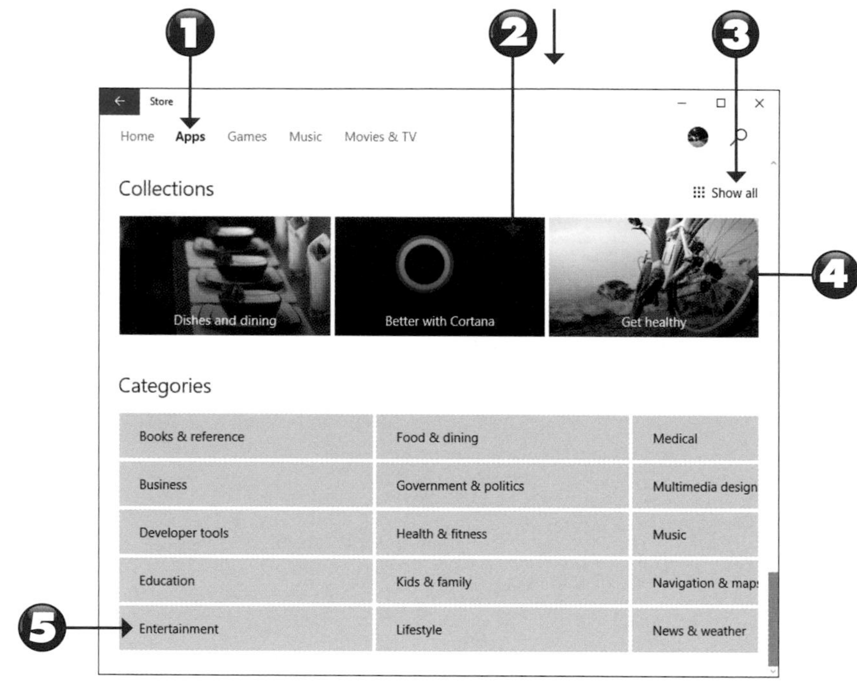

1. Click or tap **Apps** in the top-level menu.
2. Scroll down or flick up to see the Collections and Categories headings.
3. If you want to see all available collections, click or tap here.
4. If you want to see the contents of any collection, click or tap it.
5. Click or tap a category to browse it.

Continued

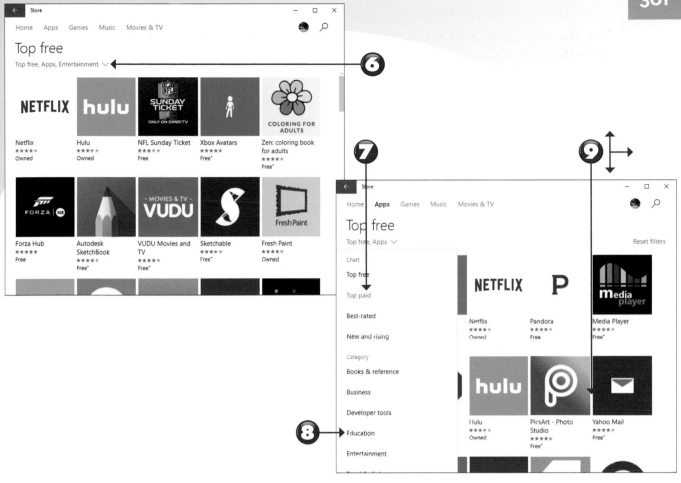

6. Click or tap to change the chart or category (if the list isn't visible).

7. Click or tap the chart desired.

8. Click or tap the category desired.

9. Scroll or flick to see more matches.

End

NOTE

Understanding Charts The Windows Store uses the term "chart" to refer to various listings of popular apps or media (top free, top paid, and so on).

INSTALLING AN APP

When you find an app you want, you can easily install it in just a few clicks. Windows 10 AE does most of the hard work for you. When you install an app, the app is added to the Windows All apps menu.

Start

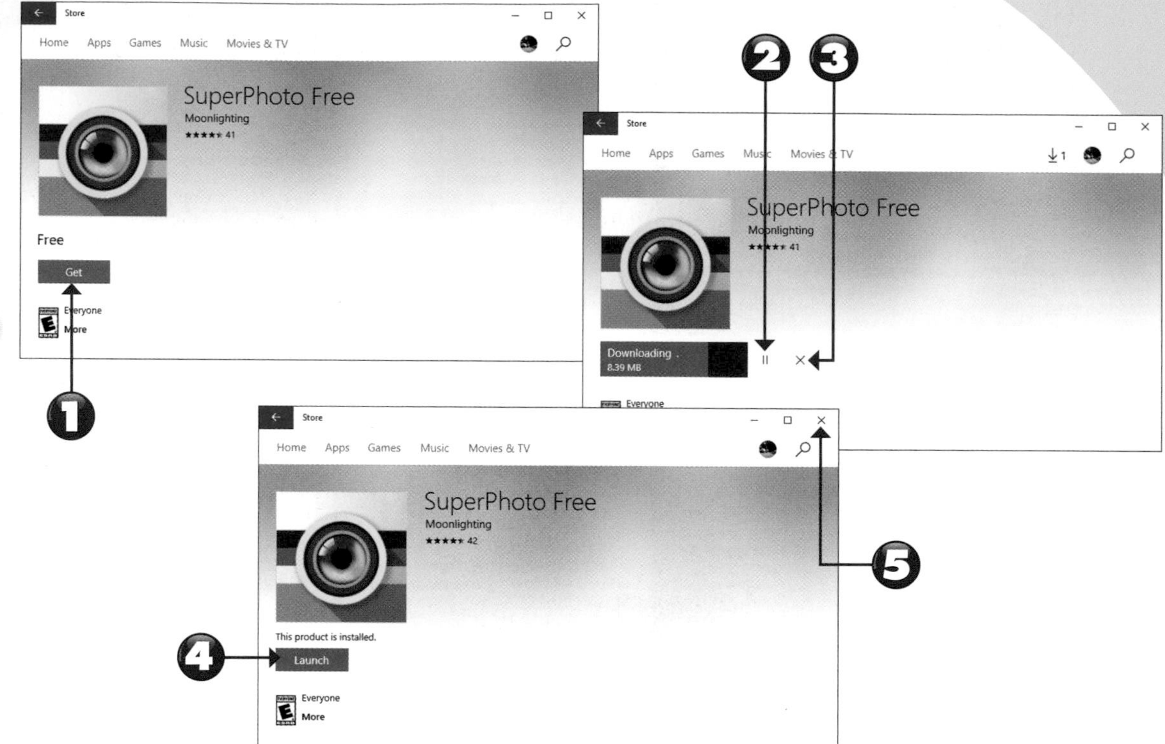

1. From the app's details page, click or tap the **Buy/Get** button.
2. If needed, you can click or tap here to pause/continue downloading and installing.
3. If you need to cancel the procedure, click or tap **X**.
4. When the download and installation are complete, you can click or tap **Launch** to open the app immediately.
5. Click or tap to close the Store window.

NOTE

Installing Paid Apps When you install a paid app, Windows 10 AE directs you to a login screen where you can log in to your Microsoft account and choose a payment method. Windows might also prompt you to log in to your Microsoft account before continuing with the download.

7

6

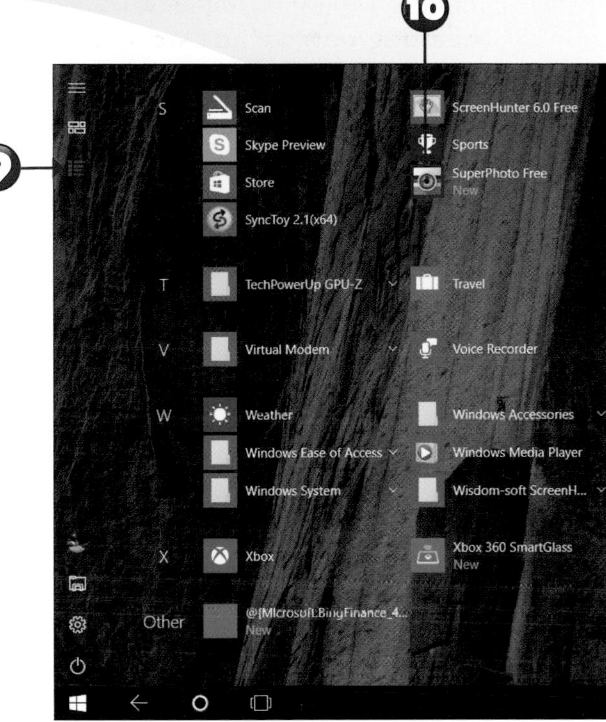

10

9

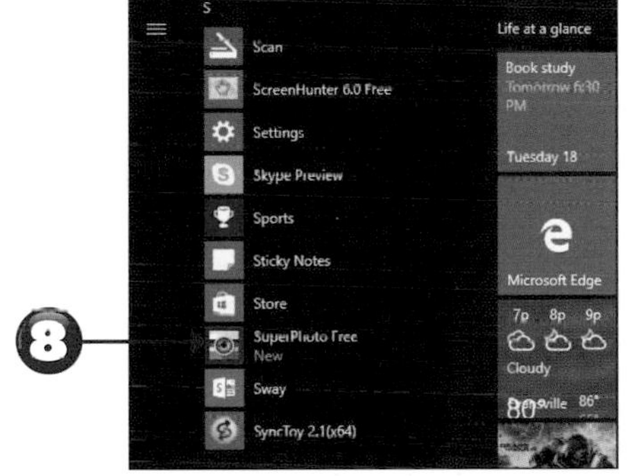

8

6. To locate the app later, click or tap **Start**.

7. In Desktop or Tablet modes, the most recently added apps are at the top of the menu, followed by most used.

8. Scroll down the list to find the app, and then click or tap to start it.

9. In Tablet mode, click or tap **All apps**.

10. If the app is not listed as recently added or as most used, flick up to locate the app, and click or tap the app to open it.

End

RATING AN APP

The Windows Store offers user reviews of apps. This information is helpful when you're deciding whether you want to try an app. By adding your rating to the app reviews, you can help other potential users know how it worked for you.

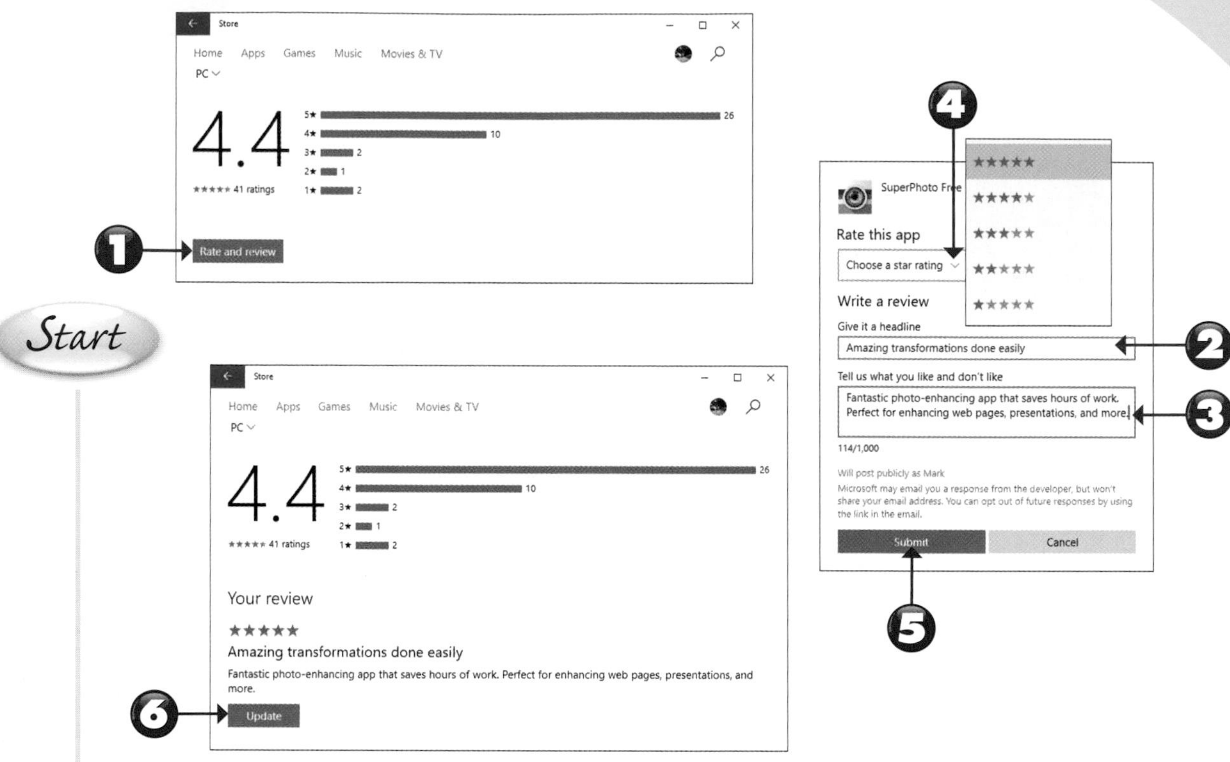

Start

1. From the app's page in the Store, click or tap **Rate and review**.
2. Enter a title for your review.
3. Enter review text.
4. Click or tap, and select the number of stars for your review.
5. Click or tap **Submit**.
6. Click or tap **Update** if you want to change your review at any time.

End

UNINSTALLING AN APP FROM THE START SCREEN

You can easily remove an app you no longer use or want. Uninstalling an app removes it from your computer and deletes the app from your Start menu. You can reinstall it at any time from the Windows Store.

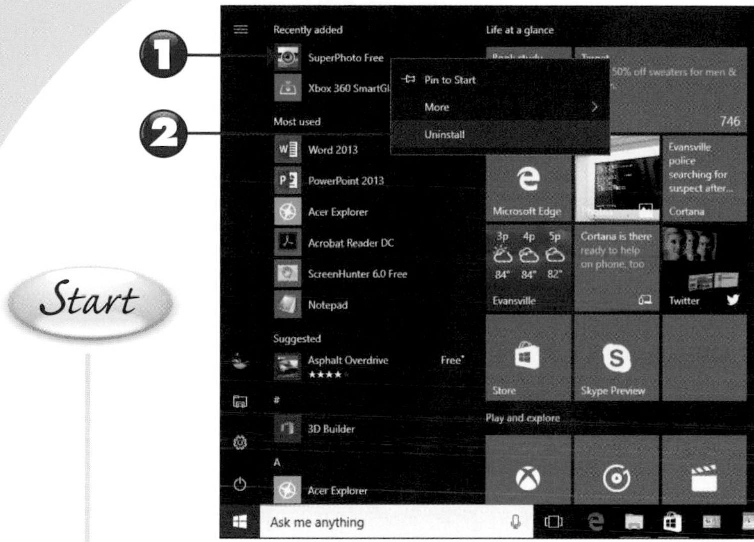

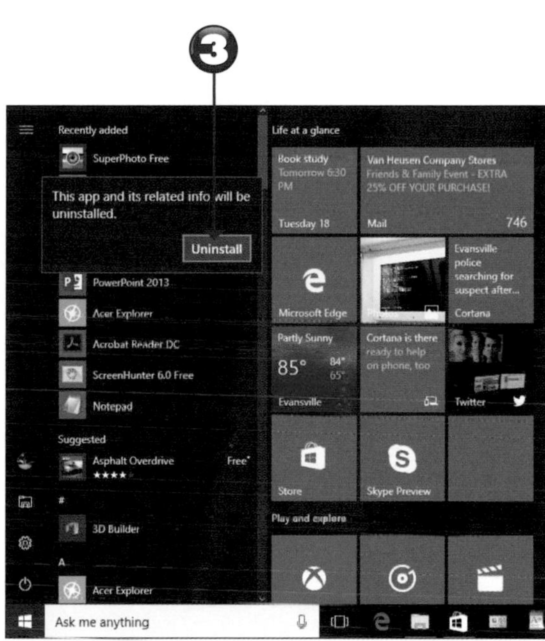

Start

1. From the Start menu, right-click or press and hold the app you want to uninstall.
2. Click or tap **Uninstall**.
3. Click or tap **Uninstall**, and the app is removed.

End

TIP

Discovering the Largest Apps If you're wondering which apps take up the most storage space on your system, use the Apps & Features dialog box in System settings. For details, see "Apps & Features" in Chapter 19, "Managing Windows 10 AE," p. 353.

GAMING

Windows 10 Anniversary Edition connects the worlds of PC and Xbox One gaming. You can download updated versions of classic Windows games from the Windows Store or buy the latest shooters, sports, or racing games for your PC or Xbox.

Xbox One and Xbox One S users can use the Xbox app to play back shared game clips from either PC or Xbox games, connect with friends, and check out the latest news in the Xbox world.

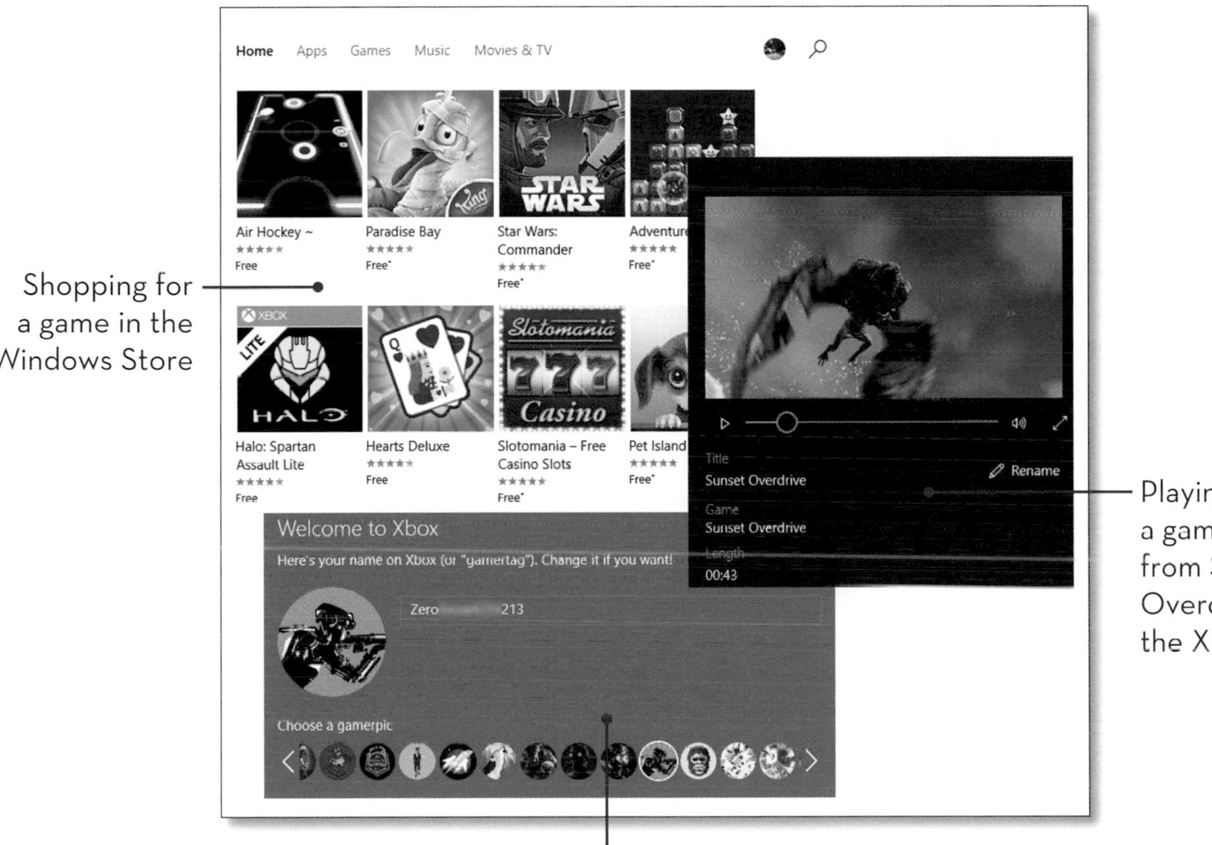
Home
Apps
Games
Music
Movies & TV
Air Hockey ~
Free
Paradise Bay
Free*
Star Wars: Commander
Free*
Adventure
Free*
Halo: Spartan Assault Lite
Free
Hearts Deluxe
Free
Slotomania – Free Casino Slots
Free*
Pet Island
Free*
Title
Sunset Overdrive
Rename
Game
Sunset Overdrive
Length
00:43
Welcome to Xbox
Here's your name on Xbox (or "gamertag"). Change it if you want!
Zero 213
Choose a gamerpic
Shopping for a game in the Windows Store
Playing back a game clip from Sunset Overdrive in the Xbox app
Creating a new Xbox account

FINDING GAMES WITH THE STORE APP

If you're looking for games to play on your computer, tablet, or Windows phone, visit the Windows Store. The Store offers all kinds of games you can download—both free and paid games for single or multiple players.

Start

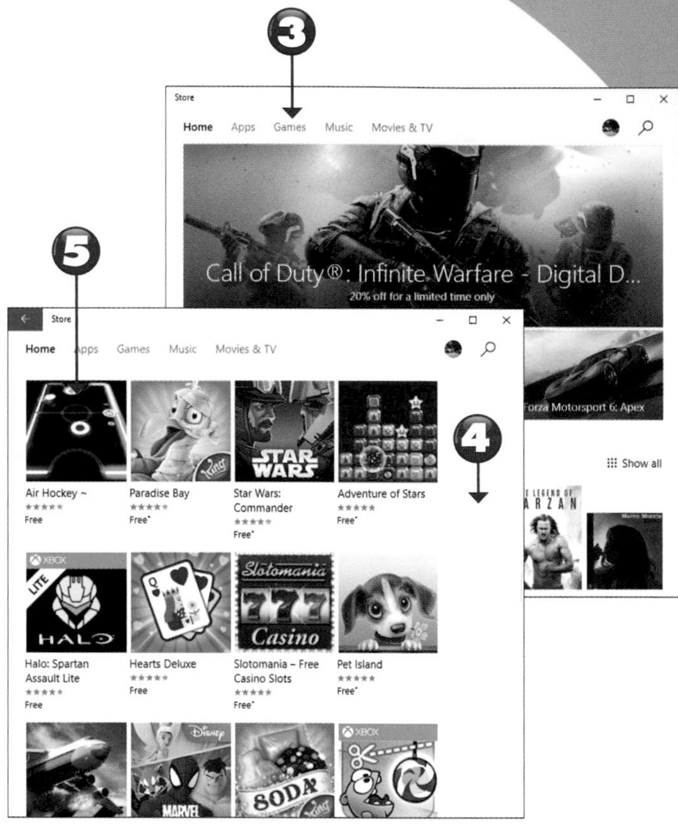

1. Click or tap **Start** (Desktop mode only).
2. Click or tap **Store**.
3. Click or tap **Games**.
4. Scroll through the list of available games to find one you like.
5. Click or tap a game to learn more about it.

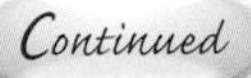

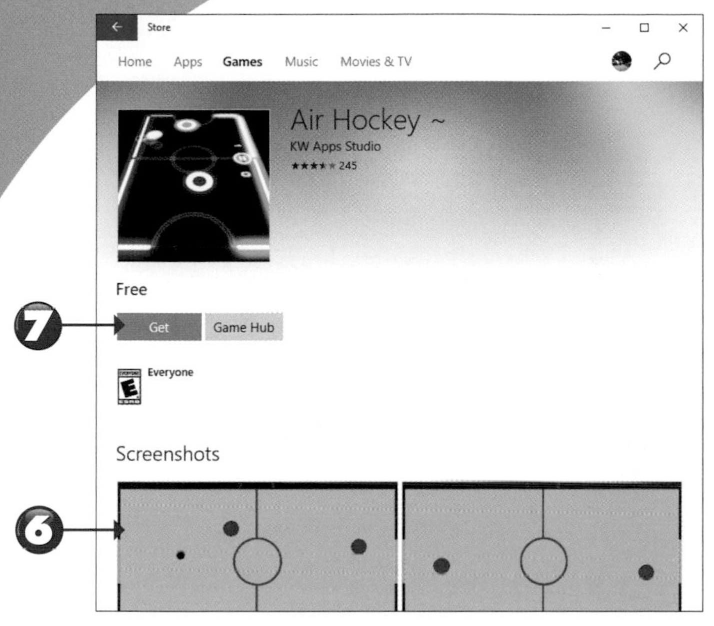

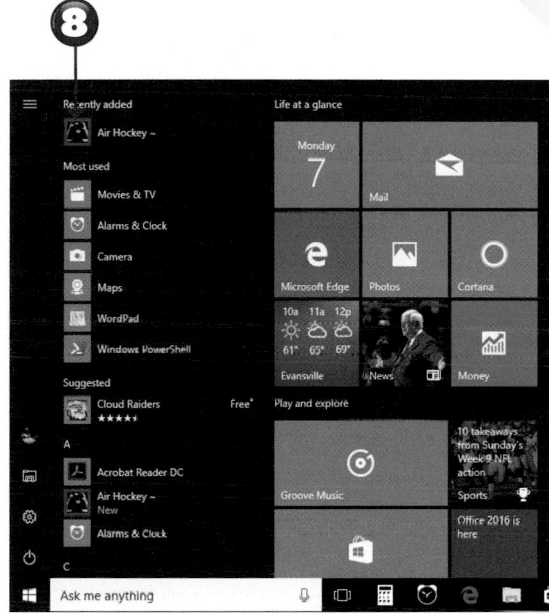

6. When you select a game to view, a description of the game opens along with screenshots of what the game looks like.

7. If it's a free game, click or tap the **Get** button to start the download.

8. Windows 10 AE installs the game automatically and adds it to the Apps list. Click or tap **Start** to see it listed under Recently added items.

End

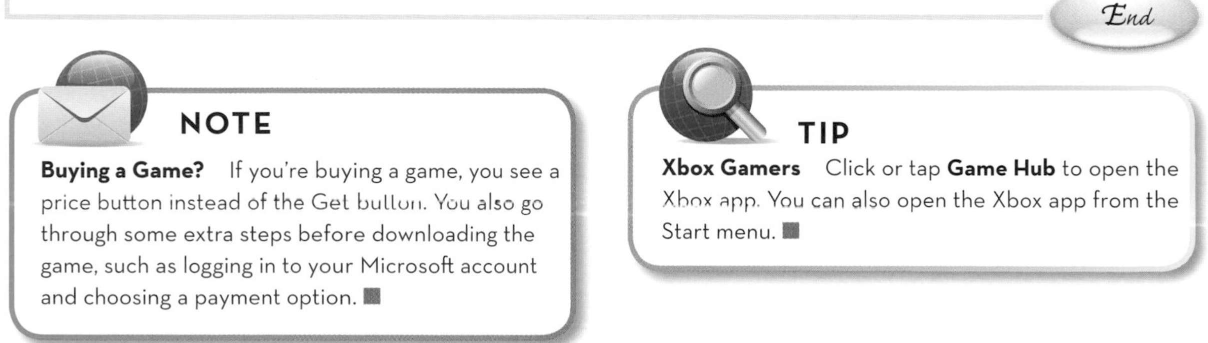

NOTE

Buying a Game? If you're buying a game, you see a price button instead of the Get button. You also go through some extra steps before downloading the game, such as logging in to your Microsoft account and choosing a payment option. ■

TIP

Xbox Gamers Click or tap **Game Hub** to open the Xbox app. You can also open the Xbox app from the Start menu. ■

CREATING A NEW XBOX ACCOUNT

You can create a new account to play games online. An Xbox account is free, and you can sign up through the Xbox app. If you already have an Xbox account, go to the next tutorial.

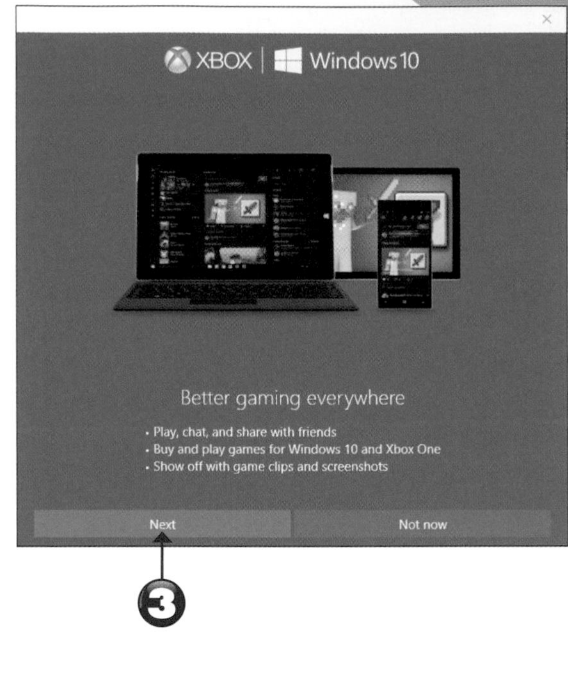

Start

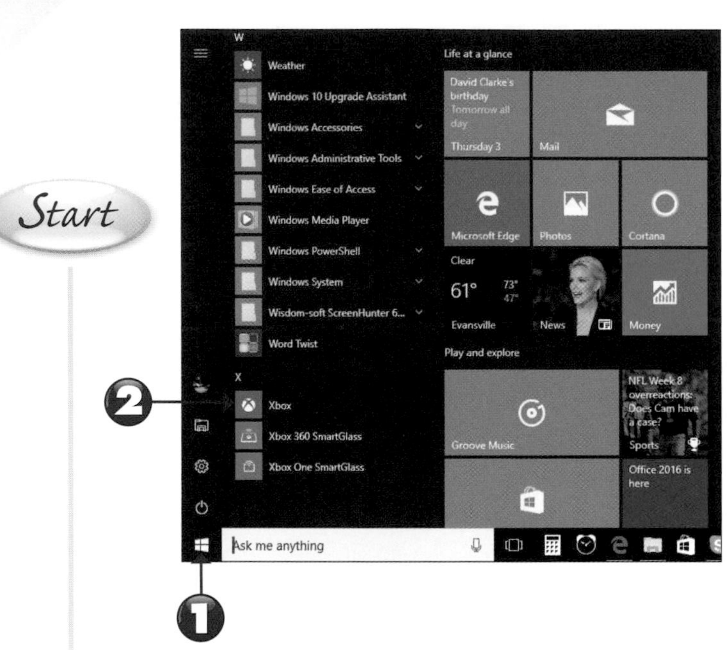

1. Click or tap **Start** (Desktop) or **All apps** (Tablet mode).
2. Click or tap **Xbox**.
3. Click or tap **Next**.

Continued

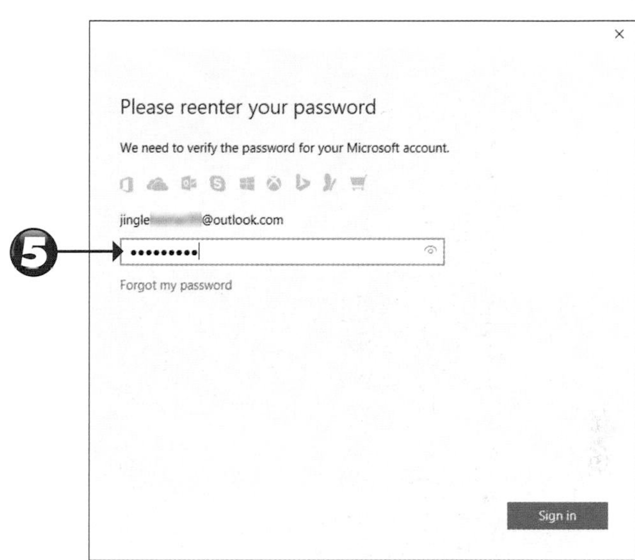

4. Click or tap the account to use.

5. The app might prompt you to sign in to your Microsoft account before proceeding; follow the instructions for entering your email, password, and verification code.

Continued

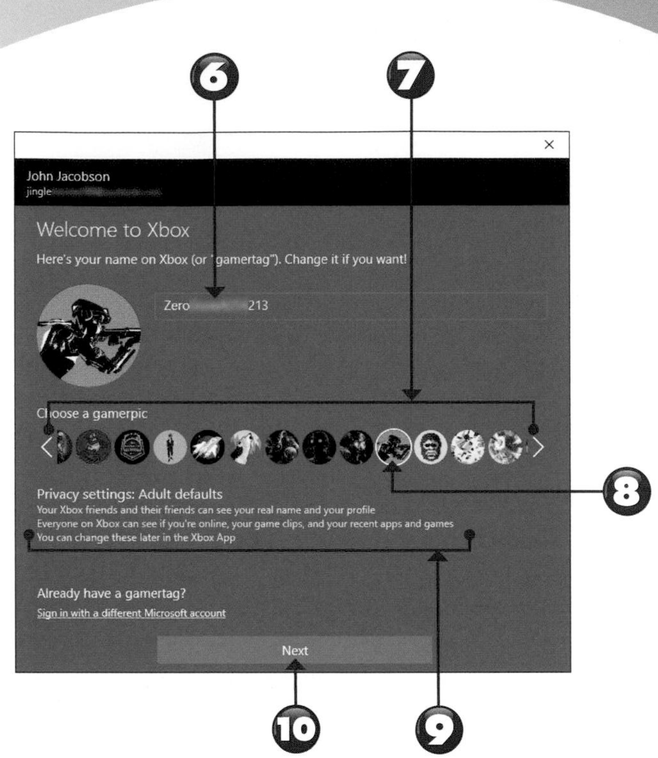

6. A default gamertag (Xbox username) is created. Click or tap to change it.
7. Scroll through the gamerpics to find a picture (also called an avatar) for your Xbox account.
8. Click or tap your favorite.
9. Default privacy settings vary by user age.
10. Click or tap **Next**.

Continued

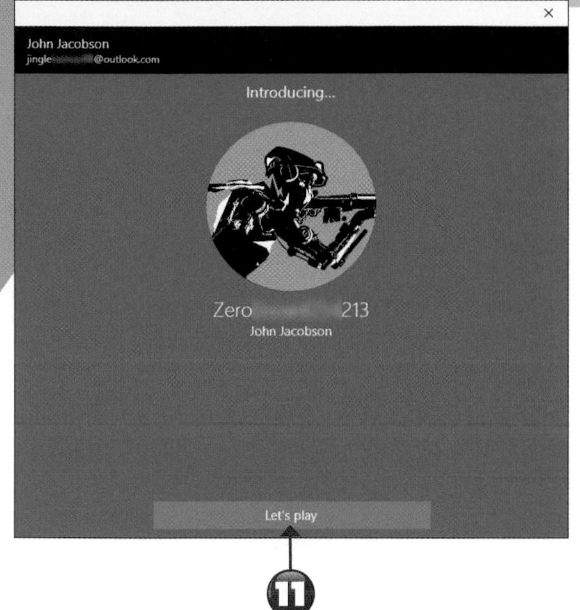

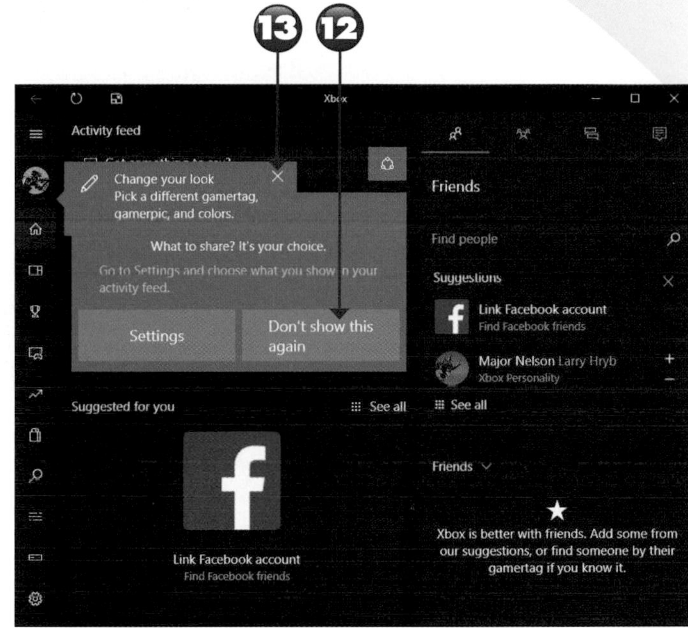

11 Click or tap **Let's play**.

12 Click or tap **Don't show this again**.

13 Click or tap the **Close** (**X**) button to close this dialog box.

End

USING THE XBOX APP

The Xbox app is your gaming headquarters for all things Xbox. You can use the app to log in to your gaming account, chat with friends, play games, track your achievements, and more. This task shows you how to get started with the app.

Start

1. Click or tap **Start** (Desktop) or **All apps** (Tablet mode).
2. Click or tap **Xbox**.
3. Click or tap **Let's play**.
4. Click or tap to expand the menu.

Continued

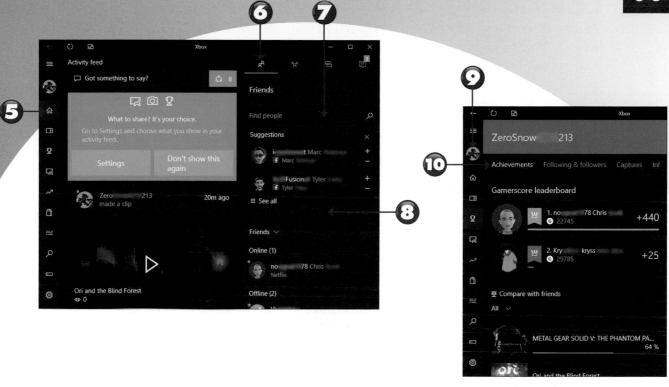

5 Click or tap **Home** to display recent activity.

6 To view friends, click or tap the **Friends** icon.

7 To find a friend online, click or tap **Find people** and type your friend's gamertag (username).

8 Friends and suggested friends are listed in this pane.

9 Click or tap your avatar picture to change settings, view achievements and followers, and more.

10 Scroll through the categories to view or change.

End

TIP

Need to Sign Out? The Xbox app keeps you signed in as soon as you start using the app unless you specify otherwise. You can find the sign-out option listed among the Xbox app's settings. Click or tap the **Settings** icon on the menu, and then click or tap **Sign Out** in the Account section to officially log off your connection.

CONNECTING TO XBOX ONE

The Xbox One and Xbox One S include several features for better integration with Windows 10 AE. To use these features, you must connect your Windows 10 AE device with the Xbox One/One S on your network from within the Xbox app. After you connect to your Xbox One/One S, you can stream compatible games from your Xbox One/One S to your Windows 10 AE device or use your Windows 10 AE device as a controller for the game.

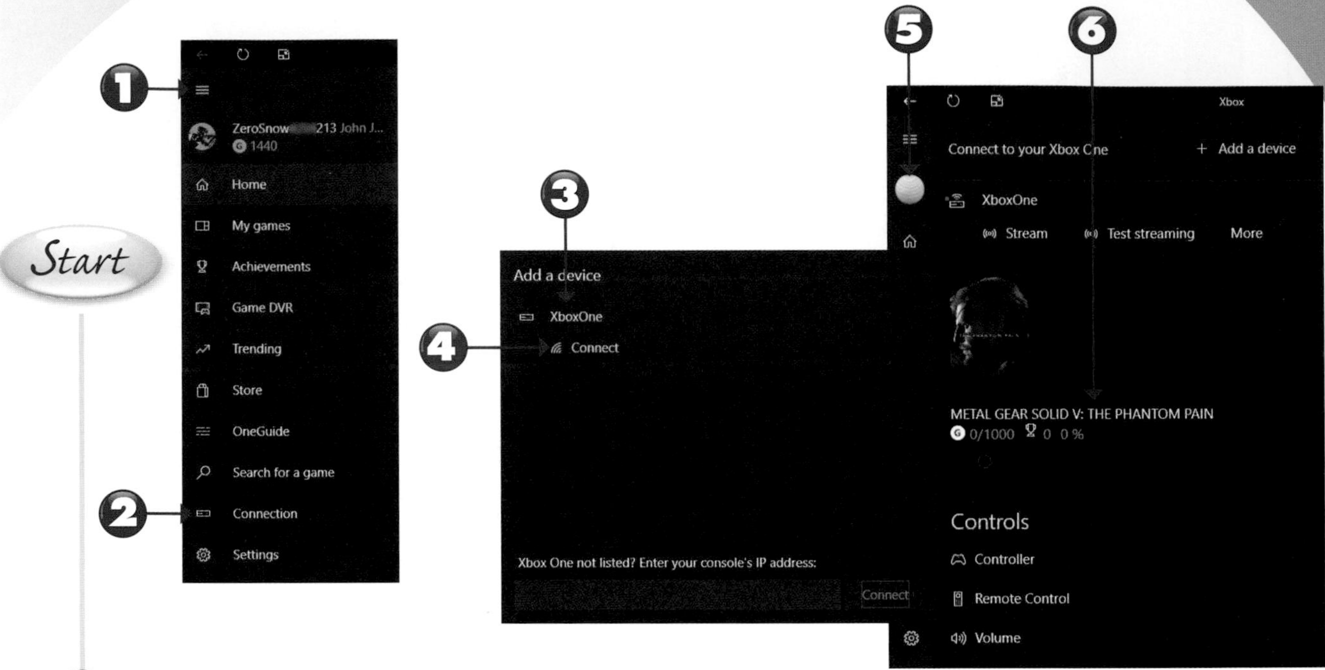

1. From the Xbox app, click or tap the **Menu** button.
2. Click or tap **Connection**.
3. Your Xbox One/One S should be listed here.
4. Click or tap **Connect**.
5. This indicates a working connection.
6. This displays your console's current activity.

End

TIP

Dealing with a "Missing" Console If your console isn't visible in step 3, enter its IP (Internet) address into the box at the bottom of the dialog box. To find your console's IP address, start your console and go to **Settings**, **Network**, **Advanced settings**. ■

VIEWING GAMING CLIPS

The Xbox One/One S can capture gaming clips, which are video files of the game recorded while you're playing. Want to show friends your marksmanship or amazing luck? Share your video clips. You can also capture gaming clips or screenshots from games you play in Windows 10 AE. Here's how to view gaming clips from either source with the Xbox app.

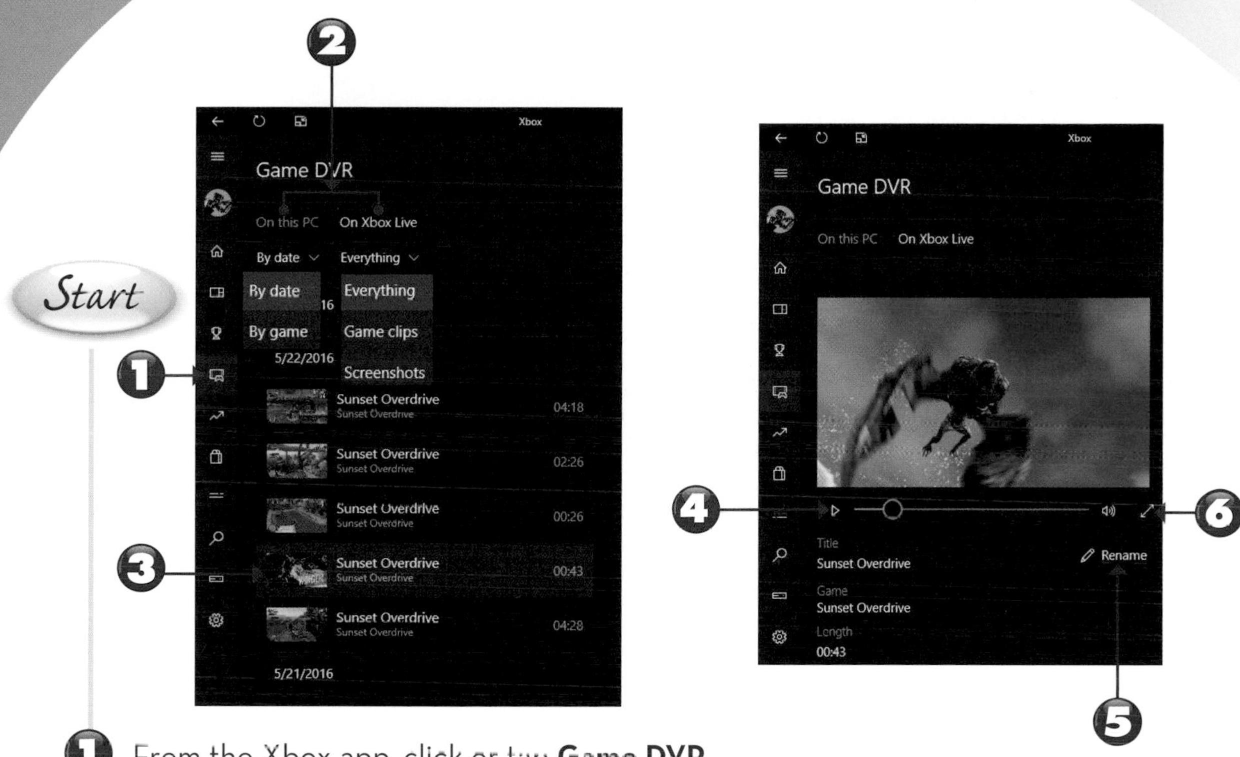

1. From the Xbox app, click or tap **Game DVR**.
2. Click or tap the source you want to use for clips. To choose by date/game or to choose game clips or screenshots only, select options from the drop-down menus.
3. Scroll down and click or tap a clip.
4. Click or tap **Play**.
5. Click or tap to rename the clip.
6. Click or tap to play it full screen.

End

TIP

Choosing a Clip Source Click or tap **On this PC** to view clips you created on your PC. Click or tap **On Xbox Live** to view clips created with your own or others' Xbox devices. ■

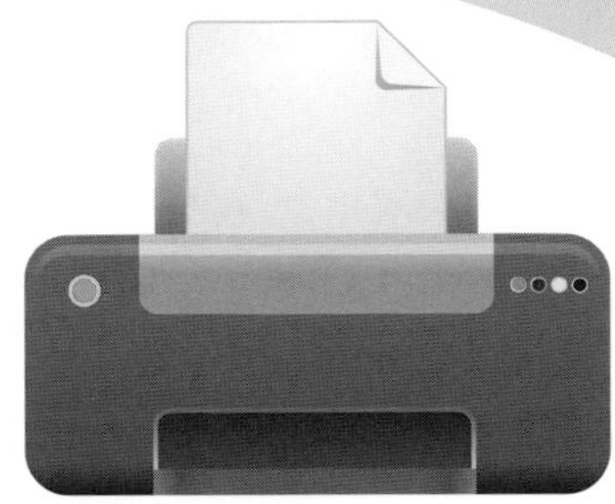

PRINTING AND SCANNING

Windows 10 AE can use most existing printers, scanners, and all-in-one units. This chapter covers how to use these various devices with Windows 10 AE's built-in apps and features.

Use the Scans folder to view scanned files
Configuring Scan
Preparing to print a photo
Selecting the paper type
Scan
Scanner
EPSON WorkForce 600 Series
Source
Flatbed
File type
JPEG
Color mode
Color
Resolution (DPI)
300
Save file to
Scans
View
Manage
Cut
Copy path
Paste shortcut
Move to
Copy to
Delete
Rename
New folder
New item
Easy access
Organize
New
Pictures › Scans
Scan_20161021 (2)
Observation Car
Scan_20161021
Copies
1
Orientation
Portrait
Paper size
4 x 6 in
Paper type
Ultra Premium Photo Paper Glossy
Photo size
Full page
Fit
Shrink to fit
Color mode
Color
More settings
Print
Cancel
Plain Paper / Bright White Paper
Ultra Premium Photo Paper Glossy
Premium Photo Paper Glossy
Photo Paper Glossy
Premium Photo Paper Semi-Gloss
Premium Presentation Paper Matte
Envelope

PRINTING A DOCUMENT

Windows 10 AE includes virtual printers that can create PDF (Adobe Reader) or XPS (Microsoft XPS) files. You can also install printers through Settings (see Chapter 19, "Managing Windows 10 AE," for details), or you can use the printer's own setup program. After your printer is installed, you can change the normal settings as needed, depending on the print job. Here's how to print a document from a typical Windows app. Depending on the app, the Print command might be found in a different location.

Start

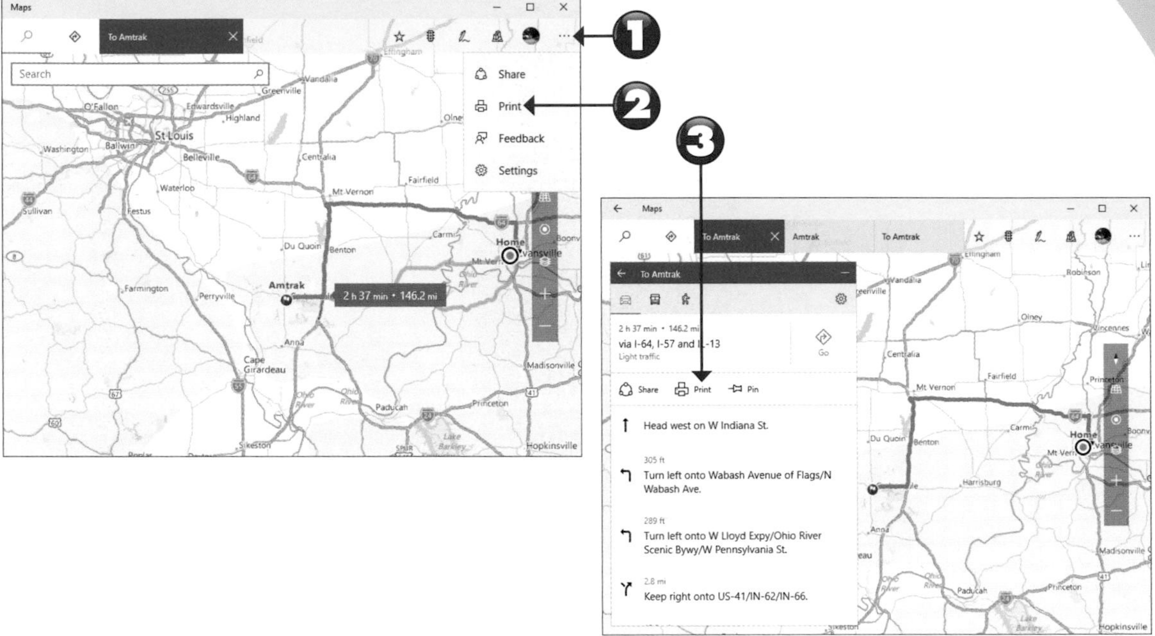

1. Depending on the app, click or tap the app's **Menu**, **Options**, or **See More** button (three-dot menu).
2. Click or tap **Print**.
3. With some apps, such as the Directions feature in Maps, the print job is started from a submenu.

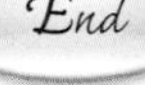

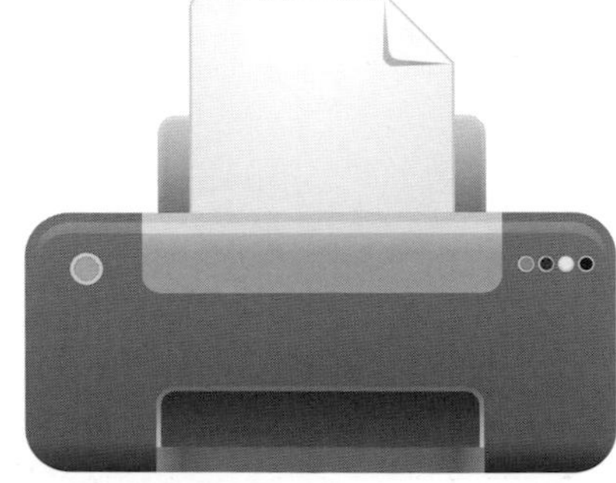

4 The Print dialog box opens with the preview area showing what the printout will look like when printed.

5 To choose a printer, click or tap and make a selection.

6 To change page orientation, click or tap **Orientation** and make a selection (portrait or landscape).

7 Click or tap to preview additional pages in the document, if applicable.

8 Click or tap **Print** to print the document.

End

TIP

Different Printer Options Don't expect to see the same print options every time you open the Print dialog box. Depending on which printer you select from the drop-down list, the options vary.

SELECTING A DIFFERENT PRINTER

Even before you install a physical printer, Windows 10 AE includes virtual printer apps that can create an Adobe Reader (PDF file extension) or Microsoft XPS (Open XML Paper, XPS file extension) file. These files can be viewed or printed to any printer. Use this lesson to learn how to choose the right printer from those installed.

Start

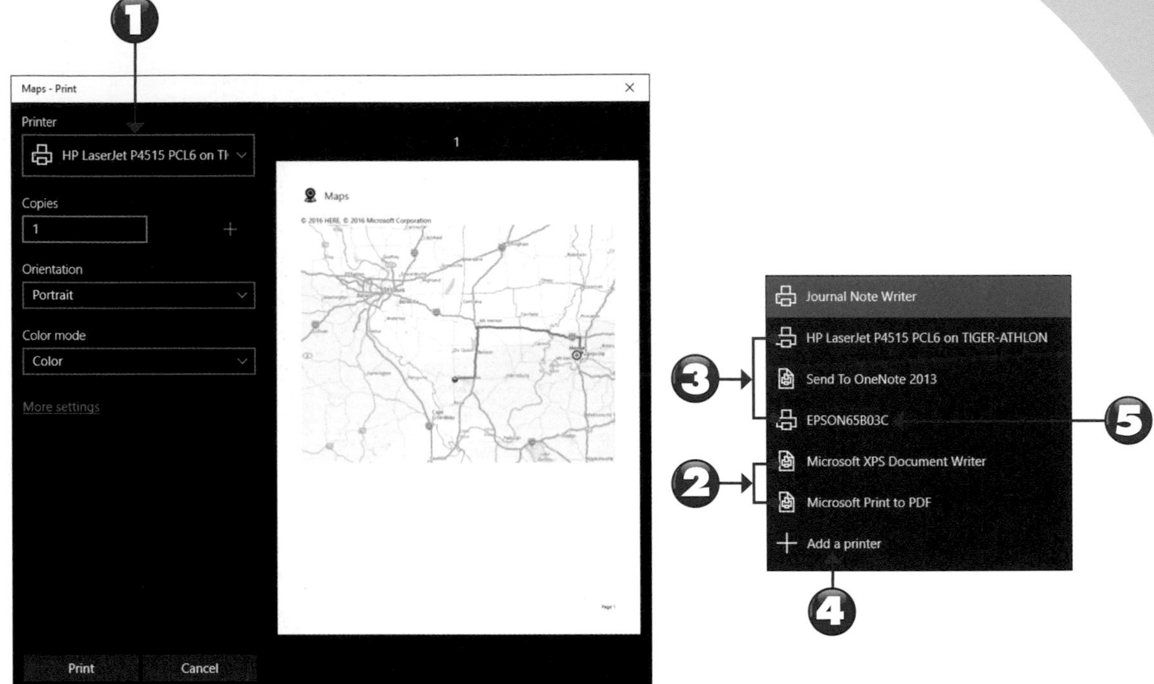

1. With the Print dialog box open, click or tap to open the printer selection menu.
2. These are software (virtual) printers included in Windows 10 AE.
3. These are user-installed printers.
4. Click or tap to install an additional printer.
5. Click or tap a printer name to choose that printer.

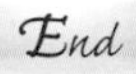

TIP

Set a Default Printer You can designate a printer as the default. When you do, the apps that allow printing list the chosen printer without needing to specify a printer every time. Conduct a Windows search for Devices and Printers (found in the Control Panel). Locate your printer, right-click or press and hold the printer name, and choose **Set as default printer**.

MORE PRINTER SETTINGS

The basic printer settings are all you need for document printing onto standard 8.5×11-inch or A4 letter-size paper. However, if you need to use a different paper size or a different type of paper, such as printing for photos, or adjust how your printer prints, you must use the More settings link. Here's what to expect with a typical inkjet printer.

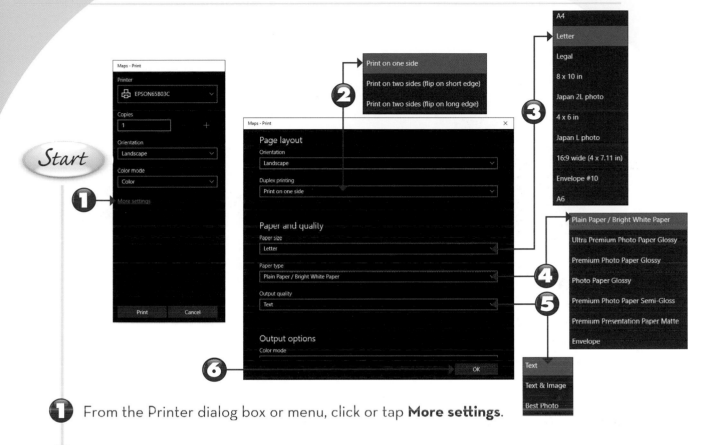

1. From the Printer dialog box or menu, click or tap **More settings**.
2. Click or tap **Duplex printing** for options for printing on both sides of the paper.
3. Click or tap **Paper size** if you need to change the paper size.
4. Click or tap **Paper type** to use matte or photo paper instead of plain paper.
5. Click or tap **Output quality** to change print quality.
6. Click or tap **OK** to return to the main print menu.

NOTE

More About Printer Options If you're printing multiple pages, select **Uncollated** in the Collation menu (if available) if you want the printer to print all copies of page 1 before page 2, and so on. Available paper sizes and paper types vary by printer.

PHOTO PRINTING SETTINGS

If you want to print a photo on 4×6-inch photo paper, you can choose from several print settings to achieve the desired printout results. You can select these options in any order, and some printers offer slightly different options or wording.

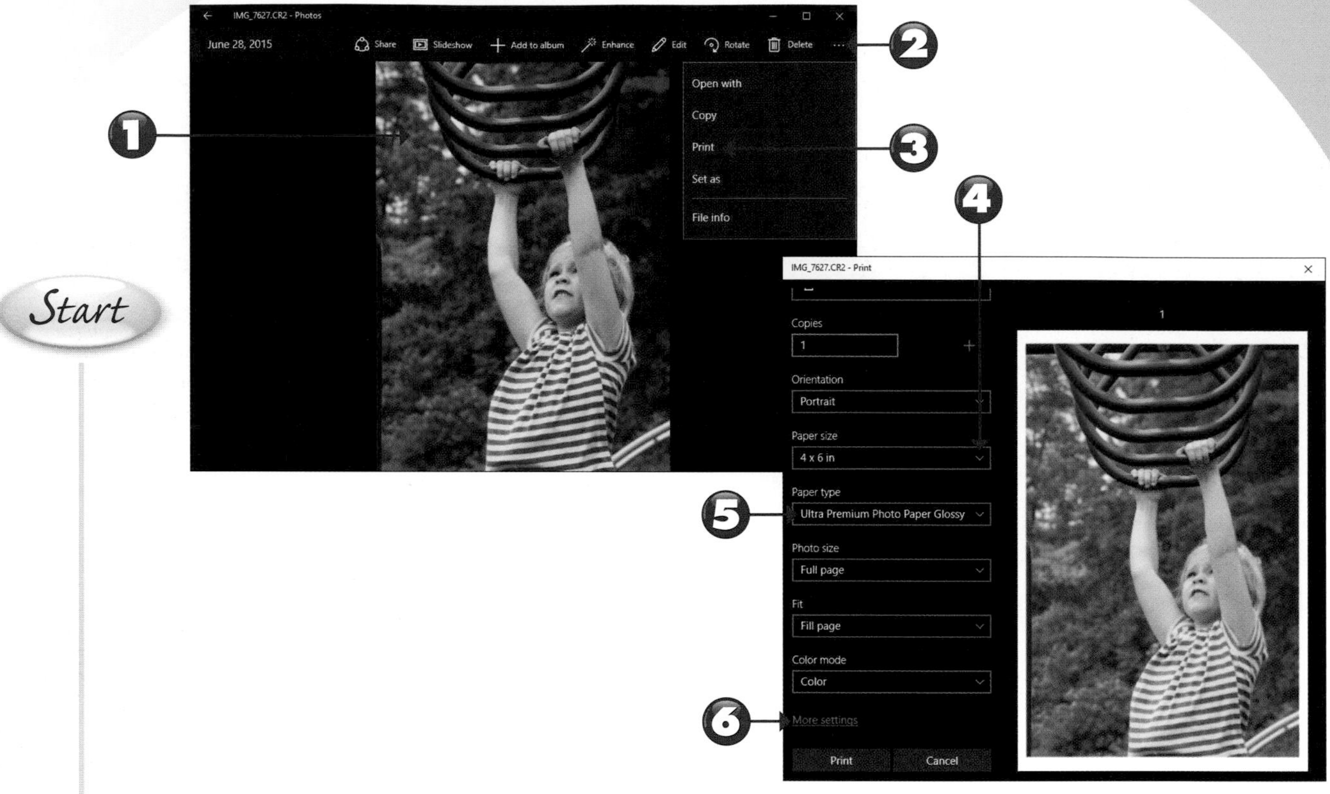

1. Open a picture in the Photos app.
2. Click or tap the three-dot menu.
3. Click or tap **Print**.
4. Click or tap the **Paper size** menu and select **4 × 6 in** or another appropriate paper size for your photo printout.
5. Click or tap **Paper type** to change paper type. Most photo paper is glossy or ultra glossy.
6. Click or tap **More settings**.

Continued

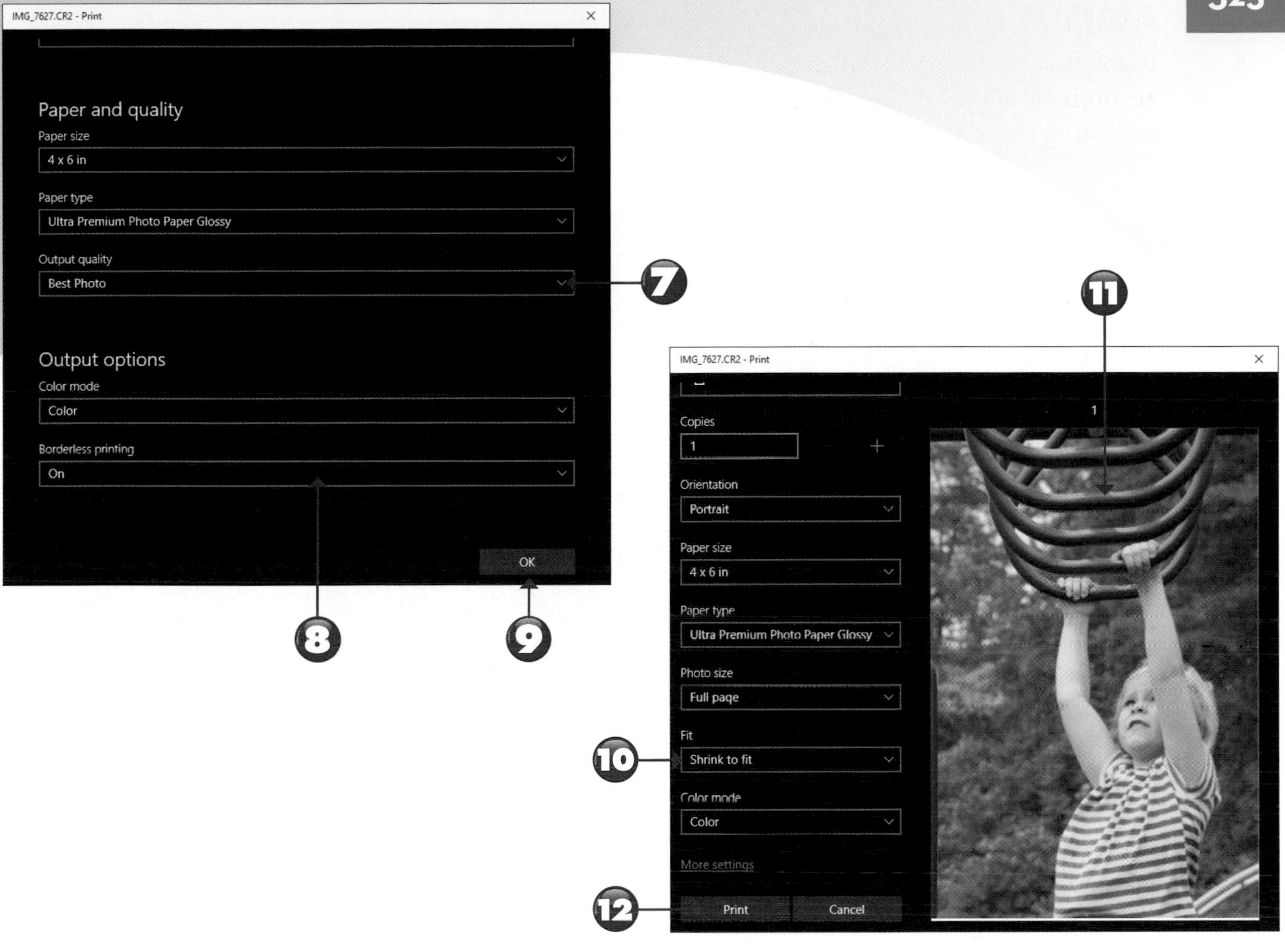

7. Click or tap the **Output quality** menu and select **Best photo** or a similar setting.

8. If you want borderless printing, turn the setting to **On**.

9. Click **OK** to return to the main print options.

10. To utilize borderless printing, you might also need to select **Shrink to fit** from the Fit menu.

11. Review the preview image here.

12. Click or tap **Print**.

End

USING SCAN

If you have a flatbed scanner or a multifunction device, you can use Windows 10 AE's simple scanning utility, called Scan, to convert prints or documents into electronic form. If the Scan app is not installed on your system, install it from the Windows Store first (it's free).

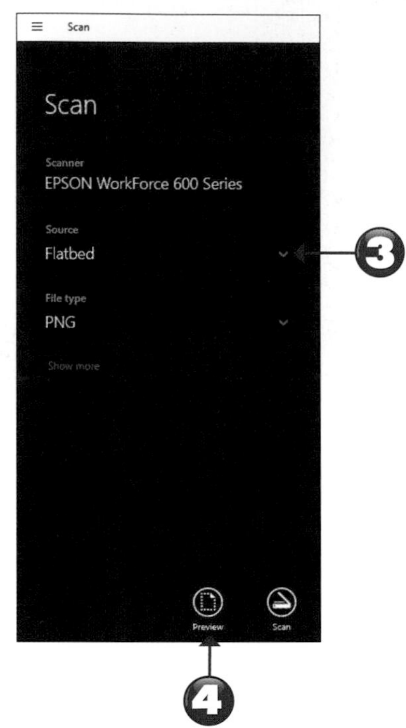

Start

1. Click or tap **Start**.
2. Scroll down or flick up, and click or tap **Scan**. (In Tablet mode, click or tap **All apps** first.)
3. If necessary, select **Flatbed** as the source.
4. After placing a photo or document face down on the scanner glass, click or tap **Preview**.

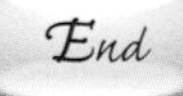

NOTE

Scan Versus Vendor-Supplied Tools The Scan app performs basic scanning with flatbed scanner or all-in-one units. However, if you need to adjust exposure or contrast, restore color to faded originals, use a sheet feeder, use a transparency unit to scan slides or negatives, or use dust or scratch removal tools, you must use software provided by the scanner vendor or third-party scanning software. Note that vendor-supplied apps available in the Store are typically much more limited than the drivers you can obtain directly from the vendors' websites. If a Windows 10 AE version is not available, you can usually install and use the Windows 8.1 version. ■

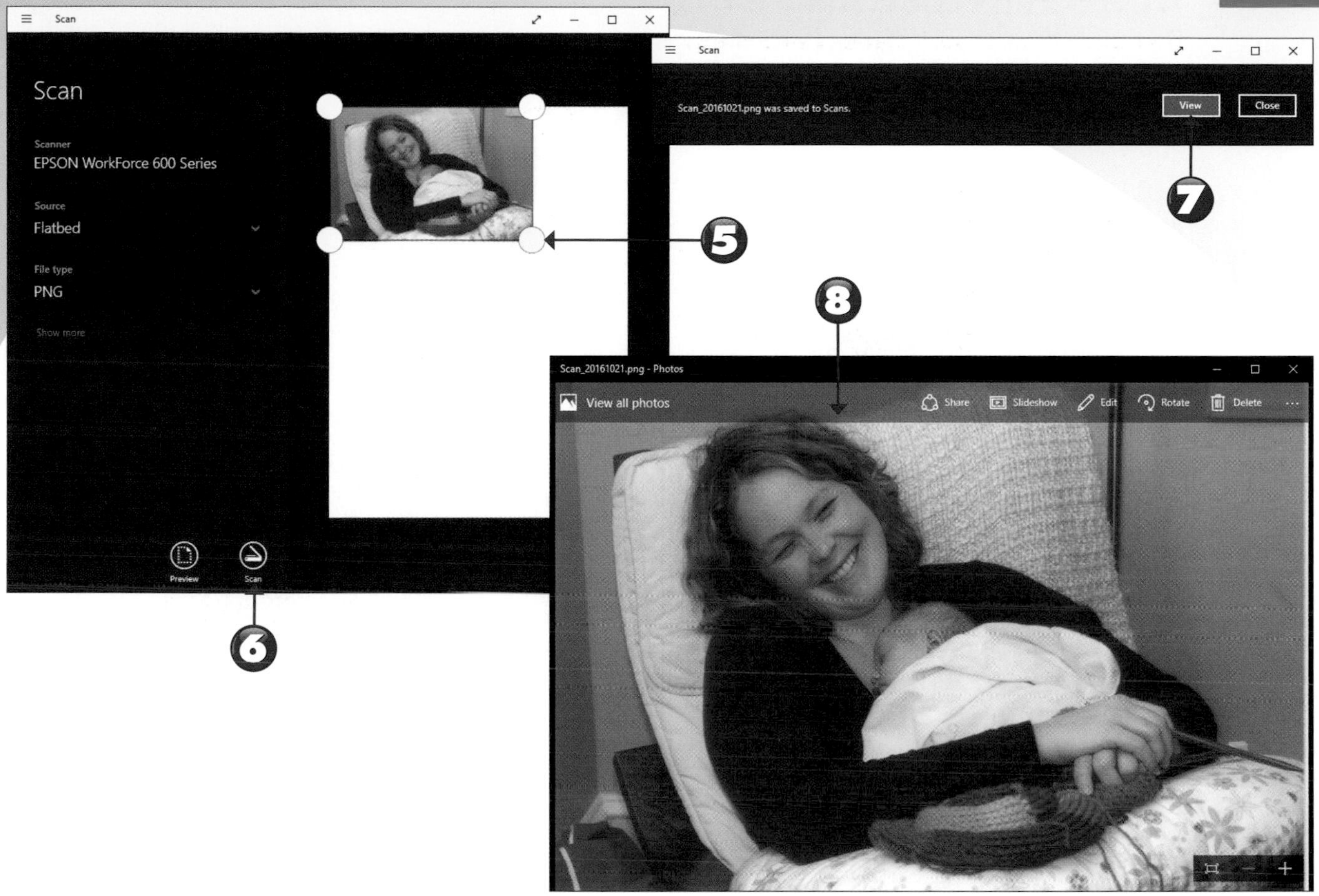

5. Drag the crop tools as desired around the preview. The area inside the rectangle will be scanned.

6. Click or tap **Scan**.

7. Click or tap **View**.

8. Your scan is opened by the default app for the file type.

End

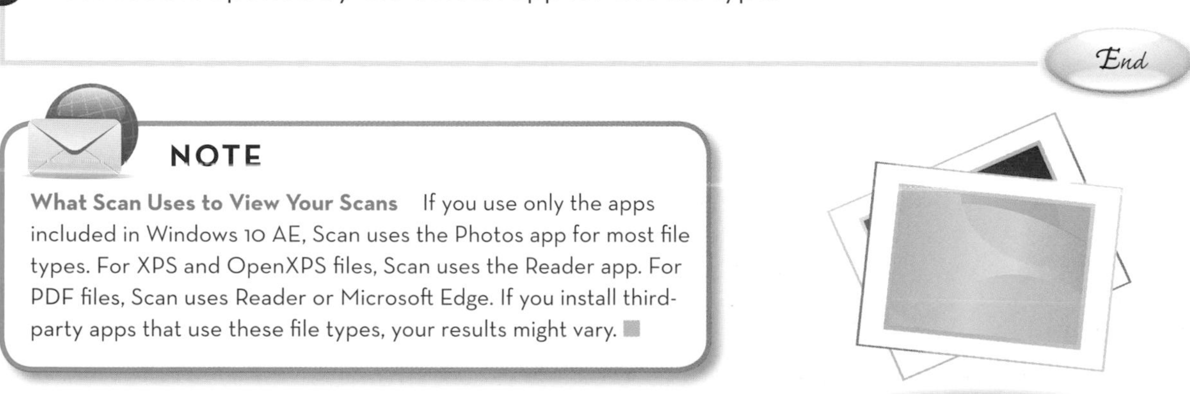

NOTE

What Scan Uses to View Your Scans If you use only the apps included in Windows 10 AE, Scan uses the Photos app for most file types. For XPS and OpenXPS files, Scan uses the Reader app. For PDF files, Scan uses Reader or Microsoft Edge. If you install third-party apps that use these file types, your results might vary.

ADJUSTING SCAN SETTINGS

By default, Scan assigns the PNG file type. However, you can select other file types if they are more suitable for your needs. Also by default, Scan uses a resolution of 100dpi (dots per inch). This is sufficient for scanning images that you plan to view or email. However, if you want to print a scan, you should use a resolution of 300dpi. To print a scan at a larger size than the original, use a resolution of 600dpi. In this lesson, you learn how to use these features.

Start

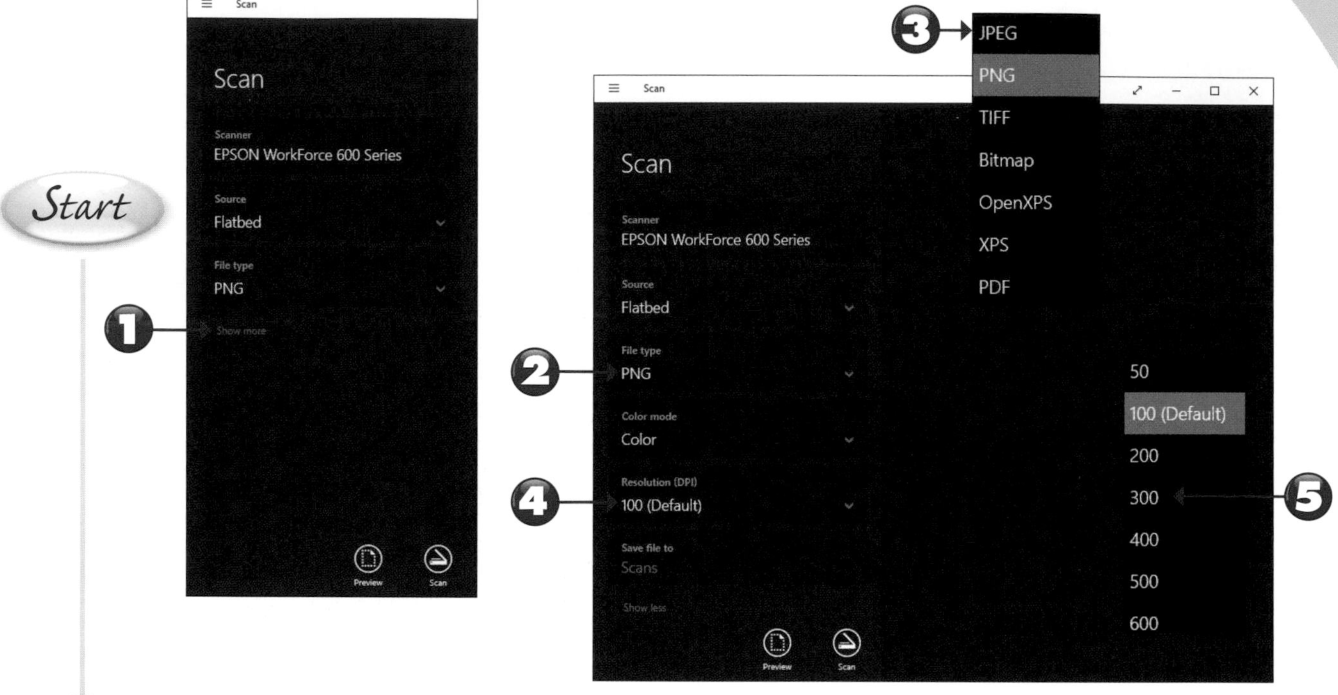

1. With the Scan app open, click or tap **Show more**.
2. Click or tap to change the file type.
3. Choose a file type. In this example, we chose JPEG because it is compatible with online photo printing services and photo-editing programs.
4. Click or tap to change the resolution.
5. Select **300** as the resolution.

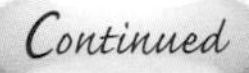

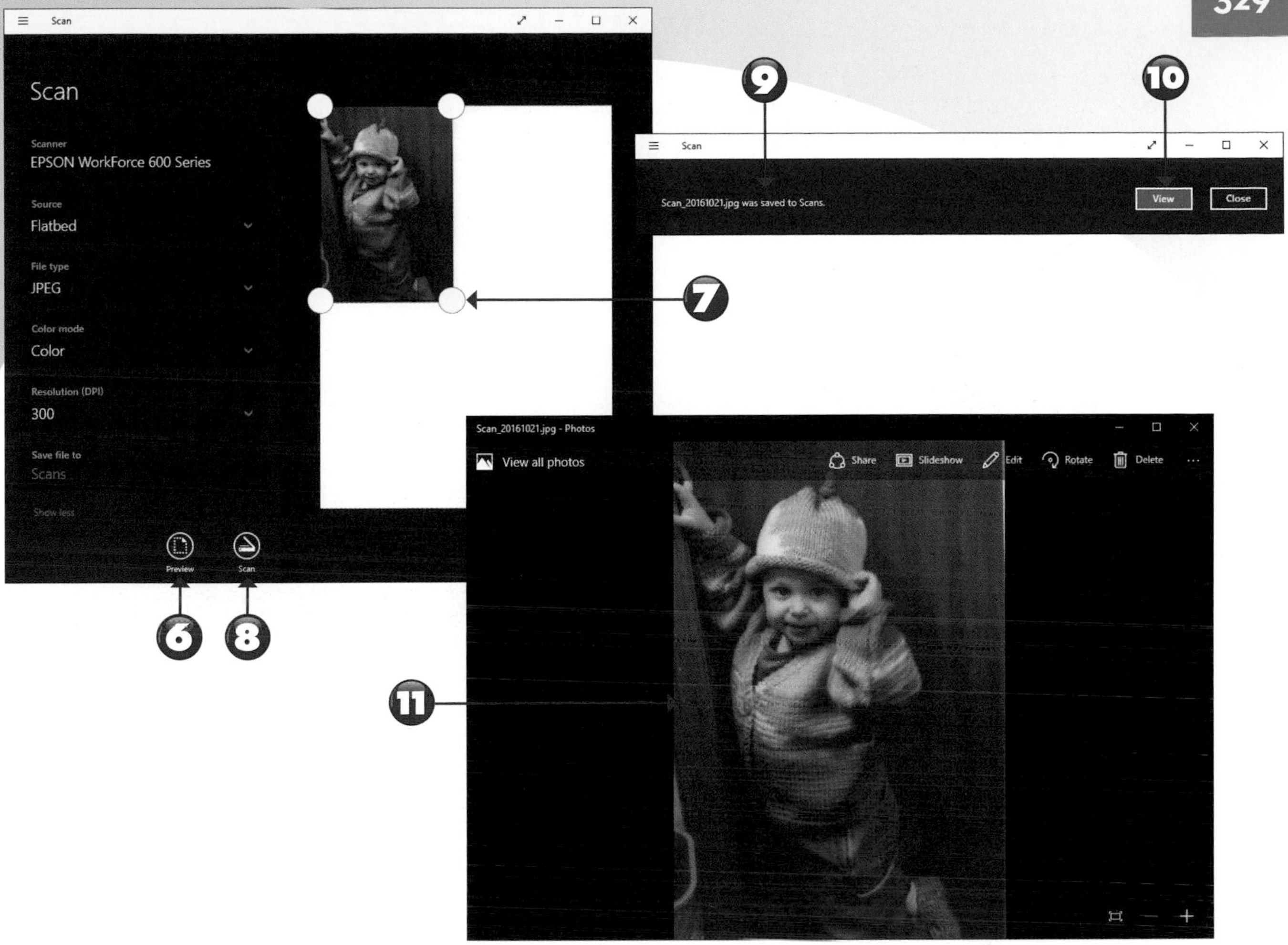

6 Place the photo face down on the scanner glass, and then click or tap **Preview**.

7 Click and drag cropping tools around the photo.

8 Click or tap to scan.

9 The scan is saved to your Scans folder.

10 Click or tap **View** to see the scanned image in its associated default app.

11 The scanned photo displayed in Photos.

End

NOTE

Choose a Folder One of the other options available among the Scan settings is choose a file destination. By default, all scans are saved to the Scans folder. Click or tap the **Save File To** link if you want to specify another folder in which to save the scanned image.

SELECTING COLOR, GRAYSCALE, OR BLACK-AND-WHITE MODES

Normally, you use the default color mode to scan color photos or documents. However, you can apply grayscale or black-and-white mode to create a colorless version of a color photo. These modes are primarily intended for scanning printed or typed documents, but as you learn in this lesson, you can turn ordinary photos into graphic designs with these colorless effects. For this example, we compare grayscale and black-and-white modes.

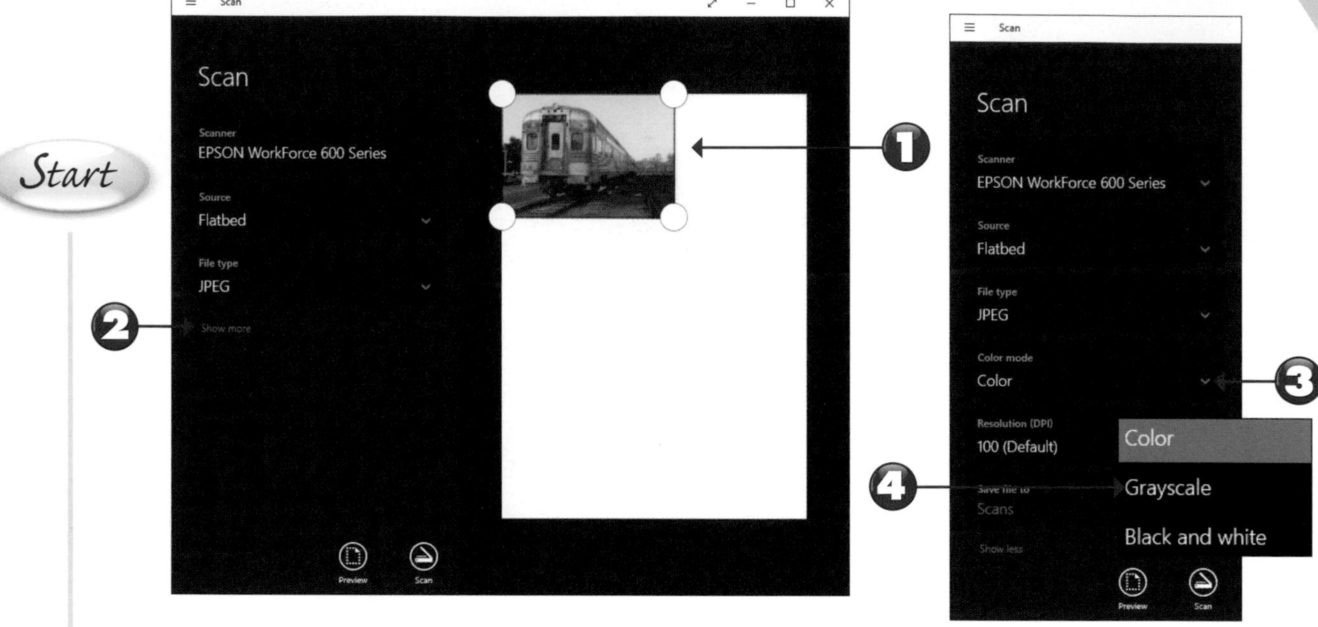

1. With the Scan app open, preview the image and adjust the cropping as needed.
2. Click or tap **Show more** (if the additional settings are not already displayed).
3. Click or tap **Color mode**.
4. Click or tap **Grayscale**.

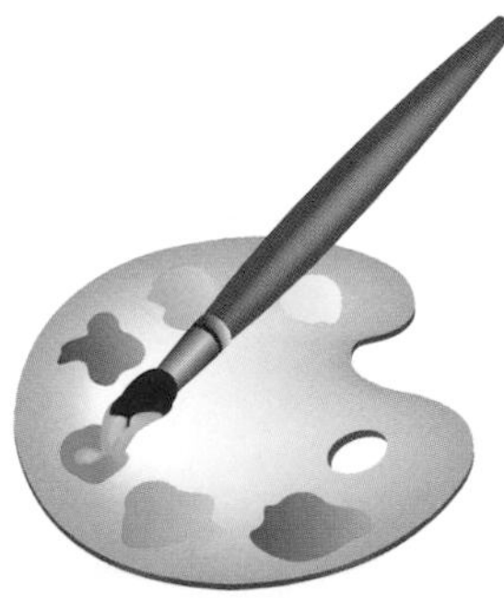

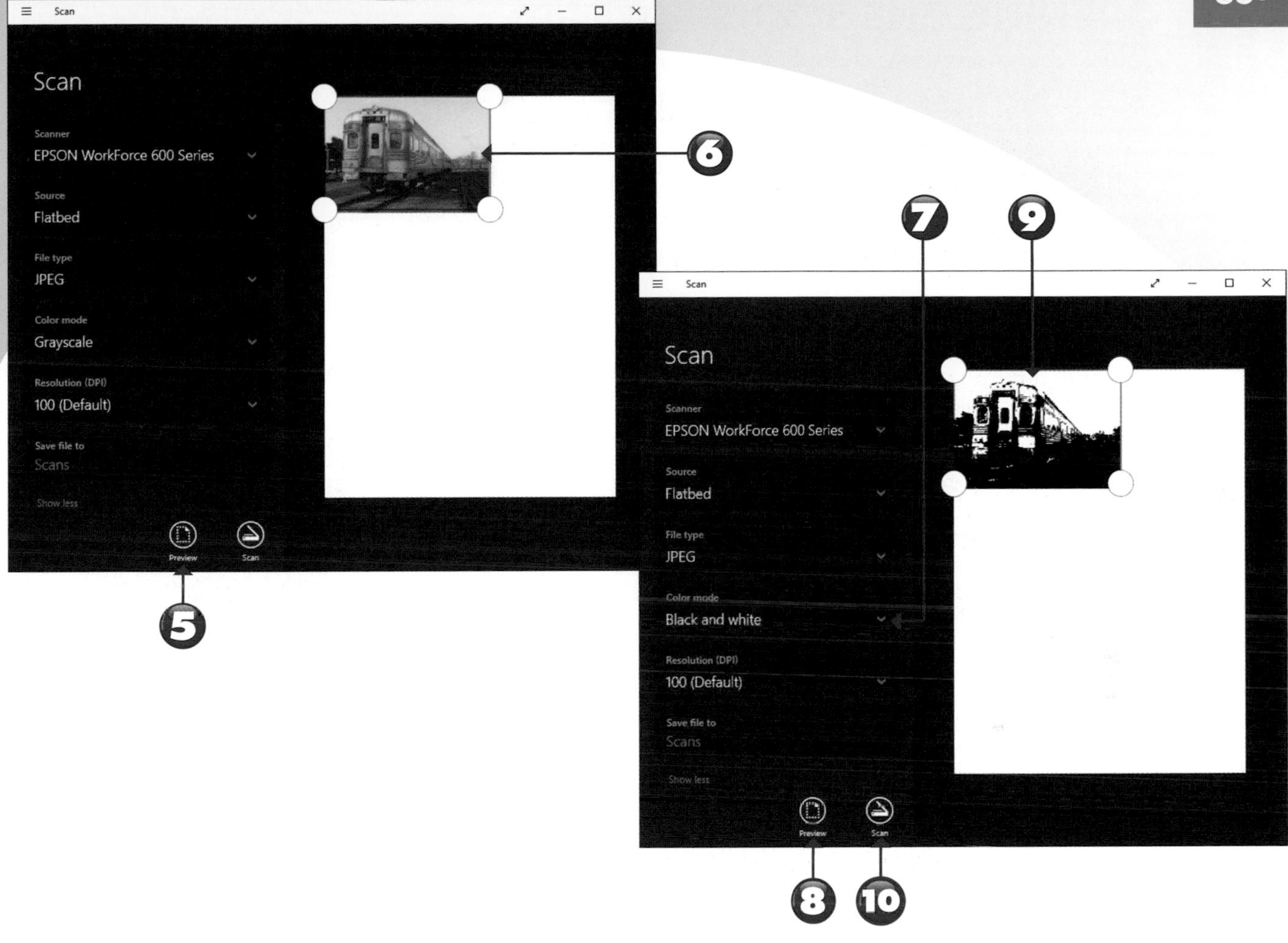

5. Click or tap **Preview**.
6. The image appears in grayscale in the preview area.
7. Change the Color mode to **Black and white**.
8. Click or tap **Preview**.
9. The image appears black and white in the preview area.
10. You can scan the image as is or reset to a preferred color mode before scanning.

End

OPENING THE SCANS FOLDER

Unless you change the default setting for Scan, all scans are stored in the Scans folder by default. You can view all your scans by opening this folder with File Manager.

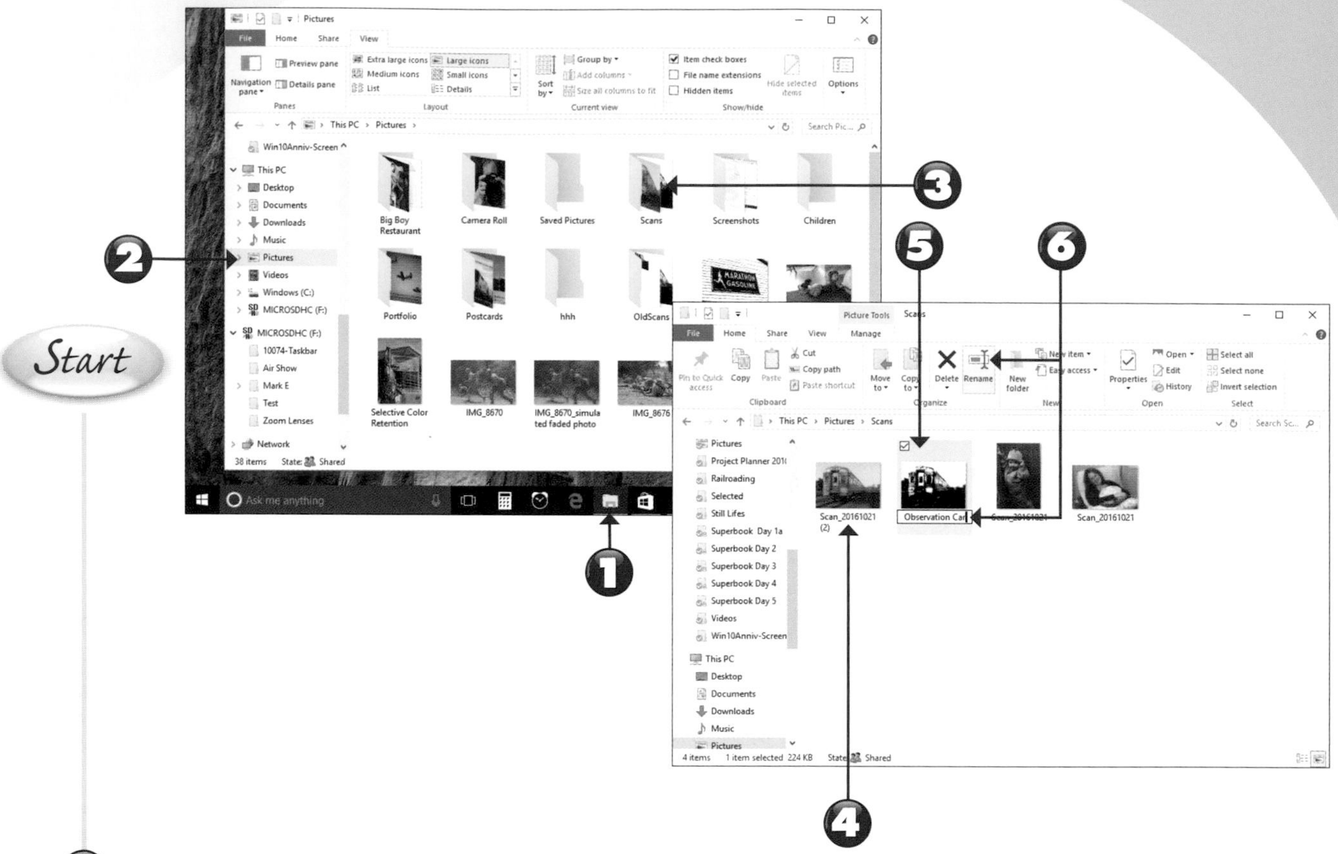

1. Click or tap **File Manager**.

2. Click or tap **Pictures**.

3. Double-click or double-tap **Scans**.

4. Scans are named with the date of the scan. If more than one file of the same type is scanned, each additional file is numbered (2), (3), and so on.

5. Click or tap a file you want to rename.

6. Click or tap **Rename** and type a more descriptive name.

Continued

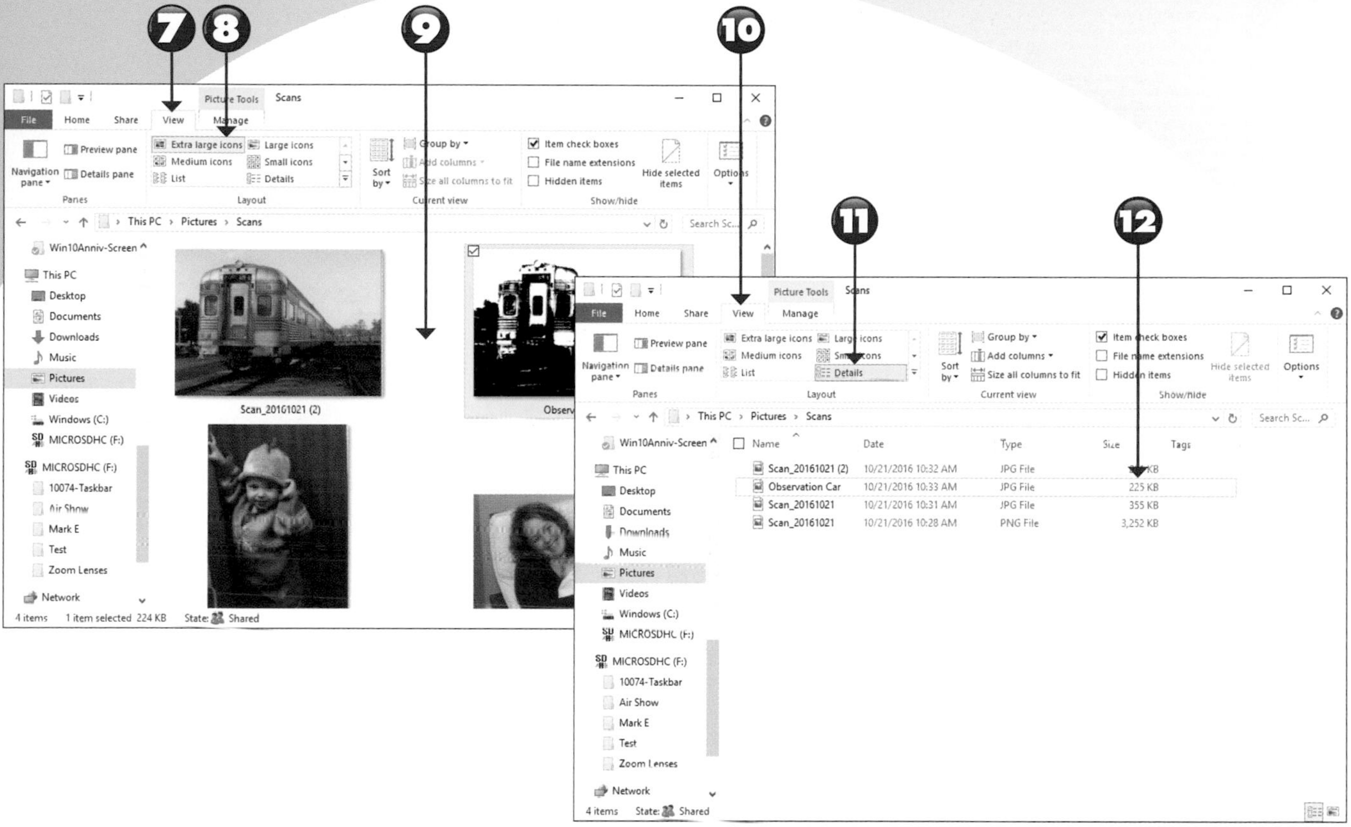

7 Click or tap **View**.

8 Click or tap a layout mode, such as **Extra large icons**.

9 File Manager adjusts the view layout.

10 To view your scans with detailed information, click or tap **View** again.

11 Click or tap **Details**.

12 The detailed information includes the date and time the image scan was created, the file type, and the file size.

End

NOTE

More About File Manager and Working with Scanned Photos To learn more about organizing, copying, moving, and deleting scans, see Chapter 14, "Storing and Finding Your Files." To learn more about editing your scanned photos, see Chapter 10, "Viewing and Taking Photos with Camera."

MANAGING WINDOWS 10 AE

The Settings dialog box in Windows 10 AE is where to go to change basic settings of all types. This chapter focuses on configuring system and privacy options as well as settings for volume and microphone control, screen resolution, battery saver options, and more.

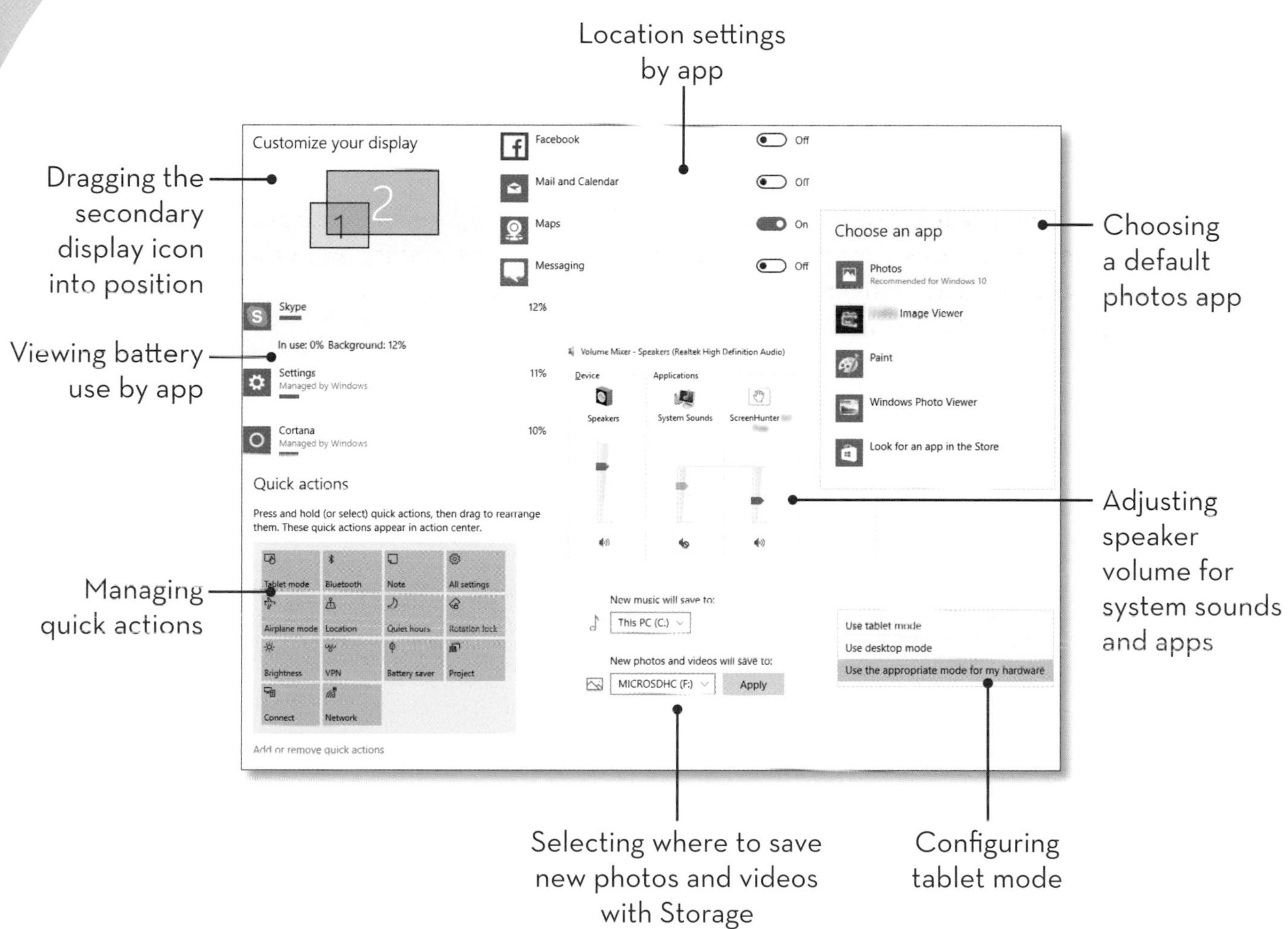
Location settings by app
Dragging the secondary display icon into position
Viewing battery use by app
Managing quick actions
Choosing a default photos app
Adjusting speaker volume for system sounds and apps
Selecting where to save new photos and videos with Storage
Configuring tablet mode
Customize your display
Facebook
Mail and Calendar
Maps
Messaging
Off
On
Skype
12%
In use: 0% Background: 12%
Settings
Managed by Windows
11%
Cortana
10%
Quick actions
Press and hold (or select) quick actions, then drag to rearrange them. These quick actions appear in action center.
Tablet mode
Bluetooth
Note
All settings
Airplane mode
Location
Quiet hours
Rotation lock
Brightness
VPN
Battery saver
Project
Connect
Network
Add or remove quick actions
Volume Mixer - Speakers (Realtek High Definition Audio)
Device
Applications
Speakers
System Sounds
New music will save to:
This PC (C:)
New photos and videos will save to:
MICROSDHC (F:)
Apply
Choose an app
Photos
Recommended for Windows 10
Image Viewer
Paint
Windows Photo Viewer
Look for an app in the Store
Use tablet mode
Use desktop mode
Use the appropriate mode for my hardware

ADJUSTING SPEAKER/HEADSET VOLUME

If your music is too loud or you can't hear the audio in the YouTube video you're playing, it's time to adjust the volume. Here's how.

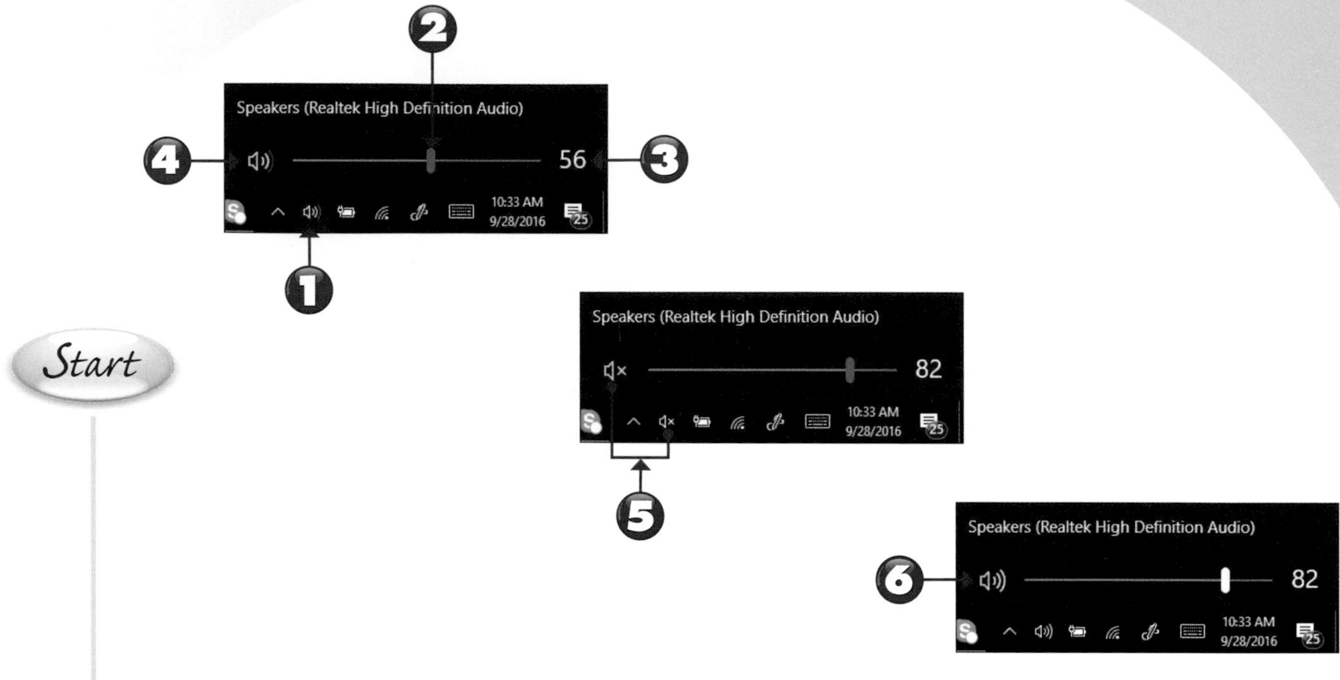

Start

1. Click or tap the **Speaker** icon on the taskbar.
2. Click or tap, and drag the slider to adjust the volume.
3. The current volume is displayed.
4. To mute audio, click or tap the **Speaker** icon.
5. Audio is muted.
6. To unmute audio, click or tap the **Speaker** icon again.

End

TIP

Changing Speaker Settings If you have just connected speakers to a different jack, or if you have connected a new display via HDMI or DisplayPort, you might not hear any audio. To select the audio source to use, search for Sound in Settings, click the Sound icon (refer to the exercise "Settings Overview" later in this chapter), and select the speaker or headset output you want to use.

ADVANCED AUDIO OPTIONS

From the Speaker icon in the taskbar, you can adjust the volume of specific apps, switch between default audio output and input sources, and select system sounds. Here's how.

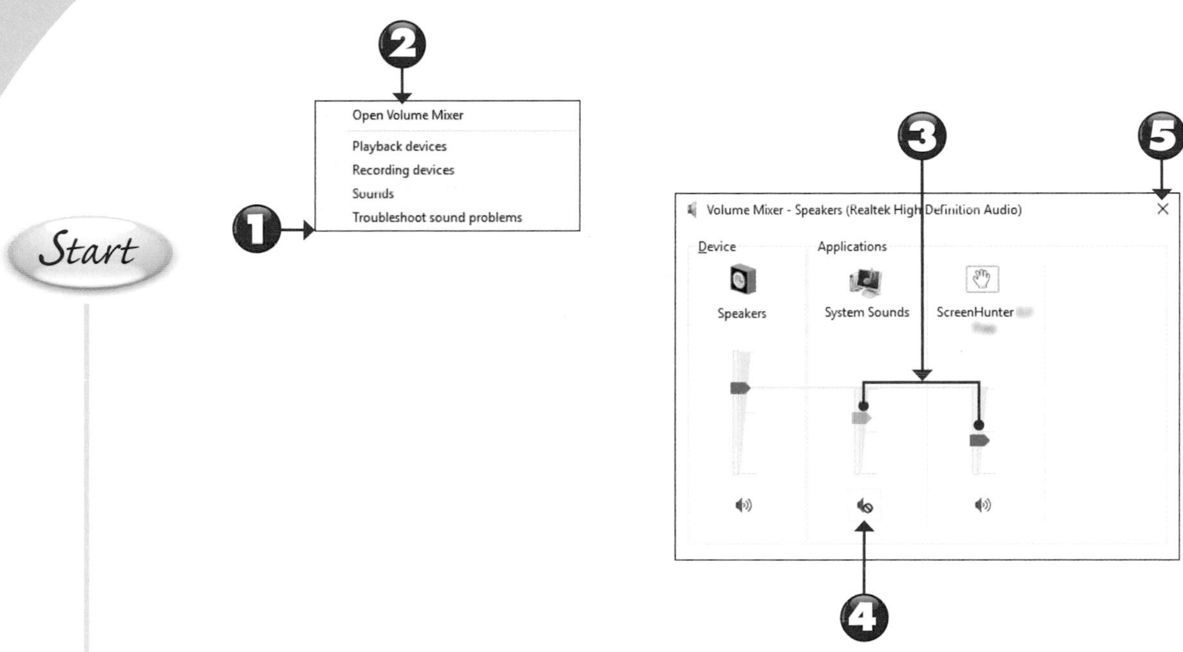

1. Right-click or press and hold the **Speaker** icon in the Notification area.
2. Click or tap **Open Volume Mixer**.
3. To adjust volume separately for audio, system sounds, or individual apps, click or press and drag the control up (louder) or down (softer).
4. To mute volume for speaker, system sounds, or individual apps, click or tap the appropriate **Speaker** icon.
5. Click or tap to close the dialog box.

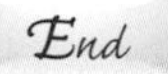

TIP

Changing Playback Devices You can click or tap Playback devices in step 2 to select and configure default speakers or other playback devices.

ADJUSTING MICROPHONE VOLUME

If you are having problems using Cortana's voice control or using Skype chat, it's time to increase the recording level on your microphone. Here's how.

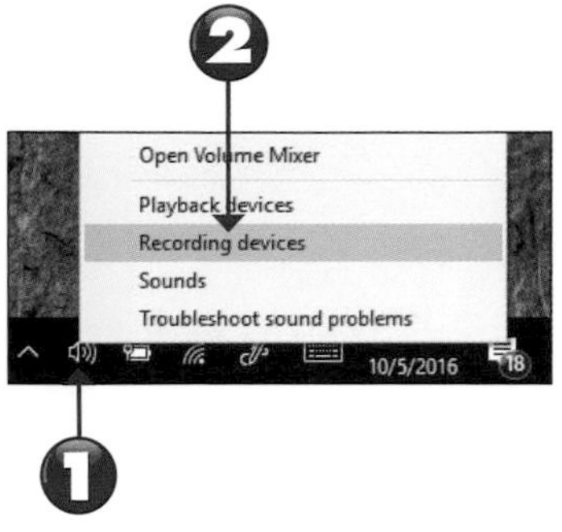

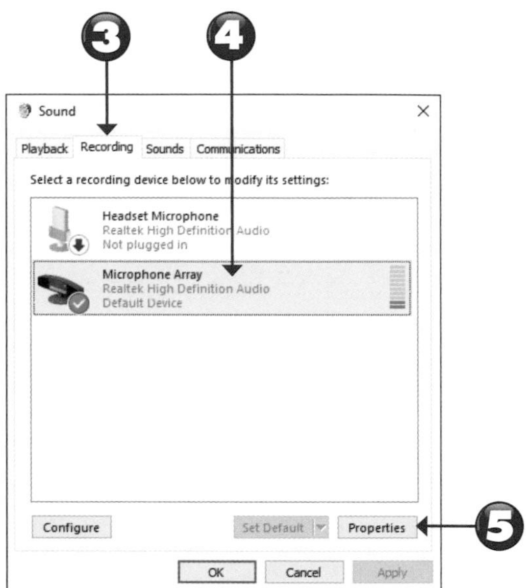

Start

1. Right-click or press and hold the **Speaker** icon in the Notification area.
2. Click or tap **Recording devices**.
3. Click or tap the **Recording** tab.
4. Click or tap the microphone you use.
5. Click or tap the **Properties** button.

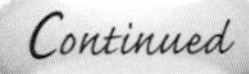

Continued

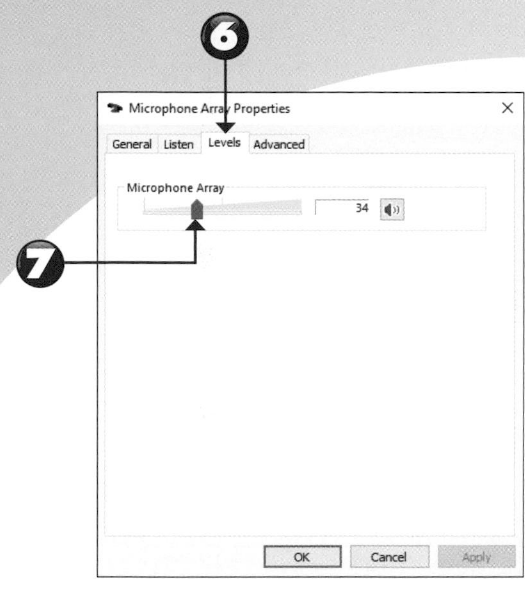

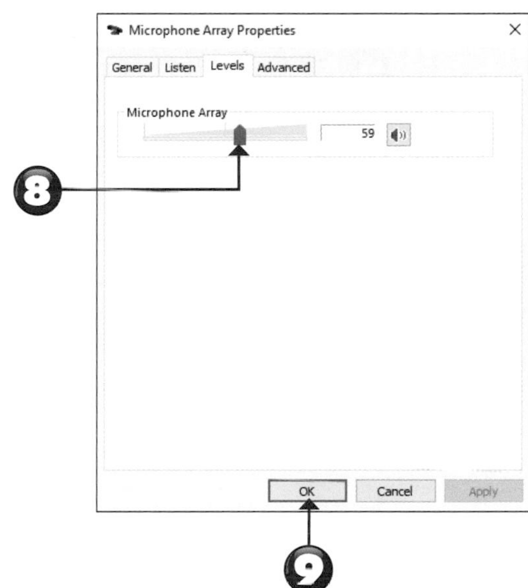

6. Click or tap the **Levels** tab.
7. Click or press and drag the slider to the right (increase volume).
8. Adjust the levels to around 55–75 for good volume without distortion.
9. Click or tap **OK**. Retry your app to verify better operation of your microphone.

End

NOTE

Better Microphone Choices If you are using the built-in microphone in a laptop or tablet and are not happy with the volume or sound quality, consider getting a headset microphone. Typical models plug in to the headset mini-jack or USB port.

ACCESSING THE SETTINGS DIALOG BOX

You use the Settings dialog box to make the most of the adjustments discussed in this chapter. Here's how to open Windows Settings.

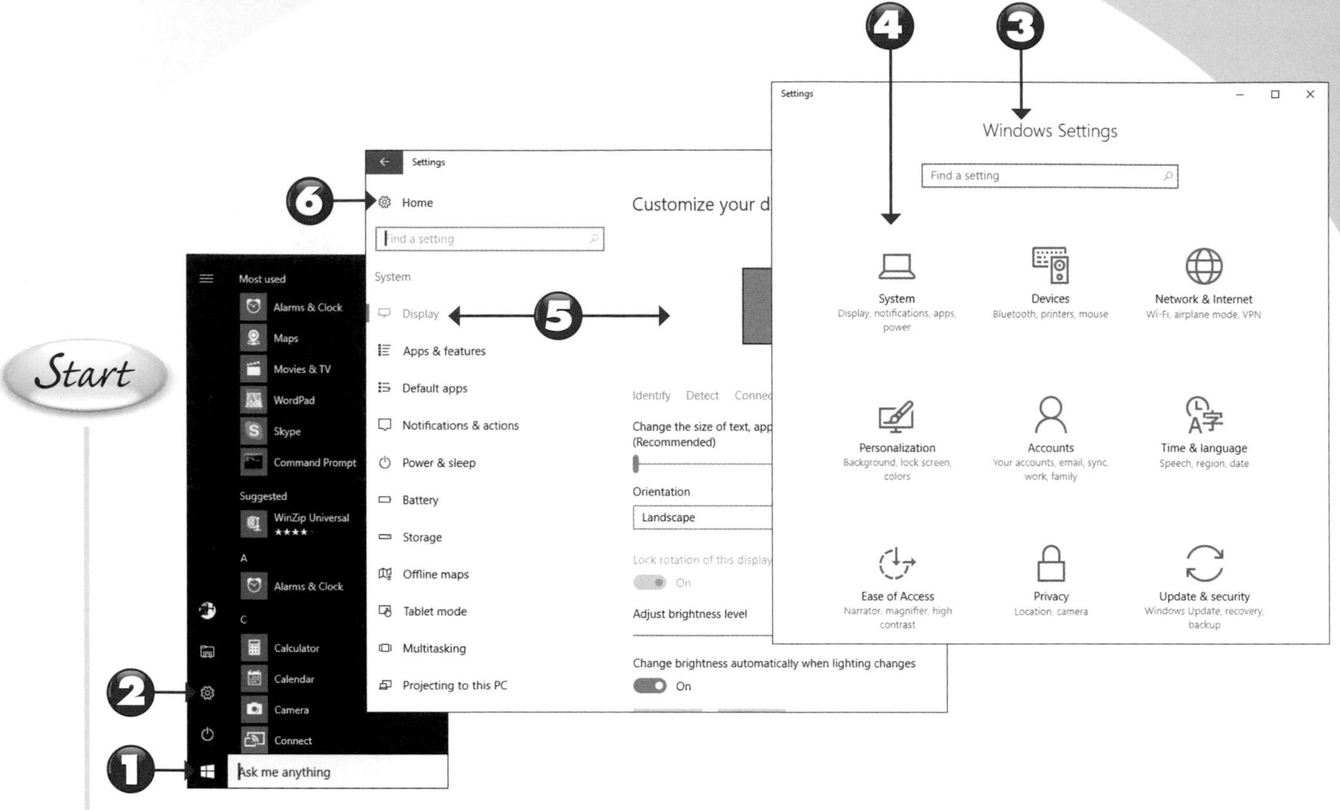

1. In Desktop mode, click or tap the **Start** button.
2. Click or tap **Settings**.
3. The Settings dialog box appears (default size).
4. Tap a category.
5. The category options appear in the left pane; the selected option appears in the right pane.
6. Tap **Home** to return to the main Settings dialog.

Continued

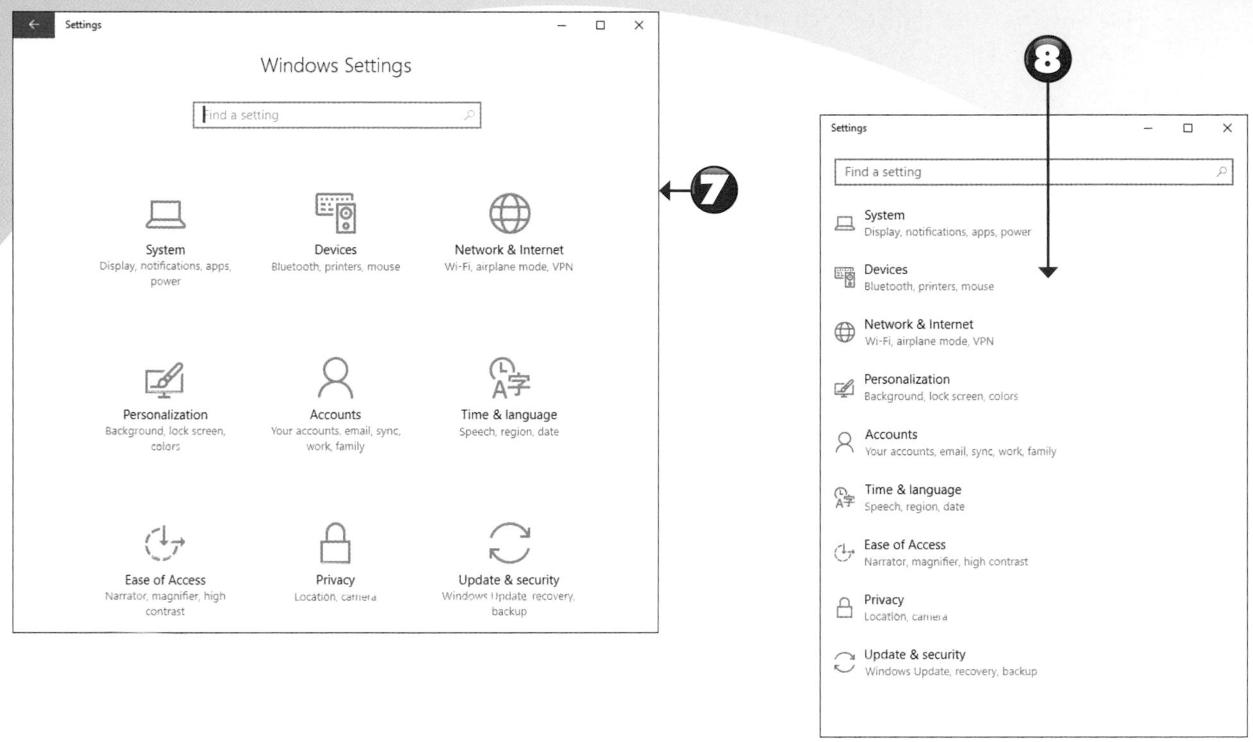

7. To reduce the size of the box, click or tap the right side and drag it to the left.

8. The Settings dialog box uses small icons when reduced in size.

End

NOTE

Resizing Settings To make most efficient use of space, this book primarily shows windowed versions of Settings dialog boxes (as demonstrated in step 8), which can be resized as desired. In Tablet mode, Settings opens full screen. ■

SETTINGS OVERVIEW

The Settings dialog box provides a useful way to access the settings you're most likely to change. Let's look at several main settings categories covered in this chapter and learn how to search for a particular setting. When you use the Settings Search box, some matches point to portions of the Control Panel, which is still present in Windows 10 AE (for example, **Sound** in step 5).

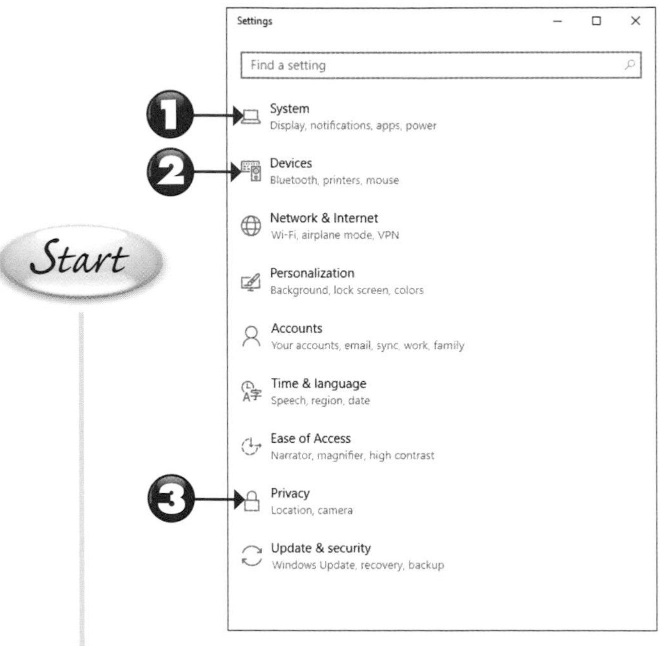

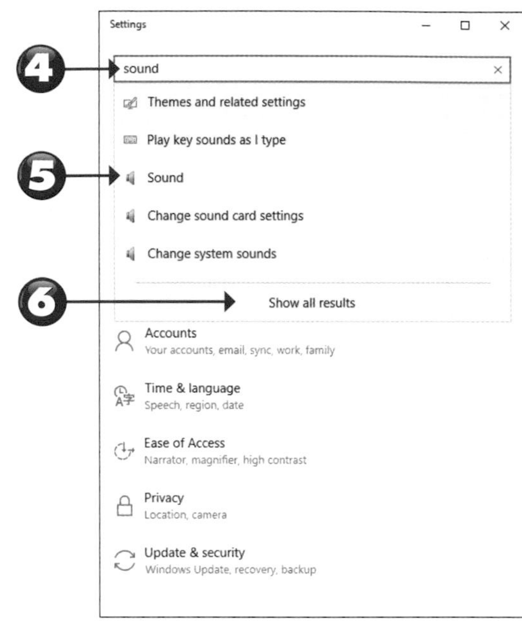

Start

1. Use the System settings to configure your computer's display, notifications, and power settings.
2. Use the Devices settings to configure your add-on hardware (printers, mouse, keyboard, and more).
3. Use the Privacy settings to protect your confidentiality.
4. To locate specific settings, enter text in the Search box. Matching settings are displayed.
5. Click or tap a setting to open its dialog box.
6. Click or tap **Show all results** for additional settings.

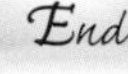

End

NOTE

Other Menus See Chapter 20, "Networking Your Home with HomeGroup," for more information on using Network & Internet. See Chapter 21, "Customizing Windows," for more information on using Personalization, Time & language, and Ease of Access. See Chapter 22, "Adding and Managing Users," for more information on using Accounts. See Chapter 23, "Protecting Your System," and Chapter 24, "System Maintenance and Performance," for more information on using Windows Update, backup, and recovery options.

ADJUSTING DISPLAY BRIGHTNESS AND ROTATION

You can change display settings, including brightness, screen orientation, and more. Adjusting brightness and rotation is easy, as this exercise points out.

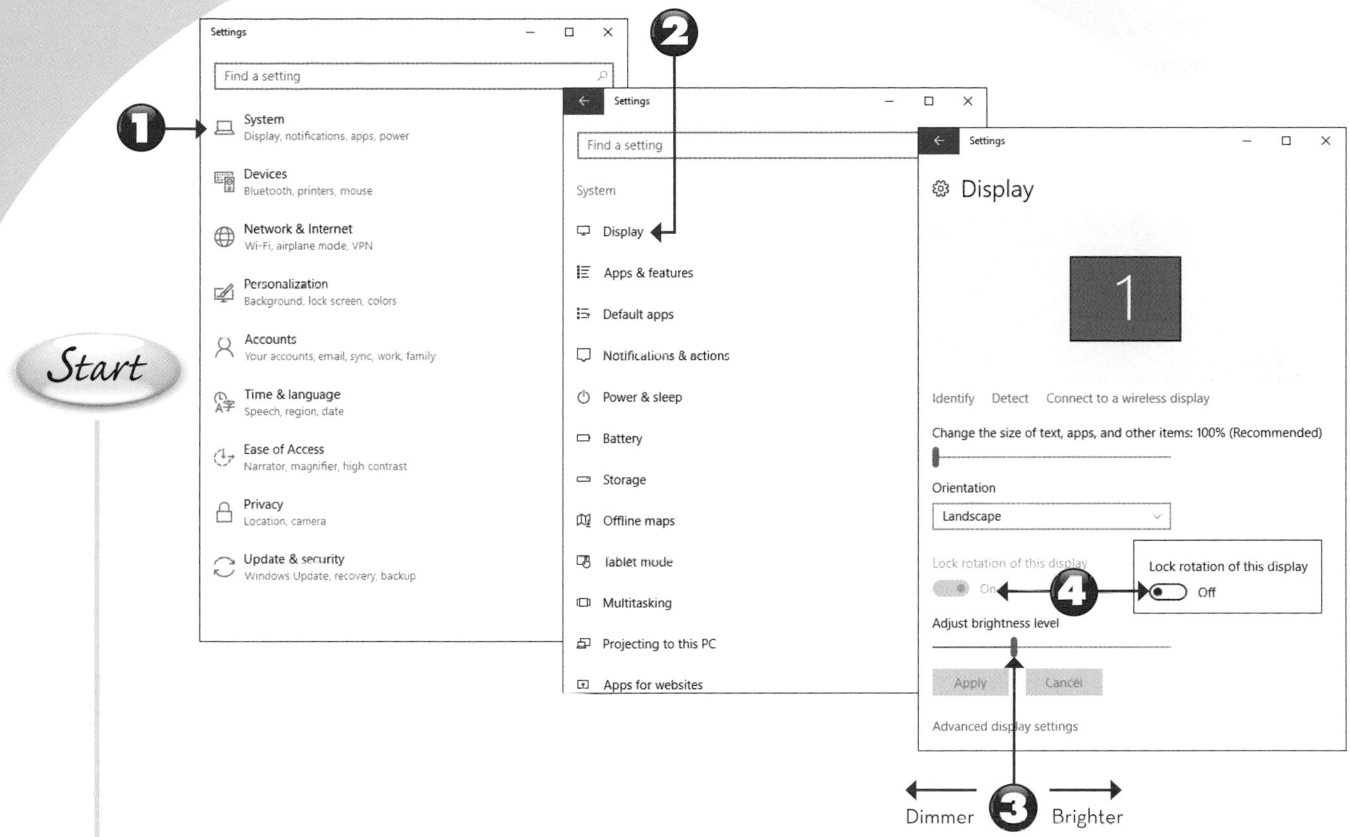

Start

1. From the Settings dialog box, click or tap **System**.
2. Click or tap **Display**.
3. Click or tap and drag the screen brightness control as desired.
4. If you want the onscreen display to rotate as you rotate your display or tablet, click or tap and drag **Lock rotation of this display** to the Off position. (This setting is disabled on laptops or convertible tablets in laptop mode.)

End

NOTE

Lock Rotation Pros and Cons The Lock rotation... option shown in step 4 is primarily intended for tablet users. Disabling rotation lock enables you to rotate your tablet from portrait (vertical) to landscape (horizontal) to view presentations or websites at the largest possible size. However, disabling rotation lock could use up battery power faster.

ADDING A SECOND DISPLAY

You can get more done more quickly and have more fun with media if you add a second display to your desktop or laptop computer. We start from the Display settings you learned about in the previous exercise to show you how it's done.

HDMI cable
HDMI port
VGA cable
VGA port
Mini DisplayPort cable
Mini DisplayPort port
Start
1
HDMI cable plugged in to HDMI port
1
VGA cable plugged in to VGA port
1
Mini DisplayPort cable plugged in to mini DisplayPort port
2
3
Display
Customize your display
1|2
Identify Detect Connect to a wireless display
Change the size of text, apps, and other items: 100% (Recommended)
Orientation
Landscape
Adjust brightness level
Multiple displays
Duplicate these displays

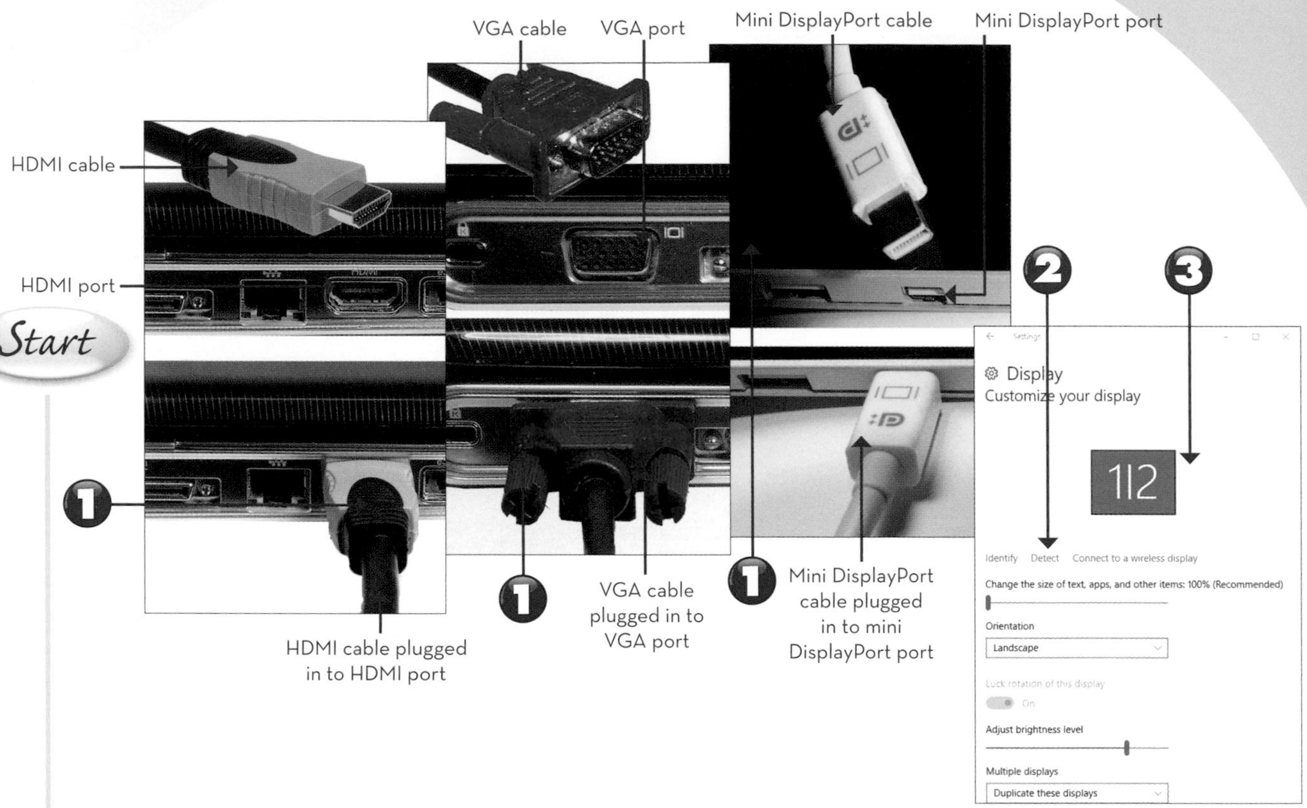

1. Plug in a display to the video port on your computer and turn it on.
2. From the Display settings, click or tap **Detect** if the second display is not detected automatically.
3. When detected, both displays appear here.

End

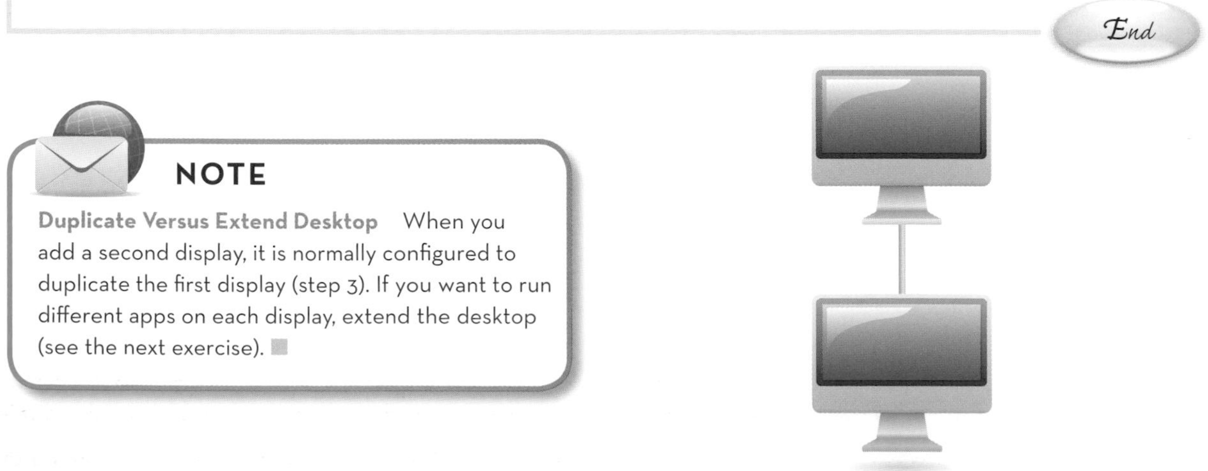

NOTE

Duplicate Versus Extend Desktop When you add a second display, it is normally configured to duplicate the first display (step 3). If you want to run different apps on each display, extend the desktop (see the next exercise).

EXTENDING YOUR DESKTOP

In most cases, if you add an additional display it's because you want more onscreen space for apps. Here's how to configure your additional display as an extended desktop.

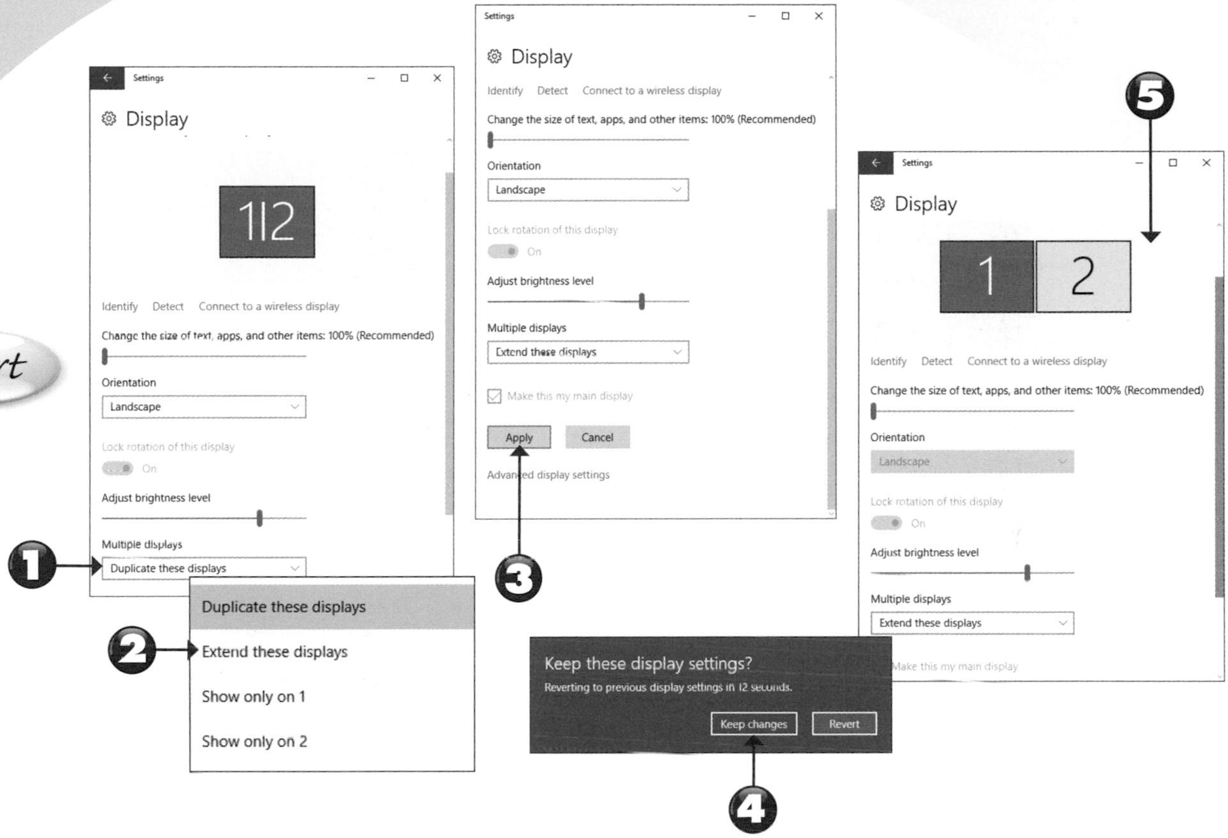

1. From the Display settings, open the **Multiple displays** menu.
2. Select **Extend these displays**.
3. Click or tap **Apply**.
4. Click or tap **Keep changes**.
5. The first and second display icons are now separate.

NOTE

Using the Extended Desktop Drag a program window to the second display, and when you close that program, Windows remembers which display was last used for the program. When you open the program again, it opens in that display.

ADJUSTING SCREEN RESOLUTION

As you view the Display settings, the relative sizes of the screen display icons shown are indicators of current resolution settings. Larger icons indicate higher-resolution displays, and smaller icons indicate lower-resolution displays. If any display is not using the recommended resolution (horizontal and vertical pixel settings), follow this procedure to change its resolution for optimal screen viewing.

Start

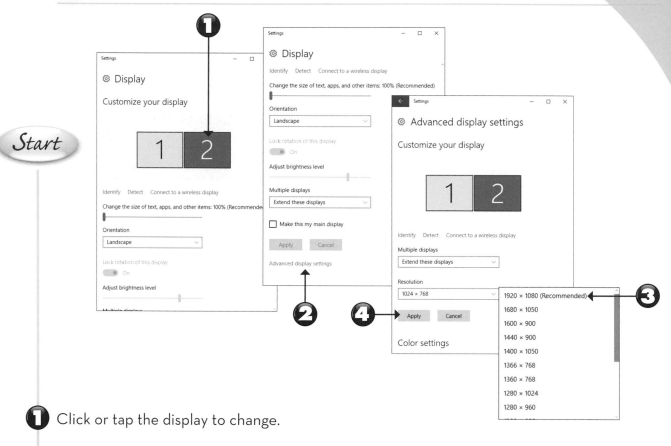

1. Click or tap the display to change.
2. Click or tap **Advanced display settings**.
3. Click or tap the **Resolution** menu and select the (Recommended) setting for your display device.
4. Click or tap **Apply**.

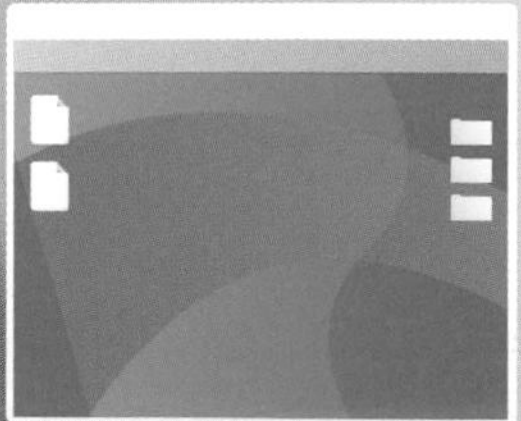

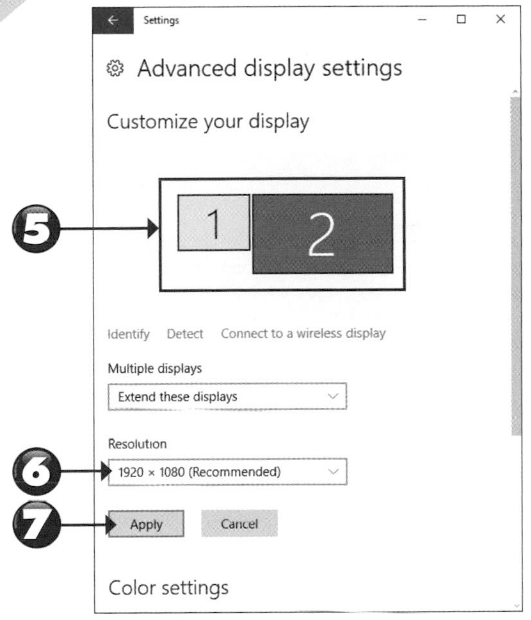

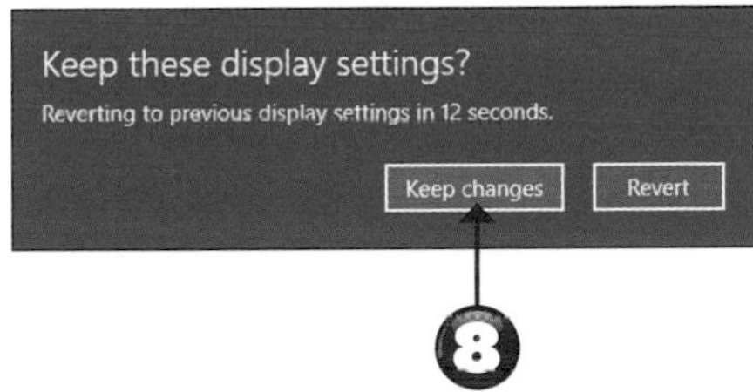

5. The display icon changes in size according to the resolution setting selected in step 3.

6. The new display resolution is now listed.

7. Click or tap **Apply**.

8. Click or tap **Keep changes**.

End

NOTE

Recommended = Optimal Windows 10 AE refers to the optimal resolution for your display as "Recommended." However, if you find the desktop objects or web pages are too small onscreen, use the Change the size of text, apps, and other items slider (found in Display settings) to choose a larger size or a lower resolution.

ADJUSTING SCREEN POSITION

When you add an additional display, Windows 10 AE assumes that it is located to the right of your original display by default. If your additional display is in some other relative position, you should move the display icon accordingly. In this example, the additional display is placed above the original. Here's how to change its position.

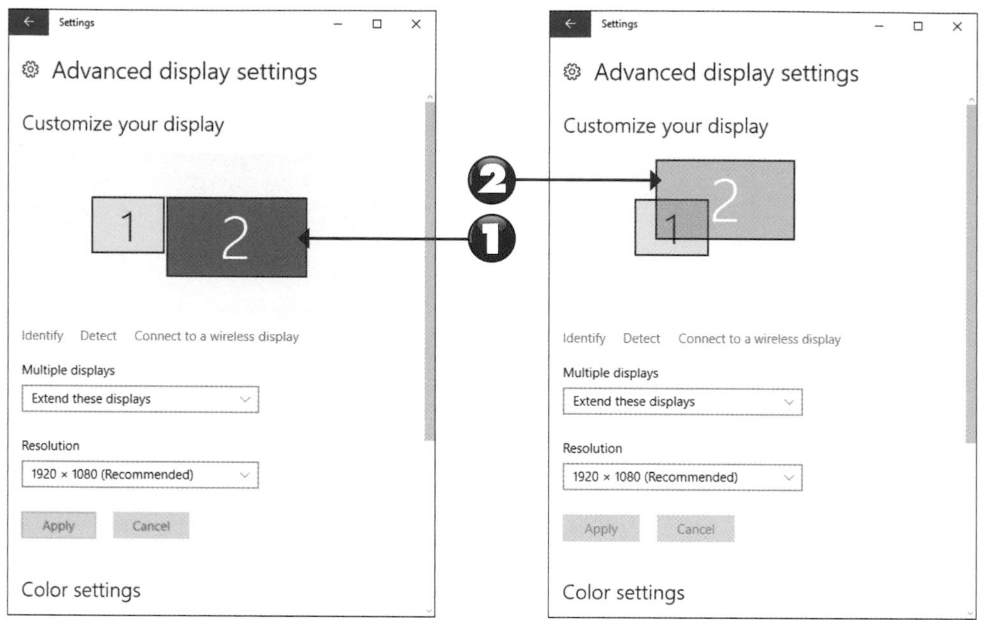

Start

1. Open Advanced display settings (see the previous task). In this example, the additional display icon (2) is not in the correct position relative to the original display (1).

2. Click or press and drag the display icon to the correct relative position.

Continued

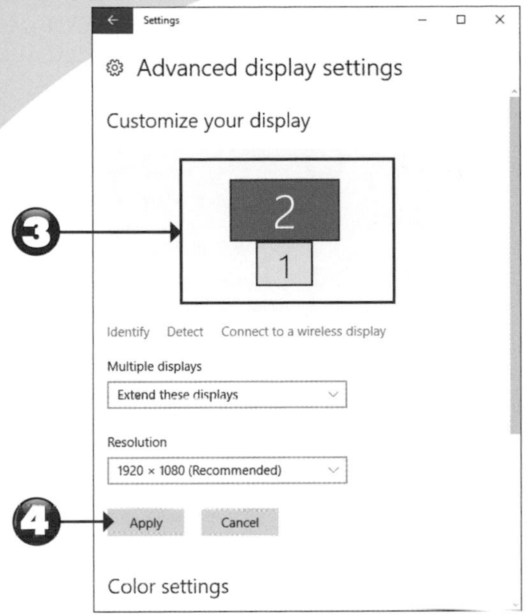

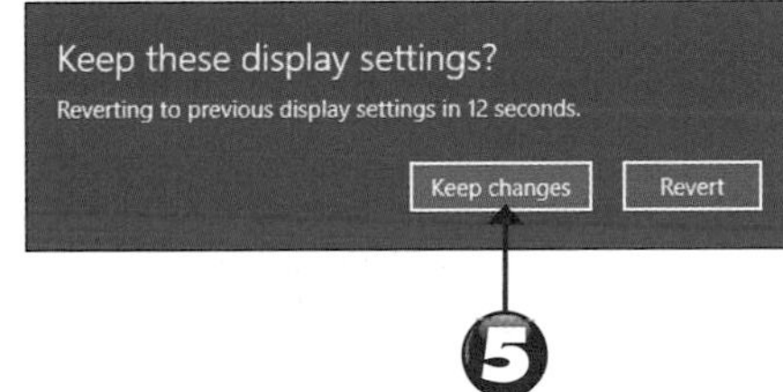

3. The additional display icon is now in the correct location.

4. Click or tap **Apply**.

5. Click or tap **Keep changes**.

End

TIP

Back Arrow and Gearbox Icons From any menu in Settings, click the gearbox icon to return to the main Settings dialog box. To return to the previous dialog box, click the back arrow. To go back two levels, click the back arrow twice.

CHANGING QUICK ACTIONS

You use the Action Center on the taskbar to get access to features you use frequently. By default, the Action Center includes icons such as network or screen brightness. Use the Notifications & Actions settings to customize the icons you prefer to display as quick actions.

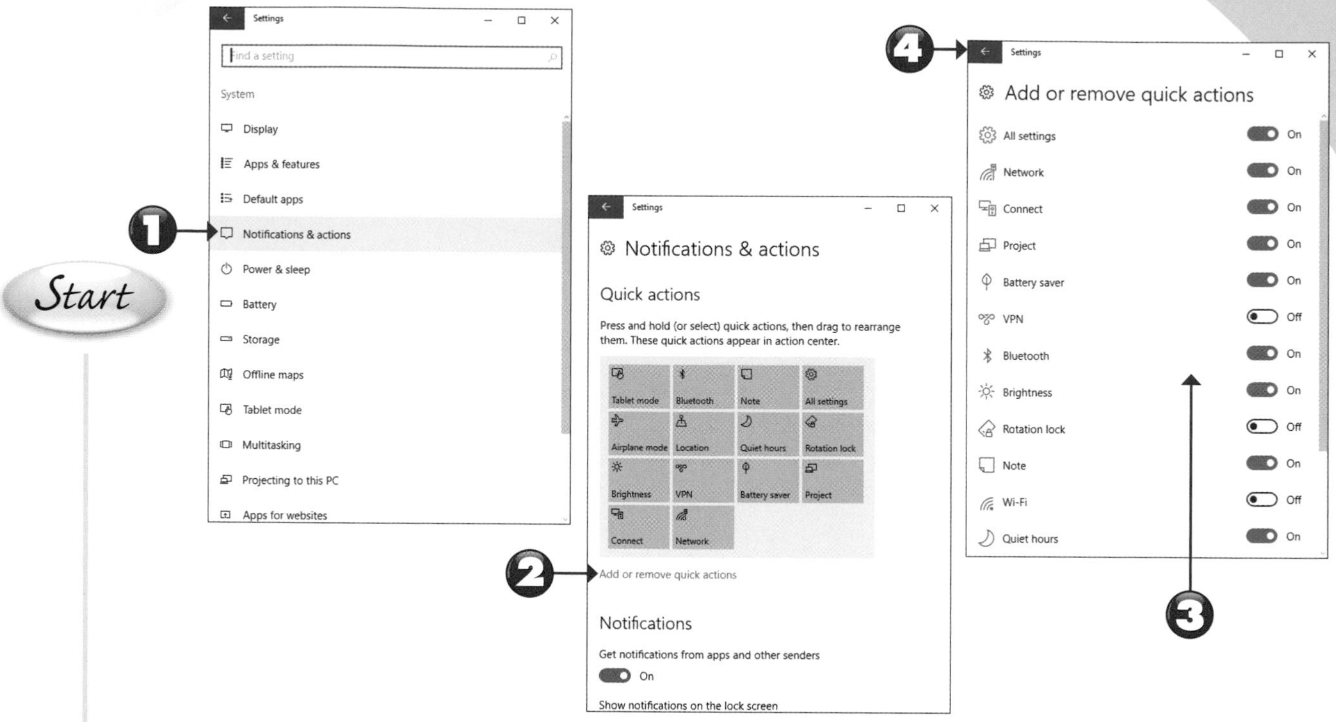

1. From System settings, click or tap **Notifications & actions**.
2. Click or tap **Add or remove quick actions**.
3. Use sliders to turn quick actions on or off.
4. Click to return to the Notifications & Actions settings.

Continued

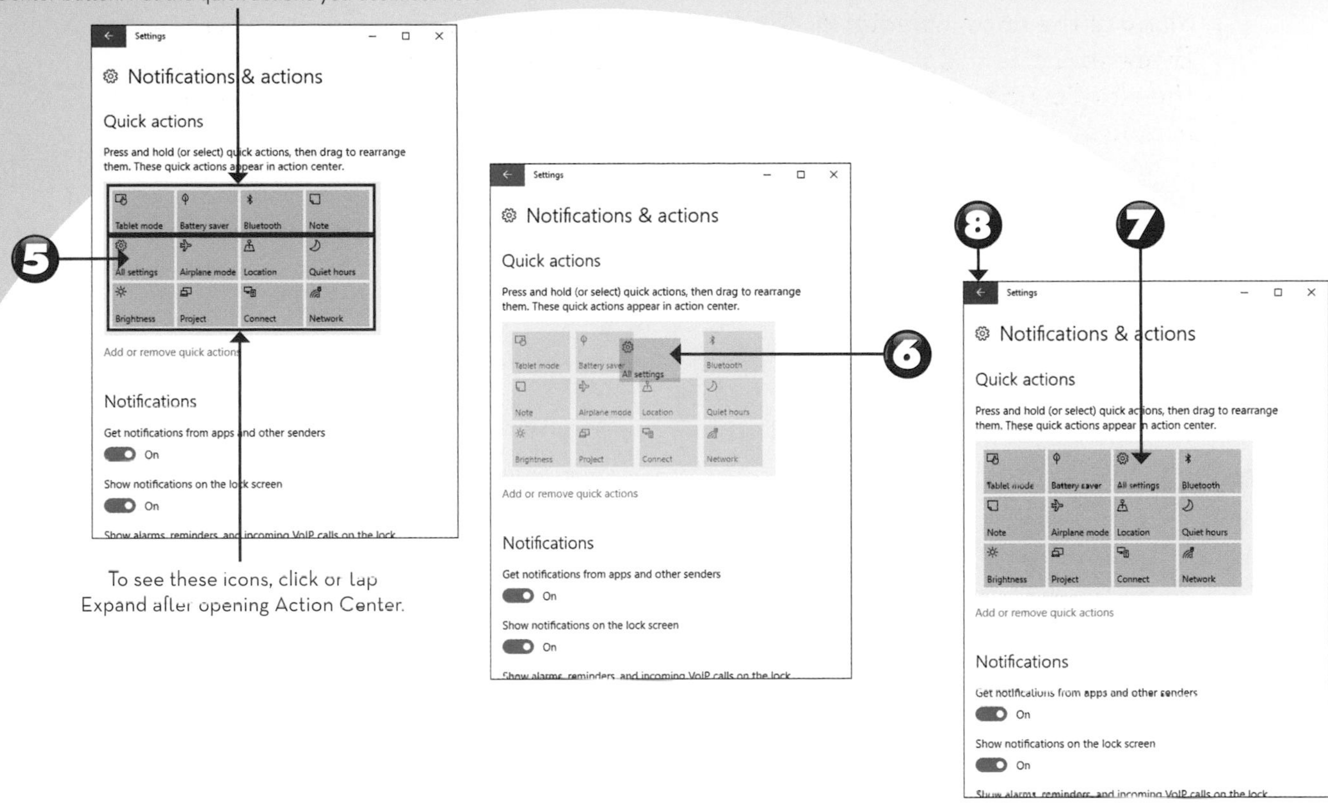

5. To move an icon to a different position, press and hold or click and hold it.

6. Drag it to the desired position. Other icons move to make room for it.

7. Release it.

8. Click or tap to return to System settings.

End

CONFIGURING APP-SPECIFIC NOTIFICATIONS

Many of the apps included in Windows 10 AE (and some you can install) can display notifications. In this exercise, you learn how to turn off notifications you do not need.

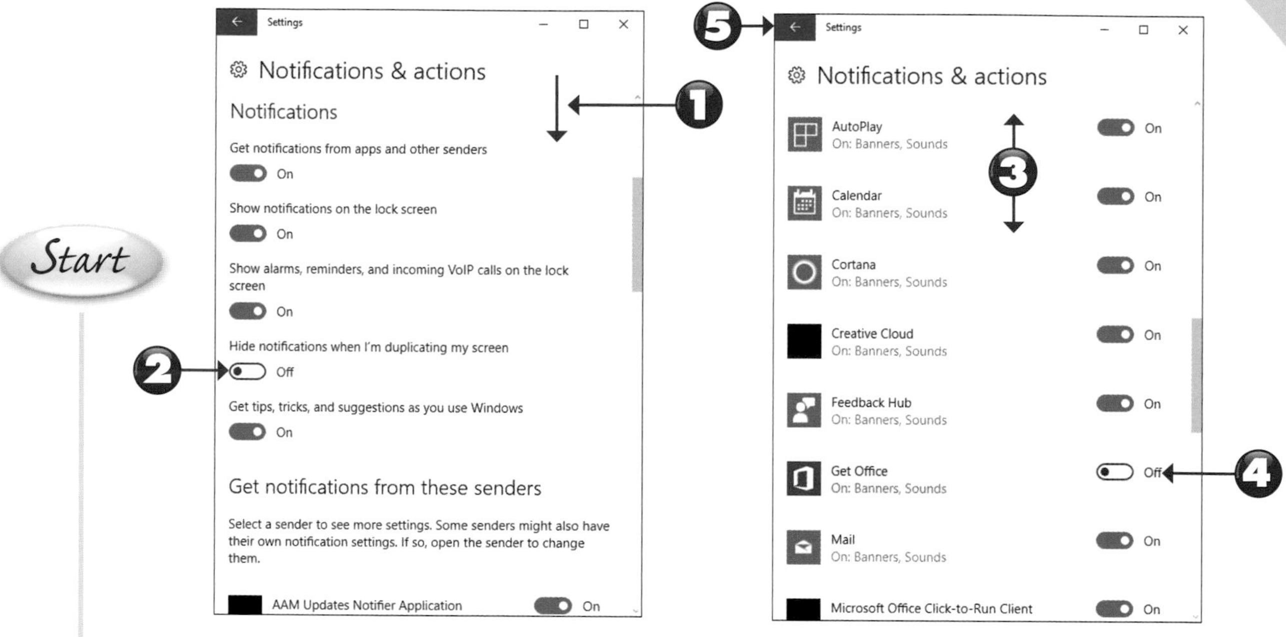

1. From the Notifications & actions settings, scroll down to the Notifications section.
2. If you want to turn off app notifications while your display is duplicated (useful when running a presentation), make sure this setting is turned **On**.
3. Scroll down or flick up to see all apps with notification options.
4. To turn off notifications for an app, click or tap to turn the switch **Off**.
5. Click or tap to return to the System settings.

End

NOTE

Notifications Where You Want Them By default, notifications occur on the Lock screen as well as from the Windows Desktop or Start menu (Notifications). Use the sliders shown in the Notifications section of the Notifications & actions settings to limit where notifications appear.

APPS & FEATURES

Particularly with Ultrabooks and tablets, both of which use small-capacity SSD storage, knowing how much space an app uses can be very helpful, especially if you also have the ability to uninstall apps that you don't need anymore. The Apps & Features dialog box provides you with both features.

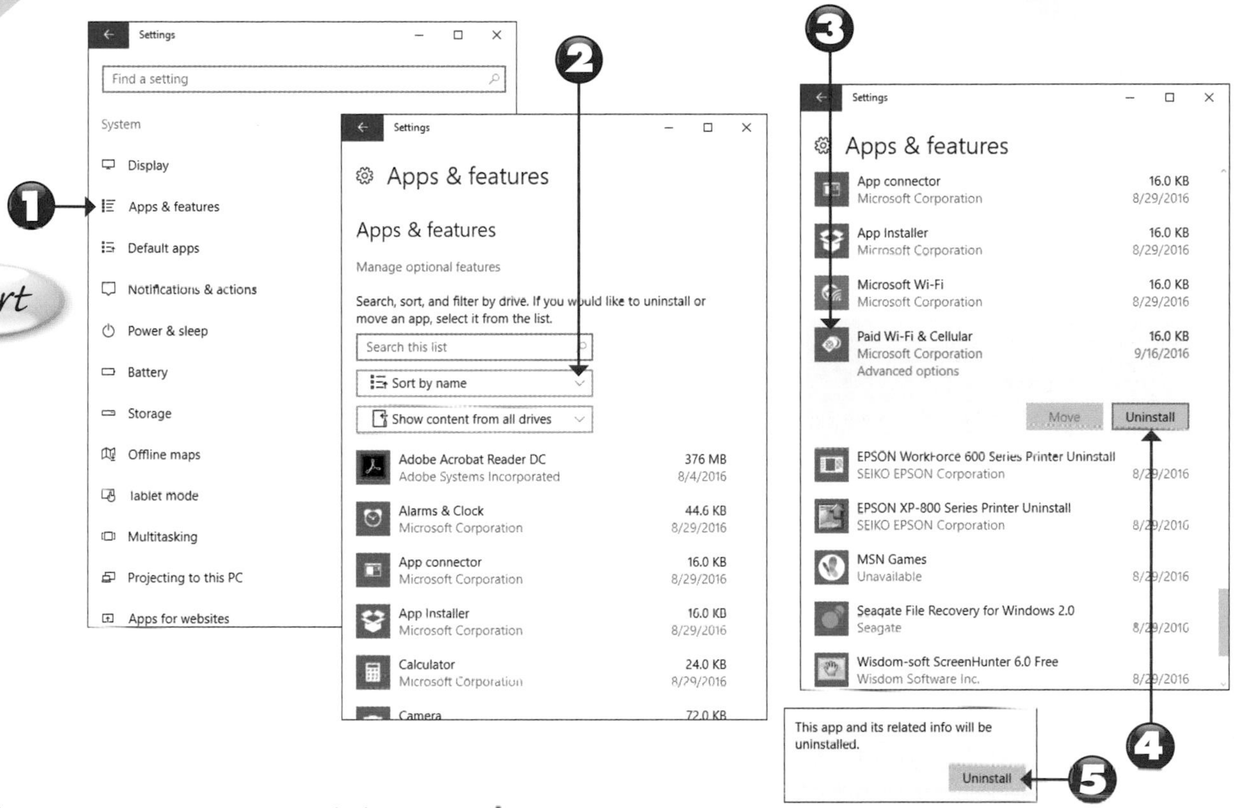

1. From System settings, click **Apps & features**.
2. Apps are listed in order from largest to smallest. Click or tap to sort by name or date.
3. Click or tap an app you want to uninstall.
4. Click or tap **Uninstall**.
5. Click or tap **Uninstall** to remove it.

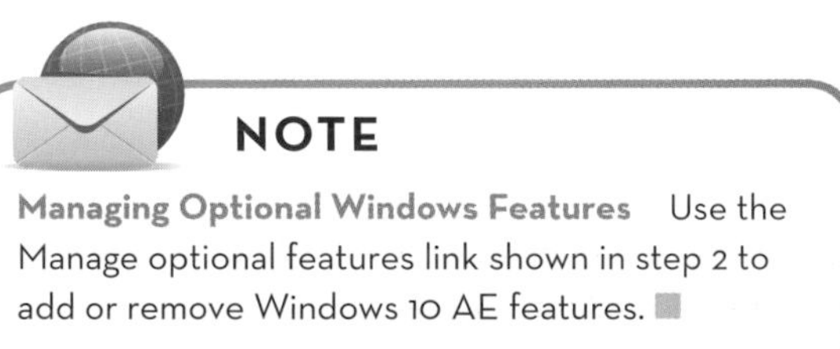

NOTE

Managing Optional Windows Features Use the Manage optional features link shown in step 2 to add or remove Windows 10 AE features.

CONFIGURING TABLET MODE

If you use a tablet or a convertible tablet/laptop device (a device with a quick-release keyboard or a keyboard that flips out of the way so you can use the touch screen as a tablet), the Tablet mode dialog box helps you optimize your device for touch use.

Start

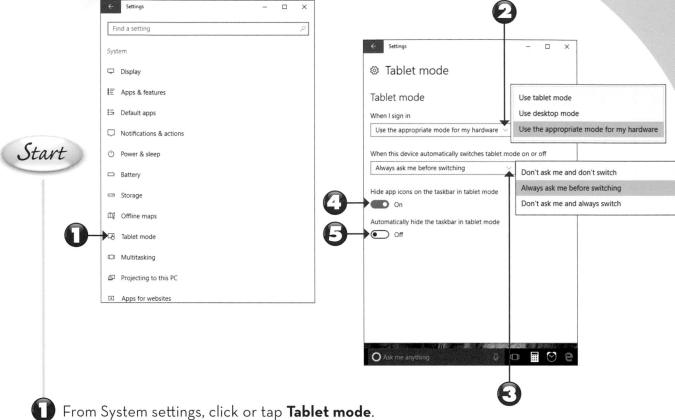

1. From System settings, click or tap **Tablet mode**.
2. By default, Windows 10 AE uses the appropriate mode for your hardware. Click or tap to change.
3. By default, Windows 10 AE asks before switching to or from tablet mode. Click or tap to change.
4. To hide app icons in Tablet mode, press and drag or click and drag to **On**.
5. To hide the taskbar in Tablet mode, press and drag or click and drag to **Off**.

Tablet mode

Multitasking

Projecting to this PC

Apps for websites

2:41 PM
10/3/2016

Tablet mode

Multitasking

Projecting to this PC

Apps for websites

2:41 PM
10/3/2016

Tablet mode

Multitasking

Projecting to this PC

Apps for websites

About

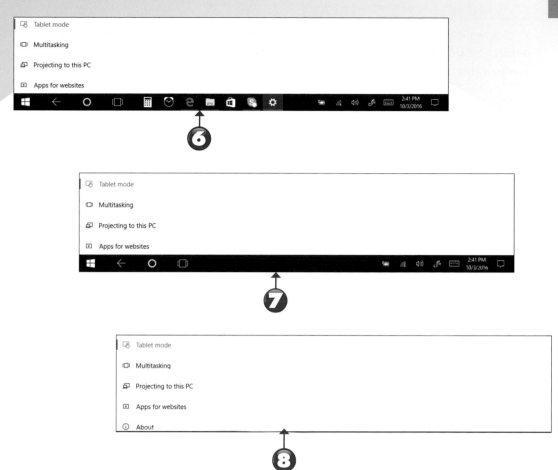

6. Here's Tablet mode desktop with taskbar and app icons visible.

7. Here's Tablet mode desktop with taskbar but no app icons.

8. Here's Tablet mode desktop without taskbar or app icons.

End

NOTE

Switching Apps in Tablet Mode To learn how to switch between apps in Tablet mode, see Chapter 6, "Running Apps."

NOTE

Start Menu in Tablet Mode To see how the Start menu looks in Tablet mode, see Chapter 3, "Logging In, Starting Up, and Shutting Down Windows 10 Anniversary Edition with a Touchscreen."

CONFIGURING SNAP

Windows 10 AE's Multitasking settings enable you to configure how your screen functions when you are using two or more apps. In this exercise, you learn how to configure the Snap feature, which controls how app windows behave.

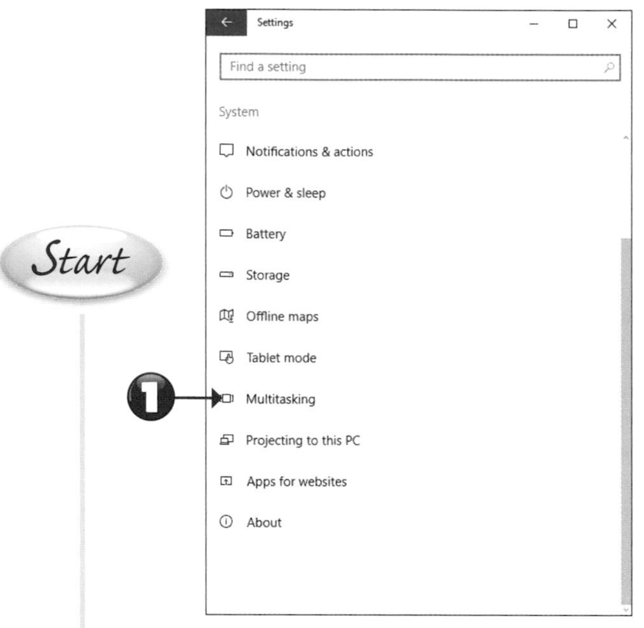

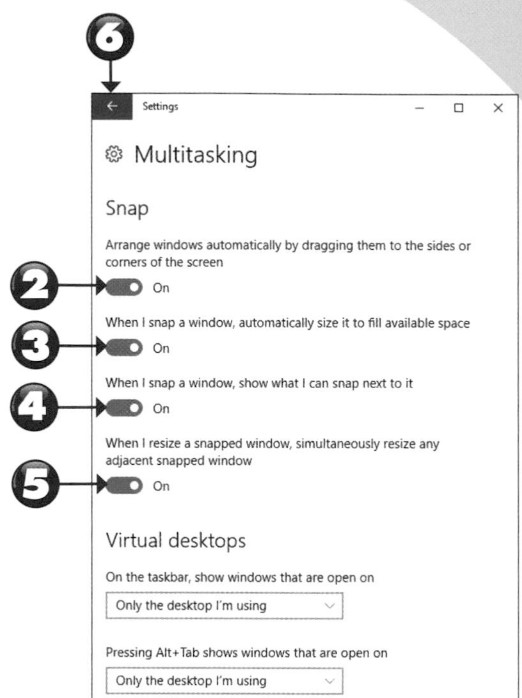

1. From System settings, click or tap **Multitasking**.
2. If you don't want a window that you drag to the top of the screen to expand to full screen, click or press and drag to **Off**.
3. If you prefer to arrange window sizes manually, click or press and drag to **Off**.
4. If you don't want to see additional running apps you can snap when you snap a window to one side, click or press and drag to **Off**.
5. If you don't want other windows to automatically resize when you resize a snapped window, click or press and drag to **Off**.
6. Click or tap to return to System settings.

End

USING BATTERY SAVER

If you use Windows 10 AE on a laptop or a tablet, Battery settings shows you how your system uses battery power. Here's how to apply battery saving settings.

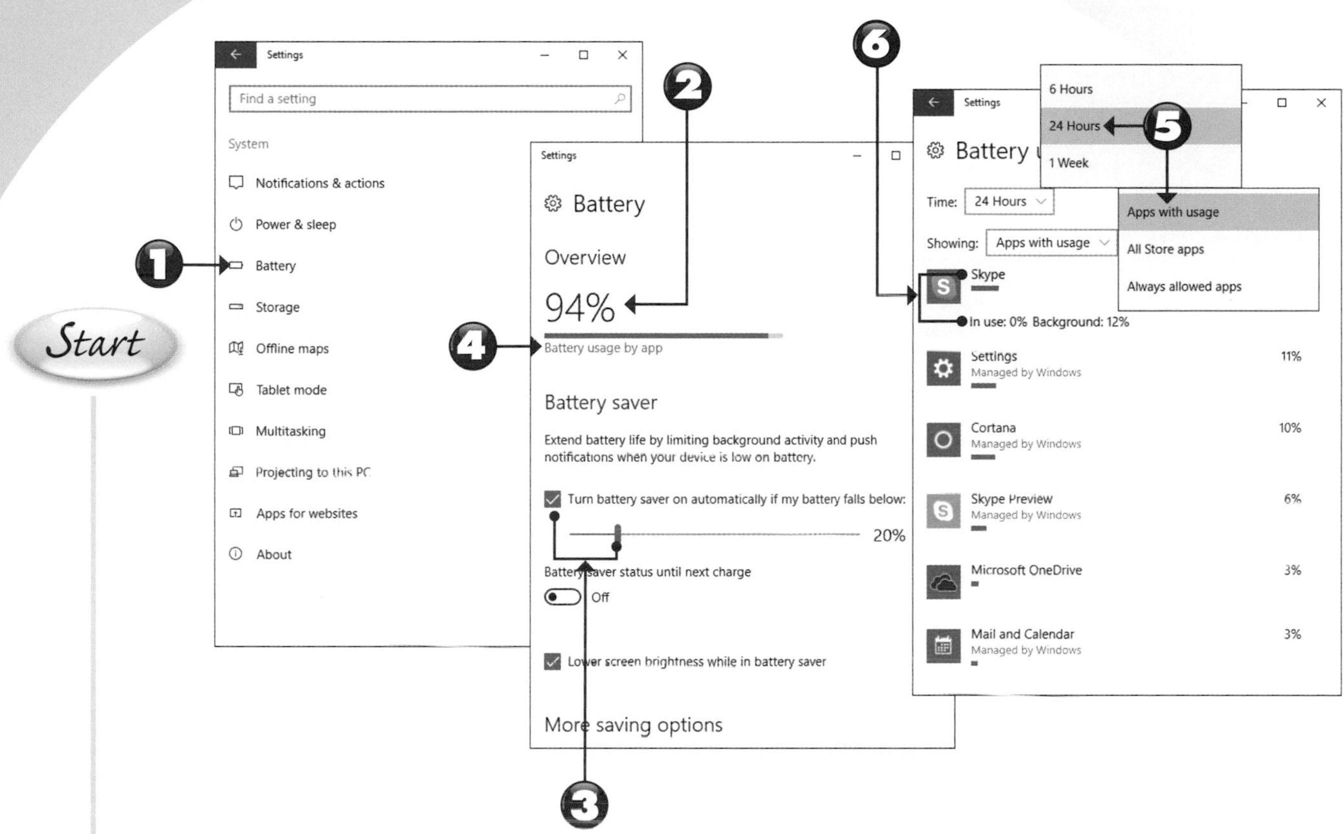

Start

1. From Settings, click or tap **Battery**.
2. View the remaining charge here.
3. Enable the battery saver checkbox, and click and drag or tap and drag the slider to adjust when the feature turns on.
4. Click or tap to see battery use by app.
5. Select the amount of elapsed time and the type of apps to view.
6. Click an app to view details.

End

POWER & SLEEP

Use the Power & sleep settings to adjust how long your device stays on when idle.

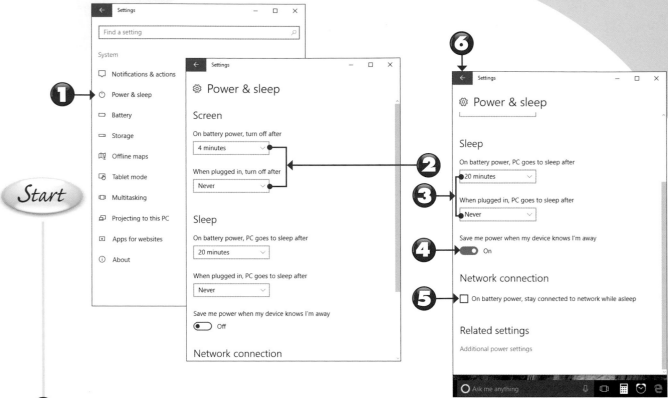

1. From Settings, click or tap **Power & sleep**.
2. Click or tap to select when to turn off the screen on battery or when plugged in (AC power).
3. Click or tap to select when to sleep on battery or when plugged in (AC power).
4. To save more power when you're away from your computer, press or click and drag to **On**.
5. Check this box to stay connected when the system is off.
6. Click or tap to return to System settings.

NOTE

Choosing a Power Plan Click the **Additional power settings** link at the bottom of the Power & sleep settings and choose the **High performance** setting if you want your device to run at top speed all the time (which uses the most power). Balanced is the normal setting. Power Saver uses the least power by running the device at a lower clock speed. Tablets support only the Balanced setting.

MAKING MAPS AVAILABLE OFFLINE

Thanks to GPS units in smartphones, tablets, and cars, real-time navigation is a great way to get around—unless you don't have a signal. If you want to use your device to navigate no matter your location or signal availability, use Windows 10 AE's downloadable offline maps feature. You can select maps for most regions of the world.

Start

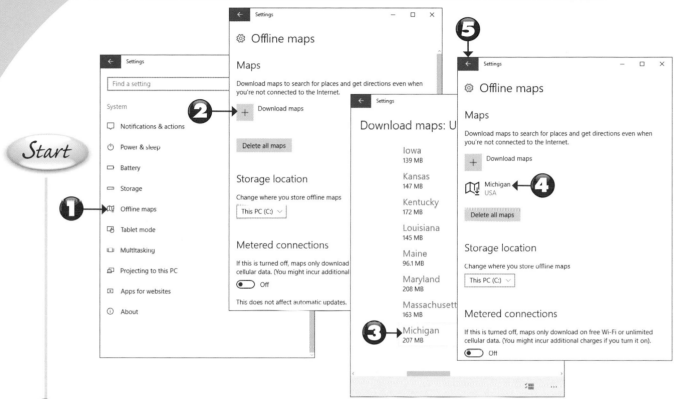

1. From Settings, click or tap **Offline maps**.
2. Click or tap + to select a map (region, country, state, or province as listed).
3. Select a map and it starts downloading to your system.
4. After you download a map, Windows 10 AE's Maps app can use it even when you're not connected to the Internet.
5. Click or tap to return to System settings.

NOTE

Maps Download in the Background Maps will continue to download while you use your computer, so as soon as you start the download (step 3), you can make other changes in Settings as needed.

CHECKING DRIVE CAPACITY WITH STORAGE

Use Storage settings to find out how much and what types of information is stored on the drives connected to your system.

Start

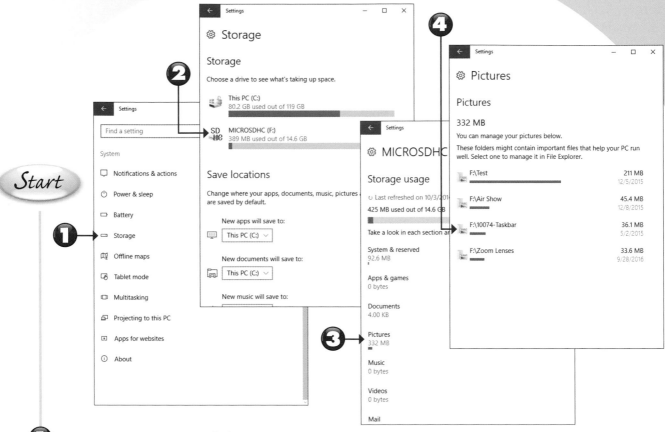

1. From System settings, click or tap **Storage**.
2. Click or tap a storage location for more information.
3. Click or tap a category to see the details.
4. Click or tap a folder you want to manage. The folder opens in File Manager.

Continued

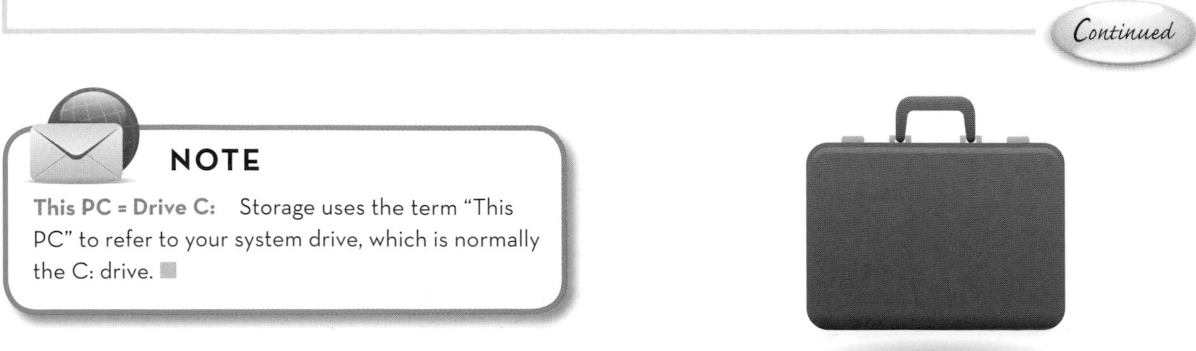

NOTE

This PC = Drive C: Storage uses the term "This PC" to refer to your system drive, which is normally the C: drive.

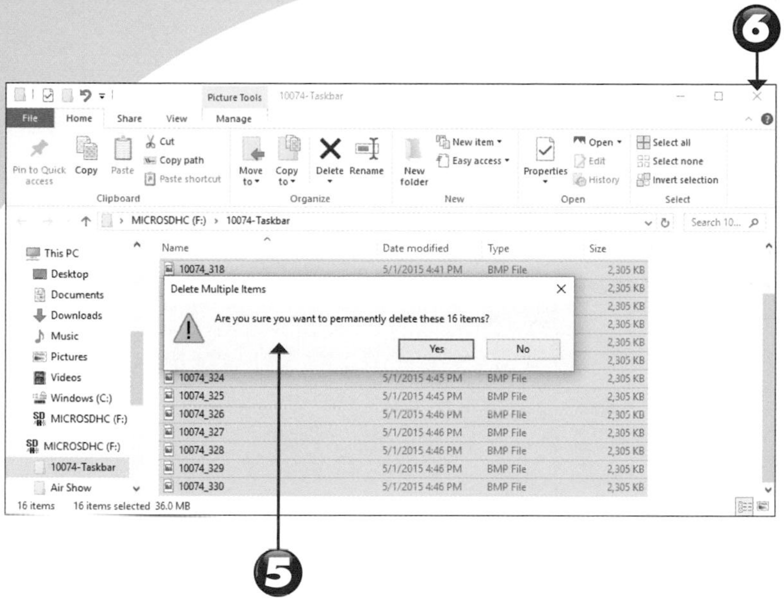

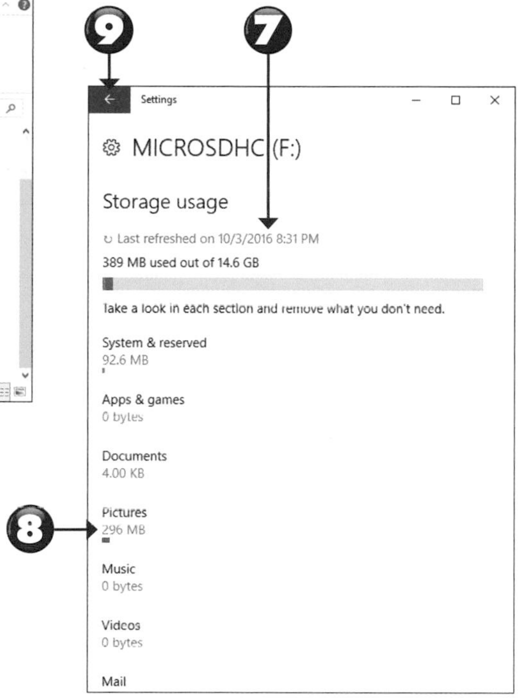

5 In this example, a folder containing unneeded photos is deleted to free up space.

6 After deleting, copying, or moving files, close the window.

7 Click or tap **Last refreshed on...** to update storage usage.

8 Review the current storage usage for the category you chose in step 3.

9 Click or tap to return to Storage settings.

End

NOTE

Copying, Moving, and Deleting Files and Folders To learn more about working with files and folders, see Chapter 14, "Storing and Finding Your Files."

CHANGING FILE LOCATIONS WITH STORAGE

Storage settings can also help you use other drives, such as additional drive letters on your internal hard drive, flash memory, or external hard disks for new apps and files. Here's how.

Start

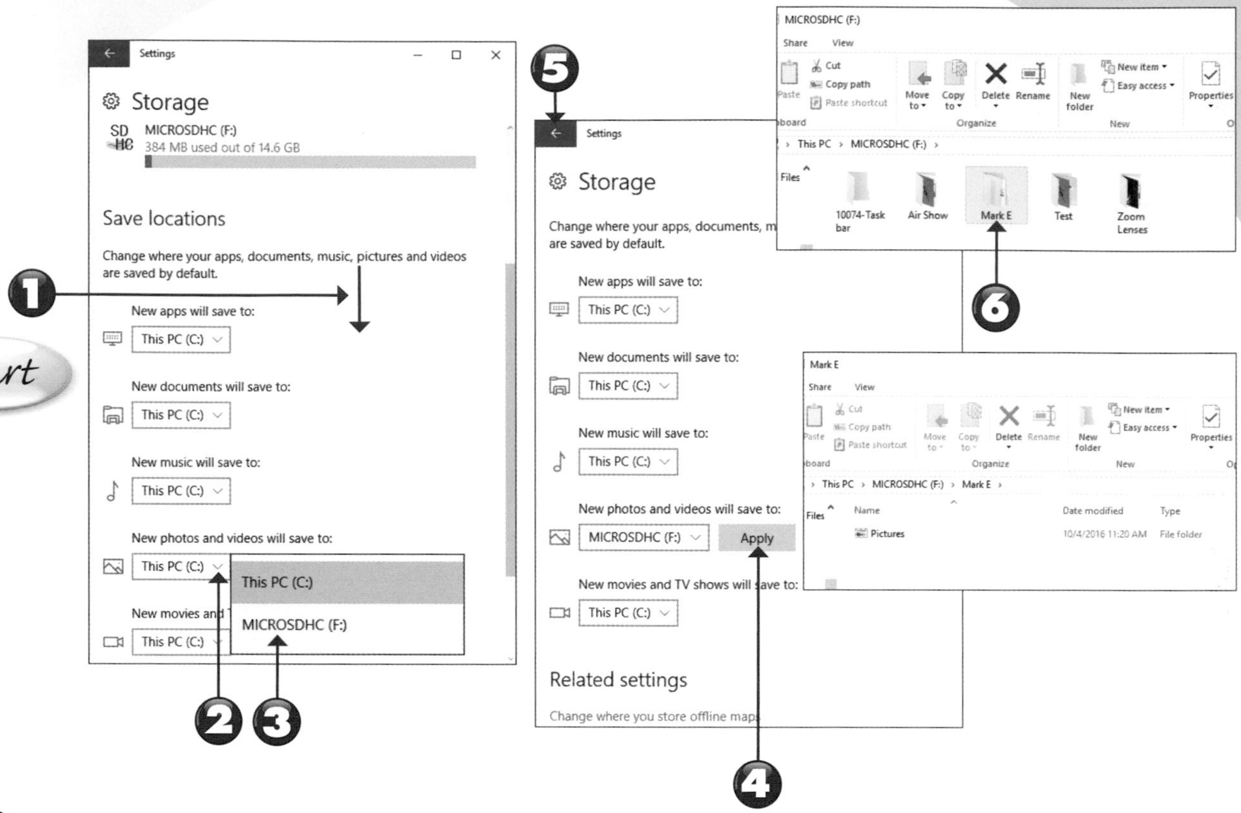

1. From Storage settings, scroll down or flick up to **Save locations**.
2. Choose a location you want to change.
3. Select a new location for the file.
4. Click or tap **Apply**. New photos and video files will be stored at the new location.
5. Click or tap to return to System settings.
6. If you choose a different drive for your files, you can view it in File Manager. Open File Manager to the drive, and click or tap your name to see the new folder.

End

CAUTION

Changed Storage Location? Don't Disconnect That Drive! If you disconnect or remove a drive that you set up for apps or files with Storage, Windows 10 AE can't find your apps or files until you reconnect or insert the drive.

CHANGING DEFAULT APPS

If you have more than one app that can be used for a particular task or to open a particular type of file, use the Default Apps settings to specify which app is the one you prefer.

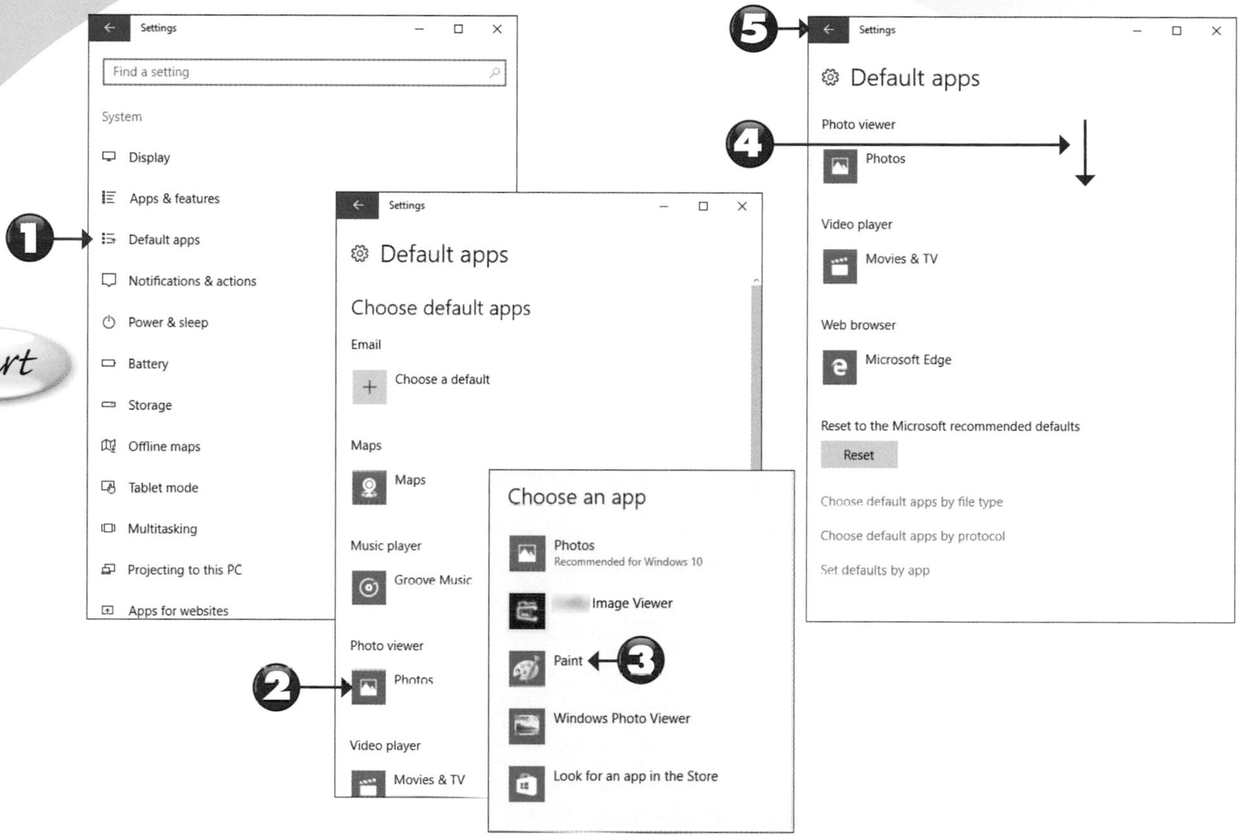

Start

1. From System settings, click or tap **Default apps**.
2. Click or tap a type of app.
3. Select the app to use, or click/tap **Look for an app in the Store** if you want more choices.
4. Scroll down or flick up for other file types and advanced settings.
5. Click or tap to return to System settings.

End

NOTE

Available Apps Vary The exact list of default apps you can choose from depends on the file or app type you choose and the apps installed on your device.

ADDING A DEVICE, PRINTER, OR SCANNER

The Devices category is used to view and add external components such as mice, keyboards, Bluetooth devices, printers, and scanners. You can also manage mouse, keyboard, pen, and AutoPlay settings in the appropriate submenus. Here's how to add a device that's plugged in or has been detected on your network.

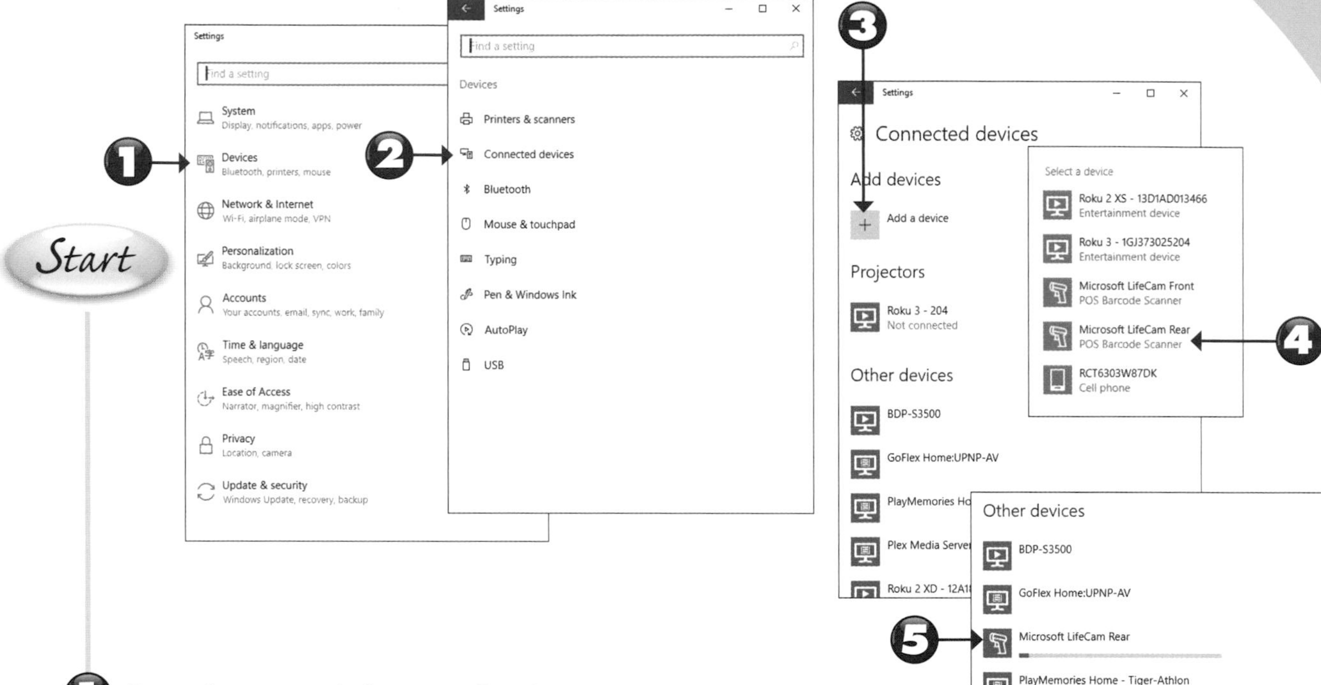

1. From Settings, click or tap **Devices**.
2. From Devices, click or tap **Connected devices**.
3. Click or tap **+** to add a device.
4. Choose a device from those available.
5. Windows 10 AE loads the device; as soon as drivers are loaded, the device can be used.

NOTE

Adding or Removing a Printer or Scanner The Printers & scanners category in Devices works the same way as the Connected Devices category. Follow these instructions to add or remove a printer or scanner.

NOTE

Directions Might Vary by Device To install some devices, you might need to install a driver disc or a downloaded installation program. If the device is connected via a network, you might need to press a physical button or click a software button on the device to finish the task.

REMOVING A DEVICE

The Connected devices settings is also the place to go to remove a device safely. Using these settings is especially important if you want to remove a storage device because it ensures that no data is being written to or read from the device when you disconnect it.

Start

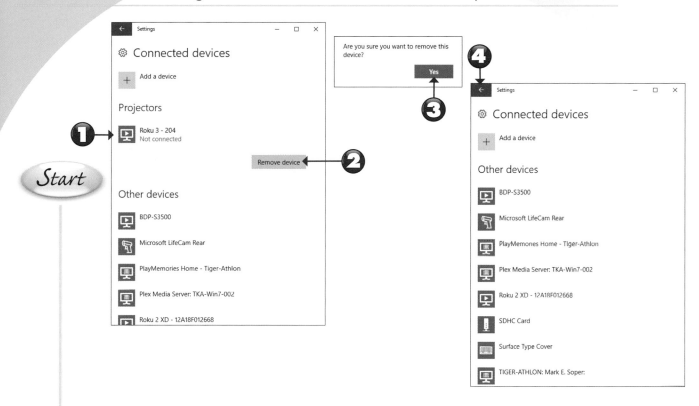

1. From the Connected devices settings (see previous task), click or tap the device to remove.
2. Click or tap **Remove device**.
3. Click or tap **Yes** to complete removal. After the device is removed from the list, you can disconnect or unplug it safely.
4. Click or tap to return to Devices.

End

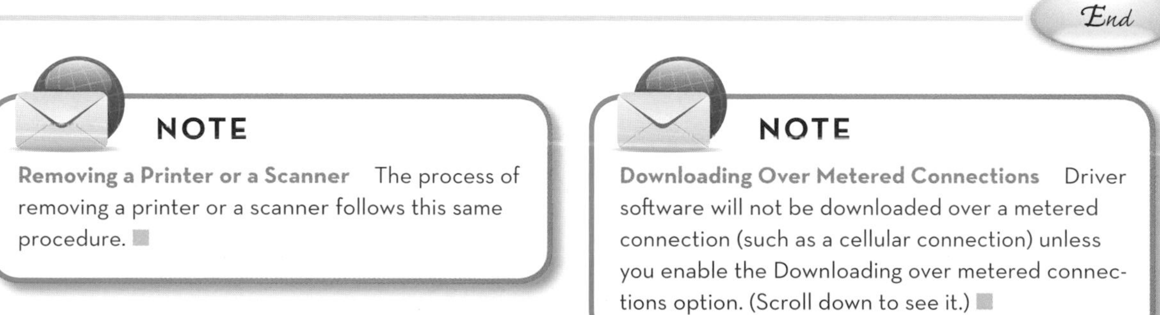

NOTE

Removing a Printer or a Scanner The process of removing a printer or a scanner follows this same procedure.

NOTE

Downloading Over Metered Connections Driver software will not be downloaded over a metered connection (such as a cellular connection) unless you enable the Downloading over metered connections option. (Scroll down to see it.)

CONFIGURING MOUSE & TOUCHPAD

Whether you use a mouse, a touchpad, or both, the Mouse & touchpad settings help you tweak your pointing devices to work the way you want.

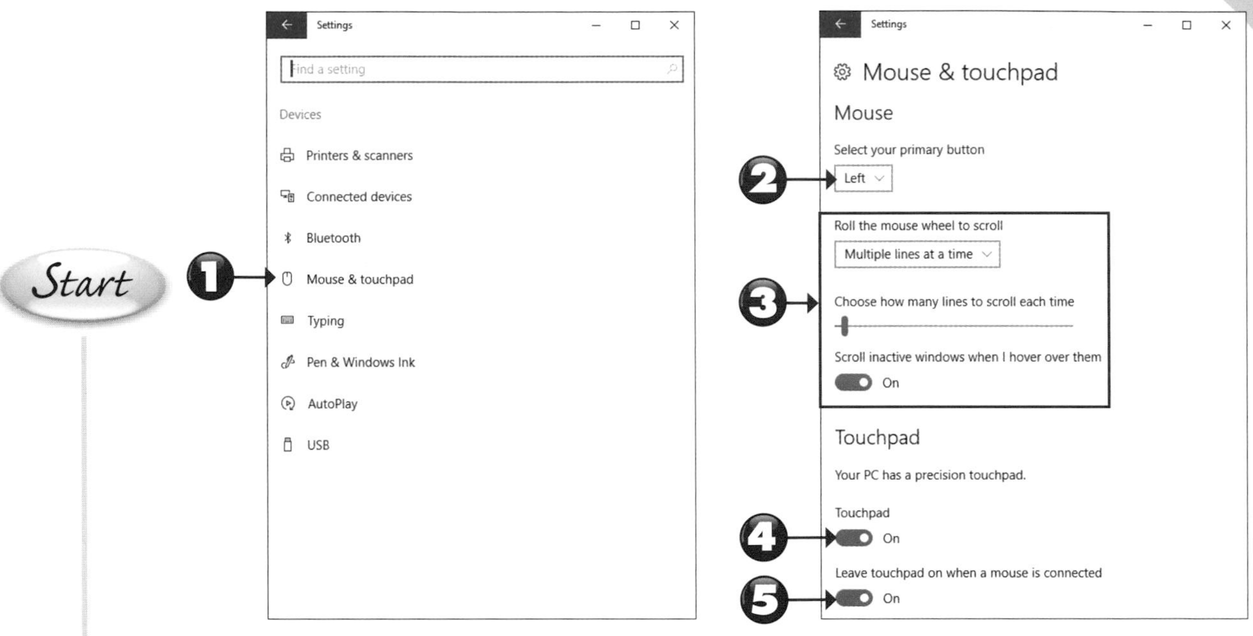

1. From the Devices settings, click or tap **Mouse & touchpad**.
2. Change to **Right** if you use your mouse with your left hand.
3. Use these settings to adjust how your scroll wheel works.
4. Hate using a touchpad? Disable it by dragging this to **Off**.
5. To disable your touchpad only when a mouse is connected (via USB or PS/2 port), turn this setting **Off**.

Continued

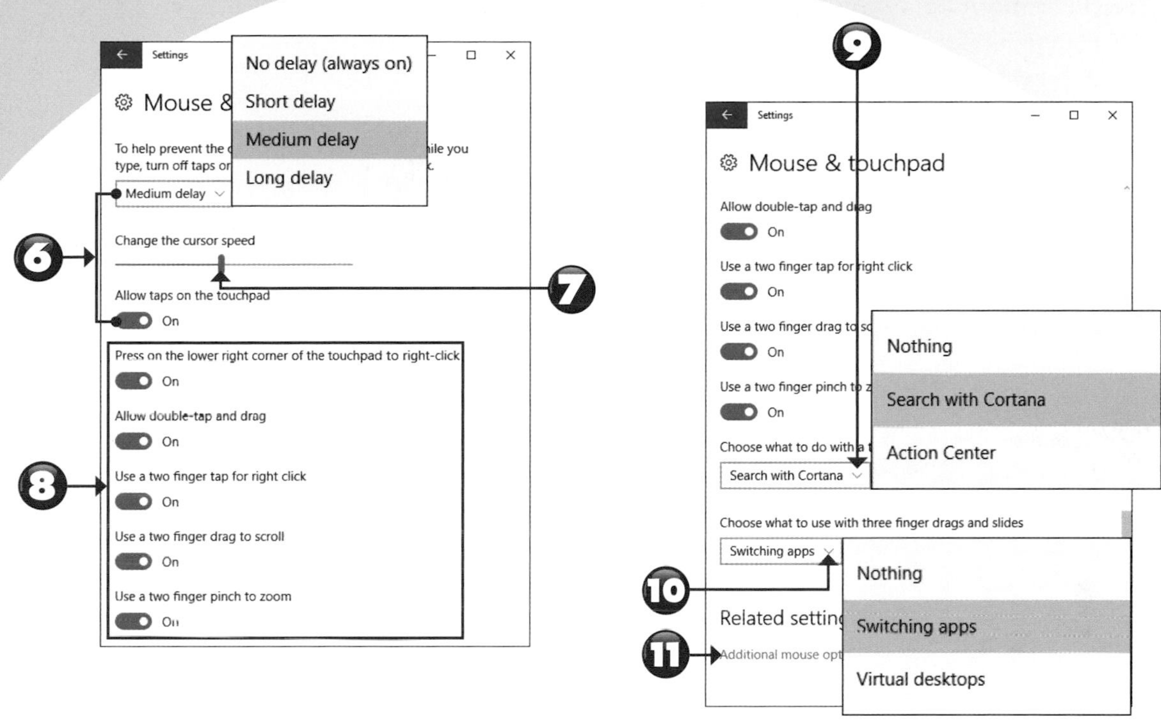

6. If you find yourself engaging your touchpad accidentally while typing, change the delay or turn off taps.

7. Drag to the left to slow down the mouse cursor; drag to the right to speed it up.

8. Use these settings to configure one-finger and two-finger touchpad operations.

9. To change what a three-finger tap does, click or tap here.

10. To change what a three-finger drag or slide does, click or tap here.

11. To change mouse pointer, pointer size, and double-click speeds, click or tap here.

End

WORKING WITH BLUETOOTH DEVICES

Use the Bluetooth settings to connect to wireless Bluetooth devices such as keyboards, mice, or media players. In this example, we'll connect a Bluetooth mouse to a tablet.

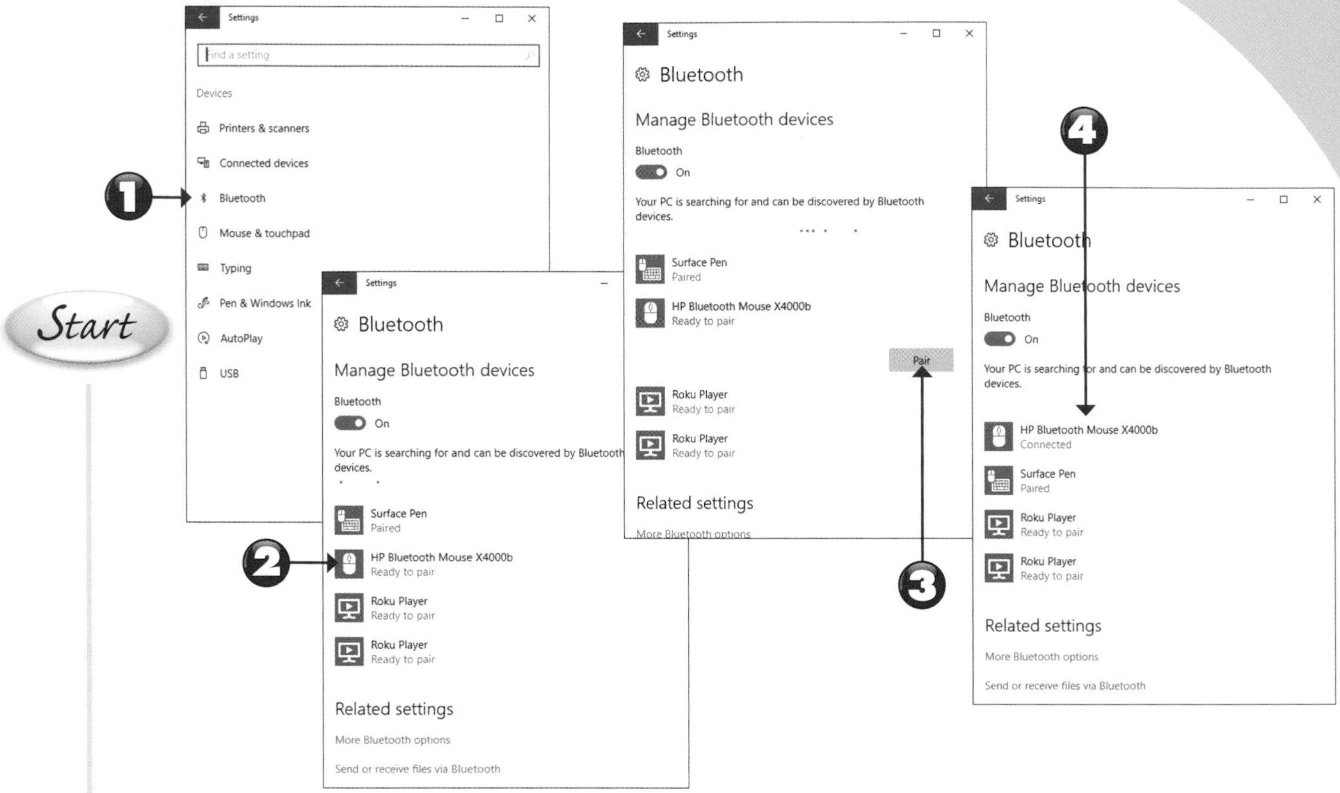

Start

1. From the Devices settings, click or tap **Bluetooth**.
2. Click or tap the device you want to pair (connect to).
3. Click or tap **Pair**.
4. After pairing is complete, the device is listed and ready to use.

End

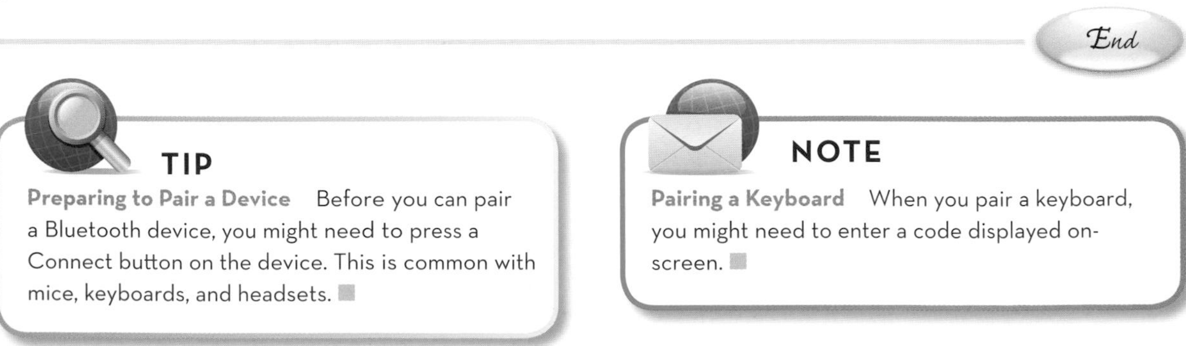

TIP

Preparing to Pair a Device Before you can pair a Bluetooth device, you might need to press a Connect button on the device. This is common with mice, keyboards, and headsets.

NOTE

Pairing a Keyboard When you pair a keyboard, you might need to enter a code displayed on-screen.

CHANGING TYPING SETTINGS

Use the Typing settings to set up spelling, typing, and onscreen keyboard options.

Settings
Find a setting
Devices
Printers & scanners
Connected devices
Bluetooth
Mouse & touchpad
Typing
Pen & Windows Ink
AutoPlay
USB

Settings
Typing
Spelling
Autocorrect misspelled words
On
Highlight misspelled words
On
Typing
Show text suggestions as I type
On
Add a space after I choose a text suggestion
On
Add a period after I double-tap the Spacebar
On
Touch keyboard
Play key sounds as I type
On

Settings
Typing
Add a space after I choose a text suggestion
On
Add a period after I double-tap the Spacebar
On
Touch keyboard
Play key sounds as I type
On
Capitalize the first letter of each sentence
On
Use all uppercase letters when I double-tap Shift
On
Add the standard keyboard layout as a touch keyboard option
On
Show the touch keyboard when not in tablet mode and there's no keyboard attached
On

Start

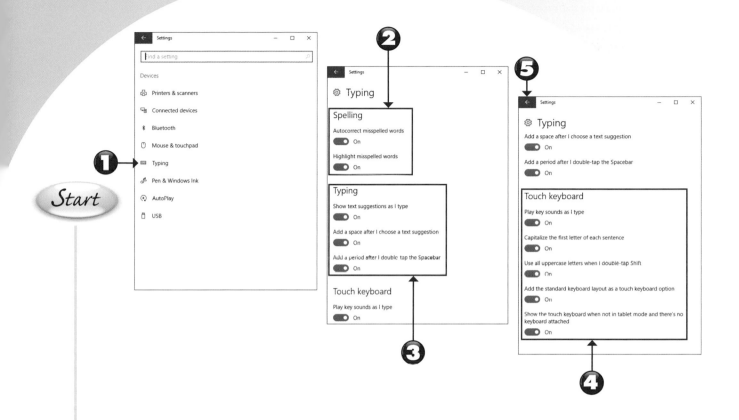

1. In Devices, click or tap **Typing**.
2. These options apply only to Modern UI/Universal apps (not desktop apps).
3. These options apply to typing with the onscreen keyboard.
4. These options apply to typing with the onscreen keyboard.
5. Click or tap to return to Devices.

CHANGING PEN & WINDOWS INK SETTINGS

If your computer or tablet uses a pen, use the Pen & Windows Ink settings to configure how you want to use it.

Start

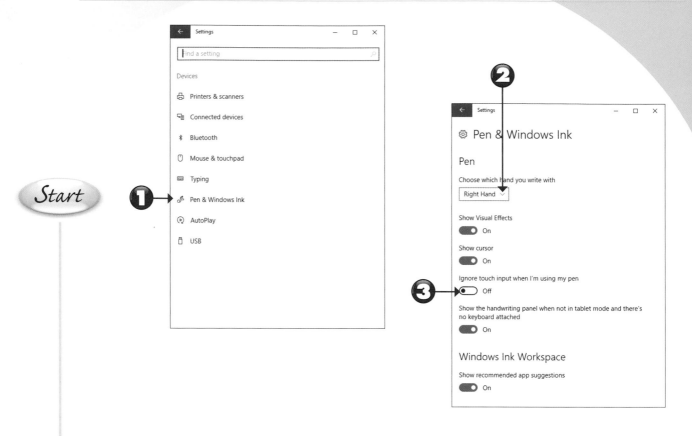

1. From the Devices settings, click or tap **Pen & Windows Ink**.

2. Select **Left Hand** if you use the pen in your left hand.

3. Turn this feature on if you find that touch input affects your use of the pen.

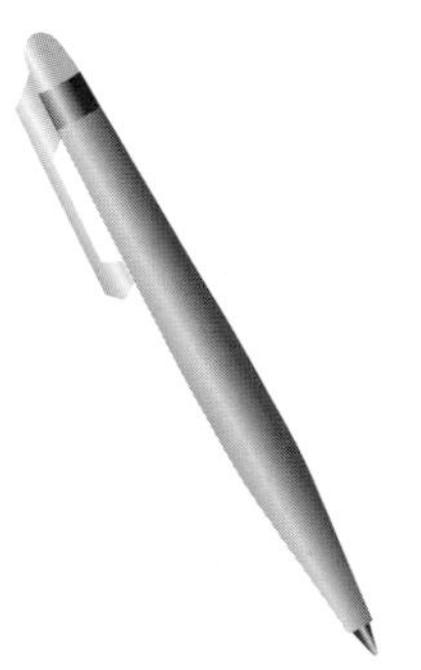

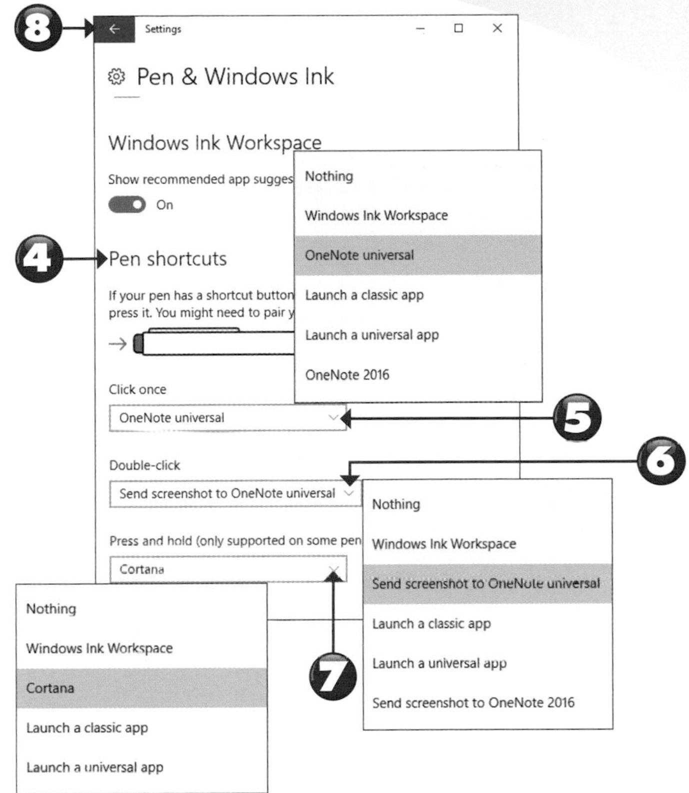

4. Scroll to the Pen shortcuts section to view default settings for a pen with a shortcut button.

5. Click or tap to choose a different one-click action.

6. Click or tap to choose a different double-click action.

7. Click or tap to choose a different press and hold action (if supported by your pen).

8. Click or tap to return to Devices.

End

NOTE

Selecting a Classic or Universal App If you select the option to run a classic or universal app in steps 5–7, a Browse button appears. Use it to navigate to the app you want to run.

CHANGING AUTOPLAY SETTINGS

Use the AutoPlay settings to determine what happens when you connect a new removable-media drive or flash memory card.

Settings
Find a setting
Devices
Printers & scanners
Connected devices
Bluetooth
Mouse & touchpad
Typing
Pen & Windows Ink
AutoPlay
USB

Settings
AutoPlay
AutoPlay
Use AutoPlay for all media and devices
On
Choose AutoPlay defaults
Removable drive
Choose a default
Memory card
Choose a default
Related settings
Default app settings

Take no action
Open folder to view files (File Explorer)
Ask me every time
Configure this drive for backup (File History)
Configure storage settings (Settings)

Import photos and videos (OneDrive)
Import photos and videos (Photos)
Play (Windows Media Player)
Take no action
Open folder to view files (File Explorer)
Ask me every time

Start

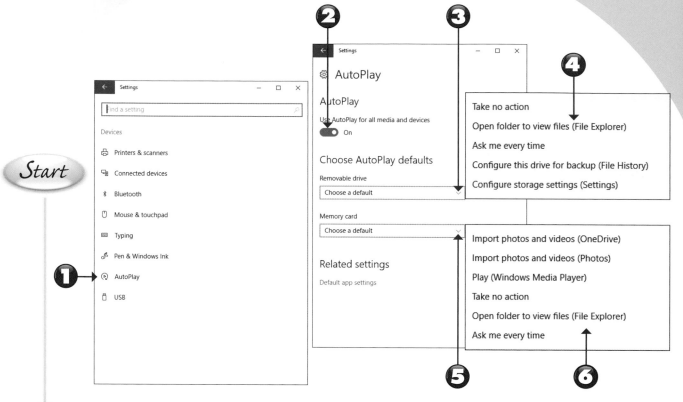

1. In Devices, click or tap **AutoPlay**.
2. To disable AutoPlay, click or press and drag to **Off**.
3. Click or tap to select an action for removable drives.
4. Click or tap to select an action for memory cards.
5. Select an action for removable drives.
6. Select an action for memory cards.

End

TIP

Dealing with Various File Types If you typically use removable drives or memory cards that contain more than one type of file, I recommend selecting **Open folder to view files** (File Explorer) or **Ask me every time**.

USB SETTINGS

The USB setting helps you troubleshoot issues with USB devices.

Start

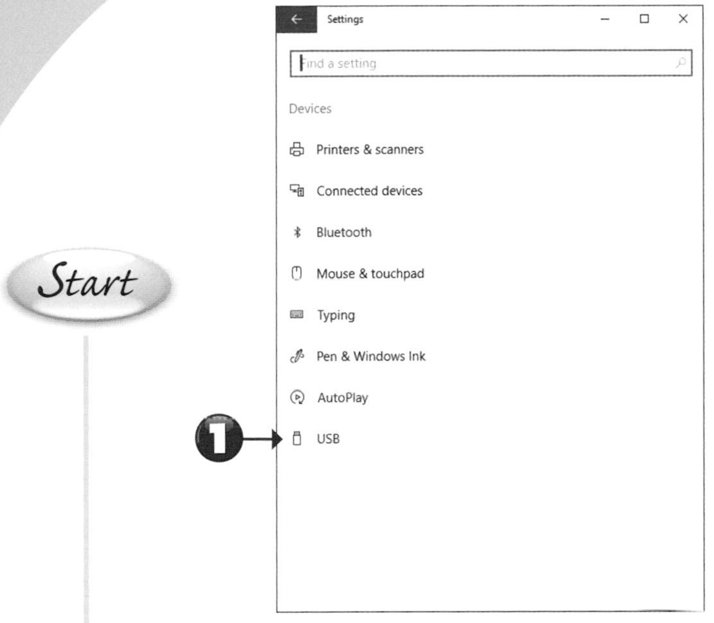

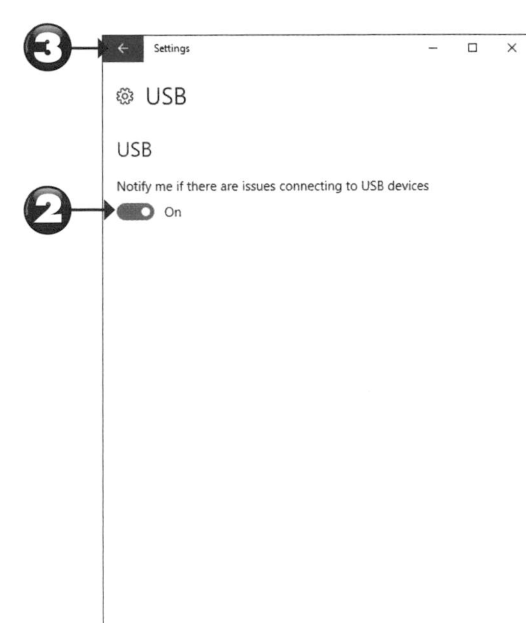

1. In Devices, click or tap **USB**.
2. Make sure the Notify me if there are issues... setting is turned **On**. If not, turn it on.
3. Click or tap to return to Settings.

End

GENERAL PRIVACY SETTINGS

In Windows 10 AE, you have much more control over how much information Windows and Windows apps can gather as you use your device than in previous versions. It's a tradeoff: the more information Windows knows about you, the more targeted the information it provides but the less privacy you have. Use the Privacy section of Settings to customize your privacy settings for apps included with Windows 10 AE or available from the Windows Store. In this example, we'll open the General privacy settings menu and see the available settings.

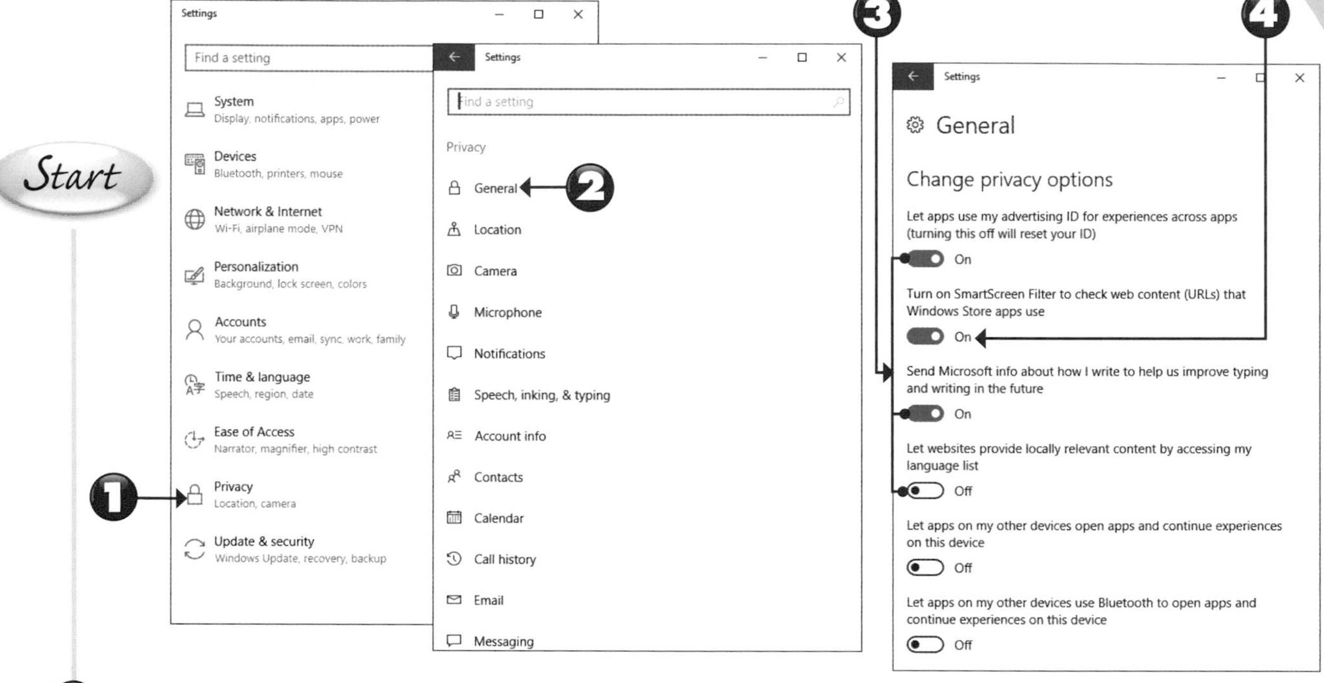

1. In Settings, click or tap **Privacy**.

2. Click or tap **General**.

3. Leaving these options enabled reduces your privacy while making searches, typing, and shopping easier.

4. Disabling SmartScreen Filter can make your online shopping less secure.

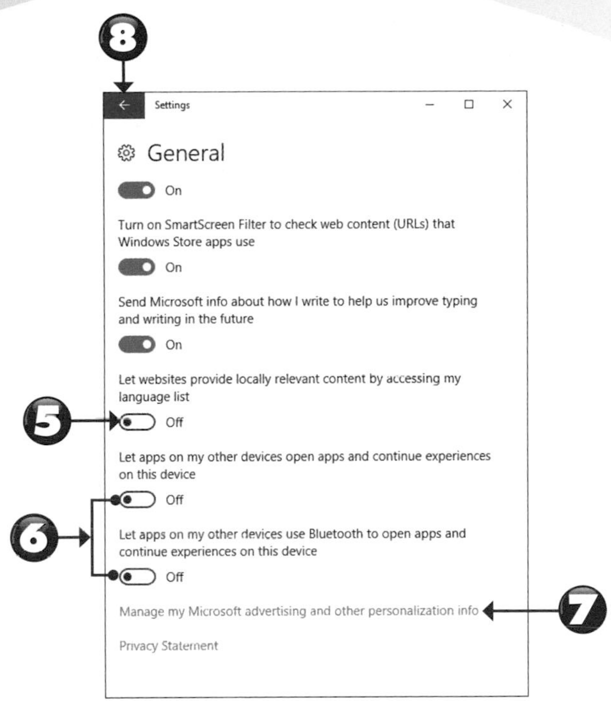

5. Enable this setting to let websites check your language list to help provide locally relevant content.

6. Enable these settings to use the new "pick up where I left off" app syncing feature.

7. To change your Microsoft personalized ad settings, click the **Manage my Microsoft advertising...** link.

8. Click or tap to return to the Privacy settings.

End

NOTE

"Handoff" Comes to Windows The app syncing feature (step 5) lets you start working on an app on one device and switch to another device and keep working with it. It is sometimes called Handoff because of its similarity to the Mac/iOS feature by the same name. ■

CONFIGURING LOCATION SETTINGS

Many apps are designed to use your location to provide you with more relevant information. If you need to change these settings, use the Location dialog box in the Privacy section of Settings.

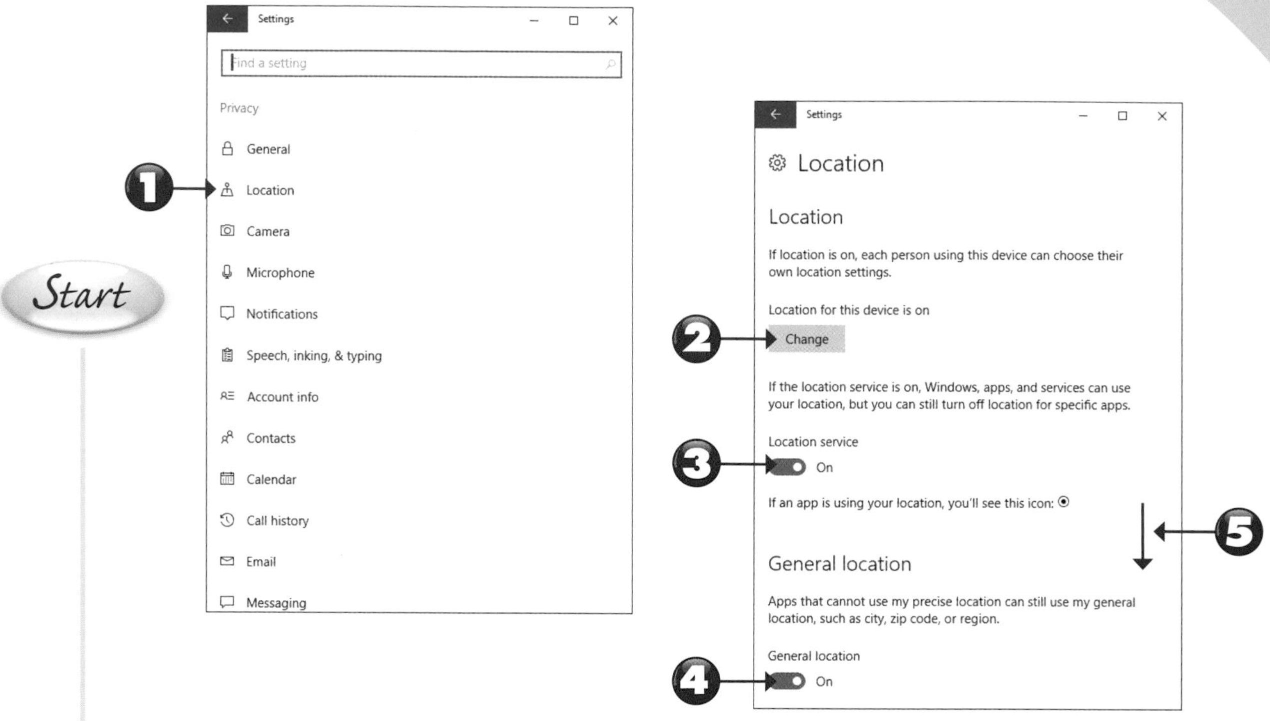

1. From the Privacy settings, click or tap **Location**.
2. If you don't want each user to set individual location settings, click or tap **Change** and select **Off** in the pop-up window.
3. To disable location settings for your account, click or press and drag to **Off**.
4. Click or tap to enable the General location setting.
5. To change location history settings by app or to see if any apps use geofencing, scroll down or flick up.

Continued

Settings

Location

Default location

Windows, apps, and services can use this when we can't detect a more exact location on this PC.

Set default

Location history

If location is on, your location history is stored for a limited time on the device, and can be used by apps that use your location.

Clear history on this device

Clear

Learn more about location settings

Privacy Statement

Settings

Location

Choose apps that can use your precise location

App connector Off

Camera Off

Cortana Location history must be on for Cortana to work On

Facebook Off

Mail and Calendar Off

Maps On

Messaging Off

Microsoft Edge Sites still need permission On

Settings

Location

Mail and Calendar Off

Maps On

Messaging Off

Microsoft Edge Sites still need permission On

News Off

Weather Off

Geofencing

Geofencing means using your location to see when you cross in or out of a boundary drawn around a place of interest.

None of your apps are currently using geofencing.

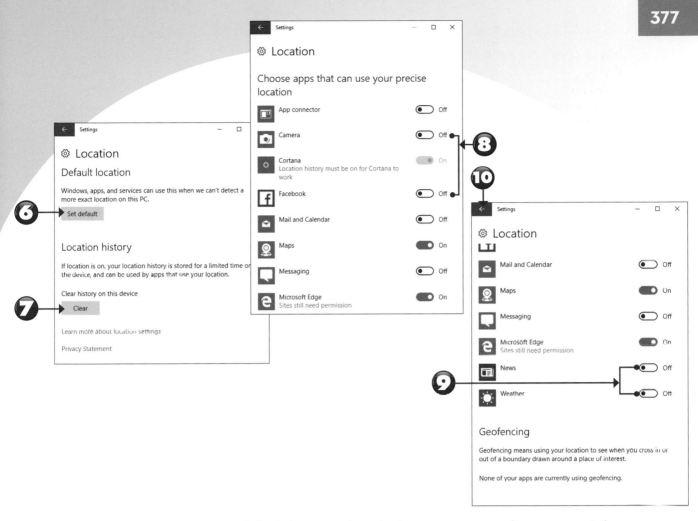

6 Click or tap to set your default location (used when your precise location can't be determined).

7 To clear location history, click or tap **Clear** and confirm your choice when prompted.

8 Enable location for these apps if you want your photos and Facebook posts to show your location.

9 Enabling location (off by default) for News and Weather can help keep you better informed.

10 Click or tap to return to Privacy settings.

End

CHANGING PRIVACY SETTINGS FOR CAMERA, MICROPHONE, CONTACTS, MESSAGING, RADIOS, AND ACCOUNT INFO

You can enable or disable privacy settings for all apps in a category or for individual apps in each category. If no apps are in a listed category, you are invited to download an app from the Windows Store. In this task, we'll see how privacy settings work for the Camera and Microphone. The same methods apply to the other apps listed in the title.

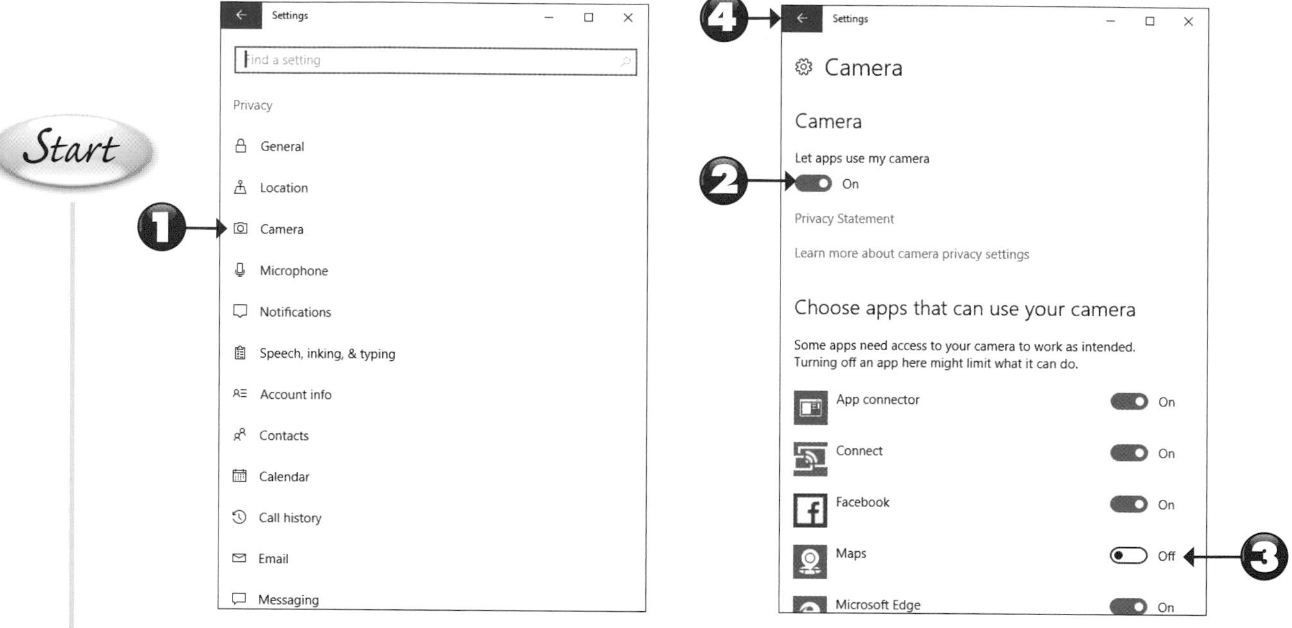

1. From the Privacy settings, click or tap **Camera**.
2. When this setting is On (the default), all listed apps can use your device's camera.
3. You can click or press and drag to turn specific app's access on or off; Maps' access to Camera has been turned off.
4. Click or tap to return to Privacy settings.

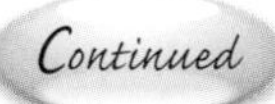

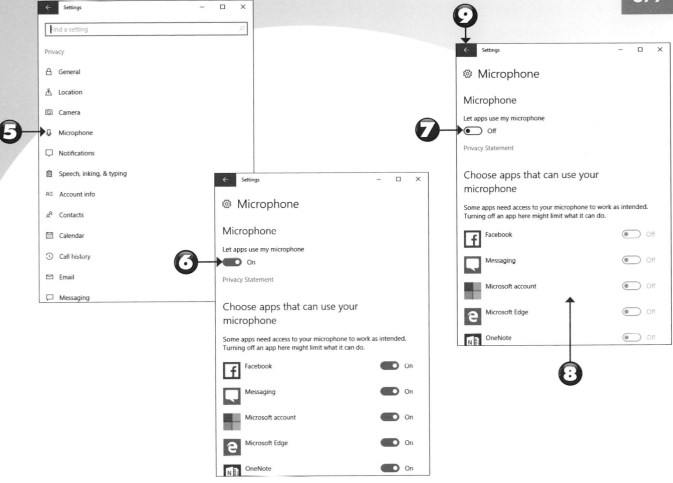

5 From the Privacy settings, click or tap **Microphone**.

6 By default, all listed apps can use the microphone.

7 To turn off app access to your device's microphone, click or press and drag the Microphone setting to **Off**.

8 Windows 10 AE changes the settings to Off; no apps can use the microphone.

9 Click or tap to return to Privacy settings.

End

CAUTION

Privacy and Cameras Even if you block listed apps from using your camera, it's possible for malware to use your camera. If you're concerned about this potential privacy risk, unplug your USB camera when you're not using it, or cover up the lenses of your devices' built-in cameras.

CHANGING SPEECH, INK, AND TYPING PRIVACY SETTINGS

The Cortana search assistant in Windows 10 AE works by learning your voice and your writing, and it collects information to serve your search and dictation needs better. If you're not interested, use the Speech, Inking, & Typing dialog box to stop the information gathering. If you change your mind later, you can restart the process. Here's how.

Start

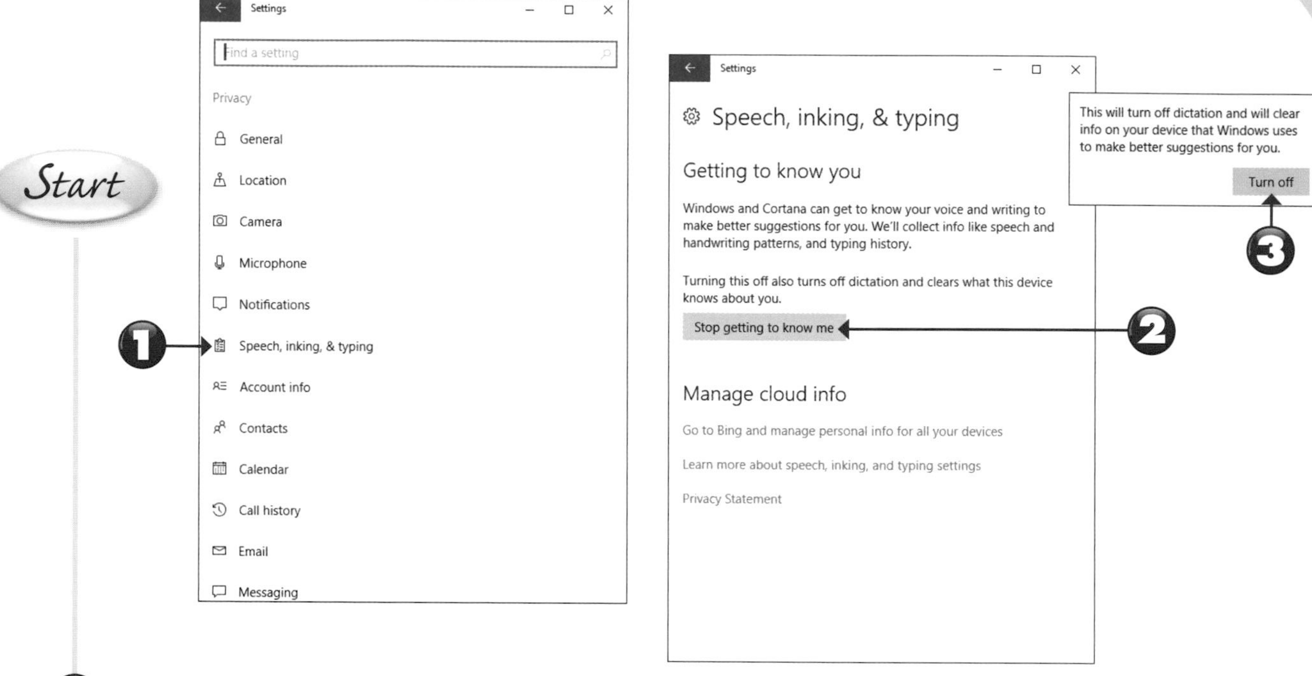

1. From the Privacy settings, click or tap **Speech, inking, & typing**.
2. Click or tap **Stop getting to know me**.
3. Click or tap **Turn off**, and you turn off dictation and clear out the information on your device that Cortana uses.

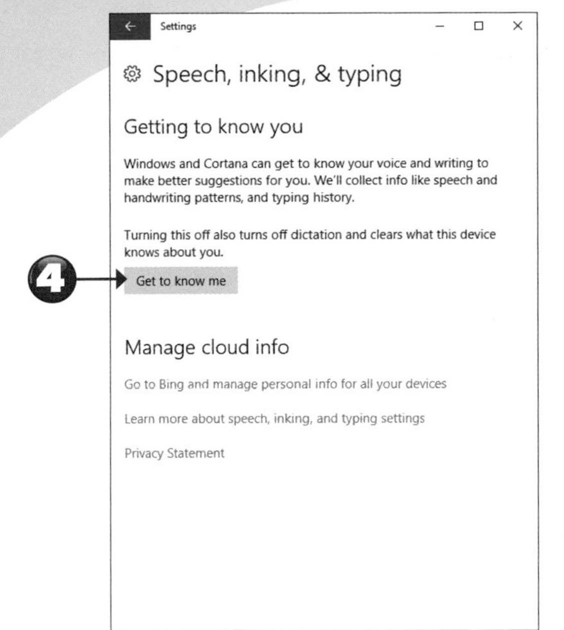

4 If you decide to enable Cortana to provide you with better information, click or tap **Get to know me**.

5 Click or tap **Turn on**, and Cortana will track speech, handwriting patterns, and typing history to improve its performance.

End

MANAGING PERSONAL INFORMATION WITH BING

In Windows 10 AE, the default Microsoft Bing search tool keeps track of a lot of information about you on every device you use with a Windows account, such as your search history. If this is a little too helpful, you can stop it. Here's how.

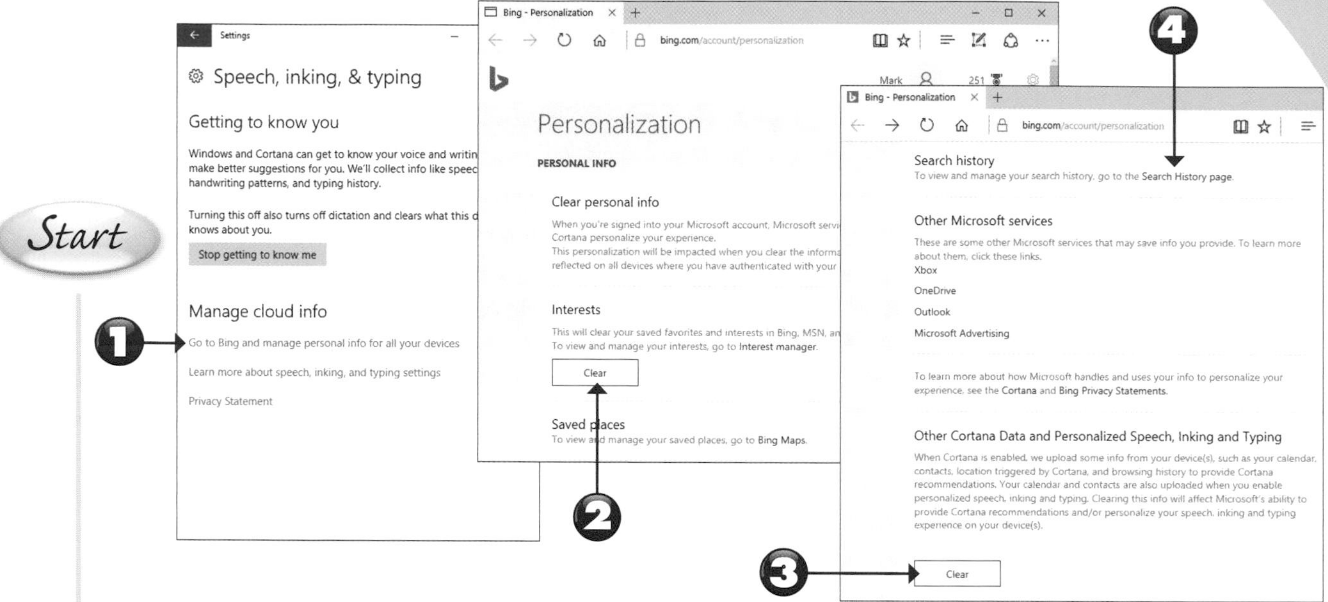

1. From the Speech, inking, & typing settings (see previous task), click or tap **Go to Bing and manage personal info for all your devices**.
2. Click or tap **Clear** to remove saved favorites and interests in Bing, MSN, and Cortana. After you confirm your choice, the information is removed.
3. Click or tap **Clear** to remove other data sent to Cortana for analysis. After you confirm your choice, the information is removed.
4. Click or tap **Search History page** to see and remove your search history.

NOTE

Enter, and Sign In Please If you use a Microsoft account on Windows 10 AE, you are already signed in to all Microsoft services. However, if prompted, provide your Microsoft account information (name and password). You must be signed in before you can make changes to your account settings.

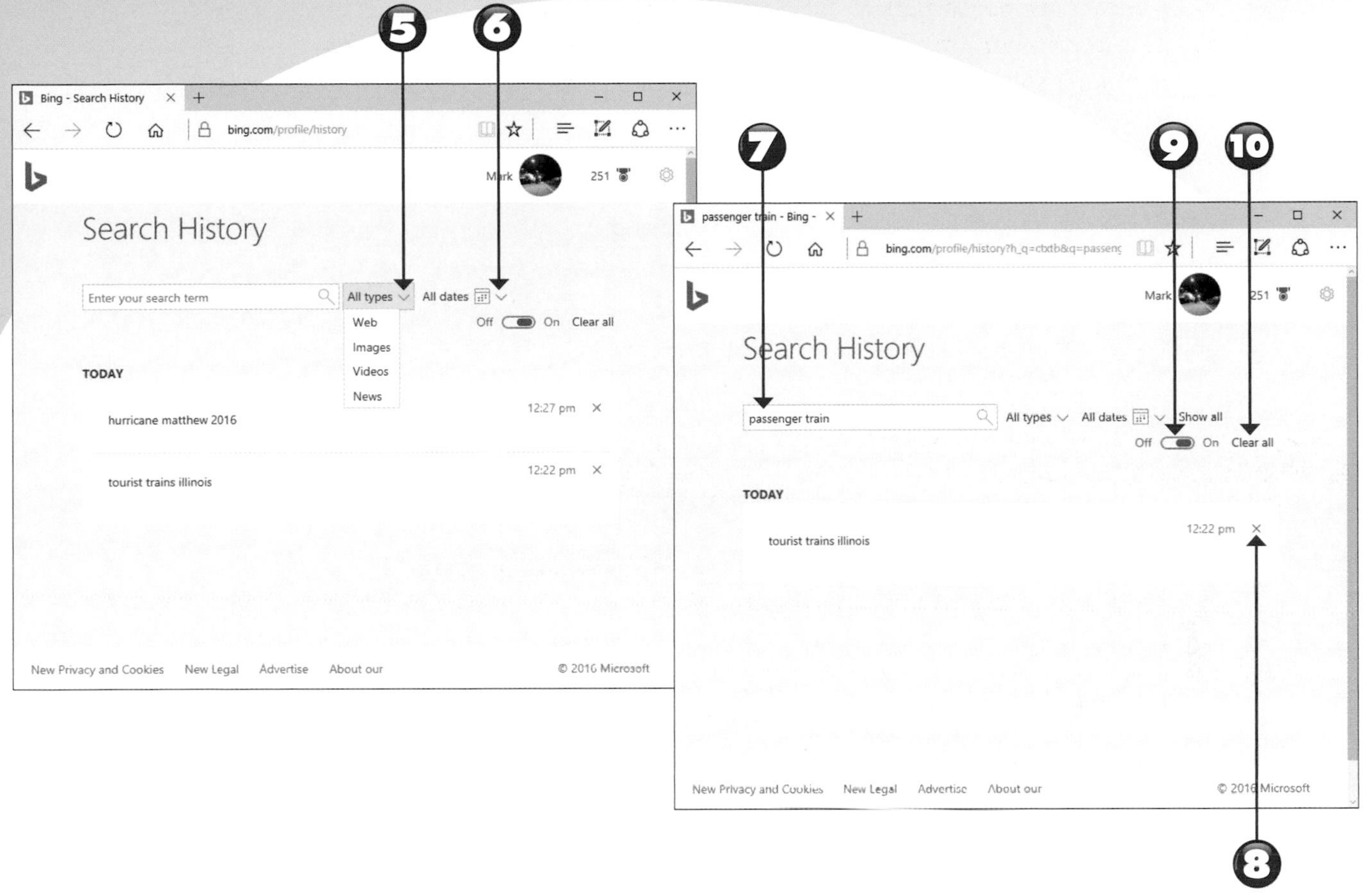

5. Click or tap to view search history by type (web, images, videos, news).

6. Click or tap to view search history by date.

7. Search for a particular item in search history here.

8. To remove a specific item from search history, click or tap the **X**. Confirm your choice when prompted.

9. To turn off search history, click or press and drag to **Off**. Confirm your choice when prompted.

10. Click or tap **Clear all** to clear search history. Confirm your choice when prompted.

End

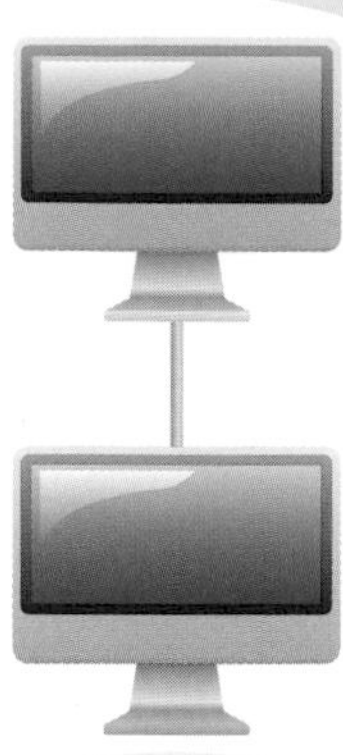

NETWORKING YOUR HOME WITH HOMEGROUP

Wireless networking (or Wi-Fi) and HomeGroup secure networking make it easy to connect your Windows 10 AE device with the rest of the world. This chapter explains how to create and leave a wireless network and how to use HomeGroup secure home networking.

Connecting to a private wireless network

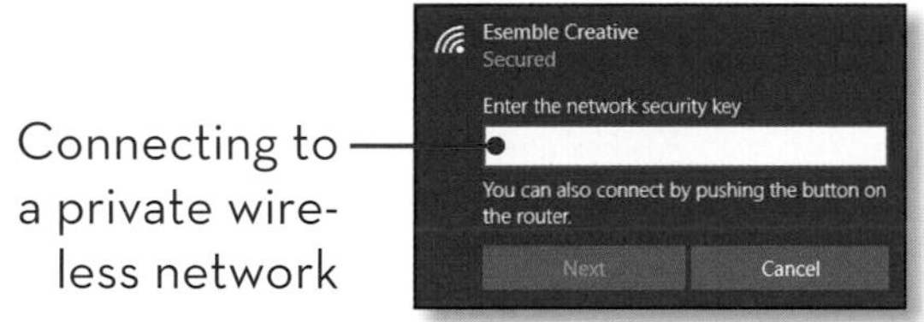

Viewing available wireless networks

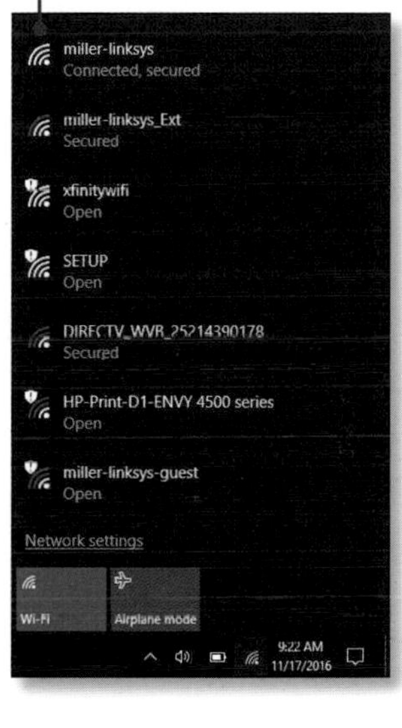

The Network & Internet menu in Settings

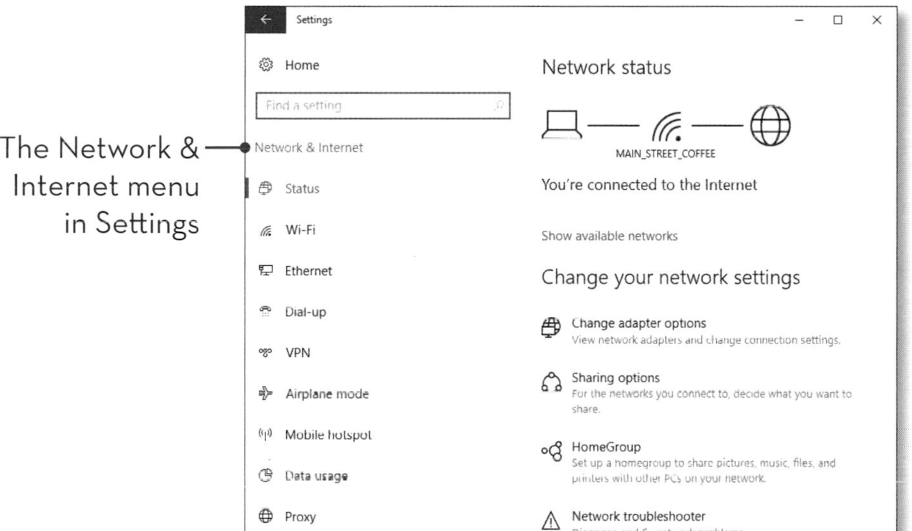

Configuring homegroup sharing

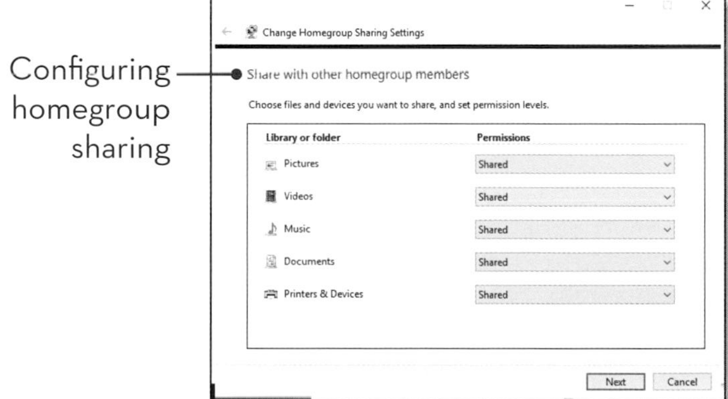

STARTING THE WIRELESS NETWORK CONNECTION PROCESS

To connect to a wireless network, use the Wireless Network button in the taskbar. Here's how.

Start

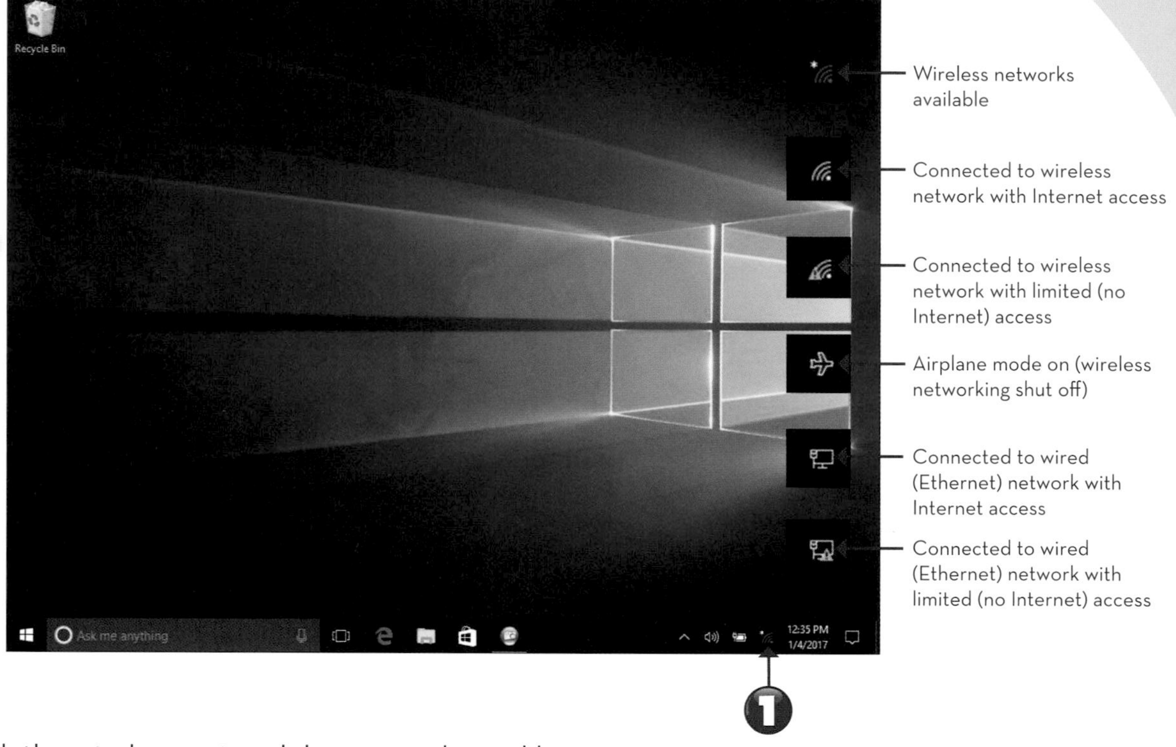

1. Click the wireless network button in the taskbar.

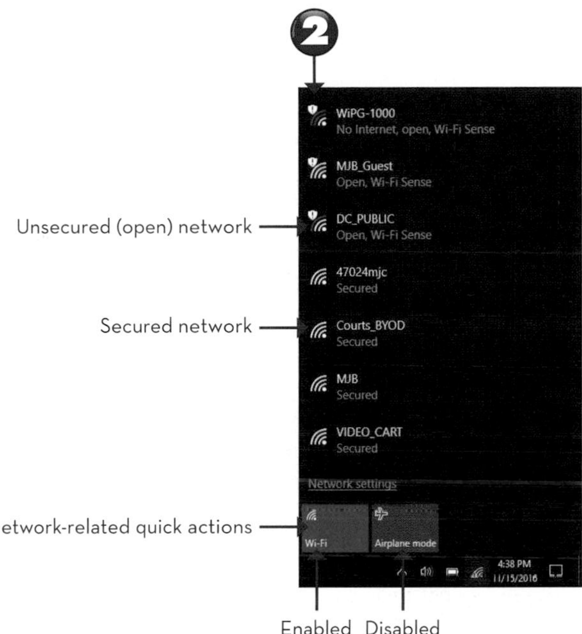

2 The Network Connections dialog appears. Choose one of the listed networks for your connection.

End

NOTE

Secure and Unsecure Network Icons Secure networks use the signal strength icon. Unsecure networks add a shield marked with an exclamation point (!) to the icon, indicating they are not secure. (See step 2.)

NOTE

Finishing Your Connection To complete the process, see "Connecting to a Secured Private Network," p. 390, or "Connecting to an Unsecured Wireless Network," p. 388.

CONNECTING TO AN UNSECURED WIRELESS NETWORK

Your home and office networks should be secure networks (in other words, you should use a password with your home Wi-Fi network; your work network is probably already secure); however, wireless networks found in locations such as coffee shops, libraries, restaurants, and hotels often are unsecured. Some of these networks also require you to use your web browser to accept the Wi-Fi service's terms. Here's how to connect to these networks using Windows 10 AE.

Start

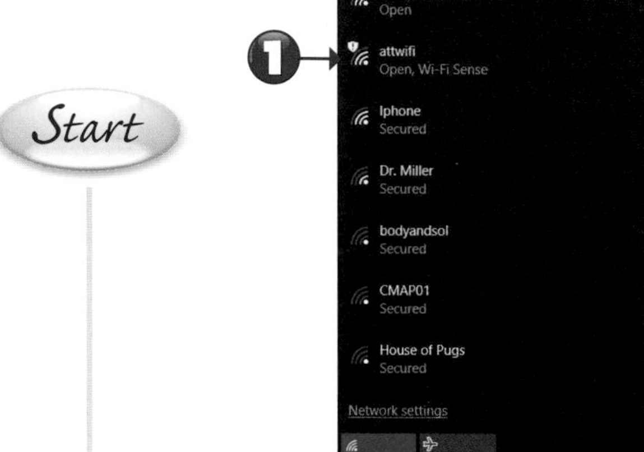

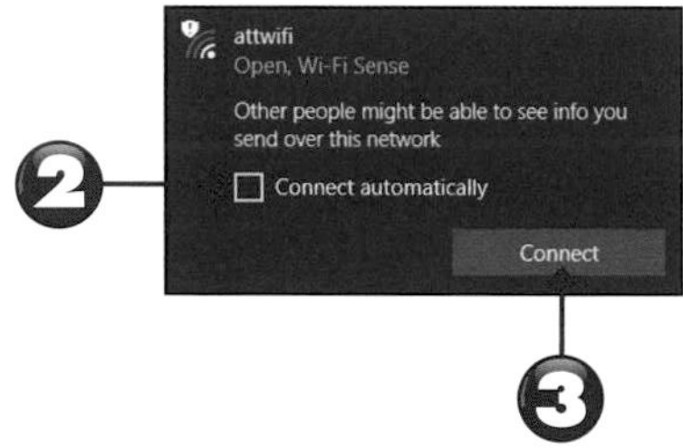

1. Click or tap the unsecured network's name (SSID) to connect to it.
2. Check **Connect automatically** if you think you'll connect to this network at some point in the future.
3. Click or tap **Connect**.

Continued

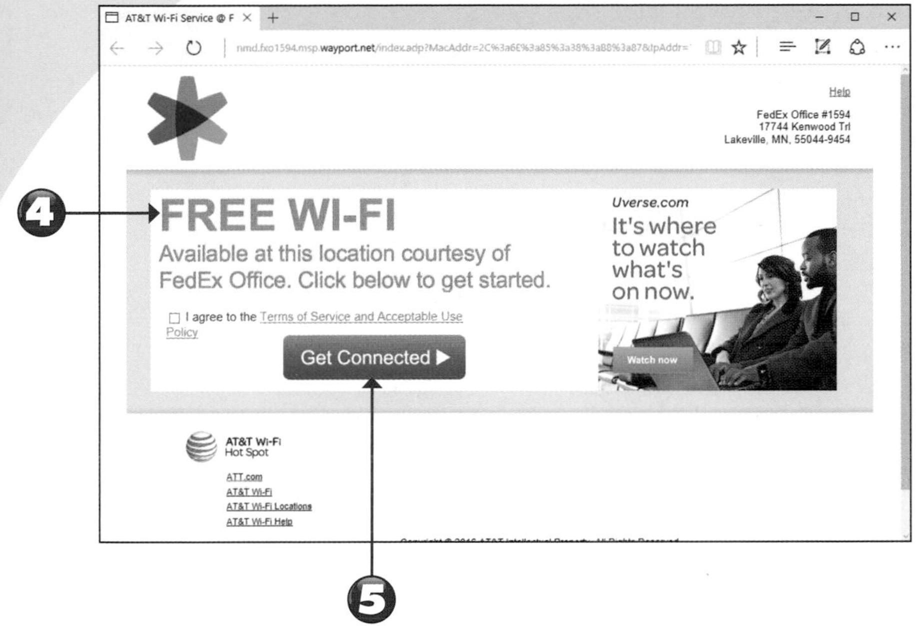

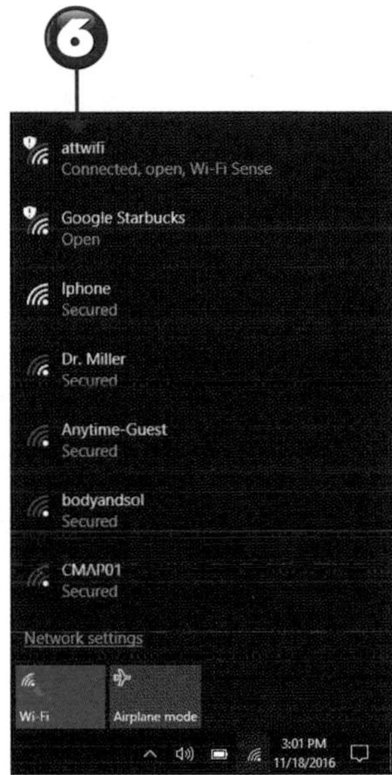

4. If the network requires you to accept terms and conditions, your browser opens the agreement page.

5. Read and agree to the terms and conditions, and click or tap the **Accept** or **Get Connected** button.

6. Your current network connection is listed first in the wireless network list and is marked "Connected."

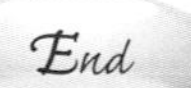

CONNECTING TO A SECURED PRIVATE NETWORK

A secured network uses a network security key, also known as an *encryption key*. The first time you connect to a secured network, you must enter the network security key. Windows 10 AE can remember your network security key and the rest of your connection details for you. Here's how this process works.

Start

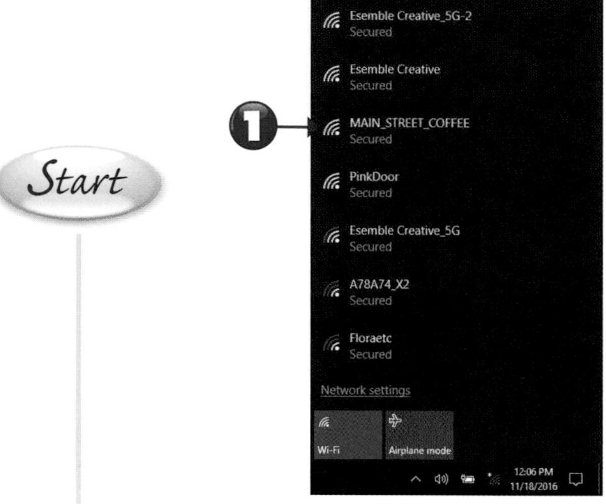

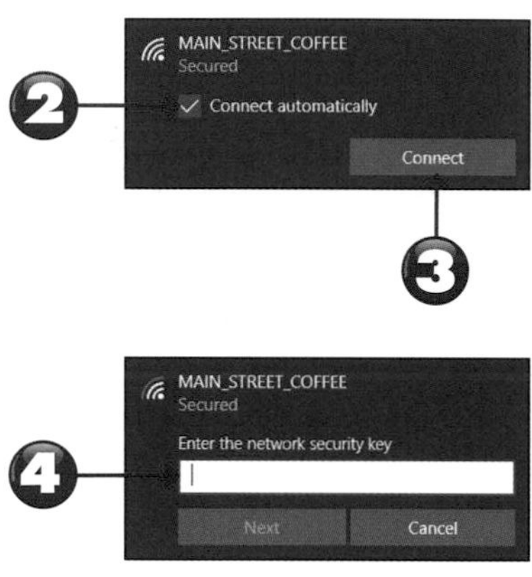

1. Click or tap a secure network.
2. If you want to connect to this network automatically in the future, check the **Connect automatically** box.
3. Click or tap **Connect**.
4. Enter the network security key.

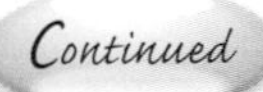
Continued

CAUTION

Learning More About Wi-Fi Sense In step 5, you have the option of sharing a network and its encryption key with your contacts, a feature called Wi-Fi Sense. To learn how to configure or disable Wi-Fi Sense, see "Managing Wi-Fi Sense," p. 397.

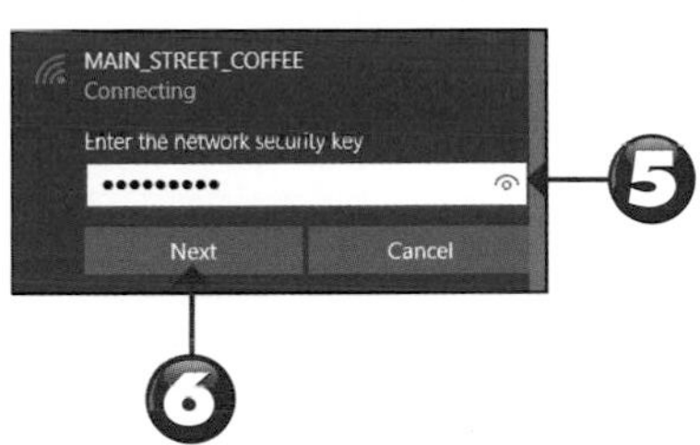

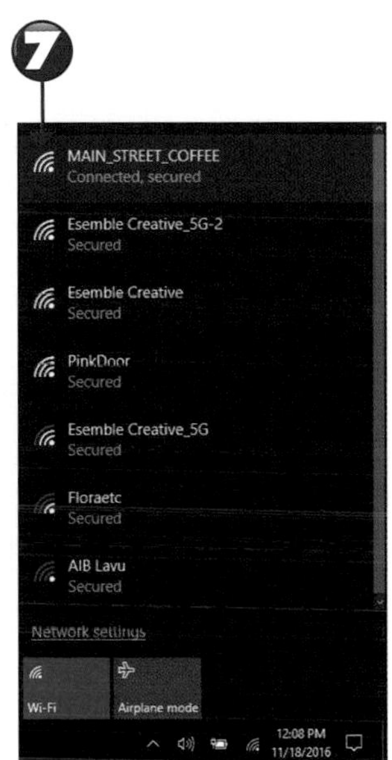

5. To see the hidden characters as you type, click or tap the eye icon.

6. Click or tap **Next**.

7. Your network connection is listed first in the wireless network list.

End

DISCONNECTING A WIRELESS CONNECTION

If you decide that you need to connect to a stronger signal or want to disconnect from Wi-Fi altogether, follow these steps to disconnect from your current Wi-Fi network.

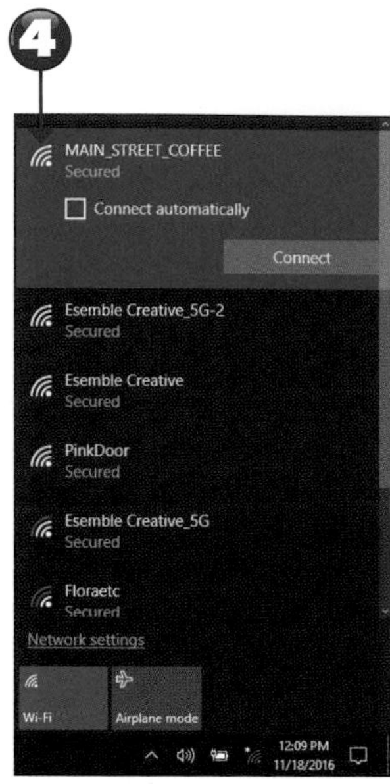

1. Click the network button in the taskbar.
2. Click or tap the current connection.
3. Click or tap **Disconnect**.
4. Your device disconnects from Wi-Fi.

End

NOTE

Disabling Automatic Reconnection In step 3, if you disconnect from a Wi-Fi network that is configured for automatic connections, the Connect button appears (as in this example). Click or tap it if you want to reconnect, click or tap a different network, or click or tap an empty part of the desktop if you don't want to connect right now.

USING AIRPLANE MODE

When Wi-Fi access is not needed, you can quickly turn off Wi-Fi (and Bluetooth) to save power. You can use the Airplane mode setting (named for air travel policies regarding radio signal frequency transmission) to quickly disable wireless transmission in Windows 10 AE. Here's how.

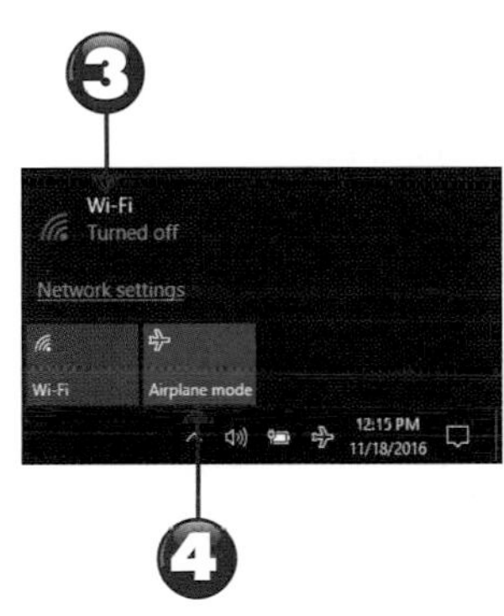

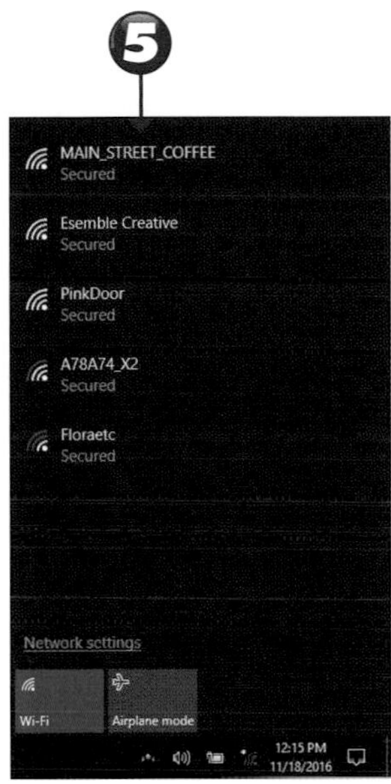

1. Click or tap the **Wireless Network** button in the taskbar.

2. Click or tap the **Airplane mode** button.

3. Wi-Fi functionality is turned off; no wireless connections are available.

4. To reenable wireless access, click or tap **Airplane mode**.

5. Wireless connections are again available.

End

CAUTION

Selecting Wi-Fi Only Using the Airplane mode quick setting is a fast way to disable Wi-Fi, but it also disables Bluetooth. If you use Bluetooth devices and want to disable only Wi-Fi, you can turn off Wi-Fi without changing Bluetooth settings. For details, see "Disabling and Enabling Wi-Fi," p. 396.

MANAGING NETWORKS

To manage wireless connections, create a HomeGroup, or manage a HomeGroup, use the Network & Internet settings available from Window's Settings. Here's how to get to the Network & Internet settings from the Start menu.

Start

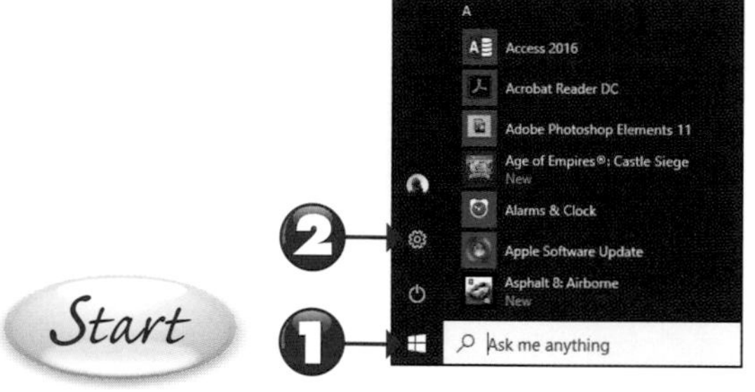

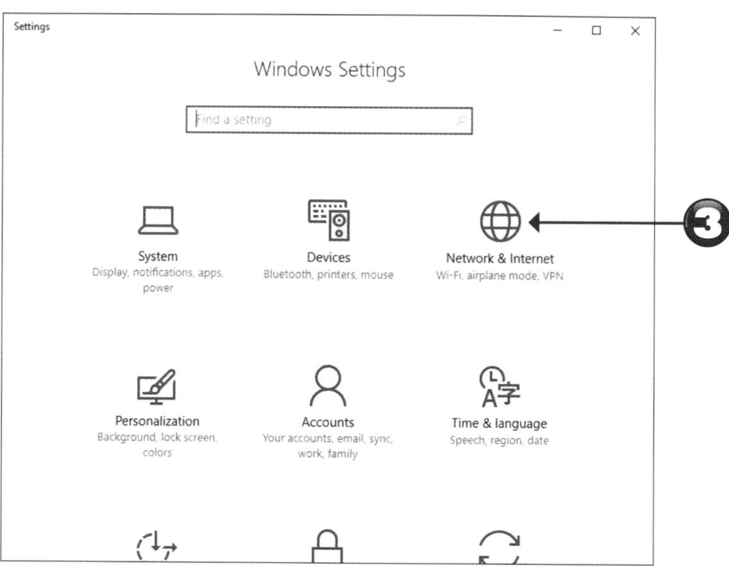

1. Click or tap **Start**.
2. Click or tap **Settings**.
3. Click or tap **Network & Internet**.

Continued

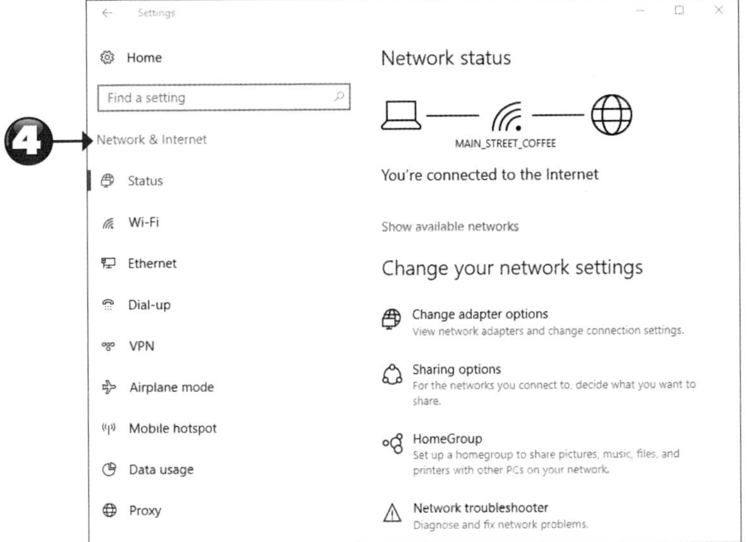

4 The Network & Internet settings.

End

NOTE

Other Network & Internet Topics This chapter focuses on the Wi-Fi and Airplane mode settings. Use the Data usage settings if you use metered connections. Use the VPN settings to help set up or manage a virtual private network (typically used to connect to corporate networks). Use the Dial-up settings to help set up or manage a modem that dials in to a telephone number for Internet connections. Use the Proxy settings if you need to set up or manage a proxy connection (typically used in corporate networks).

DISABLING AND ENABLING WI-FI

You can disable and enable Wi-Fi by using the Wi-Fi settings. By using this menu, your Bluetooth settings are unaffected.

Start

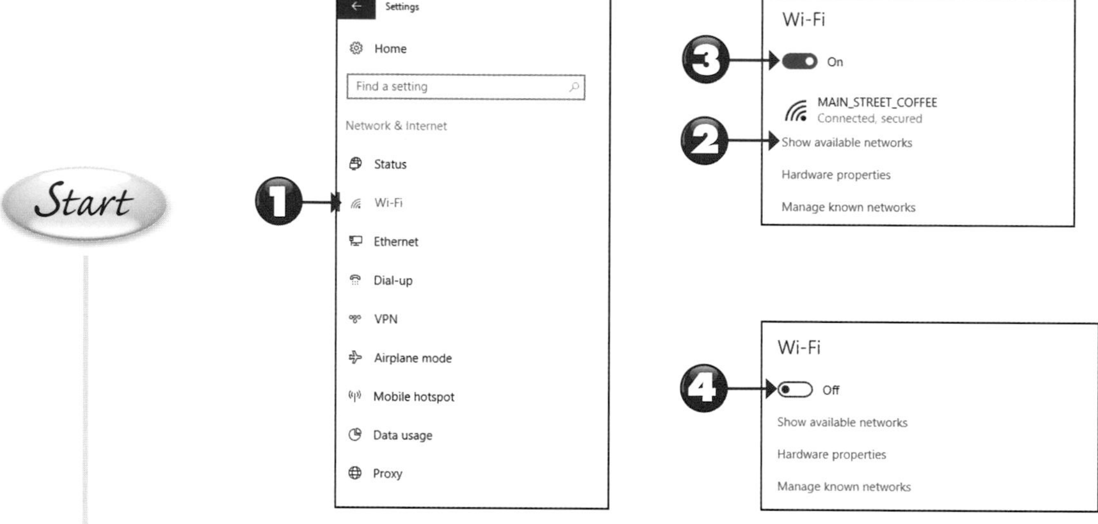

1. With Window's Settings open to the Network & Internet settings, click or tap **Wi-Fi**.
2. If you're currently connected to a network, click or tap **Show available networks** to display nearby wireless networks.
3. To disable Wi-Fi, toggle the switch to **Off**.
4. To enable Wi-Fi again, toggle the switch to **On**.

End

MANAGING WI-FI SENSE

Wi-Fi Sense is a new feature in Windows 10 AE. It enables you to automatically log in to publicly open Wi-Fi hotspots. Here's how to limit what it does.

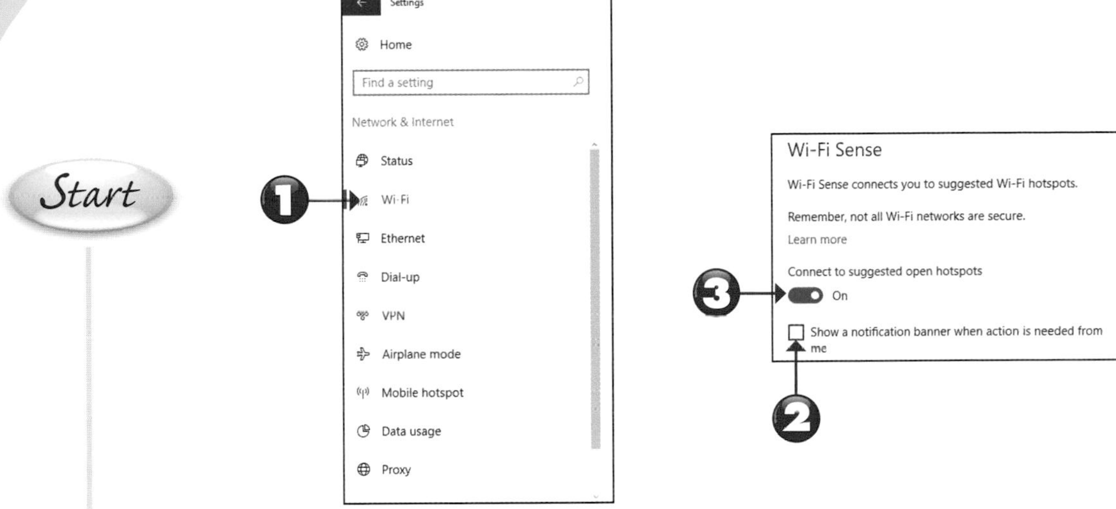

1. From the Network & Internet settings, click or tap **Wi-Fi**.

2. If Wi-Fi Sense is on, you can opt to receive notifications when action is required to connect. Check the **Show a notification banner when action is needed from me** checkbox.

3. Wi-Fi Sense is enabled by default. To disable this function, click or press the **Connect to suggested open hotspots** control and drag to **Off**.

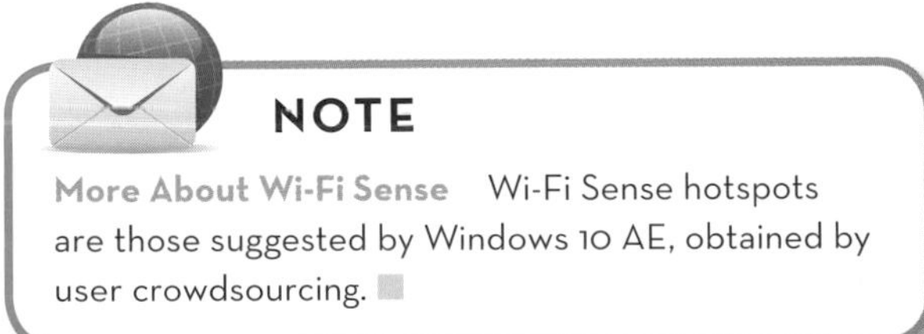

NOTE

More About Wi-Fi Sense Wi-Fi Sense hotspots are those suggested by Windows 10 AE, obtained by user crowdsourcing.

MANAGING WIRELESS CONNECTIONS

Windows 10 AE stores information about each Wi-Fi connection you create. If you travel and use different Wi-Fi networks, the list can become very long. Here's how to remove ("forget") networks you won't be using again.

Start

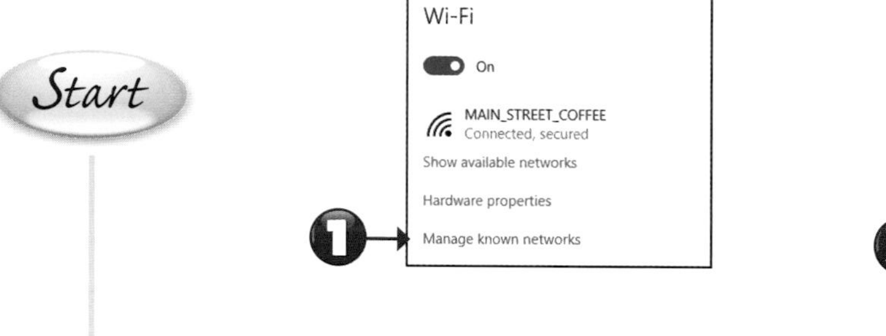

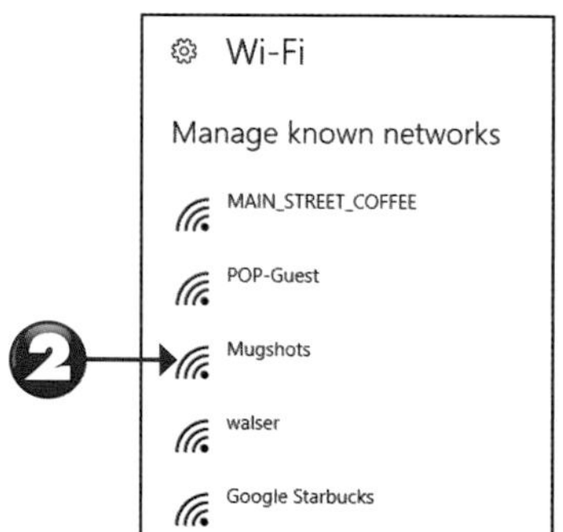

1. From the Wi-Fi settings, click or tap **Manage known networks**.

2. Click or tap a network you want to forget.

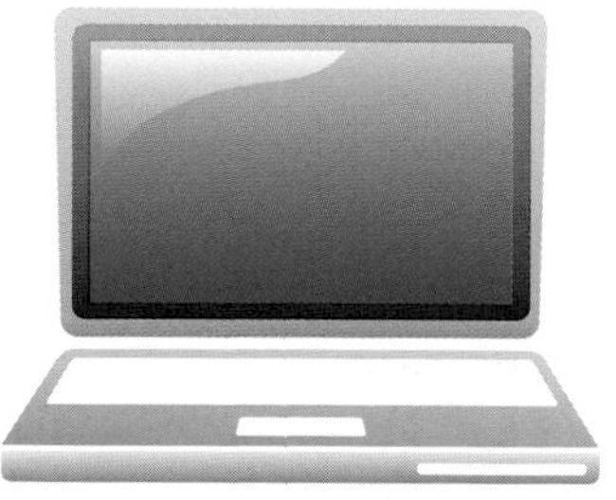

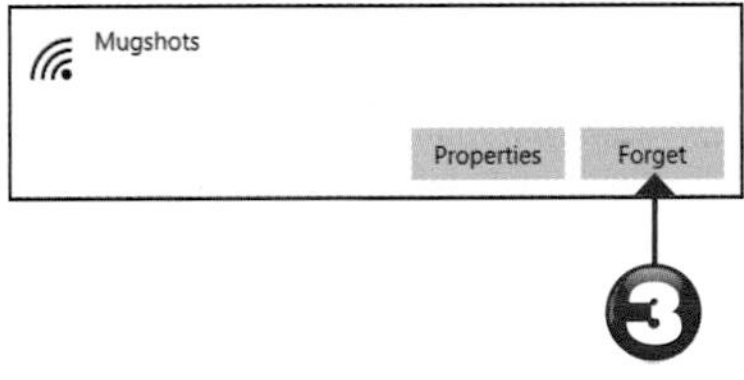

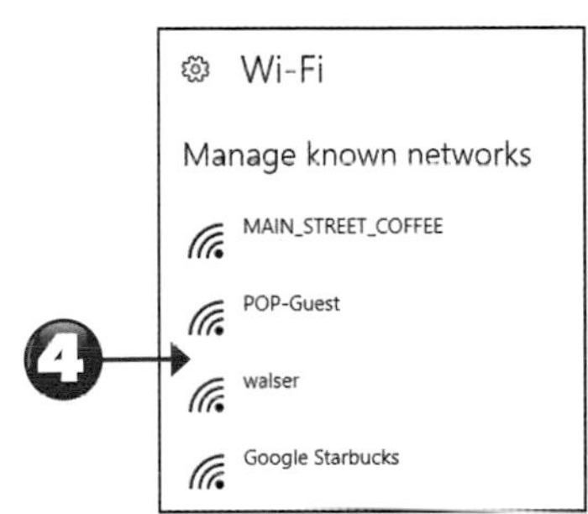

3. Click or tap **Forget**.
4. The network is removed from the list of known networks.

End

NOTE

Reconnecting to a Forgotten Network If you want to reconnect to a wireless network you forgot, you must reenter the SSID (if the network is hidden) and its encryption key (password).

CREATING A HOMEGROUP

Windows 10 AE supports an easy-to-use, yet secure, type of home and small-business networking feature called a homegroup (also available in Windows 7, 8, and 8.1). Homegroup networking enables home network users to share libraries and printers—you can specify which libraries to share and whether to share printers and devices on a particular system. All users of a homegroup use the same password but don't need to worry about specifying particular folders to share. You can create a new homegroup or join one from the Wi-Fi settings, but it's faster to start the process from the Cortana Search window.

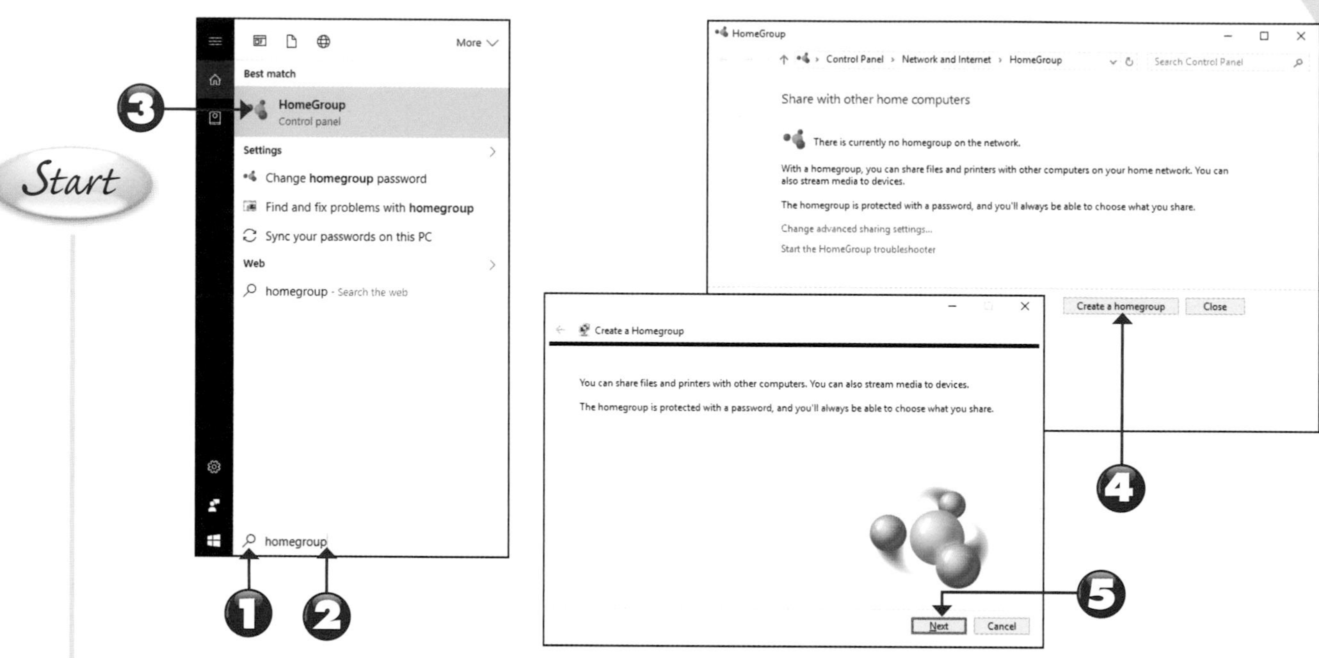

1. Click or tap the **Cortana Search** window.

2. Type **homegroup**.

3. Click or tap **HomeGroup**.

4. If there is no homegroup, click or tap **Create a homegroup**.

5. Click or tap **Next**.

Continued

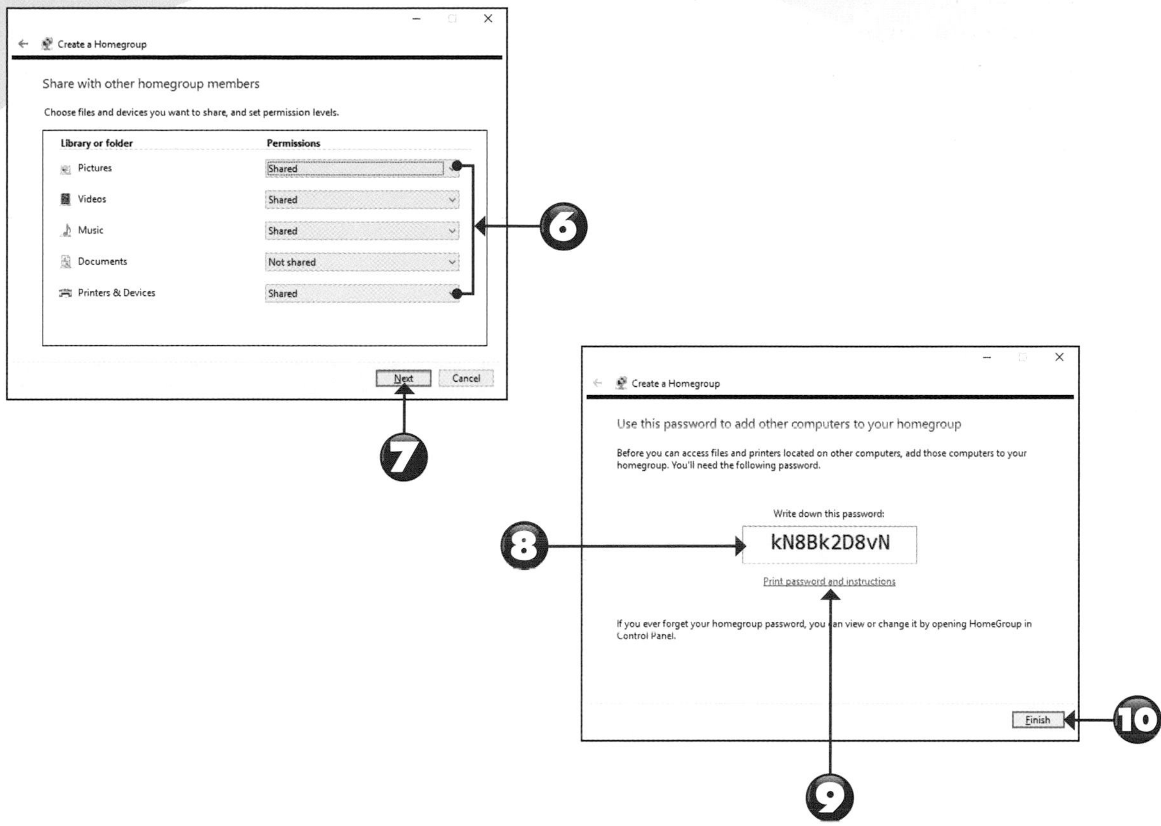

6. Select **Shared** or **Not shared** as desired for the folders and devices on your system (defaults shown here).

7. Click or tap **Next**.

8. Provide this password to others who need to connect to the homegroup.

9. Click or tap to print the password and instructions.

10. Click or tap **Finish** to close the dialog box.

End

JOINING A HOMEGROUP

Microsoft introduced homegroups in Windows 7, so if you have one or more Windows 7, Windows 8/8.1, or Windows 10 computers in your home or small office, you might already have a homegroup. Here's how to add your Windows 10 AE computer to an existing homegroup. This example starts from the Wi-Fi settings.

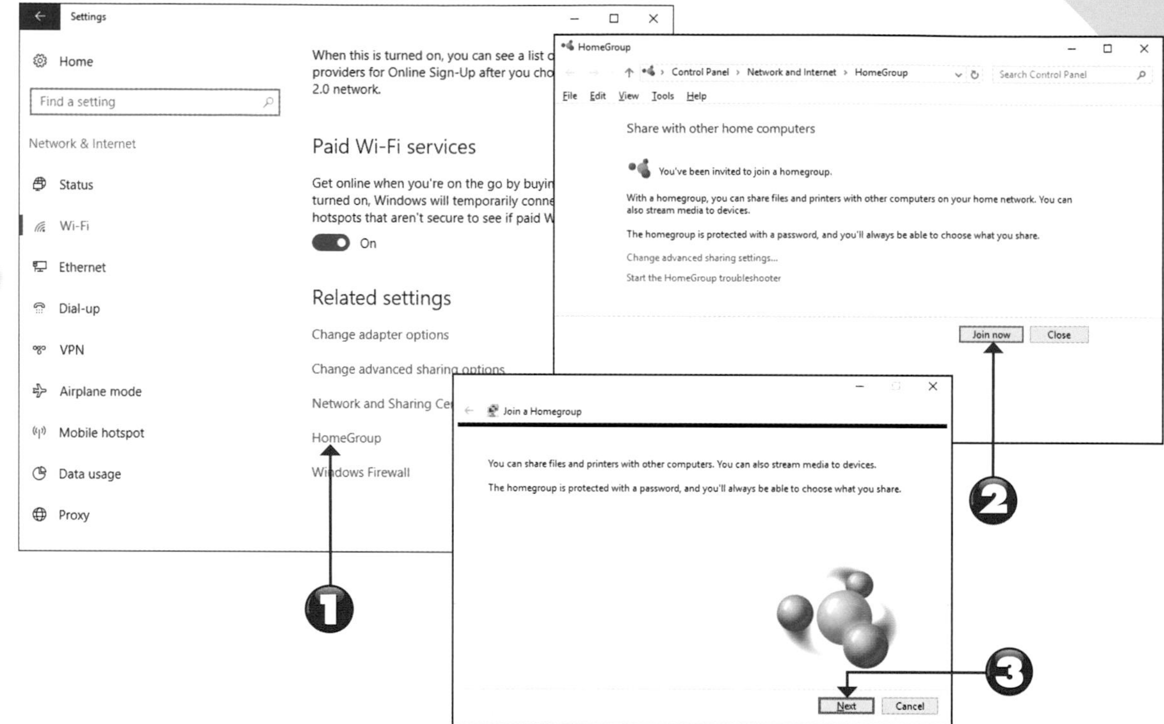

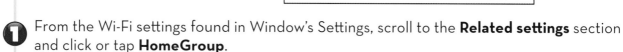

1. From the Wi-Fi settings found in Window's Settings, scroll to the **Related settings** section and click or tap **HomeGroup**.

2. If there is an existing homegroup, click or tap **Join now**.

3. Click or tap **Next**.

Continued

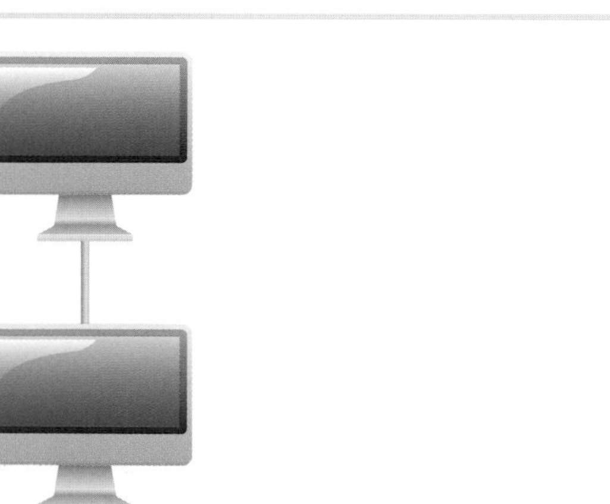

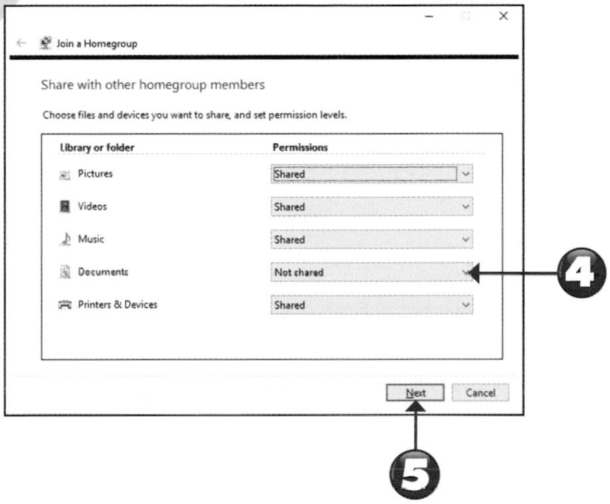

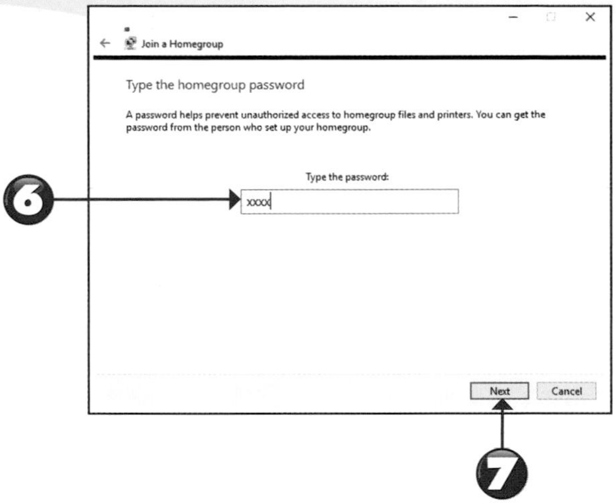

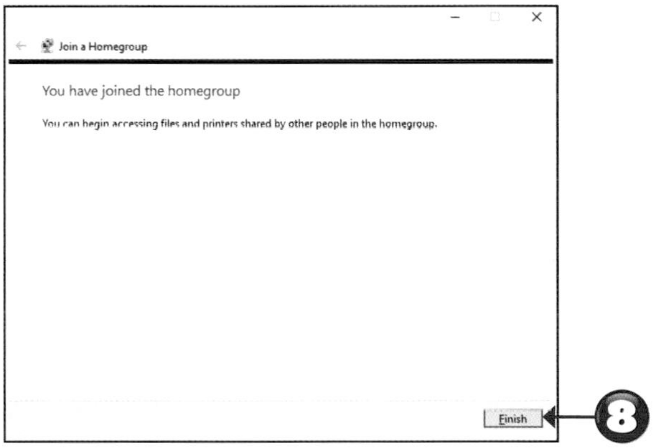

4. Select **Shared** or **Not shared** as desired for the folders and devices on your system (defaults shown here).

5. Click or tap **Next**.

6. Enter the password for the homegroup.

7. Click or tap **Next**.

8. Click or tap **Finish** to close the dialog box.

End

NOTE

Leaving a Homegroup If you want to leave a homegroup you've joined, open the HomeGroup dialog and select the link for Leave the homegroup.

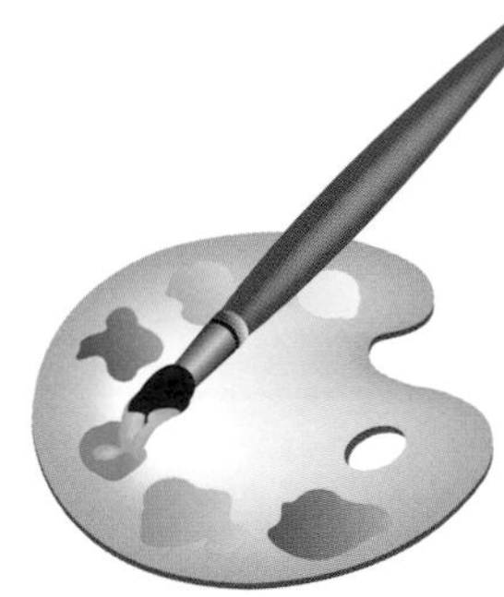

CUSTOMIZING WINDOWS

From tweaking the Start menu and the taskbar to adjusting the desktop and personalizing the Lock screen, Windows 10 AE provides many ways to make your account uniquely yours.

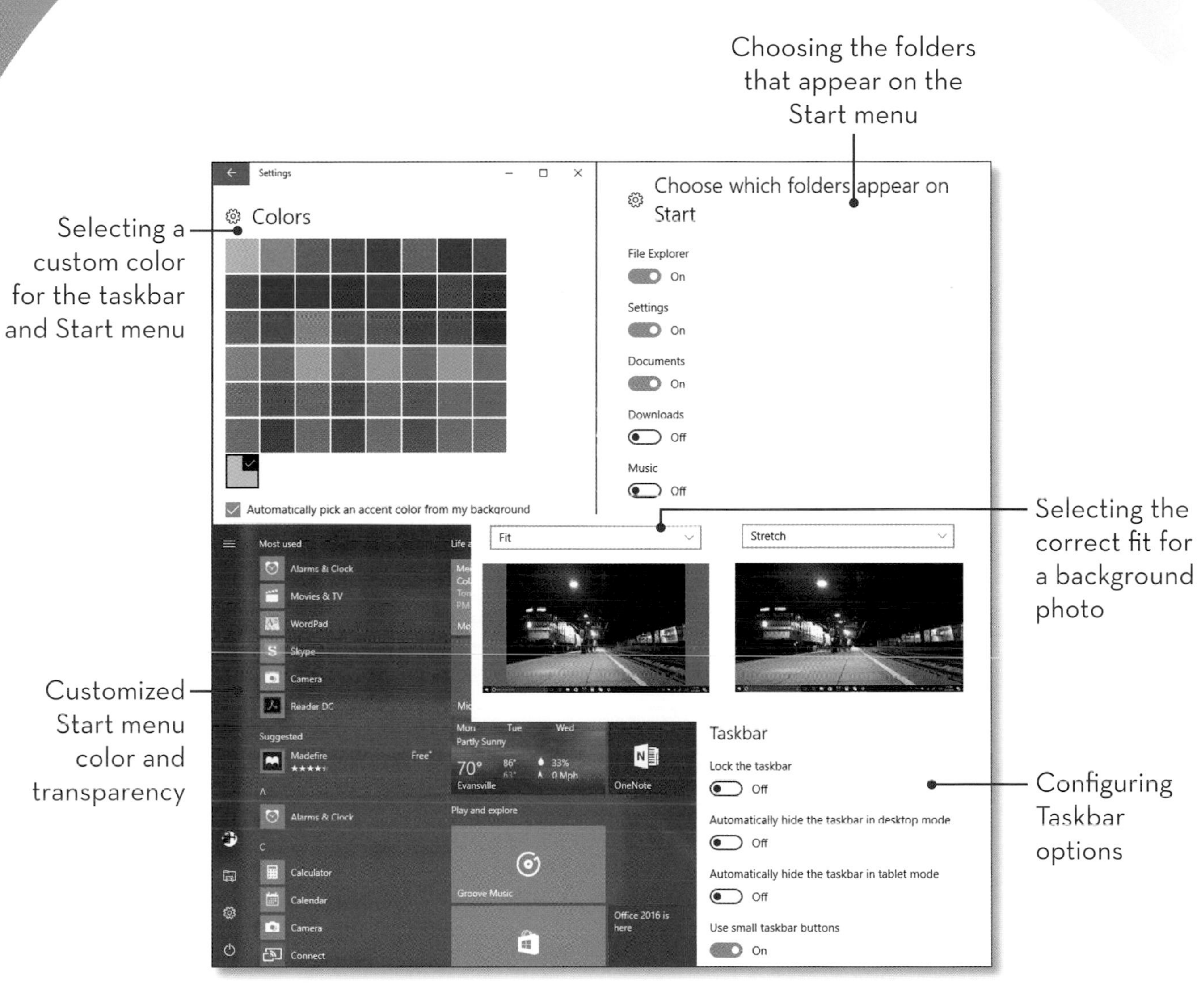
Choosing the folders that appear on the Start menu
Selecting a custom color for the taskbar and Start menu
Selecting the correct fit for a background photo
Customized Start menu color and transparency
Configuring Taskbar options
Settings
Colors
Automatically pick an accent color from my background
Choose which folders appear on Start
File Explorer
On
Settings
On
Documents
On
Downloads
Off
Music
Off
Fit
Stretch
Most used
Alarms & Clock
Movies & TV
WordPad
Skype
Camera
Reader DC
Suggested
Madefire
Free*
A
Alarms & Clock
C
Calculator
Calendar
Camera
Connect
Partly Sunny
70°
Evansville
OneNote
Play and explore
Groove Music
Office 2016 is here
Taskbar
Lock the taskbar
Off
Automatically hide the taskbar in desktop mode
Off
Automatically hide the taskbar in tablet mode
Off
Use small taskbar buttons
On

USING PERSONALIZATION SETTINGS

The Personalization settings enable you to change your desktop background, colors, Lock screen, and themes. Here's how to start the process.

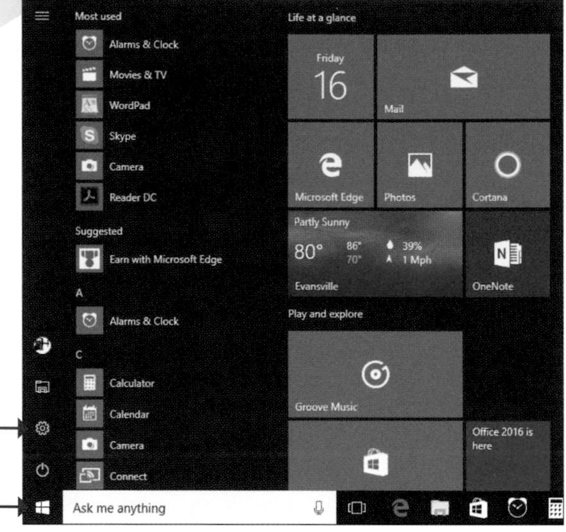

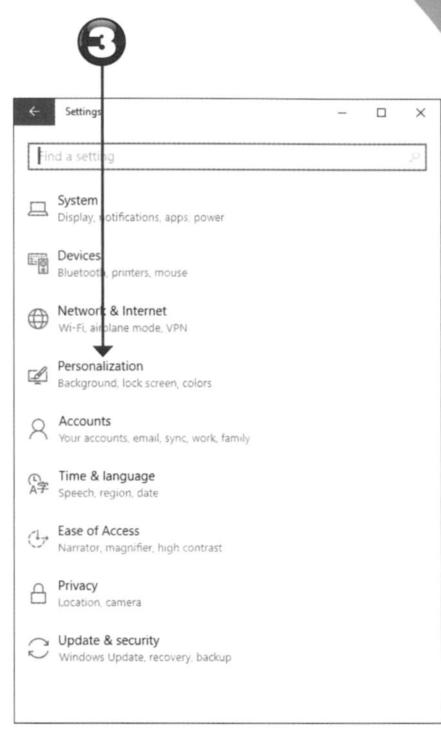

Start

1. Click or tap the **Start** button.
2. Click or tap **Settings**.
3. Click or tap **Personalization**.

Continued

TIP

Opening Settings from Quick Actions Click or tap the **Notifications/Quick Actions** button in the taskbar (far right side of taskbar), and then click or tap **All settings** to open the Settings dialog box. ■

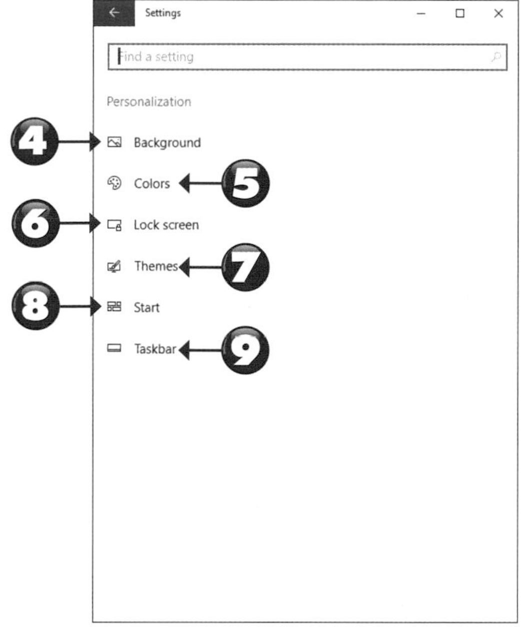

4. Click or tap to change the screen background.

5. Click or tap to change the taskbar and Start menu colors.

6. Click or tap to change the Lock screen.

7. Click or tap to change settings for sounds, mouse pointers, desktop icons, and themes.

8. Click or tap to change Start menu settings.

9. Click or tap to change taskbar settings.

End

CHANGING THE SCREEN BACKGROUND

Changing the screen background (or "wallpaper" for Windows veterans) is one of the most popular ways to personalize your system. In this exercise, you learn how to customize it, Windows 10 AE style.

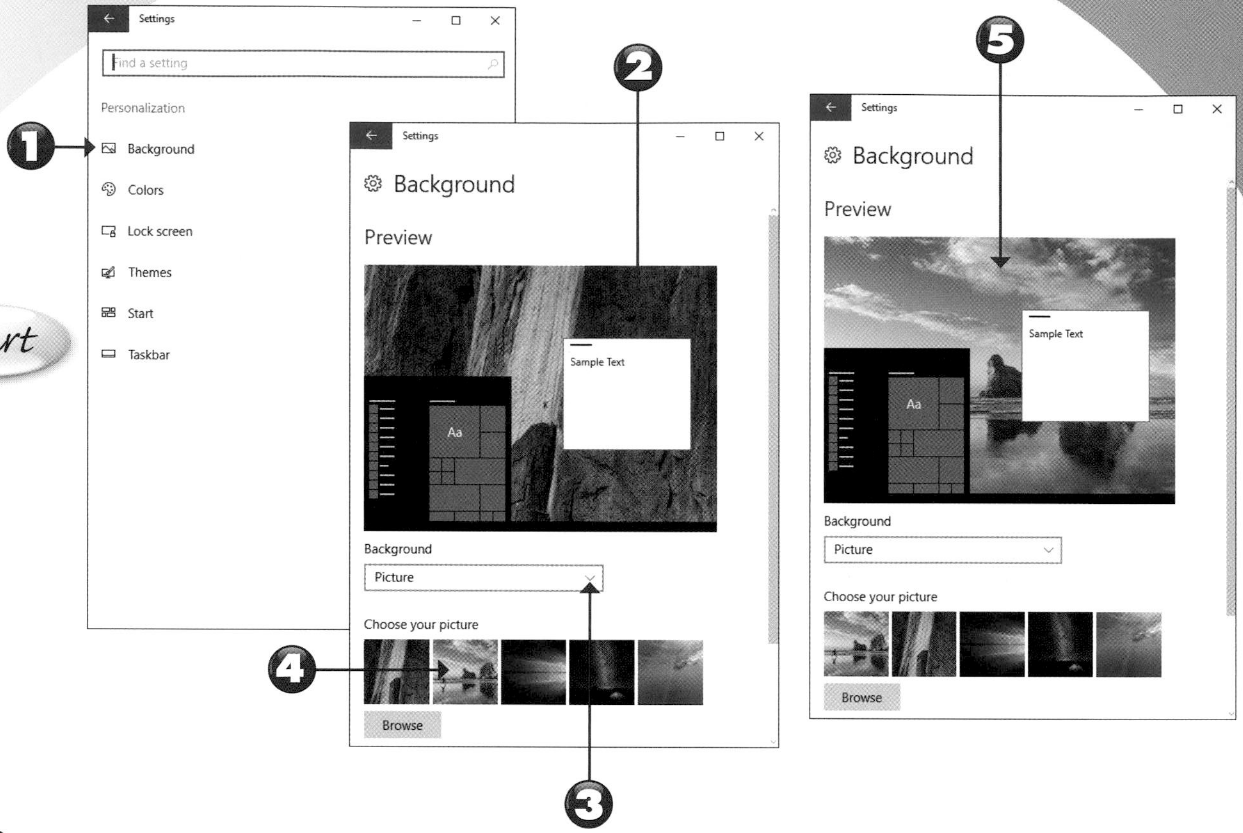

Start

1. From the Personalization settings, click or tap **Background**.
2. Preview the current background.
3. Picture is the default background type; click or tap to select from other backgrounds, including solid colors and a slide show.
4. Click or tap a different picture.
5. Preview the new selection.

End

CHOOSING YOUR OWN BACKGROUND PICTURE

Choosing one of Windows 10 AE's spectacular nature photos adds pizazz to your desktop, but if you really want to say, "This is my computer," there's nothing like adding your own photo. Here's how to do that.

Start

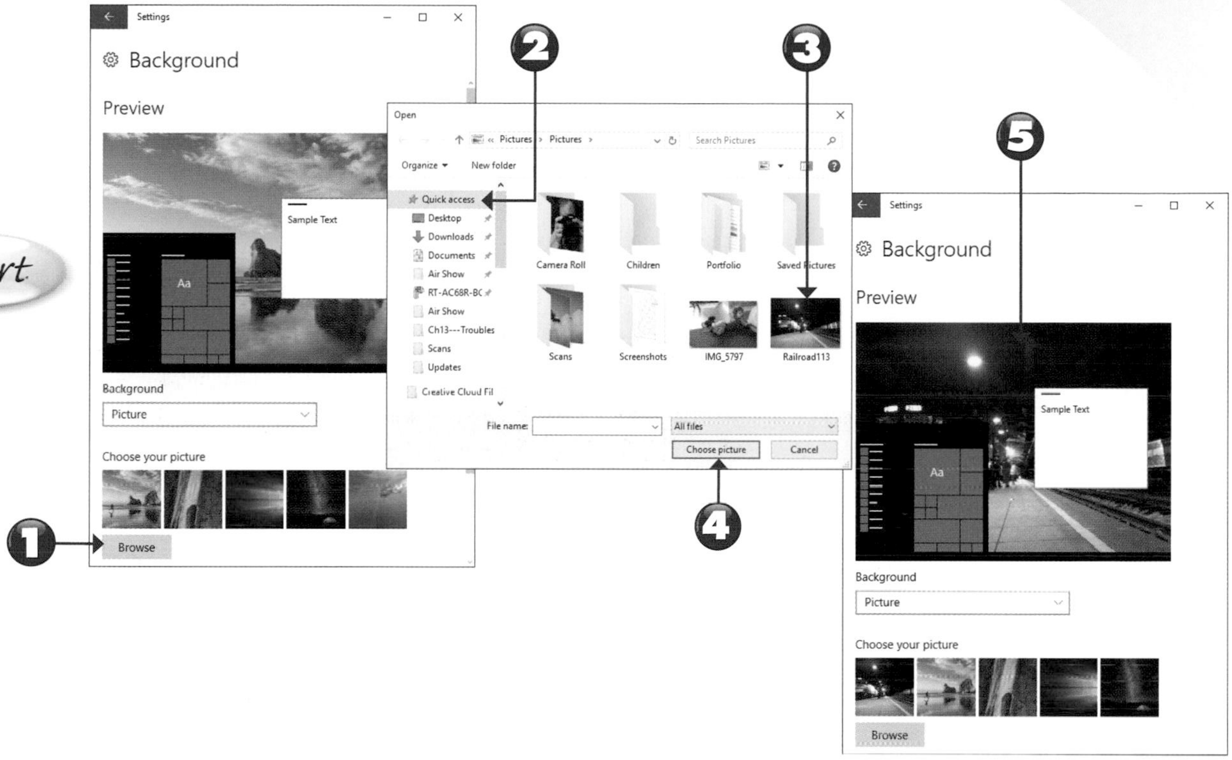

1. Click or tap **Browse** from the Background settings.
2. Navigate to the location of the photo you want to use.
3. Click or tap a picture.
4. Click or tap **Choose picture**.
5. Preview new selection.

TIP

Putting a Slide Show on Your Desktop Want to show multiple photos? Choose **Slide show** as the background type. You can then navigate to a folder and use its contents. You can also select a picture fit and determine how often to change photos. ■

CHOOSING A PICTURE FIT

Most of the time, the picture(s) you choose for your background might not be an exact fit. Here's how to use the Choose a Fit menu to select the best setting for your photo.

Start

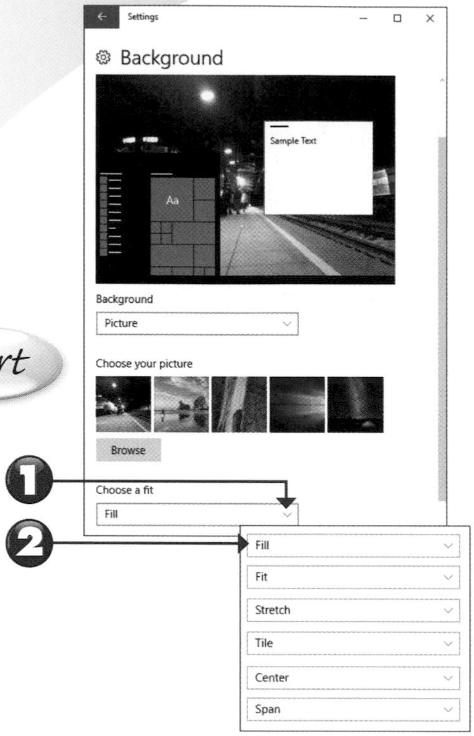

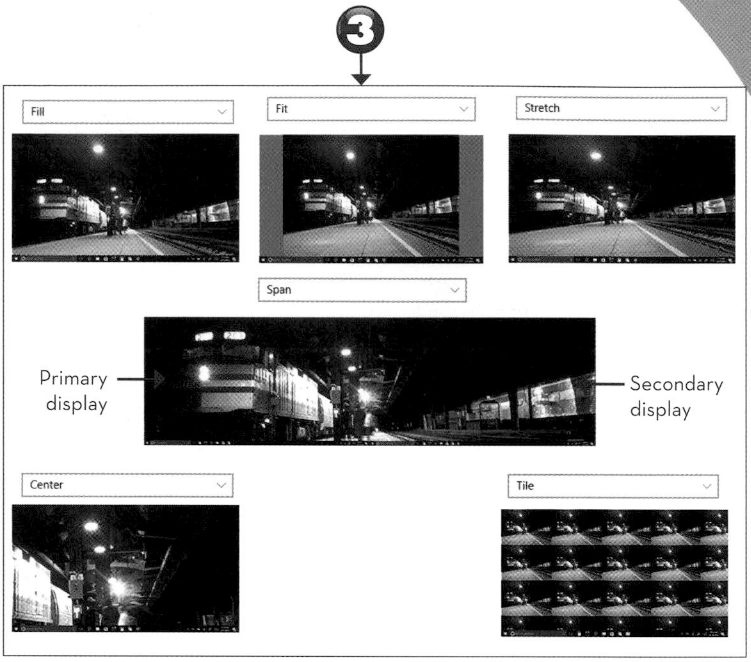

1. From the Background settings, click or tap **Choose a fit**.
2. Click or tap to choose a fit option.
3. Here's how the same image looks using different Fit settings on a widescreen display.

Continued

NOTE

Why Fill Is the Default Setting Fill does not distort the image and covers the entire desktop, so it's automatically the default. ■

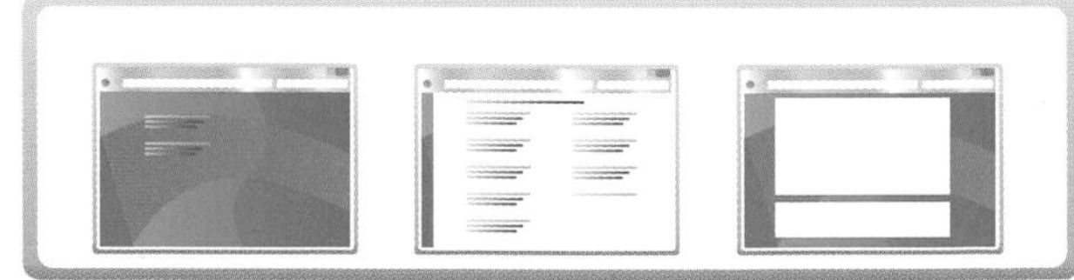

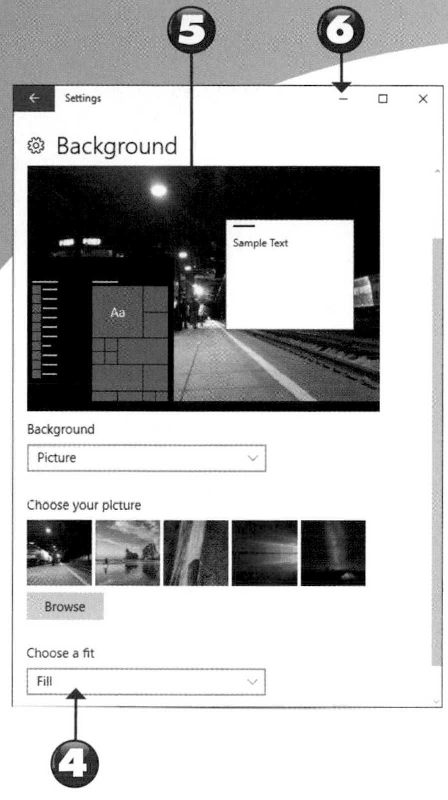

4 This is the current fit ("Fill").

5 Here's the current background preview.

6 Click or tap to minimize.

7 The Windows desktop using a personal background.

8 Click or tap to return to the Background settings.

End

NOTE

Background Fit Options When **Fit** is selected, the background will have borders on top/bottom or left/right edges if the image doesn't have the same proportions as the display setting. If the image doesn't have the same proportions as the display setting, selecting **Stretch** distorts the image to fill the desktop. **Tile** repeats an image that is smaller than the desktop to fill it. An image smaller than the desktop has a border on all four sides if **Center** is chosen. ■

CHANGING ACCENT COLORS

Windows 10 AE adds new ways to customize your taskbar and Start menu colors. Let's start by changing the accent color used for active apps and Start menu tiles from the Colors settings.

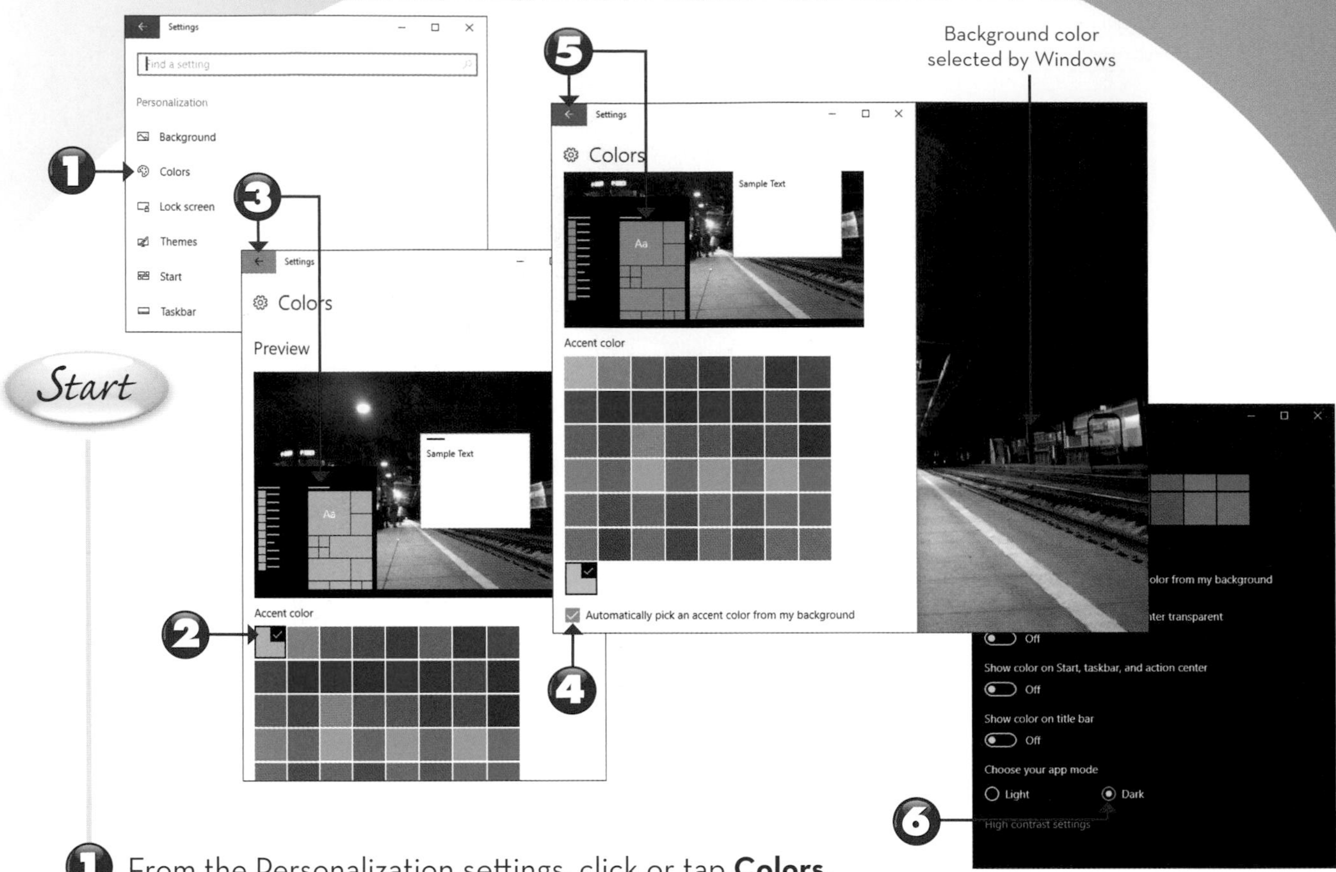

1. From the Personalization settings, click or tap **Colors**.
2. Click or tap an accent color.
3. Color is used by tiles on the Start menu, by dialog boxes (such as the color change in the navigation icon shown in this example), and by app windows.
4. Click or tap **Automatically pick an accent color from my background**.
5. An accent color is selected from your background and reflected in app windows, tiles, dialog boxes, and other screen elements.
6. Scroll down the Colors settings to view app mode options. Light mode is the default selection; click or tap **Dark** mode to apply a darker appearance to app windows, tiles, and other screen elements.

End

CHANGING TASKBAR AND START MENU COLORS AND TRANSPARENCY SETTINGS

When you select a color in the Colors settings, you can also use this color in the taskbar and Start menu. Here's how. In this example, we are using the default Light app mode.

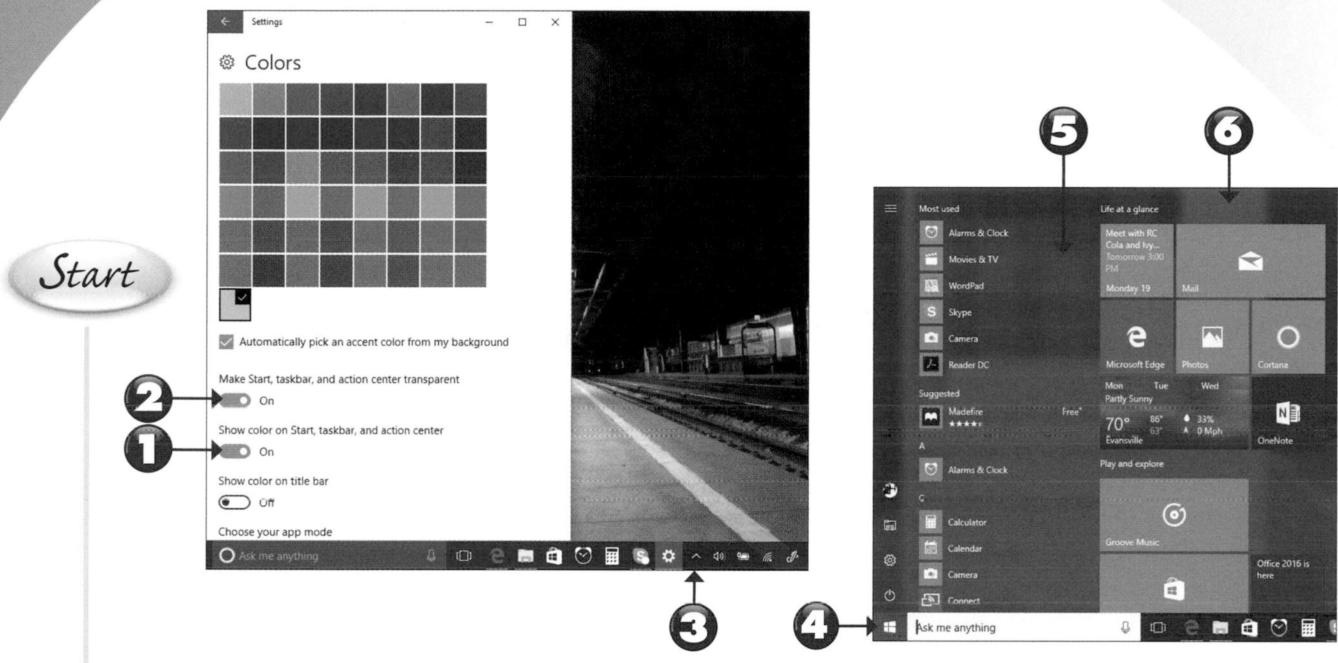

1. From the Colors settings, click or press and drag **Show color on Start, taskbar, and action center** to **On**.
2. Click or press and drag **Make Start, taskbar, and action center transparent** to **On**.
3. The taskbar changes to the selected color and displays some transparency.
4. Click or tap **Start**.
5. The Start menu changes to the selected color.
6. The Start menu displays some transparency; you can see through the menu to underlying app windows and desktop items.

End

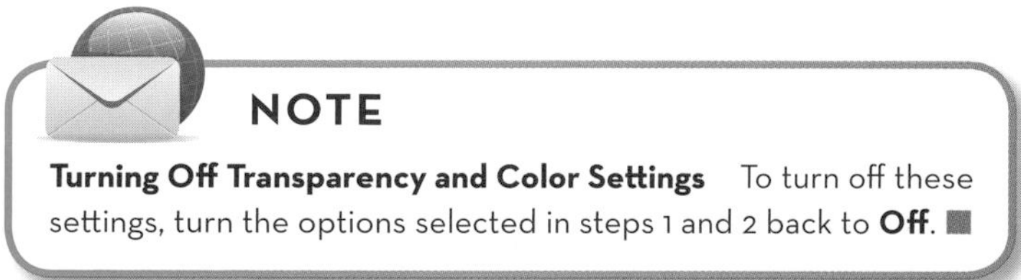

NOTE

Turning Off Transparency and Color Settings To turn off these settings, turn the options selected in steps 1 and 2 back to **Off**. ■

CHANGING START MENU SETTINGS

You can also change the items that appear on the Start menu and its onscreen size. In this lesson, you learn how to make more room for Start menu tiles and how to add folders to the Start menu.

Settings
Find a setting
Personalization
Background
Colors
Lock screen
Themes
Start
Taskbar

Settings
Start
Aa
Show more tiles
On
Occasionally show suggestions in Start
On
Show most used apps
On
Show recently added apps
On
Use Start full screen
Off
Show recently opened items in Jump Lists on Start or the taskbar
On
Choose which folders appear on Start

Settings
Choose which folders appear on Start
File Explorer
On
Settings
On
Documents
Off
Downloads
Off
Music
Off
Pictures
Off
Videos
Off
HomeGroup
Off
Network

Start

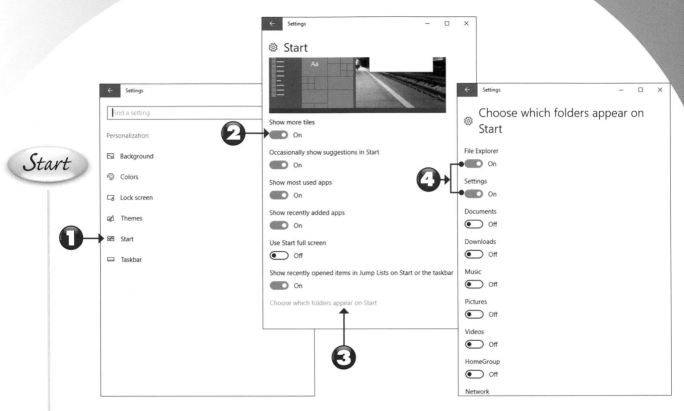

1. From the Personalization settings, click or tap **Start**.
2. Click or press and drag to **On** to show more tiles.
3. Click or tap **Choose which folders appear on Start**.
4. Default Start menu folders are already set to the On position.

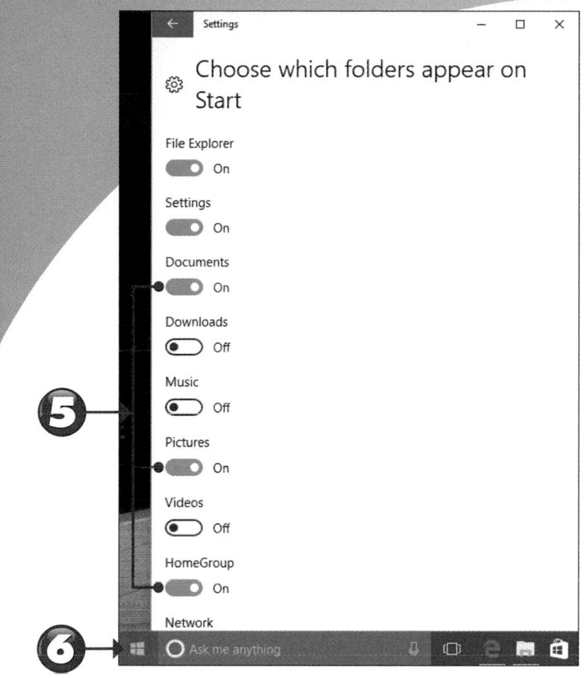

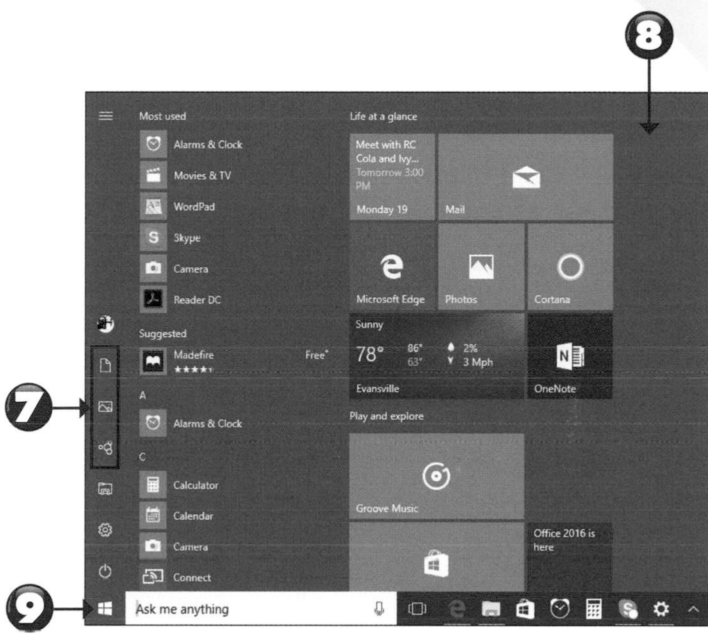

5. To add a folder to the Start menu, click or press and drag to **On**.

6. Click or tap **Start**.

7. In this example, newly added folders display in the menu.

8. More space is added for Start menu tiles.

9. Click or tap **Start** again to close the Start menu.

End

TIP

Using the Additional Start Menu Tile Space To use the additional space in the Start menu, drag or resize tiles or add programs to the Start menu. To learn more about customizing the Start menu, see Chapter 4, “Logging In to Windows 10 Anniversary Edition and Customizing the Start Menu.” ■

SELECTING A SCREEN SAVER

The Windows 10 AE screen saver function helps protect the privacy of your display when you're away from your computer. This feature also helps prevent an image from being permanently burned into your screen—still a concern if you use a plasma HDTV with your computer. This tutorial shows you how to select and customize your favorite screen saver from the Lock screen settings.

Start

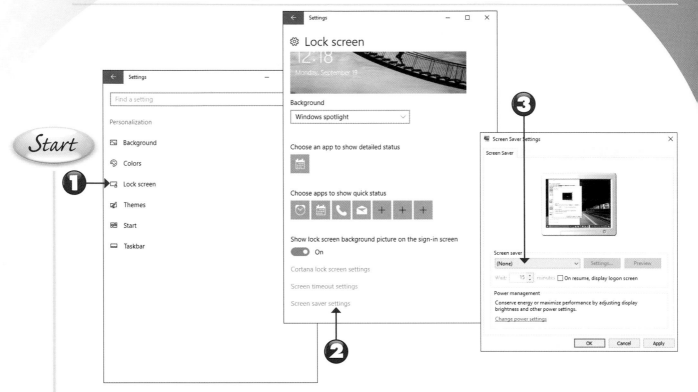

1. From the Personalization settings, click or tap **Lock screen**.

2. Click or tap **Screen saver settings**.

3. No screen saver is the default setting.

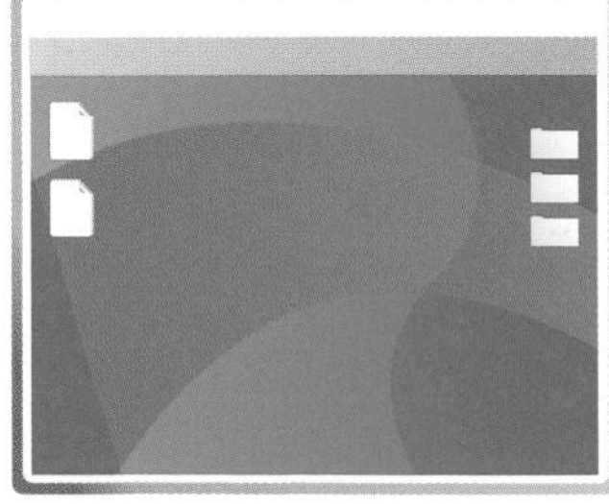

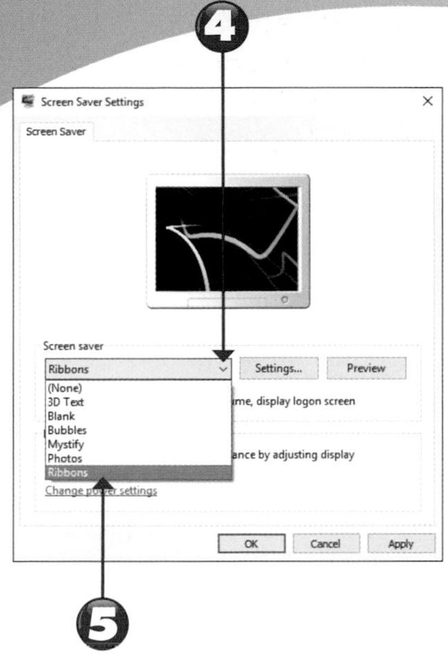

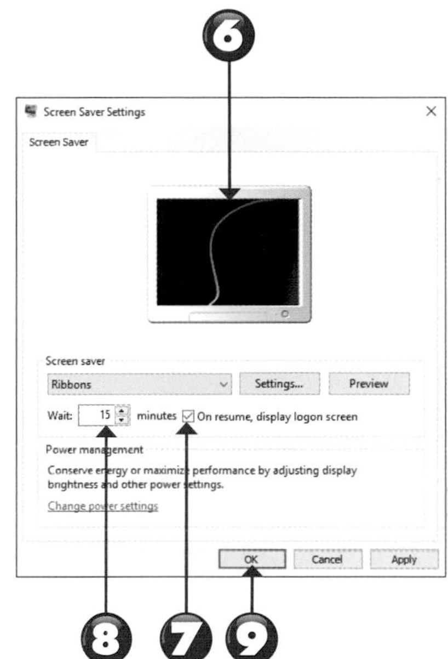

4. Click or tap the screen saver menu.

5. Select a screen saver.

6. A preview of the screen saver appears.

7. Use the checkbox to require login after the screen saver starts.

8. Adjust the wait time as desired.

9. Click or tap **OK** to apply the screen saver.

End

CUSTOMIZING THE TASKBAR

Use the taskbar customization options in Windows 10 AE to change the appearance of the taskbar. Here's how to change taskbar button label settings.

Start

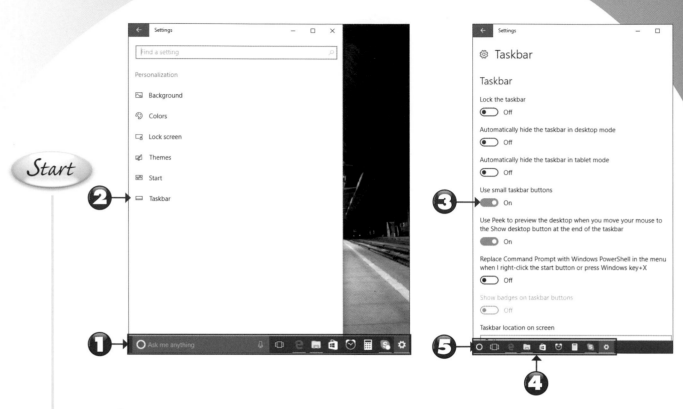

1. The default taskbar appearance is large taskbar buttons and a large Cortana search window.
2. To customize the taskbar, click or tap **Taskbar** from the Personalization settings.
3. To use small taskbar buttons, click or press and drag to **On**.
4. The taskbar buttons change to the small setting.
5. To use Cortana Search, click the round icon.

Continued

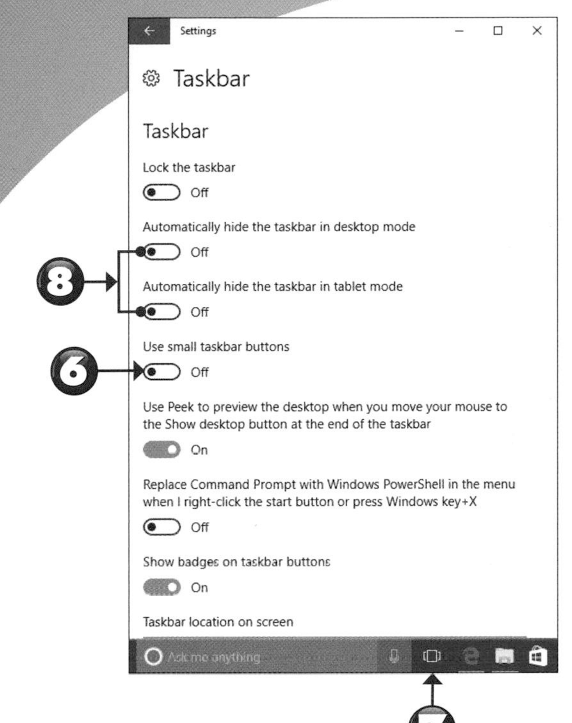

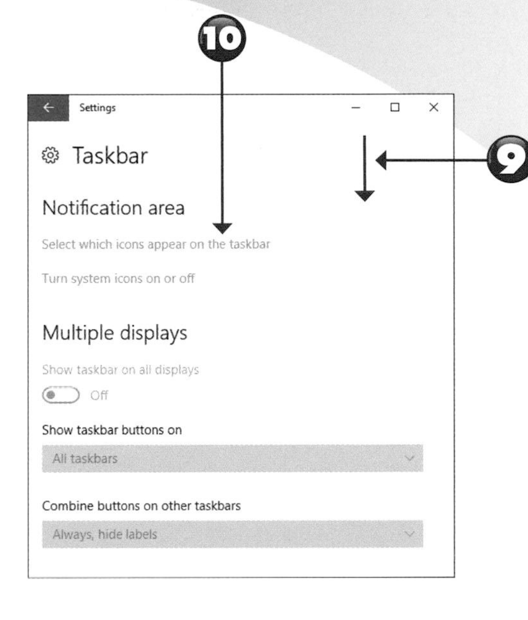

6. To return to the default (large) taskbar buttons, click or press and drag to **Off**.
7. Default taskbar appearance returns.
8. Turn **On** to automatically hide the taskbar in desktop or tablet modes.
9. Scroll down the Taskbar settings.
10. Click or tap to select the icons that appear on the taskbar.

Continued

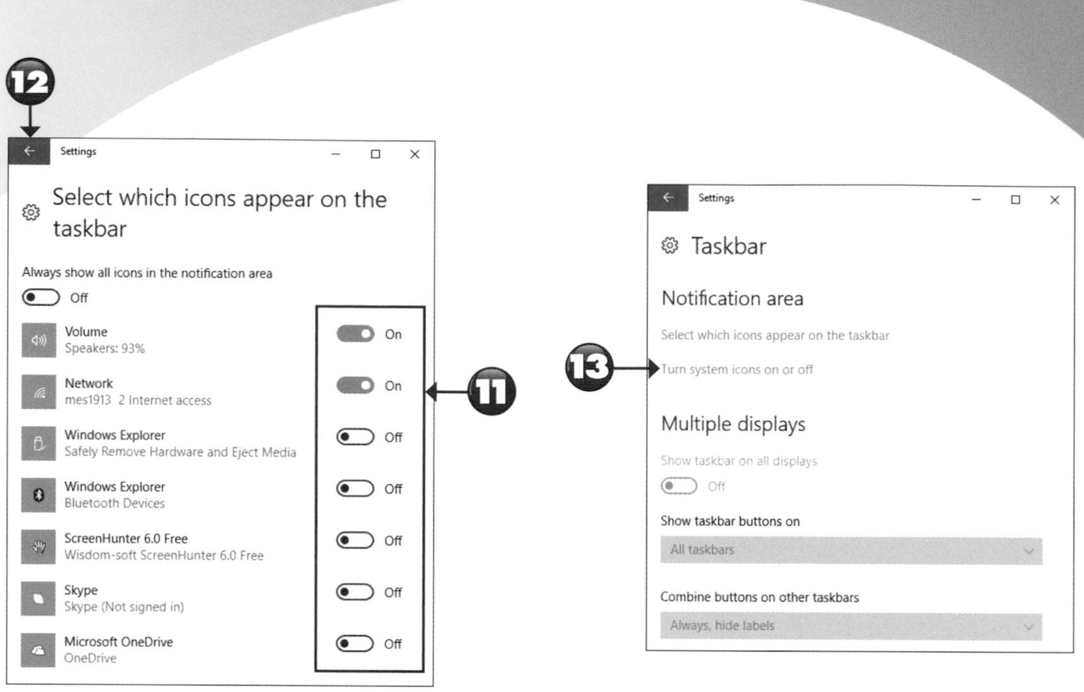

11. Select the taskbar icons you want to see with this menu.
12. Click or tap the back arrow to return to the previous settings.
13. Click or tap to turn on/turn off system icons.

Continued

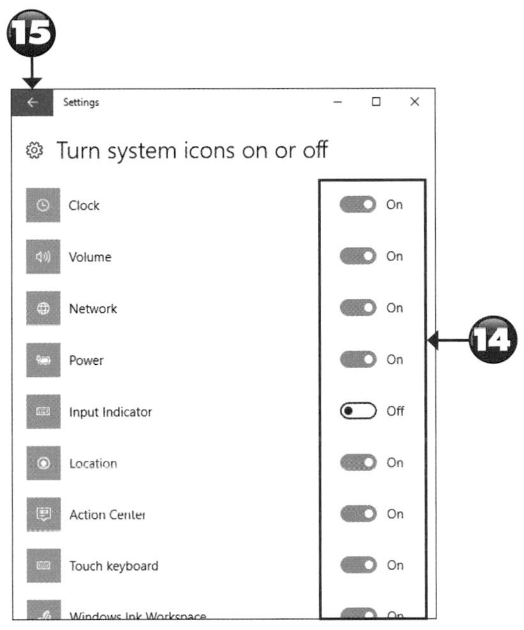

14 Select the system icons you want to see with this menu.

15 Click or tap the back arrow to return to the previous menu.

End

NOTE

Locking and Auto-Hiding the Taskbar Lock the taskbar so it can't be changed until it's unlocked. Use Auto-hide to maximize screen space; the taskbar is visible only when you move your mouse or finger to the bottom edge of the display. ■

SELECTING YOUR TIME ZONE

New computers and tablets are often set to the wrong time zone for your area when you first receive them. Fixing the problem is easy with the Settings Time & language dialog box.

Start

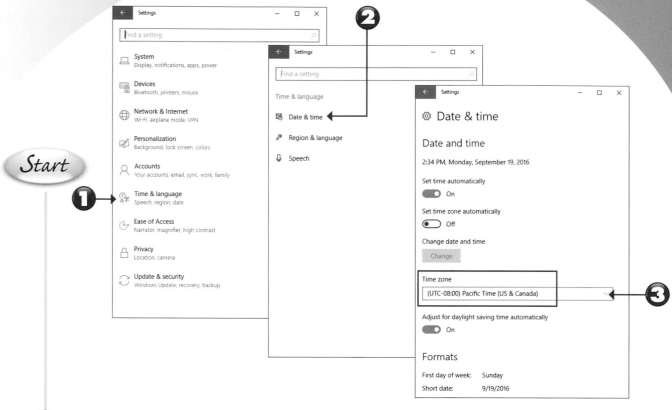

1. From the main Settings dialog box, click or tap **Time & language**.
2. Click or tap **Date & time**.
3. If the time zone shown is incorrect, click or tap to open the time zone menu.

Continued

NOTE

When to Change the Date and Time Although the time zone is listed after the date and time, you should make sure the time zone is checked (and, if necessary, changed) *before* you make any changes to the date and time. If you need to change the date and time, turn off **Set time automatically** and use the Change button shown in step 3. ■

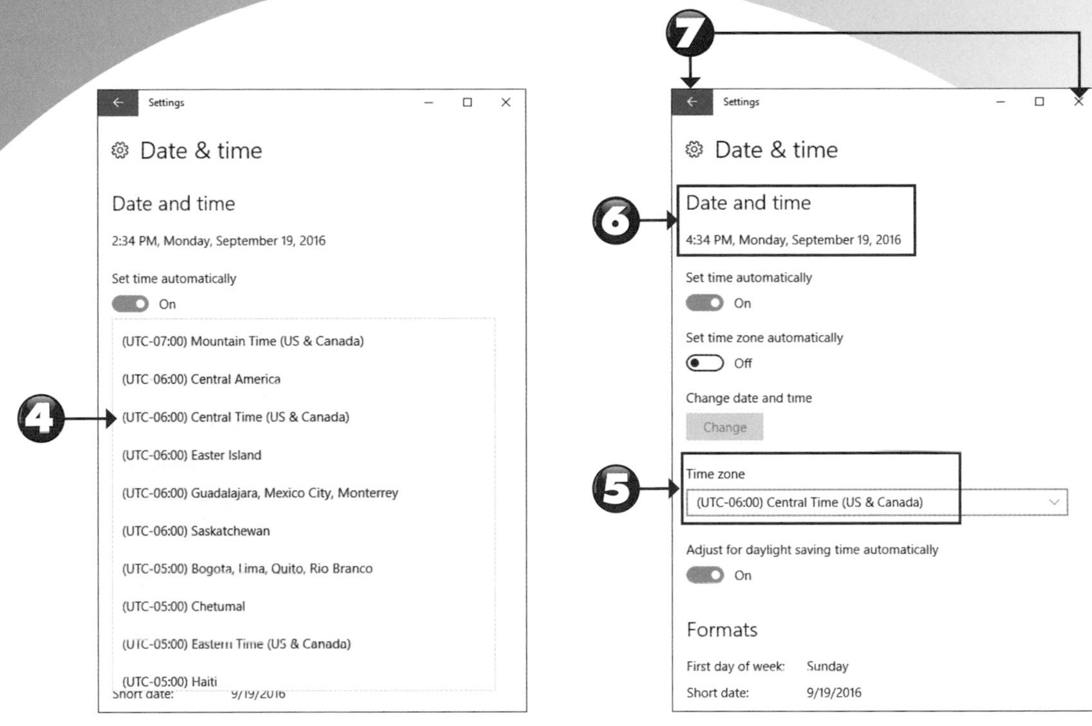

4. Select the correct time zone.

5. The correct time zone is now listed.

6. Check the date and time to be sure they are correct.

7. Click or tap twice to return to the main Settings dialog box, or click **X** to exit.

End

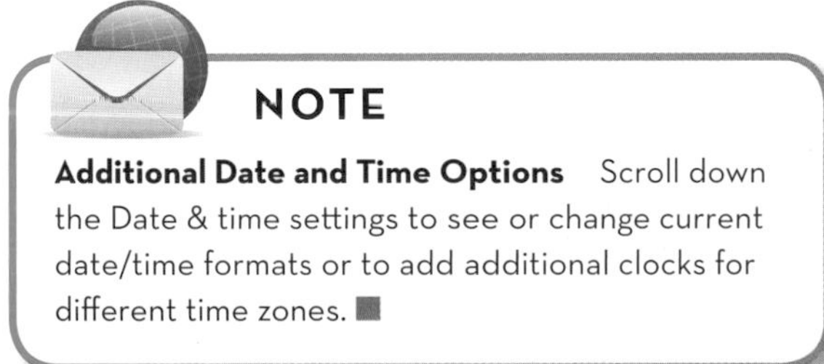

NOTE

Additional Date and Time Options Scroll down the Date & time settings to see or change current date/time formats or to add additional clocks for different time zones. ■

ADDING AND MANAGING USERS

Windows 10 AE provides new and improved ways to log in to your system and keep it secure, whether you are the only user of a device or you share it with others. Windows 10 AE also supports Microsoft Family, which permits you to set up child accounts that can be monitored and controlled.

Additional users on a device

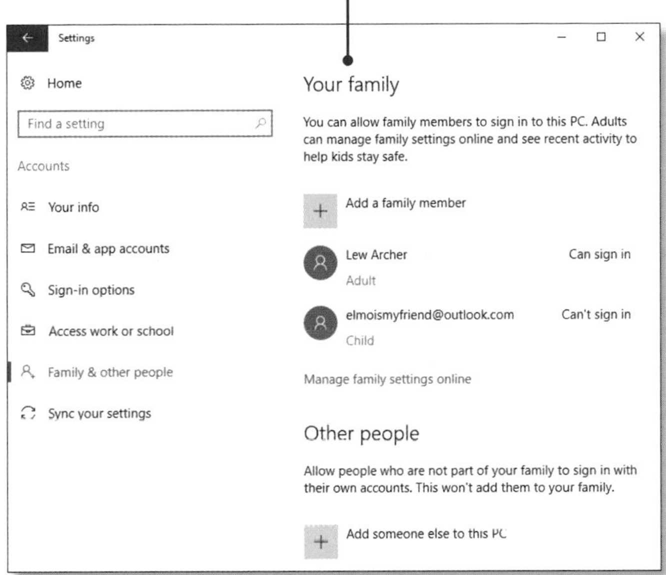

Selecting a user at startup

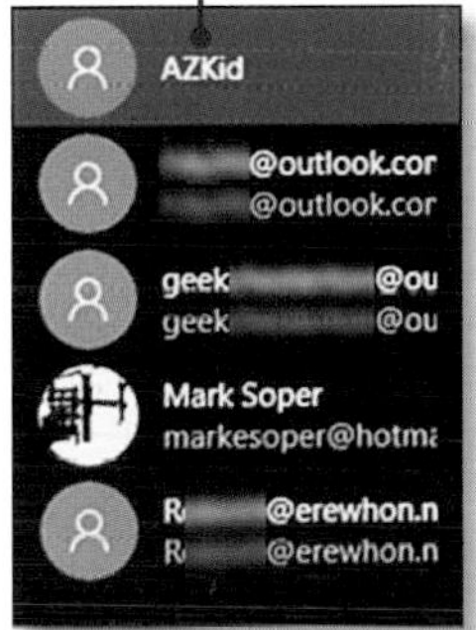

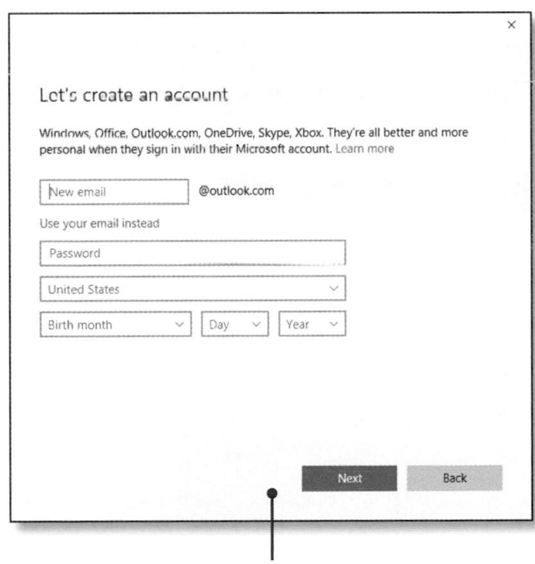

Creating a Microsoft account

PREPARING TO ADD A USER

A Windows 10 AE computer always has at least one user account. However, if you share your computer with other users at home or work, each user should have his or her own account. By using this feature, Windows 10 AE can provide customized settings for each user, and each user's information can be stored in a separate folder. In this section, you learn how to start the process of selecting the type of user to add from Windows Settings. In later sections, you learn what happens next.

Start

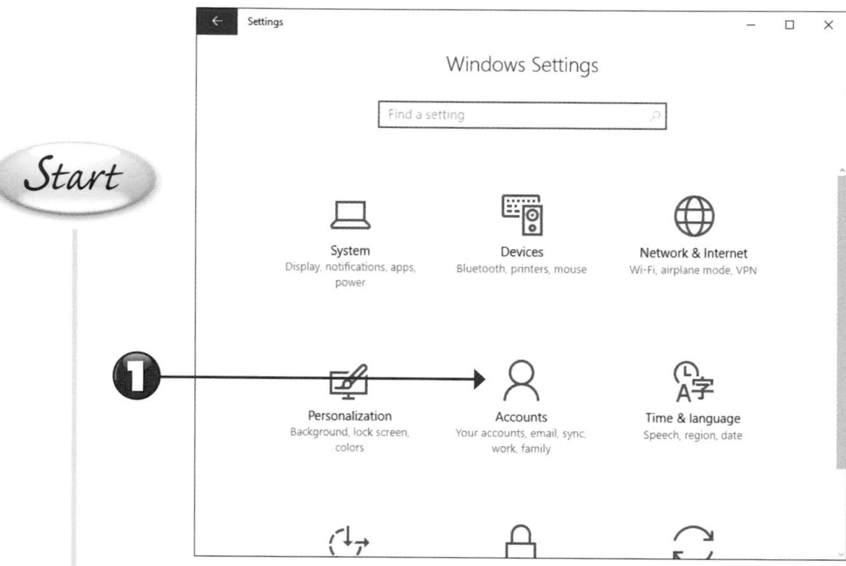

1. From Windows Settings, click or tap **Accounts**.
2. Click or tap **Family & other people**.

Continued

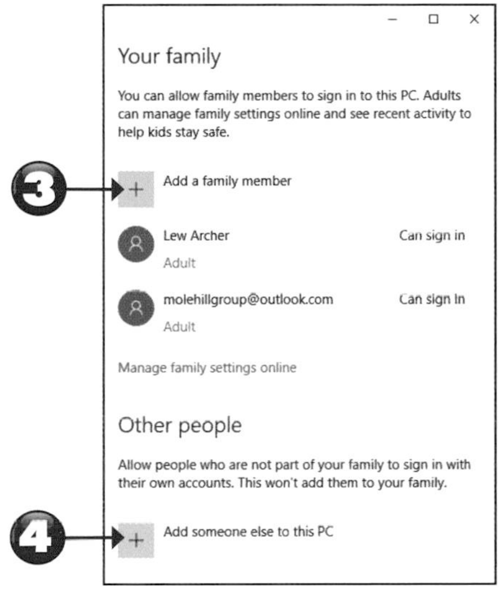

3. To add an account for a member of your family, click or tap **Add a family member**.

4. To add an account for a co-worker or a friend, click or tap **Add someone else to this PC**.

End

NOTE

Finding Windows Settings To open Windows Settings, click or tap the **Start** menu, and then click or tap **Settings**. To learn more about working with Windows Settings, see Chapter 19, "Managing Windows 10 AE."

NOTE

User Types in Windows 10 AE Use **Add a family member** to add a child's account that can be managed by Microsoft Family (Windows 10's replacement for Family Safety). To continue, see "Adding a Child as a Family Member," p. 428. To add other users, see "Adding Another User Who Has a Windows Account," p. 434 and "Adding a User Who Needs a Microsoft Account," p. 436.

ADDING A CHILD AS A FAMILY MEMBER

You can add children or adults as users to your Windows 10 AE device. In this example, we'll add a child in your household. When you add a child, you can manage her computer and Internet activity with Microsoft Family (formerly Family Safety).

Start

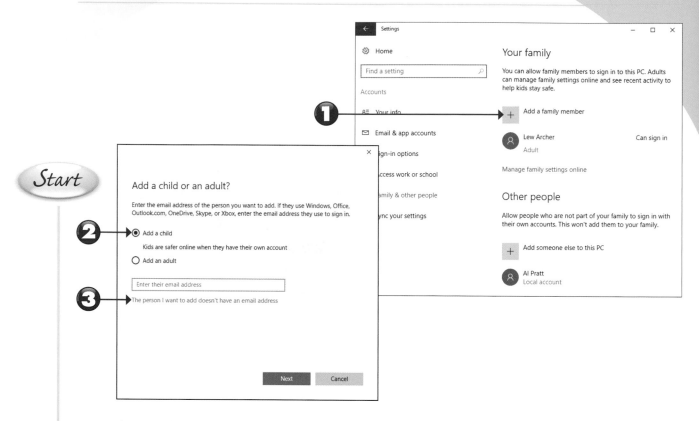

1. From the Family & other people settings (see the previous task), click or tap **Add a family member**.
2. Click or tap **Add a child**.
3. Click or tap this link to create an email address.

Continued

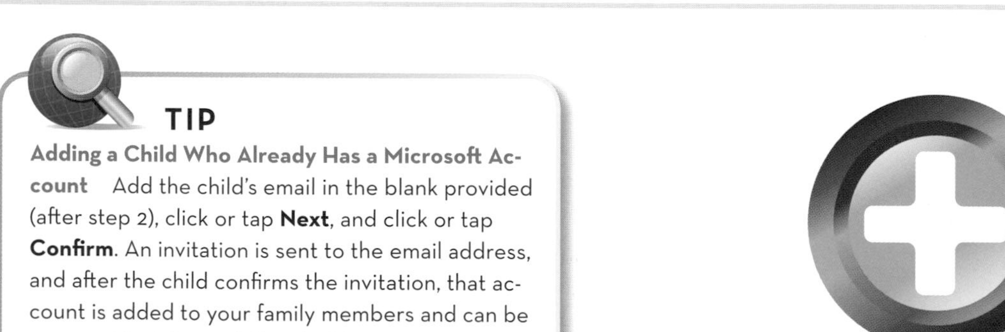

TIP

Adding a Child Who Already Has a Microsoft Account Add the child's email in the blank provided (after step 2), click or tap **Next**, and click or tap **Confirm**. An invitation is sent to the email address, and after the child confirms the invitation, that account is added to your family members and can be managed by Microsoft Family.

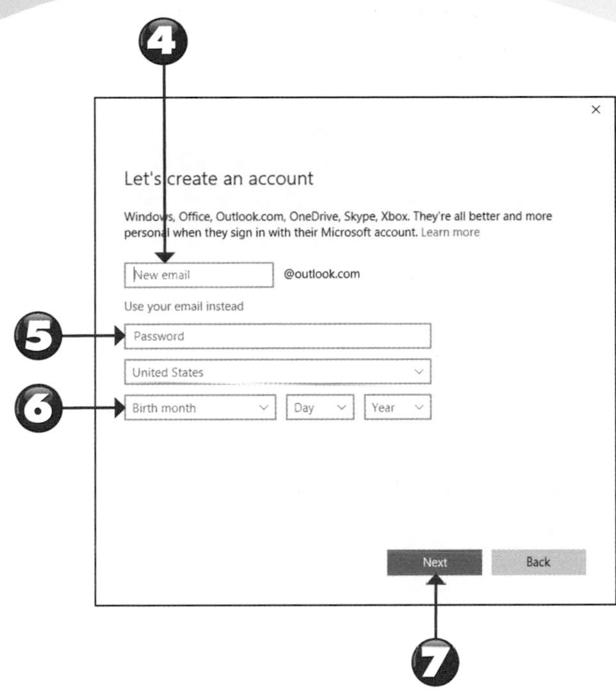

4. Enter an email address. If this address is available, continue; otherwise, try a different address until you find one that works.
5. Create a password.
6. Enter the child's birth date.
7. Click or tap **Next**.

Continued

NOTE

Email Addresses and Child Accounts Microsoft Family now requires that each account it manages has an email address. In this example, we'll create a Microsoft email address for use by the child account.

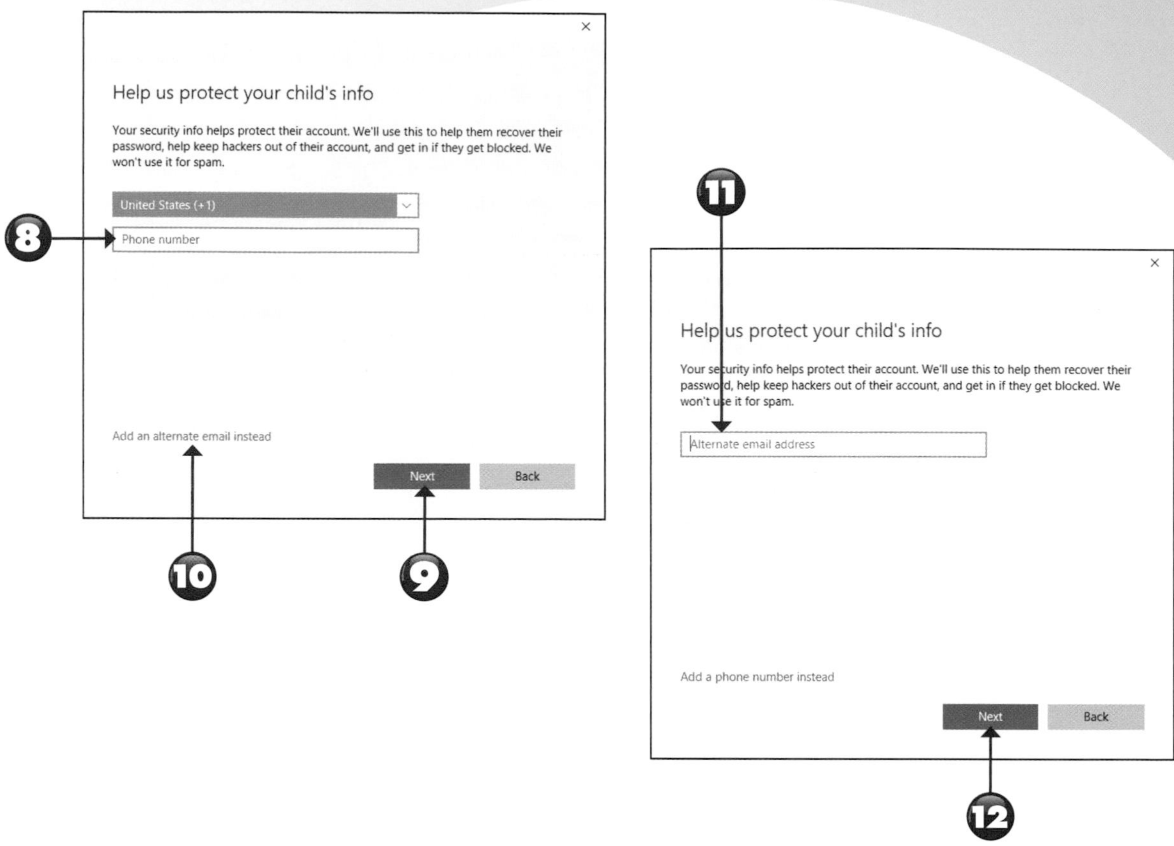

8. To add a phone number for security, click or tap here and enter it.
9. Click or tap **Next** to continue and skip to step 13.
10. To use an alternative email instead, click or tap here.
11. To add an email address for security, click or tap here and enter it.
12. Click or tap **Next** to continue.

Continued

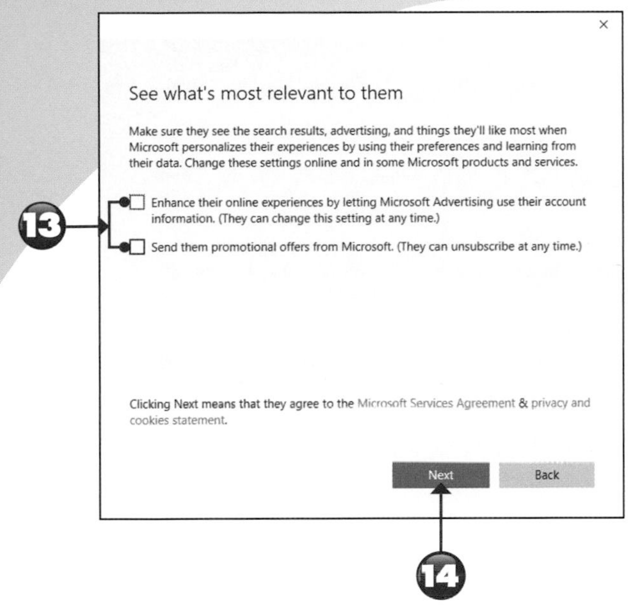

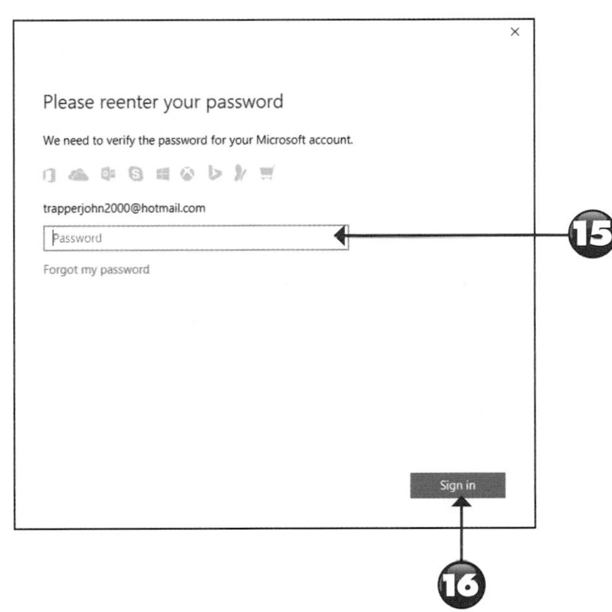

13 Click or tap the checkboxes if you want your child to receive advertising. Otherwise, leave them unchecked.

14 Click or tap **Next**.

15 Re-enter the password to your Microsoft account.

16 Click or tap **Sign in**.

CAUTION

Extra Protection for Your Child In this example, we used a made-up name and birth date for the child we added. If you are concerned about revealing your child's actual identity online, consider a similar strategy. Be sure to record this information in a safe place!

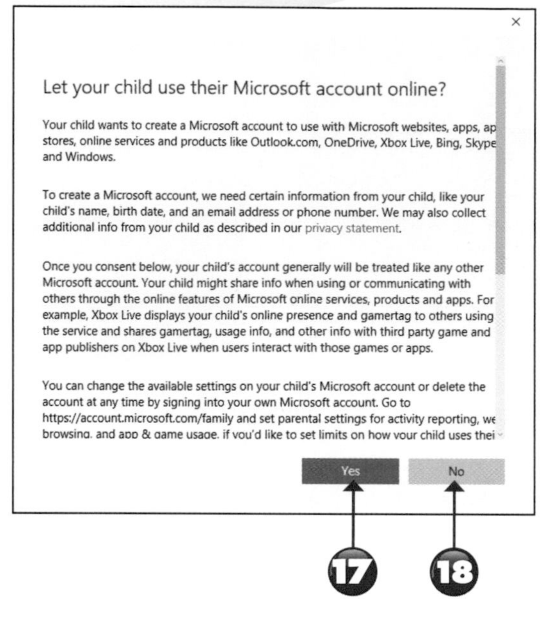

Let your child use their Microsoft account online?
Your child wants to create a Microsoft account to use with Microsoft websites, apps, ap stores, online services and products like Outlook.com, OneDrive, Xbox Live, Bing, Skype and Windows.
To create a Microsoft account, we need certain information from your child, like your child's name, birth date, and an email address or phone number. We may also collect additional info from your child as described in our privacy statement.
Once you consent below, your child's account generally will be treated like any other Microsoft account. Your child might share info when using or communicating with others through the online features of Microsoft online services, products and apps. For example, Xbox Live displays your child's online presence and gamertag to others using the service and shares gamertag, usage info, and other info with third party game and app publishers on Xbox Live when users interact with those games or apps.
You can change the available settings on your child's Microsoft account or delete the account at any time by signing into your own Microsoft account. Go to https://account.microsoft.com/family and set parental settings for activity reporting, we
Yes
No
17
18

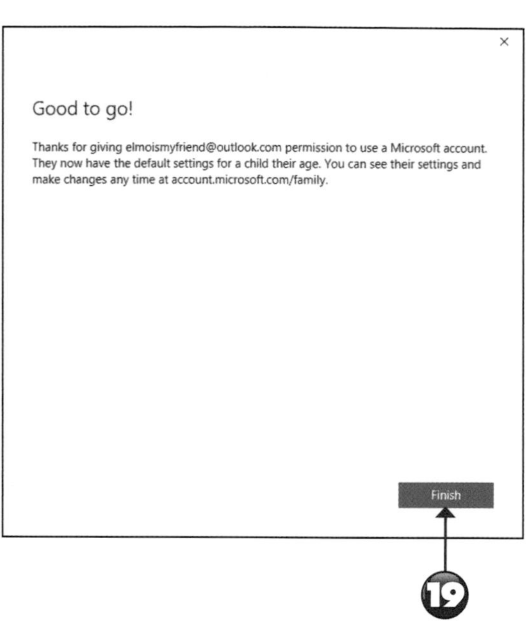

Good to go!
Thanks for giving elmoismyfriend@outlook.com permission to use a Microsoft account. They now have the default settings for a child their age. You can see their settings and make changes any time at account.microsoft.com/family.

17. Click or tap **Yes** if you want your child to use his Microsoft account online; then skip to step 19.
18. Click or tap **No** if you don't want your child to.
19. Click **Finish** to complete the account setup.

Continued

TIP

Setting Up Microsoft Family Click or tap the **Manage family settings online** link shown in step 19 to open Microsoft Family. Use it to set up usage, web browsing, and other controls for each child account. ■

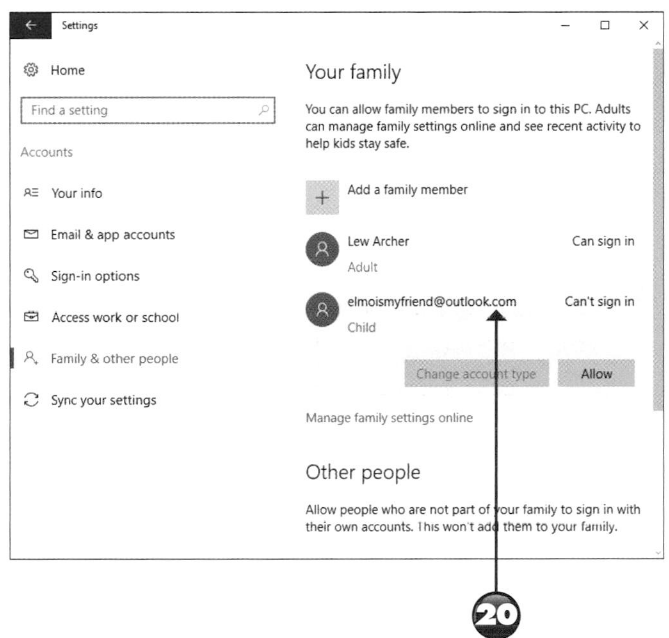

20 The new account appears in the Your Family list in Windows Settings.

End

TIP

Blocking a Child's Account After you add a child's account to a device, you can block the account from using that device: Click or tap the account name, and click or tap **Block**. You can unblock the account at any time.

ADDING ANOTHER USER WHO HAS A WINDOWS ACCOUNT

Need to share your Windows 10 AE device with a co-worker or want to set up an account for a roommate? Here's how to provide other adults with their own accounts on your system if they already have Windows accounts.

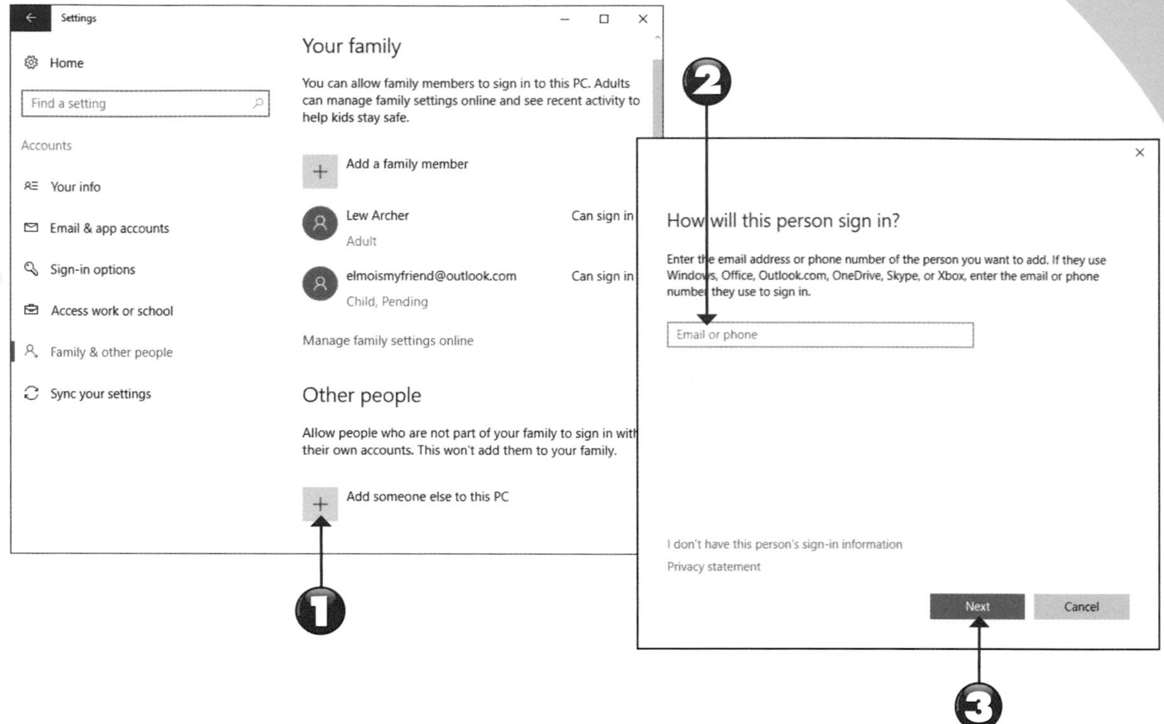

1. From the Family & other people settings, scroll to the **Other people** section and click or tap **Add someone else to this PC**.

2. Enter the email address from the user's Microsoft account.

3. Click or tap **Next**.

Continued

NOTE

Benefits of a Microsoft Account With a Microsoft account, all of a user's online email, photos, files, and settings (favorites, browser history, and so on) are available on any Windows 10 AE device that person signs in to. (As long as those files are stored on OneDrive, that is.) A Microsoft account can also be used to purchase or rent apps, music, TV shows, and movies from the Windows Store.

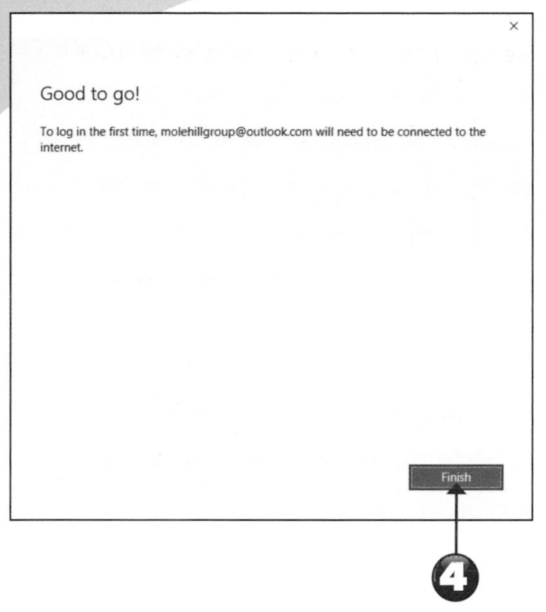

4. Click or tap **Finish**.
5. After the new user logs in to his or her account, that person is listed in the Other people section of the Family & other people settings.

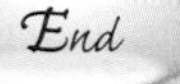

ADDING A USER WHO NEEDS A MICROSOFT ACCOUNT

As you saw in the previous exercise, there are a lot of good reasons for a user to have a Microsoft account—especially since a Microsoft account is free. Here's how to create one using an existing non-Microsoft email address.

Start

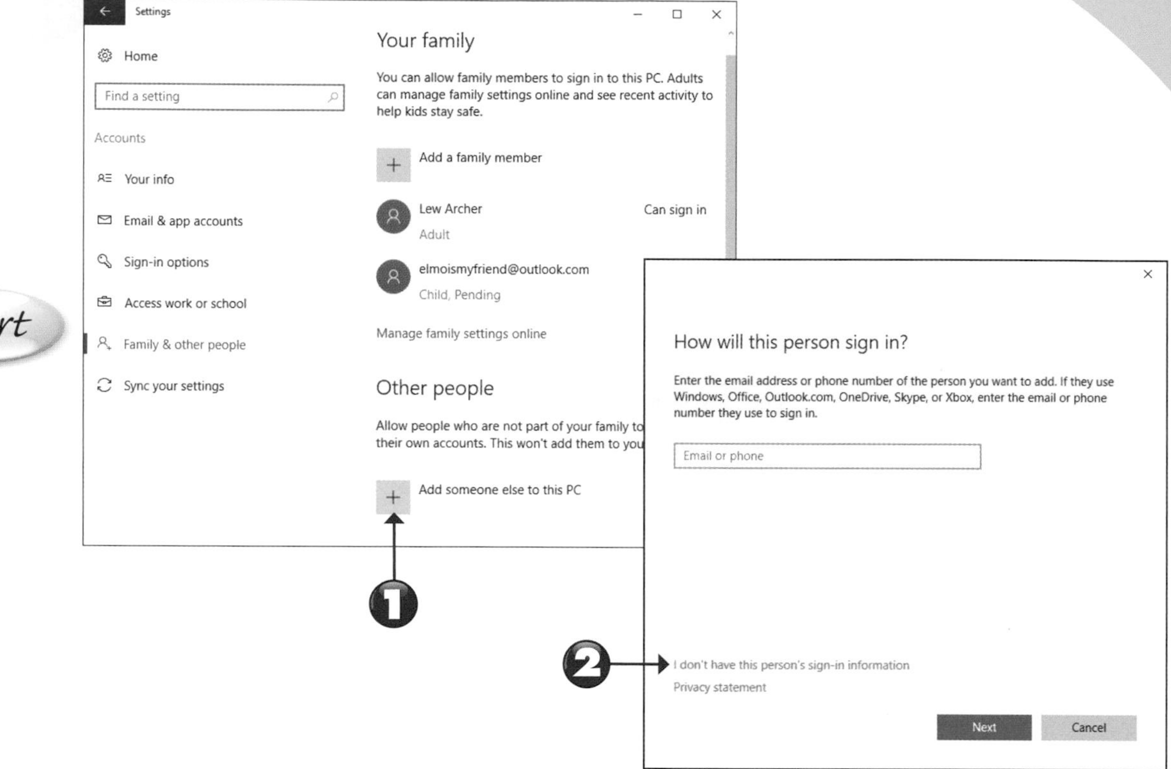

1. With the Windows Settings open to Accounts, go to the Other people section and click or tap **Add someone else to this PC**.

2. Click or tap **I don't have this person's sign-in information**.

Continued

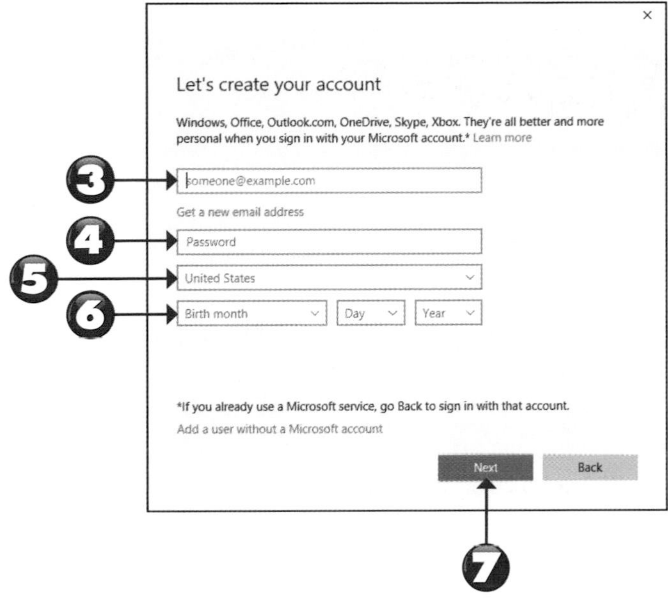

3. Enter the desired email address for this person.
4. Enter the password you want to use to log in to your system.
5. Verify or change the country where this user lives.
6. Select the user's birth date.
7. Click or tap **Next**.

Continued

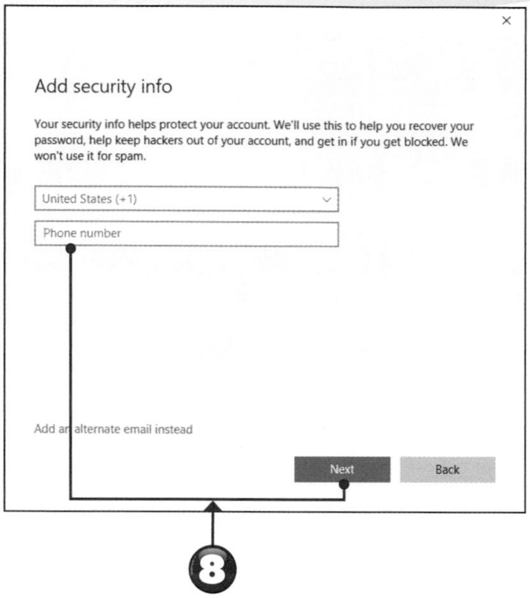

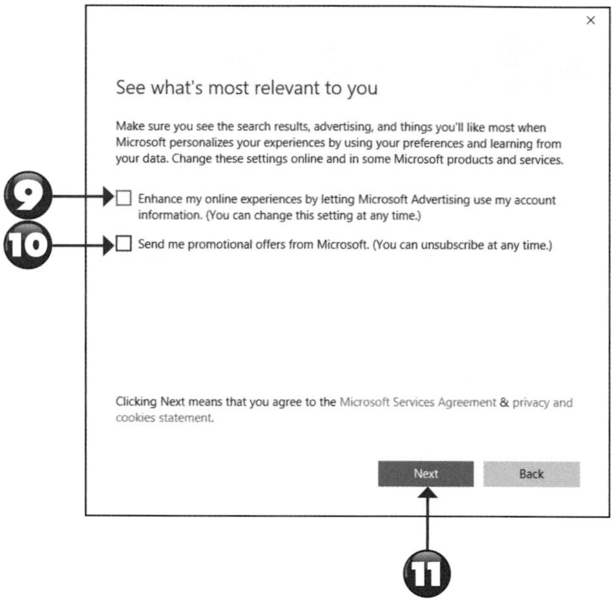

8. To add a phone number for security, click or tap here and enter it, and then click or tap **Next**. (Alternatively, click **Add an alternate email instead** to use another email address for this purpose.)

9. To opt out of letting Microsoft Advertising use your account information, clear this check-box.

10. To opt out of receiving promotional offers from Microsoft, clear this check box.

11. Click or tap **Next**.

Continued

NOTE

Country and Region Settings The country/region and country code settings are preselected based on the settings used when Windows 10 AE was installed. In most cases, it is not necessary to change them. Microsoft can use the alternative email address to help you reset your password if necessary.

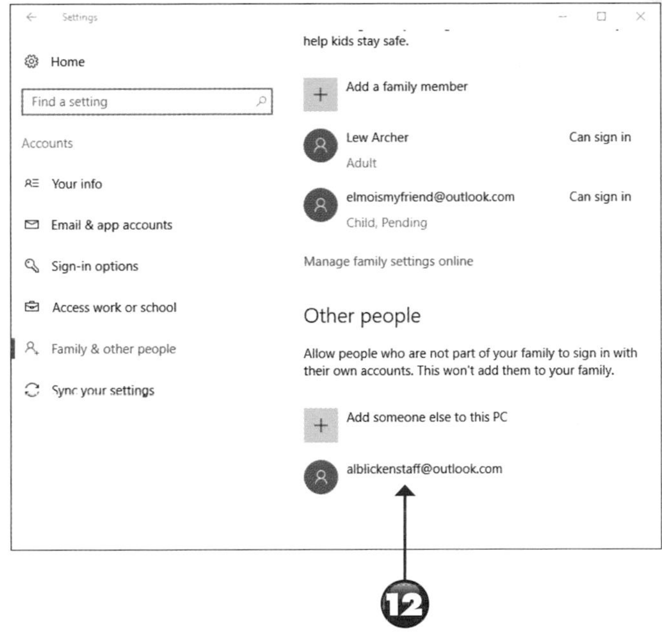

12 The new user is listed in the Other people section of the Family & other people page.

End

ADDING A LOCAL USER

Windows 10 AE is more powerful and easier to use on multiple devices if you have a Microsoft account. However, if you don't want a user to have a Microsoft account, you can set up that person as a local user. Here's how, starting from the Family & Other Users settings.

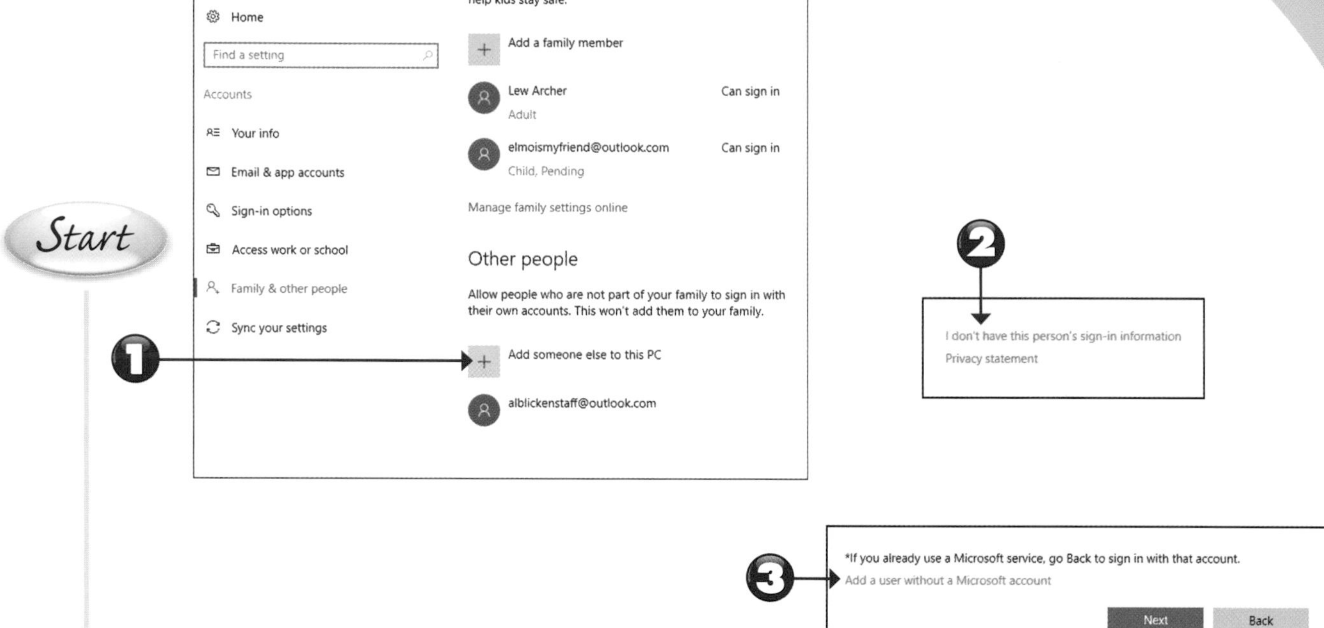

1. With the Windows Settings open to Accounts, go to the Other people section and click or tap **Add someone else to this PC**.
2. Click or tap **I don't have this person's sign-in information**.
3. Click or tap **Add a user without a Microsoft account**.

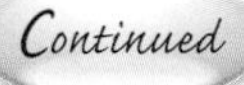

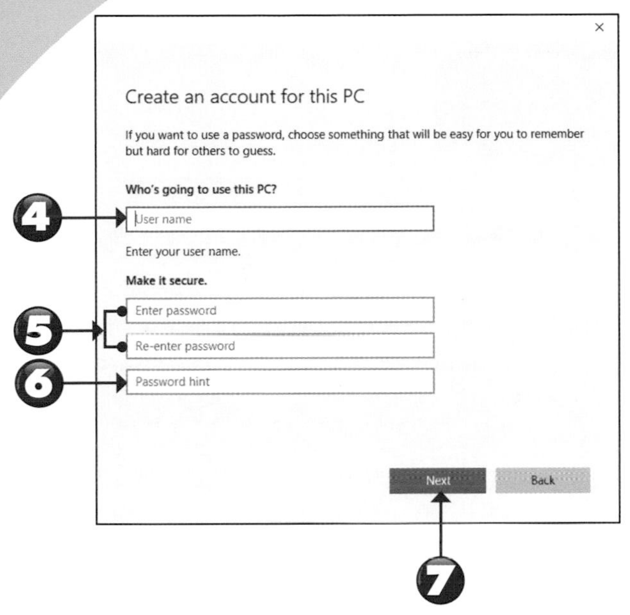

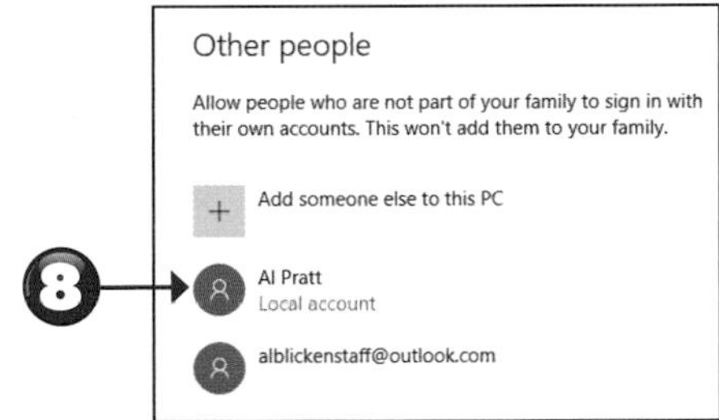

4. Enter a user name for the user.

5. Enter a password in both fields.

6. Enter a password hint.

7. Click or tap **Next** to continue.

8. The new local user appears in the Other people section of the Family & other people settings.

End

SELECTING AN ACCOUNT TO LOG IN TO

After you add one or more additional users, Windows 10 AE offers you a choice of accounts at startup or whenever the computer is locked. Here's how to choose the account you want.

1. Press any key (such as the spacebar) or swipe up on the screen (if you have a touchscreen).
2. If the account you want is displayed, log in as usual.
3. To choose a different account, scroll down.

Continued

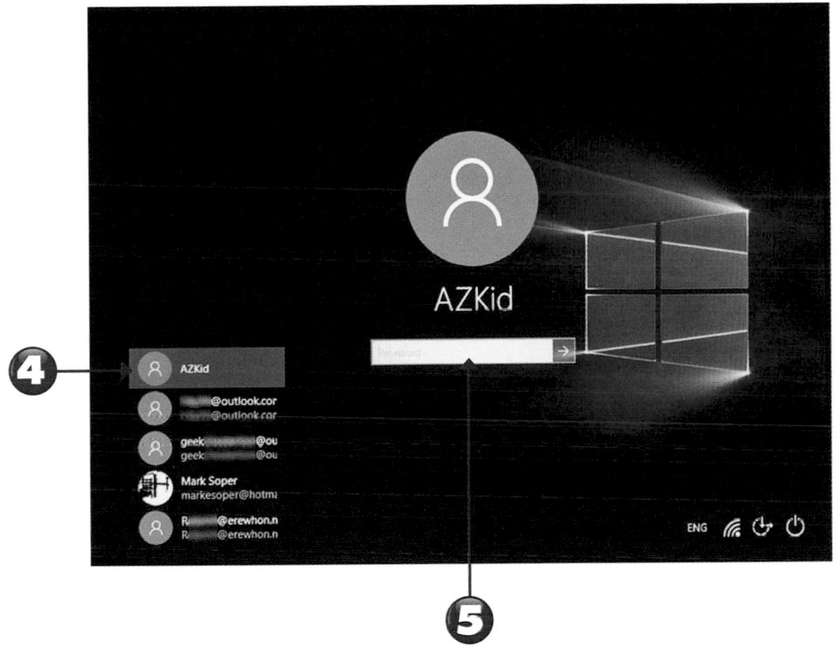

4 Click or tap the account you want to log in to.

5 Log in to the selected account.

End

CHANGING AN ACCOUNT TYPE

The first account on a Windows 10 AE computer is an administrator account. The administrator can add, change, or remove accounts and can install apps and make other changes that affect all users. When you create an additional user account in Windows 10 AE, it's a standard account. If you want another user's account to be set as administrator of the computer, follow these steps.

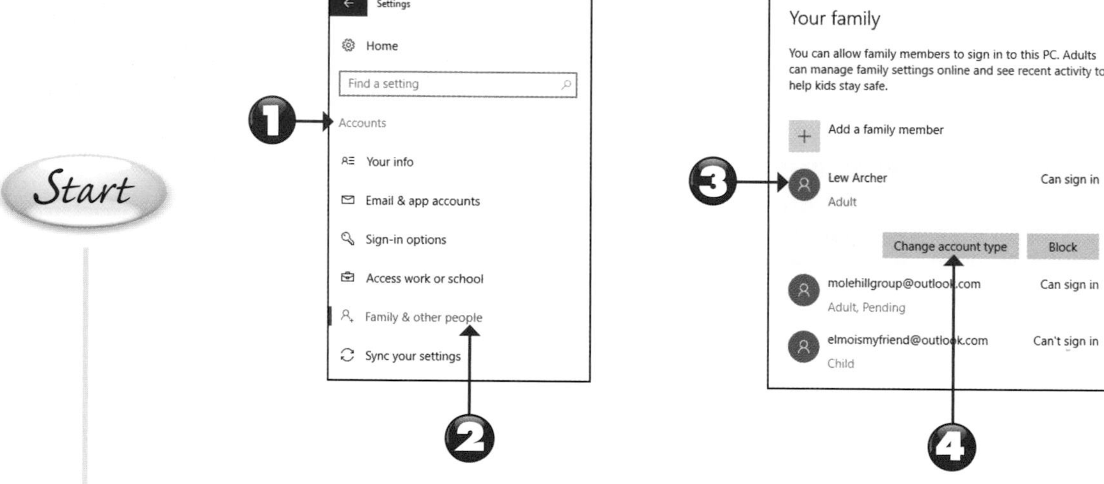

Start

1. Make sure you're logged in to your own administrator account, and then open Windows Settings to **Accounts**.
2. Click or tap **Family & other people**.
3. Click or tap the account to change.
4. Click or tap **Change account type**.

End

NOTE

Standard, Administrator, and Child Accounts A standard account needs administrator permission (given through User Account Control) to complete tasks that could change the computer. An administrator account can perform all tasks. A child account is similar to a standard account but can also be monitored by Microsoft Family.

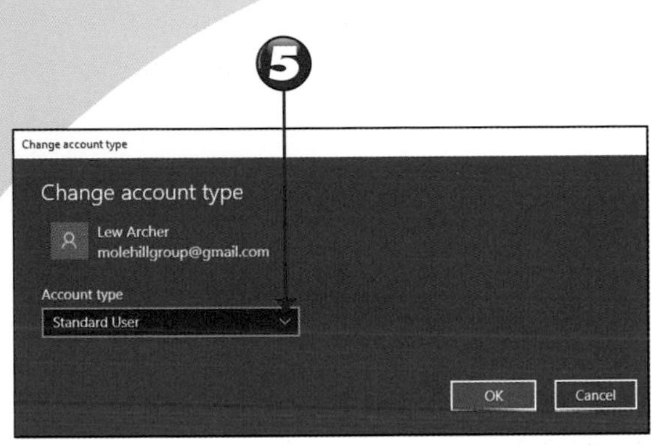

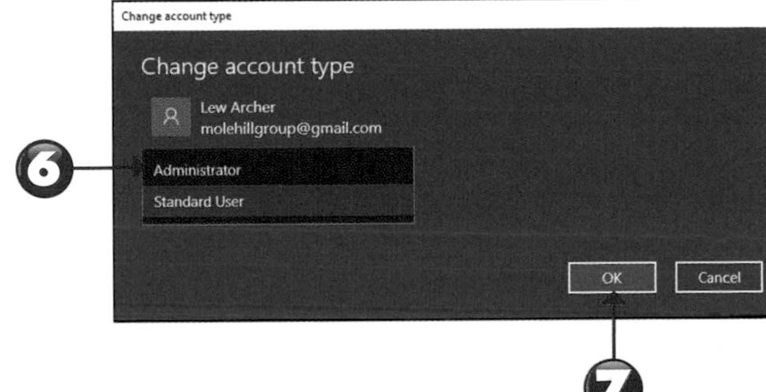

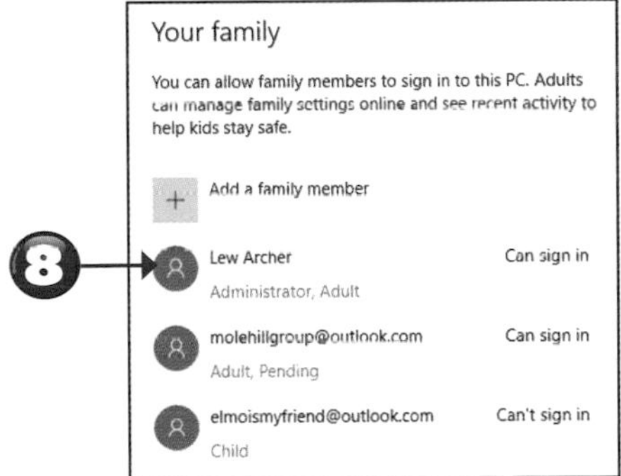

5. Click or tap to open the **Account type** menu.

6. Select **Administrator** as the account type.

7. Click or tap **OK**.

8. The new administrator account is applied.

End

NOTE

Why You Might Need Two Administrators When would you want to create more than one administrator account for a computer? There might be times when the original administrator is not available while the computer is in use and systemwide changes need to be made—such as new programs or hardware installations. Be sure that the user you select is trustworthy and not likely to mess around with the computer just for fun.

CONVERTING A LOCAL ACCOUNT TO A MICROSOFT ACCOUNT

If you've upgraded an older computer to Windows 10 AE, you might already have a local account on your computer. To get full use out of Windows 10 AE, you can convert that local account to a Microsoft account. Just log in with your local account and then follow these steps.

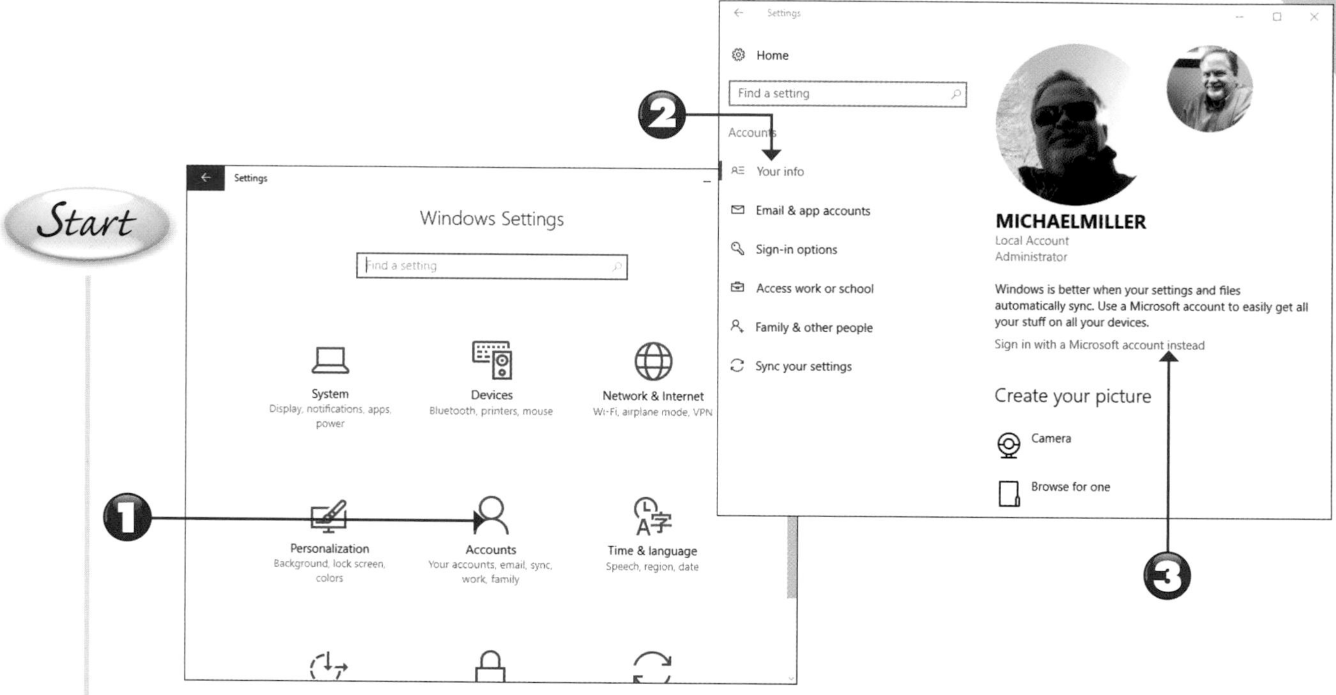

1. From Settings, click or tap **Accounts**.
2. Click or tap **Your info**.
3. Click or tap **Sign in with a Microsoft account instead**.

Continued

NOTE

Setting Up PIN Access Windows 10 AE lets you set up a PIN as an alternative to a regular password. From the Accounts settings, click or tap **Sign-in options**, and then go to the PIN section and click or tap **Add**. Enter your Microsoft account password and click or tap **Sign in** to display the Set Up a PIN dialog box. Enter and reenter your desired four-digit PIN, and then click or tap **OK**. You can now log in with either a PIN or a password from the Windows Lock screen.

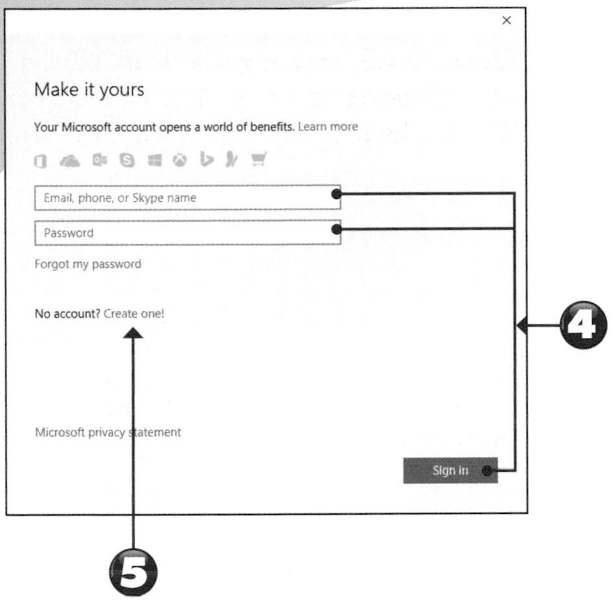

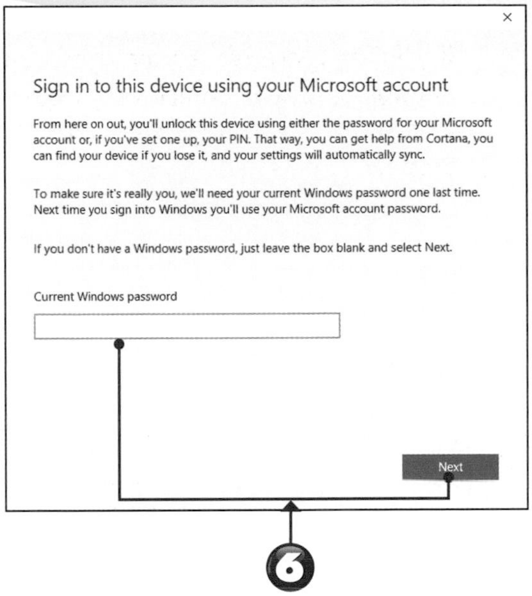

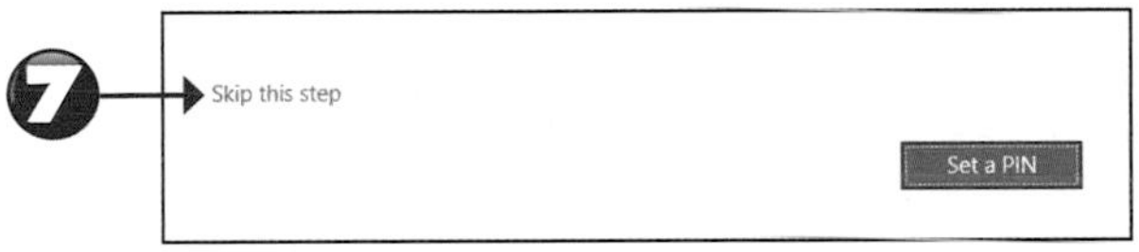

4. If you already have a Microsoft account, enter the email address and password for that account, and then click or tap **Sign in** and skip to step 6.

5. If you don't yet have a Microsoft account, click or tap **Create one!** and follow the instructions in the task, "Adding a User Who Needs a Microsoft Account," previously in this chapter.

6. Enter the password for your old local account, and then click or tap **Next**.

7. Set up a PIN if you want, or click **Skip this step** to proceed with a normal password. Your local account is now switched to a Microsoft account.

End

NOTE

Adding a Photo to Your Account To make changes to your account, including adding a photo, click or tap **Your info** from the Accounts settings. Scroll to the **Create your picture** section, where you can take your picture with your device's camera or browse for a photo stored on your computer. ■

PROTECTING YOUR SYSTEM

Computers and storage devices have never been less expensive, but the information you store on them—from documents to photos, video, and music—is priceless. In this chapter, you learn about a variety of easy-to-use features in Windows 10 AE that are designed to help you protect your computer's contents.

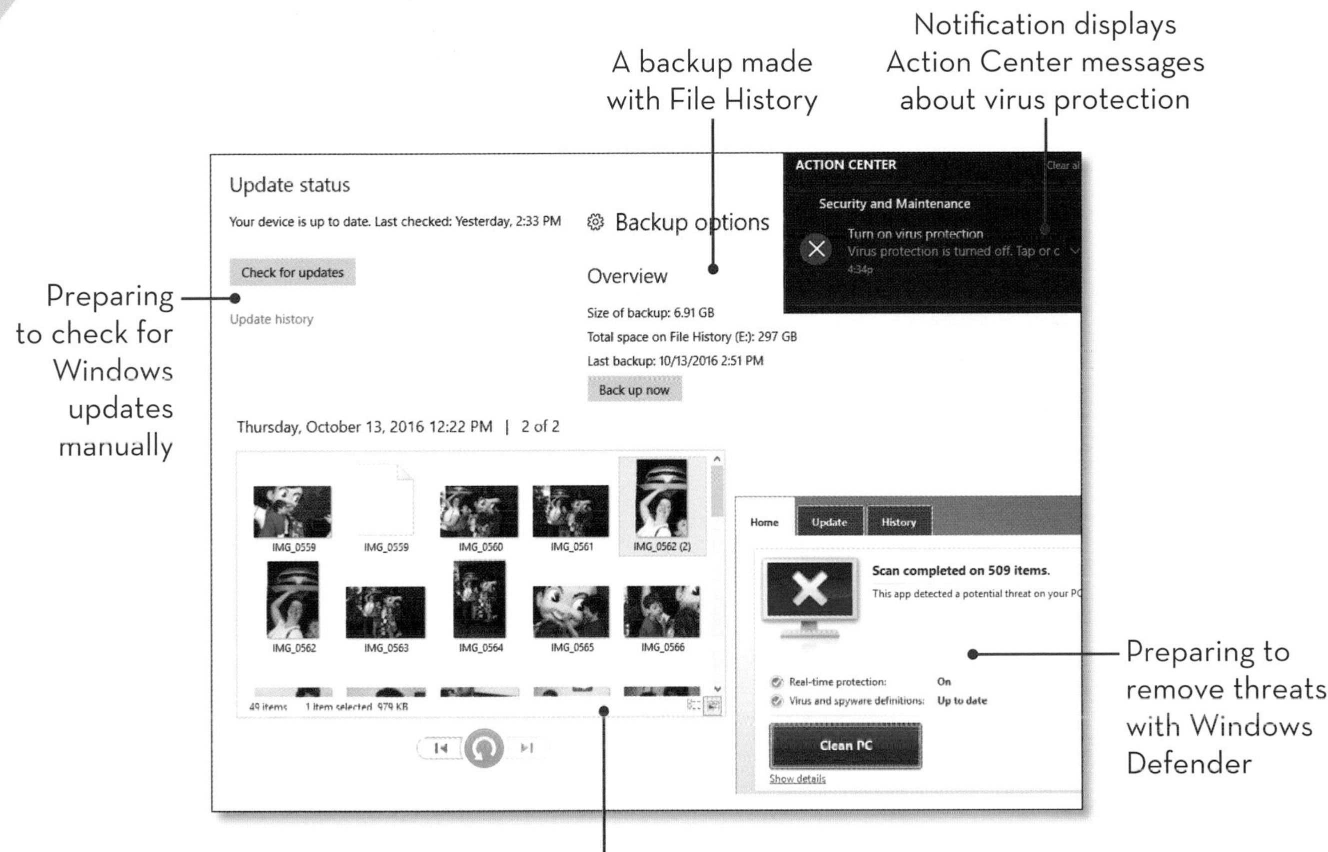

Notification displays Action Center messages about virus protection
A backup made with File History
Preparing to check for Windows updates manually
Preparing to remove threats with Windows Defender
Restoring a file with File History
Update status
Your device is up to date. Last checked: Yesterday, 2:33 PM
Check for updates
Update history
Backup options
Overview
Size of backup: 6.91 GB
Total space on File History (E:): 297 GB
Last backup: 10/13/2016 2:51 PM
Back up now
Thursday, October 13, 2016 12:22 PM | 2 of 2
ACTION CENTER
Security and Maintenance
Turn on virus protection
Home
Update
History
Scan completed on 509 items.
Real-time protection: On
Virus and spyware definitions: Up to date
Clean PC
Show details

CHECKING FOR WINDOWS UPDATES

Windows Update is your first line of defense against computer problems. It is normally set to automatically download and install updates to Microsoft Windows 10 AE and to other Microsoft apps such as Office. However, you can check for updates whenever you want using the Windows Update feature in the Settings dialog box. This is a good idea if you hear about a security problem.

Start

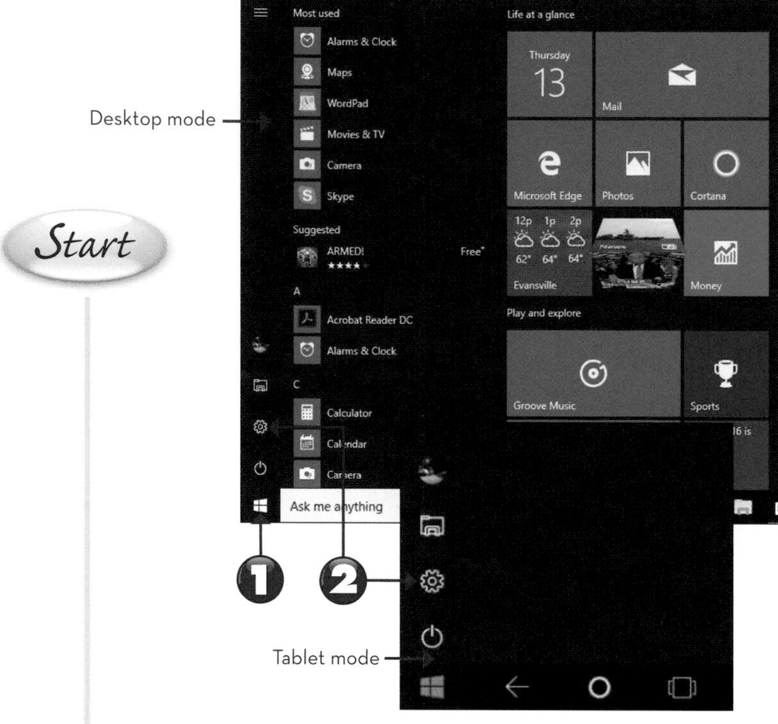

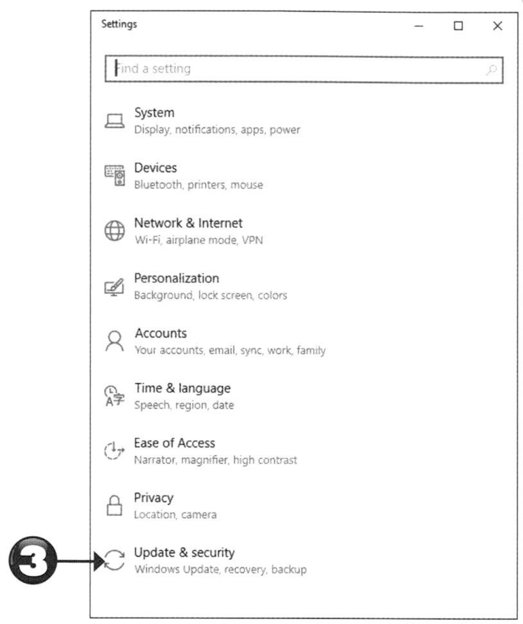

1. In desktop mode, click or tap the **Start** button.
2. Click or tap **Settings** (desktop or tablet mode).
3. Click or tap **Update & security**.

Continued

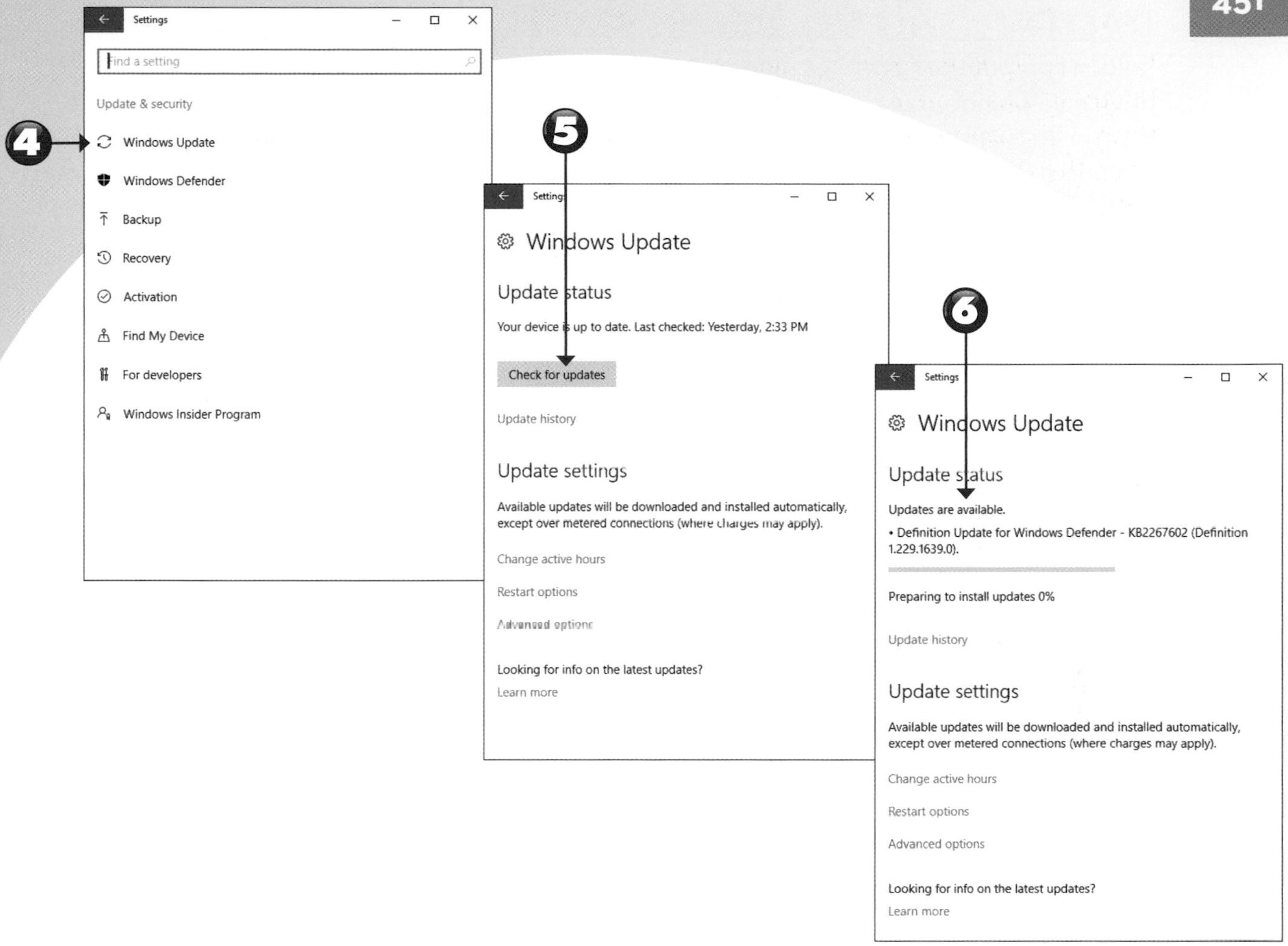

4. Click or tap **Windows Update**.

5. Click or tap **Check for updates**.

6. If there are any updates, they are downloaded and installed automatically.

End

NOTE

What Does the Update Do? Want to know more about an update? Click or tap the **Update history** link (step 6), and click or tap the **Successfully installed** link for an update to display its description. The description includes a **More info** link in case you need to learn more.

PROTECTING YOUR FILES WITH FILE HISTORY

If your computer or tablet is lost or stolen or it stops working, the information on your device is the one thing you can't replace—*unless* you make backup copies on a separate drive. File History is designed to do just that. The File History feature is part of the Backup settings in the Settings dialog box. Before starting this task, make sure you have connected a USB hard disk to your computer. (I recommend getting one that's at least twice the size of your system hard disk.)

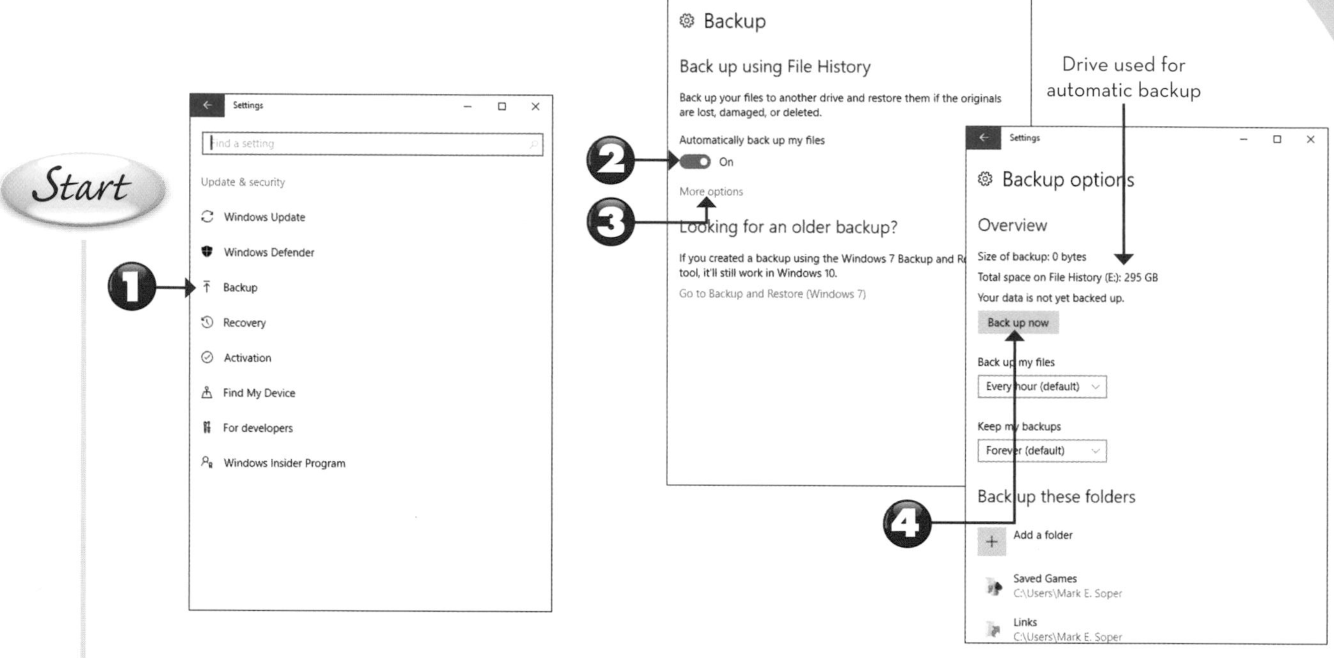

1. With the Settings dialog box still open to the Update & security settings, click or tap **Backup**. (If prompted, select a backup drive.)
2. Set **Automatically back up my files** to **On**.
3. Click or tap **More options**.
4. Click or tap **Back up now**.

Continued

NOTE

Retrieving Backups Made with Windows 7 Windows 10 AE includes the Windows 7 Backup and Restore app, so you can retrieve files from a backup you made with this tool. To learn more about using this tool, see this author's articles "Windows 7 Backup and Restore, Part 1" http://www.quepublishing.com/articles/article.aspx?p=1396503 and "Windows 7 Backup and Restore, Part 2," http://www.quepublishing.com/articles/article.aspx?p=1400869.

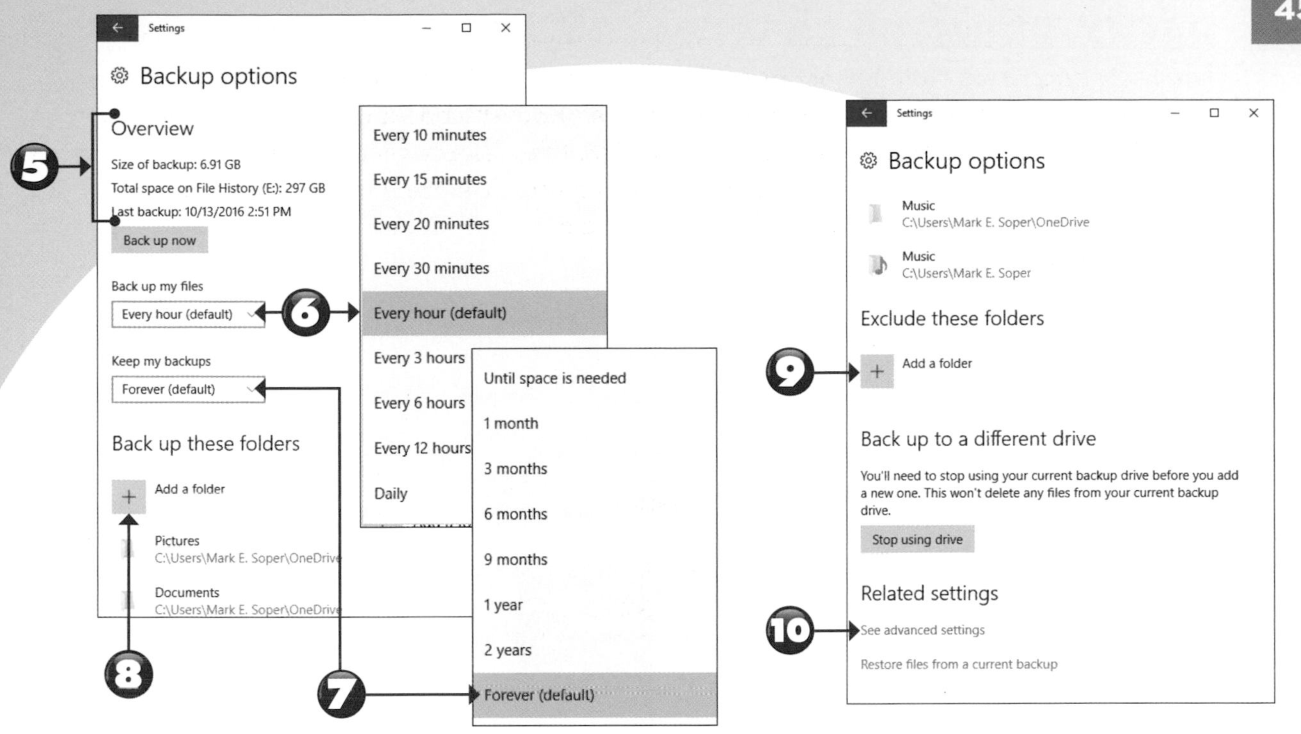

5. After the backup is over, review information about it.

6. Click or tap to change how often File History is run.

7. Click or tap to change how long to keep File History backups.

8. Click or tap to add a folder to the backup.

9. You can exclude a folder from the backup by clicking or tapping here and choosing the folder.

10. If you want to select a specific drive to use for backup, click or tap **See advanced settings**, and click or tap **Choose drive** from the File History settings in the Control Panel.

End

CAUTION

Backing Up the AppData Folder Although File History backs up all of your visible folders, hidden folders such as AppData are not backed up by default. To add a hidden folder to your backup, you must first open File Explorer, open the View tab, and make sure the **Hidden items** checkbox is checked. You can then use **Add a folder** to select AppData for backup. For more information about using File Explorer, see “Using the View Tab” in Chapter 14, “Storing and Finding Your Files.”

RECOVERING FILES WITH FILE HISTORY

File History creates backups of your files so if a file is erased or damaged, you can get it back. If you haven't yet enabled File History in Windows 10 AE and run a backup, refer to "Protecting Your Files with File History," earlier in this chapter. Here's how to retrieve a lost file or folder after it's deleted. For this exercise, we will delete a file and retrieve it.

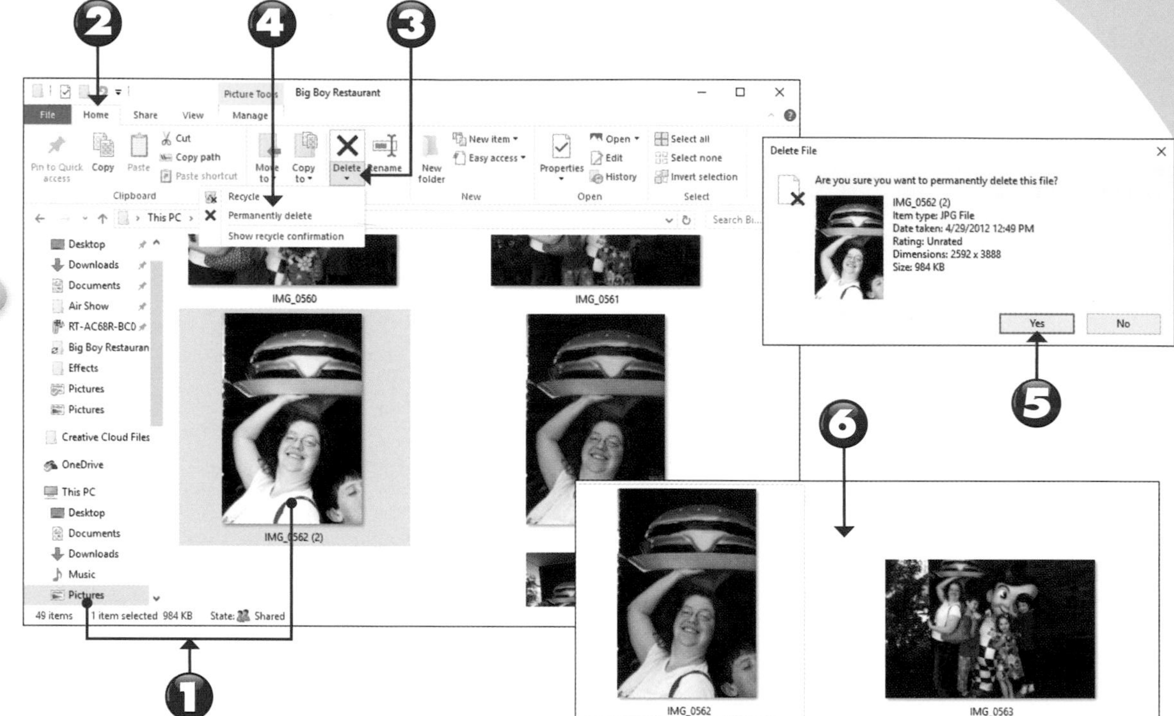

Start

1. After running a backup with File History, open File Explorer and click or tap a photo in your Pictures folder.
2. Click or tap the **Home** tab.
3. Open the **Delete** menu.
4. Click or tap **Permanently delete**.
5. Click or tap **Yes** to delete the file.
6. The file is removed.

Continued

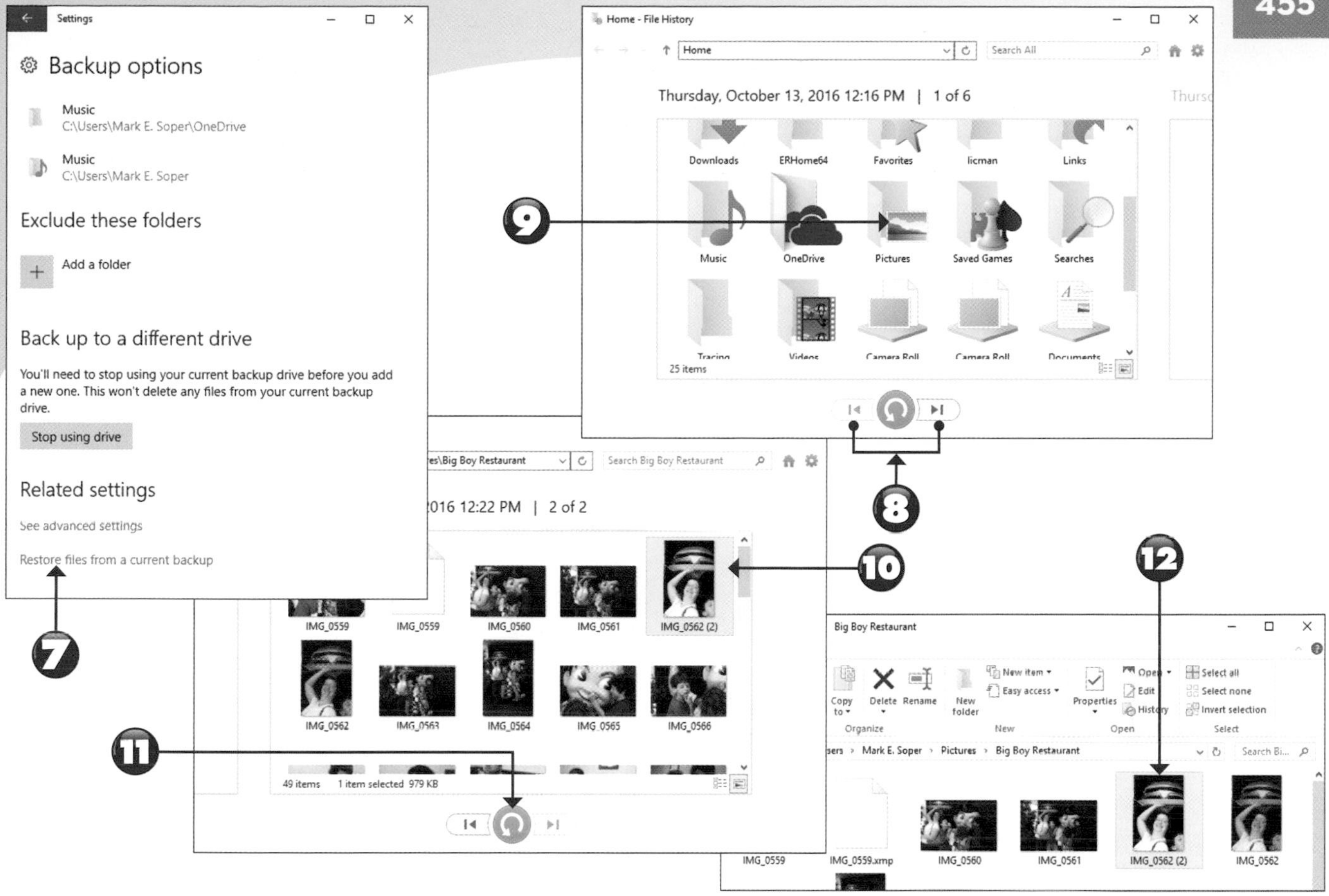

7. From the Backup options in the Settings dialog box, click or tap **Restore files from a current backup**.

8. Click or tap left or right arrows if necessary to locate the backup from which to restore.

9. Click or tap down and scroll through the folders until you reach the folder from which to restore.

10. Click or tap the file (or folder) to restore.

11. Click or tap the green **Restore** button.

12. File Explorer opens. The file or folder (and contents) is returned to its original location.

End

NOTE

Selecting a Version If the left and/or right arrows at the bottom of the File History dialog box can be clicked or tapped, you can select a different version of the folder or file. The most recent version is shown first.

TIP

Restoring Multiple Files from a Folder To restore only selected files, click the first file you want to restore, and then use Ctrl+click to select additional files. When you click or tap the **Restore** button, only the files you selected will be restored.

USING WINDOWS NOTIFICATIONS

Windows 10 AE has improved the Notifications feature, which makes it easy to see information about problems with your system or events taking place in your system. In this example, you learn how Notifications informs you of a problem with Windows 10 AE's built-in Windows Defender anti-malware program.

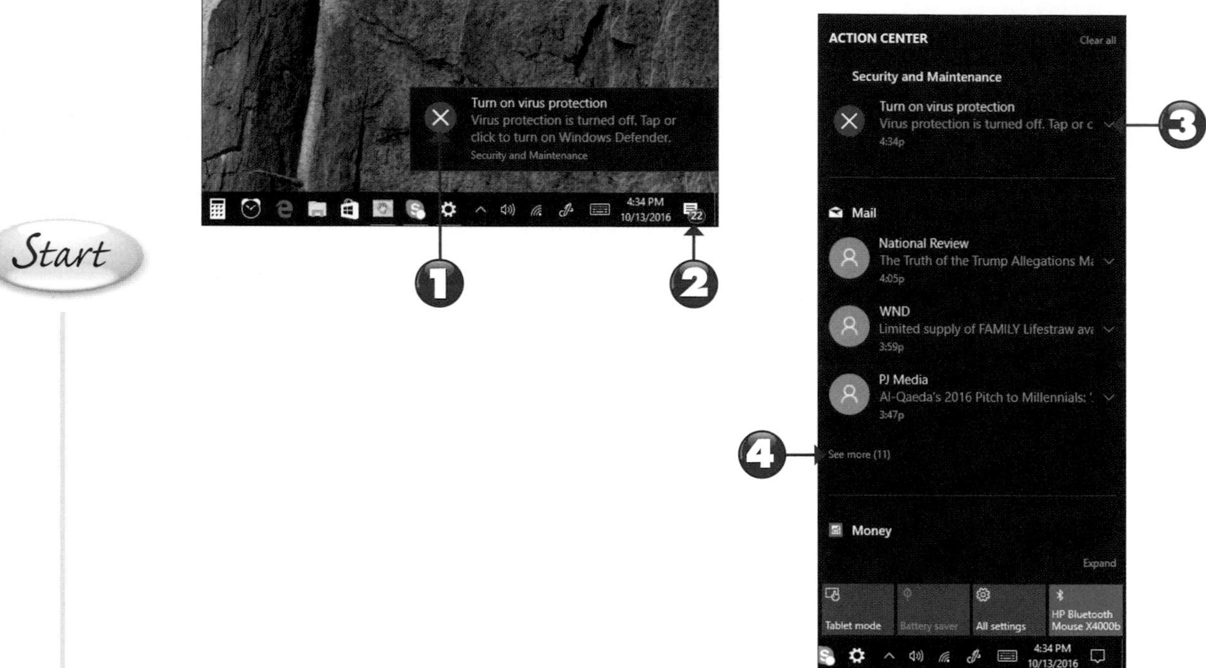

1. When a notification appears, you can click or tap it to start the recommended action. (Note: Notification pop-ups do not remain onscreen for long.)
2. The Notification/Quick Actions bubble shows the total number of notifications (22 in this example). You can also click or tap it to see them listed.
3. Click or tap a notification to act on it.
4. Click or tap to see additional notifications.

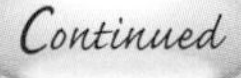

5 The problem is corrected by Action Center.

6 To remove a notification, highlight it and click or tap the **X**.

7 To remove all notifications listed, click or tap **Clear all**.

8 When you finish viewing notifications, you can click or tap an empty space on the desktop to exit Action Center.

End

NOTE

Windows Notification and Your Apps Windows 10 AE might be able to fix the problem that is responsible for the issue that Notifications displayed. In this example, when you click or tap **Turn on virus protection**, the real-time protection in the anti-malware program in use (Windows Defender) is turned on. Otherwise, Notifications opens the app so you can take action yourself. ■

TIP

What to Do Next If Your Antivirus Is Turned Off Malware running on your system can turn off an anti-malware program's real-time protection, or you might be required to turn it off to install some apps. After turning on real-time protection, scan your system, as shown later in the "Checking for Malware with Windows Defender" task. ■

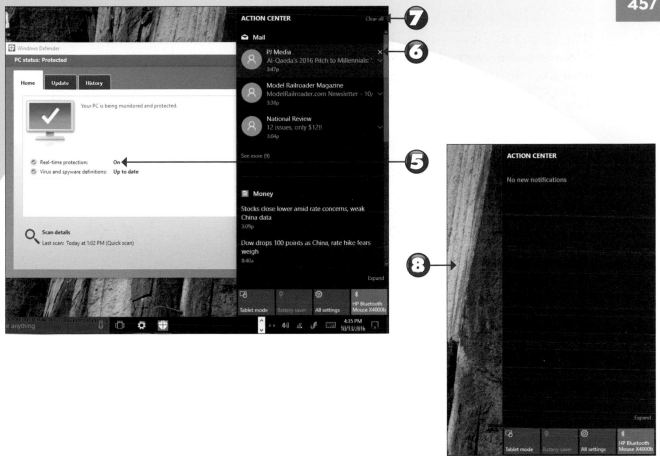

CONFIGURING AND STARTING WINDOWS DEFENDER

The Windows Defender program included with Windows 10 AE provides protection against spyware, malware, and viruses. In this task, you learn how to configure it and how to start it manually from the Update & security settings in the Settings dialog box.

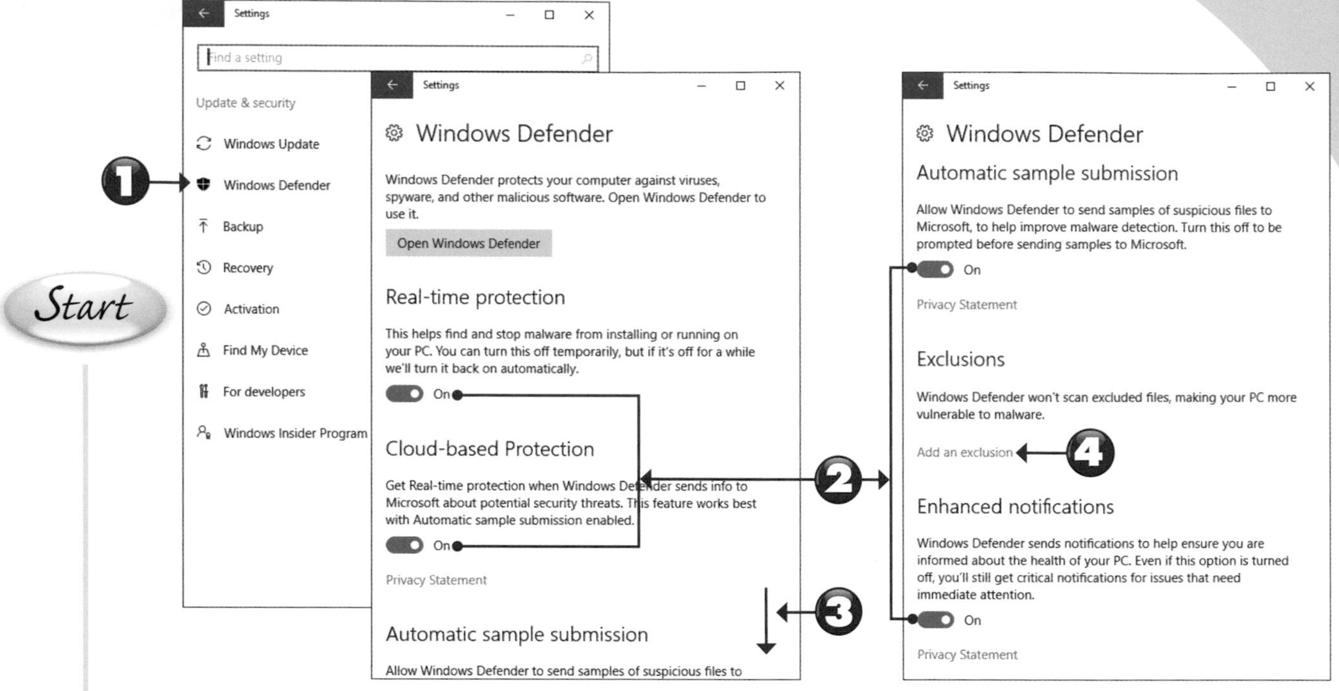

1. Open the Settings dialog box to the Update & security settings, and click or tap **Windows Defender**.
2. Real-time protection, Cloud-based protection, Automatic sample submission, and Enhanced notifications should all be turned **On** to provide maximum protection.
3. You can scroll down or flick up to view the additional settings as needed.
4. To skip scanning some files, click or tap **Add an exclusion** and specify what to skip (not recommended).

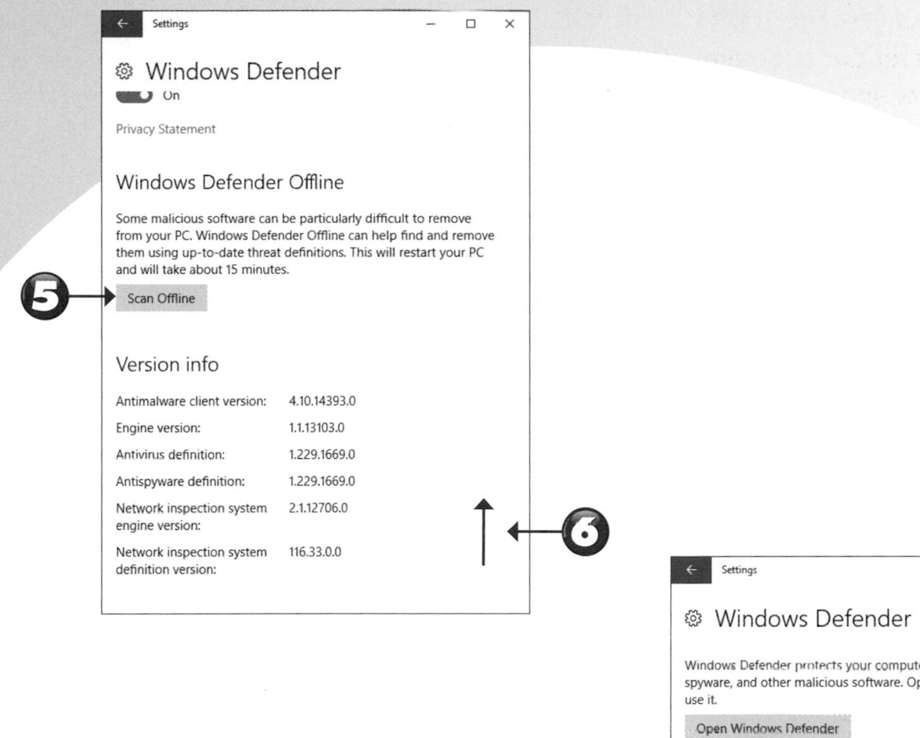

5 To remove some threats, you might need to run Windows Defender offline. Click or tap **Scan Offline** to restart the computer and run Windows Defender before launching Windows.

6 Scroll up or flick down to return to the top of the dialog.

7 Click or tap **Open Windows Defender** to scan for malware or view history.

End

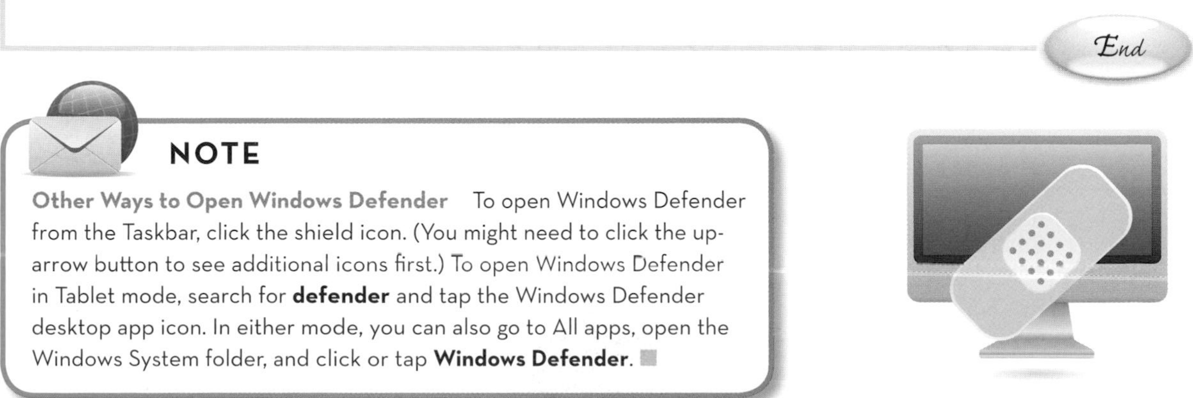

NOTE

Other Ways to Open Windows Defender To open Windows Defender from the Taskbar, click the shield icon. (You might need to click the up-arrow button to see additional icons first.) To open Windows Defender in Tablet mode, search for **defender** and tap the Windows Defender desktop app icon. In either mode, you can also go to All apps, open the Windows System folder, and click or tap **Windows Defender**.

CHECKING FOR MALWARE WITH WINDOWS DEFENDER

The Windows Defender program included with Windows 10 AE provides protection against spyware, malware, and viruses. In addition to real-time protection, Defender can scan your system for malware. In this exercise, you learn how to run a scan and what to do with malware after it is discovered.

Start

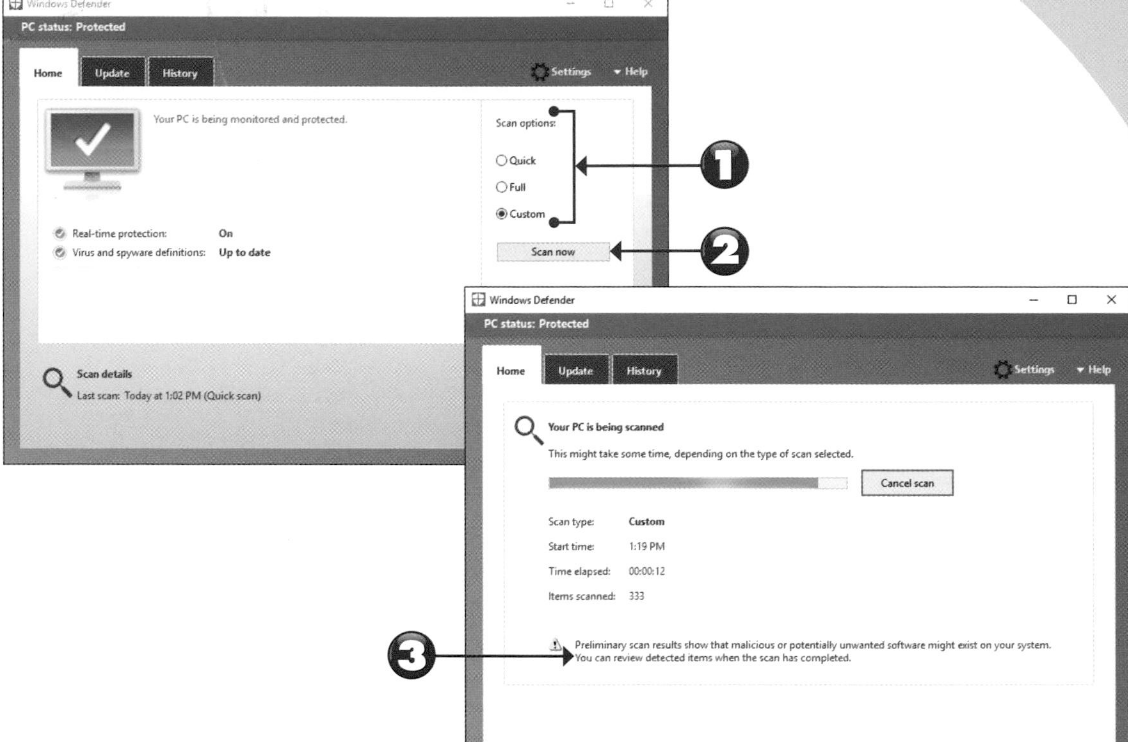

1. With Windows Defender open from the previous task, select a scan type.
2. Click or tap **Scan now**.
3. If malware is detected, you are notified before the scan is complete.

Continued

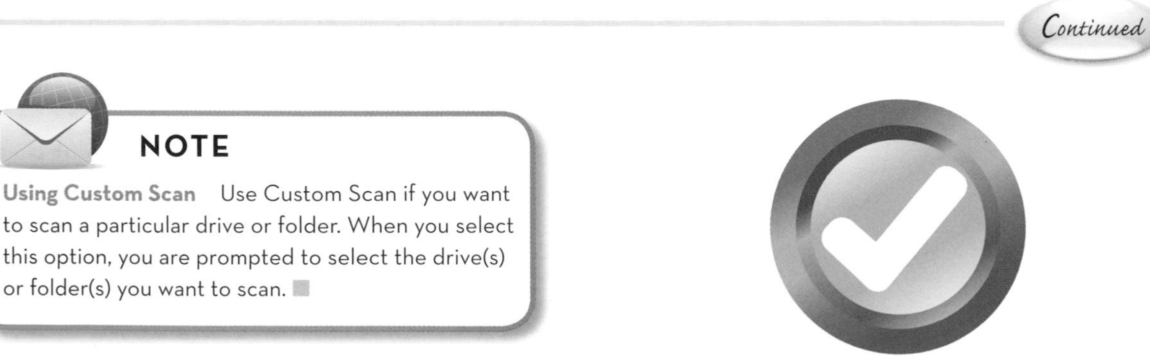

NOTE

Using Custom Scan Use Custom Scan if you want to scan a particular drive or folder. When you select this option, you are prompted to select the drive(s) or folder(s) you want to scan.

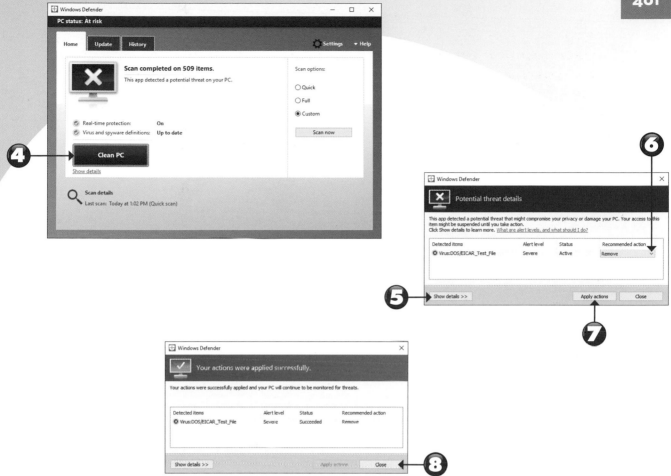

4 Click or tap **Clean PC** to remove all threats.

5 Click or tap **Show details** if you want to learn more about the highlighted threat.

6 Click or tap to change the recommended action.

7 Click or tap **Apply actions** to return to the main menu.

8 When Windows Defender completes the actions, click or tap **Close** to return to the main menu.

End

NOTE

Using the Update and History Tabs Click or tap the **Update** tab (step 1) to update Windows Defender manually. (Note that updates are normally delivered via Windows Update.) Click or tap the **History** tab (step 1) to see the malware files that have been detected and to learn more about each threat.

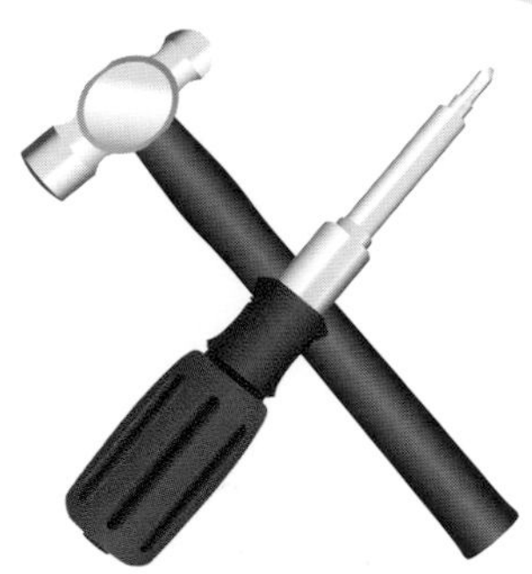

SYSTEM MAINTENANCE AND PERFORMANCE

Windows 10 AE includes a variety of tools that help solve problems and keep Windows working at peak efficiency. In this chapter, you learn how to use drive error-checking, check battery charge settings, use troubleshooters, view open apps with Task Manager, and fix Windows problems with Refresh.

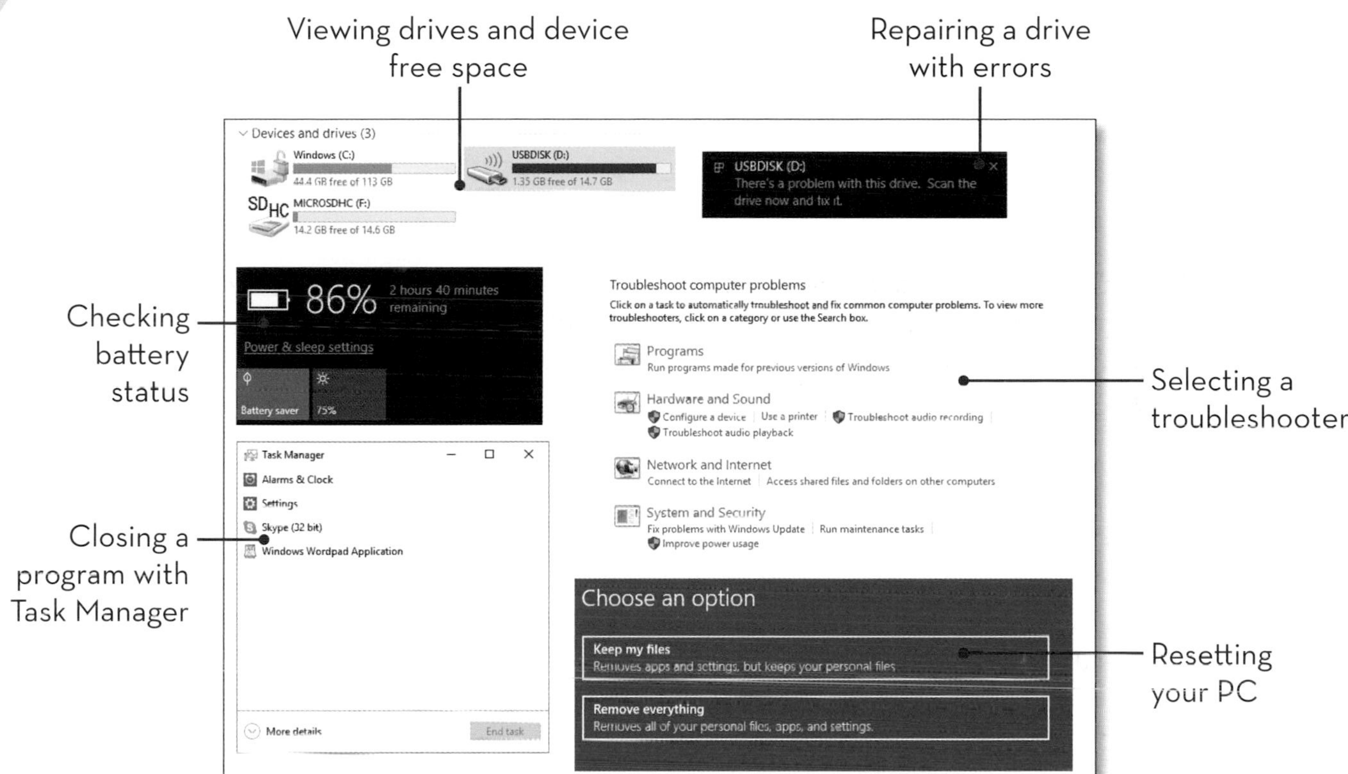

Viewing drives and device free space
Repairing a drive with errors
Checking battery status
Closing a program with Task Manager
Selecting a troubleshooter
Resetting your PC
Devices and drives (3)
Windows (C:)
44.4 GB free of 113 GB
USBDISK (D:)
1.35 GB free of 14.7 GB
MICROSDHC (F:)
14.2 GB free of 14.6 GB
USBDISK (D:)
There's a problem with this drive. Scan the drive now and fix it.
86%
2 hours 40 minutes remaining
Power & sleep settings
Battery saver
75%
Troubleshoot computer problems
Click on a task to automatically troubleshoot and fix common computer problems. To view more troubleshooters, click on a category or use the Search box.
Programs
Run programs made for previous versions of Windows
Hardware and Sound
Configure a device
Use a printer
Troubleshoot audio recording
Troubleshoot audio playback
Network and Internet
Connect to the Internet
Access shared files and folders on other computers
System and Security
Fix problems with Windows Update
Run maintenance tasks
Improve power usage
Task Manager
Alarms & Clock
Settings
Skype (32 bit)
Windows Wordpad Application
More details
End task
Choose an option
Keep my files
Removes apps and settings, but keeps your personal files
Remove everything
Removes all of your personal files, apps, and settings.

CHECKING CHARGE LEVEL

If you use a device that runs on battery power, you can quickly check its charge level from the Windows 10 AE taskbar. Here's how.

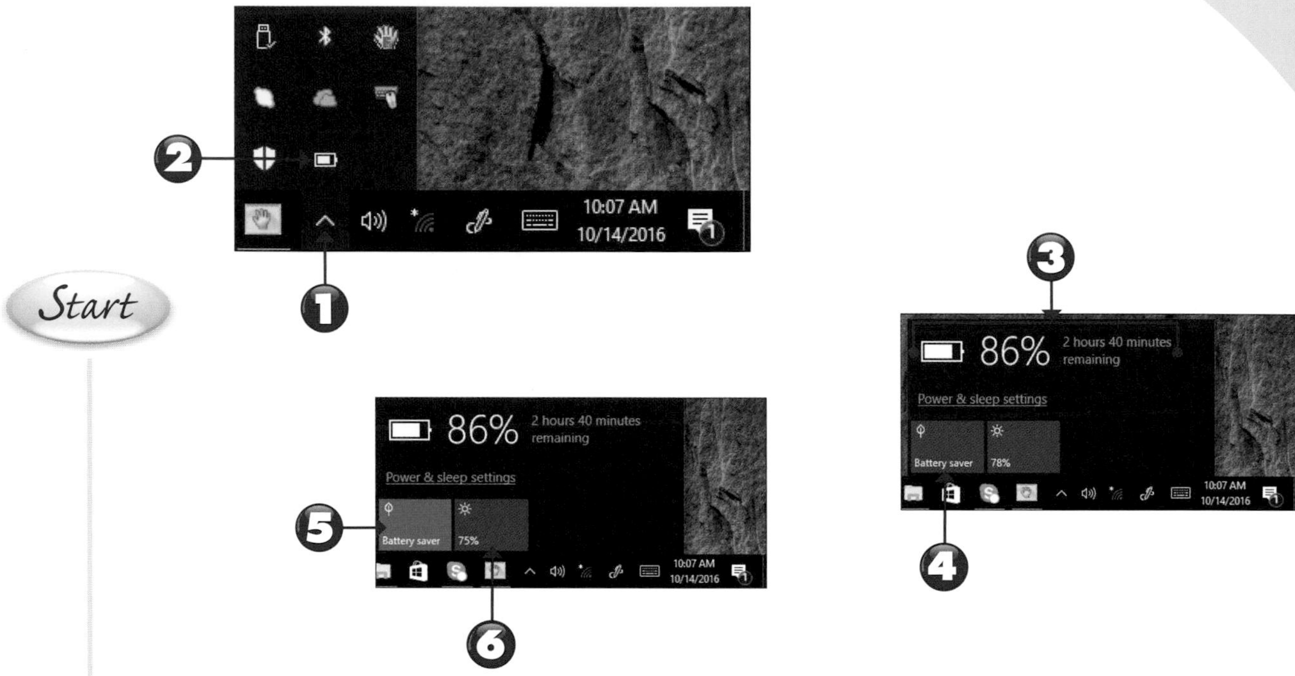

1. If the battery icon in the taskbar is not visible, click or tap the up-arrow icon.
2. Click or tap the battery icon in the taskbar.
3. The battery charge level is displayed.
4. Battery saver is off. To turn it on, click or tap it.
5. Battery saver is now enabled.
6. Tap the brightness button to move through standard brightness levels.

End

NOTE

Learning More About Battery Saver To learn more about the settings available on the Battery Saver dialog box, see "Using Battery Saver," in Chapter 19, "Managing Windows 10 AE."

SELECTING A POWER SCHEME

With laptops, desktops, and all-in-one devices, you can select a power scheme in Windows 10 AE that will stretch battery life as far as possible or keep your system running at top speed all the time. Here's how to select the power scheme you want from the Windows taskbar.

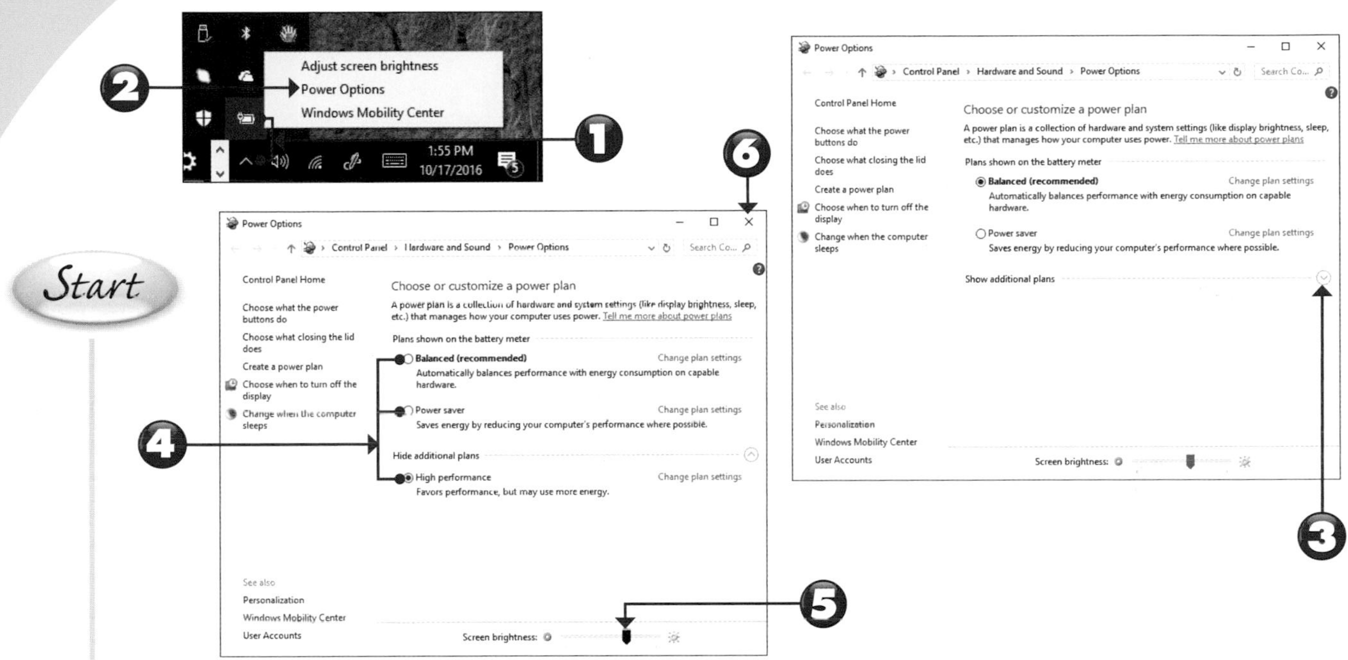

1. From the taskbar, press and hold or right-click the **power** (battery meter) icon in the notification area. Click or tap the up arrow if necessary to view the icon.
2. Click or tap **Power Options**.
3. The most common power options are shown. To see additional options, click or tap **Show additional plans**.
4. Choose a plan setting from those listed.
5. Click or press and drag to the left to make the built-in screen darker, or to the right to make the screen brighter.
6. Close the dialog box when finished.

End

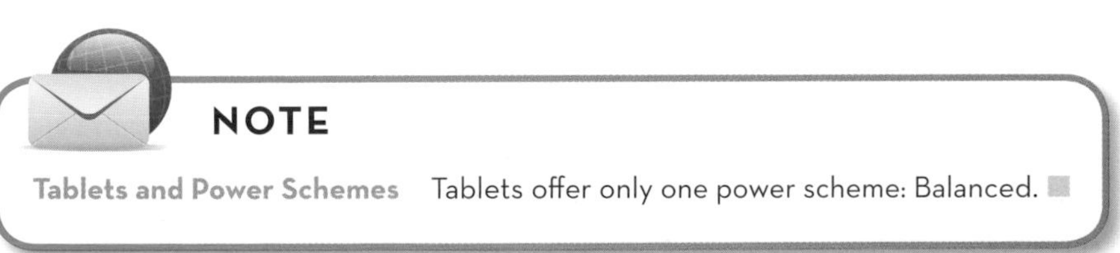

NOTE

Tablets and Power Schemes Tablets offer only one power scheme: Balanced.

VIEWING DISK INFORMATION

How much space is left on your drive? What drive letter does your external hard disk use? Use the This PC view in File Explorer for answers to these and other questions about the drives built in to and connected to your computer.

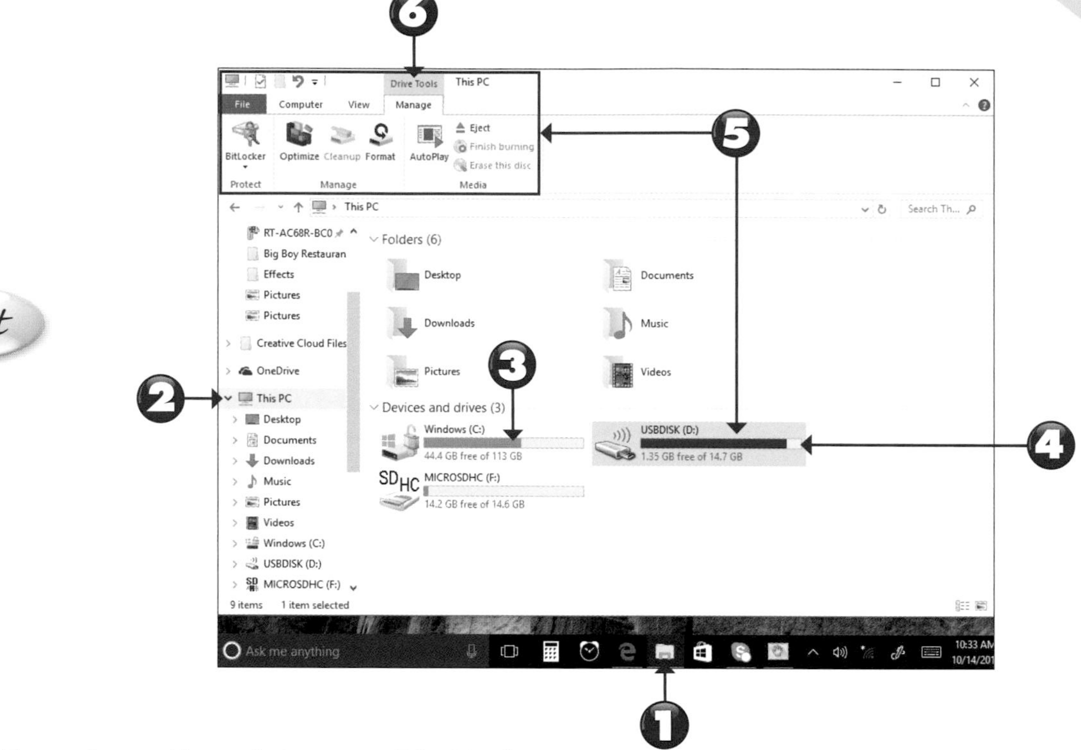

1. From the taskbar, click or tap **File Explorer**.
2. Click or tap **This PC**.
3. The blue bar indicates how much space is used on the drive.
4. The bar turns red if the drive has less than 10% free space.
5. Click or tap a drive to display the Drive Tools tab.
6. You can use the controls on the Drive Tools tab to manage your storage devices.

End

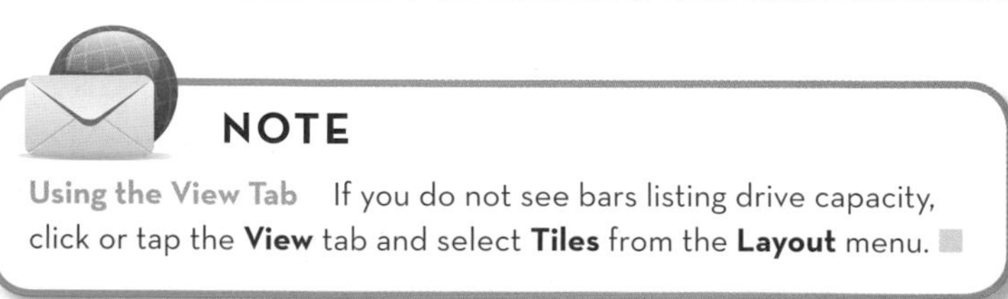

NOTE

Using the View Tab If you do not see bars listing drive capacity, click or tap the **View** tab and select **Tiles** from the **Layout** menu.

CHECKING DRIVES FOR ERRORS WHEN CONNECTED

As drives are connected to your system, Windows 10 AE watches for errors. If an error is detected, Notifications displays a message. Here's what to do next.

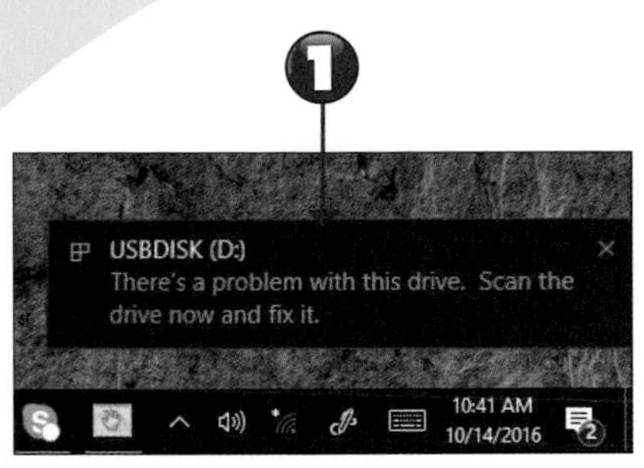

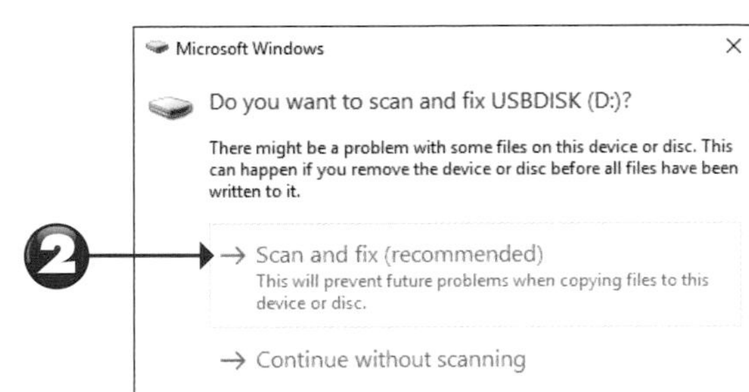

Start

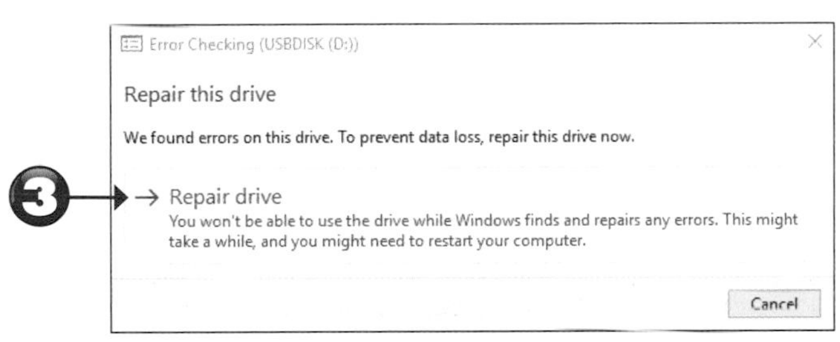

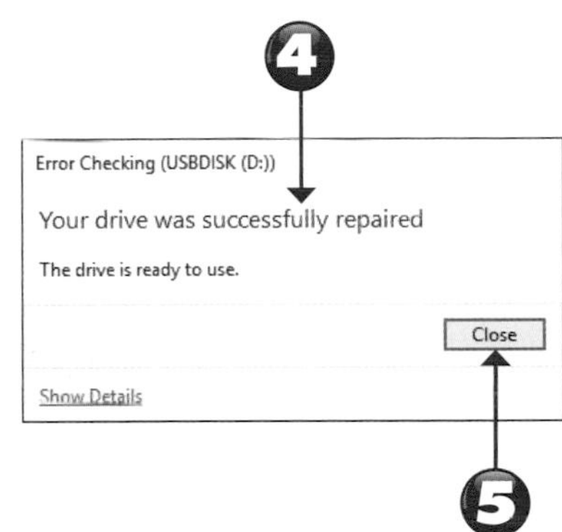

1. This just-inserted flash drive has a problem—click the notification.
2. Click **Scan and fix**.
3. Click **Repair drive**.
4. View the results. On drives with minor errors, you might see a message like this one.
5. Click or tap **Close**.

End

NOTE

Drive Error Causes Removing a drive during a data write or erase process can cause a drive error that could lead to the file being written becoming unreadable. However, if a drive that is properly used and ejected continues to have errors, it might be in danger of complete failure, causing widespread data loss. A hard drive that displays a S.M.A.R.T. error is about to fail. Use the drive vendor's diagnostic software to determine a drive's condition.

CHECKING DRIVES FOR ERRORS WITH THIS PC

You can check a drive for errors at any time using This PC. Here's how.

Start

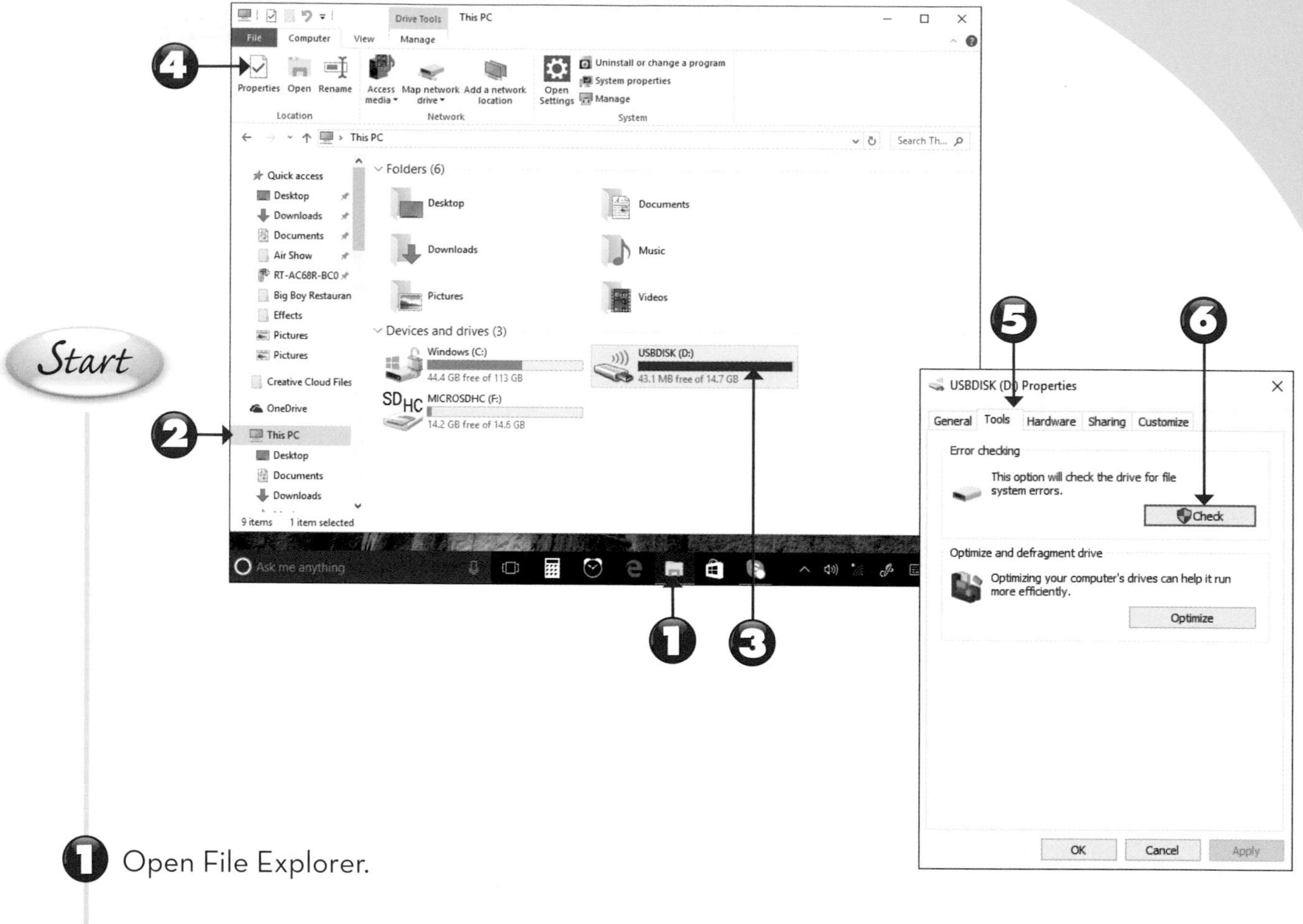

1. Open File Explorer.
2. Click or tap **This PC**.
3. Click or tap the drive you want to check for errors.
4. Click or tap **Properties**.
5. Click or tap **Tools**.
6. Click or tap **Check**.

Continued

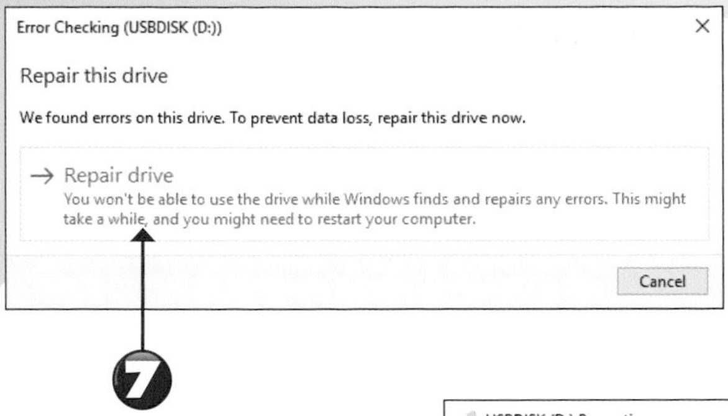

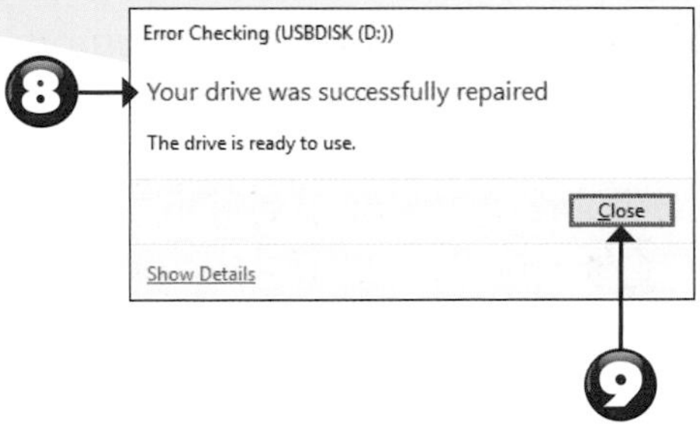

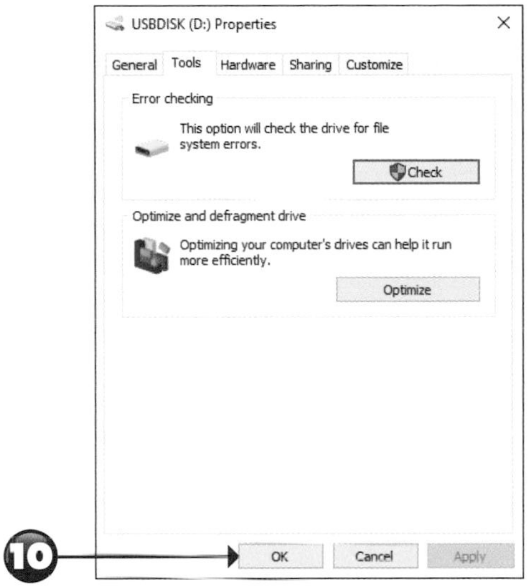

7. This drive has errors. Click or tap to repair the errors.

8. The drive has been successfully repaired.

9. Click or tap **Close**.

10. Click or tap **OK**.

End

USING WINDOWS TROUBLESHOOTERS

Windows 10 AE includes a number of troubleshooters to help solve problems with your system. Some troubleshooters are found in the menus for devices, but you can always conduct a search for troubleshooters. Here's how to search for a troubleshooter to fix an audio playback problem. In this example, the speakers were muted.

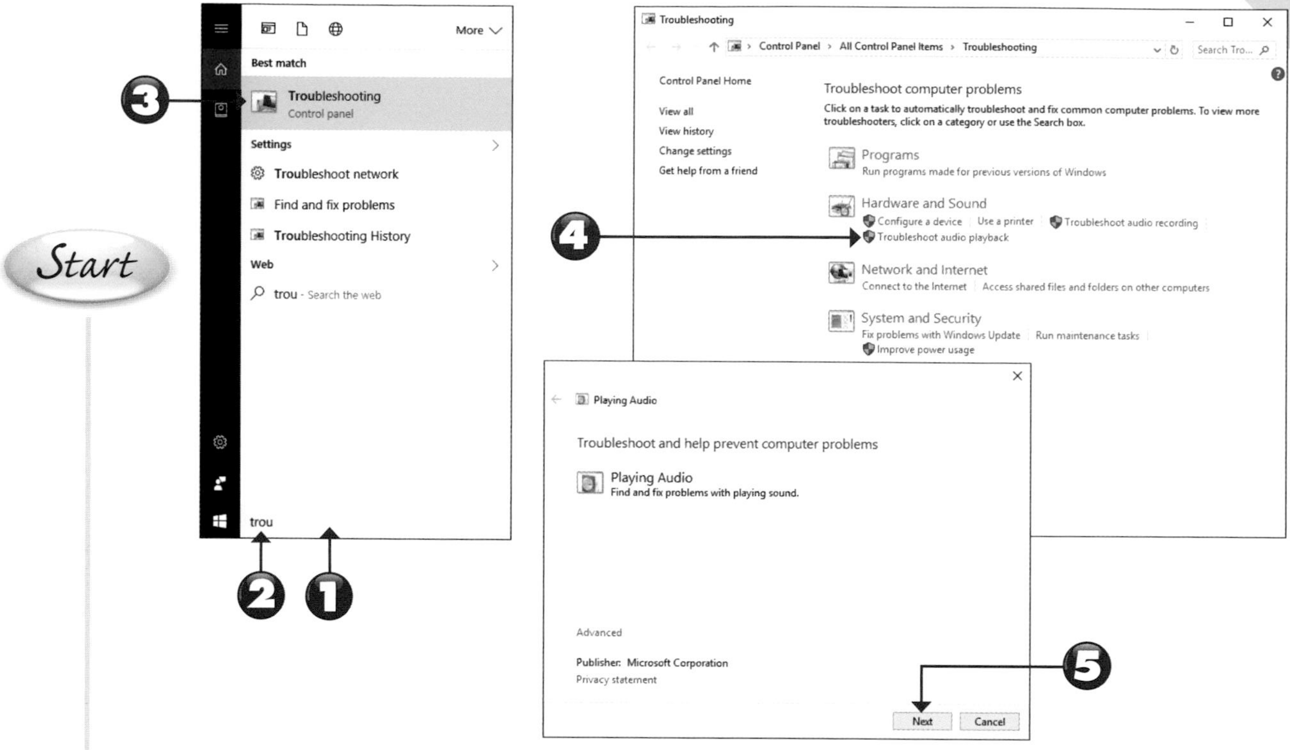

1. Click or tap the Cortana/Search window.
2. Enter part or all of the word **troubleshoot**.
3. Click or tap **Troubleshooting**.
4. Click **Troubleshoot audio playback**.
5. Click or tap **Next**.

Continued

NOTE

Choosing a Category If you don't see your exact problem in step 4, select the most likely category and choose from the troubleshooters listed there.

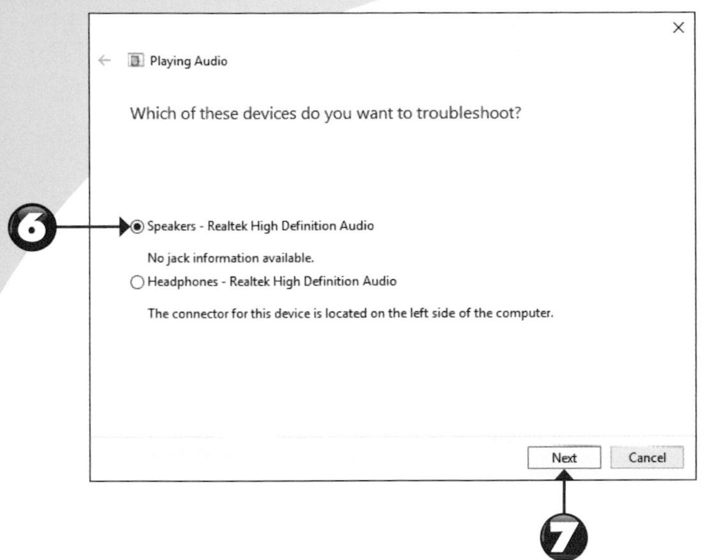

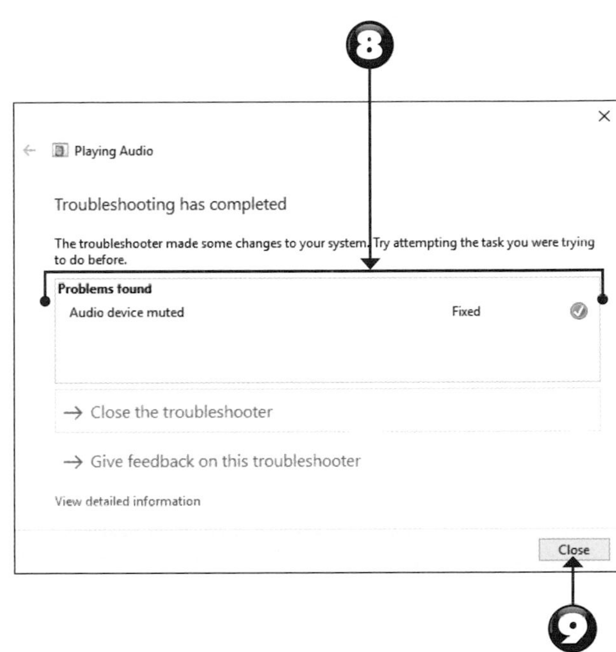

6. Choose your playback device.
7. Click or tap **Next**.
8. Review the results.
9. Click or tap **Close** to close the window.

End

NOTE

Helping the Repair Process If you need to turn on a device, plug in a cable, or make other changes to your system, you are prompted to do so during the process.

STARTING TASK MANAGER WITH A MOUSE

You can have many programs running at the same time with Windows 10 AE, even if you see only one program window visible and your taskbar is hidden. However, a running program that is not working properly can cause problems with your system. You can quickly find out what programs and apps are running at a given moment using Windows Task Manager. In this exercise, you learn how to open Task Manager with a mouse.

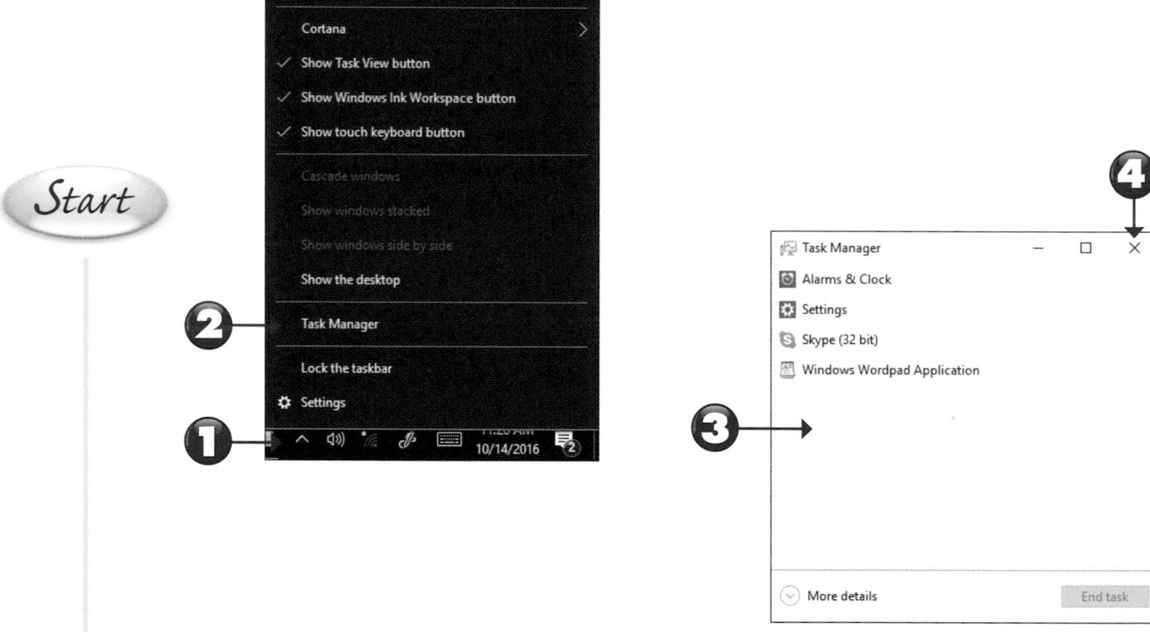

1. Press and hold or right-click an empty portion of the taskbar (if visible).
2. Select **Task Manager** (simple view shown).
3. Task Manager opens, displaying the currently open apps.
4. Close the window.

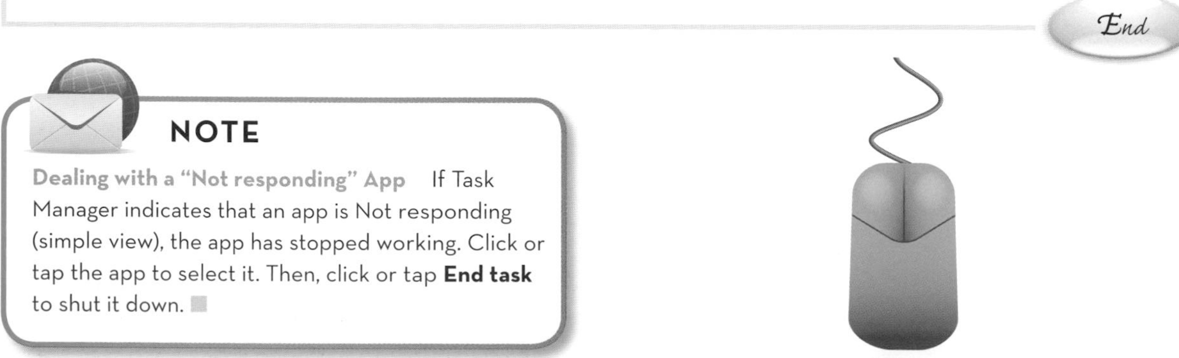

NOTE

Dealing with a "Not responding" App If Task Manager indicates that an app is Not responding (simple view), the app has stopped working. Click or tap the app to select it. Then, click or tap **End task** to shut it down.

STARTING TASK MANAGER FROM THE KEYBOARD

You can easily start Task Manager without taking your hands off the keyboard to view what programs and apps are currently running.

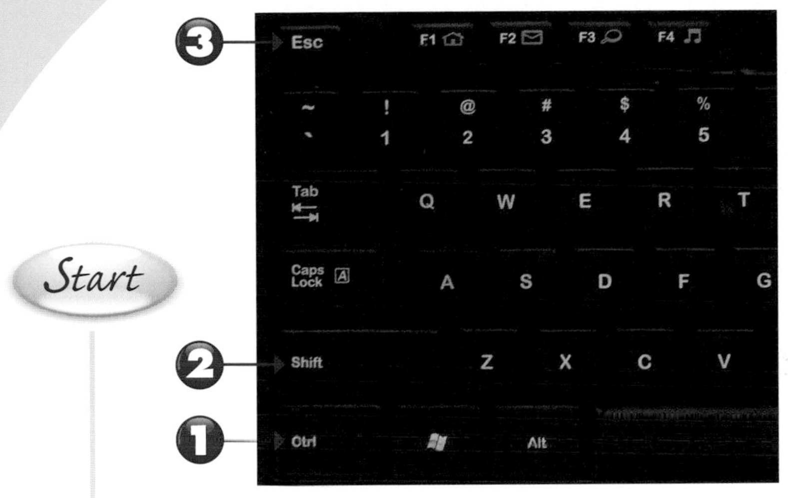

Start

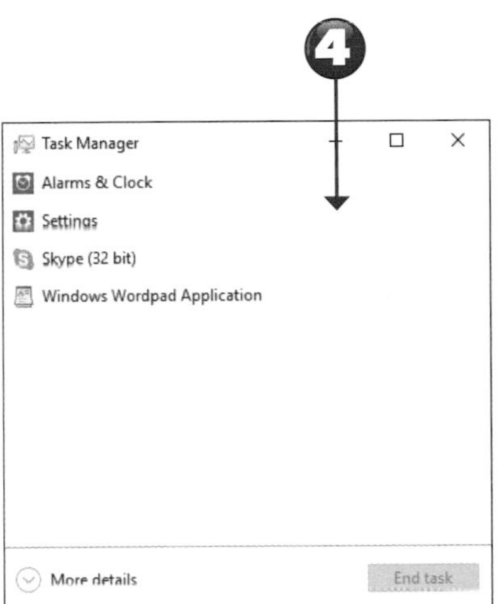

1. Press and hold the **Ctrl** key on your keyboard.
2. Press and hold the **Shift** key.
3. Press the **Esc** key.
4. Task Manager (simple view shown) displays the list of running programs and apps.

End

NOTE

More Ways to Start Task Manager The Task Manager app is known as Task Manager. You can use Windows Search to locate and run it. Task Manager's executable (program) file is called taskmgr.exe, and you can also start it by using the **Run** command.

NOTE

Simple and Detailed Views Task Manager might open in detailed view (see next task) instead of simple view. You can switch views by clicking or tapping the **More details/Fewer details** arrow at the bottom of the Task Manager window.

VIEWING AND CLOSING RUNNING APPS WITH TASK MANAGER

Task Manager displays active (running) apps. It can also provide a detailed view of services and other activities that are running. In this task, you learn how to change views and how to close a running app.

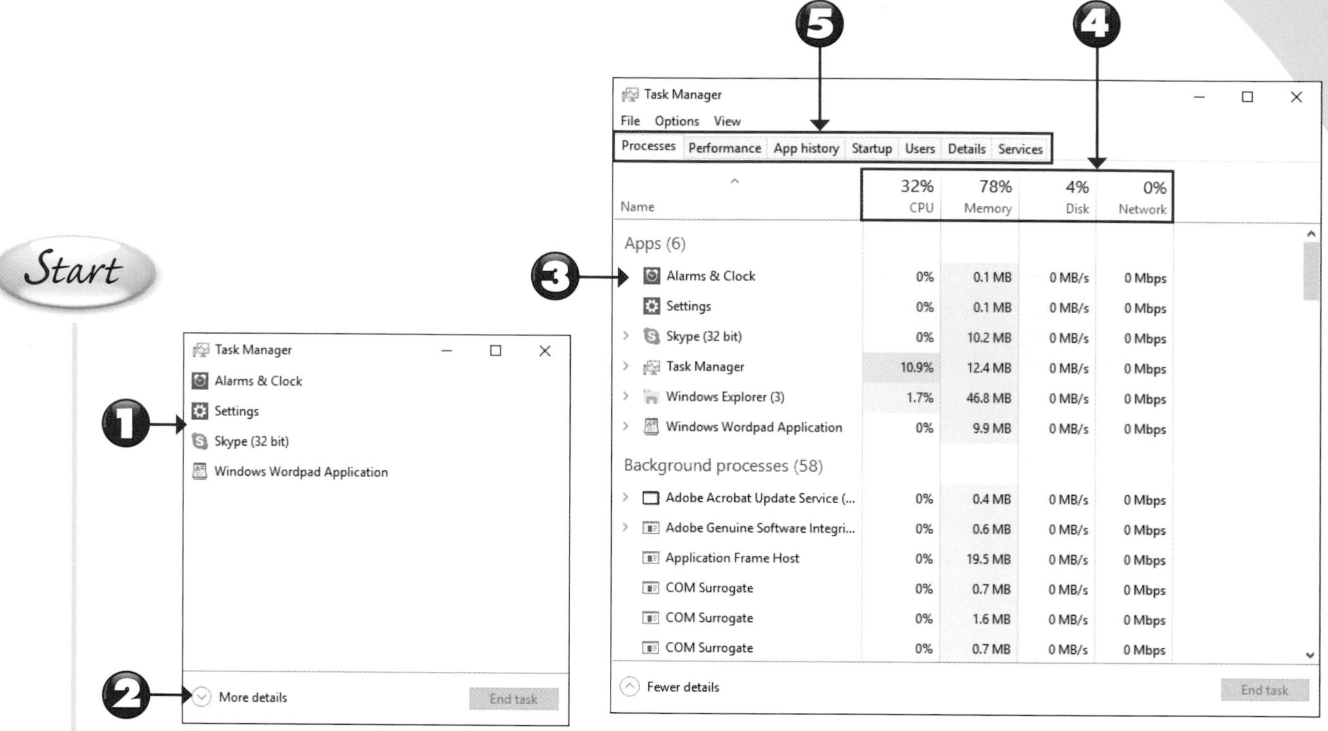

1. With Task Manager open, you can view a list of currently running apps.
2. Click or tap **More details** to switch to detailed view.
3. The Apps section lists actively running programs.
4. You can view the amount of CPU, memory, disk activity, and network activity (real time) in use.
5. Click or tap a tab to learn more.

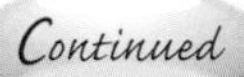

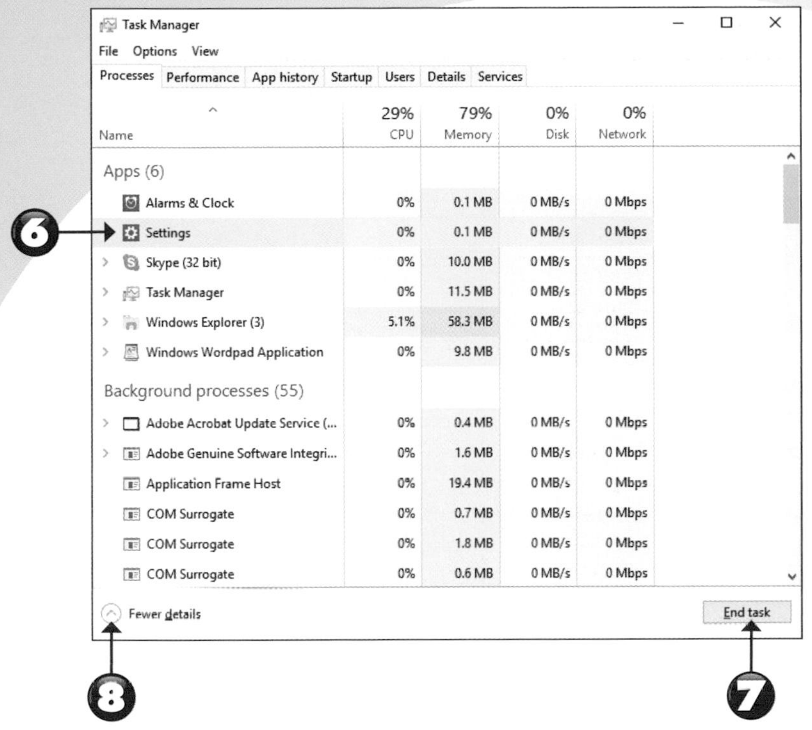

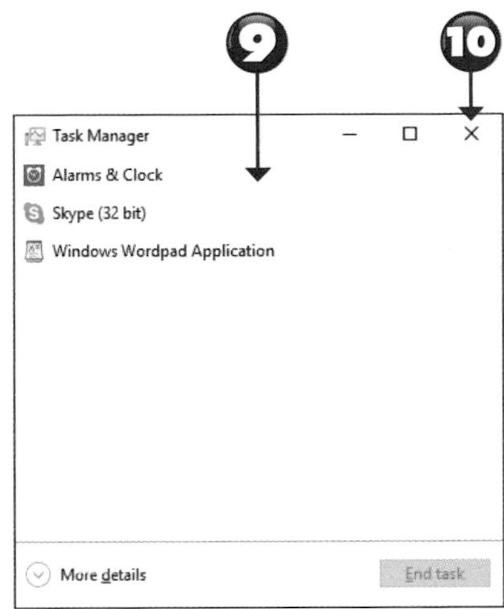

6. Click or tap an app you want to close.
7. Click or tap **End task**.
8. Click or tap **Fewer details** to return to simple view.
9. Task Manager switches back to simple view and the app you closed is no longer listed among the open apps.
10. Click or tap to close Task Manager.

End

NOTE

Apps in Detailed View Detailed view also displays apps that are not listed in simple view, such as Windows (File) Explorer and Task Manager.

NOTE

Closing Apps and Tasks In either detailed or simple view, you can close an app or process by clicking/tapping it and then clicking/tapping **End Task**.

USING RESET

If you're not sure why Windows 10 AE isn't running correctly, or your system has gradually been running more slowly, the problem could be apps and programs that didn't come from the Windows Store. You can use the Reset feature to reinstall Windows 10 AE for you while retaining your personal files. In this tutorial, you learn how to run Reset with these options.

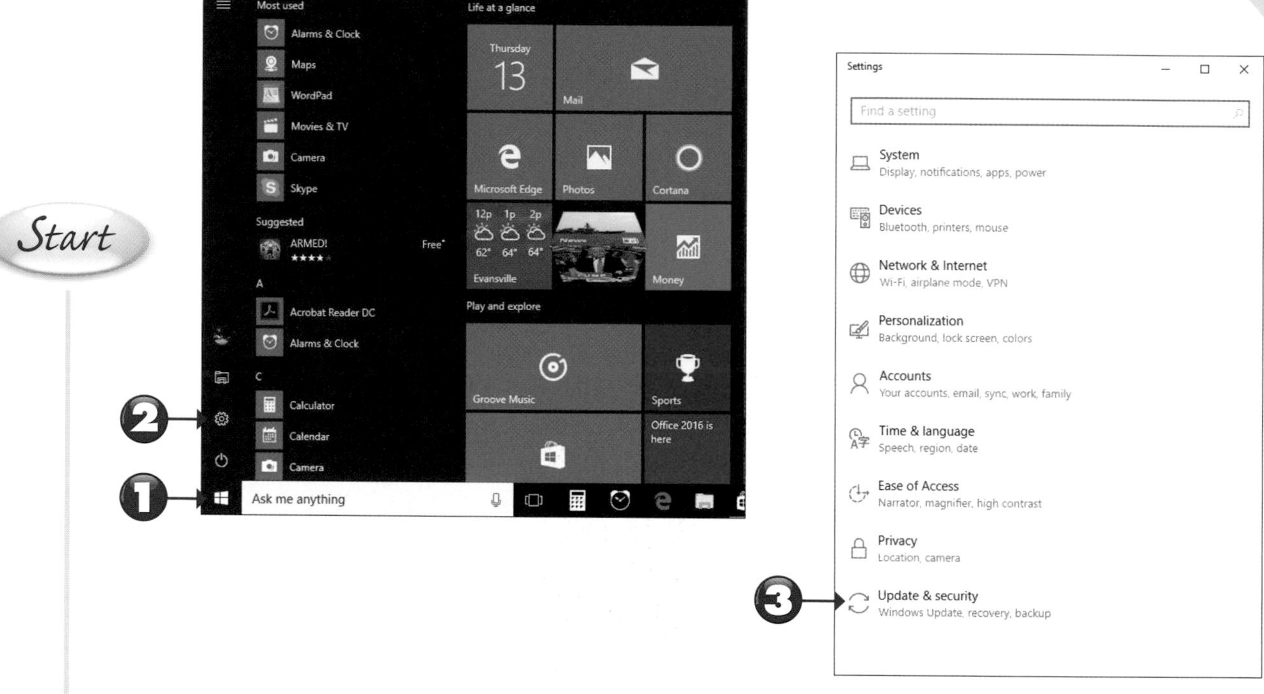

1. Click or tap **Start**.

2. Click or tap **Settings.**

3. Click or tap **Update & security**.

Continued

NOTE

Refresh and Restore Options Now Included in Reset The Refresh and Restore options included in Windows 8.1 have now been combined as Reset. ■

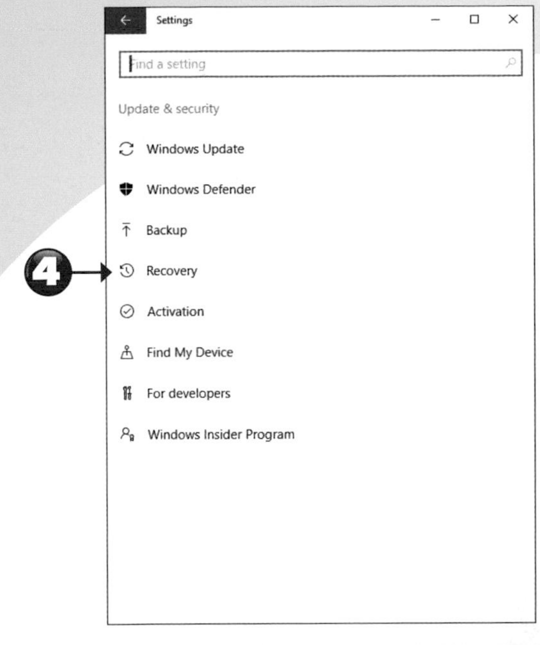

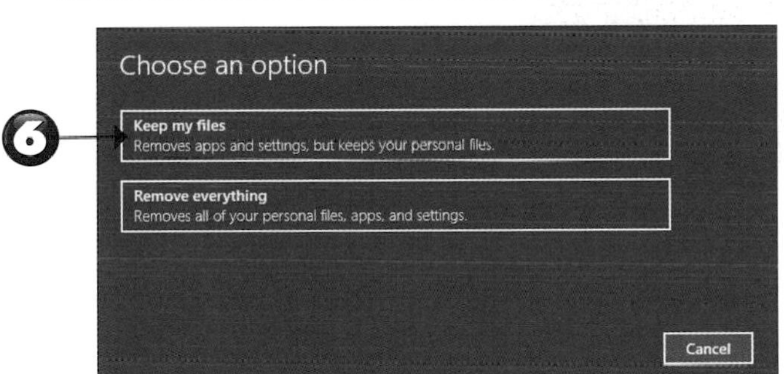

4. Click or tap **Recovery**.

5. Click or tap **Get started** in the Reset this PC section.

6. Click or tap **Keep my files**.

Continued

NOTE

Reinstalling Apps and Programs If you need to reinstall some apps, either revisit the Windows Store or use the original discs or download files to reinstall programs from other sources.

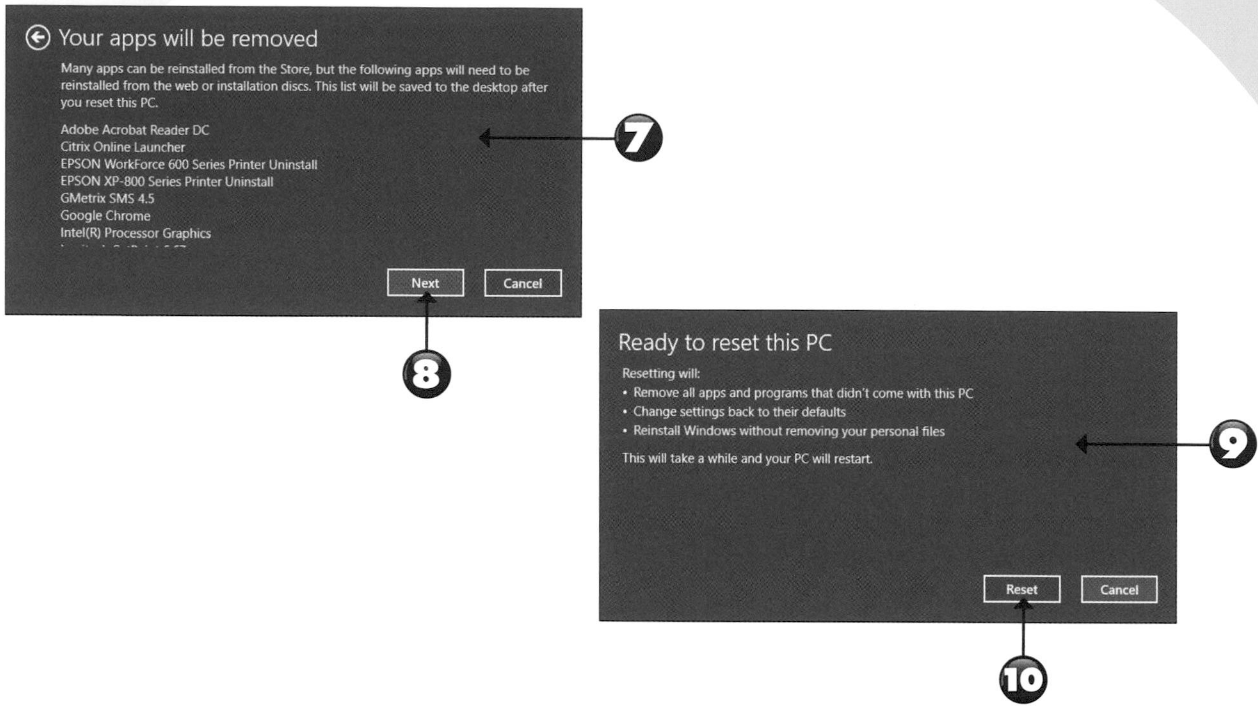

7. A list of apps that will be removed appears; if you want to use them again, you must reinstall them after Reset is finished.

8. Click or tap **Next**.

9. Review what the Reset process does.

10. Click or tap **Reset**. Windows restarts and runs the Reset process.

Continued

CAUTION

Incomplete List on the Desktop Windows 10 AE might not create a complete list of all removed apps on the desktop when the Reset process is finished. To make sure you know all the apps being removed, scroll through the list shown in step 7 and capture each section to a separate picture file you can review later. You can use the Screen sketch feature discussed in Chapter 13, "Using Windows Ink," to quickly capture the screens.

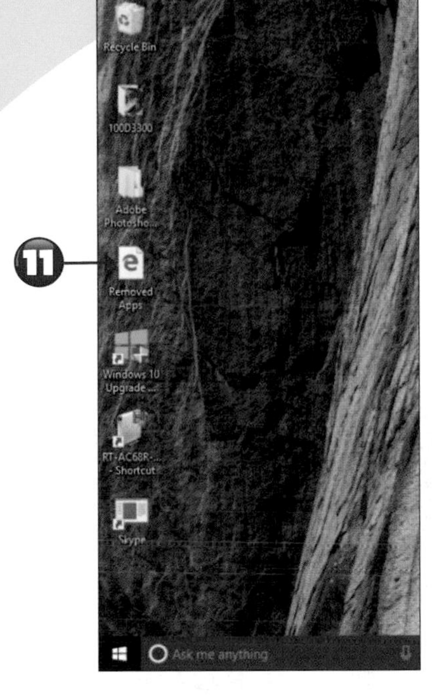

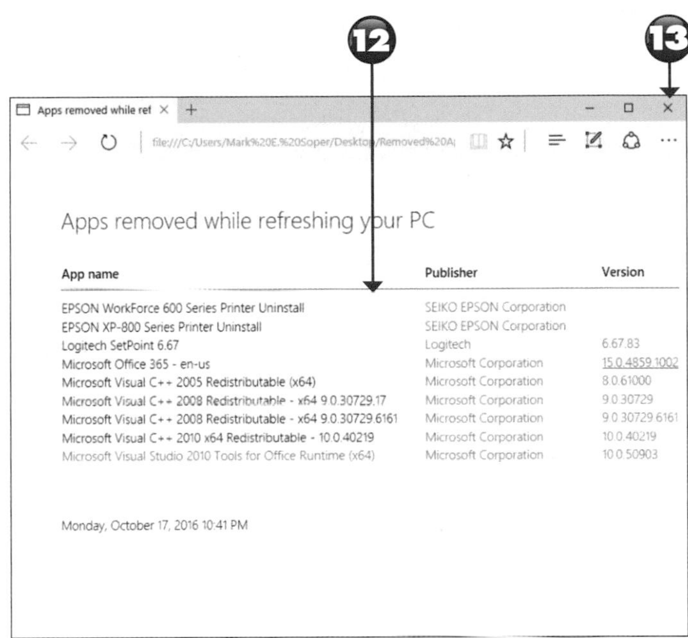

11 After Windows restarts and you log back in to your system, double-click or double-tap **Removed Apps**.

12 An HTML file displays a list of apps removed during the Reset process.

13 Click or tap to close.

End

NOTE

Finding "Hidden" Desktop Icons If you don't see any desktop icons listed among the removed programs and apps, you must first make them visible before continuing with step 12. Right-click or press and hold an empty part of your desktop and select **View**, **Show Desktop Icons**.

Use this section to bring yourself up to speed on important concepts and terms relating to Windows and your computer. Italic terms within definitions are also listed in the glossary.

A

access point A device on a Wi-Fi network that provides a connection between computers on the network. Can be combined with a router and a switch.

administrator A Windows term for the manager of a given computer or network; only users in the administrator's group can perform some management tasks. Other users must provide an administrator's name and password for tasks marked with the Windows security shield icon.

app A program that runs on Windows. Might refer to a program designed for use with touchscreens (but can also be used with a keyboard and mouse); can also refer to programs that work with Windows 7 and earlier versions. Some apps are preinstalled, whereas others are available from the Windows Store. See also *universal apps*.

application program A program used to create, modify, and store information you create. Microsoft Word, Adobe Photoshop, and CorelDRAW are all application programs. See also *app*.

B

backup A copy of a file made for safekeeping, particularly using a special program that also restores the backup when needed. Backups can be compressed to save space. A full backup backs up the entire contents of the specified drive or system; a differential backup backs up only the files that have changed since the last full backup. Windows 10 Anniversary Edition includes the *Backup and Restore (Windows 7)* and *File History* backup apps.

Backup and Restore (Windows 7) This file and system *image backup* app was originally included in Windows 7 but is also included in Windows 10 Anniversary Edition. It is primarily intended to let Windows 10 AE users retrieve backup files originally created in Windows 7 but can also be used to make a backup of the Windows 10 AE installation that can be used to restore a device to operation.

BitLocker A full-drive encryption technology used in Windows 10 Anniversary Edition Pro, Education, and Enterprise. Before you can use special boot options (such as Safe Mode), you must provide your BitLocker encryption key. Log in to https://onedrive.live.com/recovery key with your Microsoft account to obtain your recovery key.

Bluetooth A short-range wireless networking standard that supports non-PC devices such as mobile phones and PDAs, as well as PCs. Bluetooth uses frequencies ranging from 2.402GHz to 2.485GHz and is available in many versions. Range and transmission speeds vary according to transmitter strength and Bluetooth standard supported by the device. Windows 10 Anniversary Edition includes Bluetooth support.

boot Starting the computer. A warm boot involves restarting the computer without a reset or shutdown. A cold boot involves a shutdown or reset before startup.

boot disk A disk with operating system files needed to start the computer. Windows 10 AE DVDs are bootable, as is the recovery drive you can create with Windows.

broadband Internet Internet connections with rated download speeds in excess of 25Mbps download and 3Mbps upload as announced by the Federal Communications Commission in January 2015. Most common types include cable modem and fiber optic (FiOS and others).

browser A program that interprets HTML documents and enables hyperlinking to websites. Windows 10 Anniversary Edition includes Microsoft Edge (originally known as Project Spartan) as its standard (default) web browser. Windows 10 AE also includes Internet Explorer 11, mainly for corporate users.

BSOD Blue Screen of Death. This is a fatal system error in Windows that stops the system from functioning. It is also called a "stop error" and is named after the blue background and white text error message.

C

CD Compact Disc.

CD-R Recordable CD. Contents of a CD-R can be added to but not changed.

CD-ROM Compact Disc-Read-Only Memory. A standard optical drive. Most drives can read CD-R media but require multiread capability and a UDF reader program to read CD-RW media.

CD-RW Compact Disc-Rewritable. A rewritable CD. The contents can be changed. A CD-RW drive can also use CD-R media.

Compact Flash A popular flash-memory storage standard used by professional-level digital cameras. It can be attached to desktop and portable PCs by means of a card reader.

Continuum A Windows 10 Anniversary Edition feature that enables the operating system to adapt to the hardware being used to run it. For example, easy switching between touchscreen and traditional Start menus and back when the user attaches or removes a keyboard on a convertible tablet. Tablet functionality is known as Tablet mode.

Control Panel A Windows 10 Anniversary Edition feature that sets Windows options. However, Settings is the primary method of changing Windows options. See also *Settings*.

convertible tablet A tablet that converts into a laptop by attaching a keyboard with integrated touchpad. See also *Continuum*.

Cortana Microsoft's voice-enabled, integrated search and personal assistant app. Also known as Microsoft Cortana.

D

DAE Digital Audio Extraction. The process of converting tracks from a music CD to a digital format, such as MP3 or WMA, at faster than normal 1x analog speeds. Windows 10 Anniversary Edition's Windows Media Player uses DAE to rip (convert) audio into digital form.

defragment Reorganizing the files on a drive to occupy contiguous sectors to improve retrieval speed; a defragmenting utility is included in Windows 10 Anniversary Edition.

desktop Windows 10 Anniversary Edition uses the desktop for the Start menu, program shortcuts, access to components such as the Recycle Bin, and program windows.

desktop mode Windows 10 AE operating mode optimized for use with a mouse and keyboard, although touchscreens are also supported.

device driver A program used to enable an operating system to support new devices.

Device Manager The Windows portion of the system properties sheet used to view and control device configuration. This includes drivers and other configuration options.

Devices and Printers A Windows 10 Anniversary Edition feature that displays all devices and printers in a single window for quick access to the management features for each device.

dialog box An onscreen window that appears when an option is selected from a menu. Dialog boxes appear when more input is required from the user. Typical choices include Yes/No or OK/Cancel. Sometimes also known as a confirmation dialog.

drag and drop A Windows term for clicking and holding on an object (such as a file or a tile on the Start screen), dragging it to another location, and releasing it.

DVD Digital Video Disc. Also known as Digital Versatile Disc. A high-capacity replacement for CD-ROM.

DVD-R Digital Video Disc-Recordable. A recordable DVD standard developed by the DVD Forum.

DVD+R DVD+Recordable. A recordable DVD standard developed by the DVD+RW Alliance.

DVD-RAM Digital Versatile Disc-Random Access Memory. A rewritable *DVD* standard developed by Panasonic and supported by the DVD Forum. A few of these drives also support DVD-R write-once media.

DVD-ROM Digital Video Disc-Read Only Memory. Retail and upgrade editions of Windows 10 Anniversary Edition are distributed on DVD-ROM media, as are many other application and utility programs from major publishers.

DVD-RW Digital Video Disc-Rewritable. A rewritable *DVD* standard developed by Pioneer Electronics and supported by the DVD Forum. These drives also support *DVD-R* write-once media.

DVD+RW A rewritable *DVD* standard supported by the DVD+RW Alliance and sold by HP, Philips, Sony, and other vendors. Most of these drives also support *DVD+R* write-once media.

DVD±RW Refers to drives that support both *DVD-R/RW* and *DVD+R/RW* media.

E

email Electronic mail. The contents of email can include text, HTML, and binary files (such as photos or compressed archives). Email can be sent between computers via an internal computer network or via the Internet.

F

FAT File Allocation Table. The part of the hard disk or floppy disk that contains pointers to the actual location of files on the disk.

FAT16 16-bit file allocation table. FAT method used by Windows 10 Anniversary Edition and earlier versions for flash drives used for data. It allows 65,535 (2^{16}) files per drive and drive sizes up to 2GB in Windows 10 AE.

FAT32 32-bit file allocation table. The FAT method optionally available with Windows 10 Anniversary Edition and earlier versions. It allows about four million (2^{32}) files maximum per drive and drive sizes up to 2TB (terabytes). Windows 10 AE supports FAT32 for data drives only.

file attributes These control how files are used and viewed and can be reset by the user. Typical file attributes include hidden, system, read-only, and archive; Windows 10 Anniversary Edition also supports compressed and encrypted file attributes on drives that use *NTFS*.

File Explorer Windows 10 Anniversary Edition file manager. Provides access to the most-used folders and files (Quick access), *OneDrive* cloud storage, *This PC* local storage, Network, and *HomeGroup*.

file extension An alphanumeric identifier after the dot in a filename that indicates the file type, such as .html, .exe, .docx, and so on. Windows 10 Anniversary Edition does not display file extensions by default, but you can make them visible through the Control Panel's Folder Options utility.

File History The Windows 10 Anniversary Edition backup feature that automatically backs up different versions of personal file folders (photos, videos, documents, music, downloads, and optionally other folders) to a specified drive.

file system How files are organized on a drive; *FAT16*, *FAT32*, and *NTFS* are popular file systems supported by various versions of Windows.

firewall A network device or software that blocks unauthorized access to a network from other users. Software firewalls such as Zone Alarm or Norton Internet Security are sometimes referred to as *personal firewalls*. Routers can also function as firewalls. Windows 10 Anniversary Edition includes a software firewall.

font A particular size, shape, and weight of a *typeface*. For example, 12-point Times Roman Italic is a font; Times Roman is the typeface. Windows 10 Anniversary Edition includes a number of different typefaces, and you can select the desired font with programs such as WordPad, Paint, and others.

FORMAT A Windows program to prepare a drive for use; hard disks must be partitioned first.

G

GB Gigabyte. One billion bytes.

GHz Gigahertz.

GUI Graphical user interface. The user interface with features such as icons, fonts, and point-and-click commands; Windows and Mac OS are popular GUIs.

H

hard drive A storage device with rigid, nonremovable platters inside a case; also called hard disk or rigid disk.

hardware Physical computing devices.

HDD Hard disk drive. Windows 10 Anniversary Edition is typically installed to an HDD. See also *SSD*.

Hi-Speed USB Another term for USB 2.0.

high-speed Internet An Internet connection with a download speed of at least 256Kbps. Sometimes used interchangeably with broadband Internet, but broadband Internet runs at much higher speeds. Most commonly provided by cable or DSL connections, but ISDN, fixed wireless, fiber optic (FIOS and others), and satellite Internet services are also high-speed Internet services. See also *broadband Internet*.

home page The web page that is first displayed when you open a web browser; it can be customized to view any web page available online or stored on your hard disk.

HomeGroup A Windows network feature that enables two or more devices running Windows 7 or newer versions to belong to a secure, easy-to-manage *network*.

I

icon An onscreen symbol used in Windows to link you to a program, file, or routine.

image backup A backup that can be used to restore a working Windows installation in the event of system drive failure or corruption. Windows 10 Anniversary Edition includes *Backup and Restore (Windows 7)*, which can be used to create image or file backups. See also *File History*.

install The process of making a computer program usable on a system, including expanding and copying program files to the correct locations, changing Windows configuration files, and registering *file extensions* used by the program.

Internet The worldwide "network of networks" that can be accessed through the World Wide Web and by Telnet, FTP, and other utilities.

J

jump list A Windows 10 Anniversary Edition feature that enables programs and documents to offer commonly used shortcuts from the program's taskbar icon.

L

LAN Local area network. A *network* in which the components are connected through network cables or wirelessly; a LAN can connect to other LANs via a router.

landscape mode A print mode that prints across the wider side of the paper; from the usual proportions of a landscape painting.

Live Tile A Windows 10 Anniversary Edition feature that uses some tiles on the Start menu to display dynamic information being fed from local storage (Pictures) or from websites (Weather, People, News, and other tiles).

lock screen This screen appears when Windows 10 Anniversary Edition is started or locked. The user must press the spacebar, click a mouse, or press the touch interface to see the login screen. This screen displays the date, time, and a full-screen image.

logging Recording events during a process. Windows 10 Anniversary Edition creates logs for many types of events; they can be viewed through the Computer Management Console.

M

mastering Creating a *CD* or *DVD* by adding all the files to the media at once. This method is recommended when creating a music CD or a video DVD. Windows 10 Anniversary Edition's built-in CD- and DVD-creation feature supports mastering.

Microsoft account Account setup option supported by Windows 10 Anniversary Edition. Log in with a Microsoft account (for example, somebody@outlook.com), and your settings are synchronized between systems. This was previously known as a Windows Live ID. A Microsoft account is free.

Microsoft Knowledge Base The online collection of Microsoft technical articles used by Microsoft support personnel to diagnose system problems. The Microsoft Knowledge Base can also be searched by end users via the http://support.microsoft.com website.

MMC Microsoft Management Console. The Windows utility used to view and control the computer and its components. Disk Management and *Device Manager* are components of MMC.

Modern UI A user interface app made specifically for Windows 8–Windows 10 Anniversary Edition. It is touch-friendly and runs full-screen by default (can also run in a window). In Tablet mode, Modern UI apps are closed by dragging the app to the bottom of the display.

monitor A TV-like device that uses a liquid crystal display (LCD) screen or plasma screen to display activity inside the computer. The monitor attaches to the video card or video port on the system. Windows 10 Anniversary Edition supports multiple monitors.

mouse A pointing device that is moved across a flat surface; an optical or laser sensor is used to track movement.

MP3 Moving Picture Experts Group Layer 3 Audio. A compressed digitized music file format widely used for storage of music; quality varies with the sampling rate used to create the file. MP3 files can be stored on recordable or rewritable CD or DVD media for playback and are frequently exchanged online. The process of creating MP3 files from CD is called "ripping." Windows Media Player can create and play back MP3 files. Groove Music can also play back MP3 files.

MPEG Motion Picture Experts Group. MPEG creates standards for compression of video (such as MPEG 2) and audio (such as the popular MP3 file format).

multitouch A Windows feature that enables icons and windows on touch-sensitive displays to be dragged, resized, and adjusted with two or more fingers.

N

netbook A mobile computing device that is smaller than a laptop and has a folding keyboard and screen (usually no more than about 10 inches diagonal measurement). Netbooks have lower-performance processors, less RAM, and smaller hard disks (or solid state drives) than laptop or notebook computers. Windows 10 Anniversary Edition runs on netbooks as well as more powerful types of computers.

network Two or more computers that are connected and share resources, such as folders or printers.

network drive A drive or folder available through the *network*; usually refers to a network resource that has been mapped to a local drive letter.

Network and Sharing Center The Windows control center for wired and wireless networking functions.

Notifications A Windows 10 Anniversary Edition feature that displays security and maintenance messages and provides quick access to the most common settings.

NTFS New Technology File System. The native *file system* used by Windows 10 Anniversary Edition and some earlier versions of Windows. All NTFS versions feature smaller allocation unit sizes and superior security when compared to *FAT16* or *FAT32*.

objects Items that can be viewed or configured with File Explorer, including drives, folders, computers, and so on.

OneDrive A Windows online file and photo storage and sharing site formerly known as SkyDrive. Requires a free Microsoft account (formerly known as a Windows Live ID). Windows 10 Anniversary Edition provides access to OneDrive from the Start menu, All Apps menu, and File Explorer.

OS Operating system. Software that configures and manages hardware as well as connects hardware and applications. Windows 10 Anniversary Edition, Linux, and Mac OS X are examples of operating systems.

P

password A word or combination of letters and numbers that is matched to a *username* or resource name to enable the user to access a computer or network resources or accounts.

path A series of drives and folders (subdirectories) that are checked for executable programs when a command-prompt command is issued or a drive/network server and folders are used to access a given file.

personal firewall Software that blocks unauthorized access to a computer with an Internet connection. Can also be configured to prevent unauthorized programs from connecting to the Internet. Windows 10 Anniversary Edition includes a personal (software) firewall.

PIN Personal identification number. Windows 10 Anniversary Edition supports PIN codes as an optional login method.

pinning The act of locking a program or document to the Windows *taskbar* or *Start menu*. You can use this feature along with *jump lists* to create shortcuts to your most commonly used programs in either location.

POP3 Post Office Protocol 3, a popular protocol for receiving *email*. The Mail app in Windows supports POP3 email services.

portrait mode The default print option that prints across the short side of the paper; it gets its name from the usual orientation of portrait paintings and photographs.

power management BIOS or OS techniques for reducing power usage by dropping CPU clock speed, turning off the monitor or hard disk, and so on during periods of inactivity.

PowerShell A Windows utility that runs from the command prompt and enables experienced users and system administrators to write scripts (series of commands) to perform tasks. Included in most editions of Windows 10 Anniversary Edition as an optionally installed feature.

properties sheet A Windows method for modifying and viewing object properties. Accessible by right-clicking the object and selecting Properties or by using Control Panel. On a tablet or touchscreen-based device, press and hold the object until the properties sheet appears. It is located on the bottom of the screen when run from the *Start screen* or Apps menu.

Q

Quick action A Windows 10 Anniversary Edition feature that provides quick access to settings from the Notification area of the taskbar.

QWERTY The standard arrangement of typewriter keys is also used by most English or Latin-alphabet computer keyboards; the name was derived from the first six letter keys under the left hand.

R

Recycle Bin The Windows holding area for deleted files, enabling them to be restored to their original locations. The Recycle Bin can be overridden to free up disk space.

Reset A Windows 10 Anniversary Edition system recovery feature that can be used to remove non-Windows Store apps without harming user data or can be used to return the operating system to its original state, removing all user data.

resolution The number of dots per inch (dpi) supported by a display, scanner, or printer. Typical displays support resolutions of about 96dpi, whereas printers have resolutions of 600dpi to 2,400dpi (laser printers). Inkjet printers might have even higher resolutions.

Ribbon toolbar The program interface used by many Windows 10 Anniversary Edition components. Click a tab on the Ribbon to display related commands.

ripping The process of converting CD audio tracks into a digital music format, such as *MP3* or *WMA*.

router The device that routes data from one network to another. Often integrated with wireless access points and switches.

S

safe mode Windows troubleshooting startup mode; runs the system using BIOS routines only. To restart in safe mode, select Advanced Startup Options in the Settings dialog box, Restart Now, Troubleshoot, Advanced Options, Startup Settings, Restart, and select 4 (Safe Mode), 5 (Safe Mode with Networking), or 6 (Safe Mode with Command Prompt). If your device uses BitLocker encryption, you will also need to enter your BitLocker encryption key. See also *BitLocker*.

SD card Secure Digital card. A popular flash memory card format for digital cameras and other electronic devices with a capacity up to 2GB. See also *SDHC card* and *SDXC card*.

SDHC card Secure Digital High Capacity card. A popular flash memory card format for digital cameras and other electronic devices with a capacity ranging from 4GB to 32GB. Devices that use SDHC cards can also use *SD cards*; however, devices made only for SD cards cannot use SDHC cards.

SDXC card Secure Digital eXtended Capacity card. A popular flash memory card format for high-performance digital cameras and devices. Capacities range from 64GB up to 2TB. Devices that use SDXC cards can also use *SD cards* and *SDHC cards*; however, devices made only for SD or SDHC cards cannot use SDXC cards.

Settings The primary method to change settings for Windows 10 Anniversary Edition. It has largely replaced Control Panel, which was used by previous versions of Windows. See also *Control Panel*.

shared resource A drive, printer, or other resource available to more than one PC over a *network*.

shortcut A Windows *icon* stored on the desktop or in a Windows folder with an .lnk extension; double-click the icon to run the program or open the file.

SMTP Simple Mail Transport Protocol. The most common method used to send *email*.

Snap A Windows 10 Anniversary Edition feature that enables a program or app to be snapped to the top, bottom, left, or right of the display where it is running, adjusting the window size so other programs or apps are also visible. To use Snap, hold down the Windows key and then press the up arrow, down arrow, left arrow, or right arrow, or drag the app to the top, left, or right edge of the display.

software Instructions that create or modify information and control *hardware*; must be read into RAM before use. Also known as program or app.

SOHO Small office/home office.

SP Service pack. A service pack is used to add features or fix problems with an OS or application program. Windows 10 Anniversary Edition's Windows Update feature installs for Microsoft apps such as Microsoft Office automatically when standard settings are used.

spam Unsolicited *email*. Named after (but not endorsed by) the famous Hormel lunchmeat. Many email clients and utilities can be configured to help filter, sort, and block spam.

SSD Solid state drive. A storage device that uses high-speed flash memory and can be used in place of a hard disk drive (HDD). SSDs are several times faster than HDDs but are more expensive at a given capacity than HDDs. Tablets, some desktops, and many Ultrabook laptops use SSDs. See *HDD*.

SSID Service Set Identifier. The name for a wireless *network*. When you buy a wireless router, the vendor has assigned it a standard SSID, but you should change it to a different name as part of setting up a secure network.

standby The power-saving mode in which the CPU drops to a reduced clock speed and other components wait for activity.

Start menu The Windows 10 Anniversary Edition user interface that pops up from the lower-left corner of the screen when you press the Windows key or click the Windows button. The Start menu includes both desktop and Universal apps and can be customized. The Start menu works differently in Tablet mode than in normal mode.

storage Any device that holds programs or data for use, including HDDs, SSDs, flash memory cards, USB drives, DVD drives, and so on.

suspend The power-saving mode that shuts down the monitor and other devices; it saves more power than standby. Windows 10 Anniversary Edition calls suspend mode "sleep mode."

System Restore A feature built in to Windows 10 Anniversary Edition that enables the user to revert the system back to a previous state in case of a crash or other system problem. System Restore points can be created by the user and are created automatically by Windows when new hardware and software is installed or on a predefined schedule.

T

Task Manager Displays running programs, apps, and services, and enables you to disable unnecessary startup features.

Task View Switches between running apps and sets up virtual desktops. Task View replaces App Switcher. To use Task View, tap the Task View key on the Windows taskbar, use the Windows key+Tab keys (for use with virtual desktops) or use Alt+Tab keys (for app switching only).

taskbar A Windows feature that displays icons for running programs, generally at the bottom of the primary display. In Windows 10 Anniversary Edition, the taskbar also contains *jump list* shortcuts to frequently used programs.

TB Terabyte. One trillion bytes.

TCP/IP Transmission Control Protocol/ Internet Protocol. The Internet's standard network protocol that is also the standard for most networks.

This PC Displays local drives, network locations, and user folders in File Explorer. Replaces My Computer or Computer views in Windows Explorer or File Explorer in earlier versions of Windows.

tile The Windows 10 Anniversary Edition term for the Universal app icons on the right side of the *Start menu*. Tiles can be moved to different places on the Start menu by using drag and drop.

touchpad A pressure-sensitive pad used as a mouse replacement in some portable computers and keyboards.

touchscreen A touch-sensitive screen built in to tablets, many laptops, and some desktop computers.

Trojan horse A program that attaches itself secretly to other programs and usually has a harmful action when triggered. It is similar to a computer *virus* but cannot spread itself to other computers, although some Trojan horses can be used to install a remote control program that enables an unauthorized user to take over your computer. Antivirus programs can block Trojan horses as well as true viruses.

typeface A set of *fonts* in different sizes (or a single scalable outline) and weights. Times New Roman Bold, Bold Italic, Regular, and Italic are all part of the Times New Roman scalable typeface.

U

UDF Universal Disk Format. A standard for *CD* and *DVD* media to drag and drop files to compatible media using a method called "packet writing." Windows 10 Anniversary Edition supports various UDF versions.

uninstall The process of removing Windows programs from the system.

Universal apps Mobile touch-oriented apps that can run on Windows phones, laptop and desktop PCs, and tablets.

URL Uniform Resource Locator. The full path to any given web page or graphic on the Internet. A full URL contains the server type (such as http://, ftp://, or other), the site name (such as www.markesoper.com), and the name of the folder and the page or graphic you want to view (such as /blog/?page_id=38). Thus, the URL http://www.markesoper.com/blog/?page_id=38 displays the "About Mark" page on the author's website.

USB Universal Serial Bus. A high-speed replacement for older I/O ports; USB 1.1 has a peak speed of 12Mbps. USB 2.0 has a peak speed of 480Mbps, USB 3.0 has a top speed of 5Gbps, and USB 3.1 has a top speed of 10Gbps. USB 2.0 ports also support USB 1.1 devices. USB 2.0 devices can be plugged in to USB 1.1 devices but run at only USB 1.1 speeds. USB 3.0 ports support USB 2.0 and 1.1 devices, which run at their original speeds. USB 3.1 ports support USB 3.0, USB 2.0, and USB 1.1 devices, which run at their original speeds.

username Used with a *password* to gain access to network resources.

V

virtual desktop A *desktop* that includes your choice of running apps. You can switch between virtual desktops by clicking the Task View button or by pressing the Windows key plus Ctrl and left or right arrow key. See also *Task View*.

virus A computer program that resembles a *Trojan horse* but can also replicate itself to other computers.

VoIP Voice over Internet Protocol. Enables telephone calls to be transmitted or received over an IP network. Windows 10 Anniversary Edition can use Skype (available from the Windows Store). Skype technology is also available in other apps.

W–Z

WAV A noncompressed standard for digital audio. Some recording programs for Windows can create and play back WAV files. However, WAV files are very large and are usually converted into other formats for use online or for creating digital music archives.

web note A feature in the Microsoft Edge web browser that enables the user to add handwritten or typed notes and callouts to a web page. The page can be saved to local storage or OneDrive cloud storage.

WEP Wired Equivalent Privacy. A now-obsolete standard for wireless security. Replaced by *WPA*.

Wi-Fi The name for IEEE-802.11a, IEEE-802.11b, IEEE-802.11g, IEEE-802.11n, or 802.11ac wireless Ethernet devices that meet the standards set forth by the Wi-Fi Alliance.

Windows Hello A Windows 10 Anniversary Edition feature that enables users to log in to their systems using facial or fingerprint recognition.

wireless network The general term for any radio-frequency network, including *Wi-Fi*. Most wireless networks can be interconnected to conventional networks.

WLAN Wireless local area network. Instead of wires, stations on a WLAN connect to each other through radio waves. The IEEE 802.11 family of standards guide the development of WLANs.

WMA Windows Media Audio. This is the native compressed audio format created by Windows Media Player. Unlike *MP3*, WMA files support digital rights management.

WPA Wireless Protected Access. Replaced *WEP* as the standard for secure wireless networks. Original WPA uses TKIP encryption. An improved version known as WPA2 uses the even more secure AES encryption standard.

WWW World Wide Web. The portion of the Internet that uses the Hypertext Transfer Protocol (http://) and can thus be accessed via a web browser such as Microsoft Edge, Google Chrome, or Mozilla Firefox.

Zip The archive type (originally known as PKZIP) created when you use Send To Compressed (Zipped) Folder. A Zip file can contain one or more files and can be created, viewed, and opened in File Explorer. Formerly also referred to the Iomega Zip removable-media drive.

Index

A

B

C

G

N

Q–R

T

U

V

W

X

Y-Z